**Airline Management:
Strategies for the 21st Century**

Airline Management:
Strategies for the 21st Century

Paul Stephen Dempsey
University of Denver

Laurence E. Gesell
Arizona State University

With *Foreword*
by Robert L. Crandall
Chairman and CEO,
American Airlines

COAST AIRE PUBLICATIONS

Copyright © 1997, Paul Stephen Dempsey
and Laurence E. Gesell

All rights reserved. No part of this publication may be reproduced, stored in a retrieval system, or transmitted, in any form or by any means, electronic, mechanical, photocopying, recording, or otherwise, without the prior permission in writing of the copyright owners.

Library of Congress Catalog Card Number 97-69396

ISBN 0-9606874-9-1

Printed in the United States of America

COAST AIRE PUBLICATIONS
2823 North Yucca Street
Chandler, Arizona 85224-1867
Office (602) 899-6151
FAX (602) 899-7918

CONTENTS

Foreword xv

Preface xvii

CHAPTER 1.
Introduction To The Airline Industry

The Importance Of Air Transport 1
The Size And Scope Of Air Transportation 2
The World's Major Airlines 6
    U.S. Carriers 7
    Alaska Airlines 9
    America West Airlines 10
    American Airlines 10
    Continental Airlines 11
    Delta Air Lines 12
    Northwest Airlines 13
    Southwest Airlines 14
    Trans World Airlines 14
    United Airlines 16
    US Airways 17
King Of The Hill 18
Internal And External Factors
    Influencing Management 21

CHAPTER 2.
Airline Economics

Introduction	31
Supply	32
Airlines Inevitably Produce Excess Capacity	32
Airline Capacity Has A Short Shelf Life	40
Excess Capacity Is Not Easily Reduced	41
Demand	45
Demand Is Highly Cyclical And	
Highly Influenced By External Events	45
Many Consumers View Air Transportation	
As A Fungible Commodity	54
Brand Loyalty Is Soft	55
Demand Is Highly Segmented	56
Costs	59
Price	64
Other Factors Influence Economic Performance	68
Theory Of Perfect Competition	69
Theory Of Economic Regulation	84

CHAPTER 3.
Airline Finance

Profit (Loss)	95
Bankruptcies	113
Leveraged Buy-outs	119
Holding Companies	125
Asset Acquisitions And Horizontal Integration	127
Assessing Individual Carrier Performance	130
Debt: On Balance Sheet, And Off	138
Financial Risk	148
Industry Capital Requirements	153
Sources Of New Capital	160

CHAPTER 4.
Planning: Product Development

Introduction	167
Profit Differentiation	168
Airline Organization	174
Marketing And Operations Management	176
The Planning Process	179
Determining Consumer Preferences	187
Evolving Consumer Preferences	194
Traffic And Revenue Forecasting	197
Route Structures: Hub-And-Spoke vs. Linear Route Systems	200
International Alliances	213
Route Selection	213
International Routes	215
Regional Feeders And Franchisees	218
Fleet Planning	220
Cabin Configuration	225
Frequent Flyer Programs	227
Developing Synergies From Economies Of Scale And Scope	231
Innovation	232
Conservative vs. Aggressive Growth Strategies	233
Performance Monitoring And Evaluation	239
Timing: The Market Cycle	241
Competitive Response	243
Flexibility	247

CHAPTER 5.
Operations: Product Delivery

Scheduling	249
Ground Facilities	252
Maintenance	253
Security	255
The Airline Business As A Service Industry: The Importance Of Human Resources	256

Cabin Service	265
Auxiliary In-Flight Services	270
Auxiliary Non-Flight Services	271
Bundled Travel Services	272
Who's Got The Best Product ?	274

CHAPTER 6.
The Price: Revenue And Inventory Management

Terminology	280
Price And Demand	283
Yield Management	291
Overbooking	302
Types Of Fares	303
Types Of Fare Restrictions	304
Corporate Discounting	307
Liquidating Unsold Inventory	308
Consumer Savings Under Deregulation:	
The Ten Billion Dollar Myth	310

CHAPTER 7.
Promotion And Distribution

Introduction	317
The Evolution Of Airline Reservations Systems	318
The Airline Tariff Publishing Company	322
The Big Four Computer Reservations Systems	323
Public Policy Concerns	325
CRS Regulation	328
Travel Agents	330
The Airline Reporting Corporation	333
Tour Operators	335
Consolidators	336
Direct Distribution	338
Corporate Travel Departments	340
Corporate Communications	341
Advertising	341
Image	343

CHAPTER 8.
Cost Containment

The Impact Of Low-Cost Entrants	347
Overview Of Operating Costs	355
Operational And Equipment Costs	359
Service Costs	367
Labor Costs	368
Marketing And Distribution Costs	395
The Tax Burden	402
Fuel Costs	403
Air Traffic Costs	404
Airport Costs	405
Risk Management	406
Conclusion	406

CHAPTER 9.
Global Marketing And Equity Alliances

The Evolving Environment In International Aviation	407
Intercarrier Relationships	421
International Marketing Alliances	421
Code-Sharing, Blocked Space And Funnel Flights	421
Computer Reservations Systems	435
Frequent Flyer Relationships	436
International Alliances	437
Dating Versus Marriage	437
U.S. Equity Alliances	438
Foreign Equity Alliances	440
European Consolidation	441
The British Air Group	442
The Alcazar Group	445
The Air France Group	446
The Lufthansa Group	447
North American Alliances	448
Antitrust Immunity	448
Emergence Of The Global Megacarriers	450

CHAPTER 10.
Public Policy In Aviation

Introduction	453
Destructive Competition	455
The Unique Characteristics Of Commercial Aviation	459
Consumer Welfare	463
Consumer Equity	468
International Aviation	471
The Relationship Between Government And The Airline Industry In The 21st Century	481
Why Managed Competition May Be Superior To Laissez-Faire	481
Objectives Of Sound Public Policy	485
Overcoming The Financial Morass	487
Lessons To Be Learned	490
Statutory Proposals	493
Managed Competition	494
Enhanced Consumer Equity	496
Stimulating Competitive Access	498
Antitrust Enforcement	499
Prudent Procedure And Process	500
Should More Be Done	501
The Dynamics Of Commercial Aviation In The New Millennium	503

TABLES

Table 1.1—U.S. Airline Market Shares	8
Table 1.2—Major And National Airlines	9
Table 1.3—The Largest U.S. Airlines	19
Table 1.4—Airline Revenue Passenger Kilometers	19
Table 1.5—Airline Passengers Flown	20
Table 1.6—Airline Gross Revenue	21
Table 1.7—Largest Operating Profits	22
Table 1.8—Largest Cargo Carriers	23
Table 2.1—Reasons For Choosing Airlines	37
Table 2.2—Airline Selection Factors	57

Table 3.1—Net Profit Of U.S. Scheduled Passenger Airlines	98
Table 3.2—Net Profit (Loss) Of U.S. Major Airlines	101
Table 3.3—U.S. Economic Expansions	107
Table 3.4—Airline Bankruptcies	114
Table 3.5—Airline Acquisitions	127
Table 3.6—Debt As A Percentage Of Capitalization	139
Table 3.7—U.S. Airline Percentage Of Aircraft Leased	140
Table 3.8—Capitalization And Ratio Analysis	143
Table 3.9—Airline Leases And Interest Expenses As A Percentage Of Operating Expenses	145
Table 3.10—Standard And Poor's Debt Rating	149
Table 3.11—Standard And Poor's Airline Debt Rating	151
Table 3.12—U.S. Airline Fleet Ages	156
Table 3.13—Government Ownership Of Major European Airlines	164
Table 4.1—Reasons For Choosing An Airline: U.S. vs. Non-Residents	191
Table 4.2—Reasons For Choosing An Airline: Male vs. Female	191
Table 4.3—Largest U.S. Metropolitan Areas	201
Table 4.4—Ten Largest U.S. Airports	203
Table 4.5—Ten Largest Foreign Airports	203
Table 4.6—Concentrated Hub Airports	205
Table 4.7—Major Airlines Aircraft Utilization Per Day	210
Table 4.8—Top Ten Tourist Generating Nations	216
Table 4.9—Top Ten Nations Generating Airline Passenger Traffic To And From The U.S.	217
Table 4.10—Largest U.S. Flag Carriers In Domestic And International Markets	219
Table 4.11—Average Age Of Fleet	223
Table 4.12—Major Airlines Stage Three Fleet Composition	225
Table 5.1—Zagat Airline Survey: Foreign Carriers	275
Table 5.2—Zagat Airline Survey: Domestic Carriers	276
Table 5.3—Consumers Report Ranking Of Airlines	277
Table 5.4—University Of Nebraska/Wichita State Airline Quality Rating	277
Table 8.1—Upstart Airlines	350
Table 8.2—Breakdown Of Airline Operating Expenses	356

Table 8.3—U.S. Major Airlines Aircraft Trip Length And Utilization	362
Table 8.4—U.S. Major Airlines Aircraft	365
Table 8.5—Labor Costs At Major U.S. Airlines	373
Table 8.6—Employee Productivity Per Aircraft And Revenue Passenger Mile	377
Table 8.7—Airline Productivity Per Employee	377
Table 8.8—Airline Operating Revenue And Expenses Per Employee	378
Table 8.9—Airline Costs And Revenues	378
Table 8.10—Operating Costs Of Selected Foreign Airlines	380
Table 8.11—Employees Per 1,000 Revenue Passenger Kilometers Of Selected Foreign Airlines	383
Table 8.12—Major Airline Strikes Since Deregulation	388
Table 8.13—Airline Employee Stock Ownership In The 1980s	390
Table 8.14—Wage And Work Rules Exchanged For Equity At Major Airlines	390
Table 8.15—Ownership Alternatives	391
Table 9.1—TWA Funnel Flights Via New York JFK Airport	429
Table 9.2—European Computer Reservations Systems Partners	435
Table 9.3—Asian Computer Reservations Systems Partners	435
Table 9.4—Frequent Flyer Relationships	436
Table 9.5—Foreign Carrier Ownership Of U.S. Airlines	438
Table 9.6—U.S. Airline Equity Interests In Other Carriers	440
Table 9.7—Major Equity Investments Between Foreign Airlines	440
Table 9.8—The British Air Group	442
Table 9.9—The Air France Group	446
Table 9.10—The Lufthansa Group	447
Table 9.11—The Global Megacarriers	451

FIGURES

Figure 1.1—Passengers Carried By U.S. Airlines	5
Figure 1.2—Cargo Ton Miles Flown	6
Figure 2.1—U.S. Airline Load Factors	33

Figure 2.2—Hypothetical S-Curve	37
Figure 2.3—Major U.S. Airline Load Factors By Month	46
Figure 2.4—Major U.S. Airline Load Factors By Day Of Week	46
Figure 2.5—U.S Airline Domestic Intercity Passenger Miles	50
Figure 3.1—Airline Industry Operating Revenue And Profit (Loss)	96
Figure 3.2—Airline Industry Cumulative Net Profit	101
Figure 3.3—Domestic Aviation Fuel Costs	103
Figure 3.4—Percent Changes In Annual Fuel Costs	104
Figure 3.5—U.S. Airline Operating Ratios	105
Figure 3.6—U.S. Airline Industry Net Profit Margin	106
Figure 3.7—Debt As A Percentage Of Total Capital	151
Figure 4.1—Hub-And-Spoke vs. Linear Route Model	207
Figure 6.1—U.S. Airline Discount RPMs And Discount Yields	289
Figure 6.2—U.S. Airline Discount And Full Fares	304
Figure 6.3—U.S. Airline Real Yields	311
Figure 7.1—Computer Reservations Systems: U.S. Market Shares	322
Figure 7.2—World-Wide Market Share Of Computer Reservations Systems	325
Figure 8.1—U.S. Airline Operating Expenses Breakdown	356
Figure 8.2—U.S. Airlines Expenses Per Available Seat Mile	358
Figure 8.3—Airline Labor Costs As A Percentage Of Operating Expenses	370
Figure 8.4—U.S. Airline Employee Average Annual Compensation	374
Figure 8.5—U.S. Major Airlines Available Seat Mile Costs	375
Figure 8.6—Major U.S. Airlines Yield Compared To Costs	379
Figure 8.7—U.S. Airline Industry Marketing Expenses	396
Figure 8.8—Airport Charges	405
Figure 10.1—Rate Of Return On Investment	458
Figure 10.2—Interest On Long-Term Debt	465
Figure 10.3—Domestic Fuel Price	466
Figure 10.4—Yields Per Revenue Passenger Mile	468
Figure 10.5—Domestic Passenger Yields	469
Figure 10.6—The Evolution Of Economic Regulation	491

INDEX 507

About The Authors 529

FOREWORD

The business of flying has fascinated mankind for centuries. Since the dawn of commercial aviation in the early years of the 20th century it has been one of the most closely observed, and frequently commented on, of all the world's businesses.

The technical accomplishments of the world's aircraft and engine manufacturers are genuinely awesome. The notion—50 years ago—that aircraft weighing three quarters of a million pounds would one day fly 400 plus people across distances of more than 6,000 miles would have been considered the stuff of science fiction. Moreover, the idea that traveling by air would become a routine event in the lives of ordinary citizens, which we take for granted today, would have been regarded as fanciful only 40 years ago.

Despite its technological achievements and rush towards ubiquity, air transportation has been anything but a successful commercial enterprise. Measured against the standards associated with virtually every other major industry, aviation's commercial record has been abysmal!

As this book goes to press, commercial aviation is enjoying better economic health than has been true for some time and as has happened often in the past, there are many now predicting that a new confluence of circumstances—described variously by different prognosticators—have righted the industry's economic ship and that clear sailing lies ahead. While I very much doubt that view, I am certain that all those who, like myself, have spent a lifetime pursuing consistent profitability, avidly hope it's so.

Paul Dempsey, one of the co-authors of this volume, is both a seasoned observer of commercial aviation and a long-time friend and colleague. While I have not had the opportunity to share the same kind of personal relationship with Laurence Gesell, the other co-author, he too is recognized in his own right for his contributions to the air transportation industry.

In these pages you'll find a wealth of historical and statistical detail, as well as interesting arguments bearing on various aspects of the past and future of commercial aviation. While I cannot endorse all of the authors' conclusions—Professor Dempsey and I have often debated the cause and effect of various economic phenomena in the industry—I can attest to both his and Professor Gesell's long-standing interest in the mysteries of the industry's economics and their commitment to understanding and explaining them. Serious students of the subject should, therefore, find this a useful volume.

> Robert L. Crandall,
> Chairman and CEO, American Airlines

PREFACE

Few industries are as important to the economic and social wellbeing of a nation as transportation. By collapsing the time/space continuum, aviation allows the world's economies and cultures to cross-fertilize, and markets to proliferate in number and grow in size and wealth. Aviation is an integral part of the infrastructure of a global economy. It is the foundation for commercial exchange and economic growth. Because it defies national boundaries, it is uniquely international in scope.

Since their deregulation in 1978, airlines have undergone profound change. Established airlines have merged, consolidated, or acquired competitors. They established computer reservations systems as vertically integrated distribution systems, and frequent flyer programs to build consumer loyalty. New entrants emerged with a decided comparative advantage in terms of lower wages and more flexible work rules. But both incumbents and upstarts have faced serious difficulty in achieving profitability. More than 100 airlines have fallen into the abyss of bankruptcy since 1978, including such established carriers as Braniff, Pan Am, Eastern, TWA and Continental. Smaller carriers, such as National, North Central, Southern, Hughes Airwest, Frontier, People Express, Ozark, Piedmont, Western, PSA, and Air California, have been absorbed into megacarrier giants. Global marketing and equity alliances have reached across national boundaries to dominate the skies. With the European Union's deregulation in 1997, the pattern of bankruptcies, mergers and consolidations will likely repeat itself on that side of the Atlantic.

In the fiercely competitive environment deregulation unleashed, what characteristics distinguish the winners from the losers? After about two decades of deregulation, several airline survival strategies have emerged. Generally speaking, the more prudently airline management positions its airlines, the better the carrier's chances for survival in the Darwinist environment unleashed by deregulation and liberalization. The strategies for growth and survival for each carrier will differ depending upon its strengths and weaknesses—its size, fleet, route structure, market identity, and consumer affinity.

This book is a companion volume in an Air Transport Series, comprised of Volume I, *Air Transportation: Foundations for the 21st Century*, and Volume II, *Airline Management: Strategies for the 21st Century*. Together, these two volumes take readers through the dark ages and monumental losses suffered collectively by the airlines since deregulation, and into the economic reformation of the post-deregulatory era and the return of profitability. Suggested in the two books are strategies, that if used by all stakeholders in the marketplace economy, might lead to a renaissance in the next century of consistent profitability for the airlines, stable employment for labor, and continuous, reliable and fairly priced air services for consumers.

It is the purpose of this series to acquaint the reader with the principal elements of airline economics, business, finance, marketing, regulation, and management—to bring all the essential elements of commercial aviation within the two-volume series. We hope that, together, the Air Transport Series will be a solid reference for airline and aviation management, and a fundamental text for courses in air transportation, aviation management, business, law, and economics.

We are indebted to several invaluable data sources. Edmund Greenslet's comprehensive *Airline Monitor* provided much of the essential data upon which we have relied, as have the insightful Salomon Brothers' studies. Other sources have been useful, particularly the U.S. General Accounting Office, the U.S. Department of Transportation, the Air Transport Association, and the periodicals *Airline Business, Aviation Daily, Aviation Week & Space Technology,* and *Air Transport World*. We are also indebted to our research assistants, including Kevin Riant, Sam Scinta and Sheri Strailey of the University of Denver College of Law.

Our special thanks go to former Civil Aeronautics Board Chairman L. Welch Pogue, and to American Airlines CEO Robert Crandall, for their thoughtful forewords in each of the respective volumes to this series. We would also like to thank University of Denver Professor

David Barnes, KPMG Peat Marwick Senior Partner Robert Fenimore, University of Portland Professor Richard Gritta, former DOT General Counsel Steve Kaplan, former Frontier Airlines Chairman and Northwest Airlines Senior Vice President M.C. "Hank" Lund, American Airlines General Counsel Anne McNamara, former Continental Airlines Senior Vice President Bill McNamara, Lazard Freres Senior Partner Felix Rohatyn, Frontier Airlines Vice President Bob Schulman, Frontier Airlines General Counsel Art Voss, and USAirways CEO Stephen Wolf for reviewing several draft chapters and providing their constructive criticisms with respect thereto. Other air transportation experts have inspired much of what appears here. These include Frontier Airlines CEO Sam Addoms, Air Line Pilots Association President J. Randolph "Randy" Babbitt, Embry-Riddle Aeronautical University Professor Ron Clark, Airline Industry Resources President Theodore "Ted" Harris, Salomon Brothers' Senior Analyst Julius Maldutis, former Trans World Airlines CEO C.E. "Ed" Meyer, former International Association of Machinists' President John Peterpaul, and former Continental Airlines Senior Vice President Harvey Wexler. A special tribute is paid to the inspiration of the late Martin T. Farris, Regent's Professor Emeritus at Arizona State University. We thank these inspired experts for their contribution to commercial aviation and this book.

This series began with papers delivered at various aviation conferences in Europe, Asia, Australia and North America, presentations before the staffs of major airlines and aviation labor organizations, airport managers, and consulting groups; and similar relationships with various airlines and labor organizations, including Air Canada, American Airlines, Continental Airlines, Frontier Airlines, Lufthansa, the International Federation of Airline Pilots Association, the Air Line Pilots Association, the International Association of Machinists and Aerospace Workers, the Association of Flight Attendants, the Transportation Trades Department of the AFL-CIO, the state transportation agencies of California, Colorado, Iowa, Kansas, Pennsylvania, Virginia, Washington, and Wisconsin, as well as several of the nation's major airports, including Atlanta Hartsfield International, Baltimore/Washington International, Miami International, and Washington National, and other members in the Airports

Council International and the American Association of Airport Executives.

We anticipate this is but the first edition of several for this series. We therefore welcome the reader's constructive criticism. We can be reached at:

Dr. Paul Stephen Dempsey
Professor of Law &
Director, Transportation Law Program
University of Denver College of Law
1900 Olive St.
Denver, CO 80220
e-mail: pdempsey@adm.law.du.edu

Dr. Laurence E. Gesell
Professor,
Department of Aeronautical Management Technology
Arizona State University East
600 South Power Road
Sim Building - 425
Mesa, AZ 85206-6406
e-mail: gesell@asu.edu

CHAPTER 1.

INTRODUCTION TO THE AIRLINE INDUSTRY

"Science, freedom, beauty, adventure: What more could you ask of life? Aviation combined all the elements I loved." [1]
Charles A. Lindbergh, Jr.
Aviator

THE IMPORTANCE OF AIR TRANSPORT

There was a time when a person's entire universe consisted of about a 15 mile radius from his or her home, clan, or tribe. Today, the universe is global. By shrinking the planet, aviation is a principal means of intermingling and integrating disparate economies and cultures, stimulating social and cultural cross-fertilization, economic growth and diversity in an increasingly interdependent global environment. Trade and tourism are heavily reliant on this most modern means of transportation. Whole economic sectors (e.g., hotels, automobile rental firms, convention business, and tourist destinations) depend on safe, dependable, efficient and reasonably priced commercial air transportation.[2] "Just-in-time" inventory has moved to a global scale with the expeditious movement of cargo by air. The economic ripple effect throughout industrial and commercial sectors and geographic regions is profound.

---

[1] Quoted in George Seldes, The Great Quotations 429,430 (1983).
[2] George James, Airline Economics (1982).

Introduction to the Airline Industry

Air transportation facilitates the efficiency of business and government transactions, enabling a larger variety of relationships which, under the law of comparative advantage, stimulate broader economic growth.[3] As President John Kennedy observed, "A rising tide raises all ships." And as Thomas Petzinger put it, "Like bees, airlines pollinate the world's financial system with capital. They create, mobilize, and transport wealth in proportions vastly exceeding the fares paid by the passengers."[4]

As a fundamental component of the infrastructure upon which economic growth is built—the veins and arteries of commerce, communications and national defense—a healthy transportation system offering reasonable prices and ubiquitous service to the public is vitally important to the health of the nation it serves.[5] For that reason, governments the world over have promoted and encouraged its development by providing infrastructure, research and development, protective regulation, subsidies, and outright ownership of airlines. Yet by the end of the 20th Century, governmental paternalism was subsiding, giving way to deregulation, liberalization and market Darwinism. This has created new challenges and opportunities for airline management.

THE SIZE AND SCOPE OF AIR TRANSPORTATION

At the dawn of the 21st Century, more than 1,000 scheduled airlines operate more than 15,000 aircraft. The commercial airline industry carries 1.25 billion passengers and 22 million tons of cargo

---

[3] "Transportation is a fundamental component of economic growth. It is the infrastructure foundation upon which the rest of the economy is built." Paul Dempsey, The Social & Economic Consequences of Deregulation 5 (1989). "[T]ransportation has had a profound effect upon the collective economic growth and intellectual development of man." Paul Dempsey & William Thoms, Law & Economic Regulation in Transportation 1 (1986). Aviation is among the most profound of man's technological accomplishments. Like no other invention, it collapses the time/space continuum. Aviation shrinks the planet, intermingling the world's cultures and economies. It is an integral part of the infrastructure essential to commerce, and national defense. Aviation is mobility for the human race, facilitating travel and tourism, arguably the world's largest single industry. Paul Dempsey, Robert Hardaway & William Thoms, 1 Aviation Law sec. 1.01 (1993), citing Paul Dempsey, Law & Foreign Policy in International Aviation (1987).
[4] Thomas Petzinger, Jr., Hard Landing 341 (1995).
[5] For a review of the importance of transportation, see the companion to this volume, Paul Stephen Dempsey and Laurence E. Gesell, Air Transportation: Foundations for the 21st Century (1997), Chapter 1. For a review of the national defense importance of air transportation, see Richard Kane & Allan Vose, Air Transportation 1-21 to 1-24 (7th ed. 1979).

annually, about a quarter of the world's manufacturing exports based upon value.[6] An average of more than 1 million people board commercial aircraft in the United States every day.

Worldwide, civil aviation employs 22 million people[7] (3 million directly, 7 million indirectly, and 12 million induced). In the United States, more than 2 million Americans are employed in airline or airport operations.[8]

The commercial airline industry accounts for one trillion dollars a year in economic production ($250 billion directly, $250 million indirectly, and $500 billion induced).[9] In the United States, airlines and airports produce gross revenue of more than $250 billion.[10] If the industry were a nation, it would rank seventh in the world in economic production, just ahead of Canada.[11]

Air transportation is an integral part of the tour and travel industry, arguably the world's largest single industry.[12] The tour and travel industry accounts for about 5.5% of the world's gross national products [GNPs].[13] Julius Maldutis noted its tremendous economic importance:

> [The tour and travel industry] generates more than $3.5 trillion of GNP. . . . It employs 127 million people or one out of every 15 workers. It accounts for 12.9% of consumer spending and provides 7.2% of worldwide capital investment, more than $442 billion a year.[14]

In the United States, tourism-intensive industries accounted for 9.8% of all jobs in 1995, up from 6.9% two decades earlier; tourism-intensive industries' share of gross domestic product [GDP] grew from

---

[6] Economic Benefits Study Revisited, ICAO Rev. (Feb. 1994), at 19.
[7] Gunter Eser, Airlines Bleeding to Death, IATA Rev. (Apr. 1991), at 3.
[8] Transportation Research Board, Winds of Change: Domestic Air Transport Since Deregulation 21 (1991).
[9] Id.
[10] Id.
[11] Carrying the Torch Through 1992, Airline Bus., The Skies in 1992 5 (1992).
[12] Gunter Eser, Airlines Bleeding to Death, IATA Rev. (Apr. 1991), at 3.
[13] Id.
[14] Julius Maldutis, Industry Investment Requirements—Looking Beyond 2000 (address before the 7th IATA High-Level Aviation Symposium, Sept. 6, 7, 1993, Cairo, Egypt).

4.1% in 1975 to 5.8% in 1995. A weak dollar improved the attractiveness of the United States as a vacation destination. In 1995, foreign visitors poured $80 billion into the U.S. economy, more than twice what they spent in 1986.[15]

Since the first commercial flights of the 1920s, growth in air transport has been nothing short of spectacular. In 1945, nine million people traveled on scheduled airlines; by the mid-1990s, more than 1.25 billion people flew annually, representing about 25% of the world's population. It is anticipated that by the year 2001, some 1.8 billion passengers will travel, accounting for nearly a third of the world's population.

U.S. carriers transported 1.5 million passengers in 1938 (the year Congress regulated the airline industry). Within a decade, passenger demand had grown 700% (to 14.5 million passengers). The second decade of economic regulation (1948-1958) saw passenger traffic increase 338% (to 49 million passengers). Between 1958 and 1968, traffic grew another 300% (to 150 million passengers). In the last decade of regulation, traffic grew nearly 200% (to 275 million passengers). Congress deregulated the U.S. airline industry in 1978. In the first decade of deregulation (1978-1988), traffic grew by only 165% (to 455 million passengers). By the mid-1990s, U.S. airlines were carrying more than half a billion passengers annually, though traffic was growing at a slower rate than in the pre-deregulation period[16] (see Figure 1.1, "Passengers Carried By U.S. Airlines").

Another (perhaps better) measure of traffic growth is revenue passenger miles [RPMs], or the number of fare paying passengers multiplied by the miles they traveled. In 1948, U.S. airlines flew nearly 6 million domestic RPMs.[17] Within a decade, that number had increased 423% (to 25.4 million RPMs). By 1968, traffic grew 344% (to 87.5 million RPMs). During the last decade of economic regulation (1968-1978), RPMs grew 190% (to 182.7 million RPMs). In the first decade of deregulation (1978-1988), traffic growth increased only 180% (to 329.3 million RPMs). By 1994, U.S. airlines flew 378.8 million RPMs.[18] Both of these measures (decade-by-decade growth

---

[15] Tourism Role Rises, Creating Some Risks, Wall St. J., Oct. 7, 1986, at A1.
[16] Source: Air Transport Association.
[17] Source: Air Transport Association. Data for years preceding 1945 not reported.
[18] Source: Air Transport Association.

rates in passengers enplaned and domestic RPMS), belie the wide spread allegation that deregulation stimulated significant growth in the number of passengers flown.

Figure 1.1—PASSENGERS CARRIED BY U.S. AIRLINES (1938-1995)

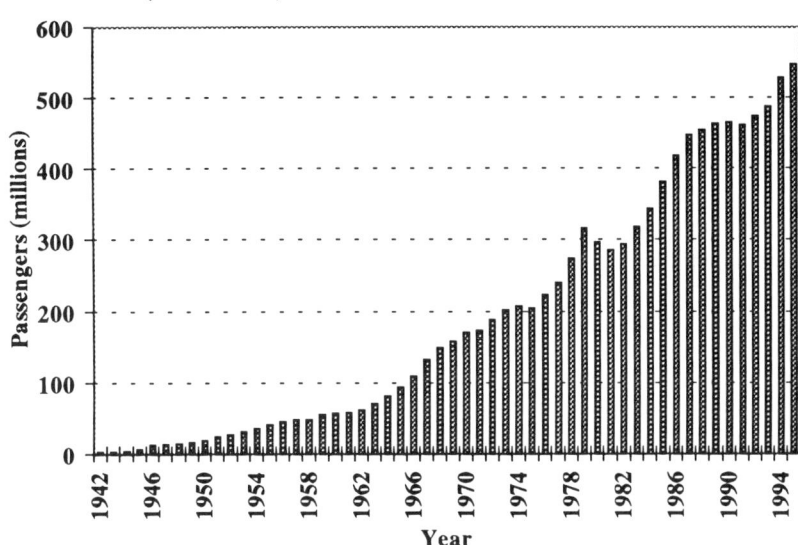

Over the past half century, 25 billion passengers have flown aboard commercial aircraft, the equivalent of nearly five times the world's current population; 350 million tons of freight have been carried by air, the equivalent of one million fully laden Boeing 747s. The world's airlines have flown 36 trillion passenger kilometers during the past half century, the equivalent of about 120,000 round-trips to the Sun.[19] Many project that commercial air transportation will double over the next 10-15 years, growing faster in under-developed nations than developed nations.[20]

Air cargo has enjoyed a robust growth rate, with 2.2 million domestic ton miles flown in 1970, growing to 5.9 million in 1994, or more than two and a half times. International cargo grew six fold

---

[19] Int'l. Civil Aviation Org., Information Kit for ICAO's 50th Anniversary (1994). Ninety-three million miles separates the Earth from the Sun.
[20] Transport Canada, The Greening of Aviation 11 (1996).

Introduction to the Airline Industry

during this period, from 1.3 million ton miles in 1970 to 7.8 million in 1994[21] (see Figure 1.2, " Cargo Ton Miles Flown").

Figure 1.2—CARGO TON MILES FLOWN

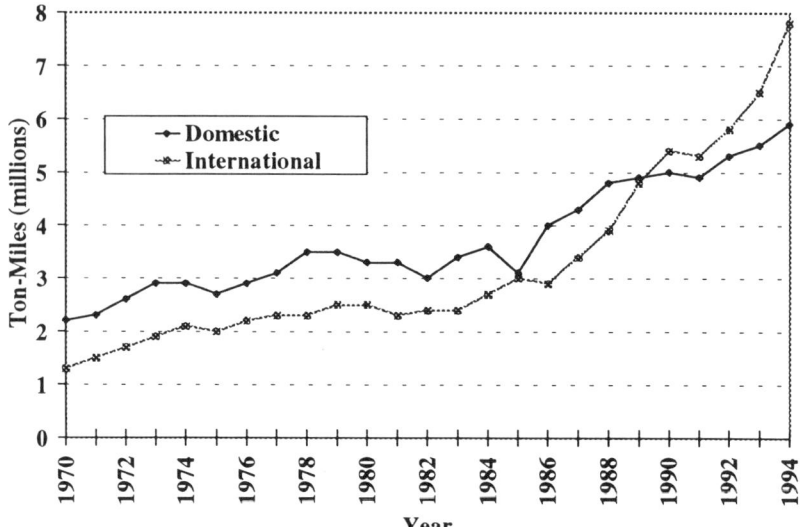

THE WORLD'S MAJOR AIRLINES

Aviation is broadly divided into three categories—military aviation, general aviation, and commercial air carriers. The emphasis of this book is on the latter category, which is sometimes referred to as "air transportation." Air transportation is the carriage by aircraft of persons or property as a "common carrier" for compensation or hire (i.e., a transport company which offers its services to the public generally).[22] A company engaged in air transportation, either directly (i.e., operates its own aircraft) or indirectly (does not operate aircraft), is an air carrier. More commonly, air carriers are referred to by their corporate name, airlines. Commercial airlines may be scheduled, or non-scheduled (charter) carriers. They may be certificated (by the

---

[21] Source: Air Transport Association. Data prior to 1970 not reported.
[22] For a glossary of air transportation terminology, see the companion to this volume, Paul Stephen Dempsey and Laurence E. Gesell, Air Transportation: Foundations for the 21st Century (1997), Chapter 10.

Chapter 1

Department of Transportation) or non-certificated commuters. They may operate over local, regional, national or international routes. They may operate large (60 seats or more) or small (less than 60 seats) commuter aircraft. They may focus their businesses on passengers, cargo transportation, or both.

U.S. CARRIERS

Part 121 of the U.S. Code of Federal Regulations (CFR)[23] defines carriers earning more than $1 billion as "Majors." Those earning more than $100 million but less than $1 billion are "Nationals." Carriers earning less than $100 million are "Regionals."

Prior to deregulation in 1978, 99% of the traffic was carried by the following 19 domestic trunk-line and local service carriers:[24]

Allegheny	Northwest
American	Ozark
Braniff	Pan American
Continental	Piedmont
Delta	Southern
Eastern	Texas International
Frontier	Trans World
Hughes Airwest	United
National	Western
North Central	

This list does not include the charter, or supplemental carriers, which had a significant share of the discretionary market before deregulation, and have been largely eradicated under deregulation.

In 1978, the eight largest airlines had a market share of 80%. However, as Table 1.1, "U.S. Airline Market Shares", reveals, the market share of the eight largest airlines exceeded 90% in the 1990s, a level unprecedented in the history of U.S. aviation. Paradoxically, under economic regulation the industry was becoming less concen-

---

[23] 14 CFR 121.
[24] The Financial Condition of the Airline Industry and the Adequacy of Competition, Hearings Before the Subcomm. on Aviation of the House Comm. on Public Works and Transportation, 102nd Cong., 2d Sess. 171 (1991) (statement of Edward R. Beauvais).

Introduction to the Airline Industry

trated, with the "big four" having 82% of the market in 1938, dropping to 68% in 1950, 66% in 1960, and 59% in 1978, the year deregulation began.[25]

Table 1.1—U.S. AIRLINE MARKET SHARES (1978-1995)[26]
(in percentage of revenue passenger miles)

Carrier	1978	1983	1984	1985	1989	1990	1991	1994	1995
United	17.4	16.0	15.5	12.5	16.4	16.7	18.5	21.0	21.0
American	12.8	12.7	12.4	13.3	17.3	17.0	18.6	19.4	19.3
TWA	11.9	10.1	9.6	9.6	8.3	7.5	6.3	4.8	4.7
Eastern	11.1	10.5	9.9	10.0	2.7	3.7	0	0	0
Delta	10.3	9.6	9.2	9.0	14.0	13.0	15.2	16.8	16.0
Pan Am	9.3	10.7	9.5	8.1	6.8	6.8	4.1	0	0
Continental	3.8	3.5	3.7	4.9	9.1	8.6	9.4	8.1	7.5
Northwest	3.1	6.6	6.7	6.7	10.8	11.3	12.0	11.2	11.7
USAir	1.8	2.7	2.8	2.9	8.0	7.8	7.7	7.5	7.2

By the mid-1990s, the four largest U.S. airlines controlled 68% of the market.[27] A doubling of an airline's market share on a particular route translates into a price increase of almost nine percent. In 1990, 76% of all passengers in domestic markets flew on routes served by three or fewer airlines; 45% flew on routes served by only one or two carriers.[28] Table 1.2, "Major And National Airlines", shows the top major and national airlines of the 1990s.

---

[25] Paul Dempsey, Robert Hardaway & William Thoms, 1 Aviation Law & Regulation §1.05 (1993).
[26] Washington Post National Weekly Edition, Dec. 10-16, 1990; Aviation Daily (Mar. 13, 1985); Aviation Daily (Feb. 5, 1986); Aviation Daily (Jan. 29, 1991), at 189; Aviation Daily (Jan. 21, 1992), at 124.
[27] See American Captures Nearly 21 Percent of Major's RPMs, Aviation Daily (Feb. 19, 1992), at 301.
[28] GAO, U.S. Airlines: Weak Financial Condition Threatens Competition 10 (1991).

Table 1.2—MAJOR AND NATIONAL AIRLINES
(during the mid-1990s)

The Major Airlines

Alaska	Northwest
America West	Southwest
American	TWA
Continental	United
Delta	USAir

The National Airlines

Aloha	Midwest Express
American Trans Air	Tower
Hawaiian	Trump Shuttle
Horizon	Westair
MarkAir	

Of the 148 new carriers reporting financial data to the U.S. Department of Transportation [DOT] since deregulation in 1978, by 1991, only 44 remained.[29] Commuter airlines, operating fewer than 30 seats, are governed by Part 135 of the Code of Federal Regulations.[30] In 1978, 210 (Part 135) commuter airlines offered passenger service; by 1991, there were but 176, and the largest 50 carried 92% of all commuter passengers.[31] Following is a brief examination of the principal characteristics of each of the major airlines:

ALASKA AIRLINES

Before airline deregulation in 1978, Alaska Airlines served primarily as a territorial carrier for the Alaska interior, but with a route segment connecting Anchorage with Seattle in the lower 48

---

[29] Transportation Research Board, Winds of Change: Domestic Air Transport Since Deregulation 31 (1991).
[30] 14 CFR 135.
[31] Transportation Research Board, Winds of Change: Domestic Air Transport Since Deregulation 31(1991).

Introduction to the Airline Industry

states. Following the onset of deregulation, Alaska Airlines established its presence as an interstate and international carrier. In 1985 the Alaska Air Group was created as a holding company. Its principal wholly owned subsidiaries are Alaska Airlines and Horizon Air.[32]

Alaska Airlines provides scheduled service to 37 airports in six states (Alaska, Washington, Oregon, California, Nevada and Arizona), three cities in Mexico, and four cities in Russia. Many of its smaller communities are served through code share agreements with local carriers, including Horizon Air. Horizon itself serves 35 cities in five states (Washington, Oregon, Montana, Idaho, and California) and four cities in Canada.

By the mid-nineties Alaska Airlines had become one of ten major airlines in the U.S. Its revenues exceeded $1.4 billion in 1995.

AMERICA WEST AIRLINES

Of the more than 200 new airlines spawned by deregulation, America West is the only one which managed both to make it into the big leagues of the majors and to survive into the 1990s. America West has significant market share at its two hubs—Phoenix and Las Vegas. After a period of rapid and optimistic expansion, it stumbled into Chapter 11 bankruptcy. America West was extricated from bankruptcy by the Bonderman group, which had also taken control of Continental.

AMERICAN AIRLINES

American Airlines is among the largest airlines in the world. American has been responsible for a disproportionate number of the industry's innovations. It pioneered computer reservations systems [CRS], and today owns the nation's largest, Sabre. In 1981, it inaugurated frequent flyer programs.[33] In 1984, American was the first airline to institute a two-tier wage structure, allowing it to expand at

---

[32] See Moody's Transportation Manual (1978/1996).
[33] Transportation Research Board, Winds of Change: Domestic Air Transport Since Deregulation 54 (1991).

Chapter 1

lower cost.[34] It transformed yield management from an art form into a science.

In addition to expanding its Dallas/Ft. Worth operations into a major hub (to which it moved its corporate headquarters from New York in 1979), it established hubs at Chicago O'Hare, San Jose, Nashville, and Raleigh/Durham, and international gateways at Miami and San Juan. American is the second largest airline at Chicago O'Hare, the world's busiest airport. Although it closed its hubs at San Jose, Nashville and Raleigh/Durham, American is the dominant carrier at Dallas/Ft. Worth, Miami, and San Juan.

American invested more than $1 billion in overseas expansion after 1989, beginning with the purchase of Eastern's Latin American routes (which Eastern had earlier bought from bankrupt Braniff). American also purchased several of TWA's routes to London Heathrow airport, and a Seattle-Tokyo route from Continental. Nonetheless, it still has a relatively weak presence in the Pacific Rim.[35] American had planned to invest $20 billion in capital spending by 1995, mostly for new, fuel-efficient aircraft, and expanded domestic facilities.[36] But as profits plummeted, American rolled back capital spending plans by $8 billion through the mid-1990s.[37] American Airlines has the largest fleet in the U.S. industry, which is among the youngest of any major U.S. airline.[38]

CONTINENTAL AIRLINES

Continental is a blend of corporate cultures and airlines. It has been described as "the product of myriad mergers, [with] a raucous recent history that sometimes bordered on the schizophrenic under former chairman Frank Lorenzo. It's a crazy quilt of airlines forged from hostile takeovers, frequent bankruptcies, employee standoffs, midnight firings, and one shocking suicide."[39]

In the early 1980s, Frank Lorenzo's Texas International acquired larger Continental in a leveraged buy-out; the two were consolidated.

---

[34] Pulley & O'Brian, Flight Plans: How the Airlines Stack Up, Wall St. J., June 17, 1991, at B1.
[35] Snapshot of the World's Major International Airlines, Wall St. J., Jan. 14, 1992, at A8.
[36] Pulley & O'Brian, Flight Plans: How the Airlines Stack Up, Wall St. J., June 17, 1991, at B1.
[37] Snapshot of the World's Major International Airlines, Wall St. J., Jan. 14, 1992, at A8.
[38] AMR, Third Quarter Report 4 (1991).
[39] Lollar, It's Not Easy Being Fourth ... Or Fifth, Frequent Flyer (Nov. 1991), at 8.

Introduction to the Airline Industry

In December 1990, Continental Airlines entered Chapter 11 bankruptcy for the second time (some call it Chapter 22 bankruptcy). It had first entered bankruptcy in 1983 (at which time it tore up its union contracts), and emerged from it in 1986, in time for Lorenzo to go on a buying binge, picking up People Express (including Frontier Airlines, Britt and PBA), Eastern Airlines, and Rocky Mountain Airways. Continental is dominant in Houston, Newark and Cleveland, and was formerly a major hub competitor at Denver. For a short while in the 1990s, it attempted to establish a hub at Greensboro, North Carolina.

Much of Continental's debt was put on in its acquisition of People Express, Frontier and Eastern, which raised its long-term debt obligations to more than 78% of its assets, almost twice the percentage of the four largest airlines.[40] In 1990, Continental Airline Holdings lost $2.34 billion on revenues of $6.23 billion; in 1991, it lost $341 million on revenue of $5.4 billion.[41] Lorenzo departed.

In 1992, Continental proposed a plan of reorganization to trade debt for equity, wiping out shareholder equity, thereby reducing the company's long-term liability from $5.1 billion to $1.7 billion, and rolling back its interest expenses by $270 million a year.[42] With the help of Air Canada, David Bonderman and partners plucked Continental out of it's second bankruptcy, installing Gordon Bethune as Chief Executive officer [CEO]. SAS, which theretofore owned nearly 19% of Continental, wrote down its investment to zero.

DELTA AIR LINES

Traditionally, Delta was regarded as providing among the highest levels of service in the industry and having the most loyal and best paid employees. It was also known as among the most conservative of airlines. Before it acquired Salt Lake City-hubbed Western Airlines for

---

[40] Continental, Aviation Daily (Dec. 19, 1990), at 525.
[41] Michelle Mahoney, Continental Ekes Out Fourth-Quarter Profit, Denver Post, Feb. 8, 1992, at 1C, 2C.
[42] Michelle Mahoney, No Layoffs in Continental Plan, Stockholders Would Lose Equity, Denver Post, Feb. 7, 1992, at 1C; O'Brian, Continental Air Reorganization Plan Erases Stock, Makes Creditors Owners, Wall St. J., Feb. 7, 1992, at A5.

$860 million in 1986, Delta had not acquired an airline since it purchased Northeast in 1972.[43]

Delta is well positioned domestically (with its hubs of Atlanta, Cincinnati, and Salt Lake City, and its purchase of Pan Am's Washington-New York shuttle), and internationally (with its purchase of Pan Am's major transatlantic and European services, hubbed in Frankfurt).[44] Delta is best positioned to capitalize on the economic growth of Eastern Europe, although with European Union liberalization, EU carriers will likely enter the type of destructive competition which characterized the domestic U.S. market in the 1980s. Delta is also expanding in Asia.[45]

In order to build global alliances and avoid a takeover attempt, in the late 1980s Delta traded blocks of 5% of its stock with both Singapore Airlines and Swissair, two of the most highly regarded airlines in the world.[46]

NORTHWEST AIRLINES

Northwest entered deregulation with perhaps the strongest balance sheet in the industry. Unfortunately, this would make it a prime candidate for a leveraged buy-out [LBO], which turned one of the industry's strongest balance sheets into one of the weakest. Until then, Northwest had produced 39 straight years of profitability, a record no other U.S. carrier could match.[47]

In 1986, Northwest acquired Republic Airlines for $884 million, itself a product of the mergers of North Central, Southern and Hughes Airwest. That gave Northwest significant domestic feed for its international routes, and control of the hubs of Minneapolis/St. Paul, Detroit, and Memphis. Of the three, Detroit is potentially the most

---

[43] Delta to Buy Western Air for $860 Million, Wall St. J., Sep. 10, 1986, at 3.
[44] See Lollar, Delta's Wild Blue Yonder, Frequent Flyer (Oct. 1991), at 8.
[45] Snapshot of the World's Major International Airlines, Wall St. J., Jan. 14, 1992, at A8.
[46] Delta Sued Again Over Pan Am Deal, Denver Post, Mar. 13, 1992, at 2C. One potential problem for Delta lies in litigation flowing from the demise of Pan Am. Pan Am folded on December 4, 1991, a day after Delta announced it would cut the flow of money it had allegedly promised. One suit, seeking $1.1 billion was filed by Pan Am employees thrown out of work. Delta counterclaimed, alleging that the demise of Pan Am was caused by its unsecured creditors. Delta Says Pan Am's Failure Was Caused By Its Creditors, Aviation Daily (Apr. 7, 1992), at 38.
[47] Smith Barney, Northwest Airlines Corp. (Sept. 8, 1994).

important, with its huge origin-and-destination [O&D] base of five million people.

Northwest "Orient" Airlines was the first airline to provide scheduled service to Japan, and has a strong presence in the fast-growing trans-Pacific market.[48] In the late 1980s, Northwest entered into a strategic equity and marketing alliance with Amsterdam-based KLM Royal Dutch Airlines.

SOUTHWEST AIRLINES

Under maverick Herb Kelleher, Southwest has been profitable by following a course alien to the other airlines. Instead of establishing a hub-and-spoke system, Southwest flies a linear route system focused on frequent, short flights with low-cost no-frills service exclusively in Boeing 737s, predominantly between smaller airports not generally served by the megacarriers.[49] "We have sort of lived off the scraps of the table of the mega-carriers," said Kelleher. "But I know lots of fat little puppies that have lived off table scraps."[50]

Southwest began in 1971 as a Texas intrastate airline flying 737s between Houston, Dallas and San Antonio. The Wright Amendment restricts service at close-in Dallas Love Airport to airlines flying from states contiguous to Texas. This has enabled Southwest to maintain a complete monopoly at Love—the world's only airport monopoly of consequence. Southwest also controls 78% of Houston Hobby Airport. Southwest has enjoyed higher profitability than any other major airline.[51] In 1995, Southwest flew a relatively young fleet of 224 Boeing 737 aircraft between 45 cities.[52]

TRANS WORLD AIRLINES

TWA entered deregulation as the nation's fourth largest airline, and the industry's most enviable route structure, although it had earlier

---

[48] Paul Dempsey & Andrew Goetz. Airline Deregulation & Laissez Faire Mythology 119 (1992).
[49] Pulley & O'Brian, Flight Plans: How the Airlines Stack Up, Wall St. J., June 17, 1991, at B1; Kahan, The Exceptional Survivor, The American Prospect (Winter 1992), at 45.
[50] American Trying to Cope With Low-Cost Success Southwest, Aviation Daily (Feb. 18, 1992), at 287.
[51] Id.
[52] Southwest Airlines Co., Annual Report (1995).

suffered from the eccentricities of its owner, Howard Hughes. Prior to deregulation, TWA diversified into several non-seasonal industries to balance its fluctuations in profitability—Hilton International, Century 21, Canteen Corporation and Spartan Foods. This diversion was to cost it market share. Ultimately, it spun off these properties.

In the mid-1980s, TWA became a leveraged buy-out target of Frank Lorenzo, then Carl Icahn. Labor was willing to surrender significant concessions to Icahn to avoid the dreaded union-buster Lorenzo. Shortly thereafter, TWA executed a pre-existing plan to acquire Ozark, giving it dominance at St. Louis Lambert International Airport.

After its acquisition, Icahn took the company private and began cannibalizing many of its properties (including its important U.S.-London Heathrow authority, which was critical to its once dominant presence on the North Atlantic). In 1992, Icahn announced a "prepackaged" Chapter 11 filing for TWA, beyond which some analysts predicted only another 18 to 36 months of life.[53] One analyst gave TWA only a 50-50 chance of reorganizing successfully.[54] In 1992, it sold off Chicago O'Hare landing slots and properties, an airport at which it once had a significant presence.[55]

In 1990, TWA carried more than $2.5 billion in debt.[56] By 1991, it was reported that TWA's debt had been reduced to $1.4 billion.[57] Interest payments exceeded 8% of operating costs at both TWA and Eastern—the highest in the industry.[58] By the mid-1990s, TWA flew the oldest fleet of aircraft of any major airline in the U.S. and, under Icahn, consistently ranked among the worst airlines in terms of consumer complaints and on-time performance. Icahn's departure in the early 1990s, employee ownership, and a third prepackaged

---

[53] Snapshot of the World's Major International Airlines, Wall St. J., Jan. 14, 1992, at A8.
[54] TWA Surprises Industry with Early Chapter 11 Bankruptcy Filing, Aviation Daily (Feb. 3, 1992), at 199.
[55] Pulley & Hirsch, TWA to Switch Bulk of Business to Midway Site, Wall St. J., May 13, 1992, at A5.
[56] Carl Icahn Considering Sale of TWA in Two-Step Process, Aviation Daily (May 7, 1990), at 247. Other sources report that TWA owed $3.2 billion in long-term debt, lease obligations and unfunded pension liability. Smith, Pan Am Stock Soars as Icahn Makes New Bid, Wall St. J., Dec. 18, 1990, at A4.
[57] Michelle Mahoney, Airline Merger Brewing, Denver Post, Dec. 13, 1991, at 1A, 14A.
[58] Aviation Daily (July 30, 1990), at 192; Aviation Daily (Feb. 19, 1991), at 326; Aviation Daily (Nov. 7, 1991), at 248.

bankruptcy gave TWA a new lease on life. Perhaps like Mark Twain, the reports of TWA's death were greatly exaggerated. TWA is the dominant carrier at St. Louis, and operated two terminals at New York's John F. Kennedy Airport. It abandoned efforts to establish a minor hub at Atlanta.

UNITED AIRLINES

United was the only major airline to support deregulation. As the nation's largest carrier, with 17% of the passenger market, it thought itself better able to grow without the benevolent presence of the Civil Aeronautics Board. But under Richard Ferris, it blundered almost immediately, by pulling out of short haul markets (selling off scores of 737s, for example), and concentrating on long-haul traffic. United soon learned that the smaller airlines were not content to feed it, inaugurating their own long-haul routes. United soon reversed course, began repurchasing smaller aircraft, and establishing hub-and-spoke systems.

United also strayed off course by buying related travel companies—it added Hertz Rent-a-Car and Hilton International Hotels to its existing Westin Hotel chain under a holding company awkwardly named Allegis. Whatever the potential value of creating a one-stop travel conglomerate, United failed to integrate the system. The corporate raiders began to circle, and United reversed course again, spinning off the non-airline properties, and dropping the Allegis label.

In the meantime, United's market share had slipped significantly. It was not able to achieve its pre-deregulation market share until 1991, by which time American had surpassed it as the nation's largest airline.

But United did several things quite right. It established hub systems radiating from San Francisco, Denver, Chicago and Washington (Dulles), covering both coasts and the interior with hubs spread about quarter way across the continent. In 1991, United announced its purchase of Air Wisconsin, which increased its number of slots at Chicago O'Hare by 16%, giving it clear dominance over American.

United also seized many of the primary international routes of a disintegrating Pan Am. United purchased Pan Am's trans-pacific operations for $715 million, its London Heathrow and fifth-freedom beyond rights for $400 million, and its Latin American operations for $135 million.[59] Although United canceled a large block of smaller aircraft,[60] it left standing orders for long-haul wide-bodied Boeing 747 and 777 planes, which will be fed into United's growing international system. United's Apollo is one of the world's two strongest computer reservations systems.

United lost $94.5 million in 1990, and a record $331.9 million in 1991.[61] As a consequence of United's unprecedented losses, it cut capital spending by $6.7 billion, or 35%, between 1993 and 1995.[62] CEO Stephen Wolf departed as labor assumed a controlling interest in the largest Employee Stock Ownership Plan (ESOP) ever consummated in any U.S. industry.

US AIRWAYS [63]

In 1987, USAir (now US Airways and formerly Allegheny Airlines) purchased Pacific Southwest Airlines for $400 million, and Piedmont for $1.56 billion. In 1989, USAir merged operations with Piedmont, although it had considerable difficulty digesting that acquisition, with both service and profitability turning south.[64] USAir suffered a record net loss of $454 million in 1990, and $305 million in 1991.[65] In order to cut costs, USAir pulled out of the competitive California markets it entered with the PSA purchase, laid off 7,000 employees, and asked the rest for 20% wage concessions.[66]

Until the mid-1990s, USAir had a relatively weak presence internationally, which it attempted to expand by purchasing TWA's authority to London from Philadelphia and Boston for $50 million.[67] It also entered into an equity and marketing alliance with British Airways

---

[59] Snapshot of the World's Major International Airlines, Wall St. J., Jan. 14, 1992, at A8.
[60] Pulley & O'Brian, Flight Plans: How the Airlines Stack Up, Wall St. J., June 17, 1991, at B1.
[61] United Lays Off 534, Warns of More Cuts, Denver Post, Feb. 22, 1992, at 1C.
[62] Id.
[63] Renamed USAirways in 1996.
[64] USAir Scaling Back Expansion Plans for 12-24 Months, Aviation Daily (Aug. 15, 1990), at 286.
[65] Pulley, USAir May Have Trouble Getting Unions to Agree to Other Workers' Concessions, Wall St. J., Oct. 7, 1991, at A4; Pulley, USAir's Vice Chairman Malin Ousted, Apparently Blamed for Carrier's Woes, Wall St. J., Feb. 5, 1992, at A12.
[66] Pulley, USAir May Have Trouble Getting Unions to Agree to Other Workers' Concessions, Wall St. J., Oct. 7, 1991, at A4.
[67] Snapshot of the World's Major International Airlines, Wall St. J., Jan. 14, 1992, at A8.

whereby USAir provided domestic feeder service into BA's long-haul wide-bodied international system. As US Airways, the carrier may also need to trim a few of its hubs east of the Mississippi.[68] It dominates Pittsburgh, Charlotte, and Baltimore (though Southwest now threatens it in Baltimore), and with the demise of Eastern and Midway has significant market share in Philadelphia. It has dismantled the once-profitable Dayton hub it inherited from Piedmont. USAir solidified its east coast operations with the purchase of Continental's new LaGuardia terminal and landing slots for $61 million, and the signing of an agreement to operate (and an option to buy) the Trump Shuttle, which flies between New York's LaGuardia, Boston's Logan, and Washington's National Airports.[69] The shuttle is saddled with some $380 million in debt, an enormous burden for such a small airline.[70] Unfortunately, US Airways must compete with mighty Delta in the shuttle market. US Airways holds 168 jet slots and 28 commuter slots at LaGuardia, and 150 jet slots and 148 commuter slots at Washington National Airport.[71]

KING OF THE HILL

Which airline is dominant? As of 1995, the largest U.S. airlines as measured by revenue passenger miles [RPMs] and available seat miles [ASMs] are shown on Table 1.3, "The Largest U.S. Airlines."

Thus, United appears to be the largest airline in terms of both RPMs and ASMs. This was not always so. For several years in the late 1980s and early 1990s, American Airlines pulled ahead of United. United was distracted by other endeavors (horizontally integrating hotel chains and car rental agencies under a single roof), while American used the B-tier wage rates[72] it had negotiated with labor to expand briskly, which enabled it to lower its average unit costs. United's management re-focused itself, and American's labor unions negotiated away the B-scale, so United has now pulled ahead again.

---

[68] Pulley, USAir May Have Trouble Getting Unions to Agree to Other Workers' Concessions, Wall St. J., Oct. 7, 1991, at A4.
[69] Takemoto, Go East, Frequent Flyer (Mar. 1992), at 8.
[70] See USAir Plan to Run Trump Shuttle Gets Approval from U.S., Wall St. J., Mar. 30, 1992, at A4.
[71] Continental Selling LaGuardia Assets to USAir, Aviation Daily (Nov. 19, 1991), at 298.
[72] On a two tiered wage-scale.

Chapter 1

Table 1.3—THE LARGEST U.S. AIRLINES (1995) [73]

Carrier	RPM%	ASM%
UAL (United)	20.954	19.994
AMR (American)	19.331	19.626
Delta	15.997	16.448
Northwest	11.744	11.052
Continental	7.523	7.713
USAir	7.154	7.414
TWA	4.678	4.789
Southwest	4.383	4.571
America West	2.501	2.454

As shown in Table 1.4, "Airline Revenue Passenger Kilometers," at this writing, United is also largest among the world's airlines. These data reveal that BA, Japan Airlines, Lufthansa and Air France are the largest non-U.S. carriers.

Table 1.4—AIRLINE REVENUE PASSENGER KILOMETERS [74]

Carrier	RPKs (billions)	
	1994	1995
UAL (United)	174	180
AMR (American)	153	166
Delta	138	139
British Airways	96	96
Northwest Airlines	94	79
Japan Airlines	64	73
Lufthansa Group	73	72
Continental Airlines	67	64
USAir Group	61	61
Air France Group	63	52

---

[73] Aviation Daily (Jan. 23, 1996), at 114.
[74] Airline Bus. (Sept. 1995), at 47; Airline Bus. (Sept. 1996), at 51.

Introduction to the Airline Industry

Another measure of size is number of passengers flown. For many years, Eastern Airlines flew the most passengers. At this writing, and by this measure, Delta is the world's largest airline (see Table 1.5, "Airline Passengers Flown").

Table 1.5—AIRLINE PASSENGERS FLOWN [75]

Carrier	Passengers (millions)	
	1994	1995
Delta	89.1	88.9
AMR (American)	81.1	79.8
UAL (United)	74.0	79.0
USAir Group	59.5	56.7
Northwest Airlines	45.6	49.3
Southwest Airlines	42.7	44.8
Lufthansa Group	37.7	40.7
All Nippon Airways	35.8	37.6
Continental Airlines	42.2	37.6
British Airways	35.6	32.3

The data in Table 1.5 reveal that airlines with relatively short average stage lengths (such as Southwest, USAir, and All Nippon Airways), tend to rank higher under this measure, for they are scheduling their aircraft for more city-pair segments per day. But a more important measure than distance and passengers is revenue. As measured by gross revenue, American is the world's largest airline (see Table 1.6, "Airline Gross Revenue").

Perhaps the most important ingredient of all in measuring performance (although at times appearing elusive to airline management) is profit. Airline profitability is highly volatile, and any snap-shot of profitability for one year may not depict the same relative performance in another. Carriers which have been consistently profitable over a long period of time include Southwest Airlines, Singapore Airlines, and Cathay Pacific.

---

[75] Id.

Table 1.6—AIRLINE GROSS REVENUE [76]

Carrier	Sales (U.S. $ billions)	
	1994	1995
AMR (American)	16.1	16.9
Japan Airlines	10.4	15.0
UAL (United)	14.0	14.9
Lufthansa Group	11.6	13.9
Delta Air Lines	12.1	12.2
British Airways	11.2	12.1
Federal Express	9.4	10.3
All Nippon Airways	9.2	10.0
Northwest Airlines	9.1	9.1
Air France	10.1	8.0

Tables 1.7 and 1.8 reveal operating profits for the world's airlines. Table 1.7, "Largest Operating Profits", shows that of the world carriers, British Airways has the largest operating profit. With the eradication of global trade barriers, and the development of "just-in-time" inventory, air cargo has become among the fastest growing areas of air transportation (see Table 1.8, "Largest Cargo Carriers").

INTERNAL AND EXTERNAL FACTORS INFLUENCING MANAGEMENT

In order to develop strategic vision for an airline, management must assess the internal and external factors which determine the potential opportunities to be seized and the problems or difficulties to be avoided or arrested. Among internal factors affecting the well-being of an existing airline, new management will have inherited a fleet of equipment, an experienced core of operational and clerical staff and management with a unique set of skills, corporate culture and labor agreements, a route structure, airport leases, maintenance facilities, market identity, consumer affinity, and a mix of debt and equity.

---

[76] Airline Bus. (Sept. 1995), at 28; Airline Bus. (Sept. 1996), at 51.

Table 1.7—LARGEST OPERATING PROFITS [77]

Carrier	Operating Profit (U.S. $ million)	
	1994	1995
British Airways	961	1,139
AMR (American)	1,006	1,015
Northwest	830	902
UAL (United)	521	829
Singapore Airlines	657	741
SAS Group	293	671
Delta	(217)	661
Alitalia	528	636
Qantas	582	635
Federal Express	591	624
Lufthansa Group	212	585
Cathay Pacific	336	467
Continental	(11)	385
Korean Airlines	339	376
Thai Airways	337	376
Japan Airlines	n.a.	325
USAir	(487)	322
Southwest Airlines	456	313
KLM	442	283

Sometimes companies reflect the intellectual and psychological strengths and weaknesses of their leaders (their depth of knowledge or analytical ability, their self-confidence or insecurity, as well as their temperament, benign or predatory), or the dehumanized impersonal atmosphere of large bureaucracies.

Rakesh Gangwal, then senior vice president of United Airlines, observed, "You have to play the cards you are dealt." Like playing a game of cards, the first task of management is to carefully assess the cards in its hand, and determine which are worth keeping, and which

---

[77] Airline Bus. (Sept. 1995), at 43; Airline Bus. (Sept. 1996), at 51; ESG Aviation Services, The Airline Monitor (Mar./Apr. 1996).

Chapter 1

Table 1.8—LARGEST CARGO CARRIERS [78]

Carrier	Freight tonne km (millions)	
	1994	1995
Federal Express	6,995	7,473
Lufthansa Group	5,688	6,235
United Parcel Service	4,269	5,367
Air France Group	4,400	4,599
Korean Air Lines	4,030	4,418
Singapore Airlines	3,472	3,918
KLM Royal Dutch Airlines	3,427	3,813
Japan Airlines	3,884	3,798
United Airlines	3,031	3,635
Northwest Airlines	3,401	3,615
British Airways	3,354	3,476

should be discarded. In other words, what are the airline's most significant strengths and weaknesses? How can it build on its strengths, and overcome its weaknesses? Can it improve its hand? Tactical and strategic planning can be important tools in helping it achieve desired objectives.[79]

Management in a new airline faces a somewhat different set of problems and opportunities in picking up a fresh hand of cards, several of its own choosing. Of course, its financial strength will significantly influence management's ability to control its own destiny.

To build an airline from scratch requires putting into place the financing, aircraft, maintenance, gates, marketing, advertising, catering, baggage handling, managerial and operational staff and their training, and satisfying the legal and regulatory hurdles necessary to begin service. It must develop a marketing plan and a strategic vision to identify a market niche likely to satisfy consumer needs and generate sufficient revenue to cover costs and produce a profit. It must be sufficiently flexible to shift course should unanticipated problems arise.

---

[78] Airline Bus. (Sept. 1995), at 47; Airline Bus. (Sept. 1996), at 51.
[79] See infra, Chapter 4.

Introduction to the Airline Industry

Management in both new and existing airlines must also make a careful assessment of external factors likely to contribute to the firm's health or illness. Among the most significant external factors are the following:

1. Management must size up its competitors and its markets, as well as their strengths and weaknesses;[80]
2. The market cycle (inflation or recession) can profoundly influence demand and revenue for air transportation services;[81]
3. Increases or decreases in fuel prices are external factors which can have profound impacts on costs and revenue, respectively, and are largely beyond the control of management;[82]
4. The legal, regulatory and political regime—safety, antitrust, tax, labor, environmental, and international policies, for example—may influence an airline's destiny;[83]
5. Management must also come to grips with the broader economic characteristics of air travel, including such concepts as derived demand, cyclical demand, price elasticity of demand, and the "S" curve relationship between capacity and frequency, on the one hand, and revenue and yield on the other;[84] and,
6. Technology also plays an important role in determining the cost and operational characteristics of the essential engines of production—aircraft.[85]

France's Institute of Air Transport has summarized the factors which exert a strong influence on air transportation, in perceived order of importance:

1. The world economy (gross domestic product, international trade);
2. World-wide geopolitics;
3. Oil prices;

---

[80] See infra, Chapter 4.
[81] See infra, Chapter 3.
[82] See infra, Chapter 8.
[83] See Paul Stephen Dempsey & Laurence E. Gesell, Air Transportation: Foundations for the 21st Century (1997), Chapter 5.
[84] See infra, Chapter 2.
[85] See Paul Stephen Dempsey & Laurence E. Gesell, Air Transportation: Foundations for the 21st Century (1997), Chapter 2.

Chapter 1

4. Environmental concerns (e.g., ecology, noise, air quality);
5. Regional development policies;
6. Impact of new communication technologies;
7. Mobility, management of time, and organization of production;
8. Technical aerospace developments;
9. Air transport organization and policy (deregulation, industry structure);
10. Air space congestion;
11. Competition from high-speed trains; and,
12. Marketing innovations (e.g., computer reservation systems, elimination of tickets, and other uses of computer technology).[86]

The initial hurdle is acquiring the salient information essential for analysis. The second is assessing it objectively. The third task is devising an appropriate strategic plan designed to achieve both short-term and long-term objectives.[87] Unfortunately, the market volatility unleashed by deregulation has led management at many airlines to focus myopically on the short-term. Moreover, change is perhaps the only constant in the dynamic airline industry. Management must be sufficiently flexible and adaptable to deal with unforeseen events. Contingency planning is crucial.[88]

The primary goal of any airline is its moral and ethical, as well as legal and regulatory responsibility to fly passengers safely. A companion goal must be to achieve profitability, for without it, no company can survive in the long-term. Of course, giving consumers a combination of price and service options that they prefer is the principal means of achieving profitability.

But the real question is often how well management can "weather the storm" in the sense that external factors (particularly the market cycle and fuel costs) are so profoundly influential. Sometimes, the best management can do during deep recession and a spike in the price of fuel is apply tourniquets to reduce the company's economic hemorrhage.

---

[86] J. Pavaux, General Introduction: Air Transport and Its Prospects, in Air Transport: Horizon 2020—Key Factors and Future Prospects (1995).
[87] See infra, Chapter 4.
[88] Charles Banfe, Airline Management 121 (1989).

Charles Banfe insists, "The best indicator of a management's success is a profitable airline."[89] While easy to measure, profitability may not always be an appropriate measure of the quality and skills of management, for the analysis is unidimensional. Certainly, an airline, or for that matter any private company, must be profitable in the long-term or it is doomed to liquidation. Thus, a balance sheet falling from black to red will send off alarms in corporate board rooms. Nonetheless, management at airlines which earn tens (or hundreds) of millions of dollars of profit in a given year may be perceived as excellent; but what if truly proficient management had been in place, and earned much more? Conversely, in years when airlines lose tens (or hundreds) of millions of dollars, management may be perceived as poor; yet, losses may have been far worse under truly deficient management.

Thus, the zero base line of red or black ink as the perceptual measure of performance, relied upon so heavily by shareholders and their Boards of Directors, may be a false reference point, particularly in an industry like aviation which is so heavily influenced by external factors, outside the control of management. Economic regulation was designed to temper the impact of such external factors; but for better or worse, that is now gone. Thus, management must attempt to swim in the sometimes stormy seas of market Darwinism without a life preserver.

Another source, Stephen Shaw, insists that "successful airlines are marketing-oriented airlines." They invest heavily in identifying their customers and their customers' requirements, and satisfying them, at a profit.[90] According to Shaw, "It is a basic rule of airline marketing that the best airlines are those that are run in order to make the best returns for their shareholders."[91] That, of course, is true of all companies.

In the post-deregulation era, ten characteristics of successful major network passenger airlines have emerged:

1. A strategically located hub-and-spoke system;[92]
2. Sophisticated yield management;[93]

---

[89] Id., at 69.
[90] Stephen Shaw, Airline Marketing & Management 2 (3rd ed. 1990).
[91] Id., at 130.
[92] See infra, Chapter 4.

3. Low debt;[94]
4. Low wages/flexible work rules;[95]
5. A computer reservations system;[96]
6. A frequent flyer program;[97]
7. Superior service;[98]
8. A young fleet of fuel-efficient and compatible equipment;[99]
9. International routes and/or alliances;[100] and,
10. A conservative growth strategy.[101]

The above characteristics are neither listed in order of importance, nor are they of equal value. But the more of them a carrier possesses, the better are itse chances for survival and growth. Direct distribution, ticketless travel, out-sourcing, and development of the air freight market are rapidly emerging developments that may well be added to the list if they withstand the test of time.[102]

Network carriers are those that focus predominantly on relatively long-haul, connecting traffic, in both dense and thin markets, many of whose passengers have complicated itineraries. However, some very successful airlines do not possess several of these characteristics. For example, cargo carriers have no need for meals or any other in-flight amenities. Moreover, the consistently most profitable U.S. carrier (in the black all but two years in the last quarter century) is Southwest Airlines. It generally does not hub (instead operating a linear-route system focused on dense, short-haul markets), and it possesses an interest in no major computer reservations system (and except for limited participation in Sabre, shuns them as a distribution vehicle).

---

[93] See infra, Chapter 6.
[94] See infra, Chapter 3.
[95] See infra, Chapter 8; See also Paul Stephen Dempsey & Laurence E. Gesell, Air Transportation: Foundations for the 21st Century (1997), Chapter 6.
[96] See infra, Chapter 7.
[97] See infra, Chapters 4 and 7.
[98] See infra, Chapter 5.
[99] See infra, Chapters 4 and 8; See also Paul Stephen Dempsey & Laurence E. Gesell, Air Transportation: Foundations for the 21st Century (1997), Chapter 2.
[100] See infra, Chapter 9.
[101] See infra, Chapters 3 and 4. Airline Economics originally developed such a list in the 1980s. But it has been modified and supplemented by the authors' assessment of the industry.
[102] See infra, Chapters 7 and 8; See also Paul Stephen Dempsey & Laurence E. Gesell, Air Transportation: Foundations for the 21st Century (1997), Chapter 7.

Southwest Airlines has developed a model quite different from the network carriers. It identified six strategies for success:

1. *Stick to what you're good at.* Since it's inception, Southwest has offered single-class service in its short- and medium-haul, high-frequency, high-density, low-fare, point-to-point market niche.
2. *Keep it simple.* Southwest offers no assigned seats or meals, and shuns interlining with other carriers. It offers only one class of seating. The focus is on the short-haul point-to-point traveler. Southwest flies only one type of aircraft—the Boeing 737—which vastly simplifies scheduling, maintenance, flight operations and activities. It was the first airline to introduce ticketless travel.
3. *Keep fares low, costs lower.* Southwest touts itself as "THE Low Fare Airline every day, everywhere we fly." Southwest is able to offer low fares because it enjoys the highest asset utilization and employee productivity of any major airline. Using a single aircraft type in a linear-route system also increases productivity and lowers costs. Shunning most computer reservations systems saves more.
4. *Treat customers like guests.* Southwest has won the annual Triple Crown repeatedly—highest customer satisfaction, best on-time record, and best baggage handling. Southwest asserts, "We provide affordable, safe air travel, and Positively Outrageous Service."
5. *Never stand still.* Southwest responded swiftly and aggressively to the efforts of the majors to replicate its model—Continental Lite and United Shuttle.
6. *Hire great people.* Southwest spends significant time hiring, training and retraining its employees, who are encouraged to be creative and have fun on the job.[103]

Thus, no single model is appropriate for every airline. Each must develop its market niche—a unique combination of price and service options designed to satiate the demands of at least some segment of the consuming public (though some carriers seek to provide alternative product lines to satisfy the needs of several segments of the public).

---

[103] Southwest Airlines Co., Annual Report (1995).

Chapter 1

Managing an airline can be both profoundly rewarding, and profoundly challenging. If history is any indication, financial success has been an extremely difficult goal to achieve under deregulation. The various chapters of this book assess these internal and external factors, as well as these survival characteristics, in an effort to stimulate managerial creativity in developing a strategic vision for success.

Introduction to the Airline Industry

CHAPTER 2.

AIRLINE ECONOMICS

"The U.S. airline industry is repeatedly plagued with prolonged periods in which it offers far more domestic seats than it can sell at compensatory prices. The airlines are not exempt from the law of supply and demand."[1]
Stephen Wolf
CEO, United Airlines

INTRODUCTION

This Chapter is divided into two major parts. Examined in the first part are the essential economic characteristics of the airline industry, focusing on supply, demand, cost and price. The economic characteristics of commercial aviation are discussed throughout this book, and certain concepts introduced here will be more fully developed elsewhere.

After a review of the basic economic characteristics of the airline industry, the focus turns to an examination of the theoretical economics which have driven the public policy dimensions of air transport, particularly regulation and deregulation. Deregulation's proponents assumed airline markets were perfectly contestable[2] and

---

[1] Stephen Wolf, Where Do We Go From Here? A Management Perspective, in Airline Labor Relations in the Global Era 18, 19 (P. Cappelli ed., 1995).
[2] Airline deregulation was a seeming attempt to return to a world of competitive capitalism, where there would be many competing companies, and where the "invisible hand" of the marketplace would drive the price of service to consumers to its lowest practical level. And if actual competition did not exist, there would be the illusion of competition created by the threat of a real competitor. See Generally Adam Smith, An Inquiry Into the Nature and Causes of the Wealth of Nations (1776). The reference here is to the "contestable market theory," that as a revived notion became a

that, if deregulated, airlines would exist in a state of nearly textbook levels of perfect competition.[3] The economic characteristics of the airline industry differ dramatically from the theoretical model of free market perfect competition. After reviewing the theories of perfect competition and contestability, the chapter concludes with a review of the literature on the theory of economic regulation, and an emphasis on destructive competition and core theory. Finally, the economic rationales for safety and environmental regulation are addressed, as well as the natural monopoly characteristics of airports.

What follows, then, is an examination of the essential economic characteristics of the airline industry which explain why supply and demand appear almost perpetually to be in disequilibrium, and cost and price often seem to intersect at an unsatisfactory level.

SUPPLY

AIRLINES INEVITABLY PRODUCE EXCESS CAPACITY

Excessive capacity is endemic to the airline industry. Whether regulated or deregulated, from the mid-1950s to present, U.S. airlines rarely have achieved an average annual domestic load factor exceeding 67% (and in most years load factors substantially worse than that, and domestic load factors worse still),[4] meaning in effect, on an

---

premise used to help justify adoption of the deregulatory policy in transportation. The contestable market theory was first identified by Adam Smith in *Wealth of Nations*. Id. The contestable market assumption is that there are no significant economies of scale or barriers to entry. Paul Stephen Dempsey, Killer Trucks: Put brakes on deregulation, The Arizona Republic (October 1988). Because there are no barriers to entry, the market, even in the absence of actual competition, is threatened (i.e., "contested") by a prospective new entrant. Hence, the market is expected to behave in a perfectly competitive way. Assumed is that potential entrants are as viable in the competitive marketplace as actual competitors. Kyle and Phillips summarize the contestable market theory as follows:

> Put simply, this theoretical framework indicates that in markets characterized by relatively costless entry and exit, the potential for entry, regardless of the actual number of incumbent competitors, will result in competitive behavior and performance. Thus, if (airline) markets are highly contestable, fares should approximate marginal cost, even in a market served by one carrier.

[3] Michael Levine, The Legacy of Airline Deregulation, Av. Week & Space Tech. (Nov. 9, 1987).
[4] Domestic load factors for U.S. carriers ranged between 60.5% and 62.6% between 1987 and 1993, while international load factors ranged between 65.6% and 67.0% during the same period. Julius Maldutis, Quarterly Global Aviation Review 2d Quarter 1994 10, 11 (1994). The

Chapter 2

annual basis, about one-third of available inventory consistently has remained unsold. As Figure 2.1, "U.S. Airline Load Factors" reveals, in the airline industry, supply exceeds demand by a wide margin.

Figure 2.1—U.S. AIRLINE LOAD FACTORS (1950-1995)[5]

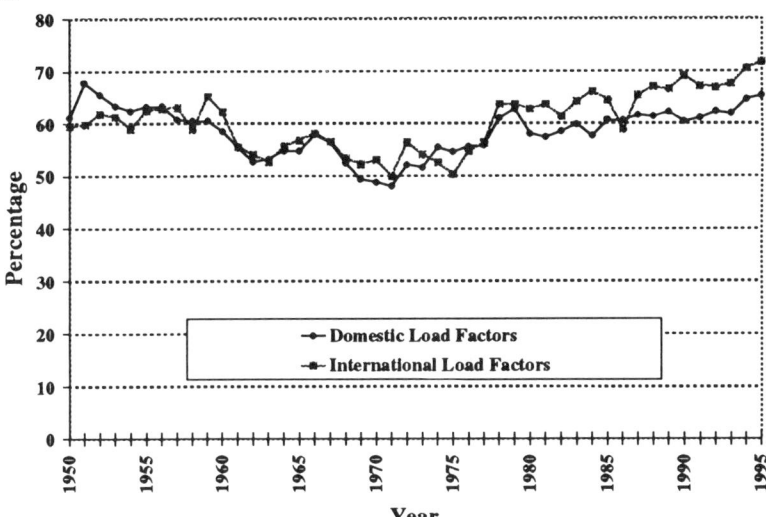

The airline industry has always, will always, and probably should always produce excessive capacity, for if airline load factors approached 100%, many people who wanted to fly would be prohibited from doing so. Studies by Boeing show that when load factors average 60%, 7% of flights will be full and unavailable for late-booking passengers. When load factors reach 70%, 21% of flights will have to turn away prospective passengers.[6] Thus, the higher the load factor, the more likely it is that some passengers will experience service inconvenience by finding their preferred departure fully booked.[7] Moreover, demand is highly cyclical, peaking and re-

---

Association of European Airlines reported load factors between 56.7% and 63.8% during the same period. Id. at 15.
[5] Air Transport Association.
[6] Michael Tretheway & Tae Oum, Airline Economics: Foundations for Strategy and Policy 5, note 3 (1992).
[7] Melvin Brenner, The Significance of Airline Passenger Load Factors, in Airline Economics 35 (G. James ed. 1982).

gressing at different hours of the day, days of the week, and months of the year. Demand can also ebb and flow, on a directional basis, depending on the season.

As a service industry, airlines are subject to constraints different from that of manufacturing. Professor Newal Taneja notes three differences: "(a) an airline's output (a seat on a flight) cannot be inventoried to match fluctuations in demand, as can most physical products; (b) air services, unlike manufactured goods and products, are produced and consumed at the same time; and (c) the customer participates in the service delivery system."[8]

On the question of why the airline industry produces excess capacity, airline industry expert Melvin Brenner notes:

> The industry has always had excess capacity, even during boom times. Overcapacity results from:
> (a) The competitive importance of schedule frequency. Since schedule convenience is one of the most important differentiating characteristics of the airline product, all airlines strive for high scheduled frequency on every important route, and
> (b) the fact that airlines have very high fixed costs and are therefore incentivized to fly their aircraft as much as possible, even if incremental flying does not produce enough revenue to cover fully allocated costs. Whenever a flight covers variable costs and contributes to overhead, the individual carrier is better off flying rather than not flying. However, the cumulation of the many marginally-justified schedules creates over-capacity for the industry as a whole.[9]

---

[8] Newal Taneja, Civil Aviation 131 (2d ed. 1989).
[9] Melvin Brenner, Program for Improving Airline Outlook 5 (unpublished monograph 1993).

American Airlines' CEO Robert Crandall has looked carefully and critically at the factors which suggest that airlines are unique among major industries. On the point of excessive capacity, he observed:

> [E]ach time a network-based airline offers a new flight, it commits an additional city to all the others served by the hub and, thus, introduces a number of new products. Additionally, by widening the reach of its network, it strengthens its entire existing product line [of] origin-departure city-pairs, time of departure, airport used and type of service (nonstop versus connecting) . . . .
>
> In most industries, increased production, by itself, does not enhance an individual competitor's sale potential or competitive position. However, in the airline industry, the fact that more capacity represents more frequency—and thus a more desirable product—gives every airline an incentive to use every airplane as intensively as possible. While this strategy makes sense for each individual carrier, it produces a tendency toward perpetual oversupply.[10]

Professors Michael Tretheway and Tae Oum give an example of how adding spokes to the hub network geometrically increases the number of city-pair markets which can be sold to consumers: "by increasing the number of stations connected to a hub from 9 to 14 (total stations including the hub rise 50% from 10 to 15), the number of [origin-and-destination] pairs served more than doubles from 45 to 105."[11] Thus, in this example, a 50% increase in capacity (the number of cities added to a hub network) results in a 122% increase of product lines (city-pairs) which can be sold to consumers. Coupled with an ability to satiate consumer demands for increased frequencies

---

[10] Robert L. Crandall, The Unique U.S. Airline Industry, in Handbook of Airline Economics 4 (D. Jenkins ed. 1995).
[11] Michael Tretheway & Tae Oum, Airline Economics: Foundations for Strategy and Policy 25 (1992).

Airline Economics

by banking flights through the hub several times a day, an airline which adds connecting points to its hub network enjoys not only an arithmetic, but a geometric, increase in product lines, which stimulates passenger and revenue growth.[12] This phenomenon prompted American Airlines to increase the spokes it flew from Dallas from 32 in 1978, to 73 in 1983, or 128%, while increasing its flights from 111 to 278, or 150%.[13] The larger the network, the more attractive it is to "one stop shoppers" who wish to hold transaction costs to a minimum, and to frequent flyers collecting points for free travel.

Hubbing also allows airlines to take advantage of economies of scope.[14] By offering a flight from city A to hub H, the carrier serves not only the origin-and-destination passenger in the local market, but also serves incremental additional connecting passengers traveling beyond H to destinations throughout the carrier's network.

Tretheway and Oum point to the "S-Curve" effect of flight frequency on demand and revenue, the essential premise of which is that a carrier which offers consumers a disproportionately larger number of flights in a market vis-à-vis its competitors will enjoy an even greater disproportionate advantage in terms of both passenger load factors and revenue.[15] The S-Curve phenomenon was first identified by economist William Fruhan in 1972. Fruhan explained that travelers tend to contact the dominant carrier in the market first, due to its marketing dominance and its greater choice of scheduling options. By virtue of this advantage, carriers are incentivized to add flights to the market. But unless the market for air travel grows, excessive overscheduling harms all competitors in the market by increasing the number of empty seats[16] (see Figure 2.2, "Hypothetical S-Curve").

Tretheway and Oum posit that a carrier with 60% of the flights may receive 80% of the passengers, and even more of the revenue.[17] This is because of consumers' preferences for schedule convenience. Table 2.1, "Reasons For Choosing Airlines", reveals domestic and international passenger preferences in selecting a carrier to serve them.

---

[12] Dan Reed, The American Eagle 160 (1993).
[13] Melvin Brenner, James Leet & Elihu Schott, Airline Deregulation 77, 78 (1985).
[14] A firm enjoys economies of scope when the unit cost of producing one more item is diminished because the scope of activity broadens.
[15] William E. O'Connor, An Introduction to Airline Economics 107-09 (5th ed. 1995).
[16] William Fruhan, The Fight for Competitive Advantage (1972).
[17] Michael Tretheway & Tae Oum, Airline Economics: Foundations for Strategy and Policy 27 (1992).

Chapter 2

Figure 2.2—HYPOTHETICAL S-CURVE

Table 2.1—REASONS FOR CHOOSING AIRLINES[18]
(percentage of passengers)

Reason	U.S. Residents	Non-Residents
Schedule	20.3	17.5
Price	13.8	11.2
Frequent Flyer Program	11.1	5.1
Airline Loyalty	8.7	11.9
Safety Reputation	8.4	11.5
Cabin Service	7.3	9.5
On Time Performance	6.4	7.3
In-Flight Comfort	5.5	7.5
Airport Facilities	3.3	3.1
Aircraft Type	2.9	3.7
No Choice	12.3	11.7

---

[18] Aviation Daily (Oct. 1, 1991), at 23.

Flight schedule is a secondary issue for discretionary travelers (for whom price is paramount), but a primary issue for high-yield business travelers. A person traveling for business typically values his or her time highly, and purchases air travel from the carrier able to offer flights throughout the day to and from important destinations, so that if business plans change, s/he can catch an alternative flight. Because they value their time greatly, business travelers typically are willing to pay more for air transportation than do discretionary travelers. Frequent flyer programs also create a motivation to accumulate miles on the airline with the widest route network, not only because miles can be accumulated faster, but the potential destinations for mileage redemption are more attractive.[19] Moreover, because of the tendency of every airline to follow the price leader, pricing differences are less of a factor in product differentiation than is schedule rivalry.[20]

A carrier with a larger presence in a market ordinarily has relatively lower informational costs in distributing its products to consumers, and consumers have lower transaction costs in doing business on a "one stop shopping" basis with the dominant carrier, which has the ability to fly the consumer to most of his or her preferred destinations. Many travelers tend to economize in their search; calling the airline with the most frequencies reduces transaction costs by reducing the likelihood of needing to make a second call. Thus, the carrier with significantly more frequencies and destinations in a market enjoys a disproportionately higher level of passengers and an even greater level of revenue. According to economist Severin Borenstein, "an airline that carries a large share of the traffic originating at an airport will be able to attract a disproportionate share of the traffic on any particular route from that airport."[21] The S-Curve phenomenon incentivizes carriers to offer more capacity in important markets.

---

[19] See Michael Levine, Airline Competition in Deregulated Markets: Theory, Firm Strategy, and Public Policy, 4 Yale J. Reg. 393, 443 (1987).
[20] Melvin Brenner, James Leet & Elihu Schott, Airline Deregulation 93 (1985).
[21] Severin Borenstein, The Dominant-Firm Advantage in the Multiproduct Industries: Evidence From the U.S. Airlines, Quarterly J. of Economics 1237, 1239, 1260 (1991).

Thus, excessive capacity is a product of several factors:

- *Consumer demand for schedule frequency is high, particularly among high-yield business travelers.* As a general rule, the carrier which enjoys a disproportionate comparative advantage in the number of flights in a given market enjoys an even greater disproportional advantage in terms of passenger volume and revenue. Moreover, high-yield business travelers tend to select an airline on the basis of departure and arrival time. These demand factors will be discussed in greater detail below.
- *Adding spokes to a hub network geometrically increases product lines.* Increasing the number of cites served from a hub geometrically increases the number of city-pairs served, vastly increasing the number of products which can be sold. Thus, carriers are incentivized to build ubiquitous hub networks. These competing hub networks offer duplicative and overlapping service, resulting in vigorous price competition for connecting long-haul traffic.
- *New aircraft orders must be placed years ahead of delivery.* There is an old maxim in the industry that "airlines order new planes in good times, and take delivery in bad times." Aircraft prices range from about $35 million for a new 737, to about $170 million for a 747. Air transport demand is highly cyclical, on a daily, weekly, seasonal and recession/inflation market cycle basis. This means that airline management, attempting to create capacity to satiate peak demands, will have a difficult time gauging real future demand.
- *Investment is often irrational.* The evolutionary economists recognize that market decisions are not always rational. Given the anemic profit margins plaguing the airline industry since deregulation, it is remarkable that new sources of capital have been found, for returns on investment have been extremely poor, and many debt and equity investments have disappeared in bankruptcy. Airlines in the 1980s went through a period of relentless addiction to market share and territorial invasion, each believing it would emerge as King of the Hill, even when it became apparent that the nation was vastly over-hubbed. Airlines remain a glamorous industry, and new airline ventures appear regularly,

despite a high infant mortality rate among new firms. Further, aircraft equipment leases enjoy special treatment under the bankruptcy laws, and as a somewhat fungible vehicle of production, may easily be transferred from one carrier to another.
- *Airlines have high fixed costs.* Because most costs are incurred whether aircraft are parked on the ground or not, airlines tend to send their fleets aloft even during periods of poor demand.

Airlines are not unique in producing excess capacity. For example, telecommunications networks have enormous excess capacity (particularly after having laid fiber optics), a relatively fungible product, and relatively high fixed costs. Hotels and radio and television broadcasting produce excess capacity as well; but among hotels, radio and television broadcasting, there appears to be more room for product differentiation. For airlines, the very means of product differentiation—additional city-pair options, and frequency of service—compel the industry to offer ever more frequency. Adding capacity in the telecommunications industry does not create a geometrical explosion in the number of product lines which can be offered to consumers (in part, because federal regulatory agencies and courts insist on "seamless" connections between rival telecommunications companies, allowing each firm to serve the customers of the other). Furthermore, telephone customers tend to dedicate their local and long-distance business to individual firms for long periods of time (months or years), while purchasers of transportation services may freely shift business between competitors on a trip-by-trip basis, thus generating enormous incentive for pricing competition among transport providers.

AIRLINE CAPACITY HAS A SHORT SHELF LIFE

Airline capacity has an exceptionally short shelf life. Once a scheduled flight pulls back from the jetway, any empty seats are lost forever. Stephen Wolf has observed:

> When supply exceeds demand, perishable commodities are sold for what they will bring. A seat on a specific flight is no exception.

> When the flight departs with a seat unsold, the commodity has perished. As a result of trying to fill too many such seats, yields in the airline industry have sunk to the lowest common denominator.[22]

In contrast, if a manufactured good cannot be sold, it can be left on the shelf or placed in a warehouse for a sunnier day. Hotel rooms are perishable too, but not nearly as perishable as airline seats, for everyone sleeps at the same time; not everyone travels from Boston to Pittsburgh at the same time. A hotel room need be sold only once a day. A domestic aircraft has a fresh inventory of perishable seats every few hours.

Seeking to sell as much of that perishable inventory as possible, carriers offer the price of the lowest price provider in an effort to grasp an ascending and, too often, elusive break-even load factor and to preserve market share. As another source noted, "In a high fixed cost, price sensitive, commodity type business such as this, excess capacity has a devastating effect because it motivates carriers to fill aircraft by cutting prices. Other carriers are forced to match, and fare wars erupt."[23]

EXCESS CAPACITY IS NOT EASILY REDUCED

As noted above, the acquisition of essential assets involves long lead times.[24] Thus, new aircraft orders must be placed years ahead of delivery, meaning that turning off the valve of growing inventory is difficult and costly, even when passenger demand softens as the market cycle turns south. Further, if demand slackens modestly, an airline cannot reduce capacity by shrinking the size of its aircraft. For example, if demand falls 10% in the Omaha-St. Louis market, an airline cannot reduce its costs appreciably by taking 10% of the seats off of each of its aircraft. Aircraft configurations are relatively static (although sometimes smaller aircraft can be substituted in markets where traffic declines). A carrier might be able to take the capacity

---

[22] Stephen Wolf, Where Do We Go From Here? A Management Perspective, in Airline Labor Relations in the Global Era 18, 19 (P. Cappelli ed., 1995).
[23] J.P. Morgan Securities, The U.S. Airline Industry (1993).
[24] Newal Taneja, Civil Aviation 132 (2d ed. 1989).

out of the Omaha-St. Louis market and reposition it in another city-pair market if demand is growing elsewhere (in the winter, for example, carriers adjust their fleets to add capacity in the north-south Sunbelt markets). But if the 10% decline in demand is a national phenomenon because of recession, an airline cannot curtail its costs significantly by parking 10% of its fleet on the ground, for fixed costs are relentlessly high in the airline industry. A 10% reduction in a carrier's flights reduces the appeal of its product in the markets where service is reduced, weakening its network relative to its rivals, and causing a significant forfeiture of revenue to them, while contributing little to arresting the overcapacity on the remaining 90% of its network.[25]

Former TWA CEO Ed Meyer put it this way:

> Since most of the fixed costs could not be eliminated easily you were aggravating your losses by grounding those flights [on which revenue exceeded variable costs, but did not cover fully allocated costs]. We were more often than not talking in terms of real cash losses. The decision to ground a flight became a difficult one, particularly if you thought the situation temporary or you felt the route to be of great strategic value.[26]

Another source echoed these sentiments with an evaluation of airline price, capacity, as well as variable, fixed, and marginal costs:[27]

> All the airlines set the same price and have excess capacity. The price they set is above the market clearing price, but they still do not make any money because their cost function

---

[25] Robert L. Crandall, The Unique U.S. Airline Industry, in Handbook of Airline Economics 5 (D. Jenkins ed. 1995).
[26] C.E. Meyer, Cabotage, Foreign Ownership and International Marketing Alliances (address before the University of Denver/Smithsonian Air & Space Museum Conference on Airlines, Airports & Aviation, Washington, D.C., May 29, 1992).
[27] Variable costs are costs that fluctuate depending on the firm's level of output. Fixed costs remain the same irrespective of the level of output. Marginal costs are the costs necessary to produce one additional unit of output.

c(*) is too large. Since the demand for air travel is basically elastic, any attempt to increase price to increase revenue will fail. In any other industry, participants would, at the next time the first stage rolls around merely decrease capacity. Such behavior is more difficult in the airline industry. If United sets capacity at 100 seats going from Denver to Cedar Rapids, and only 50 people fly there, United has 50 seats of excess capacity. If United knows that only 50 people will fly to Cedar Rapids, it should reduce capacity to 50 in the next first-stage. United may not be able to do that because aircraft have a (more or less) fixed number of seats. If excess capacity is 5 seats, taking those 5 seats out at the next first-stage really doesn't make any difference. Marginal cost for each passenger is minuscule, except for one passenger. In this example, the 101st person who wants to fly to Cedar Rapids creates a huge marginal cost for United; they must get another aircraft, fill it with fuel, staff it, feed the passenger, etc. Every passenger after that again has low marginal costs.[28]

Additionally, network carriers have enormous difficulty downsizing hubs in order to take account of demand declines, because every spoke in the hub feeds passengers to every other spoke in the hub, and vice-versa. Eliminating a spoke has a marginal detrimental impact throughout the system, for passengers from each spoke connect with flights from virtually every other spoke. Instead, carriers typically maintain hub capacity but drop prices during demand downturns in an effort to cover variable costs,[29] deferring the day when prices can be raised until demand improves. In one sense, it is sometimes preferable for a carrier to abandon a hub than to downsize it.

---

[28] James Lanik, Stopping the Tailspin: Use of Oligopolistic and Oligopsonistic Power to Produce Profits in the Airline Industry, 22 Transp. L.J. 509, 522 n. 76 (1995).
[29] Variable costs are costs that change with the level of output, such as raw materials, wages and fuel. Paul Samuelson & William Nordhaus, Economics 74 (14th ed. 1992).

Airline Economics

But abandoning a hub may be an invitation for a competitive carrier to enter the market.

New airline ventures seem to spring up like dandelions. While some excess capacity disappears with the collapse of major airlines (e.g., Eastern and Pan Am) and the downsizing of others, many used aircraft and skilled labor simply are recycled into the fleets of new entrants and growing carriers. For example, Delta sold a large number of aging DC-9s, only to see them re-emerge in Atlanta in the fleet of low-cost ValuJet.

Chapter 11 bankruptcy also offers wounded airlines a respite from most creditors (except aircraft manufacturers and lessors), allowing them to re-group and shed themselves of shareholder obligations and much debt. Because airlines are networks, their liquidation values are relatively low, making continued operation and cash flow preferable to asset liquidation. The present value of future streams of cash flows generated by the integrated use of equipment, facilities and labor exceed the liquidation value of even an unprofitable airline network.[30]

Financing is available via the equipment manufacturers for both new entrants and carriers emerging from Chapter 11. While the leasing companies may have been disciplined by the profligate decade of the 1980s, public sources of capital, in the form of state and local contributions and guarantees, have become increasingly available—to TWA (from Missouri), Northwest (from Minnesota), United (from Indiana), and American (from North Carolina). Foreign airlines also continue to inject significant capital into U.S. firms to take advantage of the domestic feed they provide into their lucrative long-haul wide-bodied international networks (e.g., KLM-Northwest, British Airways-USAir, and SAS-Continental and Air Canada-Continental). For a growing number of airlines, labor has also become the lender of last resort (e.g., TWA, Northwest, and United).

---

[30] Robert L. Crandall, The Unique U.S. Airline Industry, in Handbook of Airline Economics 6, 7 (D. Jenkins ed. 1995).

Chapter 2

DEMAND

DEMAND IS HIGHLY CYCLICAL AND HIGHLY INFLUENCED BY EXTERNAL EVENTS

Long-term and short-term market cycles play a profound role in airline economics. Demand for air transport services has always been highly cyclical, with greater or lesser demand depending on time of day, day of week, and season, and on broader market fluctuations, year to year. For example, discretionary, leisure traffic (which has grown to be the dominant traffic base) peaks in the Summer months, thereby allowing the industry to enjoy higher load factors for the second and third calendar quarters, while demand in the first quarter is typically poor. East-west traffic is heaviest in the Summer; north-south traffic is heaviest in Winter. Business traffic peaks between 7:00 to 9:00 on week day mornings, and between 4:00 and 6:00 on week day afternoons. Leisure traffic peaks during Thanksgiving, Christmas, New Year's, Easter, Labor Day and Memorial Day weekends.[31]

The seasonal variation is so profound that the peak month (August) has about 20-25% more traffic than the trough month (January, domestically, and February, internationally). Domestically, the strongest months are June, July and August, while internationally, the strongest months are July, August and September. For both domestic and international travel, the weakest months are December, January and February (see Figure 2.3, "Major U.S. Airline Load Factors By Month"). On a daily basis, the peak day (Sunday, because for many passengers, Saturday night restrictions compel Sunday travel), is 26% stronger than the weakest day, Tuesday (see Figure 2.4, "Major U.S. Airline Load Factors By Day Of Week"). And on a hourly basis, in many markets, peak periods of 9:00 a.m. and 5:00 p.m. far outpace demand at other hours of the day.[32]

---

[31] Newal Taneja, Civil Aviation 131 (2d ed. 1989).
[32] William E. O'Connor, An Introduction to Airline Economics 100 (5th ed. 1995). See also, Melvin Brenner, The Significance of Airline Passenger Load Factors 35 (G. Jamed ed. 1982).

Figure 2.3—MAJOR U.S. AIRLINE LOAD FACTORS BY MONTH[33]

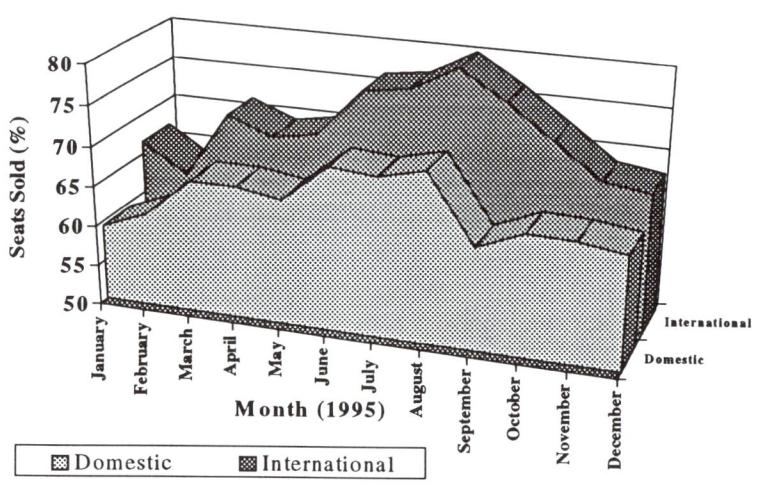

Figure 2.4—MAJOR U.S. AIRLINE LOAD FACTORS BY DAY OF WEEK[34]

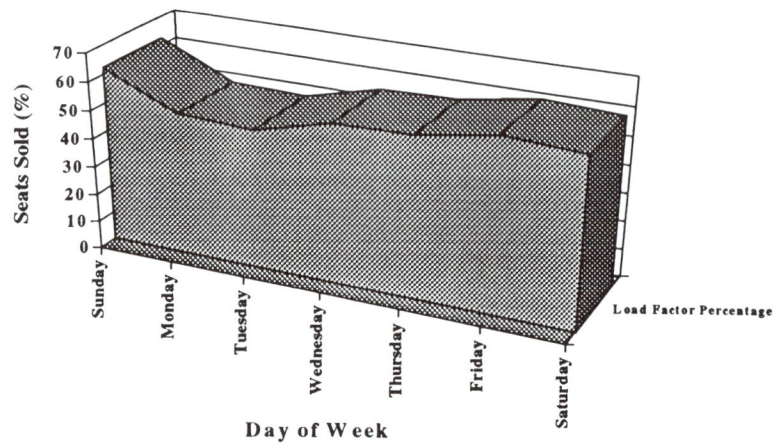

---

[33] Source: Salomon Brothers.
[34] Id.

The airline industry is highly sensitive to the business cycle, with economic performance correlating strongly with fluctuations in personal disposable income and gross domestic product.[35] When the economy is growing and consumer confidence is strong, air transport demand grows, often improving airline load factors, and allowing carriers to raise yields and profitability. When the economy falls into recession, unemployment grows, and consumer confidence declines, individuals postpone discretionary travel and other luxury purchases (e.g., recreational vehicles), and airline load factors, yields and profitability decline. Dan Reed summarized how external factors can combine to cause an airline extreme difficulty:

> When the economy is good, when passenger demand and fares are high, and when fuel prices are relatively low, an airline can be an incredibly productive cash cow. Because its fixed costs are so high and virtually impossible to pare down without major negative ramifications, an airline beset by a recession, slack demand, insane price competition, high labor costs, and fuel prices or international terrorism can be bled dry very quickly. All it really takes to kill a cash-poor airline is one relatively strong or long recession, one particularly frightening act of international terrorism, one major maintenance-related accident, or one major fare war. The actual death may be years in coming, depending on how skillfully the carrier can manage the bankruptcy process and/or its creditors. But any one of those circumstances can determine its fate.[36]

In addition, airline economic performance drops more deeply during recession than does the rest of the economy. Air Line Pilots

---

[35] Philip Baggaley, Assessing An Airline's Credit Quality, in Handbook of Airline Economics 239 (D. Jenkins ed. 1995).
[36] Dan Reed, The American Eagle 39, 40 (1993).

Association President Randy Babbitt notes the hyper-cyclical nature of airline economic performance on a macro-economic basis:

> On the macro-economic level, we have a hyper-cyclic situation. Our lows are lower and longer—and our highs are lower and shorter—than the general economy.
>
> During good economic times, new entrant airlines proliferate, skimming off enough passengers to damage the established airlines. Then when an economic downturn hits, the new-entrants declare bankruptcy and operate in Chapter 11 or go out of business altogether, but always manage to prevent the established airlines from making much of a profit.[37]

On the issue of the corrosive effect Chapter 11 carriers have on yields, both Bob Crandall of American Airlines and Stephen Wolf (then) of United Airlines, agreed. Said Wolf:

> In a truly free market . . . oversupply would be temporary. That is, the least efficient producers will exit the market. U.S. bankruptcy laws, however, in effect displace the realities of the marketplace and have now become a barrier to exit. Carriers are able to operate literally for years without repaying their debt obligations; consequently, their capacity is artificially retained in the system and the result is economic havoc for all.[38]

Pointing to the fact that leisure travelers are accounting for an increasing share of the air transport market, and that leisure travelers have greater income elasticity than do business travelers, Professors

---

[37] Randolph Babbitt, Saving the Golden Goose, AIR LINE PILOT (Feb. 1995), at 10, 11.
[38] Stephen Wolf, Where Do We Go From Here? A Management Perspective, in Airline Labor Relations in the Global Era 18, 19 (P. Cappelli ed., 1995).

Tretheway and Oum concluded: "Air travel is . . . not just cyclical but procyclical. This procyclic behaviour has likely been exacerbated by airline deregulation."[39] Professor O'Connor makes essentially the same point: "To the extent that deregulation-inspired low discount fares have increased the proportion of leisure to business passengers, the average income elasticity has risen and with it the degree of vulnerability of airlines to recessions."[40]

Traditionally, passenger traffic has grown at about 2.25 times the rate of gross domestic products [GDP] growth; thus, if the world economy grows by 2%, passenger demand should grow by approximately 4.5%. World air travel growth averaged 7.4% a year during the boom 1983-1989 period.[41] But worldwide, traffic fell 4% in 1991, the first decline since records have been kept.[42]

Many experts predict that global passenger demand will average 5-6% annually over the next two decades,[43] although it will be spread unevenly, with intra- and inter-Asian markets growing at 8-9% annually,[44] and North American, transAtlantic, and European markets growing at only 4% annually.[45] Some analysts predict that traffic will have to grow about 8% in order for the U.S. airline industry to

---

[39] Michael Tretheway & Tae Oum, Airline Economics: Foundations for Strategy and Policy 15 (1992).
[40] William E. O'Connor, An Introduction to Airline Economics 98 (5th ed. 1995).
[41] Richard Evans, Why the World's Airlines Can't Seem to Get Enough Cash, Global Finance (May 1993), at 48.
[42] Data, Airline Bus., The Skies in 1992 72 (1992).
[43] See Economic Benefits Study Revisited, ICAO Rev. (Feb. 1994), at 19.
[44] The Asia-Pacific region is growing fastest. In 1990, it accounted for about 31% of the world's total, and 132 million passengers. By the year 2000, IATA estimates the region will account for 189 million passengers, or 39% of the world's total; by 2010, it will account for 375 million passengers, or 51% of the world's total. IATA predicts that the doubling of traffic in the region over the past six years will be repeated, with China, Malaysia, Thailand and Indonesia expected to be growing fastest. Asia-Pacific, Airline Bus., The Skies in 1992 55 (1992). For Asian markets, the Orient Airlines Association predicts 7.5% traffic growth through the year 2000; IATA predicts between 7% and 8.6% growth through the year 2010; OECD predicts 8.5% traffic growth in the Asia/Pacific region during the next two decades; and McDonnell Douglas predicts 9.7% through the year 2010. See Has the Asian Bubble Burst? Airline Bus. (Oct. 1993), at 7; and Int'l Civil Aviation Org., Air Traffic to the Year 2003 (Oct. 1994). No matter who is making the predictions, all are tremendously optimistic for the Asia-Pacific passenger market. Seven of the ten most profitable airlines in the world in 1993 operate in this region. Airline Business 100 Data, Airline Bus, The Skies in 1994 (Supp. 1994), at 59. The year before, twelve of the twenty most profitable airlines were domiciled in the Asia-Pacific Region. Has the Asian Bubble Burst? Airline Bus. (Oct. 1993), at 7.
[45] OECD, New Policy Approaches to International Air Transport 4 (1992).

achieve sustained profitability, something it is not likely to do.[46] Others predict that the airline industry must earn operating margins of 8.5%, something it has never done, in order to finance its needed aircraft.[47]

U.S. domestic traffic growth softened significantly beginning in 1986,[48] which is remarkable in light of the unrealistic and destructive price wars of the era, and the fact that the recession did not begin to set in until 1989-1990. This raises concern among some that the U.S. domestic passenger market may have matured. One source notes, "the big U.S. and European markets have not reached maturity yet, but the rate of growth has been falling ever since the double-digit growth of the 1960s"[49] (see Figure 2.5, "U.S. Airline Domestic Intercity Passenger Miles").

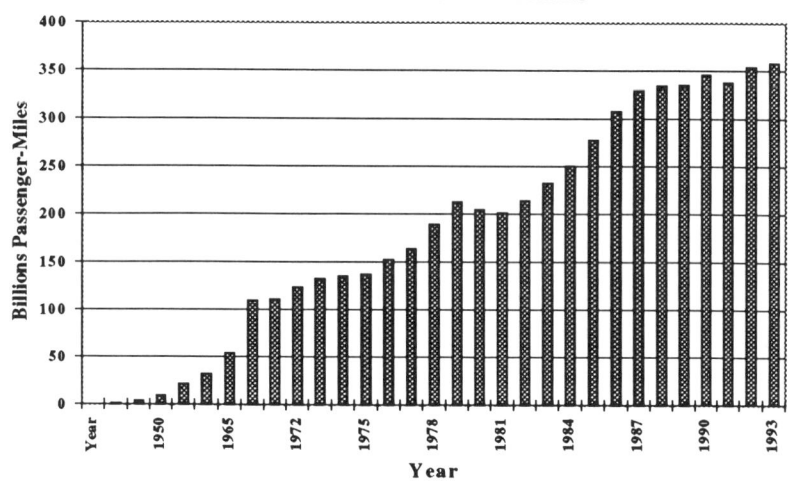

Figure 2.5—U.S. AIRLINE DOMESTIC INTERCITY PASSENGER MILES

---

[46] Richard Evans, Why the World's Airlines Can't Seem to Get Enough Cash, Global Finance (May 1993), at 48, 53.
[47] Homi Mullan, Financing the Future, in IATA, A Vision of the Future 69, 80 (1995).
[48] Julius Maldutis, Industry Investment Requirements -- Looking Beyond 2000 (address before the 7th IATA High-Level Aviation Symposium, Sept. 6, 7, 1993, Cairo, Egypt).
[49] Richard Evans, Why the World's Airlines Can't Seem to Get Enough Cash, Global Finance (May 1993), at 48, 52.

Why does U.S. domestic passenger growth appear to be stagnant? Dr. Julius Maldutis advanced four reasons:

1. Some in the academic community are beginning to raise the question, Is it a mature industry? In 1994, 255 million Americans flew, making 460 million trips. How many more times can you travel? That's one possible answer.
2. The second possible answer is globalization. Every U.S. company buys or sells or competes in the global arena. Perhaps the business traveler to Cleveland didn't disappear but now is going to Copenhagen to buy the milling machine; namely, a diversion from domestic to international [travel].
3. The third possibility: At the end of 1993, the United States had 15,000 video teleconferencing centers. In my company, every Monday morning, we have a general sales meeting that is televised to all our branch offices around the globe. IBM is demonstrating a PC that has a video camera, and now all IBM executives can be in a video teleconference via their computers. Or the chief executive of an engine manufacturer says that he has constructed two video teleconferencing centers and now has no employees who need to travel between East Hartford and the Florida plant. Thus, technology may be affecting intracorporate business travel.
4. But the fourth reason is perhaps the most important reason of all in assessing what is happening to the airline industry. In the last four years 1.6 million Americans have been restructured . . . . One and a half

> million white-collar, middle-management frequent flyers have lost their jobs. To me, this is the fundamental cause of the airline industry's difficulty. The lack of growth is a function of the fact that corporate America is undergoing vast structural change, and this vast structural change is affecting the airline industry travel market.[50]

Many small businesses simply have been priced out of the passenger market by aggressive yield management, and no longer fly. With corporate downsizing constricting the white collar labor force and trimming travel budgets, and communications technologies improving robustly, business travel fell to 37% of traffic in 1992, 48% in 1993, 47% in 1994 and 41% in 1995.[51] In the late 1980s, business traffic accounted for between 52% and 60% of domestic traffic and 75% of revenue.[52] The shift of demand to the price-sensitive leisure market erodes carrier yields, for leisure travelers are much more sensitive to price than are business travelers.[53]

But others resist the notion of market maturity in the domestic airline industry. While conceding that exponential growth cannot continue *ad infinitum,* Adam Pikarski and Paul Thomas, former senior economists with the Douglas Aircraft Company, insist that maturation has not occurred in the U.S. market.[54]

Thomas Gallagher of Chase Manhattan notes the effect market maturation has on demand:

---

[50] Julius Maldutis, Why Aren't the Airlines Profitable?, AIR LINE PILOT (Jan. 1995), at 26-28.

[51] Julius Maldutis, Industry Investment Requirements—Looking Beyond 2000 (address before the 7th IATA High-Level Aviation Symposium, Sept 6, 7, 1993, Cairo, Egypt); Julie Schmit & Del Jones, Jittery Airlines Need Business Travelers, USA Today (Int'l. Ed., May 23, 1994); Air Trasnport Ass'n., Annual Report 11 (1996).

[52] Richard Evans, Why the World's Airlines Can't Seem to Get Enough Cash, Global Finance (May 1993), at 48, 51.

[53] The decline in business traffic appears to be a global phenomenon, reflected in the reduction of the number of first and business class seats by, for example, KLM, British Airways, Japan Airlines, ANA, American Airlines and Northwest.
See James Hirsch, First-Class Cabins Are Shrinking On a Growing Number of Flights, Wall St. J., Dec. 21, 1993, at B1.

[54] Adam Pikarshi & Paul Thomas, Maturation in Air Transportation, in Handbook of Airline Economics 175 (D. Jenkins ed. 1995).

> We know that the leading determinant of air traffic growth is the rate of economic growth. As economic activity increases, measured by the rate of Gross Domestic Product [GDP] growth, air traffic increases as well. Historically, the relationship between the rate of economic growth and the rate of traffic growth has exceeded a multiple of one. Depending upon the relative maturity of the aviation sector and its related economy, the relationship has ranged between two and four times the rate of GDP growth. But this factor, called the traffic-income multiplier, has experienced a gradual, but continuous, decline. In the first cycle of the jet age (1965-1972), traffic increased at about twice the rate of GDP growth. By the fourth cycle (1987-1993), traffic was climbing at about one and one-half times the economic growth rate....
>
> In addition to observing a continuous worldwide decline in the income-traffic growth multiplier, we also observe that—while the world's economies continue to grow—they are doing so at a decreasing rate. So, the economic activity components of global traffic growth are experiencing both a declining rate of economic growth and a declining multiplier: economic growth rates in decline are having a diminishing influence on traffic growth rates.[55]

On the other hand, there is evidence of significant market stimulation by Southwest Airlines and its short-haul low-fare clones, taking travelers out of their automobiles and busses, and inducing them to fly more, suggesting there is much price elasticity and significant pent-up demand for low-priced air service. Because of the high cost of hubbing and other overhead, many major airlines (par-

---

[55] Thomas Gallagher, Aircraft Finance and Airline Financial Analysis in the Fifth Cycle of the Jet Age, in Handbook of Airline Economics 223, 227 (D. Jenkins ed. 1995).

ticularly the large network carriers) are unable to offer prices as low. One must, however, caution such optimism with a realization that Southwest-type service (in short-haul high-density nonstop markets) cannot replace the overwhelming portion of the larger long-haul and connecting market, which will continue to be served by the network carriers. Thus, such traffic stimulation is likely limited to high-density short-haul markets.

MANY CONSUMERS VIEW AIR TRANSPORTATION AS A FUNGIBLE COMMODITY

By advertising a one-way rather than a round-trip price, and by launching what sometimes seems to be an endless series of fare wares, airlines have conditioned consumers to hold unrealistic expectations of what a ticket should cost, and to withhold discretionary spending until price wars erupt, as they eventually and inevitably do. Carriers typically match the prices of their competitors. All carriers fly essentially the same aircraft, and increasingly, most offer less service, and thus, relatively little service differentiation; hence most consumers view air travel as a fungible commodity (i.e., one carrier's service is easily replaced by another airline).

Airline service is in the nature of a credence good. Unlike a manufactured product, which can be picked up off its retail shelf, turned over, plugged in, and generally inspected before purchase, it is difficult for a prospective passenger to know how pleasant the airline trip will be—the leg room, the meal, the courtesy of the cabin crew, the cleanliness of the aircraft, whether it will arrive and leave at its scheduled time, the smoothness of the flight, the size and personal hygiene of the passenger seated in the next seat, and so on.[56] Thus, it is difficult for an airline to differentiate its product on the basis of quality.

Having said that, one must concede that business class and first class is available for the passengers willing to pay the relatively higher differential cost. But even here, business and first class cabins have been flooded with coach-class upgrades, filling what once were empty seats (a positive development for passengers who would otherwise sit in the coach cabin; a somewhat negative development

---

[56] Paul Dempsey & Andrew Goetz, Airline Deregulation & Laissez Faire Mythology 276 (1992).

for the passengers paying the full price)—in essence, an egalitarian integration of the proletarian and bourgeois classes in confined quarters.

BRAND LOYALTY IS SOFT

Passengers select an air carrier to serve their transportation needs based principally on the basis of schedule and price. Since most major airlines fly essentially the same aircraft, the product is deemed by many consumers as virtually indistinguishable, unlike hotels, which are able to differentiate their product by location, type of building, and quality of room. When a consumer purchases air transportation, s/he rents a seat for a few hours, sometimes receives a meal, and shares a public closet-like toilet. When a consumer purchases a hotel room, s/he rents a bed, shower, sink, closet, television and telephone for an entire evening. On the fungible nature of airline service, Professor O'Connor notes:

> Airline service tends to be what economists call an undifferentiated product—that is, to many passengers the service of one airline is rather hard to differentiate from the service of another. Modern aircraft are very much alike, at least within any given size range. The speed, comfort, and safety aspects of a journey are likely to be much the same, whichever airline a passenger selects . . . . [Usually a carrier is chosen] simply by the most convenient times of departure and arrival. In a sense, flight scheduling is a form of product differentiation, and it would appear to be the most important one.[57]

Some airlines have attempted to differentiate their product by offering better service—better food or more seat pitch, for example. Among new entrants, Midwest Express appears to be the most successful of these experiments. But most airlines have concluded that

---

[57] William E. O'Connor, An Introduction To Airline Economics 5 (5th ed. 1995).

consumers still prefer schedule or price over service. Most flights are short in duration, and this limits the amount of meaningful product differentiation that can be accomplished.[58] Major airlines offer three classes of service on international and trans-continental routes, at a much higher price than coach. Frequent flyer awards have also been created to attempt to induce consumer loyalty among high-yield business traffic, with some success. But most carriers tend to offer the same range of prices as their competitors (although the number of seats for which individual fares are offered may vary from one carrier to another), often making schedule the paramount means of product differentiation, particularly for business travelers.

DEMAND IS HIGHLY SEGMENTED

Air transportation is an intermediate good, the demand for which is derived demand, for the overwhelming number of passengers fly not for the sake of flying, but in order to travel somewhere and do something (e.g., consummate a business agreement, or lie under a palm tree, sip a cold margarita, and watch the Sun set). Thus, in order to assess passenger demand, it is useful to discern why people are traveling.[59]

As a consequence of the foregoing, there is not one market for air transportation services; there are several. Because business travelers typically need to travel on short notice, and pay for air transportation with pre-tax dollars, they are less sensitive to price than are discretionary travelers. Again, schedule is often the determining factor in carrier selection.

In contrast, leisure/vacation travelers are relatively sensitive to price, and will take their discretionary dollars elsewhere with relatively small increases in price. They are less influenced by schedule, and are typically able to plan their trips several weeks ahead of departure. Thus, there appear to be significant price elasticities of demand in the discretionary market.[60]

Leisure travelers who visit friends and relatives [VFR] can also be price sensitive, depending on the reason which prompts the travel.

---

[58] Robert L. Crandall, The Unique U.S. Airline Industry, in Handbook of Airline Economics 4 (D. Jenkins ed. 1995).
[59] William E. O'Connor, An Introduction to Airline Economics 97 (5th ed. 1995).
[60] Id. at 98.

Individuals who need to travel great distances on short notice because of friend or family illnesses, deaths or other crises tend to be relatively price insensitive.[61]

Table 2.2, "Airline Selection Factors", reveals the relative preferences of the two broad classes of passengers.

Table 2.2—AIRLINE SELECTION FACTORS [62]
(mean value on a ten point scale)

Factor	Leisure Travel	Business Travel
Price	3.9	2.1
Schedule Convenience	3.2	4.5
Frequent Flyer Program	1.5	2.0
Airline Reputation	1.5	1.5

The business travel market can also be divided into two broad segments.[63] Large purchasers of air travel (e.g., Fortune 1000 companies) can and do play airlines off against one another to extract contractual concessions on ticket prices which assure their employees are flown for the discretionary traveler's price, or something close to it, without the advance purchase, non-refundability, and Saturday-night-stay-over requirements. The chronic overcapacity from which the airline industry suffers affords unusually strong bargaining leverage to relatively larger purchasers of air travel, such as the U.S. government.[64] One might describe this as oligopsony power exerted by a small number of purchasers unilaterally able to dictate price—in this instance a price above variable costs, but below fully allocated costs.[65] Ironically, large businesses are relatively less price elastic than small businesses.

In contrast, small businesses pay significantly higher prices for air transportation. Thus, small businesses seeking mid-week travel on

---

[61] Michael Tretheway & Tae Oum, Airline Economics: Foundations for Strategy and Policy 17 (1992).
[62] P.L. Ostrowski & T.V. O'Brien, Predicting Customer Loyalty for Airline Passengers (1991)
[63] Paul Dempsey, The Disintegration of the U.S. Airline Industry, 20 Transp. L.J. 19, 20 (1991).
[64] Robert L. Crandall, The Unique U.S. Airline Industry, in Handbook of Airline Economics 6 (D. Jenkins ed. 1995).
[65] Fully allocated costs are variable (or out-of-pocket) costs plus an appropriate allocation of fixed (or overhead) costs.

short notice are expected to bear the fixed cost burden. However, small businesses also are constrained by limited travel budgets from paying exorbitant prices for air travel (this reflects their price elasticity of demand), and will take fewer trips if forced to pay a price significantly above fully allocated costs. To the extent that small businesses are dissuaded from sending their sales force aloft to sell their products (vis-à-vis their larger competitors), one wonders whether this result is desirable from a public policy perspective, since small businesses create 90% of the nation's jobs.

Airlines have attempted to build brand loyalty, particularly among business travelers, with frequent flyer programs. Consumers who take more than 10 trips a year constitute only 8% of the air travel market, but account for 45% of the trips taken and a disproportionate amount of revenue.[66] By giving the reward directly to the flying employees rather than the firm by which they are employed (and which is paying for their transportation), airlines incentivize repeat business with relatively less concern for price.

The market is also segmented according to distance. A passenger traveling only a few hundred miles ordinarily has surface transportation alternatives—bus, rail or automobile. Thus, s/he is very sensitive to the relative price of alternative modes of transport. In contrast, a passenger traveling distances of more than about 1,500 miles is likely to be more concerned with time than price. But beyond a thousand miles, duplicative and overlapping hub networks tend to compel airlines to price the IR product below fully allocated costs, despite the relative lower elasticity of demand of the long-distance traveler. For example, a passenger flying from Seattle to Philadelphia has a number of alternative airline competitors from which to choose to route her over their respective hubs (e.g., Delta over Salt Lake City or Cincinnati, Northwest over Minneapolis or Detroit, United over Denver or Chicago, American over Chicago or Dallas, USAir over Pittsburgh, or TWA over St. Louis), each of which has ample excess capacity it would like to dispose of at a level above variable costs.

Most airlines attempt to tailor the price of travel to the demand elasticities of each of these demand segments. Through yield management, carriers offer various "buckets" of seats from lower to higher prices, the lowest fares usually encumbered with the most onerous

---

[66] Air Transport Ass'n., The Airline Handbook (1995).

restrictions (e.g., advance purchase, non-refundability, Saturday night stay), extracting a higher proportion of fixed costs from relatively demand inelastic travelers. Fewer than 10% of passengers pay the full fare, which has risen well above the rate of inflation; the average discount is about 65% off the full fare.

COSTS

As noted above, airlines have relatively low variable, or out-of-pocket costs (typically fuel and labor), accounting for less than 25% of fully allocated costs. Fully allocated costs consist of all variable costs, plus some appropriate share of the fixed cost burden.[67] Fixed costs, or constant costs (which do not change depending on the amount of traffic served), are the dominant costs in the industry. The dividing line between fixed and variable costs is not always clear. Once aircraft are purchased, crews trained, and flights scheduled, arguably almost all costs are fixed.

One other difficulty is ascribing joint, or common, costs to particular passengers, particularly for network carriers, which must attempt to determine how much of the cost of flying from A to B must be attributed to the passengers connecting at B to the flight taking them on to C, or how much of the flight's cost should be attributed to the transportation of belly cargo, for example. As Michael Levine observed:

> [A]irline production in the face of indivisibilities resembles the joint product production of different cuts of meat along with hides from a single animal[68] . . . . [A]irline hub flights are a joint product on which many categories of traffic are carried at many fares. It is no more possible to know the "cost" of carrying any particular passenger across a hub than it is to know the cost of producing a pound of steak from a carcass that yields many

---

[67] William E. O'Connor, An Introduction to Airline Economics 97 (5th ed. 1995).
[68] Michael Levine, Airline Competition in Deregulated Markets: Theory, Firm Strategy, and Public Policy, 4 Yale J. Reg. 393, 449 (1987).

> salable products. To make things worse, different airline hubs generate different mixes of local and overhub traffic, leisure and business traffic, and peak and off-peak traffic. To cope, airlines vary the capacity available at any given fare level day by day and flight by flight.[69]

Thus, airlines suffer from the problem that most of their costs are joint costs, spread over an array of originating, destination and connecting passengers and freight moving throughout their networks. Actual costs are obfuscated and difficult to ascribe to particular passengers. Rather than cost-based pricing, airlines tend to price on the basis of demand (imposing higher fares on less price elastic traffic, and offering lower fares to more price elastic traffic), and competition (following the price leader in a given market, or offering predatory prices to drive a competitor out).

As noted above, costs in the airline industry are typically measured in terms of available seat miles, since seats and distance are what is being sold. As a general rule, large aircraft tend to have lower available seat mile [ASM] costs than smaller aircraft. In addition, the industry enjoys a cost taper over distance, so that shorter flights ordinarily have higher ASM costs than longer flights.[70] This is because fuel consumption increases on takeoff and landings, and the aircraft preparation costs for both short and long stage lengths are similar. With more miles over which to spread these inputs, ASM costs decline over longer distances.[71]

Another way to measure airline costs is on a per passenger basis. Since most flight costs are fixed regardless of the number of passengers flown, higher load factors results in lower per passenger costs.[72] In sum, larger aircraft, flying longer distances, with higher load densities enjoy lower costs vis-à-vis smaller aircraft, flying shorter distances, with lower load densities. Thus, the wide-bodied aircraft, like the 747, which flies more passengers over longer distances, have

---

[69] Id. at 487
[70] William E. O'Connor, An Introduction to Airline Economics 71 (5th ed. 1995).
[71] Michael Tretheway & Tae Oum, Airline Economics: Foundations for Strategy and Policy 4 (1992).
[72] Michael Tretheway & Tae Oum, Airline Economics: Foundations for Strategy and Policy 5 (1992).

significantly lower ASM costs than do narrow-bodied aircraft like the 737.

Network economies of scale and scope[73] have motivated most major airlines to increase the number of routes served from a centralized connecting airport—the infamous hub-and-spoke systems. On the marketing side of the equation, it allows carriers to offer a geometrically increasing array of city-pair products with every additional spoke. It also allows carriers to satiate consumer desires for frequent flights to that wide array of destinations. Hubs generate higher revenue, and can create barriers to market entry.[74] But on the cost side of the equation, the impact is quite different.

This brings up a comparison of Southwest Airlines, which embraces the linear-route model, versus the major network airlines, which distribute passengers according to the hub-and-spoke model. Southwest offers high frequency point-to-point service in dense short-haul markets. By offering several non-stop flights a day between city-pairs, it satiates consumers' desires for frequent service. By utilizing its gates and ground services at both end points throughout the day, Southwest enjoys economies of density.[75] Because it shuns connections, and avoids congested airports wherever possible, it is able to enjoy greater productivity in the utilization of its aircraft and labor, and consume relatively less fuel vis-à-vis the network carriers.

While building an extensive network has enormous marketing and revenue advantages, it imposes significant costs. Hub-and-spoke carriers do enjoy economies of density at the hub airport; the recur-

---

[73] *Economies of scale* are realized when increases in total production simultaneously decrease unit costs; long-run average cost decreases as output increases. As the scale of production grows, the enterprise becomes more efficient. For example, a large capital-intensive piece of equipment operating at full capacity (such as a Boeing 747) can allow significantly lower ASM costs vis-à-vis a smaller aircraft (such as a Boeing 727). A related concept is *economies of scope*. The unit cost of producing one more item may be diminished when the scope of activity broadens. For example, advertising costs per unit of serving a particular city-pair market are lower the more city-pairs served, for the same ad can offer several city-pair product lines. Similarly, combination carriers airlines can offer "belly" cargo service in their passenger markets.

[74] Philip Baggaley, Assessing An Airline's Credit Quality, in Handbook of Airline Economics (D. Jenkins ed. 1995).

[75] Yet another related concept to economies of size, or scale, is *economies of density*. By combining passengers and groups of passengers, an airline can carry the aggregation of passengers more cheaply than if it carried those passengers separately. Through careful scheduling of flights, consolidating operations, and routing passengers through its hub, an airline streamlines its system, making it more dense, and thereby reducing costs per passenger. Airline deregulation was predicated on the assumption that there were no scale economies in the airline industry.

ring banks of passengers allow enhanced utilization of gate and ground personnel and equipment, at least at the hub, although hubbing requires the leasing of many more gates than does a linear route system. By attempting to land and take-off large waves of aircraft at a central point, congestion causes delay (worsened when the weather becomes inclement), resulting in poorer aircraft and labor utilization, and increased fuel consumption.

Hubbing has also led airlines to invest in relatively smaller aircraft than was the trend before deregulation. In the early 1980s, enthusiasm for the relatively small 737 replaced orders for larger aircraft such as the 747, for in hubbing, carriers do not need large aircraft to fly long distances; instead, they need small aircraft to fly relatively short distances. Thus, both the economies of aircraft size and stage length have been significantly sacrificed by hubbing. According to Brenner:

> The deregulation-encouraged emphasis on smaller planes means that the industry will be losing the unit-cost efficiencies of larger aircraft. Many of the costs involved in aircraft operation do not increase proportionately to increased plane size. The result is that larger planes normally provide greater seat-mile cost efficiency.[76]

In sum, that which drives the airline industry to produce excess capacity (the frequent overlapping ubiquitous hub-and-spoke networks) has forced an erosion of systemwide efficiency and productivity in the post-deregulation period. This has forced airlines to slow the pace of price decreases significantly from pre-deregulation trends, despite conventional wisdom to the contrary. From 1950 to 1978, pro-ductivity improvements (primarily attributable to the economies of scale of larger and larger aircraft flying longer distances, as well as advances in engine technology) allowed real yields to decline 2.5% per year on average. In contrast, from 1979 to 1993 real yield fell only 1.7% per year.[77]

---

[76] Melvin Brenner, James Leet & Elihu Schott, Airline Deregulation 95 (1985).

[77] ESG Aviation Services, 7 Airline Monitor 1 (Nov. 1994).

Chapter 2

Many carriers have inaugurated comprehensive efforts to cut costs. They have reduced or eliminated meals, reduced seat pitch, and deferred new aircraft purchases, for example. But in fact, most airline costs, including variable costs, are extremely difficult to manage. There is little an airline can do, for example, if the cost of Persian Gulf and West Texas crude begins to soar. Airline labor costs are theoretically pliable, except that most major airlines are highly unionized, and their work force is, and must be, highly skilled. Labor laws do not allow a unilateral lowering of wages or change of work rules by management without the kind of economic warfare and deterioration in labor-management relations no service industry can easily endure. Airlines have used their oligopsony power to roll back travel agent commissions.[78] But for many airlines, even variable costs are either outside the company's control, or extremely difficult to manage.[79] New entrant airlines, not burdened with union agreements, and with a junior work force, have a comparative cost advantage in terms of lower wages and less restrictive work rules.

Nonetheless, large airlines enjoy several economies of size vis-à-vis small airlines. One of the principal advantages of size consists of economies of information and transaction costs. An individual passenger knows a large network carrier can fly her to virtually any conceivable point. In contrast, it is costly for a new airline to inform the public it has opened a new route to Des Moines, and for the public to learn that there is now a new competitor in the Des Moines market.

As noted above, airlines appear to enjoy significant economies of density. Adding more flights or seats to an existing city-pair market will result in lower ASM costs, for it has only a modest impact on airport station costs (i.e., ticket counters, baggage handling, mechanics, and ground crew) and marketing costs (e.g., advertising).[80]

While the principal focus of this book is on the passenger market, it would be inappropriate not to address cargo issues, for air cargo is an important stream of revenue for the combination carriers (accounting for nearly 10% of revenue),[81] and the air cargo industry

---

[78] James Lanik, Stopping the Tailspin: Use of Oligopolistic and Oligopsonistic Power to Produce Profits in the Airline Industry, 22 Transp. L.J. 509, 530, 531 (1995).
[79] Robert L. Crandall, The Unique U.S. Airline Industry, in Handbook of Airline Economics 5 (D. Jenkins ed. 1995).
[80] Michael Tretheway & Tae Oum, Airline Economics: Foundations for Strategy and Policy 10 (1992).
[81] Air Transport Ass'n., The Airline Handbook (1993).

itself is a tremendously important mode of moving the world's commodities on a "just-in-time" inventory basis. Air cargo can also be divided into three principal segments—air mail, air express, and air freight.[82] Air express typically consists of small, high-value, time-sensitive shipments. Federal Express [now FedEx] grew in response to the need for the overnight shipment of documents which the U.S. Postal Service was seemingly unable to perform. By the mid-1990s, FedEx was flying more than 500 aircraft, handing 2.4 million packages daily, and transporting 40 million tons of freight monthly. Compared to air express, air freight usually consists of relatively larger shipments which are somewhat less time-sensitive.[83]

Other characteristics of air freight differ from passenger transportation. Air freight movements tend to be uni-directional, while most passengers travel round-trip. Cargo is far less concerned with circuity of movement, number of stops or transfers, schedule, cold weather, or the need to be fed, than are passengers, who prefer nonstop flights departing and arriving at convenient times, a warm and dry environment, hot food and cold drinks. Of course, hubbing forces passengers to endure circuity, delay, and transfer from one aircraft to another, while cost cutting has eliminated the hot meals—or in other words, treating passengers as if they were cargo.

PRICE

The airline industry exhibits a relentless tendency both to produce excess capacity and to price its product below fully allocated costs. The demand of consumers for schedule frequency produces tremendous excess capacity with no shelf life, pushing costs up. The widespread price elasticity of demand of discretionary travelers creates an environment where lowering prices will sell highly perishable inventory. The demand of consumers for low prices and a perception that air transportation is virtually a fungible commodity, as well as the desire of producers to sell as much of their abundant and perishable inventory as possible, drives prices down to levels which often fail to cover fully allocated costs.

---

[82] See the companion to this volume, Paul Stephen Dempsey and Laurence E. Gesell, Air Transportation: Foundations for the 21st Century (1997), Chapter 7.
[83] Michael Tretheway & Tae Oum, Airline Economics: Foundations for Strategy and Policy 29, 30 (1992).

Airlines are labor intensive and fuel intensive.[84] Unlike most service industries, airlines are also capital intensive, requiring tremendous investment in operating equipment and facilities, which regularly needs servicing, overhaul, and replacement.[85] Historically, airlines have spent 15% of annual revenue on capital equipment, more than double the average for manufacturing companies.[86] Also of note, the airline industry has relatively high fixed costs. Excessive capacity coupled with perishable inventory creates a tendency toward variable cost pricing. The incremental costs of adding a passenger to a scheduled flight are nil (e.g., a bag of peanuts, a cup of Coca-Cola, a few gallons of kerosene in the wings, and sometimes, a sales commission and other distribution costs). But industry costs are disproportionately fixed, with fixed costs comprising between 80% and 90% of total costs.[87] As Melvin Brenner has observed, "in air transport economics, the variable costs of filling an otherwise empty seat is close to zero. Thus, there is ever-present in this situation the encouragement of a pricing level that is less than compensatory in relation to fully allocated costs."[88]

In the long run, carriers must recover their fixed costs or face bankruptcy (as scores of airlines have learned). Individually, carrier behavior is rational. If one carrier lowers its price in a city-pair market (either because it wants to stimulate demand, consume excess capacity, or attract market identity), each competitor is faced with a Hobson's choice—either meet the lower fare, even if it fails to cover fully allocated costs, or hold its prices firm, which will cause it to lose even more market share and revenue than if it met the new low price. Selling a seat below fully allocated costs is manifestly unprofitable over the long-term. But any ticket sold at a price above the relatively low variable cost level makes some contribution to fixed costs, however small; an empty seat makes absolutely no contribution.[89] The result is that both the price leader and the price follower

---

[84] Newal Taneja, Civil Aviation 132 (2d ed. 1989).
[85] Air Transport Ass'n., The Airline Handbook (1993).
[86] Gerald Arpey, The Challenge of Airline Finance, in Handbook of Airline Economics 235 (D. Jenkins ed. 1995).
[87] Robert L. Crandall, The Unique U.S. Airline Industry, in Handbook of Airline Economics 3 (D. Jenkins ed. 1995).
[88] Melvin Brenner, James Leet & Elihu Schott, Airline Deregulation 86 (1985).
[89] Robert L. Crandall, The Unique U.S. Airline Industry, in Handbook of Airline Economics 5 (D. Jenkins ed. 1995).

sometimes raise their break-even load factors beyond attainable levels. Thus, capacity and pricing behavior of competing firms is sometimes individually rational, but collectively irrational. On this point, American Airlines' CEO Bob Crandall has observed:

> While each participant's actions make sense within its particular framework, the cumulative result is severe price instability for the industry as a whole . . . . [The cumulative impact of high fixed costs, low variable costs, and highly perishable inventory] encourages airlines to dispose of excess seats at almost any price. And all too often, that is exactly what airlines do, wreaking havoc as competitors scramble to match one sale after another . . . . As with decisions to add or sustain capacity, the pricing decisions of individual carriers usually make economic sense from the carrier's perspective. But for the industry as a whole, these decisions contribute to the continual price erosion which has restricted the ability of all carriers to increase revenues to keep up with rising costs.[90]

These factors cause cost and price to fail to achieve equilibrium at a level which covers fully allocated costs and allows an adequate profit. In the absence of government oversight or market concentration, the inherent primordial economic characteristics of the airline industry appear often to propel it to engage in below-cost pricing.

One major U.S. airline described the inability of airlines to avoid selling a seat for less than fully allocated costs even to consumers who otherwise would be willing to pay more for air travel:

> Airline seats are a perishable commodity whose costs include a very high proportion of fixed charges. As a result, there has al-

---
[90] Id. at 4, 5.

ways been a financial incentive for airlines to sell seats that would otherwise depart empty for any price that exceeds variable costs; i.e., expenses for passenger ticketing, baggage handling, food service and incremental fuel.

As simple and reasonable as this sounds, prices based on variable costs cannot, in the real world, be limited to seats that would otherwise depart empty. The highly competitive airline marketplace ensures that whatever price is set will be made available for a large percentage of all seats, including many that could have been sold at higher fares.

The problems associated with variable cost pricing become particularly acute when demand for air travel slackens. The lead time for new aircraft orders is two to three years, and airlines cannot quickly reduce their capacity without putting planes on the ground, a move than invariably means losing business to their competitors and—because fixed costs continue—forces up average unit costs. Thus, in periods of reduced economic activity, there are many more empty seats, a circumstance that leads to heightened temptation on the part of airlines to fall into the variable cost pricing trap.[91]

Unlike most industries, in commercial aviation computers (computer reservations systems) transmit real-time pricing information regarding schedule and price between any conceivable city-pair market anywhere in the world. Because a small difference in price can inspire a vast difference in sales, airlines are strongly incentivized to match the lowest fare in every city-pair market in which it competes (at least, on a capacity-controlled basis). As Dan Reed noted, "In the airline industry, it's said that fare prices in any market

---

[91] AMR Corporation, 1992 Annual Report 12 (1992).

will go only as high as the weakest—or, in some cases, the dumbest or most suicidal—participant in that market will allow them to go."[92]

Because industry costs are disproportionately fixed, selling seats at a loss often sacrifices less revenue than parking aircraft in the desert, because parked planes still generate costs but produce no revenue. Hence, excessive capacity (which the industry inevitably produces) too often remains aloft even when the highly cyclical demand curve turns downward.

Carriers attempt to cover their fixed costs through cross-subsidization—by imposing relatively higher prices on inelastic travelers (e.g., small business travelers) or in less competitive markets (e.g., hub origin and destination [O&D] passengers) through yield management. According to economist F.M. Scherer, "Price discrimination can be practiced profitably only if the discriminator possesses some monopoly power."[93] The existence of monopoly power in some markets (and destructive competition in others) is antithetical to the theoretical notions of perfect competition and contestability, which fueled the engine of airline deregulation.

OTHER FACTORS INFLUENCING ECONOMIC PERFORMANCE

Certain other factors influence airline economic performance. For example, the industry remains highly regulated and highly taxed by government. Airlines are highly dependent on governmental institutions for infrastructure, including airports and air traffic control, the efficiency of which directly effects the efficiency, productivity and pro-fitability of airlines. Technology turnover in the airline industry has been high. Technological breakthroughs by airframe or engine manufacturers can vastly improve airline performance. The airline industry is highly leveraged, financially and operationally. A modest improvement or decline in load factors can have a profound impact on profitability.[94] Cumulatively, all of the factors described above make commercial aviation unique among industries.

---

[92] Dan Reed, The American Eagle 149 (1992).
[93] F.M. Scherer, Industrial Market Structure and Economic Performance 323 (2d ed. 1979).
[94] Newal Taneja, Civil Aviation 131-33 (2d ed. 1989).

Chapter 2

THEORY OF PERFECT COMPETITION

Economic theory is examined here as it pertains to the question of regulation and deregulation. Emphasize are the writings of three economists—Alfred Kahn, Elizabeth Bailey, and Michael Levine—who were most responsible both for providing an intellectual justification for deregulation, and implementing it. Kahn, a Cornell University economist, served as Chairman of the Civil Aeronautics Board and President Carter's Chairman of Economic Advisors; Bailey, a Bell Labs economist, served as a member of the CAB; Levine, a University of Southern California law professor, was Director of the CAB's Bureau of Pricing and Domestic Aviation. (After deregulation, both Kahn and Levine assumed prominent positions in Frank Lorenzo's Texas Air empire). At this writing, Levine is a vice president at Northwest Airlines. While not the first economists to criticize economic regulation of the airline industry,[95] these "Three Marketeers" were the individuals most responsible for deregulation of the airlines, and the destruction of the Civil Aeronautics Board.

Economic theory has been an important catalyst in shaping U.S. aviation policy, and providing an intellectual justification for the philosophical movement of free market *laissez-faire*, which has manifested itself *inter alia*, in deregulation. As Elizabeth Bailey noted:

> Just as economic theory was useful in laying the foundation for reform, so economics has played a large role in its implementation . . . . Prior to regulatory reform, economic theory was ahead of policymakers in critiquing the existing system of regulation and was instrumental in providing the framework for change.[96]

Before they were deregulated, airlines were believed to be potentially naturally competitive, without economies of scale, scope or density, or significant barriers to entry. As Alfred Kahn said in 1977,

---

[95] See e.g., Lucille Keyes, Federal Control of Entry in Air Transportation (1951); Richard Caves, Air Transportation and Its Regulation (1962).
[96] Elizabeth Bailey, David Graham & Daniel Kaplan, Deregulating the Airlines 3 (1985).

"every study we have ever made seems to show there are not economies of scale [in the airline industry]."[97] Thus, deregulation was deemed likely to produce neither undisciplined concentration nor destructive competition, despite the allegations of most airlines to the contrary.[98] According to Kahn, aircraft were merely "marginal costs with wings."[99] The Austrian economist, Joseph Schumpeter, observed, "Analytical work begins with material provided by our vision of things, and this vision is ideological almost by definition."[100] *Laissez-faire* ideology was a powerful force fueling the movement toward deregulation.

Many of the problems which are endemic to the airline industry—excessive capacity and inadequate profitability, for example—were deemed by free market economists to have been created by regulation. According to Kahn, "the answer to the fear of excessive capacity and low load factors, I am convinced, is to revise the process that produces this kind of wasteful, cost-inflating competition, by opening the door to price competition."[101] Yet, excess capacity remains a chronic and inescapable problem for the airline industry. And, as will be seen in the next chapter, the industry's financial performance is profoundly worse under deregulation.

In articulating a theoretical justification for deregulation of the airline industry, deregulation proponents embraced neoclassical economic analysis, first using the model of perfect competition, and later, the more recently developed contestability theory.[102] A perfectly functioning market requires several ingredients. Property rights must be privately held, exclusive and transferable. Individual actors in the market must act independently, have perfect information and behave rationally. Transaction costs and externalities must be insignificant. No single producer or consumer may have market power; none may

---

[97] Aviation Regulatory Reform, Hearings Before the Subcomm. on Aviation of the House Committee on Public Works and Transportation, 5th Cong., 1st Sess. 1137 (1977).
[98] Paul Dempsey & Andrew Goetz, Airline Deregulation & Laissez Faire Mythology 179-87, 221-34 (1992).
[99] Said Kahn, with characteristic irreverence, "I really don't know one plane from the other. To me they are just marginal costs with wings." Barbara Sturken Peterson, & James Glab, Rapid Descent 77 (1994). Marginal costs are the costs of producing one extra unit of output, given a particular level of production. Paul Samuelson & William Nordhaus, Economics 74 (14th ed. 1992).
[100] Joseph Schumpeter, History of Economic Analysis 42 (Elizabeth Schumpeter, ed. 1954).
[101] Aviation Week, Mar. 20, 1978, at 41.
[102] See Michael Levine, Airline Competition in Deregulated Markets: Theory, Firm Strategy, and Public Policy, 4 Yale J. Reg. 393, 399 (1987).

Chapter 2

have the ability to unilaterally influence price (all are price takers, and the market has an atomistic structure). Each firm faces a horizontal demand curve, along which it may sell as much or little as it chooses.[103] Entry and exit barriers must be absent, and resources employed or potentially employable must be mobile. Given these assumptions, the market will clear at a price and level of output which reflects the optimum allocation of society's resources. Consumers purchase goods at prices closely approximating their marginal and average costs of production.[104]

A more formal definition of the theory of perfect competition has been proffered by several economists:

1. *The product is homogeneous.* In other words, the product sold by each firm is perfectly substitutable for the product sold by every other firm in the industry.
2. *The number of buyers and sellers is large*, each one of whom buys or sells only a small fraction of the products bought and sold in the market. No single buyer or any one seller can influence price. Each acts independently.
3. *Barriers to entry and exit in the market are relatively small.*
4. *All participants in the market, buyers and sellers, are adequately informed* about prices, quality, quantity, and other essential facts.[105]

In one sense the product is, indeed, relatively homogeneous—airlines fly essentially the same aircraft, with similar seat configurations and in-flight amenities. In another it is not—carriers can differ significantly in the quantity and schedule (timing) of flight frequencies they offer, and the number and array of destinations they serve. Quality can also differ marginally between carriers.

The number of buyers of air transportation is extremely large (450 million a year in the United States alone); the number of sellers is relatively large on a national basis, providing a wide array of connecting alternatives for trips more than about 1,000 miles. However,

---

[103] Paul Samuelson, Economics 484 Fig. 1(a) (1985).
[104] See generally, George Stigler, Essays On the History of Economics 234-67 (1965); F.M. Scherer, Industrial Market Structure and Economic Performance 10, 11 (2d ed. 1980).
[105] See Roger Miller, Economics Today 474-57 (5th ed. 1985); Edwin Dolan, Economics 551, 552 (4th ed. 1986).

the economics of aircraft size dictate that most city-pair markets can only serve one or two carriers on a nonstop basis,[106] and most hubs are dominated by a single airline, which can and do extract monopoly rents (the ability to raise prices above competitive levels, which produces a wealth transfer from consumers to producers, and thereby a regressive misallocation of resources). Thus, many air transportation markets are dominated by relatively few sellers. Oligopolists tend to compete on the basis of advertising or product differentiation, rather than price.[107] There is relatively little room for product differentiation in airline service except on the basis of schedule, and airlines tend to offer their product up at a fairly standard price (all airlines tend to meet the lowest price in the market, at least on some portion of its inventory, so as to not suffer a diversion of revenue to competitors). Because capacity is excessive and revenue is inadequate, the airline oligopoly functions poorly as wealth-maximizer, except in markets where exceptionally high levels of concentration exist.

Further, buyers with significant annual travel (typically Fortune 1000 companies) can and do exercise their oligopsony power to influence price downward. Many successfully negotiate a discretionary traveler price contract, without the advance purchase and Saturday night stay over restrictions.

The issue of barriers to entry and exit in the market is a more complicated one, and closely related to contestability theory, to be discussed below.

Finally, large carriers which own computer reservations systems have real-time information regarding sales of various product lines in various city-pair markets at particular prices, and can shift seats from one category to another, perhaps in a more agile fashion than can their competitors. Further, many consumers lack perfect information because, with hundreds of thousands of pricing changes daily, many laden with complicated restrictions, the labyrinthine pricing system raises the transaction costs for individual consumers of finding the most desirable combination of fare and restrictions. The fare, or the number of seats for which discounted fares are available, may change radically between the time the trip is booked and the journey is begun, meaning that a passenger who locked into a particular price

---

[106] Elizabeth Bailey, David Graham & Daniel Kaplan, Deregulating the Airlines 4 (1985).
[107] Robert Heilbroner & Lester Thurow, Understanding Micro-Economics 179 (1975).

with a nonrefundable ticket may pay more or less than the person seated next to him or her who purchased their ticket subsequently. Major airlines also encourage travel agents to obfuscate the better bargains by offering them commission overrides. The "halo effect" of computer reservations system [CRS] ownership allows a carrier which owns a CRS to enjoy more sales on its system than its competitors.

And what of the free market economists' view of rational economic man? Why does he seem not to dwell in the land of commercial aviation? Is it the industry's glamour, defiance of gravity, or just sex appeal that draws investors to this industry with such remarkably poor returns on investment? While most free marketeers assume rational behavior in terms of individual maximization of self-interest (broadly defined) and consistency (narrowly defined), a new generation of economists is adopting a more realistic and comprehensive view of man's behavior. Some, such as economist Herbert Simon, have redefined rationality to acknowledge it is "bounded"—the ability of people to make self-interested choices is limited by a lack of information of the cost of gathering and interpreting it. Economist Kevin Murphy assumes people make rational choices, but their range of options and preferences is often influenced and limited by factors outside their control. Others, such as economist Richard Thaler, attempt to devise economic models based of individual behavior which is rational most, but not all, of the time.[108] Economist Brian Arthur says the problem with mainstream economics is that it assumes people possess vast deductive abilities. A game of chess between two rational-expectations economists, he says, would consist of a couple of hours of silence while the players worked out all the moves, until one would resign. In fact, people play chess (and tackle other complex tasks) by spotting patterns and employing predictive rules of thumb. People also tend to pay excessive attention to recent data and insufficient attention to long-run averages and statistical odds.[109] From a macro-economic perspective, the swing in the business cycle appears to be a collectively irrational phenomenon. Keynes

---

[108] Richard Thaler, The Winner's Curse (1994).
[109] Rational Economic Man, The Economist (Dec. 24, 1994), at 90.

blamed these swings in the mood ("animal spirits") of entrepreneurs.[110]

Aside from the above-described excessive exuberance for new airline ventures, there is a lot of lemming-like behavior in the ranks of airline management. In the post-deregulation period, major airlines have gone through a series of waves of building hubs, acquiring smaller rivals, purchasing international routes, micro-managing yield, creating linear route "airlines within an airline," entering into global alliances, closing hubs, and cost cutting, in a frantic struggle to be King of the Hill (at one moment), or simply a surviving life form (at another). What one group of carriers does the others seem compelled to emulate. This seems to fit with Kevin Murphy's view that people may rationally choose to adopt irrational social norms.

Because of the economies of scale related to aircraft size, as well as the fact that thin markets cannot accommodate multiple competitors successfully, it was clear that deregulation would not produce a proliferation of a large number of sellers (carriers) in individual markets (nonstop city-pair routes). In fact, the overwhelming majority of nonstop city-pair markets are so thin as to suggest they may be natural monopolies. Hence, the success of deregulation could not be measured according to the theory of perfect competition.[111] This led proponents of airline deregulation to embrace a modified version of the perfect competition model—the theory of contestable markets.[112] Although it has had various formulations,[113] the essential components are three: (1) costless entry and exit (no sunk costs); (2) price sustainability; and (3) equal access to economies of scale and technology[114]—in essence, costless entry and exit at efficient scale.[115] According to Alfred Kahn:

---

[110] A Vicious Cycle, The Economist (Mar. 18, 1995), at 14.

[111] Elizabeth Bailey, David Graham & Daniel Kaplan, Deregulating the Airlines 4 (1985).

[112] Elizabeth Bailey & John Panzar, The Contestability of Airline Markets During the Transition to Deregulation, Law & Contemp. Problems 809 (1981); William Baumol, John Panzar & Robert Willig, Contestable Markets and the Theory of Industry Structure 7 (1982).

[113] Actually, the foundations of contestability theory, particularly costless entry and exit at efficient scale, were laid in Harold Demsetz, Why Regulate Utilities?, 11 J. L. & Econ. 55 (1968).

[114] See William Baumol, John Panzar & Robert Willig, Contestable Markets and the Theory of Industrial Structure (1982); William Baumol, John Panzar & Robert Willig, Contestable Markets: An Uprising in the Theory of Industrial Structure: Reply, 73 Am. Econ. Rev. 491 (1983). A different formulation was offered by Elizabeth Bailey and her co-authors: "(1) all factors of production are mobile among markets, (2) consumers are willing and able to switch quickly among suppliers, and (3) existing firms are unable to change their prices quickly in response to the entry of

> Almost all of this industry's markets can support only a single carrier or a few: their natural market structure, therefore, is monopolistic or oligopolistic. This kind of structure could still be conducive to highly effective competition if only the government would get out of the way; the ease of potential entry into those individual markets, and the constant threat of its materializing, could well suffice to prevent monopolistic exploitation.[116]

A decade after deregulation, 64% of nonstop U.S. city-pair markets were monopolies—they were served by only a single carrier—while 85% were (perhaps natural) monopolies or duopolies.[117] Unlike the theory of perfect competition, contestability theory does not require that a number of firms compete in a given market in order to produce efficient performance.[118] Since entry was thought to be costless, an airline which raised prices above or restricted output below competitive levels would be faced with new competitors attracted like sharks to the smell of blood—"hit-and-run" entry, as it was described.[119] Since incumbent airlines knew this to be the case, or would be quickly educated by new entrants, they would be dissuaded by the threat of entry materializing from extracting monopoly rents. According to Bailey:

> Actual competition in the market along with potential competition for the market would be effective in guaranteeing that supernormal profit would not be achieved. Thus, even in markets with substantial natural monopoly characteristics, the framers of deregulatory

---

a new firm." Elizabeth Bailey, David Graham & Daniel Kaplan, Deregulating the Airlines 153, 154 (1985).

[115] Michael Levine, Airline Competition in Deregulated Markets: Theory, Firm Strategy, and Public Policy, 4 Yale J. Reg. 393, 405 (1987).

[116] Alfred Kahn, Talk to the New York Society of Security Analysts 24 (Feb. 2, 1978).

[117] Paul Dempsey & Andrew Goetz, Airline Deregulation & Laissez Faire Mythology 233 (1992).

[118] Michael Levine, Airline Competition in Deregulated Markets: Theory, Firm Strategy, and Public Policy, 4 Yale J. Reg. 393, 404 (1987).

[119] Elizabeth Bailey, David Graham & Daniel Kaplan, Deregulating the Airlines 153 (1985).

> policy felt that carriers would not be able to set fares substantially above costs without inviting entry.[120]

Contestability theory posits that entry and exit are costless. But neither are costless in the airline industry, and sustained entry is quite difficult. Certainly, aircraft are mobile, and can land wherever there is a landing strip of adequate length (assuming an available gate and landing slot). But it takes more than a takeoff and landing to start an airline. A firm must make a substantial investment in pre-operating costs—assembling the financing, securing FAA and DOT regulatory authorizations (most of a safety and fitness nature), assembling management and operational employees and training them, securing office space and equipment, aircraft, ground equipment and services, airport gates, maintenance facilities, and the like. Even an existing airline incurs "ramp up" costs in opening a new market, marketing the new city-pair product, generating consumer familiarity with the carrier, and establishing patronage, which can consume several months of operation before break-even load factors are achieved.[121] Most of these pre-operating and "ramp up" costs are sunk costs; they are not recoverable if an airline leaves the market.[122]

Consumers have greater familiarity with an incumbent's service, reliability and schedule than a new entrant's. In order to generate some level of consumer interest in and familiarity with the new service, a new airline typically enters a market with a heavily advertised promotional fare, which may be below fully allocated costs unless an exceptionally high load-factor is achieved. But computer reservations systems allow almost instantaneous matching of the discount fare (some airlines have programmed their yield management software to automatically match new competing fares in a given market). The fact that the incumbent's prices are not "sticky" increases the cost of new entry.[123] New carrier entry typically does drive down prices, at least in the short run (until the new rival is driven from the market). Since sunk costs are not trivial, and an incumbent can respond in

---

[120] Id. at 4.
[121] Id. at 154 (1985); Russell Klingaman, Predatory Pricing and Other Exclusionary Conduct in the Airline Industry, 4 DePaul Bus. L.J. 281 (1992).
[122] Michael Levine, Airline Deregulation: A Perspective, 60 Antitrust L.J. 687 (1991).
[123] See Elizabeth Bailey, David Graham & Daniel Kaplan, Deregulating the Airlines 154 (1985).

price and quantity as quickly as a new competitor can enter, the mere threat of hypothetical new entry materializing apparently has little effect on an incumbent's pricing, contrary to the essential tenet of contestability theory.[124]

An incumbent airline can respond to new entry in a predatory fashion, for example, by matching its low fares on frequencies in close proximity to the new entrant's departures, meeting the new competitor's introductory fares and locking them in (i.e., refusing to follow the new price leader's fares up after the promotional period), dumping additional capacity (flights) into the market, or sandwiching the new competitor's frequencies (with a departure within a few minutes on both sides of the new entrant's departure) until the new entrant is financially exhausted and withdraws.[125] As Borenstein notes, airport dominance may intensify the retaliatory threat:

> Besides the advantage in attracting customers to its flights over a competitors', airport dominance might also allow an airline to deter entry of competitors. This could be done with a threat of retaliation, possibly made more credible due to airport dominance, or by blocking access to scarce gates or landing slots at an airport.[126]

Predatory pricing has been defined as pricing below an appropriate measure of cost for the purpose of eliminating competitors in the short-term and reducing competition in the long-term.[127] Under neo-classical free market theoretical beliefs, such predation is irrational, for the dominant firm engaging in the predatory behavior must be able to recover the short-term losses it incurs in the longer term after it has driven the new entrant from the market; since it can never hope to recover its short-term losses, it will not likely engage in such predation, at least in theory. Hence, many neo-classical econ-

---

[124] See id. at 164 (1985); See Severin Borenstein, The Evolution of U.S. Airline Competition, 6 J. Econ. Perspectives 45, 53 (1992).
[125] See Michael Levine, Airline Competition in Deregulated Markets: Theory, Firm Strategy, and Public Policy, 4 Yale J. Reg. 393, 417 (1987).
[126] Severin Borenstein, The Dominant-Firm Advantage in Multiproduct Industries: Evidence From the U.S. Airlines, Quarterly J. of Econ. 1237, 1248 (1991).
[127] Cargill, Inc. v. Monfort of Colorado, Inc., 479 U.S. 104 (1986).

omists argue that predatory pricing schemes are rarely attempted, and even more rarely are they successful.[128]

Despite the theoretical opposition to predation based on its hypothetical irrationality, airline observers have seen numerous examples of predatory behavior in the airline industry attempted since deregulation, with various degrees of success. Evaluating the post-deregulation experience, during which he served as CEO of a small airline (New York Air), Levine concluded, "I believe predation is possible and that it occurs . . . . [I]t is possible for an incumbent to impose on prospective entrants nonrecoverable costs by pricing in a way that seeks to ensure that they do not attract a significant share of passengers regardless of the incumbent's own costs."[129] Kahn concurred, criticizing Northwest Airlines for its "scorched-earth" policy of substantially undercutting People Express' price while simultaneously increasing the number of flights in the market, saying:

> If predation means anything, it means deep, pinpointed, discriminatory price cuts by big companies aimed at driving price cutters out of the market, in order then to be able to raise prices back to their previous levels. I have little doubt that is what Northwest was and is trying to do.[130]

An established carrier which finds its spokes assaulted by a new entrant typically will cut prices to meet the competition. Both will lose money, but deeper-pocketed large carriers have the ability to cover short-term revenue losses from profits derived from less competitive markets.[131] Typically, the major airlines offer the low fare

---

[128] See e.g., Robert Bork, The Antitrust Paradox 149-55 (1978); Areeda & Turner, Predatory Pricing and Related Practices Under Section 2 of the Sherman Act, 88 Harv. L. Rev. 697, 699 (1975); Easterbrook, Predatory Strategies and Counterstrategies, 48 U. Chi. L. Rev. 263, 268 (1981). This view was embraced by the U.S. Supreme Court in Matsushita Electric Industrial Co. v. Zenith Radio Corp., 475 U.S. 574 (1986).
[129] Michael Levine, Airline Deregulation: A Perspective, 60 Antitrust L.J. 687, 689 (1991).
[130] Alfred Kahn, The Macroeconomic Consequences of Sensible Microeconomic Policies, Soc'y. Gov't. Economists Newsletter (May 1985), at 6.
[131] Peter Cartensen, Evaluating 'Deregulation' of Commercial Air Travel: False Dichotomization, Untenable Theories, and Unimplemented Premises, 46 Wash. & Lee L. Rev. 109, 126 (1989); Russell Klingaman, Predatory Pricing and Other Exclusionary Conduct in the Airline Industry, 4 DePaul Bus. L.J. 281 (1992).

only on local O&D traffic on a large volume of seats on flights in close time proximity to the new entrant's, extracting higher yields from passengers connecting to the assaulted spokes. This revenue advantage may neutralize the new entrant's cost advantage and will deleteriously impact its staying power.[132] Levine notes, "The ability of an incumbent to respond rapidly and cheaply to the prices and output of new entrants contradicts perhaps the most critical assumption of contestability theory."[133]

Although many neo-classical economists continue to cling to the notion that predation is irrational and therefore highly unlikely to exist, modern economics literature has developed a theoretical model which supports the notion that dominant firms may attain monopoly power by placing their competitors at a competitive cost disadvantage.[134] In the airline industry, this may be reflected in vertical agreements between airlines and airports which tie up gates in long-term leases, and/or prohibit airport expansion through majority-in-interest clauses, allowing the incumbent to charge monopoly rents for gate sub-leases, or vertical ownership of computer reservations systems, which charge rivals prices far above any reasonable measure of costs. Raising rivals costs may also be reflected in a dominant hub carrier's refusal to enter into ticketing-and-baggage, joint-fare, and/or code-sharing with smaller regional jet carriers, and other violations of the "essential facilities doctrine." As Professors Krattenmaker and Salop note:

> There have been a number of criticisms made of the plausibility of predatory pricing, but these arguments do not apply to the exclusionary strategies we analyze. Raising rivals' costs can be a particularly effective method of anticompetitive exclusion. This strategy need not entail sacrificing one's own profits in the short run; it need not require classical market power as a prerequisite for its success; and it

---

[132] Michael Levine, Airline Competition in Deregulated Markets: Theory, Firm Strategy, and Public Policy, 4 Yale J. Reg. 393, 451 (1987).
[133] Id. at 393, 452 (1987).
[134] Thomas Krattenmaker & Steven Salop, Anticompetitive Exclusion: Raising Rivals' Costs To Achieve Power Over Price, 96 Yale L.J. 209 (1986).

> may give the excluding firm various options in exercising its acquired power.[135]

In one sense, barriers to entry appear deceivingly small, and were deemed inconsequential by deregulation's architects. As former DOT Assistant Secretary Matt Scocozza said, "in 1978 we envisioned that there would be a hundred airlines flying to every major hub."[136] A large used aircraft leasing market and a large number of skilled workers (individuals who had been laid off by the major airlines or lost their jobs because of major carrier liquidation) were available in the early 1990s. Despite their financial collapse, airlines remain a glamorous industry. Coupled with investor and lender enthusiasm for new airline ventures, this led to the emergence of a number of new airlines. But entering and surviving are two entirely different things.[137] More than a hundred new airlines have emerged since deregulation, and the overwhelming majority have collapsed in bankruptcy. Even entering a single market where the incumbent enjoys supra-competitive profits is difficult, given that the overwhelming number of nonstop city-pair routes appear able to support only a single airline, and that new entry must manifest itself inflexibly in plane-load lots.[138]

Barriers to entry have been defined as "any factor that prevents a new firm from competing on a equal footing with existing firms."[139] These factors are numerous in the airline industry, ranging from the consumption by incumbent airlines of airport gates and landing slots, to computer reservations systems.

Economies of scale, scope and density also appear to exist in the airline industry, although the fact that new entrant airlines have lower ASM costs than established major airlines might suggest the contrary to those who do not look more deeply. Larger aircraft, and larger fleets of aircraft, afford carriers scale economies in terms of lower unit operational and maintenance costs. There are the informational economies associated with incumbency—a small carrier must invest in relatively higher advertising, marketing and ramp up costs in

---

[135] Id. at 223.
[136] The Frenzied Skies, Bus. Week, Dec. 19, 1988, at 70, 71.
[137] William O'Connor, An Introduction to Airline Economics 7 (5th ed. 1995).
[138] Melvin Brenner, James Leet & Elihu Schott, Airline Deregulation 50 (1985).
[139] Edwin Dolan, Economics 602 (4th ed. 1986).

introducing its service to a city-pair market, while a large established carrier adding that city-pair to its existing hub network has relatively lower start-up costs. Likewise, there are the economies of scope that are achieved as a carrier increases frequency in a market (spreading more customers over its station costs, for example), as well as the impact enhanced frequency has on demand for its product (the carrier with more frequency enjoying a disproportionately larger share of passengers and higher-yield revenue). And, there are the network economies a hub carrier enjoys by adding a spoke to an existing hub network, offering a vast increase in the number of city-pair products it can offer. According to Levine, "We have seen the creation of a large number of hub monopolies because of the economies of scale and scope at the hubs."[140] Kahn has insisted, "We advocates of deregulation were misled by the apparent lack of evidence of economies of scale."[141]

Add to network economies the vast increase in product lines that are added when large networks are joined together in code-sharing relationships, relationships from which new entrants are generally excluded. In fact, some carriers, such as United, refuse to enter into joint-fare and code-sharing relationships with virtually all regional jet airlines in the continental United States.

Then there are the "induced" scale and scope effects, including frequent flyer programs (for which larger network carriers have a manifest advantage vis-à-vis their smaller competitors) which attract higher-yield business travelers, and travel agent commission overrides, which essentially bribe agents to steer business toward the carrier which offers them. These have been described in the literature as the "principal-agent" problem.[142] As Levine has noted, "by constructing incentive commission programs and by inventing frequent flyer programs, big airlines learned to create economies of scope and scale that are not present in the basic technology."[143]

---

[140] Michael Levine, Airline Deregulation: A Perspective, 60 Antitrust L.J. 687, 693 (1991).
[141] Alfred Kahn, Surprises from Airline Deregulation, 78 AEA Papers and Proceedings 316, 318 (1988).
[142] See Ross, The Economic Theory of Agency: The Principal's Problem, 63 Am. Econ. Rev. 134 (1973).
[143] Michael Levine, Airline Deregulation: A Perspective, 60 Antitrust L.J. 687, 690 (1991); See Michael Levine, Airline Competition in Deregulated Markets: Theory, Firm Strategy, and Public Policy, 4 Yale J. Reg. 393, 419 (1987).

Levine cataloged the multitude of developments not anticipated by the pro-deregulation economists—mergers and consolidations, vertical integration, hub-and-spoke systems, complicated fare structures, frequent flyer programs, travel agent commission overrides, computer reservations systems, slot and gate monopolies, predation, and the high mortality rate among new entrants. From these developments, he concluded:

> [T]hese unanticipated effects of deregulation seem to stem from the economics of information and from related economies of scope and scale, and from production indivisibilities (such as the problems of providing frequent and convenient service in city-pair markets with small traffic flows) . . . . Frequent flyer programs, the importance of travel agents and travel agent incentive programs, computer reservations systems, and hub and spoke systems all are techniques of utilizing economies of scale and scope to take best advantage . . . of the costs of communicating a complex web of service and service attributes to consumers . . . . The information and transaction costs are real . . . .[144]

Finally, equal access to technology essentially exists on the operations side of the equation—if it has adequate financial resources, a new airline can buy or lease a 737 or an MD-80 nearly as easily as an established airline can (albeit not at the same price). But on the distribution side of the equation, the largest airlines, which own the computer reservations systems, through which the vast majority of flights are sold, have superior access to proprietary information regarding their competitors' sales, and are incentivized to display their competitors' flights more poorly (for example, CRSs add the equivalent of 24 hours in time to non-code sharing connections so as to push them off the first page of the screen, where 85% of seats are

---

[144] Michael Levine, Airline Competition in Deregulated Markets: Theory, Firm Strategy, and Public Policy, 4 Yale J. Reg. 393, 423 (1987).

Chapter 2

sold), and earn significant revenue from their competitors' CRS bookings and sales. Some newer entrants have responded by attempting to sell their products directly to consumers through 800 toll-free telephone numbers and heavy advertising.

Most empirical studies have demonstrated that deregulated airline markets are not perfectly contestable,[145] and that there is a positive relationship between concentration and fares.[146] While ticket prices in city-pair markets with two competitors were about 8% lower than in monopoly markets, and markets with three competitors were another 8% less still, a potential competitor has one-tenth to one-third the competitive impact of an actual competitor.[147] The exit of a competitor results in a 10% average price increase for the remaining incumbents.[148] Other studies reveal that the number of competitors is not nearly as significant as their identity (e.g., Southwest's presence in a market creates deeper pricing competition than, say, Delta's).[149] Some deregulation apologists have insisted that the airline industry is "imperfectly contestable."[150] Without doubt, imperfection is an appropriate adjective to describe airline economics.

Although an early proponent of the application of contestability theory to the airline industry, deregulation advocate Elizabeth Bailey has concluded that airline ". . . markets are not perfectly contestable, so that carriers in concentrated markets are able to charge somewhat higher fares than carriers in less concentrated markets."[151] Michael Levine, another of deregulation's principal architects, said it even more strongly: "Unfortunately, those theories turned out to be wrong as they applied to the airline industry . . ."[152] and "airline markets cannot be modeled by any reasonably pure version of contestability

---

[145] The first article to cast doubt on the applicability of contestability theory to the airline industry was D. Graham, D. Kaplan, and D. Sibley, Efficiency and Competition in the Airline Industry, Bell J. Econ. 118 (1983).
[146] See sources cited in James Brander, Dynamic Oligopoly Behavior In the Airline Industry, 11 International Journal of Industrial Organization 407, 409 (1993).
[147] Severin Borenstein, The Evolution of U.S. Airline Competition, 6 J. Econ. Perspectives 45, 53 (1992).
[148] Id. at 54.
[149] See sources cited in William Evans & Ioannis Kessides, Structure, Conduct, and Performance in the Deregulated Airline Industry, Southern Econ. J. (1991).
[150] Steven Morrison & Clifford Winston, Empirical Implications and Tests of the Contestability Hypothesis, 30 J.L. & Econ. 53 (1987).
[151] Elizabeth Bailey, David Graham & Daniel Kaplan, Deregulating the Airlines 153 (1985).
[152] Michael Levine, Airline Deregulation: A Perspective, 60 Antitrust L.J. 687 (1991).

theory."[153] Levine concluded that new industrial organization theory better describes the airline industry.[154] Assistant Attorney General Charles Rule concluded, "Most airline markets do not appear to be contestable, if they ever were . . . . [D]ifficulties of entry, particularly on city pairs involving hub cities, mean that hit-and-run entry is a theory that does not comport with current reality."[155]

The consensus among economists today is that the airline industry does not reflect theoretical notions of perfect competition or contestability. The high degree of pricing discrimination between consumers and markets suggests that the industry may better reflect economist Joan Robinson's theory of "imperfect competition"[156] or Edward Chamberlin's theory of "monopolistic competition."[157] But the strikingly inadequate level of industry profitability in the post-deregulation environment suggests either that airlines have not yet transformed themselves into an efficient competitive model, or that they cannot (because relentlessly excessive capacity prohibits pricing at a level able to generate reasonable profitability), further suggesting that the "destructive competition" model may best describe the airline industry.

THEORY OF ECONOMIC REGULATION

The phenomenon of destructive competition has long been recognized as an appropriate rationale for government regulation.[158] In fact, destructive competition was a primary rationale for airline economic regulation in the 1930s.[159] Although imperfect, regulation attempted to solve the problem by attempting to rationalize capacity and stabilize pricing. (Nonetheless, as the national route network expanded

---

[153] Michael Levine, Airline Competition in Deregulated Markets: Theory, Firm Strategy, and Public Policy, 4 Yale J. Reg. 393, 405 (1987).
[154] Id. at 393, 418 (1987).
[155] Charles Rule, Antitrust and Airline Mergers: A New Era 15, 18 (speech before the International Aviation Club, Washington, D.C., Mar. 7, 1989).
[156] Joan Robinson, The Economics of Imperfect Competition (1933).
[157] Edward Chamberlin, The Theory of Monopolistic Competition (1933).
[158] See e.g., Paul Dempsey, Market Failure and Regulatory Failure As Catalysts for Political Change: The Choice Between Imperfect Regulation and Imperfect Competition, 46 Wash. & Lee L. Rev. 1 (1989).
[159] See Paul Dempsey, Robert Hardaway & William Thoms, 1 Aviation Law & Regulation sec. 1.03 (1993).

Chapter 2

during the ensuing decades, passenger traffic grew and real prices fell at faster rates than in the post-deregulation era).

In the mid-1970s, two lawyers—Phil Bakes (subsequently a lieutenant of CAB Chairman Alfred Kahn, and Texas Air's Frank Lorenzo) and Stephen Breyer (now a U.S. Supreme Court Justice)— were architects of Congressional airline deregulation as aides to Senator Ted Kennedy. In reviewing the allegation that "competition would force the airlines to charge prices that covered only variable, but not fixed, costs," they concluded that there was no evidence that destructive competition did (prior to regulation) or would (subsequent to deregulation) occur.[160]

As Chairman of the Civil Aeronautics Board, Alfred Kahn also dismissed allegations that deregulation would lead the industry to engage in destructive competition, saying, "the assumption that you are going to get really intense, severe, cut throat competition just seems to me unrealistic when you are talking about a relatively small number of carriers who meet one another in one market after another. We don't find in American industry generally when you have a few relatively large carriers competing with one another that they engage in bitter and extended price wars."[161] Kahn saw no differences between airlines and other major industries. As CAB Chairman, Kahn defied anyone to identify meaningful differences between airlines and grocery stores. But imagine a grocery store that had relentlessly high fixed costs, excessive capacity, and highly perishable inventory. A grocer who was selling a store full of commodities which had the spoilage properties of open jars of unrefrigerated mayonnaise would have to have a fire sale every few hours to rid himself of unsold inventory, for it could not be warehoused and sold another day.[162]

Before deregulation, Kahn adamantly denied that deregulation would "depress profits, render the industry unable to raise capital, and so cause a deterioration in the service it provides."[163] But after only a decade of deregulation, Kahn would confess, "There is no denying that the profit record of the industry since 1978 has been

---

[160] See U.S. Senate Comm. on the Judiciary, Subcomm. on Administrative Practice and Procedure, Civil Aeronautics Board Practices and Procedures 60, 61, 94th Cong., 1st Sess. (1975).
[161] Aviation Regulatory Reform, Hearings Before the Subcomm. on Aviation of the Committee on Public Works and Transportation, 95th Cong., 1st Sess. 178 (1977).
[162] Paul Dempsey, Running On Empty; Trucking Deregulation and Economic Theory, 43 Admin. L. Rev. 253, 306 (1991).
[163] Alfred Kahn, Talk to the New York Society of Security Analysts 14 (Feb. 2, 1978).

dismal, that deregulation bears substantial responsibility, and that the proponents of deregulation did not anticipate such financial distress —either so intense or so long continued."[164]

By the mid-1990s, some were alarmed by the fact that the industry had lost all the profits it had earned since the inauguration of commercial aviation in the 1920s.[165] With the benefit of a decade and a half of real world experience with deregulation, Kahn appeared to have changed his mind on the issue of whether the airline industry is subject to bouts of destructive competition. When asked about whether his vision of deregulation in the late 1970s included the steep financial nose dive that resulted from it, Kahn replied, "No. I talked about the possibility that there might be really destructive competition, but I tended to dismiss it. And that certainly has been one of the unpleasant surprises of deregulation."[166]

One need only revisit Alfred Kahn's 1971 treatise on economic regulation to find a definition of an industry which exhibits the tendency to engage in destructive competition. Wrote Kahn:

> The major prerequisites [of destructive competition] are fixed or sunk costs that bulk large as a percentage of total cost; and long-sustained and recurrent periods of excess capacity. These two circumstances describe a condition in which marginal costs may for long periods of time be far below average costs. If in these circumstances the structure of the industry is unconcentrated—that is, its sellers are too small in relation to the total size of the market to perceive and to act on the basis of their joint interest in avoiding competition that drives price down to marginal cost—the possibility arises that the industry as a whole, or at least the majority

---

[164] Alfred Kahn, Airline Deregulation—A Mixed Bag, But a Clear Success Nevertheless, 16 Transp. L.J. 229, 248 (1988).
[165] Because the numbers were not adjusted for inflation, they overstated the magnitude of the financial collapse in relation to accumulated industry profit.
[166] Anthony Velocci, Jr., Kahn Tells Airlines: Sit Tight, Cut Costs, Av. Week & Space Tech. (Aug. 16, 1993).

of its firms, may find themselves operating at a loss for extended periods of time.[167]

Kahn described the post-deregulation airline industry almost perfectly. Fixed costs outweigh variable costs, by a margin of about four to one. The airline industry suffers from relentless excess capacity. On a national basis the industry is unconcentrated, leading to tremendous network competition for connecting traffic, often driving prices down to variable costs. Under deregulation, the airline industry has operated at a loss for extended periods of time.

Another individual who may have explained why competitors sometimes tend to engage in individually rational, but collectively irrational, behavior is Garrett Hardin, a student of population and environmental problems. In his powerful essay, *The Tragedy of the Commons*, Hardin wrote:

> Picture a pasture open to all. It is to be expected that each herdsman will try to keep as many cattle as possible on the commons. Such an arrangement may work reasonably satisfactorily for centuries because tribal wars, poaching, and disease keep the numbers of both man and beast well below the carrying capacity of the land. Finally, however, comes the day of reckoning, that is, the day when the long-desired goal of social stability becomes a reality. At this point, the inherent logic of the commons remorselessly generates tragedy.
>
> As a rational being, each herdsman seeks to maximize his gain. Explicitly or implicitly, more or less consciously, he asks, "What is the utility to me of adding one more animal to my herd?" This utility has one negative and one positive component.

---

[167] Alfred Kahn, II Economics of Regulation 173 (1971) [citation omitted].

> 1) The positive component is a function of the increment of one animal. Since the herdsman receives all the proceeds from the sale of the additional animal, the positive utility is nearly +1.
> 2) The negative component is a function of the additional overgrazing created by one more animal. Since, however, the effects of overgrazing are shared by all the herdsmen, the negative utility for any particular decision-making herdsman is only a fraction of 1.
>
> Adding together the component partial utilities, the rational herdsman concludes that the only sensible course for him to pursue is to add another animal to his herd. And another . . . . But this is the conclusion reached by each and every rational herdsman sharing a commons. Therein is the tragedy. Each man is locked into a system that compels him to increase his heard without limit—in a world that is limited. Ruin is the destination toward which all men rush, each pursuing his own best interest in a society that believes in freedoms of the commons. Freedoms in a commons brings ruin to all.[168]

Substitute airlines for herdsmen, aircraft for cattle, and the airways and airports for the commons and you can see how the airline industry propels itself toward destruction, particularly in a market in which consumers value frequency. Airlines have a tendency to "over graze" city-pair "fields" with an excessive number of aircraft feasting on a limited number of passengers.

It is the inability to capture the commons (for airlines: the airports and airways) through private ownership that creates a relentless ten-

---

[168] Garrett Hardin, The Tragedy of the Commons, Science, Dec. 13, 1968, at 1243; See also Laurence E. Gesell, Airline Re-Regulation 126,127 (1990).

dency toward excessive consumption of its resources. Hardin points out that the tragedy of the commons can be avoided where private property rights exist. The problem is dividing the skies into parcels of property. Domestically, economic regulation attempted to parcel the commons into property rights by issuing certificates of public convenience and necessity to only that number of airlines the market could profitably support. In international markets, the bilateral air transport agreements effectively do that by limiting the number of entrants; capacity limitation agreements discipline firms from their primordial tendency to flood the market with excessive capacity; and price regulation attempts to restrain carriers from pricing below average fully allocated costs. Airlines operating in regulated international markets traditionally have enjoyed higher load factors and yields than in unregulated domestic markets, although consumers in most regulated international markets have been denied the opportunity to buy air travel below the cost of providing it.

Other economists have examined the airline industry and concluded that it does not fit the perfect competition model. As Robert Kuttner observed, airlines are "a highly capital-intensive industry with a standard product [which] cannot stand pure price competition—for all the profits would soon be competed away. Airlines dwell not in an Adam Smith world but in a world more reminiscent of economist Joseph Schumpeter's model in which 'efficiency' depends more on technical advances than on price wars."[169] Schumpeter was an Austrian-school lawyer/economist who argued that "perfect competition is not only impossible but inferior, and has no title to being set up as a model of ideal efficiency."[170] Professor Scherer concurs in Schumpeter's view that "perfect competition has no title to being established as the model of dynamic efficiency."[171]

Schumpeter believed productive efficiency was a superior measure of market performance than the perfect competition model, with its objective of creating allocative efficiency in terms of consumer welfare. According to Schumpeter, with sufficient profits, firms would be incentivized to create technological breakthroughs, and such

---

[169] Robert Kuttner, Flying in the Face of Reason: Why the Skies Need Regulating, Bus. Week (May 3, 1993), at 18.
[170] Joseph Schumpeter, Capitalism, Socialism and Democracy 106 (1942); F.M. Scherer, Industrial Market Structure and Economic Performance 438 (2d ed. 1980).
[171] F.M. Scherer, Industrial Market Structure and Economic Performance 438 (2d ed. 1979).

technological advances are the driving force in spurring economic growth. With airlines in distress (and with a the dominant hub-and-spoke route structure), the aircraft manufacturers have less ability to pursue the next generation of larger and faster aircraft.

But even among those who embrace allocative efficiency as the proper goal of a market economy, one finds serious doubt as to whether commercial aviation is able to achieve it. One school of economics which suggests that the perfect competition/allocative efficiency model is inappropriate for aviation centers around core theory. Core theory grew out of game theory, which uses formal mathematical models to evaluate different types of conflict between two categories, noncooperative (e.g., the prisoner's dilemma[172]), and cooperative.[173] The "core" is a key notion of cooperative game theory.[174] Cooperative game theory assumes that players communicate with each other, and are free to bargain or form coalitions with other players in order to maximize their personal benefit. A game has an empty core whenever each and every coalition can be outbid by a rival coalition. Games without a core lack the possibility of achieving a stable competitive equilibrium or a Pareto optimal result[175]—prices and output fluctuate incessantly.[176]

---

[172] Attributed to Thomas Hobbes (1588-1679), the prisoner's dilemma considers two prisoners suspected of criminal complicity. They are confined in separate cells and cannot communicate. The prosecutor confronts each individually with the following proposal: "Confess to the more serious charge and you will be treated leniently. Your partner in crime will be jailed for ten years, you for one. If you fail to confess but your partner does, the sentences will be reversed. Should both of you confess, each will be sentenced to five years. Yet should neither of you confess, evidence now suffices to convict both only on a lesser charge drawing three-year sentences each." If both prisoners are rational and committed to minimizing their own sentences, each will reason thus: "I don't want to confess, but the other person might. If he confesses and I do not, I get ten years and he one. So, I should confess. For then, if he fails to confess, I get one year, and if we both confess, we each get five." So, if rational, both will confess. See David Theo Goldberg, Ethical Theory And Social Issues 57 (2d ed. 1995).

[173] See John von Neumann & Oskar Morgenstern, The Theory of Games and Economic Behavior (1953).

[174] For an application of game theory to the airline industry, see James Lanik, Stopping the Tailspin: Use of Oligopolistic and Oligopsonistic Power to Produce Profits in the Airline Industry, 22 Transp. L.J. 509 (1995).

[175] Pareto optimality ia a utilitarian function; to satisfy a majority of the population. It differs from other utilitarian processes in that there are to be no losers when resources are distributed in a Pareto optimal fashion (i.e., anyone's gain cannot be to someone else's loss). When the distribution is "optimized", there is no way of making someone better off without making someone else worse off. Hence, in the airline scenario, Pareto optimalization occurs when just the right number of seats are sold in each of the seating classes—first, business, and coach. As a result, a first-class or business-class passenger, willing to pay extra, receives superior service, but not at the expense of coach passengers who, for whatever reason, do not pay the premium. Equity and efficiency, nor the

University of Chicago economist Lester Telser has applied core theory to the airline industry, and found its core to be empty. He identified six characteristics of markets with empty cores:

1. demand is uncertain or periodic;
2. plant capacities are large relative to demand;
3. plants have increasing returns of scale;
4. plants have fixed, or rigid, capacity;
5. there exist unavoidable fixed costs; and
6. it is costly to store unsold inventory.[177]

As already observed above:

1. demand for air travel is highly cyclical;
2. airline capacity exceeds demand by a wide margin;
3. airlines exhibit economies of scale, scope and density;
4. aircraft have fixed capacity;
5. airline fixed and sunk costs bulk dispropor-tionately large vis-à-vis variable costs; and
6. airline seat inventory is highly perishable and effectively cannot be warehoused.

Telser points out that the transportation industry is comprised of firms with fixed operating costs not dependent on the number of passengers, but on the length of travel and size of the vehicle. According to Telser, "Fixed costs of an airline depend on the distance the plane goes, or whether it takes off or not, but they don't vary based on the number of passengers."[178] Because of the nature of the airline industry's cost functions, the market lacks a core.[179] In a chapter entitled "Sufficient Conditions for Natural Monopoly or

---

relative value received, are not at issue. See Jeffrie Murphy and Jules Coleman, The Philosophy of Law 212-18 (1984).

[176] John Wiley, Jr., Antitrust and Core Theory, 54 U. Chi. L. Rev. 556 (1987); Abagail McWilliams, Rethinking Horizontal Market Restrictions: In Defense of Cooperation In Empty Core Markets, Q. Rev. Econ. & Bus. 3 (Sept. 22, 1990); Lester Telser, The Usefulness of Core Theory in Economics, 8 J. of Econ. Perspectives 151, 155 (1994).

[177] Summarized in Abagail McWilliams, Rethinking Horizontal Market Restrictions: In Defense of Cooperation In Empty Core Markets, Q. Rev. Econ. & Bus. 3 (Sept. 22, 1990).

[178] Timothy Smith, Why Air Travel Doesn't Work, Fortune, Apr. 3, 1995, at 45.

[179] Lester Telser, Competition and the Core, 104 J. Political Economy 85, 106 (1996).

Natural Monopsony," Telser observes, "The operating cost of an airplane depends primarily on its size and hardly at all on the number of passengers aboard." According to Telser, average cost in the transportation sector "is a decreasing function of output per plant."[180]

Economist William Sjostrom has also applied core theory to the transportation industry, focusing on ocean shipping. According to Sjostrom, "An empty core arises whenever capacity, defined here as the output associated with minimum short-run average avoidable cost, in the industry exceeds the quantity demanded at the price equal to that minimum average cost . . . . [W]henever there is short-run excess capacity, there is unlikely to be a competitive equilibrium."[181] The bottom line, according to Sjostrom, is that core theory "really amounts to saying that competition just isn't possible in some industries . . . ."[182]

According to economist Abagail McWilliams, "The policy implications of the empty core theory are clear. It is unrealistic to expect firms to act like perfect competitors in markets where the underlying supply and demand conditions make such behavior disastrous. The issue, then, is not whether some means should be used to achieve a nonempty core. The issue is what form the fix-up will take and how much inefficiency consumers should have to support for the sake of competition."[183] Telser concludes, "Eventually what happens is, the situation gets so bad that people realize that some very drastic reforms are necessary."[184] The drastic reforms that emerged in the 1930s from what was perceived to be destructive competition in the airline industry was economic regulation of entry, pricing and business practices. Telser suggests that long-term contracts or vertical integration might resolve the problem. According to Telser:

---

[180] Lester Telser, Economic Theory and the Core 45 (1978). See also, Lester Telser, Competition, Collusion and Game Theory (1972); Lester Telser, Cooperation, Competition and Efficiency, 28 J. L. & Econ. 271 (1985).

[181] William Sjostrom, Antitrust Immunity for Shipping Conferences: An Empty Core Approach, 8 Antitrust Bull. 19 (1993). See also, William Sjostrom, Collusion in Ocean Shipping: A Test of Monopoly and Empty Core Models, 97 J. Pol. Econ. 1160 (Oct. 1989)

[182] Timothy Smith, Why Air Travel Doesn't Work, Fortune, Apr. 3, 1995, at 46.

[183] Abagail McWilliams, Rethinking Horizontal Market Restrictions: In Defense of Cooperation In Empty Core Markets, Q. Rev. Econ. & Bus. 3 (Sept. 22, 1990).

[184] Id. A less pessimistic view is advanced by J.A. Donoghue, Discovering the Center, Air Transport World, June 1, 1995, at 5.

> [A] general method of resolving an empty core requires suitable upper bounds on the quantities that may be sold by certain sellers....
>
> It may seem that a proposal for restricting output must be inefficient, since it has the character of a profit-maximizing cartel. However, in the situation where no core exists, such upper bounds can be efficient, if suitably chosen....[185]

Finally, and succinctly, other economic characteristics of aviation require different types of governmental supervision. The airports themselves are natural monopoly bottlenecks (with declining costs over a large range of output), and are owned by local governments. Where they have been privatized, as in the United Kingdom, economic regulation has been imposed to prohibit monopolistic exploitation of tenants, for airports hold monopoly power over airlines. Externalities such as noise require environmental regulation, for without it, airlines would have little incentive to purchase quieter, but more expensive, aircraft. Safety regulation is mandated largely for social welfare reasons. While the tort litigation system motivates producers to higher levels of accident avoidance, it often works imperfectly. A firm close to bankruptcy, for example, might devote its limited resources keeping marginal aircraft aloft, rather than maintaining aircraft at the levels demanded for a near-zero accident objective. Public policy considerations will be addressed in the concluding chapter of this book.

---

[185] Lester Telser, The Usefulness of Core Theory in Economics, 8 J. of Econ. Perspectives 151, 159 (1994).

CHAPTER 3.

AIRLINE FINANCE

"Maybe it's sex appeal, but there's something about an airplane that drives investors crazy." [1]
Alfred Kahn
Chairman, Civil Aeronautics Board

"He whose investment banker neglects to mention the lessons of history, may be forever condemned to part with his money." [2]
Captain Dave Bates
Allied Pilots Association

"If we want a competitive airline system, we must allow the market to finish the painful process of eliminating whatever number of carriers are surplus to the market's needs." [3]
Robert L. Crandall
CEO, American Airlines

PROFIT (LOSS)

Profit, of course, is the margin between revenue and cost. In the airline industry, it is a thin margin indeed, with net profits hovering within only a relatively few percentage points (or fractions thereof) on either side of zero. The principal revenue streams for combination car-

---

[1] Quoted in Thomas Petzinger, Jr., Hard Landing 111 (1995).
[2] Dave Bates, Debunking the Myth, Flight Line (Apr. 1996), at 7.
[3] Briget O'Brian, Predatory Pricing Issue Is Due to Be Taken Up In American Air's Trial, Wall St. J., July 12, 1993, at A1.

Airline Finance

riers are passenger fares (first, business, and coach classes), cargo and mail, with additional revenue earned from in-flight amenities (e.g., liquor, movie head-sets, in-flight telephones, duty free and catalog sales), and non-flight services (e.g., sales of frequent flyer mileage, ground handling, maintenance, management services), non-operating (e.g., interest) income, and, for vertically integrated airlines, CRS booking fees. Major costs include labor salaries and benefits, fuel, maintenance, rentals, commissions and other distribution costs, food, landing fees, advertising, and interest, roughly in that order. Another way to divide costs is along functional lines: flight operations, aircraft and traffic servicing, promotion and sales, maintenance, general and administrative costs, and depreciation and amortization, roughly in that order. The difference between the two clusters of revenue and operating expenses is net income (or net loss). Although the airline industry has long enjoyed a generally upward sloping operating revenue curve (by 1995, reaching $87 billion), its operating expenses have also been quite high, leaving operating profit to hover within a relatively narrow range of zero (see Figure 3.1, "Airline Industry Operating Revenue And Profit [Loss])".

Figure 3.1—AIRLINE INDUSTRY OPERATING REVENUE AND PROFIT (LOSS)[4]

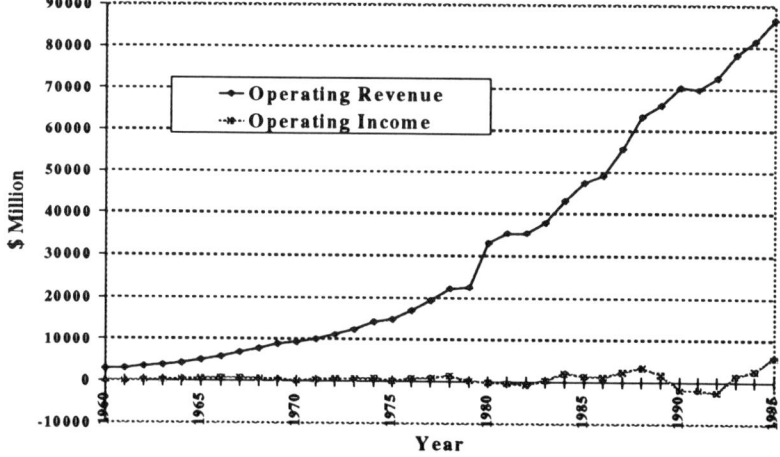

[4] Source: Air Transport Association.

Chapter 3

As noted in the previous chapter, the airline industry's economic performance is highly correlated with the market cycle, particularly rises and falls in disposable income and gross domestic product. Also noted was that as an economy matures, the multiple in air traffic growth declines over time. Moreover, as business traffic declines relative to leisure traffic, price elasticity of demand increases.

Among the major criticisms of economic regulation was that it allegedly produced excessive service competition, excess capacity, and bloated costs, and that these were the principal causes of inadequate profitability for the airline industry. Airline profit margins before deregulation were poor relative to the performance of other industries; but they deteriorated to even lower levels under deregulation. Airlines have sustained unprecedented financial losses since the advent of deregulation and liberalization.[5]

U.S. airlines were deregulated in 1978. Paradoxically, despite the fact that the industry has become very highly concentrated under deregulation, the first decade of deregulation produced an extremely modest net profit for U.S. carriers of $800 million on revenue of more than $400 billion. In the ensuing five years, net losses totaled $14 billion.[6] By the mid-1990s, the U.S. airlines alone carried a debt burden of $35 billion, or more than eight times the industry's total accumulated profit from the beginning of commercial aviation in the 1920s, until 1988.[7]

During the first decade of deregulation, the U.S. airline industry's profit margin declined 74%, from already unsatisfactory levels, to a paltry 0.6% (compared with between 3.0% and 6.0% for all manufacturers).[8] Table 3.1, "Net Profits Of U.S. Scheduled Passenger Airlines", reveals profit margins in the airline industry pre- and post-deregulation.

---

[5] See Paul Dempsey & Andrew Goetz, Airline Deregulation & Laissez Faire Mythology (1992).
[6] Julius Maldutis, Industry Investment Requirements—Looking Beyond 2000 (address before the 7th IATA High-Level Aviation Symposium, Sept. 6, 7, 1993, Cairo, Egypt).
[7] See Lisa Burgess, International Community Wants Action on Panel Report, Commercial Aviation News (Aug. 23, 1993), at 21. Actually, the amount of accumulated profit is overstated since it has not been adjusted for inflation. Despite the popular perception, in real dollars, the airline industry has not lost all the profit it ever made since the inception of commercial aviation.
[8] US Airline Deregulation a Financial Disaster, AFN Study Shows, Commuter Regional Airline News (Apr. 8, 1991), at 8.

Airline Finance

Table 3.1—NET PROFITS OF U.S. SCHEDULED PASSENGER AIRLINES[9]

Year	Return on Investment (%)	Net Profit ($ million)	Net Profit Margin (%)
1955	11.8	76	5.6
1956	9.4	80	4.6
1957	4.9	44	1.9
1958	6.3	50	3.0
1959	7.3	73	3.4
1960	2.8	9	0
1961	1.5	(38)	(1.7)
1962	4.1	52	0.4
1963	4.3	78	0.5
1964	10.0	223	4.8
1965	11.2	367	6.8
1966	9.7	427	6.5
1967	6.9	415	5.5
1968	4.9	210	2.5
1969	4.3	53	1.8
1970	1.4	(200)	(1.6)
1971	3.3	28	0
1972	5.1	215	2.5
1973	4.7	227	1.8
1974	7.8	322	2.1
1975	2.5	(84)	(1.8)
1976	8.5	563	2.0
1977	10.2	752	2.7
1978	13.3	1,197	3.6

(beginning of the deregulatory era)

---

[9] 1955-70: Melvin Brenner, Need for Continued Economic Regulation of Air Transport, 41 J. Air L. & Com. 793, 810 (1975). 1971-78: Melvin Brenner, Airline Deregulation—A Case Study in Public Policy Failure, 16 Transp. L.J. 179, 202 (1988). 1979-89: Melvin Brenner, Analysis of Airline Concentration Issue 84 (unpublished monograph, 1990). Air Transport Association; ESG Aviation Services, 9 Airline Monitor (Sept. 1996), at 12.

Table 3.1 (Cont'd.)

Year	Return on Investment (%)	Net Profit ($ million)	Net Profit Margin (%)
1979	6.5	347	1.3
1980	5.3	17	0.1
1981	4.7	(301)	(0.8)
1982	2.1	(916)	(2.5)
1983	6.0	(188)	(0.5)
1984	9.9	825	1.9
1985	9.6	863	1.8
1986	4.9	(235)	(0.5)
1987	7.2	593	1.0
1988	10.8	1,686	2.6
1989	6.3	128	0.2
1990	(6.0)	(3,921)	(5.1)
1991	(0.5)	(1,940)	(2.6)
1992	(9.3)	(4,791)	(6.1)
1993	(0.4)	(2,136)	(2.5)
1994	5.2	(344)	0.4
1995	11.9	2,314	2.4
1996	11.5	2,824	2.8

The two year period ending June 30, 1989, was the most profitable period in airline history.[10] But the industry's best net profit margin of the decade (2.6% in 1988) compares poorly with the Standard and Poor's 500 index which averaged 4% to 5%.[11] Philip Baggaley of Standard & Poor's offered a comparative analysis of airline performance vis-à-vis that of other industries:

> The Standard and Poor's 500 list of industrial, utility, and transportation companies has had

---

[10] Hearings on Leveraged Buyouts and Foreign Ownership of United States Airlines Before the Aviation Subcomm. of the House Comm. on Public Works and Transp., 101st Cong., 1st Sess. 14 (1989) (statement of Timothy Pettee).
[11] Business Is Picking Up for Airline Industry, Wall St. J., Mar. 27, 1995, at A1, A10.

> net profit margins averaging 4-5 percent over the past 10 years. The worst year saw a margin of 1.8 percent, and the best year 6.1 percent.
>
> By contrast, the scheduled passenger airlines have lost money in 6 of the last 10 years. Their best year, a 2.6 percent margin in 1988, would have qualified as the second worst year for the S&P 500.[12]

In the 1980s, returns of the Standard & Poor's Airline Index (consisting of American, Delta, United and USAir), lagged behind those of the S&P 500 in all but three years.[13]

Profitability turned sharply south in 1990, when the domestic airline industry suffered an unprecedented net loss of $3.9 billion—the worst losses in its history, until 1992, when it lost $4.8 billion.[14] The world's commercial airlines lost $2.7 billion in 1990 and $4 billion in 1991 on international routes alone.[15] One would anticipate that such dismal economic performance would force the airline industry to load up with debt. That, it has done.

Table 3.2, "Net Profit (Loss) Of U.S. Major Airlines", reveals the economic performance of the nation's major carriers during the worst economic period in their history.

By the end of 1991, the U.S. airline industry had lost all the profit it had earned since the Wright Brothers flew at Kitty Hawk, plus nearly $2 billion more. The net cumulative earnings of the U.S. airline industry is reflected in Figure 3.2, "Airline Industry Cumulative Net Profit".

---

[12] The Financial Condition of the Airline Industry, Hearings Before the U.S. House Subcomm. on Aviation, 104th Cong., 1st Sess. 48 (1995) (testimony of Philip Baggaley).
[13] Gerald Arpey, The Challenge of Airline Finance, in Handbook of Airline Economics 235, 236 (D. Jenkins ed. 1995).
[14] Laurie McGinley, Airline Industry Seen Posting Losses in Fourth Quarter, Wall St. J., Oct. 8, 1991, at A16. Few Bright Spots in 1991 for U.S. Carriers, Aviation Daily (Dec. 16, 1991), at 466; U.S. Airlines Will Lose Another $1.8 Billion in 1991, Aviation Daily (Dec. 10, 1991), at 429.
[15] Will They Ever Fly Again?, Economist (Mar. 7, 1992), at 67.

Chapter 3

Table 3.2—NET PROFIT (LOSS) OF U.S. MAJOR AIRLINES[16]
(in $ million)

Airline	1988	1989	1990	1991	1994	1995
AmWest	9.4	20.0	(74.7)	(213.8)	62.2	53.8
American	449.4	423.1	(76.8)	(239.9)	172.2	162.0
Continental	(315.5)	3.1	(1,236.4)	(305.7)	(613.0)	224.0
Delta	344.5	473.2	(154.0)	(239.5)	(258.0)	422.0
Eastern	(335.4)	(852.3)	(1,115.9)	--	--	--
Northwest	162.8	355.3	(10.4)	(317.0)	317.2	694.0
Pan Am	(118.3)	(414.7)	(638.1)	(309.2)	--	--
Southwest	57.4	71.4	47.1	26.9	179.3	182.6
Trans World	249.7	(298.5)	(237.6)	197.5	(435.8)	(227.5)
United	589.2	358.1	95.8	(331.9)	252.0	669.0
USAirways	217.2	2.1	(410.7)	(305.3)	(763.0)	34.4
TOTAL	1,310.4	140.8	(3,811.8)	(2,037.9)	(1,054.6)	2,214.3

Figure 3.2—AIRLINE INDUSTRY CUMULATIVE NET PROFIT[17]

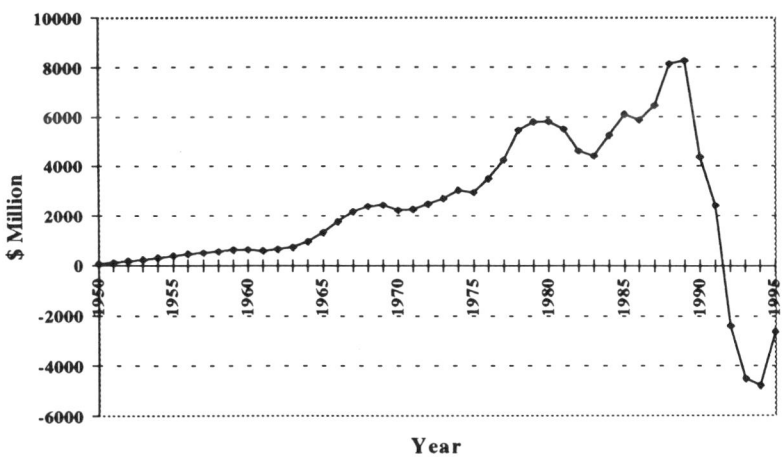

[16] Frank Mulvey, Airline Concentration and Competition At the Nation's Airports 19 (unpublished monograph 1992); Julius Maldutis, Update—August 1996 (Sept. 9, 1996), at 14.
[17] Source: Air Transport Association.

Anemic economic performance has forced more than 100 airlines into bankruptcy since deregulation began in 1978. Some entered Chapter 11 reorganization bankruptcy, continuing operations while seeking to restructure debt. Because they are shielded from their creditors while in Chapter 11, many "trash" the fares in the markets in which they compete, much to the chagrin of carriers operating outside of Chapter 11. Executives at United, American and Delta have urged the DOT to revoke the certificates of airlines in bankruptcy on grounds that they fail to satisfy the fitness obligations of the Federal Aviation Act.[18] Yet Steven Morrison and Clifford Winston allege that the bankrupt carriers have not constituted a source of significant revenue erosion for the major airlines. Never reticent to attach extravagant dollar numbers to their findings, they insist that the airline industry actually gained $1.6 billion from these bankruptcies by tarnishing the images of the Chapter 11 carriers and allowing their competitors to raise fares.[19] Morrison and Winston's claims of consumer benefits allegedly resulting from airline deregulation were extraordinary.

By the early 1990s, the airline industry had placed approximately $80 billion in orders for new aircraft—two to three times the total invested capital in the industry.[20] The industry needs to raise between $130 billion and $200 billion by the end of the decade for new aircraft (investing between $15 billion and $20 billion annually), and another $50 billion for airport and infrastructure improvements.[21] Bear in mind that the airline industry as a whole had operating cash of less than $5 billion and operating earnings of $2.3 billion in 1988, which was a very good year.[22] Excessive debt can have a debilitating effect on the ability of airlines to make new aircraft purchases, expand operations, maintain competition, or withstand the vicissitudes of the market cycle.

---

[18] Delta Executive Echoes Crandall Remarks On Bankrupt Airlines, Aviation Daily (Feb. 19, 1992), at 296.
[19] Steven Morrison & Clifford Winston, The Evolution of the Airline Industry 108 (1995).
[20] The Financial Condition of the Airline Industry and the Adequacy of Competition, Hearings Before the Subcomm. on Aviation of the House Comm. on Public Works and Transportation, 102nd Cong., 2d Sess. 589 (1991) (statement of Timothy Pettee).
[21] Laurie McGinley, Airline Industry Seen Posting Losses in Fourth Quarter, Wall St. J., Oct. 8, 1991, at A16; U.S. Airlines Will Lose Another $1.8 Billion in 1991, Aviation Daily (Dec. 10, 1991), at 429.
[22] Hearings on Leveraged Buyouts and Foreign Ownership of United States Airlines Before the Aviation Subcomm. of the House Comm. on Public Works and Transp., 101st Cong., 1st Sess. 3 (1989) (statement of Philip Baggaley); Id. at 73 (statement of Timothy Pettee).

Some blamed the financial collapse of the late-1980s and early-1990s on the Persian Gulf crisis, the spike in fuel costs it produced, an excessive amount of new aircraft capacity, and recession.[23] The Persian Gulf crisis and recession exacerbated, but did not create, inadequate profitability. Fuel actually cost the airline industry more per gallon in the early 1980s (reaching $1.06 a gallon in 1981—or, adjusted for inflation, between $1.40 and $1.47 a gallon) than in the late 1980s (reaching a high point of $0.80 a gallon in 1990)[24] (see Figure 3.3, "Domestic Aviation Fuel Costs"). In the early 1970s, the airlines confronted a more profound spike in fuel costs (with the Arab Oil Embargo of 1973, causing aviation fuel costs to rise 89% in 1974, compared with a 29% increase in 1990) and a severe recession, as well as an influx of new capacity (with the advent of the 747s, DC-10s and L-1011s) (see Figure 3.4, "Percentage Changes In Annual Fuel Costs").

Figure 3.3—DOMESTIC AVIATION FUEL COSTS

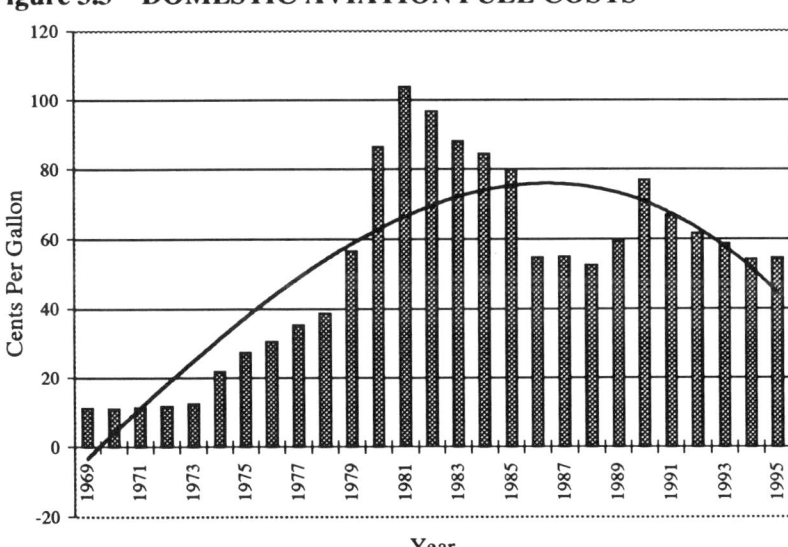

---

[23] See e.g., James Ott & Raymond Neidl, Airline Odyssey (1995); Transportation Research Board, Winds of Change: Domestic Air Transport Since Deregulation (1991).
[24] Samuel Buttrick, Airline Industry Database (1992); Flint, Don't Blame It All On Fuel, Air Transport World (Feb. 1991), at 32.

Figure 3.4—PERCENTAGE CHANGES IN ANNUAL FUEL COSTS

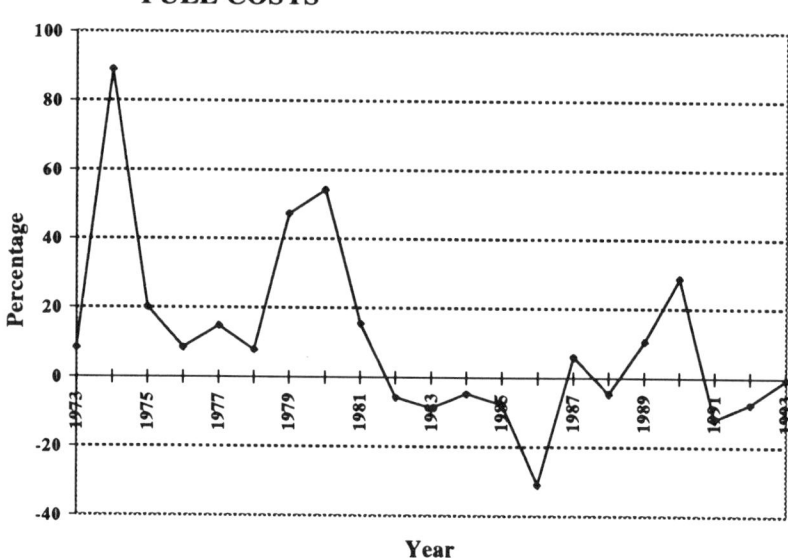

Recession hit the nation hard in the 1970s as well. But a comparison of industry profitability in the late 1980s and early 1990s with these nearly identical events in the 1970s, under regulation, contrasts sharply.

One widespread measure of operational performance by transportation firms is *Operating Ratio* [OR], which is pre-tax and pre-interest operating expense divided by operating revenue.[25] Operating ratio can be used as a direct measure of business risk.

Although counter-intuitive, the *lower* the OR the better for firm's performance. A company with an OR in excess of 100 is spending more money than it is generating. For example, a firm with an OR of 104 is spending $1.04 in expenses for every $1.00 of income it earns. As the following chart reveals, before deregulation, the airline industry had never experienced an operating ratio in excess of 100 (though it likely did during the pre-regulation period before 1938 for which, unfortunately, we have no data). Yet in six of the 18 (one-third of the) post-deregulation years (1978-1995), the industry has had operating

---

[25] Richard Kane & Allan Vose, Air Transportation 15-22 (7th ed. 1979).

Chapter 3

ratios in excess of 100. The average annual operating ratio in the 18 regulated years for which we have data (1960-1977) was 94.2; the average annual operating ratio for the 18 deregulation years (1978-1995) was 98.3, a deterioration of 4.1 (see Figure 3.5, "U.S. Airline Operating Ratios"). In other words, in the regulated period, the airline industry had 5.8% of operating revenue with which to pay interest, taxes and profit. In the deregulation period, that margin dropped to 1.7%. With such a razor thin margin, it should come as no surprise that net profit margins have collapsed under deregulation.

Figure 3.5—U.S. AIRLINE OPERATING RATIOS[26]

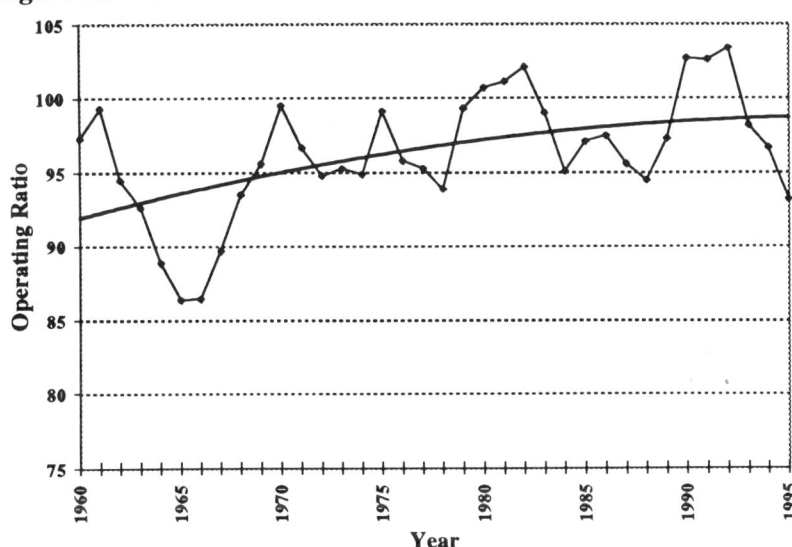

From 1977 to 1992, the global air transport industry earned gross revenue of just over $2 trillion, while operating expenses were $1.96 trillion; operating profit was 2% of revenue, and net profit was a meager 0.6% of revenue.[27] Worldwide, airlines experienced a $15 billion shortfall from 1989 to 1994.[28]

---

[26] Source: ESG Aviation Services.
[27] Richard Evans, Why the World's Airlines Can't Seem to Get Enough Case, Global Finance (May 1993), at 48.
[28] Pierre Jeanniot, The Balancing Act, IATA Rev. (Mar./Apr. 1994), at 4. The world's airlines lost $6.7 billion in 1991, $4.8 billion in 1992, $2 billion in 1993, and are projected to lose another $1.5 billion in 1994. Ian Verchere, IATA Expects World Airline Losses to Total $2 Billion,

Airline Finance

Historically, on an industry-wide basis, manufacturers rather consistently have earned a net profit margin between 4% and 6%. As shown on Figure 3.6, "U.S. Airline Industry Net Profit Margin", the U.S. airline industry's net profit margin averaged a modest 2.8% from 1955-1977, then collapsed to 0.5% from 1978-1987, deregulation's first decade. Add in 1988-1995, and the average after deregulation drops to a *negative* 0.3% (the airline industry's net profit margin averaged 1.6% in its ten profitable post-deregulation years, and -2.6% in its eight unprofitable post-deregulation years).

Figure 3.6—U.S. AIRLINE INDUSTRY NET PROFIT MARGIN

Commercial Aviation News (Aug. 23, 1993), at 18; Julius Maldutis, Industry Investment Requirements—Looking Beyond 2000 (address before the 7th IATA High-Level Aviation Symposium, Sept. 6, 7, 1993, Cairo, Egypt.
[28] Air Transport Ass'n., Annual Report (1994); Little Progress On Profits, Airline Bus., The Skies in 1994 60 (Supp. 1994). Julius Maldutis, Industry Investment Requirements—Looking Beyond 2000 (address before the 7th IATA High-Level Aviation Symposium, Sept. 6, 7, 1993, Cairo, Egypt); New Data Boost 1992 Losses, Airline Bus., The Skies in 1994 58 (Supp. 1994).

Since demand is cyclical, dependent on rises and falls in disposable income and consumer confidence, to some extent airline performance correlates with the rise and fall of the economy. Table 3.3, "U.S. Economic Expansion", shows periods of U.S. economic expansion

Table 3.3—U.S. ECONOMIC EXPANSIONS[29]
(since World War II)

Begin	End	Duration
(Month/Year)		*(Days)*
October 1945	November 1948	37
October 1949	July 1953	45
May 1954	August 1957	39
April 1958	April 1960	24
February 1961	December 1969	106
November 1970	November 1973	36
March 1975	January 1980	58
July 1980	July 1981	12
November 1982	July 1990	92
March 1991	July 1997*	75

* date of this writing

If one examines the historical trend there is evidence of several distinct cycles since the inauguration of the modern jet era (the introduction of the Boeing 727 and Douglas DC-9) in the early 1960s.

- *1961-1970*—On the heels of the 1960 recession, airline net profit margins hit a low of -1.2% in 1961 (when the industry lost $38 million), then rose to a high of 7.4% in 1965 and 1966 (when airlines earned their best operating and net profit margins ever, and made a net profit of more than $400 million each of the two years). Much of this high level of profitability resulted from a 7.3% annual productivity growth in 1961-1966, after the introduction of

---

[29] Jacob Schlesinger, The Business Cycle Is Tamed, Many Say, Alarming Some Others, Wall St. J., Nov. 15, 1996, at A1.

Airline Finance

jet aircraft.[30] The U.S. economy was expanding from early 1961 until late 1969. Turbo jets like the 707 and DC-8 had begun service in the late 1950s; the first generation turbofans entered service in the early 1960s, and by the mid 1960s, were abundant throughout the U.S. fleet. The recession which began in the fourth quarter of 1969 ended the cycle, so that by 1970 the U.S. airline industry suffered a net margin of -2.2% (as the industry lost $200 million).

- *1970-1982*—Operating profits nearly disappeared in 1970, as the industry's operating ratio hit 99.5. The negative impact of an influx of a large number of wide-bodied aircraft (i.e., the Boeing 747, Douglas DC-10 and Lockheed L-1011), dampened passenger demand caused by recession (from late 1973 until early 1975), and a sharp spike in fuel costs after the Arab Oil Embargo of 1973 was blunted by the Civil Aeronautics Board's route moratorium and capacity limitation agreements (activities which were viewed as anticompetitive, and served as catalysts for the regulatory reform movement), lasting from 1970-1975. Fuel prices increased 89% in 1974 alone, then another 20% the following year.[31] Carriers were forced to engage in operating changes to conserve fuel, resulting in an annual productivity improvement of 5.4% from 1975-1979.[32] Technology helped, with the introduction of the second generation high bypass ratio turbofan jet engines in the 1970s. Beginning in 1977, pricing and entry liberalization (regulatory reform) allowed carriers to rationalize their route systems and tap the elasticities of demand to fill seats which otherwise would fly empty. These factors contributed to a net profit margin of 5.4% in 1978 (when it earned an operating and net profit of more than $1 billion for the first time in its history). Perceived as a win-win situation for both the airline industry (which enjoyed better profits than seen in more than a decade) and consumers (which saw air fares plummet), Congress promulgated the Airline Deregulation Act of 1978, which eliminated pricing and entry

---

[30] David Swierenga & Mark Caldwell, Airline Revenues, Costs, and Productivity, in Airline Economics 3, 19 (G. James ed. 1982).

[31] Kathleen Argiropoulos, The Airline Fuel Crisis of the 1970s, in Airline Economics 99, 104 (G. James ed. 1982).

[32] David Swierenga & Mark Caldwell, Airline Revenues, Costs, and Productivity, in Airline Economics 3, 19 (G. James ed. 1982).

regulation of domestic air transportation. Recession again hit the national economy in 1980-1982. Without economic regulation to shield the fierce winds of recession, the airline industry suffered the first operating losses in modern history in 1980 (-$221 million), with new records set in 1981 (-$401 million) and 1982 (-$738 million). This cycle brought the airline industry to a new net profit low of -2.5% in 1982 (when it lost about $900 million net).

- *1982-1992*—The market cycle reached its zenith in 1988, when the airline industry enjoyed a net profit margin of 2.7% (earning $1.7 billion net). Late that year, Pan Am flight 103 was blown up over Lockerbie, Scotland, by a bomb planted in the baggage compartment, killing all 259 passengers aboard. Fear of terrorism as well as recession caused demand to drop in 1990. Fuel costs fell dramatically between 1982 and 1988, then rose in 1989 (14%) and 1990 (29%), particularly after Iraq's Saddam Hussein invaded Kuwait in August 1990. This drove up unit costs 8.8% in 1989 and 7.3% in 1990.[33] Coupled with a 7.9% increase in capacity in 1990, and national recession in 1990-1991, this caused the airline industry to reach a new record net loss in 1990, of -5.1% (when it lost nearly $4 billion net). But unlike earlier cycles, the last cycle did not bottom out promptly and dragged on for several years, as the industry suffered a net loss of -2.6% in 1991, -6.1% in 1992 (when its losses approached $5 billion), -2.6% in 1993, and -1% in 1994. The 1992 losses were exacerbated by the fare wars which began with American Airline's Value Pricing in April that year, and Northwest's response with "Grownups Fly Free" in May, which caused yields to spiral downward in a blood bath of red ink. The ripple effects crossed the oceans, with IATA carriers reporting net losses of -5.1% in 1990, -3.3% in 1991, -8.1% in 1992, and -3.8% in 1993. Never in the history of commercial aviation have so many airlines lost so much money.
- *1993-*   —Massive cancellations (in the late 1980s and early 1990s) of new aircraft orders began to slow the glut of capacity. Seven hundred aircraft were parked in the desert. Fuel prices stabilized (by 1994, aviation fuel was selling for nearly 30% less

---

[33] ESG Aviation Services, 9 Airline Monitor (Sept. 1996), at 1.

than its 1990 high), and the economy improved. Cost cutting, equipment deferrals and improvement in the overall economy began to be felt by the mid-1990s. Airlines began to pull out of their tailspin in 1993-1994, and the upward swing of the market cycle put them in the black by 1995-1996.[34] The major airlines enjoyed profitability, although a host of low-cost new entrant airlines were beginning to make their presence felt. The majors were no longer in adequate financial condition to engage in widespread price wars, and instead focused on surgical fare increases. Airline industry profitability was further enhanced by an extended exemption from the 4.3 cents a gallon excise fuel tax (until late 1995), and by a Congressional-White House budget impasse which caused the 10% ticket tax to lapse until the third quarter of 1996. By November, 1996, 68 months of sustained economic expansion contributed not only to the re-election of President Clinton, but to a significant improvement in airline economic health. The airlines began ordering billions of dollars in new aircraft, though this time insisting the new planes were predominantly for aging aircraft retirement and fleet simplification. In 1996, American Airlines signed an agreement with Boeing to purchase 103 jets valued at $6.5 billion, and to purchase Boeing aircraft exclusively until the year 2018 at the lowest aircraft price sold to any airline.[35] United ordered 51 Boeing and Airbus aircraft worth $4.4 billion.[36] USAirways ordered $4.5 billion in new aircraft from Airbus.[37] Of course, these are list prices. Major airlines enjoy discounts significantly below list. But once again, it was likely that airlines were ordering new aircraft in good times (the top of the market cycle), for delivery in bad (the bottom). According to British Airways' Chief Executive, Robert Ayling, "The penalties for insanity are higher than they used to be."[38]

---

[34] Some Unloading Heavy Baggage, U.S. News & World Rep. (Sept. 25, 1995), at 73.
[35] Scott McCartney & Jeff Cole, American Airline Signs Exclusive Pact To Buy Boeing Jets for Two Decades, Wall St. J., Nov. 22, 1996, at A3.
[36] Jeff Cole, United Air Places $4.4 Billion in Orders For 51 Jetliners From Boeing and Airbus, Wall St. J., Aug. 23, 1996, at C16.
[37] Susan Carey, USAir Weighs Ordering Up to 120 Jets To Simplify Its Fleet and Reduce Costs, Wall St. J., Oct. 14, 1996, at A3.
[38] Statement Before Salomon Bros. Transportation Conference (New York, N.Y., Nov. 14, 1996).

Thus, airline economic performance in each of these cycles has grown progressively worse, with generally declining highs (7.4% in 1965-1966; 5.4% in 1978; 2.7% in 1988; and, though with tax relief, it improved to 2.8% in 1996), and progressively deeper lows (-1.2% in 1961; -2.2% in 1970; -2.5% in 1982; and -5.6% in 1990).[39] Most of these profitability cycles correlate somewhat with the rise and fall in GDP and fuel costs, as well as fluctuations in fleet capacity. But the airline industry is hyper-cyclical. In good years, it has done nearly as well as other industries; in bad years, it has performed far worse. Individual airlines exhibit operational leverage—wide swings in performance based or relatively small changes in demand or costs. For example, in the 1980s, a one cent increase in fuel cut TWA's earnings by $14 million, while a single additional passenger booked on each of TWA's aircraft increased revenue by $12 million.[40]

The average net profit margin for U.S. airlines has fallen each decade. From 1955-1960, its net profit margin was 3.1%; from 1961-1970, the net profit margin was 2.7%. It fell to 2% from 1971-1980, then to -0.3% from 1981-1990, and then to -1.6% from 1991-1995.[41] Much traffic growth and corresponding revenue improvement is stimulated by declining yields. But the decline in real yields has slowed during the post-deregulation era, in part because of the relative dearth of major aircraft productivity improvements since 1978, in part because the grim U.S. air carrier financial condition has not allowed the airline industry to re-place fully its aging fleet with the newest generation of fuel efficient aircraft, and in part because hubbing has led airlines to fly relatively smaller aircraft shorter stage lengths (vis-à-vis the pre-deregulation trend of larger aircraft flying longer distances), thus depriving the industry of the economies of scale inherent in larger aircraft flying longer distances. Thomas Gallagher summed up the secular historical trends influencing the airline industry:

> Taken together, all these historical data argue that the macro drivers of air traffic growth, consisting of economic activity or income growth, its traffic multiplier, the real cost of air

---

[39] Data from ESG Aviation Services and the Air Transport Association.
[40] Mark Stevens, King Icahn 203, 204 (1993).
[41] ESG Aviation Services, The Airline Monitor 8 (June 1995).

travel, and its multiplier, are becoming increasingly less favorable each cycle. During the last four, real yields have steadily declined, spurring higher and higher levels of traffic. But over the same period, the rate of decline in real yields has, in itself, *decreased.* Here is the equally familiar notion of diminishing marginal returns: the yield phenomena resulting from improvements in efficiency, largely due to the introduction of modern jet aircraft, have shown a diminishing rate of influence.[42]

Homi Mullan, managing director of London's Chase Investment Bank, studied the cyclical trends of air traffic and airline operating margins, finding the two correlated closely with each other and with spikes in fuel costs and recession. But he objects to the complacency that "cyclical industry" theory has created, noting that "although we still have good years followed by bad, the good years are not as good as they used to be and the bad years are a lot worse than they used to be. Put another way, the industry's performance is steadily getting worse."[43]

Despite the conventional wisdom to the contrary, deregulation has *not* resulted in increased industry productivity.[44] In fact, hubbing, the primary means of rationalizing the market after deregulation, appears to have reduced efficiency and productivity as measured by labor and equipment utilization, and fuel consumption. Hubbing also has increased airport congestion, increased travel circuity, and been a catalyst for the purchase of smaller aircraft, ending the pre-deregulation trend toward larger and larger aircraft (with their corresponding lower ASM costs).[45] Despite squeezing seat pitch tighter and (for many airlines) reducing the number of flight attendants to FAA minimums, "in the ten

---

[42] Thomas Gallagher, Aircraft Finance and Aircraft Financial Analysis in the Fifth Cycle of the Jet Age, in Handbook of Airline Economics 223, 228 (D. Jenkins ed. 1995).

[43] Homi P. R. Mullan, Financing the Future, in Int'l Air Transport Ass'n., A Vision of the Future 69 (1995).

[44] "Any business that produces an ever smaller amount of physical product for each dollar of cost had better be able to raise its prices at will. Needless to say, this is not an option generally available to the airlines." ESG Aviation Services, 7 The Airline Monitor 5 (Sept. 1994).

[45] See Paul Dempsey & Andrew Goetz, Airline Deregulation & Laissez Faire Mythology 317, 318 (1992).

years after 1983, despite deregulation and intensified competition, neither cabin crew nor flight crew productivity appear to have improved in North America!"[46]

BANKRUPTCIES

More than 100 airlines have gone bankrupt since promulgation of the Airline Deregulation Act of 1978.[47] Beginning in 1989, several major airlines entered Chapter 11 (reorganization) bankruptcy, including Eastern, Pan Am, Midway, Continental, America West and TWA.

Several carriers found themselves in and out of bankruptcy. Continental emerged in 1986, then reentered in 1990. Eastern Air Lines, the nation's oldest (which began operations as Pitcairn Aviation on May 1, 1927) ceased operations on January 18, 1991. Midway Airlines, a creature born of deregulation, ceased operations on November 14, 1991.[48] Pan Am, which began flying on October 28, 1927, ceased operations on December 5, 1991. One would have anticipated that their elimination from the data base would improve the industry's aggregate performance. But by and large, it has not.

Several executives at the healthier airlines (e.g., American and Delta) have urged the Department of Transportation to revoke the certificates of airlines operating in Chapter 11 bankruptcy on grounds that they fail to satisfy the statutory standard of "fitness" required by section 401 of the Federal Aviation Act.[49] To date, DOT has shown little enthusiasm for the idea. Anemic profitability has been a major catalyst for bankruptcy. As a percentage of total capitalization, Eastern's debt climbed from 79% of total capitalization in 1980 to 473% in 1988, its last year before bankruptcy. TWA's debt increased from 62% in 1980 to 115% in 1989. Continental's rose from 62% in 1980 to 96% in 1989. Pan Am's debt (created in part by a changing regulatory environment, and in part by poor management) soared from

---

[46] Rigas Doganis, Fariba Alamdari & Andrew Lobbenberg, Who is Lean & Mean?, Airline Bus. (Nov. 1994), at 22, 31.
[47] Uchitelle, Off Course, N.Y. Times Magazine (Sept. 1, 1991), at 12, 14.
[48] Asra Nomani, Midway Airlines Grounds Fleet as Accord Fails, Wall St. J., Nov. 14, 1991, at A; Pan Am Shutdown Sets Up Bid War for Latin American Route Authority, Aviation Daily (Dec. 5, 1991), at 399, 400.
[49] Asra Nomani & Briget O'Brian, Healthy Airlines Lash Out at Their Struggling Rivals, Wall St. J., Mar. 17, 1992, at B4.

Airline Finance

62% in 1980 to 273% in 1989.[50] Congressman Byron Dorgan aptly noted, "I'm not so alarmed if they load up a lipstick company with debt and it fails. But if you do that to an airline, it's a real blow to the public interest."[51] It is difficult to argue that a company whose debt has been downgraded to "junk" or which has collapsed into bankruptcy can satisfy any legitimate test of "financial fitness." Nonetheless, DOT has never promulgated financial fitness standards, perhaps because any meaningful such standards would require the revocation of the operating certificates of a number of airlines, large and small.

Prior to deregulation, no major airline collapsed into bankruptcy. Weak airlines were bolstered by a paternalistic Civil Aeronautics Board with lucrative route awards. Like banking regulators, if all else failed, larger, the CAB encouraged healthier carriers to absorb the weaker birds. Thus did Delta acquire Northeast Airlines in the 1960s.

As revealed in the rather incomplete list in Table 3.4, "Airline Bankruptcies", since deregulation, more than 100 carriers have collapsed into bankruptcy.

Table 3.4—AIRLINE BANKRUPTCIES[52]

Carrier	Filing Date	Type of Filing	Successfully Reorganized?
1. **New York Airways**	5/18/79	Chapter 11	No
2. Aeroamerica	11/19/79	Chapter 11	No
3. Florida Airlines	1/24/80	Chapter 11	No
4. Indiana Airways	3/3/80	Chapter 11	No
5. Air Bahia	12/15/80	Chapter 11	No
6. Tejas Airlines	12/31/80	Chapter 11	No
7. Mountain West	3/6/81	Chapter 11	No
8. LANICA	3/16/81	Chapter 11	No
9. Coral Air	7/13/81	Chapter 11	No
10. Pacific Coast	9/11/81	Chapter 11	No

---

[50] Aviation Daily, Feb. 13, 1991, at 297.
[51] Smith, Trump Bid $7.54 Billion to Acquire American Air, Wall St. J., Oct. 6, 1989, at A3.
[52] The Aviation & Aerospace Almanac 102, 103 (1995).

Table 3.4 (Cont'd.)

Carrier	Filing Date	Type of Filing	Successfully Reorganized?
11. Swift Aire Line	9/18/81	Chapter 7	No
12. Golden Gate	10/9/81	Chapter 11	No
13. Pinehurst Airlines	1/26/82	Chapter 11	No
14. Silver State	3/3/82	Chapter 11	No
15. Air Pennsylvania	3/26/82	Chapter 11	No
16. Air South	4/2/82	Chapter 11	No
17. Cochise Airlines	4/16/82	Chapter 11	No
18. **Braniff International**	5/13/82	Chapter 11	No
19. Astec Air East	7/8/82	Chapter 11	No
20. Will's Air	8/19/82	Chapter 11	No
21. Aero Sun International	10/5/82	Chapter 11	No
22. Aero Virgin Islands	10/19/82	Chapter 11	No
23. Altair	11/9/82	Chapter 11	No
24. North American	12/9/82	Chapter 11	No
25. Island Empire	2/1/83	Chapter 11	No
26. State Airlines	2/14/83	Chapter 11	No
27. Golden West	4/18/83	Chapter 11	No
28. **Continental Air Lines**	9/24/83	Chapter 11	Yes
29. National Florida	12/2/83	Chapter 7	No
30. Air Vermont	1/30/84	Chapter 11	No
31. **Pacific Express**	2/2/84	Chapter 11	No
32. Dolphin	2/8/84	Chapter 11	No
33. Combs Airways	4/9/84	Chapter 11	No
34. New York Helicopter	5/1/84	Chapter 11	No
35. **Air Florida**	7/3/84	Chapter 11	No
36. Excellair	7/17/84	Chapter 7	No
37. **American International**	7/19/84	Chapter 11	No
38. **Emerald**	8/21/84	Chapter 11	No
39. Hammonds Commuter	8/29/84	Chapter 11	No
40. Air North	9/4/84	Chapter 11	No
41. Wright Air Lines	9/27/84	Chapter 11	No
42. Oceanaire Lines	10/2/84	Chapter 7	No
43. Atlantic Gulf	10/10/84	Chapter 11	No

Airline Finance

Table 3.4 (Cont'd.)

Carrier	Filing Date	Type of Filing	Successfully Reorganized?
44. Connectaire	10/10/84	Chapter 7	No
45. **Air One**	10/26/84	Chapter 11	No
46. Capitol Air	11/23/84	Chapter 11	No
47. **Wien Air Alaska**	11/28/84	Chapter 11	No
48. Northeastern Int'l.	1/8/85	Chapter 11	No
49. Pompano Airways	1/22/85	Chapter 11	No
50. Far West Airlines	2/22/85	Chapter 11	No
51. American Central	3/8/85	Chapter 11	No
52. Provincetown Boston	3/13/85	Chapter 11	No
53. Sun West Airlines	3/19/85	Chapter 11	No
54. Wise Airlines	5/1/85	Chapter 11	No
55. Cascade Airways	8/19/85	Chapter 11	No
56. Wheeler Airlines	10/7/85	Chapter 11	No
57. Pride Air	12/2/85	Chapter 11	No
58. Southern Express	1/21/86	Chapter 11	No
59. Imperial Airlines	1/30/86	Chapter 11	No
60. **Arrow Airways**	2/11/86	Chapter 11	No
61. Sea Airmotive	4/9/86	Chapter 11	No
62. SFO Helicopter	4/18/86	Chapter 11	No
63. Trans Air	8/19/86	Chapter 11	No
64. **Frontier Airlines**	8/28/86	Chapter 11	No
65. Chicago Airlines	2/19/87	Chapter 11	No
66. **McClain Airlines**	2/23/87	Chapter 11	No
67. Rio Airways	2/27/87	Chapter 11	No
68. Air Puerto Rico	3/6/87	Chapter 11	No
69. Gull Air	3/10/87	Chapter 11	No
70. Royal West Airlines	3/12/87	Chapter 11	No
71. **Air Atlanta**	4/3/87	Chapter 11	No
72. Air South Inc.	6/17/87	Chapter 11	No
73. Royale Airlines	9/9/87	Chapter 11	No
74. Sun Coast Airlines	1/5/88	Chapter 11	No
75. Air New Orleans	1/14/88	Chapter 11	No
76. Air Virginia	1/15/88	Chapter 11	No

Table 3.4 (Cont'd.)

Carrier	Filing Date	Type of Filing	Successfully Reorganized?
77. Mid Pacific Airlines	1/19/88	Chapter 11	No
78. Exec Express	3/4/88	Chapter 11	No
79. Caribbean Express	5/6/88	Chapter 11	No
80. Pocono Airlines, Inc.	5/25/88	Chapter 11	Yes
81. Virginia Island Seaplane	6/20/88	Chapter 11	No
82. Princeton Air Link Corp.	8/11/88	Chapter 7	No
83. Qwest Air	9/14/88	Chapter 11	No
84. Southern Jersey Airways	9/27/88	Chapter 11	No
85. **Eastern Air Lines**	3/9/89	Chapter 11	No
86. Big Sky Airlines	3/14/89	Chapter 11	No
87. Air Kentucky	7/19/89	Chapter 7	No
88. **Braniff, Inc.**	9/28/89	Chapter 11	No
89. **Presidential**	10/26/89	Chapter 11	No
90. Resort Commuter	11/17/89	Chapter 11	No
91. Pocono Airlines	1/23/90	Chapter 11	No
92. SMB Stage Lines	5/10/90	Chapter 11	No
93. CC Air	7/5/90	Chapter 11	No
94. Britt Airways	12/2/90	Chapter 11	No
95. Rocky Mountain Airways	12/2/90	Chapter 11	No
96. **Continental Airlines**	12/3/90	Chapter 11	Yes
97. **Pan Am World Airways**	1/8/91	Chapter 11	No
98. Pan Am Express	1/8/91	Chapter 11	No
99. L'Express	1/9/91	Chapter 11	No
100. **Eastern Air Lines**	1/18/91	Chapter 7	No
101. Bar Harbor Airlines	1/20/91	Chapter 11	No
102. Northcoast Executive	1/29/91	Chapter 7	No
103. **Midway Airlines**	3/25/91	Chapter 11	No
104. Grand Airways	3/26/91	Chapter 11	No
105. Metro Airlines	4/1/91	Chapter 11	No
106. Mohawk Airlines	4/1/91	Chapter 11	No
107. Jet Express	5/20/91	Chapter 11	No
108. Metro Airlines Northeast	5/30/91	Chapter 11	No
109. **America West**	6/27/91	Chapter 11	Yes

Airline Finance

Table 3.4 (Cont'd.)

Carrier	Filing Date	Type of Filing	Successfully Reorganized?
110. **Midway Airlines**	11/7/91	Chapter 7	No
111. Flagship Express	12/31/91	Chapter 11	No
112. Virgin Island Seaplane	1/22/92	Chapter 11	No
113. **Trans World Airlines**	1/31/92	Chapter 11	Yes
114. L'Express	2/28/92	Chapter 7	No
115. **MarkAir**	6/8/92	Chapter 11	Yes
116. Hermans/Markair Exp.	6/8/92	Chapter 11	Yes
117. States West Airlines	12/15/92	Chapter 11	No
118. **Hawaiian Airlines**	9/21/93	Chapter 11	Yes
119. Florida West	10/18/94	Chapter 11	Yes
120. USAfrica Airways	2/8/95	Chapter 11	No
121. **MarkAir**	4/15/95	Chapter 11	No
122. **Trans World Airlines**	6/30/95	Chapter 11	Yes
123. Business Express	1/22/96	Chapter 11	No
124. GP Express	1/22/96	Chapter 11	No
125. Jet Aspen	2/24/96	Chapter 11	No
126. **Kiwi International**	9/30/96	Chapter 11	?
127. Conquest	11/23/96	Chapter 11	No
128. Air 21	1/6/97	Chapter 11	?
129. Sun Jet International	6/18/97	Chapter 11	?

Bold = Airlines operating under FAR 121 and 14 CFR 401.[53]

Of the 50 largest regional airlines in 1983, by 1996, 42% had filed bankruptcy, and 50% had been merged with or acquired by other carriers.[54] As the list in Table 3.4 reveals, while there have been several significant successful airline reorganizations in bankruptcy (e.g., America West once, Continental twice, and TWA thrice), the overwhelming majority of airline reorganizations have failed. If one defines success for a new company as surviving a decade without bankruptcy,

---

[53] Part 121 carriers operate aircraft with fewer than 30 seats.
[54] Aviation Daily, Nov. 15, 1996.

the post-deregulation failure rate for start-up carriers is about 97%.[55] Moreover, the financial impact on investors and creditors has been unkind, even for the few carriers able to successfully reorganize under Chapter 11.

Chapter 11 has become a popular means of washing airlines clean of debt, a process which continues to erode the economic health of carriers not eligible for Chapter 11's debt shield. While in bankruptcy reorganization, a Chapter 11 airline can hold all creditors (except for airport proprietors and aircraft lenders and lessors) at bay, giving it a lower cost structure with which to price its product. This places non-Chapter 11 carriers, which must make current payments to all creditors, at a competitive cost disadvantage. As Chapter 11 has become more common over time, passenger demand has been less effected by it, so that load factors remain high for deeply discounted low-cost seats. Given the 20 to 30 year life of airline capital assets (aircraft), and the high cash flows generated from ticket sales, an airline can go through a very long period of chronic illness before it is deceased. With a bit of hyperbole, one airline executive referred to these anemic airlines as the "un-dead."

LEVERAGED BUY-OUTS

Deregulation freed corporate raiders, like Frank Lorenzo (at Continental and Eastern), Carl Icahn (at TWA), Alfred Checchi (at Northwest) and David Bonderman (at Continental and America West) to laden airlines with an enormous debt burden. The Airline Deregulation Act of 1978 removed governmental review of an airline acquisition by individuals unless they were "substantially engaged in the business of aeronautics."[56] Although the DOT has ample "financial fitness" jurisdiction to prevent the corporate raiders from saddling airlines with enormous debt, it has declined to do so. In fact, DOT affirmatively assisted the leveraged buy out [LBO] of Northwest, both by raising the amount of non-voting equity foreign carriers could invest, and according antitrust immunity to the marriage.

---

[55] Dave Bates, Debunking the Myth, Flight Line (Apr. 1996), at 3, 5.
[56] Paul Dempsey & William Thoms, Law & Economic Regulation in Transportation 242 (1986).

Airline Finance

But the LBO phenomenon began much earlier, while the Civil Aeronautics Board was steering the ship of deregulation. Frank Lorenzo took control of Texas International Airlines in a 1972 LBO. Shortly after deregulation began, Texas International's Frank Lorenzo asked the CAB's Mike Levine what the Board might do if one airline began a hostile takeover of another. Levine replied, "I thought the Board would have no view one way or another."[57] This gave Lorenzo the green light he needed, so off he flew.

Lorenzo's first target was National Airlines, a company three times the size of Texas International. He began buying at $26 a share, figuring the stock was undervalued relative to its assets, and that he would be buying aircraft at a steep discount. Other airlines jumped into the bidding war, including Pan Am, Eastern and Air Florida. National's management preferred Pan Am to Lorenzo, and sold the company for $55 a share to Pan Am, for a total of $400 million (from which it was to suffer a fatal bout of indigestion). Lorenzo earned $46 million in arbitrage on National's stock. He then set his sights on TWA (a company ten times the size of Texas International), inviting TWA's Chairman, Edwin Smart, to breakfast at New York's Hotel Carlyle. Lorenzo offered to buy TWA. Smart left abruptly without eating.[58]

Rebuffed by TWA, Lorenzo put Continental Airlines in his crosshairs. Fighting off Lorenzo's LBO of Continental Airlines, Continental CEO Alvin Feldman warned Lorenzo:

> Your proposal hardly seems fair. But, more important, the resulting company would be very weak. I believe its chances for survival would be poor. Even before it purchased Continental's stock, Texas International was a highly leveraged company with $183 million in debt and only $53 million in equity. When you add to Texas International the burden of additional borrowings you made to purchase the Continental stock, the situation becomes almost intolerable. The combined company would have

---
[57] Barbara Peterson & James Glab, Rapid Descent 78 (1994).
[58] Paul Dempsey & Andrew Goetz, Airline Deregulation & Laissez-Faire Mythology 26, 27 (1992).

> long term obligations of $642 million, and equity of only $142 million. This results in an 82:12 debt to equity ratio, which is worse than Braniff Airways at the end of 1979. More importantly, the debt service coverage requirement, including the dividend on the preferred stock you propose, approaches $150 million annually. The operating profit required to service this debt is more than our two companies together have ever earned.[59]

Feldman had previously headed Frontier Airlines, where he had been only one of two airline CEOs (Dick Ferris of United Airlines was the other) to support airline deregulation. Deregulation unleashed the corporate raiders to prey on the airline industry. Lorenzo was not dissuaded by Feldman's dire warnings, and succeeded in taking over Continental. Feldman was so distraught, he committed suicide. Within two years, Feldman's prophesy proved true. Continental found itself in Chapter 11 bankruptcy, where Lorenzo tore up the union contracts. Continental would find itself in Chapter 11 bankruptcy a second time before the decade was done. Eastern would be liquidated in Chapter 7, after Lorenzo stripped it of major assets at tens of millions of dollars less than fair market value.[60]

Lorenzo made another run at TWA in the mid-1980s. But the employees naively viewed Carl Icahn as their "white knight," surrendering significant wage and work rule concessions to persuade Icahn to acquire the struggling airline. (Frontier Airlines also found itself in Lorenzo's near grasp, where its employees too made significant concessions to their "white knight", People Express' Donald Burr).[61] Labor was duped at both airlines. Carl Icahn paid $440 million for 22 million shares of TWA in a 1986 LBO, then subsequently took the company private. Re-leveraging its assets, Icahn pursued raids on USX, Texaco and USAir. By 1989, it was estimated

---

[59] Quoted in Paul Dempsey & Andrew Goetz, Airline Deregulation & Laissez Faire Mythology 68, 69 (1992).
[60] Paul Dempsey & Andrew Goetz, Airline Deregulation & Laissez Faire Mythology 109-116 (1992); see also Aaron Bernstein, Grounded (1990).
[61] Paul Dempsey & Andrew Goetz, Airline Deregulation & Laissez-Faire Mythology 28, 29 (1992).

that TWA had a net worth of only $30 million, long-term debt of $2.5 billion, and a debt-to-equity ratio of 15-to-1. That year, Icahn sold $300 million of TWA high-interest junk bonds, secured on the airline's spare parts (e.g., light bulbs, gaskets) and landing slots. Junk bond holders found themselves stiffed as their investments were diluted in Chapter 11 bankruptcy.[62] Indeed, TWA would find itself in Chapter 11 three separate times.

Unfortunately, low debt has subjected some airlines to leveraged buy outs. Low debt suggests that there are lots of assets owned which can be sold to pay off the debt assumed during the acquisition. For example, Northwest had one of the lowest percentages of aircraft leased (4%) and one of the industry's most pristine balance sheets prior to its acquisition of Republic in 1986; it consistently earned an operating profit every year from 1983 through 1989[63] Among major airlines, only Delta had a more favorable debt-to-equity ratio.[64]

Denver oil king Marvin Davis began a hostile takeover bid for Northwest Airlines in 1989, offering $2.7 billion. He was out-bid by Alfred Checchi and associates, offering $3.7 billion.[65] In 1989, the Checchi group put up $40 million, while persuading KLM to put up $400 million (since written down to zero on KLM's books), while Northwest was saddled with more than $3 billion in debt. DOT ignored the financial fitness consequences, and liberalized the foreign ownership rules to facilitate the LBO.[66] More specifically, the transaction, which increased Northwest's debt-to-equity ratio from 0.42/1 to 5.85/1, allowed Wings Holdings, Inc., to acquire control of Northwest with 81.5% debt and 18.5% equity. Wings' debt was $3.1 billion, almost two-thirds of which was put up by Japanese banks. Equity was $705 million, of which Alfred Checchi, Gary Wilson and Frederic Malek put up only $40 million (for which they received about half the voting and nonvoting common stock), KLM (a Netherlands airline) put up $400 million (or 57% of the equity, for which KLM received 70% of Wings' nonvoting preferred stock, 31% of its nonvoting common stock, and 4.9% of its voting common stock, as well as a warrant

---

[62] Id. at 31-34.
[63] Aviation Daily, November 6, 1986.
[64] Transportation Research Board, Winds of Change: Domestic Air Transport Since Deregulation 72 (1991).
[65] Paul Dempsey & Andrew Goetz, Airline Deregulation & Laissez-Faire Mythology 14 (1992).
[66] Paul Dempsey, Robert Hardaway & William Thoms, 1 Aviation Law sec. 2.07 (1993).

allowing it to convert up to $50 million of its preferred stock into common stock, some of which could be voting), and Elders IXL (an Australian company) put up $80 million (or 11% of the equity, for which it received 10% of Wings' nonvoting preferred stock, 16% of its nonvoting common stock, and 15.4% of its voting stock).[67]

Northwest spent more than $3 billion on the LBO. That is more than the purchase price of Pan Am's trans-Pacific division (bought by United for $715 million), Western Airlines (bought by Delta for $860 million), Ozark Airlines (bought by TWA for $250 million), Eastern Airlines and People Express (bought by Texas Air for $676 million and $112 million, respectively), and Air Cal (bought by American for $225 million), *combined*. For these purchases, these airlines acquired significant operating assets and market share. For its purchase, Northwest acquired the talents of Alfred Checchi and associates.

By the early 1990s, Price Waterhouse concluded that Northwest was at a "critical juncture" and was facing "significant hurdles."[68] Most stem from the $3.65 billion leveraged buy-out of the company by Alfred Checchi and partners (Wings Holdings, Inc.) in 1989, which saddled an almost debt-free company with enormous debt.[69] Both mergers and route sales have been explored to shore up its financial condition and strategic position.[70] Northwest has among the oldest fleets of aircraft in the industry, and was unable to replace aging aircraft, instead choosing to "husk-kit" them to comply with Stage 3 noise requirements.

According to one source, the heavy debt burden put on by the Checchi LBO, coupled with these tremendous losses, caused Northwest's debt-to-equity ratio to soar to an unbelievable 30 to 1 ($4.2 billion in debt versus $141 million in equity).[71] Others estimated that Northwest carried $1.4 billion in debt.[72]

After the Checchi LBO, annual interest expenses at Northwest rose to $7,835 per employee, compared to $2,534, $1,612 and $928 at

---

[67] In the matter of the Acquisition of Northwest Airlines by Wings Holdings, Inc., DOT Order 91-1-41 (1991), at 2.
[68] Snapshot of the World's Major International Airlines, Wall St. J., Jan. 14, 1992, at A8.
[69] Asra Nomani, NWA Weighs Sale of Routes, Merger Option, Wall St. J., Feb. 11, 1991, at A3.
[70] Id.
[71] Laing, Losing Altitude: Heavy Debt Load, a Legacy of Its LBO, Weighs Down NWA, Barron's (Feb. 17, 1992), at 8.
[72] Lollar, It's Not Easy Being Fourth... Or Fifth, Frequent Flyer (Nov. 1991), at 8, 12.

United, American and Delta, respectively.[73] However, Northwest's deteriorating cash position was bolstered by an infusion of $790 million by the state of Minnesota to lure the construction of maintenance bases in the state.

The LBO so loaded Northwest with debt that, in order to avoid Chapter 11, Northwest deferred aircraft deliveries, persuaded banks to defer loan payments, and convinced labor to take deep wage cuts in exchange for stock. In 1993, labor surrendered $886 million in concessions over three years, in exchange for 33% of the company's stock. By 1994, despite several profitable quarters, Northwest was still struggling to refinance $4 billion in debt, with a $1.7 billion note due in 1997.[74] A balloon payment of $731 million due in the year 2000 was rescheduled to be paid out over three years beginning in 2005; that debt was taken off the books as long-term debt and treated as a minority interest in an affiliated company.[75]

Other raids ensued. Marvin Davis took his $30 million of arbitrage on the Northwest raid and put a siege on United Airlines. United CEO Stephen Wolf put together a management/pilot bid (partnering with British Airways) for $300 a share, or nearly $7 billion. Management would have owned 10%, British Airways 15%, and the employees 75%.[76] In October 1989, Donald Trump, a former suitor of United and purchaser of the Eastern Airlines' Boston-New York-Washington shuttle, bid $7.5 billion for American Airlines. Financing for the $7 billion bid collapsed on Friday, October 13, 1989, and Trump withdrew his bid for American.[77]

In order to thwart potential LBOs (and deal with a declining flow of operating profit, constricting their ability to finance capital investment from internal resources), some airlines have sold aircraft and leased them back, a strategy which reduces the inventory of aircraft which could finance an LBO, but nonetheless increases the long-term costs of doing business, whether the debt shows up on the books of the airline

---

[73] Laing, Losing Altitude: Heavy Debt Load, a Legacy of Its LBO, Weighs Down NWA, Barron's (Feb. 17, 1992), at 8.
[74] Steven Lifin & Carl Quintanilla, NWA May Turn to Modest Loan Plan, As Larger Credit Is Said to Worry Banks, Wall St. J., Oct. 17, 1994, at A4.
[75] Aviation Daily (Oct. 27, 1995), at 155.
[76] James Ott & Raymond Neidl, Airline Odyssey 27 (1995).
[77] Paul Dempsey & Andrew Goetz, Airline Deregulation & Laissez-Faire Mythology 14, 20 (1992).

or not. Delta traded blocs of stock with Swissair and Singapore Airlines to dissuade the LBO artists, and forge a marital relationship with two of the world's best carriers. According the Edmund Greenslet, the impact of LBOs has been profoundly unfortunate, by 1990 reducing industry equity by $6.2 billion:

> Leveraged buyouts may have worked in companies with a large free cash flow . . . . But in an industry where every dollar of cash flow is needed for capital investment, and where even this is not enough to supply all of the investment needs, a leveraged buyout is the height of folly.[78]

David Bonderman's LBOs were somewhat different than the rest; his group would pluck Continental and America West out of bankruptcy. Bonderman's group, Air Partners L.P., in cooperation with Air Canada, put up $450 million for 28% of Continental in 1992.[79] In 1994, Bonderman's AmWest Partners L.P. invested $220 million for 37.5% of America West.[80]

There appears to be a significant correlation between the aging fleets of aircraft and LBOs, suggesting that debt leverage impedes a carrier's ability to finance capital equipment needs. Thus, the oldest fleets of aircraft are operated by TWA, Northwest and Continental, all of which have been subjected to LBOs. Nonetheless, DOT has shown no interest in exerting its financial fitness jurisdiction to prohibit corporate raiders from loading up airline balance sheets with exorbitant debt.

HOLDING COMPANIES

The airline industry is a highly cyclical business. In an effort to ameliorate the fluctuations of the market cycle, beginning in the 1960s,

---

[78] ESG Aviation Services, The Airline Monitor 9 (May 1994).
[79] Michelle Mahoney, Continental, Air Canada Link Up, Denver Post, Nov. 10, 1992, at 1A.
[80] James Hirsch, America West Picks One Bid; Creditors Back Another Offer, Wall St. J., Feb. 28, 1994, at B12; Michelle Mahoney, America West Accepts Partners, Denver Post, Feb. 26, 1994, at D1.

TWA purchased several non-airline businesses, including Hilton International Hotels, Century 21 real estate, Canteen Corporation and Spartan Foods. Trans World Corporation was established as the parent holding companies of these subsidiaries, as well as TWA.

Diversification did temper the cyclical fluctuations in corporate financial performance. But it had two deleterious impacts. First, when the airline's losses were offset with non-airline profits, labor was less persuaded that wage and work rule concessions were necessary. Second, in the "junk bond" LBO frenzy of the 1980s, TWA looked more profitable to corporate raiders as the sum of its parts, rather than as an integrated whole. With corporate raiders on the horizon, TWA jettisoned its non-airline properties. The same occurred at United, when its Allegis (UAL) parent cut loose Hertz, Hilton International, and Westin Hotels.

Quite a different motivation for the holding company structure in the 1980s was manifested by Frank Lorenzo's Texas Air Corporation, the holding company for a number of subsidiaries, the most prominent of which were Continental, New York Air, People Express, Frontier, and Eastern Airlines. With a holding company, Lorenzo could create a "double breasted" non-union subsidiary to influence labor negotiations at its unionized sibling, Continental Airlines. (Frontier did the same in the 1980s with the creation of non-union Frontier Horizon). Moreover, one Texas Air subsidiary owned many of the aircraft Continental leased. In order to get pilots to cross the picket line after the 1983 bankruptcy and strike, Continental promised "profit sharing." Yet so long as Continental had a positive cash flow and could satiate even inflated lease prices, the profits could be upstreamed to Texas Air, leaving Continental's coffers relatively empty. Once Continental was in Chapter 11 bankruptcy, Lorenzo could funnel aircraft into non-bankrupt New York Air.

Once in control of Eastern Airlines, the holding company structure enabled Lorenzo to strip important assets out of Eastern (including, notably, the System One computer reservations system, numerous aircraft, and gates), and transfer them to other Texas Air subsidiaries at between $285 and $400 million less than fair market value, according to Eastern's bankruptcy examiner.[81]

More recently, American Airlines split its powerful Sabre CRS from the airline, making both companies subsidiaries of the AMR holding company. Sabre's enormous profits had obfuscated the somewhat mediocre performance of the airline, making labor negotiations more difficult.

ASSET ACQUISITIONS AND HORIZONTAL INTEGRATION

Yet another source of airline debt has arisen because of a large number of airline and airline asset acquisitions during the 1980s. Table 3.5, "Airline Acquisitions", summarizes the major purchases during this period, and the reported costs.

Table 3.5—AIRLINE ACQUISITIONS
(in $ millions)

Year	Acquired Airline Properties	Acquiring Entity	Price
1979	National	Pan Am	374
1980	Seaboard	Flying Tigers	unknown
1982	Continental	Texas International	100
	Braniff (Latin America)	Eastern	30
1985	Frontier (half its fleet)	United	360
	Frontier	People Express	307
	Muse	Southwest	61
1986	Pan Am (trans-Pacific)	United	715
	Republic	Northwest	884

---

[81] Paul Dempsey & Andrew Goetz, Airline Deregulation & Laissez-Faire Mythology 109-116 (1992).

Table 3.5 (Cont'd.)

Year	Acquired Airline Properties	Acquiring Entity	Price
	Ozark	TWA	250
	Eastern	Texas Air	676
	People Express	Texas Air	112
	Hilton International	United	980
	Western	Delta	860
	PARS CRS (50%)	Northwest	400
1987	Air Cal	American	225
	Pacific Southwest	USAir	400
	Piedmont	USAir	1,590
1988	TWA	Carl Icahn	unknown
	Flying Tigers	Federal Express	800
1989	Eastern (NY shuttle)	Donald Trump	365
	Northwest	Checchi Group	3,650
	Eastern (Philadelphia)	Midway	210
1990	Midway (Philadelphia)	USAir	68
	Eastern (Latin America)	American	471
	Eastern (LaGuardia slots)	American	10
	Eastern (Canadian routes)	American	10
	Continental (Seattle-Tokyo)	American	150
	TWA (Chicago)	American	83
	TWA (partial interest in PARS)	Delta	38
	TWA (D.C. slots)	United	19
	Pan Am (London)	United	400
	Pan Am (Berlin)	Lufthansa	150
1991	Midway (21 Chicago gates)	Northwest	22
	Eastern	United	90

Table 3.5 (Cont'd.)

Year	Acquired Airline Properties	Acquiring Entity	Price
1991	(Chicago & D.C. gates & slots) Eastern	Continental	54
	(LaGuardia gates & slots) Eastern	Delta	243
	(Canadian routes) Eastern	Delta	63
	(Atlanta and L.A. gates) Pan Am	Delta	416
	(European routes and NY shuttle) Pan Am (NY shuttle)	Delta	113
	Pan Am	United	135
	(Latin America) Air Wisconsin	United	72
	Pan Am Express	TWA	28
	TWA	American	445
	(LAX, JFK, BOS-Heathrow) TWA	American	110
	(Chicago-London) TWA	USAir	50
	(Philadelphia and Baltimore-London)		
1992	Continental	USAir	61
	(LaGuardia terminal and slots) TWA (Chicago)	American	500
1994	Morris Air	Southwest	133
	America West	AmWest Partners	220
1997	Frontier	Western Pacific	37
	AirTran	ValuJet	66
	Trump Shuttle	American	300

This trend may not be over. In 1996, Continental encouraged Delta to acquire it. Such an acquisition would create the world's largest airline, with 852 aircraft and $18 billion in combined revenue, and likely set off a new round of mergers with USAirways, TWA and American West as likely targets.[82]

Among the criticisms levied at economic regulation was its high cost. Whatever the direct and indirect costs of economic regulation over its 47 year history, they pale in significance compared with the above expenditures.

Even beyond its cost, acquiring another airline is a painful process. It requires integrating different corporate cultures, equipment types and labor seniority lists.

ASSESSING INDIVIDUAL CARRIER PERFORMANCE

Whether measured in terms of operating profits, net profits, return on investment, or return on equity, airline industry performance has been poor under deregulation, although some carriers have performed worse than others.

Thus, Southwest has consistently outperformed the rest of the industry. USAirs' performance was superior to most of the industry prior to 1989; Delta and Northwest also performed well before 1989. United's performance has been highly volatile. American initially adjusted well to deregulation, performing extremely well from 1984 through 1989. Continental adjusted poorly, suffering massive losses until its 1983 bankruptcy. Eastern also had difficulty adjusting. Pan Am performed poorly both before and after deregulation. The one airline created after deregulation in this group, America West, performed below-par nearly every year.[83]

How does one assess carrier performance among its peers? Most airlines are publicly traded; all commercial airlines must secure DOT certification. The requirements of the Securities and Exchange Commission [SEC] and the Department of Transportation [DOT] for public disclosure of financial and other performance data allow a glimpse of an airline's performance. *Form 41* reports are the various financial and traffic forms and reports required to be filed with the DOT pursuant to Part 241 (hence "41") of the DOT's Economic Regulations comprising the Uniform System of Accounts and Reports

---

[82] See Scott McCartney & Martha Brannigan, Behind Talks of Delta, Continental Are Fears Of Being Left Behind, Wall St. J., Dec. 5, 1996, at A1.
[83] See Steven Morrison & Clifford Winston, The Evolution of the Airline Industry 29 (1995).

[USAR] for certificated air carriers. Many of Wall Street's major investment houses (e.g., Lehman Brothers, Morgan Stanley, Salomon Brothers, Smith Barney, and Standard & Poor's) also periodically assess the strengths and weaknesses of individual airlines or peer groups of carriers.

But these are less than perfect portraits. It is said of airlines that they produce three sets of financial data (income statements and balance sheets)—one for the federal government, another for shareholders, and a third for internal use by management.[84] Nonetheless, accounting is the language of business, of reporting, measuring and communicating its performance. The principal financial statements are the *Balance Sheet* (which reveals assets, liabilities and owners' equity) and the *Income Statement* (which reveals revenue, expense, profit and loss over a period of time covered by the statement). Because of the emphasis on earnings, the income statement is usually considered to be the more important of the two.[85] Net worth and cash reserves are important indicia of performance, although the credit card companies typically restrict sufficient cash to cover passenger tickets sold but not yet flown.

A group of entrepreneurs typically will launch an Initial Public Offering [IPO] by securing an underwriter who will market the shares of stock, options and warrants, via a Prospectus. The *Prospectus* describes the new company, its strategic plan, how many shares will be issued, at what price, how many shares are held by the company's founders and its management, their identity and positions in the airline, the risks of investing in the new venture (as well as the risks inherent of investing in airlines generally), a description of the company's capitalization, how the capital proceeds are to be used, the business and marketing strategy, personnel, aircraft, their maintenance, facilities, a description of the securities, and the role of the underwriter.[86] The Prospectus typically will be written with a comprehensive (and perhaps draconian) description of investment risks, so as to avoid shareholder litigation on the issue of whether they were misled.

The underwriter will escort the company's founders and managers around to investment houses for a "road show" where they will attempt

---

[84] Charles Banfe, Airline Management 156 (1992).
[85] Richard Kane & Allan Vose, Air Transportation 15-1 (7th ed. 1979).
[86] See e.g., Prospectus of Frontier Airlines, Inc. (1994).

to entice investment by defining the market niche they perceive and how the new airline will fill it. Underwriters are also sometimes employed for "private placements," or the sale of large blocks of stock to a small number of investors at discounted prices.

New airline ventures are highly speculative endeavors. Nevertheless, in the early 1990s, several were launched. In 1994 and 1995, 22 new airlines were certificated by the DOT. Airlines are one of the few industries where a business can be built to $100 million in gross annual revenue in a relatively short period. Initial capital requirements are relatively small—between $70,000 and $100,000 per month to lease a Boeing 727, depending on its age and condition. With carriers such as Pan Am and Eastern liquidating their fleets, and some 700 aircraft parked in the desert, aircraft were plentiful. Skilled workers were also plentiful, and willing to work at entry grade wages, which made the new entrants' cost structures superior to the established majors. They rode the wave favoring IPOs, and the shift of capital away from the NYSE to the NASDAQ. Typically, IPOs involve the issuance of a mix of common and preferred stock, options and warrants. The new ventures were able to get off the ground quickly because of the ability to "outsource" such functions as maintenance, reservations, distribution, training, and such.[87]

Once the company is aloft, it will provide its shareholders with Quarterly and Annual Reports (although several major airlines ceased mailing Quarterly Reports to shareholders beginning in the mid-1990s). Typically, the *Annual Report* begins with a letter to shareholders from the CEO describing the fiscal year's accomplishments, and some vision of how the company is attempting to position itself to deal with its challenges. This is followed by detailed financial data, including a consolidated balance sheet, and statements of income, stockholders' equity, and cash flows, usually over several recent years. Typically, the financial data has been audited by an outside accounting firm, which will include an independent opinion (with new start-ups, sometimes reserving judgment as to whether the company will survive as a going concern). Nonetheless, these data are not entirely reliable, given the obfuscation of debt allowed by aircraft operating leases permitted by generally accepted accounting practices.

---

[87] Scott McCartney, Conditions Are Ideal For Starting an Airline, Wall St. J., Apr. 1, 1996, at A1.

The SEC requires quarterly production of a Form 10-Q, and annual production of a Form 10-K. Part 1 describes the firm's overall structure, lines of business and subsidiaries. The *10-Q* includes balance sheets, statements of operations, statements of cash flows, and management's discussion and analysis of the airline's plan of operations.

The *10-K* is perhaps the most useful public document of all. It describes the airline's overall structure, and it's lines of business. Among the items typically addressed are market share, route structure, employees, competitors, strategic plan of operations, aircraft and fleet acquisition plans, environmental considerations, capitalization, financing and liquidity, as well as an identity of the legal proceedings in which the airline is involved. Subsequent parts of the 10-K provide financial and operational data. Much of the 10-K information will be included in the firm's Annual Report.[88]

Subsequently, the exercise of outstanding warrants requires issuance of SEC Form *SB-2*, an Addendum to the Prospectus, which updates much of the information contained in the original Prospectus, with the addition of actual financial and operating information, its financial condition, plan of operation, its liquidity and capital resources, as well as the history and future of its operations.

The investment houses typically provide assessments of carrier performance vis-à-vis its competitors, although objectivity may be compromised where it underwrites or facilitates private placement of a portion of the capital issuance. These several sources, coupled with trade and general press accounts, provide a qualitative look at an airline's performance.

To determine the financial strength of a company and assess its potential for survival and growth, a detailed quantitative analysis is necessary. Solvency, financial stability and profitability are essential factors to be considered.[89] One must assess the airline's *liquidity,* or the debts due over the next year compared with current assets. The difference between current assets and current liabilities is *working capital.*[90] Given the cyclical nature of airlines, several rules of thumb have been suggested to describe a cash horde sufficient to weather the storm of a financial downturn. Some suggest $2 million per aircraft is

---

[88] Charles Banfe, Airline Management 156, 157 (1992).
[89] Richard Kane & Allan Vose, Air Transportation 15-20 (7th ed. 1979).
[90] Charles Banfe, Airline Management 159 (1992).

sufficient; others insist the carrier should have cash on hand sufficient to cover 90 days of operation without revenue.

The ability of an airline to meet its current obligations is defined by its *current ratio,*[91] or current assets (cash, securities, receivables, inventories and prepaid expenses) divided by current liabilities (liabilities that must be paid within one year). Current ratio reveals the short-term debt paying ability of the firm. Current assets are those expected to be realized in cash or consumed in the production of revenue within the year. Current liabilities are those debts or obligations due within the year. Firms prefer to maintain a current ratio of 1:1, with current assets equal to or greater than current liabilities. Because unearned ticket revenue (tickets sold to passengers not yet flown) is treated as a current liability, most airlines maintain a smaller ratio.[92] *Quick ratio* is a company's quick assets (highly liquid assets such as cash, receivables and securities) divided by its current liabilities; it reveals the firm's short-term liquidity.

Capitalization, or the relative relationship between debt and equity, is also an important measure of financial strength. An excessive *debt-to-equity ratio* suggests the company has higher risk, for even in a downturn, lenders must be paid; shareholders need not. A debt/equity ratio of 2.5:1 should raise a red flag.[93] A debt/equity ratio of 1:1 is considered healthy. Excessive debt creates a troublesome problem for an airline during downturns in the market cycle, for adding new debt can become prohibitively expensive. In 1993, Felix Rohatyn of the Wall Street investment firm of Lazard Freres estimated that the airline industry would have to earn a profit of $15 billion annually through the year 2000 to achieve a 1:1 debt/equity ratio.[94]

The *debt-to-capital ratio* consists of long-term debt (debts and obligations due after one year, including bonds, notes payable, mortgages, and lease obligations) divided by total invested capital (the sum of stockholder's equity, long-term debt, capital lease obligations, deferred income taxes, investment credits and minority interest). It reveals how highly leveraged the company is.[95]

---

[91] Richard Kane & Allan Vose, Air Transportation 15-22 (7th ed. 1979).
[92] Charles Banfe, Airline Management 160 (1992).
[93] Id.
[94] Address of J. Randolph Babbitt Before the Salomon Brothers Ninth Annual Transportation Conference (New York, N.Y., Nov. 17, 1994).
[95] Standard & Poors, Industry Surveys (June 30, 1994), at A47.

Net income is revenue from all sources minus expenses, taxes and fixed charges, and not including extraordinary items or dividend payments. *Return on equity* consists of net income, minus preferred dividend requirements, divided by the common shareholder's equity. *Return on assets* is net income divided by average total assets. This measures the company's efficiency in asset use.[96]

Net worth, or stockholder's equity, is the difference between total assets and total liabilities. It consists of funds raised from investors, plus retained earnings. If the firm has suffered net losses, these are subtracted from investors' capital. If net worth becomes negative, survival of the company becomes doubtful.

The *Statement of Cash Flow,* required in financial statements, includes an entry entitled "Total sources of funds from operations", which is computed by adding to net income or loss any expenses that were deducted in computing net income that did not require or provide cash, such as depreciation (which is deducted from revenue as an expense item, but requires no cash outlay). Cash flow typically consists of three items—cash from operations (cash from customers less cash paid to suppliers and adjustments for depreciation and amortization), cash from investments, and cash from financing. When total sources of funds from operations is negative, operations are a cash drain which may require the firm either to sell assets or raise new capital in order to survive.[97]

The *Income Statement* offers another vehicle for assessing an airline's financial performance. Have revenue or expenses been rising or falling over the last several years? *Operating Profit* or *Operating Loss* is the difference between operating income and operating expenses. *Operating Margin* is calculated by dividing operating profit by operating revenue. As noted above, historically, profit margins have been extremely weak in the airline industry. Each item of cost should be compared with the preceding years' to determine which are falling, and which are rising. The most revealing non-operating expense item is interest, which reflects the firm's debt. One particularly useful measure of airline performance is net operating profit or loss minus the net of

---

[96] Id.
[97] Charles Banfe, Airline Management 161 (1992).

interest income and expense.[98] Net profit margin includes this item as well as taxes paid.

Two items of particular attraction to bottom feeding corporate raiders is accumulated capital and *cash flow*. Carl Icahn became interested in acquiring TWA because of its $400 million of accumulated cash (built up to offset the threat of a flight attendants' strike), and heavy cash flow. According to Icahn,

> It's the old Graham Dodd philosophy. He wrote the book in the thirties where you really buy these things when nobody wants them, and you have to sort of see that there is value there . . . . The value is there. I think it can be appreciated. [TWA] has a very good cash flow and the cash flow is very important in this situation. When you really analyze these companies, to get into it more deeply, depreciation isn't always true depreciation, and so when you look at earnings, it isn't always a true picture . . . and TWA has good cash flow.[99]

But Marty Whitman, another financial bottom fisherman, warned Icahn, "[Airlines] look pretty good to people who don't distinguish between gross cash flow and net cash flow."[100]

Each of the above factors must be assessed to determine the financial strength and viability of a particular airline, and compared with the historic performance of the carrier during prior years, as well as with the performance of those carriers with which it may reasonably be compared.[101]

One rather imperfect reflection of individual carrier performance is the value and performance of their stock on the major stock exchanges. Airlines tend to outperform the general market during a bull market, because its high capital leverage implies that a large share of revenue earned after break-even load factors are achieved goes to the bottom

---

[98] Id. at 161-63.
[99] Mark Stevens, King Icahn 173 (1993).
[100] Id. at 172.
[101] Richard Kane & Allan Vose, Air Transportation 15-22 (7th ed. 1979).

line. During a bear market, airlines tend to underperform the general market.[102]

In 1990 and 1991, the stock value of all U.S. major airlines combined ranged from a low of about $9 billion (in December 1990) to a high of $14 billion (in May 1990, and May 1991). The value of all national airlines ranged from a low of about $550 million (in November 1990), to a high of about $1.2 billion (in December 1991).[103] The stock value of the regional airlines combined ranged from a low of $75 million (in September 1990) to a high of $187 million (in December 1991).[104] The stock value of the all-cargo airlines combined ranged from a low of $1 billion (in November 1990) to a high of $3.8 billion (in April 1990).[105] The combined value of all cargo and passenger airlines ranged from a high of $18.7 billion in May 1991 to a low of $15.6 billion in November 1991.[106]

During 1995, the stock value of the majors rose from a low of about $15 billion, to a high or $27 billion; the nationals rose from $1.5 billion to a high of $2.5 billion; the regionals ranged from a low of $250 million to a high of $450 million; the cargo carriers rose from $5 billion to a high of $6.7 billion.[107]

Other measures of stock performance include the following:

- *Yield*—The percentage of dividend paid on a common or preferred stock. A stock selling for $60 with an annual dividend of $3 would have a yield of 5%. This definition of "yield" is in no way related to the concept of passenger yield discussed elsewhere in this book (particularly Chapter 6).
- *Price-Earnings Ratio*—The PE Ratio is the stock's market price divided by its profits per share. It measures how well or how poorly investors value a stock. It is typically a trailing ratio, using reported profits from the preceding year. It reveals the value investors place on the company's earnings.

---

[102] Newal Taneja, Airline Planning: Corporate, Financial, and Marketing 49 (1982).
[103] Value of Airline Stocks Soar Despite Financial Losses, Aviation Daily (Jan. 8, 1992), at 36.
[104] Id.
[105] See Aviation Daily (Dec. 4, 1991), at 396, and Aviation Daily (May 3, 1991), at 235.
[106] U.S. Carriers' Market Value Declines to Lowest Point of Year, Aviation Daily (Dec. 4, 1991), at 392.
[107] Aviation Daily (Feb. 15, 1996), at 260.

- *Projected PE Ratio*—Same as above, except it uses a consensus of Wall Street analysts' opinions of what earnings will be in the next year.
- *Market Capitalization*—The corporation's total worth, as calculated by the price of the stock and the number of shares outstanding.

DEBT: ON BALANCE SHEET, AND OFF

Healthy corporations have an appropriate balance of debt and equity. The advantage of equity in its usual form—common stock—is that its dividends do not have to be declared during unprofitable periods. This source of capital acts as a cushion for the carrier during economic downturns, and reduces risk for lenders. Preferred stock may also be issued. Without diluting the interests of common stockholders, it carries less risk than debt, but more risk than common stock.[108] Loading up the balance sheet with excessive debt results in a growth in interest obligations, and because the debt is placed at higher risk, increases the cost of capital for new debt.[109] In a highly cyclical industry like commercial aviation, significant fixed-interest payments may constitute an equally significant financial burden for the airline.[110]

Since deregulation, the balance sheets of U.S. airlines have been polluted with enormous debt, caused by grossly inadequate profitability and, at several airlines, leveraged buy-outs [LBOs] and profligate asset acquisition.[111] By the mid-1990s, total debt to capital ratios exceeded 65% at virtually all the major U.S. airlines, and would have been worse still if operating leases had been capitalized. Total debt at the major airlines was $62 billion by the end of 1995.[112] As a consequence, Wall Street downgraded the debt of virtually every major airline to speculative, or "junk" status (meaning that Wall Street believes that firms so categorized have about a 28% default rate).[113] As

---

[108] Newal Taneja, Airline Planning: Corporate, Financial, and Marketing 40, 51 (1982).
[109] See generally, Stephen Shaw, Airline Marketing & Management 138 (3rd ed. 1990).
[110] Newal Taneja, Airline Planning: Corporate, Financial, and Marketing 53 (1982).
[111] Paul Dempsey & Andrew Goetz, Airline Deregulation & Laissez Faire Mythology 11-40 (1992).
[112] Aviation Daily (Apr. 17, 1996), at 102.
[113] The Financial Condition of the Airline Industry, Hearings Before the U.S. House Subcomm. on Aviation, 104th Cong., 1st Sess. 48 (1995) (testimony of Philip Baggaley).

Wall Street analyst Julius Maldutis aptly noted, if the airlines were savings and loan institutions, the government would put them into receivership and liquidate them.

Table 3.6, "Debt As A Percentage Of Capitalization", reveals the total debt/total capitalization ratios for selected major airlines.

Table 3.6—DEBT AS A PERCENTAGE OF CAPITALIZATION[114]

Carrier	1978	1980	1983	1986	1989	1990	1992	1993	1994	1995
AmWest	--	--	44.7	81.5	84.5	96.7	183.6	43.9	43.9	36.5
American	54.4	63.4	51.2	45.1	33.5	46.7	70.1	63.9	70.0	65.5
Continental	46.7	62.3	308.9	97.3	96.3	n.a.	(212.3)	69.8	88.5	73.8
Delta	13.3	10.6	45.0	33.4	18.3	49.8	53.6	65.6	63.7	57.3
Eastern	n.a.	78.5	93.2	90.7	(52.9)	(21.8)	--	--	--	--
Northwest	11.2	5.4	8.2	50.8	23.1	43.5	129.8	133.8	114.6	79.7
Pan Am	n.a.	62.0	71.9	99.0	272.9	n.a.	--	--	--	--
Southwest	59.1	38.0	29.6	35.3	33.4	35.1	45.0	37.7	32.0	31.7
TWA	64.2	61.8	65.4	94.2	114.8	140.6	309.0	98.7	140.7	73.7
United	49.3	45.2	41.5	45.8	46.1	42.5	83.7	74.6	109.6	104.8
USAirways	41.7	44.0	31.8	24.8	44.8	55.8	84.9	81.7	105.0	102.9
AVERAGE	44.8	53.5	57.3	56.8	56.2	74.3	95.2	76.5	81.9	70.9

As can be seen in Table 3.6, the period of the late-1980s and early-1990s showed a very sharp increase in debt-to-equity ratios. By the mid-1990s, the balance sheets of United, USAirways, Northwest and TWA, although improving, were still poor. By 1995, the average debt-to-capital ratios, though significantly improved from their 1992 depths, still were significantly worse than their pre-deregulation levels, even with the removal of Eastern and Pan Am from the data base.

Debt is the source of 65% of airline capital spending, compared with 40% in all U.S. industry.[115] Debt is on-balance sheet, and off.

---

[114] Data: ESG Aviation Services and U.S. General Accounting Office. See also Transportation Research Board, Winds of Change: Domestic Air Transport Since Deregulation 72 (1991); ESG Aviation Services, 8 Airline Monitor (June 1995), at F6.
[115] Paul Proctor, ATA Predicts Record Year for U.S. Airlines, Aviation Week & Space Tech. (May 13, 1996), at 33.

Airline Finance

Off-balance sheet debt appears primarily in the form of aircraft operating leases.[116] The magnitude of the leasing phenomenon is reflected in Table 3.7, "U.S. Airline Percentage Of Aircraft Leased". The lease burden has grown enormously since deregulation. While U.S. major airlines leased an average of 19% of their fleets in 1969, some 25 years later, the average had jumped to 51%—more than a 250% increase. In contrast, British Airways leases only one third of its fleet.[117]

Table 3.7—U.S. AIRLINE PERCENTAGE OF AIRCRAFT LEASED[118]

Carrier	1969	1986	1992	1995
Alaska	--	--	n.a.	69
America West	--	--	n.a.	80
American	22	41	40	40
Braniff	28	100	--	--
Continental	2	25	78	84
Delta	0	21	48	42
Eastern	33	30	--	--
National	13	--	--	--
Northeast	83	--	--	--
Northwest	0	4	46	47
PanAm	n.a.	50	--	--
People Express	--	31	--	--
Republic	--	18	--	--
Southwest	n.a.	8	48	53
TWA	19	25	61	74
United	19	21	51	48
USAirways	--	17	48	49
Western	8	50	--	--

---

[116] Frequent flyer liability is also a significant source of off-balance sheet liability for airlines, but because of capacity limitations, usually consumes seats which otherwise would be flown empty.
[117] Julius Maldutis, British Airways Plc—The Crown Jewel (Aug. 23, 1993), at 11.
[118] Richard Gritta, Ellen Lippman & Garland Chow, Lease Capitalization and the Effect on the Debt Ratios of the Major U.S. Airlines, 22 Transp. L.J. 1, 3 (1994); Julius Maldutis, The U.S. Airline Industry, 1994-2000 (Aug. 18, 1995); Aviation Daily (Nov. 6, 1986). See also Julius Maldutis, The U.S. Airline Industry, 1993-99: Aircraft Fleet Analysis (Jan. 28, 1994); Julius Maldutis, The U.S. Airline Industry, 1992-98 (July 14, 1993).

In 1969, 87% of the leases were long-term agreements. Healthy carriers leased few, if any aircraft (Delta and Northwest leased none). Financially distressed carriers, such as Eastern, TWA and Northeast, leased a large percentage of their fleets.

Owned aircraft have large residual values. In 1970, Northwest's Don Nyrop began selling off his fleet of 707s (then about 12 years old, on average), and used the proceeds to purchase new aircraft, particularly DC-10s. Between 1971 and 1978, these proceeds from the sale of old aircraft provided more than a third of the total capital cost of the purchase of new aircraft. During this period, nearly a third of Northwest's pre-tax earnings came from these sales.[119] A sale/leaseback results in an immediate capitalization of these values on a discounted basis with a loss of these long-term residual values. In other words, the short-term benefits of leasing results in a sacrifice of the long-term values of ownership.

By the early 1990s, airlines had shifted strongly from capital leases to operating leases. Operating leases typically have five year terms and generally convey no residual value at the end of their term; from an accounting standpoint, they are treated as operating costs. Such leases, although a form of *de facto* financing of capital goods, do not appear as such on carrier balance sheets. Financial leases have terms of 12-25 years, and are considered a form of capital financing. Capital leases appear on airline balance sheets as long-term financing. Where residual values are not retained, the airline foregoes the opportunities for long-term capital gains. In the 1960s and early 1970s, virtually 100% of major carrier aircraft were financed by debt and internal capital; by 1990, half of the aircraft were financed through operating leases.[120]

Professor Richard Gritta and his colleagues attribute the shift from capital to operating leases to management concerns about the appearance of their balance sheets: "Because of the increased usage of operating leases, non-capitalization of operating data distorts the financial condition of the firms, particularly the debt burden, since the vast majority of leases classified as operating leases are really long term

---

[119] ESG Aviation Services, 8 The Airline Monitor 7 (Feb. 1996).
[120] Transportation Research Board, Winds of Change: Domestic Air Transport Since Deregulation 68 (1991).

Airline Finance

debt."[121] Capital leases are revealed on airline balance sheets; operating leases are not.

Thus, leasing is merely a surreptitious form of debt financing, which increases financial leverage and the risk it entails.[122] Among the Big-3 U.S. airlines, operating leases rose from 35% of total capital in 1987, to 55% in 1992.[123] If the long-term operating leases were put on the airlines' balance sheets, they would look considerably worse than they already do.

But accounting changes have made an independent assessment of true leverage extremely difficult. In 1976 the Financial Accounting Standards Board issued SFAS No. 13 which established new criteria for the capitalization of new financial type leases. According to Gritta, in response "many firms structured their lease agreements to strategically violate the requirements for capitalization of many noncancellable leases."[124] Also in 1980, the Civil Aeronautics Board dropped Schedule B14 from its Form 41 requirements. The cold reality of enormous debt and inadequate profitabililty in the post-deregulation environment means that many airlines no longer have the ability to finance their new equipment requirements with internal revenue, and must look elsewhere for capital.

Adding an estimated capitalized lease burden to the balance sheets of airlines has a profound effect, as the data calculated by Professor Gritta and his colleagues shows in Table 3.8, "Capitalization And Ratio Analysis".

Of course, leases must be paid, requiring *de facto* debt service. But astonishingly, between 1980 and 1990, as a percentage of airline operating expenses, equipment rentals (primarily aircraft leases) increased 781%.[125]

---

[121] Richard Gritta, Ellen Lippman & Garland Chow, Lease Capitalization and the Effect of the Debt Ratios of the Major U.S. Airlines, 22 Transp. L.J. 1, 10 (1994).
[122] Id. at 1, 3.
[123] Jeffrey Long, The U.S. Airline Industry 25 (J.P. Morgan, Jan. 8, 1993).
[124] Richard Gritta, Ellen Lippman & Garland Chow, Lease Capitalization and the Effect of the Debt Ratios of the Major U.S. Airlines, 22 Transp. L.J. 1, 6, 7 (1994).
[125] Comparison of Selected Airline Industry Expenses, Aviation Daily (July 29, 1991), at 176.

Table 3.8—CAPITALIZATION AND RATIO ANALYSIS (1991)[126]

Carrier	Long Term Debt/Total Capital		Total Debt/Net Worth	
	Before	After	Before	After
Alaska	70%	81%	3.26	5.03
America West	120%	109%	-7.67	-13.59
American	67%	82%	3.27	5.66
Continental	--	--	-2.56	-4.31
Delta	60%	81%	2.36	5.12
Southwest	60%	71%	1.92	2.96
United	61%	87%	5.19	10.55
USAirways	71%	87%	3.90	8.39

Leveraged lease financing was an extremely popular financing vehicle in the 1980s. According the Edmund Greenslet:

> Leasing was the great financing development of the 1980's and the industry embraced it with enthusiasm. What they seemed not to recognize was that by using leasing to accelerate capital spending growth they were undermining their long term earning power. The reason is that the total return on assets was not rising, so in effect aircraft rent was substituted for pretax earnings among the sources of internal funds . . . . The airlines were given an almost unlimited new line of credit and it is the height of understatement to say that they did not use it wisely . . . .
>
> There are good and sound reasons to use leases in a capital intensive industry, which the airlines certainly are. However, leasing does not increase the amount of total capital investment can prudently support. If aircraft rent replaced interest costs among the sources of internal

---

[126] Id. at 1, 13.

'Airline Finance

> funds then all would have been well, but that was not the case here. Interest also increased rapidly after 1985 and the combined growth of this and aircraft rent means that now about 60% of the internal funds in an average earnings year must be paid out in cash to service past capital spending. That leaves just 40% for depreciation and pre-tax earnings, the funds available for new investment [compared with 75% between 1978-85]....
>
> This grim mathematical fact will, for a number of years, limit the ability of the U.S. airlines to grow and to replace obsolete equipment.[127]

In 1980, the airline industry devoted 1.8% of its operating expenses to equipment (predominantly aircraft) rentals; by 1995, that figure had grown to 15.7%. Table 3.9, "Airline Leases And Interest Expenses As A Percentage Of Operating Expenses", demonstrates the amount of operating expenses devoted to rentals and interest by the major airlines (most of which reflects aircraft rentals). Rental and interest expenses are consuming an extremely large percentage of operating expenses. Jeffrey Long of J.P. Morgan Securities gave his assessment as to why lease financing has become so popular in the airline industry:

> The value of leases at the Big Three has tripled [by 1992]. These carriers have traditionally preferred ownership but have significantly increased their lease commitments. This growth was fueled by:
>
> - demand for tax shelters from tax-paying corporations and investors after 1986 tax reform;
> - the non-tax paying status of most U.S. airlines;

---
[127] ESG Aviation Services, The Airline Monitor 3 (May 1994).

- the relative security and preferences afforded operating lessors in bankruptcy; and
- the airlines' ability to profit from sale/leaseback transactions.[128]

Table 3.9—AIRLINE LEASES AND INTEREST EXPENSES AS A PERCENTAGE OF OPERATING EXPENSES (1995)[129]

Carrier	Rentals	Interest	Total
America West	17.97	3.91	21.88
American	7.96	3.64	11.60
Continental	13.58	3.81	17.39
Delta	8.72	2.38	11.10
Northwest	7.54	2.77	10.31
Southwest	10.17	1.04	11.21
TWA	7.36	3.08	10.36
United	10.53	2.20	12.73
USAirways	10.19	4.55	14.74
AVERAGE	10.45	3.04	13.49

Yet another rationale for sale/leasebacks is that it allows the company to improve its cash position by leveraging its fleet, thereby improving its liquidity, giving the carrier greater flexibility as to how to invest its capital in new equipment, routes or other assets.[130] The heavily leveraged airline industry has removed equity from its balance sheets in the form of sales of residual aircraft values (the estimated value of the aircraft at the end of the lease term), while leasing back the planes.[131] For example, adding the debt equivalent of aircraft leases to Delta's 1989 balance sheet debt (about $3 billion to the on balance

---

[128] Jeffrey Long, The U.S. Airline Industry 25 (Jan. 8, 1993).
[129] Aviation Daily (Jan. 29, 1996), at 146; Aviation Daily (Jan. 25, 1996), at 130.
[130] Dan Reed, The American Eagle 40 (1993).
[131] The Financial Condition of the Airline Industry and the Adequacy of Competition, Hearings Before the Subcomm. on Aviation of the House Comm. on Public Works and Transportation, 102nd Cong., 2d Sess. 589, 590 (1991) (statement of Timothy Pettee).

sheet debt of $1.2 billion), increases the debt-to-equity ratio to 61%.[132] About fifty percent of the aircraft in the U.S. fleet are owned and leased by equipment leasing companies.[133] Frequent flyer liability, totaling more than $100 million at some airlines, is also omitted from the balance sheets. But leasing is not without its costs, including a debt burden which can be suffocating, and an absence of sufficient internal capital to invest in new equipment.

Philip Baggaley of Standard & Poor's [S&P] concluded that the prospectus for returning many of the major U.S. airlines to investment grade was grim:

> The required operating margins are well above any historical performance and the required new equity actually exceeds the total market capitalization of these companies. Basically, the problem is that airlines are carrying a much heavier burden of debt and leases now than they were in the 1980's. For example, AMR had about $6 billion of debt and leases in 1988, their operating margin high point. The total now is about $18 billion![134]

By 1993, Delta Air Lines had some $12 billion in on and off balance sheet debt.[135] In 1995, United Airlines had $16 billion in debt and fixed obligations. USAir had $7.7 billion in debt and fixed obligations.[136] By 1996, the U.S. General Accounting Office reported that United Airlines had net equity of approximately $76 million, and debt of about $12 billion.[137]

---

[132] Hearings on Leveraged Buyouts and Foreign Ownership of United States Airlines Before the Aviation Subcomm. of the House Comm. on Public Works and Transp., 101st Cong., 1st Sess. 3 (1989) (statement of Philip Baggaley).
[133] Aircraft Lessors Concerned About Stage 2 Phaseout, Aviation Daily (Oct. 10, 1991), at 69.
[134] Philip Baggaley, Unpublished Address Before the Chicago Convention 50th Anniversary Conference (Oct. 31, 1994).
[135] Briget O'Brian, Once-solid Delta Air Is Burdened by Cost of European Foray, Wall St. J., June 25, 1993, at A1.
[136] UAL's Board Votes Against Proceeding With Bid for USAir, Wall St. J., Nov. 14, 1995, at A6.
[137] U.S. General Accounting Office, Denver Airport: Operating Results and Financial Risks 5, 6 (1996).

Several carriers have attempted to pay down debt in attempt to have their debt elevated to investment grade status (so as to reduce their cost of capital). For example, Delta's on-balance sheet debt was $3.6 billion in June 1993; by November 1996, it was down to $1.7 billion.[138]

Some airlines also have seriously underfunded pension plans. TWA's pensions were underfunded by $190 million in 1990, $440 million in 1991, and $933 million in 1992.[139] Concern over Carl Icahn's privatization of TWA, and the potential that the taxpayer might be stuck with paying its underfunded pension liability led Congress to pass legislation making Mr. Icahn personally responsible for the bill.[140] In 1990, United's pension was underfunded by $57 million; Northwest's was underfunded by $78 million.[141] Continental's was underfunded by $183 million, and the Pension Benefit Guarantee Corporation [PBGC] filed a claim in Continental's bankruptcy seeking to recover $752 million in underfunded Eastern Air Lines liability.[142]

In January 1992, the Pension Benefit Guaranty Corporation filed to block Continental's $290 million sale of Air Micronesia to an investor group on grounds that Continental Airline Holdings owes approximately $700 million in underfunded pension liability.[143]

A number of carriers which have ceased operating left the PBGC holding the bag. These included Pan Am ($914 million underfunded), and Eastern ($752 million underfunded).[144] It has been predicted that underfunded pension plans left high and dry by the disintegration of airlines may ultimately cost the U.S. taxpayer $1.7 billion.[145]

---

[138] Statement of Delta CEO Ron Allen Before the Salomon Bros. Transportation Conference (New York, N.Y., Nov. 13, 1996).

[139] Three Majors Among Top 50 Firms With Underfunded Pensions, Aviation Daily (Nov. 26, 1991), at 355; TWA Surprises Industry With Early Chapter 11 Bankruptcy Filing, Aviation Daily (Feb. 3, 1992), at 199.

[140] Bill Binding TWA Chairman to Pensions Passed in Congress, Aviation Daily (Dec. 2, 1991), at 372.

[141] Three Majors Among Top 50 Firms With Underfunded Pensions, Aviation Daily (Nov. 26, 1991), at 355.

[142] Continental Withholds $17 Million Pension Payment, Aviation Daily (Oct. 10, 1991), at 67.

[143] PBGC Moves to Block Sale of Continental's Stake in Air Micronesia, Aviation Daily (Jan. 23, 1992), at 139.

[144] Three Majors Among Top 50 Firms With Underfunded Pensions, Aviation Daily (Nov. 26, 1991), at 355.

[145] Airline Financial Woes Trigger Pension Underfunding Crisis, Aviation Daily (Feb. 21, 1991), at 339. See PBGC Asks Court for Ruling On 'Danforth Amendment', Aviation Daily (Apr. 23, 1992), at 136.

FINANCIAL RISK

The airline industry is capital intensive, labor intensive, has high fixed costs, and low returns on capital. The airline industry suffers from severe business risk in the form of high fixed costs, highly cyclical demand, and intensive competition; it suffers severe financial risk in the form of high debt-to-equity ratios, which increases the variability of earnings and the chances of insolvency.[146] The industry has a high beta coefficient (high earnings volatility), given its high level of capital intensiveness and high operating leverage.[147] By the end of the 1980s, airline equity and asset betas rose sharply.[148] Because of the level and intensity of business and financial risk in the industry, one would expect that airlines, in order to attract adequate investment, should earn more than other industries.[149] But in fact, airlines earn less. According to Professor Gritta, "It is a sound and very well-tested principle of finance that companies high in business risk (because they are cyclical, high or fixed and/or constant costs) should follow conservative debt policies (that is, utilize low levels of financial leverage)."[150] With massive capital equipment requirements coupled with anemic profitability (plus LBOs and preferential treatment for aircraft under bankruptcy law), both well and poorly managed airlines have loaded their balance sheets up with oppressive levels of debt.

Standard and Poor's evaluates debt to determine the degree of risk. These measures and those of other Wall Street rating services provide a benchmark of the carrier's ability to compete for capital in the marketplace, and the cost of debt capital to them.[151] Investment grade

---

[146] "The net result of overleverage can be explosive changes in rates of return to stockholders resulting from small changes in revenues." Richard Gritta, Garland Chow & Todd Shank, The Causes and Effects of Business and Financial Risk in Air Transportation Operating and Financial Leverage and the Volatility in Carrier Rates of Return, 6 J. Transp. Management 127 (1994). See also, Richard Gritta, Ellen Lippman & Garland Chow, Lease Capitalization and the Effect on the Debt Ratios of Major U.S. Airlines, 22 Transp. L.J. 1 (1994).
[147] Newal Taneja, Airline Planning: Corporate, Financial, and Marketing 49 (1982).
[148] Transportation Research Board, Winds of Change 78, 311 (1991).
[149] Despite the sharp decline in the industry's profit margin since deregulation, capital continued to flow into the industry, with a proliferation of equipment leasing companies eager to purchase aircraft for airlines able to pay from robust cash flow, and from the glamour of the industry, which attracts new entrepreneurs. There are three businesses everyone seems to believe they can run -- restaurants, ball clubs, and airlines.
[150] Letter from Richard Gritta to Paul Dempsey, Nov. 14, 1996.
[151] See Newal Taneja, Airline Planning: Corporate, Financial, and Marketing 39 (1982).

debt has a default rate of about 3.5%; speculative grade (more commonly known as "junk") debt has a 28% default rate. Any rating below BBB is considered non-investment grade, or "junk." Table 3.10, "Standard And Poor's Debt Ratings", lists the different rating categories.

Table 3.10—STANDARD AND POOR'S DEBT RATINGS[152]

Investment Grade
AAA
AA
A
BBB

Speculative Grade
BB
B
CCC
CC

Default
D

Assessing airline risk is a complex task, requiring a review not only of industry risk, but firm position, operations analysis, management quality and innovation, earnings, cash flow, equipment financing, and other issues. Accounting methodology must also evaluate depreciation methods (most U.S. airlines depreciate on a straight-line basis over 20 to 25 years, while many non-U.S. carriers depreciate on a more conservative basis, which understates their earnings and equity), amortization of intangibles (including goodwill, operating rights—particularly international routes—and pre-operating costs), employee benefits, and operating leases (S&P uses a discounted present value model to reflect this off-balance sheet financial burden).[153]

---

[152] The Financial Condition of the Airline Industry, Hearings Before the U.S. House Subcomm. on Aviation 70 (Mar. 22, 1995) (statement of Philip Baggaley).
[153] Philip Baggaley, Assessing An Airline's Credit Quality, in Handbook of Airline Economics 239, 243 (D. Jenkins ed. 1995).

Airline Finance

A few other airline accounting practices warrant parenthetical consideration. One is that airlines typically run working capital deficits, taking advantage of the fact that most passengers pay for their travel days or weeks before they consume it. The short-term cash advantage is offset by an accounting entry termed "air traffic liability." Rental expenses are shown on airline balance sheets as operating expenses, although they are in reality a capital outlay. Airlines using a high proportion of off-balance sheet leases appear to have higher operating costs per ASM, but lower interest expenses, than airlines which own their fleets.[154]

Total debt as a percentage of capitalization is deemed by airline financial experts as the most useful measure of a firm's financial leverage (see Figure 3.7, "Debt As A Percentage Of Total Capital"). Unlike most industries, lease obligations (both capitalized and off-balance sheet) form a large portion of the airline capital structure. In making the debt-to-capitalization calculation, the present value of off-balance sheet operating leases is added to the debt.[155]

In early 1990, Standard and Poor's rated the 15 largest U.S. airlines as follows: six were investment grade; one (Eastern Airlines) was in bankruptcy; and eight were speculative grade. In 1992, several investment houses downgraded the debt of most of the nation's airlines and observed that the industry would have increased difficulty obtaining financing.[156] By 1995, Standard and Poor's rated 10 airlines, only one of which (Southwest Airlines) was rated investment grade.[157] Table 3.11, "Standard And Poor's Airline Debt Rating", reveals the declining rating of five of the nation's largest airlines.

---

[154] Id. at 239, 242, 244.
[155] Id. at 239, 244.
[156] Limited Access to Capital Could Be Longer Term Problem, Aviation Daily (Apr. 24, 1992), at 147; Michelle Mahoney, Brutal War Punishes Airlines, Denver Post, June 2, 1992, at 1C, 3C.
[157] The Financial Condition of the Airline Industry, Hearings Before the U.S. House Subcomm. on Aviation 48 (Mar. 22, 1995) (testimony of Philip Baggaley).

Figure 3.7—DEBT AS A PERCENTAGE OF TOTAL CAPITAL[158] (U.S. Major Airlines)

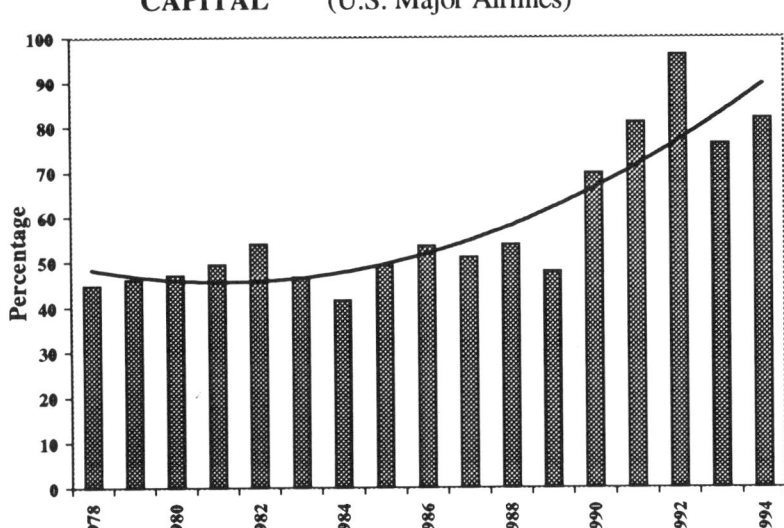

Table 3.11—STANDARD AND POOR'S AIRLINE DEBT RATING[159]

Carrier	1988	1994
American Airlines	A	BB+
Delta Air Lines	A-	BB
United Airlines	BB	BB
USAirways	BBB	CCC+
Northwest Airlines	B+	B+

Such downgrading raises the cost of capital. This has led some airlines to shift financing of traditionally tenant improvements to airports, which have a higher debt rating, and a correspondingly lower cost of capital. Thus, Denver International Airport financed the bag-

---

[158] Source: EGS Aviation Services.
[159] Gerald Arpey, The Challenge of Airline Finance, in Handbook of Airline Economics 235, 236 (D. Jenkins ed. 1995).

gage system, flight kitchen, air freight facility, and hangars for United Airlines.[160]

Despite anemic financial performance, airlines have been able to secure access to capital well beyond what their balance sheets suggest. According to Standard & Poor's Philip Baggaley, "This reflects the liquidity, high value retention, and ability of creditors to repossess and re-deploy an airline's principal asset: its aircraft. Unlike most other industries, the value of an airline's assets have little necessary relationship to its operating performance."[161] He elaborated as to the reasons why this is true:

> A large pool of unencumbered assets helps assure availability of bank, equipment and lease financing.... [A]ircraft are readily salable and financeable, reflecting:
>
> 1. Aircraft can be transferred easily from one operator to another in an active, liquid and global market.
> 2. The value of an aircraft does not decline substantially when the operating airline is in financial distress....
> 3. Lessors and secured creditors can repossess aircraft financed under Section 1110 of the bankruptcy code if the airline does not continue rentals or debt service in reorganization proceedings.[162]

Since deregulation, more than 100 airlines have collapsed into bankruptcy.[163] Given the preferential treatment aircraft receive in bankruptcy, coupled with the virtual fungibility of equipment between

---

[160] Paul Dempsey, Andrew Goetz & Joseph Szyliowicz, Denver International Airport: Lessons Learned (1997).
[161] Philip Baggaley, Assessing An Airline's Credit Quality, in Handbook of Airline Economics 239, 241 (D. Jenkins ed. 1995).
[162] Id.
[163] More specifically, there were 118 bankruptcy filings between 1979 and 1994. Aviation & Aerospace Almanac 102, 103 (1994).

carriers, airlines can use equipment trust certificates to reduce investor risk, and thereby lower their cost of capital.[164]

Major airlines attempt to reduce business risk somewhat by developing risk management programs to lessen earnings volatility and insulate the company against sharp increases in commodity prices and currency and interest rate fluctuations. Among the tools used are (1) currency hedging (foreign currency exchange agreements), (2) fuel hedging (fuel swap contracts), and (3) interest rate management (interest rate swap contracts).[165]

In 1978, various public opinion polls revealed that airlines ranked at the very top of all industries in terms of consumer confidence and satisfaction.[166] But in 1989, when the *Wall Street Journal* polled Americans to discern the industries in which they had most, and least, confidence, the largest number by far, 43%, said they had least confidence in the airline industry.[167] The disapproval ratings for the industries which followed—insurance (27%), banking (23%), oil and gas (22%), and stockbrokers (22%)—was not nearly as high as that for airlines.[168] It is not clear whether consumer dissatisfaction with the airline industry was based on financial stability, service, perceptions of safety, or all three.

The goals of management must be to improve their airline's capital structure, reduce interest expense, and maximize shareholder return, rather than attempting to enhance market share in vicious competitive, and primordial territorial battles.

INDUSTRY CAPITAL REQUIREMENTS

By the mid-1990s, fuel costs and interest rates were relatively benign, and consumer confidence was relatively high. Nonetheless, even as the economy improves, debt service consumes much of po-

---

[164] See Raymond Neidl, Equipment Trust Certificates: An Insurance Policy for Investors, in Handbook of Airline Economics 251 (D. Jenkins ed. 1995).
[165] Gerald Arpey, The Challenge of Airline Finance, in Handbook of Airline Economics 235, 238 (1995). See e.g., UAL Corporation, 1994 Annual Report 25 (1994); AMR Corporation, 1994 Annual Report 60 (1994).
[166] Callison, Airline Deregulation—Only Partially a Hoax: The Current Status of the Airline Deregulation Movement, 45 J. Air L. & Com. 961, 964 n. 4 (1980), citing 236 Aviation Daily 118 (1978).
[167] Winans and Dahl, Airlines Skid on Bad Moves, Bad News, Wall St. J., Sept 29, 1989, at B1.
[168] Id.

tential operating profit. The recommendations of the U.S. National Commission to Ensure a Strong Competitive Airline Industry for meaningful tax reform will not likely be implemented by a Congress already fearful of its own debt burden (although for the first several months of 1996, the 10% ticket tax expired, but because of an impasse between the White House and Congress, rather than because of empathy for the airline industry).[169] Carriers have a tendency to bid up travel agent commissions in an effort to buy traffic (although caps on agent commissions seek to roll them back).[170] The potential for spinning off short haul feeder routes and ancillary services (as United proposed in 1993) has been met with labor antagonism and a consequential deterioration of service.[171] Some carriers have used Chapter 11 to trade debt for equity (e.g., Continental and TWA). Trading wage and work rule concessions for equity (as TWA, Northwest and United have done, and USAirways and American would like to do) seems the primary opportunity for reducing costs.[172] And in fact, the comparative lower cost advantage thereby given TWA, Northwest and United likely will cause the remaining major network carriers to follow suit or risk gradual erosion of market share.

The capital needs of the airline industry are enormous. While the world's airlines spent $147 billion in the 1980s, the industry is projected to need $815 billion by the year 2000.[173] Airbus, Boeing and Douglas predict the industry will need between $40 billion and $50 billion for new aircraft each year over the next decade.[174] Boeing

---

[169] See The National Commission To Ensure A Strong Competitive Airline Industry, Change, Challenge and Competition (1993).

[170] As a portion of total operating expenses, travel agent commissions rose 308% between 1980 and 1990. Paul Dempsey, Robert Hardaway & William Thoms, 1 Aviation Law & Regulation § 2.19 (1993).

[171] As one commentator noted, "The only other option [to trading equity to labor for wage and work rule concessions] is slash-and-burn restructuring with labor war and significant disruptions of the national travel system." Joseph Conn, Expert: United Plan Sets Pattern for Others, Denver Post, Dec. 28, 1993, at 4C.

[172] In late 1993, United reached an agreement with its pilots and machinists whereby labor would take 52% of voting equity in exchange for $5.1 billion, partly in terms of wage and work rule concessions. In mid-1993, employees at Northwest surrendered billions of dollars in wage and work rule concessions for 37.5% of the airline. Earlier, TWA, emerging from bankruptcy, gave employees 45% of equity in the airline for significant concessions.

[173] Julius Maldutis, Industry Investment Requirements -- Looking Beyond 2000 (address before the 7th IATA High-Level Aviation Symposium, Sept. 6, 7, 1993, Cairo, Egypt); The Balancing Act, Airline Bus., The Skies in 1992 16 (1992).

[174] Philip Baggaley, Unpublished Address Before the Chicago Convention 50th Anniversary Conference (Oct. 31, 1994).

predicts the world's airlines will need about 16,000 aircraft, valued at about $1.1 trillion in the 20 year period between 1996-2016. Only 3,900 of this projected total will replace aging jets; the rest will be required to accommodate anticipated growth in air travel. Intra-Asia traffic is projected to grow by 7.1% a year; Trans-Pacific 6.4%; Asia-Europe 6.7%; and North America 3.6%.[175] ESG Aviation Services predicts that the total value of more than 20,000 aircraft to be delivered between 1995-2020 will be $1.8 trillion, compared with $345 billion between 1947-94.[176]

In the late 1980s and early 1990s, billions of dollars in new equipment were deferred by many carriers (although this creates a problem for phasing out Stage Two aircraft), and more than 700 aircraft were parked in the desert. Older aircraft are being "hush-kitted" (i.e., outfitted with sound attenuated engines) rather than retired. Meanwhile, the U.S. fleet ages (see Table 3.12, "U.S. Airline Fleet Ages").

Unfortunately, aircraft fleet age has had a direct correlation with the amount of productivity attributable to fuel consumption, the maintenance costs per block hour, the hours of aircraft utilization, and real ownership costs.[177]

The International Civil Aviation Organization predicts the world will need between $250 billion and $350 billion in new airport infrastructure by the year 2010.[178] Admittedly, some of that infrastructure will come from land-side sources—taxpayers, concessions, parking and such. But the bulk of it must come from air-side sources—the airlines, directly or indirectly, in the form of landing and air traffic control fees, gate, counter and hanger leases, passenger facility charges, fuel and other taxes, and ground services fees. Airports account for between 4% to 6% of airline operating costs.

---

[175] Jeff Cole, Boeing Raises Its Projection of Jet Demand, Wall St. J., Mar. 7, 1996, at A4.
[176] ESG Aviation Services, The Airline Monitor 18 (Jan. 1996).
[177] ESG Aviation Services, The Airline Monitor 7, 17 (Feb. 1996).
[178] Int'l. Air Transport Ass'n., The Economic Benefits of Air Transport 20 (1992).

Table 3.12—U.S. AIRLINE FLEET AGES [179]

Carrier	1990	1991	1992	1993	1994	1995	1996
				(years)			
Tans World	16.3	17.5	17.9	18.3	18.0	18.6	19.0
Northwest	15.5	15.9	15.4	15.8	16.8	18.3	19.2
Continental	12.6	13.5	14.6	15.0	14.7	13.6	14.3
USAirways	8.9	9.0	9.8	10.4	10.6	10.9	12.9
Delta	8.9.	9.2	8.9	9.1	10.1	10.8	11.5
United	12.3	11.2	10.3	9.8	10.0	10.7	10.9
America West	6.7	6.0	6.7	8.1	9.1	9.9	10.5
American	9.6	8.9	8.4	7.7	7.6	8.0	9.0
Southwest	5.8	6.6	6.9	7.3	7.5	7.8	7.9
Alaska	8.9	8.7	6.8	6.5	5.8	6.6	7.5
PanAm	15.9	--	--	--	--	--	--
Eastern	14.2	--	--	--	--	--	--
Midway	13.0	--	--	--	--	--	--

According to Thomas Gallagher, in addition to the industry's exaggerated reaction to world economic activity, "The wide variation of external capital needs and the industry's extraordinary dependence upon large amounts of external capital are two other features that distinguish global aviation from other forms of economic endeavor."[180]

In the 1960s, the world's airlines spent $20 billion on capital equipment, raising 40% from internal cash flow and the rest from the capital market. In the 1970s, the industry spent $48 billion on capital equipment, raising 52% from cash flow. At the time of deregulation, the industry financed their capital equipment needs approximately 30% through external sources, 60% through internal sources, and 10% from deferred taxes.[181] In the 1980s, the industry spent $143 billion on capital equipment, raising 51% from internal cash flow, much of the rest

---

[179] Julius Maldutis, The U.S. Airline Industry, 1994-2000 4 (Aug. 18, 1995); Julius Maldutis, The Airline Industry, 1996-2002 4 (Apr. 5, 1997).
[180] Thomas Gallagher, Aircraft Finance and Airline Financial Analysis in the Fifth Cycle of the Jet Age, in Handbook of Airline Economics 223, 224 (1995).
[181] Newal Taneja, Airline Planning: Corporate, Financial, and Marketing 34 (1982).

financed by leasing companies. From 1990 to 1993, capital spending totaled $127 billion, but cash flow covered only 17% of that.

It has been projected that cash flow will cover only 37% of capital spending throughout this decade, while capital expenditures will double to $511 billion by the year 2003.[182] It has also been estimated that, given the tremendous debt burden created by inadequate profitability and LBOs, the world's airlines need operating margins of 4% just to service debt, and 6% if they are to generate sufficient profit to pay for fleet modernization.[183] Edmund Greenslet concluded, "The really critical question is whether the airlines can, over time and on average, reverse the decline in net profit margins . . . . [I]n the end it will be capital, and the need for cash flow to support it, that is likely to be the primary driver of airline economic trends in the 1990s and beyond."[184]

The airline industry's annual financing need is defined as the amount of external capital needed to finance new aircraft deliveries that cannot be financed by internal cash flow. During the 1960s and 1970s, the industry appeared to be generating sufficient cash to finance new aircraft. By the end of 1979, the cumulative annual shortfall was about $9 billion. But during the 1980s and 1990s, it increased fourteen-fold, to $135 billion. The cumulative financing requirements, which remained consistently below 30% of annual operating revenue in the 1960s and 1970s, rose to 37% in the 1980s, and to 75% by the mid-1990s. This has caused the world's airlines to laden their balance sheets with $135 billion in debt, more than 85% of the industry's invested capital. According to Homi Mullan, "This mountain of debt is the millstone round the industry's neck. It is what makes the industry today different from what it has been at any other time in its history."[185]

In evaluating whether the airline industry can finance the $50 billion in new aircraft it needs, Mullan notes that in recent years, the industry has generated annual cash flow of about $15 billion (in 1994

---

[182] Edmund Greenslet, World Airline Capital Requirements (address to the Chicago Convention 50th Anniversary Conference, Oct. 31, 1994).
[183] Richard Evans, Why the World's Airlines Can't Seem to Get Enough Cash, Global Finance (May 1993), at 48, 53.
[184] Id.
[185] Homi P. R. Mullan, Financing the Future, in Int'l Air Transport Ass'n., A Vision of the Future 69 (1995).

dollars). Even if debt service remained steady at $10 billion, this would leave only $5 billion a year with which to purchase new aircraft without more external financing. Assuming (1) the industry's annual cash flow grows to $25 billion, (2) the industry is never obliged to pay the principal off of its debt, and merely services interest, and (3) interest rates remain at 7.5%, the industry will be able to add about $200 billion in additional debt, meaning that (even under these optimistic assumptions) the airline industry will be able to finance new aircraft requirements with new debt only until the turn of the century. The minimum level of operating margin needed to sustain such a cash flow would be 8.5%, according to Mullan, higher than the industry has ever earned in its entire history.[186] He concludes:

> First, that the industry today is in worse shape than it has ever been. Its profitability has been steadily declining over time. This worsening performance, together with the massive over-purchasing of aircraft in the recent past, has caused debt to rise to imprudent levels.
>
> Second, the industry is simply not in a position to finance $50 billion worth of aircraft each year for the next decade and beyond.
>
> The industry's accumulated debt has increased the break-even point for profitability to a level which is arguably beyond reach in the medium term. If the industry is to acquire new aircraft at this rate, an extraordinary improvement in profitability is required.[187]

Average industry performance has been so poor in the post-deregulation period that a study of the Transportation Research Board concluded:

> The apparent financial performance of the major air carriers has been sufficiently weak

---
[186] Id. at 69, 79.
[187] Id. at 69, 80.

since deregulation to raise questions about the long-run health of the industry. These concerns have focused on three areas: the thin profit margins of the industry, the increase in industry leverage, and the airlines' low return on equity capital. Of particular concern is what the airlines' financial condition implies for their ability to withstand periods of recession and to attract capital for the long-term investment in replacement and expansion of their current fleets.[188]

Shortly after deregulation began, Charles Glass observed that "a capital intensive industry or company cannot continuously replace its assets without meaningful profits."[189] The same is true today. Without the ability to finance its aircraft needs, the industry as a whole will be forced to watch helplessly as its fleet ages, raising maintenance costs, and depriving the industry of newer generation fuel-efficient aircraft. Yet some carriers will be profitable, and their aircraft needs will be met. Some carriers may become effectively "assetless" in nature, contracting out for aircraft, maintenance, reservations, distribution, and even "wet leased" flight crews.[190] Only the aircraft livery, airline name and management team may form the airline core. If air transport truly is a "fungible" commodity in the eyes of discretionary travelers, then perhaps it matters little who performs what function. And given the dismal financial performance of most airlines in the post-deregulatory environment, perhaps many airlines will be unable to possess significant capital assets.

---

[188] Transportation Research Board, Winds of Change: Domestic Air Transport Since Deregulation 57 (1991).
[189] Charles Glass, Financial Planning for Fleet Acquisition, in Airline Economics 253, 259 (G. James ed. 1995).
[190] See James Ott & Raymond Neidl, Airline Odyssey 207, 208 (1995).

SOURCES OF NEW CAPITAL

The enormous losses suffered since deregulation and liberalization have so polluted the balance sheets of many of the world's airlines that it will be difficult to finance investment out of earnings or raise significant new equity.[191] Nevertheless, in addition to excusing themselves of equity and significant debt with the aid of the bankruptcy courts, troubled carriers have found several alternative sources of new capital. Eight of these alternatives are described below:

1. *Asset Sales*—Many airlines have cannibalized assets to stay aloft. Pan Am sold its Intercontinental Hotel chain ($500 million), its Manhattan skyscraper ($400 million), its trans-Pacific ($750 million), London Heathrow ($400 million) and intra-German ($150 million) routes to raise operating capital.[192] TWA sold its Hilton International Hotel chain, Century 21 real estate company, Spartan Foods, and its operating authority across the Atlantic to serve London's Heathrow Airport.[193] Air France sold its 57% interest in Meridien Hotels.[194] Many carriers also have sold and leased back their aircraft, although in so doing, they sacrifice residual values, and thereby, their long-term financial strength.

2. *Additional Investment From Existing Investors, Debt Holders, or Equipment Manufacturers*—Northwest approached KLM, and USAir approached British Airways, unsuccessfully, about injecting more capital into these U.S. carriers. Several carriers have also been able to shed debt via Chapter 11 bankruptcy.

The equipment manufacturers have been an intermittent source of capital for airlines. Anxious to break into the U.S.-flag market, Airbus put together an extremely attractive package for Eastern Air Lines by subsidizing the acquisition of A-300s. Rolls Royce/Lockheed provided financing to Pan Am to move L-1011s. Boeing did much the same with the sale of 767s to Pan Am.[195] The engine manufacturers assisted Continental's exit from bankruptcy by injecting capital and trading debt for equity. In its second Chapter 11 reorganization in less than

---

[191] The Balancing Act, Airline Bus., The Skies in 1992 16 (1992).
[192] Paul Dempsey & Andrew Goetz, Airline Deregulation & Laissez Faire Mythology 129 (1992).
[193] Id. at 137.
[194] Air France Sells Meridien, Aviation Daily, Sept. 15, 1994, at 439.
[195] Newal Taneja, Airline Planning: Corporate, Financial, and Marketing 57, 58 (1982).

five years, TWA removed $500 million in debt from its books and reduced interest expenses by $50 million annually by trading debt for equity with creditors. Creditors ended up owning 65% of the company, while employee ownership declined from 45% to 30%.[196] While America West was in bankruptcy, it negotiated $130 million in debtor-in-possession financing from GPA Group, Ansett, Northwestern, Kawasaki Leasing and other Phoenix lenders, and $215 million in financing by Air Partners (Continental Airlines, Mesa Airlines, Fidelity Investments, and the Bonderman group).[197]

3. *New Investors*—Despite anemic profitability, the airline industry still attracts capital from those seeking a piece of a high-profile glamour industry. According to Alfred Kahn, there is something about airplanes that makes investors crazy.[198] There are three industries everybody thinks they can run: (1) a restaurant; (2) a baseball team; or (3) an airline. The defiance of gravity, the sweaty palms some passengers get on takeoff or landing, the magnificence of cutting edge technology, images of exotic destinations, the prestige of owning a franchise fewer in number than those of the National Football League, and the opportunity to become Lord of a city whose hub it dominates have always attracted men with huge egos.[199] In the 1980s, major airlines became targets of corporate raiders, such as Carl Icahn (TWA), Frank Lorenzo (Continental, People Express, and Eastern), Alfred Checchi (Northwest), and David Bonderman (Continental and America West). Even rapidly descending Pan Am was able to tap the capital markets with new stock issuances in the 1980s, despite the fact it was drowning in a sea of red ink. Aircraft lessors are willing to lease planes to struggling carriers because of the special protection such assets enjoy under the bankruptcy laws, allowing them to be recaptured and leased to other carriers.

4. *New Airline Partners*—Several foreign airlines have gained feed from the world's largest passenger and air freight market by buying equity in U.S. carriers. For example, British Air effectively turned USAir into a regional feeder airline, funneling short-haul connecting

---

[196] Aviation Daily (Aug. 25, 1995), at 315.
[197] Danna Henderson, America West Airlines: Making Reorganization Work, Air Transport World (Feb. 1, 1995), at 26.
[198] The Financial Condition of the Airline Industry, Hearings Before the U.S. House Subcomm. on Aviation, 104th Cong., 1st Sess. 29 (1995) (testimony of Gerald Greenwald).
[199] Paul Dempsey & Andrew Goetz, Airline Deregulation & Laissez Faire Mythology 11 (1992).

traffic into its lucrative, long-haul, wide-bodied, trans-Atlantic system, to be fed throughout its beyond-Heathrow network. KLM invested in Northwest. SAS and Air Canada invested in Continental. However, the extremely poor performance of these U.S. carriers led most of these foreign carriers to write down their U.S. airline investments on their books to zero.

5. *Trading Labor Concessions for Equity*—Wage and work rule concessions were traded for equity at Eastern Airlines in the 1980s, and at TWA, Northwest and United in the 1990s. However, the amount of capital required to finance an Employee Stock Ownership Plan [ESOP] can be formidable, making an ESOP a mixed blessing. For example, United Airlines paid shareholders $2.1 billion to fund its ESOP. That reduced its cash reserves by $1 billion, and saddled it with $741 million in long-term debt and $410 million in preferred stock; equity decreased by $1.7 billion.[200]

6. *Governmental Economic Assistance*—A study performed by the European Community Commission conservatively estimated that, during the 1970s and 1980s, the U.S. government gave the airline industry between $33.5 billion and $41.5 billion in direct and indirect support.[201] The investment includes between $12.4 billion and $20.2 billion in aeronautics R&D from the U.S. Defense Department, between $1 billion and $1.2 billion in independent R&D reimbursed by the U.S. Department of Defense [DOD], and $17 billion from NASA programs. It also estimated that total tax deferrals and exemptions granted the industry have exceeded some $3.5 billion since 1976.[202]

One criticism levied at the U.S. Department of Transportation is that it accumulated some $16 billion dollars in the Airport and Airway Trust Fund during the Bush Administration,[203] using it to offset a $16 billion piece of the $3 trillion U.S. budget deficit. Some noted that if this were a private trust, the trustees would be sent to jail for misuse of trust funds. But putting Congress and the Administration in jail would be a difficult endeavor.

---

[200] UAL Corporation, 1994 Annual Report 4, 17 (1994).
[201] EC Study: U.S. Gave Up to $41.5 Billion to Aircraft Industry, Aviation Daily (Dec. 5, 1991), at 401.
[202] EC Study: U.S. Gave Up to $41.5 Billion to Aircraft Industry, Aviation Daily (Dec. 5, 1991), at 401.
[203] See Aviation Daily (Jan. 2, 1992), at 7; Aviation Daily (Apr. 26, 1991), at 190; Aviation Daily (Jan. 24, 1991), at 159; Aviation Daily (Aug. 17, 1990), at 248.

Chapter 3

From 1977 to 1992, governments gave $3 billion to state-owned airlines.[204] Many nations of the world view airline investment as analogous to building a road—basic transportation infrastructure essential to the well being of the nation. Although the U.S. industry is privately owned, the U.S. National Commission to Ensure a Strong Competitive Airline Industry recommended that several taxes be rolled back on U.S. airlines, and that the Strategic Petroleum Reserve be tapped to aid airlines when fuel costs rise significantly. Congress exempted aviation fuel from a new 4.3 cents a gallon gasoline tax until October 1995.[205] The state of Minnesota agreed to sell $250 million in bonds on behalf of Northwest Airlines to finance construction of a maintenance facility in Duluth, and $100 million for an engine repair facility in Hibbing.[206] In 1991, the state of Minnesota gave an incentive package worth $838 million to Northwest Airlines to build an aircraft maintenance complex in the state.[207] Included was $320 million in low-interest loans provided by the Metropolitan Airports Commission, operator of the Minneapolis/St. Paul Airport, as well as $350 million in bonds to construct the complex. The complex was expected to add approximately 1,900 new jobs to the state, on top of the 18,000 Northwest already employed in Minnesota.[208]

Many states have subsidized airlines, or provided them with debt at favorable rates, including Indiana (United) and North Carolina (American). Some cities also have subsidized air service from time to time. The federal government also authorized the sale by airlines of billions of dollars of public assets in the form of airport landing slots and international routes. As liquidation of public resources, these are indirect forms of taxpayer subsidy.

This phenomenon proceeds robustly abroad, where most airlines enjoy significant governmental ownership, and a paternalistic relationship which forbids airline collapse. Table 3.13, "Government

---

[204] Richard Evans, Why the World's Airlines Can't Seem to Get Enough Case, Global Finance (May 1993), at 48.
[205] Lisa Burgess, International Community Wants Action on Panel Report, Commercial Aviation News (Aug. 23, 1993), at 21.
[206] Debra Werner, Northwest Airlines, Minnesota Put Maintenance Hubs Back on Agenda, Commercial Aviation News (Aug. 23, 1993), at 10.
[207] Minnesota Legislature Gives Final Approval to Northwest Incentive Package, Aviation Daily (Dec. 17, 1991), at 474.
[208] Id.

Ownership Of Major European Airlines", shows the level of governmental ownership in the major airlines of western Europe.

Table 3.13—GOVERNMENT OWNERSHIP OF MAJOR EUROPEAN AIRLINES (1993)[209]

Carrier	Government Stake (%)
Aer Lingus	100.00
Air France Group	99.38
Alitalia	84.90
Austrian Airlines	51.90
British Airways	0.00
Iberia	100.00
KLM	38.20
Lufthansa	59.16
Olympic Airways	100.00
Sabena	88.00
SAS Group	50.00
Swissair	20.40
TAP Air Portugal	100.00

In 1991, the Belgian government wrote off $250 million in debt for its flag carrier, Sabena.[210] In 1992, Spain injected $922 million into Iberia.[211] In 1993, the Portuguese government granted $230 million in aid to TAP Air Portugal.[212] Air France and Olympic Airways also turned to their governments for billions of dollars of subsidies.[213] Nonetheless, governmental assistance is becoming more difficult under the European Union's [EU] state aid rules. Ironically, the problem is circular, for with every EU Commission reluctantly approving state

---

[209] Airline Bus. The Skies in 1992 74 (1993).
[210] George Richmond, Sabena, Labor Agree on $152 Million Lifeboat, Commercial Aviation News (Aug. 23, 1993), at 3.
[211] Carlta Vitzthum, Iberia Air Lines Realizes Limitations, Cutting Costs After Years of Expansion, Wall St. J., Sept. 24, 1993, at B5D.
[212] Public Approval, Airline Bus. (May 1993), at 12.
[213] Brian Coleman, SAS Turns Around With Pretax Profit During First Half, Wall St. J., Aug. 18, 1994, at A4.

capital infusions, the Commission imposes conditions insisting on still more competition, exacerbating the downward financial spiral.

Recently privatized carriers entered the market with a significant comparative advantage—relatively clean balance sheets, and therefore superior access to the capital markets. For example, the Philippine government wrote off $560 million of Philippine Airlines debt before its privatization in 1992.[214] It was little problem for recently privatized British Airways to tap the capital markets to finance major equity investments in USAir and Qantas.

7. The Traditional Debt and Equity Markets—Many on Wall Street believe the airline industry's long-term prospectus is for a severe capital shortfall.[215] Though the world's airlines are expected to generate $1.6 trillion in gross revenue between 1996-1999, most will go to paying down the massive debt with which they are burdened; only 45% will likely be available for capital expenditures.[216] According to Philip Baggaley:

> [A]irlines face less hospitable capital markets than they did in the late 1980s. While banks and capital market lenders have returned to aviation financing, they do so with a more cautious appraisal of airline credit fundamentals and aircraft residual values. Japan's financial institutions, at one time a source for more than half of all aircraft funding, are constrained by problems elsewhere in their loan portfolios. GPA Group Ltd., one of the two largest operating lessors of aircraft, is shrinking after a near brush with insolvency.[217]

8. Aircraft Lessors—In 1986, 41% of the world's airlines owned all their equipment, 15% leased all their equipment, and 44% operated

---

[214] The Balancing Act, Airline Bus., The Skies in 1992 16 (1992).
[215] See e.g., Philip Baggaley, Assessing An Airline's Credit Quality, in Handbook of Airline Economics 239, 245 (D. Jenkins ed. 1995).
[216] Anthony Velocci, Jr., GECAS Study Reveals Leasing Paramount to Aircraft Acquisition, Aviation Week & Space Tech. (Nov. 25, 1996), at 44.
[217] Philip Baggaley, Assessing An Airline's Credit Quality, in Handbook of Airline Economics 239, 245 (D. Jenkins ed. 1995).

a mix of owned and leased aircraft. A decade later, 16% owned all their equipment, 42% leased all, and 42% used a mix of the two. Airlines will need an average of 500 to 600 aircraft a year to satisfy needs for growth and retirement of aging aircraft. Leasing will be essential to acquisition of such vast capital resources.[218]

GPA Group PLC, the giant Irish aircraft-leasing company, has a fleet of 440 aircraft.[219] GPA came close to collapse in 1993, restructuring with a $1.35 billion financial rescue from GE Capital Corp., and selling $4 billion of asset-backed securities through a complicated transaction handled by Morgan Stanley.[220] Though aircraft lessors like GPA took a beating in the early 1990s, leasing will continue to be a major (perhaps *the* major) source of aircraft financing because airline capital resources may preclude outright purchases, while equipment trust certificates and bankruptcy laws accord the lessor special protection not accorded to other creditors. Thus, aircraft with relatively generic interiors will be circulated and recirculated through various carrier fleets. Sadly, the United States of America, the world's largest air travel market, will continue to fly the oldest and most repainted fleet of any developed nation.

---

[218] Anthony Velocci, Jr., GECAS Study Reveals Leasing Paramount to Aircraft Acquisition, Aviation Week & Space Tech. (Nov. 25, 1996), at 44.
[219] Troubles of a Lessor of Jet Airliners Touch Many Parts of Industry, Wall St. J., Dec. 17, 1992, at A1.
[220] Charles Goldsmith, Ireland Offers Green Pastures for Aviation, Wall St. J., Aug. 15, 1996.

CHAPTER 4.

PLANNING: PRODUCT DEVELOPMENT

"An airline seat is probably the closest thing to a real commodity."[1]
Stephen Wolf
CEO, United Airlines

INTRODUCTION

In the preceding chapters, such essential concepts as supply, demand, price and cost were introduced, along with their relationship to profit, loss, debt and equity. These concepts provide a foundation for what follows in the ensuing chapters, which divide the industry along functional lines. Introduced in this Chapter and Chapter 5, are concepts of marketing, planning and operations, with an emphasis on the *product* offered. More specifically, strategic planning issues for route selection, fleet composition, utilization, scheduling, and operations are presented.

The topic of Chapter 6 is revenue, or yield, management, with an emphasis on the *price* for which the product is offered. It is the combination of price and service options that differentiate one airline product from another, and are the primary generators of revenue for the firm.

Chapter 7 addresses the issue of *sales*, with an emphasis on advertising and distribution. Advertising alerts the consuming public to the price and service differences between carriers. Distribution is prin-

---

[1] Michael McCarthy & Carl Quintanilla, Holders of UAL Approve Bold Buyout That Gives Workers Majority Control, Wall St. J., July 13, 1994, at A3.

cipally through travel agents and computer reservations systems, though distribution directly to consumers is a growing phenomenon.

Chapter 8 is an examination of *cost* considerations, particularly labor and distribution costs, which may directly influence the type of service being offered, and bottom-line profitability. Cost containment has become an overriding concern of airline management in the 1990s.

Yet another contemporary concern is the emergence of inter-carrier marketing and equity alliances, particularly in international markets, the subject of Chapter 9. As can be seen, these concepts are inextricably intertwined. A comprehensive understanding of the airline business requires an understanding of each of these concepts and how they are related to each other.

PRODUCT DIFFERENTIATION

Among the difficulties airlines have in marketing their product is the very nature of the product itself—it isn't a product at all; it's a service, an intermediate good, and a fungible commodity. J.L. Grumbridge observes that the difference in marketing products and marketing services is a result of four characteristics of services: (1) the service cannot be inventoried during the downward slope of the demand cycle; (2) a service is usually personalized; (3) there is no equivalent of replacing an unsatisfactory product; and (4) it is difficult for a consumer to appraise the quality of a service before it is consumed. Grumbridge continues to identify the characteristics of commercial aviation which make the marketing of air transportation different from marketing other services: (1) demand for air transportation is derived demand; (2) the airline industry is heavily regulated by government; (3) delivery cannot be guaranteed because of inclement weather or mechanical problems; and (4) the service can only be produced in batches rather than individually.[2]

One of the most difficult problems facing airline management is that there is relatively little room for meaningful product differentiation, particularly for flights of less than two hours. Airlines fly essentially the same aircraft. The soft drinks are essentially the same.

---

[2] J.L. Gumbridge, Marketing Management in Air Transport (1966), also summarized in Newal Taneja, The Commercial Airline Industry 61 (1976).

The peanuts taste the same. Airlines can offer better food, complimentary drinks, more leg room, and other so-called "frills," but will consumers pay for them, or steer their business toward the competitor which offers a lower fare without these amenities? Air transportation is in the nature of a credence good, for which payment must be made prior to consumption. Thus, it is difficult for a prospective passenger to know whether carrier A's trip will be better than carrier B's—which will leave on time, which will have the better food, the friendlier flight attendants, the empty seat on which to lie one's brief case, as opposed to sitting next to an individual with physical hygiene deficiencies. Airline management is faced with the disturbing fact that, to many consumers, air transportation is essentially a fungible commodity.

Edmund Greenslet described the problem of the intermediate and fungible nature of air transportation this way:

> Unlike almost every other consumer service air transportation is not an end produced but is an intermediate step used only when it is necessary for someone to satisfy another personal or business need. No one gets up in the morning and says that today I am going to take an airplane ride . . . . That means that the airplane ride is not the important activity but rather it is the desire to reach a vacation resort or a place where business can be conducted. Taking a vacation or doing business is the real object; the airplane trip is just a necessary intermediate activity to achieve that end.
>
> The intermediate nature of air transportation is the reason that it is considered, in economic terms, a commodity. An analogy can be made to a bushel of wheat which is a commodity for two reasons. First, nobody wants a bushel of wheat, what they want is a loaf of bread or a cake and so, like air transportation, wheat is an intermediate material needed to achieve the desired end product. Second, every bushel of wheat is just like every other bushel so no

producer can make his different from any other. In the same manner every airplane seat is just like every other seat. There are, of course, different grades of wheat and there are first class and business class seats, but for the mass market a seat is a seat.[3]

What is the product being offered? Airline management sometimes refers to it as an Available Seat Mile [ASM], or Kilometer (or Ton Mile, or Ton Kilometer), something which, so defined, appears quite fungible. But consumers do not ordinarily go to a ticket counter and ask for a few hundred ASMs. To a passenger, the product is air transportation between desired city-pairs at a certain departure and arrival date and time.

Passengers tend to select among carriers providing service between desired cities primarily on the basis of schedule and price. Research reveals that 75% of passengers base their choice of airlines on schedule and price, and 13% on their affiliation with the carrier's frequent flyer program.[4] Frequency therefore becomes a critical means of product differentiation—the carrier with a larger number of flights in a market usually enjoys an even greater number of passengers than its competitors, and superior revenue (a product of the "S-curve" phenomenon). Nonstop service is preferred to one-stop service, and one-stop service is preferred to connecting service. On-line connections are preferred to off-line connections, although the nefarious practice of code-sharing fraudulently identifies off-line connections as on-line connections, thereby thwarting another of consumer preferences—jets over turboprop aircraft.

Business and first class sections are different products, though some would argue that, at most airlines, the price premium vastly exceeds the difference in the value of the product. Nonetheless, the inelasticity of demand for the business and first class products (whose purchasers are the wealthy, or business travelers paying with pre-tax dollars, often someone else's dollars) allows airlines to price them well above any objective measure of qualitative difference. Frequent flyer

---

[3] ESG Aviation Services, 9 Airline Monitor 1 (Oct. 1996).
[4] Bridget O'Brian, Continental's CALite Hits Some Turbulence In Battling Southwest, Wall St. J., Jan. 10, 1995, at A1, A16.

programs have become another means of product differentiation, particularly for those individuals who fly regularly.

Charles Banfe has observed that the key to survival in the airline industry is finding the right niche in the market, and airlines which knew or learned how to carve out that specific niche were characterized by good management and economic resources to fill it.[5] Another way to view the objective is one of market segmentation—differentiating one's product from one's competitors to satiate a specific area of consumer demand. Professor Newal Taneja summarized the approaches used by the post-deregulation new entrant airlines:

> The changed environment in the airline industry encouraged new airlines to fill special niches in the marketplace. Each new entrant analyzed the marketplace to identify a particular price or service option that would satisfy the needs of a particular segment of the marketplace and produce a profit for the airline. Price and service options offered after deregulation ranged from the no-frills service offered by People Express to the all-frills service offered by Regent Air. Between those two extremes, other airliners experimented with various price/service options, such as first-class travel at standard coach fares and service from secondary airports. Some new airlines attempted to create new markets, while others attempted to divert traffic from existing airlines.[6]

Among the models which have been attempted include the following:

1. *High Fare, Full Service Network Carriers*—These are carriers which offer ubiquitous national and international connecting service distributed through computer reservations systems [CRS] pre-

---

[5] Charles Banfe, Airline Management 84 (1992).
[6] Newal Taneja, Civil Aviation 139 (2d ed. 1989).

dominantly by travel agents. Examples are the big four U.S. airlines—United, American, Delta and Northwest.
2. *Low Fare, High Service Network Carriers*—These carriers which offer widespread connecting service distributed via CRS. An example is Continental, which under Frank Lorenzo had degenerated into a low fare, low service network carrier, but post-Lorenzo, has much improved its service.
3. *Low Fare, Low Service Network Carriers*—These are carriers which offer widespread connecting service generally distributed outside CRS and travel agents. Examples include WesternPacific.
4. *High Fare, High Service Point-to-Point Carriers*—Midwest Express has embraced an apparently successful formula of spacious seating, and gourmet meals, at relatively high prices.
5. *Low Fare, High Service Point-to-Point Carriers*—These are carriers which offer good service (ample leg room, meals) in city-pairs, distributed by CRS and travel agents. Examples include the new Frontier Airlines. If high frequencies and low consumer complaints were added to the service analysis, one might add Southwest Airlines to this list, though its seat configuration is tight, and its in-flight amenities are nil.
6. *Low Fare, Low Service Point-to-Point Carriers*—These are carriers which offer bare bones in-flight amenities with direct product distribution. Examples include ValuJet, and the belated People Express, Air Florida, and MarkAir. Though Southwest ranks high in customer satisfaction, it provides its clientele "bare bones" in-flight service.

Like any effort to simplify categories of complicated phenomena, these categories oversimplify to a degree. Thus, the network carriers carry lots of passengers on a point-to-point basis; the point-to-point carriers handle some connecting traffic (for example, only about 10%-15% of Southwest's traffic is connecting).[7] But the purpose here is to segregate them along three essential dimensions of service—price, in-flight service, and route systems—with a focus on their primary product. A full service carrier is, by the definition used in this text, one

---

[7] Address of Pete McGlade Before the Fifth Annual Phoenix International Aviation Symposium (Apr. 18, 1996).

which offers seat assignments, frequent flyer mileage, interlining, and is displayed in CRS. Other salient features of service not fully reflected in these categories are age and reliability of fleet, flight frequency, and multiple classes of service. And generally speaking, each carrier offers a wide portfolio of products (i.e., city-pairs and fare categories) designed to attract a range of customers with different demand characteristics.

Further, there are a number of points across which one carrier can differentiate its product from another's. The following list provides the most prominent alternatives:

- High Frequency/Low Frequency
- High Cost/Low Cost
- Full Service/De Minimus Service [8]
- High Price/Low Price
- Network Carrier/Point-to-Point Carrier
- Long Haul Routes/Short Haul Routes
- Jet Carrier/Turboprop Carrier

For example, one might characterize United as a high frequency, high cost, full service, high price, network jet carrier flying relatively long-haul routes. One might characterize Continental as a high frequency, low cost, de minimus service, low price network jet carrier flying relatively long haul routes. Southwest is a high frequency, low cost, de minimus service, low price, point-to-point jet carrier flying short haul routes. Mesa Airlines is a low frequency, high cost, de minimus service, high price, connecting feeder turboprop carrier flying short haul routes. This is a fairly subjective assessment, and the carriers taken as examples may disagree with the authors' characterizations. Moreover, the grass always seems to be greener on the other side. Note that most established airlines focus heavily on cost containment, while most upstart airlines focus heavily on yield improvement.

All in all, airline management has several critical choices to make, which cumulatively will differentiate its product from its competitors, albeit sometimes in subtle ways. These include:

---

[8] This criterion includes such features as food, reserved seats and CRS distribution of product.

Planning: Product Development

1. Between which city-pairs will it operate?
2. How frequently, and at what times, will it provide service between these points?
3. Will it serve connecting traffic, or instead focus on origin-and-destination passengers?
4. Which aircraft types will it fly?
5. Will it offer multiple classes of service (for example, dividing the cabin into first, business, and economy classes), and what will be its seat pitch? [9]
6. What will it offer in terms of in-flight amenities (e.g., beverages, meals, movies)?
7. At what price will it offer its product, and with what restrictions?
8. Will it distribute its product via the four major CRS?

All but the last two of these questions is the subject of this Chapter. The seventh question will be discussed in the next Chapter. The eighth question is the subject of Chapter 7. But before exploring means of differentiating one's product, the structural and procedural templates under which such decisions are made are examined.

AIRLINE ORGANIZATION

The best organizational structure is the simplest structure that works. Some companies divide themselves into small, entrepreneurial units with lean staffs and specific direction to get things done.[10]

According to Charles Banfe, the two principal factors governing the ability of airlines to pursue their goals efficiently and effectively are (1) the intelligence of the organizational structure, and (2) the intelligence of the organization's management.[11] Typically, an airline is headed by a Chief Executive Officer [CEO] and President, to whom several vice presidents (heads of key departments) report. These may include departments of marketing, operations, finance, law, industrial

---

[9] "Seat pitch" means the distance from a given point on a seat to the corresponding point on the seat in front or behind it. This distance is generally standard from one row of seats to the next in an aircraft for each class of service. Seats in a first-class service area of an aircraft generally have a greater pitch than those in the coach service area. See Paul Stephen Dempsey and Laurence E. Gesell, Air Transportation, Foundations for the 21st Century 557 (1997).

[10] Thomas Peters & Robert Waterman, Jr., In Search of Excellence (1982).

[11] Charles Banfe, Airline Management 60 (1992).

relations, purchasing, and scheduling, reflecting the various functional activities of the airline.[12] The CEO will set the tone of the place depending on his level of intelligence, creativity, stamina, ability to know what and when to delegate, and lead and motivate subordinates to perform at their highest levels of productivity and efficiency. He will have greatest influence on the company's corporate culture. But like any large institution, a large airline will have a soul of its own.

Major airlines are huge institutions with tens of thousands of dispersed employees. Typically they may have a corporate structure with the Chairman of the Board of Directors and the CEO at the top of the pyramid, followed by a President, Chief Operating Officer [COO] and Chief Financial Officer [CFO]. Below them will be a host of vice presidents, dealing with such functions as these:

- Marketing
- Planning
- Revenue Management
- Flight Operations
- Maintenance & Engineering
- Legal and General Counsel
- Financial Planning & Analysis
- Human Resources/Employee Relations
- Customer Service
- Reservations
- Advertising and Promotions
- Corporate Communications/Public Relations
- Properties and Facilities/Airport Affairs
- Purchasing
- In-Flight Services
- Government Affairs
- International
- Catering
- Flight Standards and Training
- Safety and Security
- Regional/Area Management

---

[12] Robert Kane & Allan Vose, Air Transportation 13-14 (7th ed. 1979).

Planning: Product Development

- Cargo
- Controller and Treasurer
- Secretary

Before deregulation, the operations and government affairs functions were dominant. Since deregulation, the marketing and finance functions have become dominant.

One airline that encountered significant difficulty in establishing a consistent corporate culture was Continental Airlines. Prior to the mid-1990s, Continental had ten CEOs and Presidents in as many years, which, coupled with awkward mergers, gave it an eclectic internal environment, and contributed to its poor service levels.[13] At the other end of the spectrum is American Airlines, where Robert Crandall has served as CEO since the mid-1980s.

MARKETING AND OPERATIONS MANAGEMENT

The early airlines were dominated by pilots, engineers, and brash entrepreneurs, such as Eddie Rickenbacker (Eastern), Bob Six (Continental), Howard Hughes (TWA), and C.E. Woolman (Delta). As Ron Davies noted, these men were "giants among a band of intuitive executives who counted few pygmies in their numbers."[14] Dr. Julius Maldutis observed, "the industry was started and grew because it attracted risk takers and entrepreneurs of the highest caliber."[15] As aviation grew, demand exceeded supply, so the operations team became the dominant airline managers. With the focus on production, schedulers and route planners became central players. But as capacity grew, and leisure traffic began to dominate demand, the marketing managers became dominant, particularly in the post-deregulation era.

Airlines have two major line functions: (1) marketing (selling and servicing the product of available seat miles); and (2) operations (delivering the product to the consumer).[16] Airline marketing essentially includes all of the airline's activities associated with the demand side of the coin. Demand, is highly volatile, fickle, and constantly evol-

---

[13] Bridget O'Brian, Continental Air Ousts Its Chief, Wall St. J., Oct. 26, 1994, at A3.
[14] R.E.G. Davies, Airlines of the United States Since 1914 532, 533 (1972).
[15] Julius Maldutis, The Airlines: $99 Forever 5 (Apr. 1993).
[16] Robert Kane & Allan Vose, Air Transportation 13-17 (7th ed. 1979).

ving. An airline's marketing department typically includes the functions of market research and analysis, traffic, reservations, advertising and sales.[17] The marketing mix, or the 4Ps of marketing—Product, Price, Place (or distribution), and Promotion—correspond roughly with the organization of these several Chapters.

Operations focuses on supply, is deterministic, and can be quantified with reasonable accuracy.[18] The operations department typically includes the functions of flight operations, ground operations, and aircraft engineering, overhaul and maintenance.[19] According to Banfe:

> Marketing describes the demand, defines a market niche, outlines strategy in type of service, highlights market characteristics, develops a capacity penetration plan, analyzes the competition, plans revenues, and maps a path to profitability.
>
> Operations crunches numbers to determine whether or not it can support the plan. Operations is on the ground floor of every strategic planning decision. Some details left to operations include determining fleet strategy in number and type of aircraft; describing the potential for fleet expansion; deciding on engine types and spares requirements; and determining crew and training requirements to meet growth scheduled in the strategic plan.[20]

The functional areas of planning, forecasting, scheduling, fleet acquisition, and operations require coordination between two of the central organizational areas of an airline—marketing and operations.[21] One source emphasizes the danger in allowing either to become dominant: "If the operations structure is dominant, an increased integrity of supply results but only with added costs and decreased revenue. If

---

[17] Id.
[18] Charles Banfe, Airline Management 80 (1992).
[19] Robert Kane & Allan Vose, Air Transportation 13-18 (7th ed. 1979).
[20] Charles Banfe, Airline Management 114, 115 (1992).
[21] Robert Kane & Allan Vose, Air Transportation 13-17 (7th ed. 1979).

marketing is dominant, capacity and revenues increase, but operating costs rise measurably."[22] The challenge, therefore, for the airline's Chief Executive Officer is to balance priorities and encourage cooperation between the company's departments of operations and marketing (and, of course, finance, for no service can be provided without adequate financial resources), so that they not become competing turfs. For that reason, these overlapping functions are blended here.

Marketing has been defined as "the process of planning and executing the conception, pricing, promotion, and distribution of ideas, goods, and services to create exchanges that satisfy individual and organizational objectives."[23] Academics view exchange as the most important component of the definition, while managers view consumer satisfaction as the most important ingredient.[24] The managers are right, for the company's growth, even its survival, depends upon satisfying its customers.

A *marketing strategy* consists of identifying the target market (the consumers the firm wants to reach), and creating an appropriate market mix (product, price, distribution, and promotion) that will satisfy them.[25] The firm begins by establishing an information system to discern consumers' true preferences, and uses the information to create products that satisfy them.[26] Nor does the process stop there. The firm must continue to monitor consumer tastes and alter existing products and develop new ones designed to satiate consumers' evolving preferences.[27]

Typically, the marketing department has three principal divisions—sales, advertising, and market research. Research and planning are addressed in this Chapter. The pricing dimension of sales is addressed in Chapter 6; advertising and distribution is addressed in Chapter 7. The operations department also typically has three divisions—flight operations, maintenance & engineering, and ground operations. It is responsible for compliance with the Federal Aviation Regulations [FARs], supervising flight personnel and their line flying operations, purchasing fuel, evaluating schedule performance, maintaining the flight and

---

[22] Charles Banfe, Airline Management 62 (1992).
[23] AMA Board Approves New Marketing Definition, Marketing News (Mar. 1, 1985), at 1.
[24] William Pride & O.C. Ferrell, Marketing Concepts and Strategies 8 (6th ed. 1989).
[25] Id. at 19.
[26] Id. at 18.
[27] Id. at 15.

ground equipment, and administering the station and ground facilities.[28]

THE PLANNING PROCESS

Professor Lester Digman describes the essential components of *strategic planning*:

> Conceptually, strategic planning is very simple. Stripped of its complexities, a strategy consists of the *means* an organization chooses to move it from point A (where it is now) to point B (where it must be at some time in the future) . . . . [T]he organization must first assess where it is at present. In reality, this step is not so simple: "where we are" includes defining the market; the industry; the competitors; our resources, strengths, and weaknesses; technology; economic factors; customer needs and preferences; demographics; international effects; regulatory influences, and a host of other factors. Determining "where we must be" and "when we must be there" is even more difficult, because it requires us to predict changes in all of the previously mentioned factors. Choosing the "best way to get from A to B" is obviously a judgmental matter, and is only as good as our ability to assess points A and B.[29]

A *strategic plan* is a comprehensive assessment of where the company can best position itself over the longer-term, including certain tactical and marketing plans to be implemented over the short-term. The rational model of corporate planning involves defining the firm's objectives, missions and policies over a defined planning horizon. The

---

[28] Charles Banfe, Airline Management 104-07 (1992).
[29] Lester Digman, Strategic Management 6, 7 (1990).

Planning: Product Development

structure for developing marketing and strategic plans may be summarized as follows:

1. Defining corporate objectives;
2. Performing a situation analysis of the strengths and weaknesses of the airline and its competitors, and environmental opportunities and threats;
3. Forecasting future events;
4. Evaluating various alternatives, and their risk/reward probabilities;
5. Establishing broad strategies to satisfy corporate objectives;
6. Formulating specific plans to implement strategies and integrating plans through all departments;
7. Executing plans effectively;
8. Appraising results; and
9. Modifying plans as experience dictates.[30]

After broad corporate objectives (e.g., improved yields and market share) have been defined, the airline should undertake a *situation analysis*—a candid, objective and detailed appraisal of its strengths and weaknesses and those of its competitors, no matter how painful an honest assessment may be. Among the factors to be considered are the following:

1. Customers (business and discretionary passengers, corporations, the government, travel agents, tour operators, consolidators, shippers and freight forwarders);
2. Market Identity (high or low service, high or low price);
3. Route Structure (connecting or point-to-point, dense or thin city-pairs, domestic/international);
4. Schedule (stage length, flight frequency, aircraft and gate utilization, load factors, fuel consumption);
5. Fleet (age, composition, Stage 3, heterogeneous/homogenous, maintenance, reliability);
6. Marketing (market share, yield management, distribution network, product lines);

---

[30] See Robert Crandall, Marketing Planning, in Airline Economics 231 (G. James ed. 1982); and Newal Taneja, Airline Planning: Corporate, Financial and Marketing 11-28 (1982).

7. Finance (return on investment, cash flow, debt/equity ratio, interest coverage, fleet age and percentage leased, working capital, credit availability);
8. Cost structure (labor, fuel, distribution);
9. Personnel (salary levels, unionization, turnover, training, morale); and
10. Environment (demographic, social, economic, regulatory).[31]

Both in the short and long-term, the analysis should be focused on capitalizing on the airline's strengths, and compensating for its weaknesses.[32] A useful starting point is an evaluation of the profit contribution of each subsidiary, division or route (of course, the latter becomes more difficult when one attempts to ascribe the costs and revenue of connecting passengers to particular routes).

The airline must also objectively evaluate the strengths and weaknesses of its existing and potential competitors in its markets, as well as competition from alternative modes (e.g., rail or automobile transport) and technologies (e.g., video-conferencing). The economic environment also has a profound impact on airline profitability, so that it must be assessed as well, including such factors as consumer confidence, recession/inflation, interest rates, employment levels, foreign-exchange rates and fuel prices.[33] The development of a market plan requires the assessment of both macro-economic factors (e.g., demography, economy, environment, technology, regulation, seasonality) and micro-economic factors (e.g., size of market, competition, cost, revenue, business/discretionary mix, fit with existing route structure and corporate objectives).[34] This process is employed in designing a route structure, selecting specific routes, assembling a fleet of aircraft to serve those routes, scheduling the aircraft, maintaining them, and acquiring ground facilities, all with an keen eye on cost and revenue. A market plan can be short-term (a few months, or a year) or long-term (several years).

Though predicting the future is a difficult game, forecasting is essential, perhaps with several scenarios identified—best case, worst

---

[31] See Newal Taneja, Airline Planning: Corporate, Financial, and Marketing 18, 19 (1982).
[32] Id. at 15-17.
[33] Id. at 20, 21.
[34] See Charles Banfe, Airline Management 96-97 (1992).

case and most probable case. Planning must include a description of objectives and the means to achieve them. Multiple objectives should be both internally consistent and prioritized. Different scenarios pose differing degrees of risk. Risk assessment does not mean that management should be risk averse, for risk-free paths are unrewarding, but only insists that the degree of risk be properly evaluated, and that greater risk alternatives have greater rewards.[35] According to Banfe:

> A strategic plan is the allocation of resources, over time, that will optimize the position of the airline and maximize profitability. The planning process includes definition of the ends to be achieved, a time frame with milestones to measure progress, and a description of how the airline can meet those milestones.
> Strategic planning is systematic and should be formalized, It is optimal when written. It must take into account the power, political, and social forces within the airline.
> Planning strategically is broad, conceptual, and consists of policy-making. It establishes corporate philosophy, expectations, and goals . . . . Altogether, a coherent set of appraisal, mission, planning, and execution functions defines the scope of a strategic plan.[36]

Development of a strategic plan involves consideration of several factors, including:

1. *Designate the planning horizon*—Over what time period is the plan to address?
2. *Identify goals and objectives*—What are the quantifiable data by which to measure the airline's progress over time?
3. *Perform a position audit*—What are the airline's current strengths, weaknesses, and opportunities?

---

[35] Newal Taneja, Airline Planning: Corporate, Financial, and Marketing 14, 21, 22, 24 (1982).
[36] Charles Banfe, Airline Management 110 (1992).

4. *Identify the "do nothing" case*—Where will the airline be at the end of the planning horizon if present policies are unaltered?
5. *Identify strategic alternatives*—Identify the most promising alternatives building on the airline's strengths and/or shoring up its weaknesses. This requires an evaluation of such factors as customer requirements, demand forecasts, the competition, controllable vs. uncontrollable costs, government regulation, infrastructure capacity, fleet composition, financing, and market identity.
6. *Evaluate alternatives*—Which of the strategic alternatives appear most or least promising? Which produces the highest levels of net revenue?
7. *Perform sensitivity analysis*—The different options should be assessed using pessimistic assumptions.
8. *Define the marketing plan*—Identify the specific goals to be achieved, and means by which they are to be achieved.
9. *Implement the marketing plan.*
10. *Monitor its performance*—Evaluate how well the plan performs and modify it, if necessary, to improve its performance.[37]

While planning should not be intuitive, and should be based on as much objective information as can be made reasonably ascertained, it is a process of informed analysis and experienced judgment rather than one of empirical science. Inevitably, it requires making assumptions about future macro-economic and competitive conditions beyond the control of the airline.

A comprehensive and cohesive strategy should be developed to allow coordinated implementation by each department. According to Professor Taneja:

> Initially, the planner can examine a broad list of alternative strategies at each level—corporate, business, functional, and operational. The alternatives to be examined should be creative, imaginative, and consistent with the style and philosophy of management. At the

---

[37] Stephen Shaw, Airline Marketing & Management 118-24 (3rd ed. 1990).

corporate level, for instance, expansion into other businesses could be examined by a large airline, particularly where there is synergy or expansion by acquisition. At the business level, an airline with heavy passenger orientation could explore the feasibility of expanding its airfreight operations. In this case, examination of supporting strategy alternatives at the functional and operating level is needed....

For a smaller airline... a marketing-attractiveness strength matrix is available to identify and formulate strategies. Several options are available, even for a small airline with a small fleet: (1) new markets for existing fleet and services; (2) new services in existing markets; (3) new services for new markets; or (4) improved existing services in existing markets. Regarding the possibilities of just the last alternative, the airline could focus on any one of the four elements of the marketing mix—service, price, promotion, or distribution; each of these elements, in turn, allows for multiple possibilities. The consideration of modifying price alone presents three different strategies—market penetration, market skimming, and unbundling of the total service.[38]

Taneja also offers a list of questions used to narrow the multitude of strategic choices available to the planner:

1. How do the alternatives rank in terms of offering the strongest competitive advantage?
2. Which alternatives are most vulnerable to an effective strategic counterattack from existing and potential competitors?
3. Which alternatives are flexible in terms of allowing for responses to unforeseen events?

---

[38] Newal Taneja, Airline Planning: Corporate, Financial and Marketing 22, 23 (1982).

4. Which alternatives could lead to substantial confrontation among various groups within the airline?
5. Do any of the alternatives fail to exploit the airlines' distinctive strengths?
6. How do the alternatives mesh with other strategies being pursued?[39]

Inevitably, the rational model of strategic planning meets resistance on a number of fronts.[40] Managers may question the time and resources it consumes. Some of the most effective strategic managers may be intuitive and creative, and many strategic decisions tend to be "event driven." But as General Dwight Eisenhower observed, the planning process is far more important than the plan itself, for while the plan may have to be amended many times because of unforeseen circumstances or events beyond one's control, the process will have forced careful evaluation of strategic alternatives and development of back-up contingency plans.

Every company has a planning process. It may be formal and structured, or informal and unstructured. The formal planning process and systematized implementation of strategies tends to produce better performance. Nonetheless, formalized planning is not necessarily more effective planning, though formalization ensures the process will not be ignored.[41] Professor Digman observed:

> The reason we do formal planning is that we *have* to in order to manage the process in complex organizations, even though it is somewhat detrimental to the making of the most effective strategic decision—it is a necessary evil. The goal is to make the correct strategic decisions, not the development of detailed plans.
>
> The best strategists tend to have a *vision* of their organization—a clear understanding of

---

[39] Id. at 24, 25.
[40] For a criticism of the rational planning model, see Paul Dempsey, Andrew Goetz & Joseph Szyliowicz, Denver International Airport: Lessons Learned Chapter 10 (1997).
[41] Lester Digman, Strategic Management 27, 28 (1990).

what the firm is about and where it is headed. This vision is the "glue" that holds things together through turbulent times and business fluctuations. It guides competitive strategy, and does not require exhaustive analysis. In fact some managers consider this vision to be at the very core of strategic planning—defining it as helping your organization "create, maintain, and implement a long-term or strategic vision."[42]

While they have the knowledge, skill and ability to lead the strategic planning process, typically, a carrier's Chairman, CEO, President and COO can be too immersed in the day-to-day operations of their airlines to be able to devote the time and attention to long-term strategic planning it deserves. The person who heads the corporate planning function must be compatible with the personality of the CEO, and have his trust and confidence. He or she must also have a special set of skills—the ability to communicate, sell ideas, inspire confidence and trust, and understand the internal politics of the corporation. Diplomatic skills can help diffuse conflicts among competing executives with different levels of competence, ambition, and aggression, and point them in a direction in their collective best interest. Proficient "people skills" can also be used to avoid getting caught in the "cross fire" between line managers.[43]

No single individual can possess all the in-depth knowledge of a complex corporate enterprise like an airline, so the corporate planner should develop a small staff, preferably on an *ad hoc* basis, recruiting from each of the airline's major departments. The task-force approach can be extremely effective if it includes field managers in the process of strategic planning, for they will have greater incentive to implement a plan if they consider it theirs.[44]

The objectives identified in a strategic plan must be both realistically achievable, and acceptable to the individuals who must

---

[42] Id. at 12.
[43] Newal Taneja, Airline Planning: Corporate, Financial, and Marketing 27 (1982).
[44] Id. at 27.

implement it.[45] Development of a strategic plan should involve as wide a cross-section of the airline's line management as possible, with interaction between top level and lower level employees, for it is the line managers who are in closest contact with the marketplace, and it is they who shall implement it. Their enthusiasm for the plan will be enhanced if they are involved in developing it.[46] Key management must also affirmatively support the objectives if line employees are to be expected to implement the plan effectively.[47]

Unionized carriers face another set of limitations on strategic planning—the scope clause in their union contract. It may restrict flexibility on aircraft and route decisions as well as alliances with other carriers. Labor representation of the airline's Board of Directors may inhibit managerial flexibility in some areas, while creating opportunities in others.

Once implemented, performance of the plans must be monitored. This requires the development of management information systems, including regular reports of flight profitability and revenue analysis, for example, so that management has a "hands on" view of performance. Both the marketing plan and the strategic plan must be sufficiently agile, flexible and dynamic so that they can be "fine-tuned," amended, or even jettisoned, should they either become inconsistent with the internal or external environment, or fail to fulfill their objectives.[48] For example, external factors such as evolving demand patterns or government regulatory priorities may jeopardize projected revenue and costs, respectively. Back-up, or contingency, planning is helpful in enabling the airline to shift its resources expeditiously.

DETERMINING CONSUMER PREFERENCES

The most successful companies tend to be "customer driven," producing goods and services designed to satisfy consumer preferences.[49] Although prudent strategy, reliable information systems, dedi-

---

[45] Id. at 13.
[46] Stephen Shaw, Airline Marketing & Management 118 (3rd ed. 1990).
[47] Newal Taneja, Airline Planning: Corporate, Financial, and Marketing 14 (1982).
[48] See id. at 14, 20.
[49] Thomas Peters & Robert Waterman, Jr., In Search of Excellence (1982); Milind Lele & Jagdish Sheth, The Customer is Key: Gaining An Unbeatable Advantage Through Customer Satisfaction (1987); Donald Clifford, Jr. & Richard Cavanaugh, The Winning Performance: How America's

Planning: Product Development

cated employees, and excellent implementation all are important in making a business successful, it is critically important that the business be dedicated to sensing, serving and satisfying consumers in a well-understood and identified target market.[50] In determining how to design a product to satiate consumers' wants and needs, among the key questions to be asked are:

1. What business are we in?
2. Who are the customers we wish to serve?
3. What are their needs and wants?

Commercial aviation is a derived demand business, dependent on individuals' needs for transportation to conduct a business transaction, take a vacation, or visit friends and relatives [VFR]. Each of these market segments has different demand characteristics. Management must determine whether the airline is serving the business traveler, the leisure traveler, or both. A combination carrier must also be sensitive to the demand characteristics of freight, for it will also account for a sizable stream of revenue (usually around 10% of operating revenue).

Sometimes the customer (the individual who selects the carrier and purchases air transportation services) is not the passenger at all. For business travel, a secretary, or the corporation's travel department may be the customer. For business or leisure travel, the customer may be a travel agent, for agents wield enormous influence over certain purchases. For leisure travel, the husband, or the wife, or a tour operator, may be the primary carrier selector for the family. For cargo, an air freight forwarder may be the customer. Thus, the customer is not necessarily the passenger or the shipper.

Moreover, an airline must be cognizant of "Pareto's Law"—80% of the profits are often derived from only 20% of the customers.[51] The relative elasticities of demand of business (employees of large or small corporations) and leisure (vacation or visiting friends and relatives travelers) are very different. Basically, business travelers tend to have less price elasticity of demand than do leisure travelers. Frequency and

---

High-Growth Mid-Size Companies Succeed (1985); Valarie Zeithaml, A. Parasuraman & Leonard Berry, Delivering Quality Service (1990).

[50] Philip Kotler, Marketing Management 3 (7th ed. 1991).

[51] Stephen Shaw, Airline Marketing & Management 15-29 (3rd ed. 1990).

schedule are the most important criteria for high-yield business travelers; price is most important for discretionary travelers. But more on price elasticity later in the book. For present purposes, the concern is with the product that consumers prefer.

Prudent management begins by attempting to ascertain consumer preferences. In order to assess consumer preferences, the marketing department should engage in environmental scanning and analysis. Scanning is the process of collecting information about the market—observation, examination of secondary sources such as trade and governmental periodicals and publications, and marketing research efforts. Analysis involves interpreting the information so gathered.[52] Information is essential in assessing the market and tailoring a product to fit consumer preferences, and elevates decision making above the realm of the intuitive.[53]

Jan Carlzon transformed SAS into a carrier that high-yield business travelers prefer simply by identifying their preferences and satisfying them. Surveys revealed the top priority for European businessmen was on-time arrival; they also preferred expeditious baggage check-in and retrieval. SAS devoted resources to training its front-line customer-service personnel (regarded by Carlzon as the most important people in the company) and managers (whose responsibility was to help the front-line employees perform well). Within four months, SAS was the most punctual airline in Europe. Baggage check-in and unloading procedures were expedited. Passengers were allowed to check baggage in at SAS affiliated hotels. The result was an 8% increase in European full-fare sales, and a 16% increase in full-fare transcontinental sales. As one source noted, "Carlzon's impact on Scandinavian Airlines illustrates the customer satisfaction and profits that a corporate leader can achieve when he or she creates a vision and mission for the company and gets the personnel to swim in the same direction—namely toward satisfying the target consumers."[54]

In identifying market opportunities, airline management typically evaluates historical data on the number of passengers or volume of freight between city-pairs. Several sources of data exist. Existing sche-

---

[52] William Pride & O.C. Ferrell, Marketing Concepts and Strategies 42 (6th ed. 1989).
[53] Robert Waterman, Jr., The Renewal Factor: How the Best Get and Keep the Competitive Edge (1987).
[54] Philip Kotler, Marketing Management 23 (7th ed. 1991).

dules are published in the Official Airline Guide, a ready source of information regarding frequency and capacity, as well as the identity of the competitors, in any city-pair market. The CAB/DOT *Handbook of Airline Statistics* provides historical data on the industry. Further, Form 41 data provides essential information revealing the characteristics of competitors in the market. The U.S. Department of Transportation also collects a 10% ticket sample, an origin-destination survey, which reveals useful information such as the number of passengers traveling between city-pairs on any date, or time, and the fare they paid. In addition, computer reservations systems include detailed information concerning passenger flows and pricing. These data must be made available to competitors of the airlines which own CRSs, though the price is steep. The cost of domestic market information tapes are about $10,000 per month for each of the four systems (Sabre, Apollo, System One and Worldspan), a prohibitive fee for many upstart airlines.

Certain polls of consumers can reveal information about their preferences. The American Automobile Association surveyed Americans to identify their principal concerns. Dubbed the "Hassle Index", in 1992 it found that 23% said the cost of air service was their principal concern (only 7% said that in 1990). Safety rated second at 22%, while 10% were concerned about the condition of the aircraft, and 8% with traffic congestion. Forty-two percent believed that fares became worse during 1991 (compared with 34% in 1990).[55] A poll conducted in late 1992 by the Roper Organization revealed that 37% approved of the current level of government regulation of fares and service, while 33% thought there was not enough; 51% of Americans believe that safety regulation is not strong enough, while 21% believe that safety regulation is sufficient.[56]

Most important to airlines is why passengers select one carrier over another. Table 4.1, "Reasons For Choosing An Airline: U.S. vs. Non-Residents", provides some insight as to consumer preferences between U.S. residents and nonresidents. Men and women also differ as to the

---

[55] Cost of Air Travel Replaces Safety As Main Concern to Travelers, Aviation Daily (Jan. 7, 1992), at 28.
[56] Union Releases Survey on Deregulation With Mixed Findings, Aviation Daily (Nov. 25, 1991), at 342.

reasons they choose a particular carrier, as shown on Table 4.2, "Reasons For Choosing An Airline: Male vs. Female".

Table 4.1—REASONS FOR CHOOSING AN AIRLINE: U.S. vs. NON-RESIDENTS[57]
(in percentage of passengers)

Reason	*U.S. Residents*	*Non-Residents*
Schedule	20.3	17.5
Price	13.8	11.2
Frequent Flyer Program	11.1	5.1
Airline Loyalty	8.7	11.9
Safety Reputation	8.4	11.5
Cabin Service	7.3	9.5
On Time	6.4	7.3
In Flight Comfort	5.5	7.5
Airport Facilities	3.3	3.1
Aircraft Type	2.9	3.7
No Choice	12.3	11.7

Table 4.2—REASONS FOR CHOOSING AN AIRLINE: MALE vs. FEMALE[58]

Reason	*Rank for Men*	*Rank for Women*
Routes	1	2
Timeliness/Reliability	2	4
Service	3	6
Price	4	1
Frequent flyer program	5	5
Comfort	6	7
Safety	7	3
Food	8	8

---

[57] Data are for the second quarter, 1991. Aviation Daily (Oct. 3, 1991), at 23.
[58] According to the 1990 Zagat Airline Survey. Travel Tips, San Diego Union-Tribune, Dec. 2, 1990, at G9.

Besides data systems, airlines can survey consumers directly. A concise written survey can be distributed to passengers on certain flights, asking demographic and attitudinal information. While in-flight surveys convey useful information concerning how pleased or displeased passengers may be with their flight, their limitation is that they are distributed to people who have already decided to purchase the airline's product.[59] Airlines also mail surveys, particularly to their frequent flyers, asking them such questions as how many domestic or international flights they will take during a given year. Airlines attempt to improve the response rate by giving the consumer additional frequent flyer mileage as an inducement to complete and return the form. Another method is for airlines to station employees at airports to conduct personal surveys.

Airlines regularly receive letters from consumers, either praising the carrier's performance, or condemning it. Some complaints may be unjustified, made to induce some refund of a portion of the ticket price or recovery of lost or damaged baggage, and can be discounted.[60] But if the airline receives repeated complaints about some aspect of its service, it should investigate to determine the cause and devise a remedy. Because commercial aviation is a service industry, management should attempt to reply to all complaints, and resolve as many as possible satisfactorily. Customer contact line personnel should also be listened to, for many will have heard individual passenger oral complaints or praise. They too, can be an invaluable source of information concerning consumer preferences.

Yet another means of determining consumer preferences is to "test market" a new product. This is less expensive than introducing a new product line system-wide should consumers not respond favorably to it.

What are the needs (essential characteristics of air transport) as opposed to wants (desirable, but not essential characteristics) of the various traveler segments? First and foremost, all travelers need safe air transportation. Since they do not fly often, leisure travelers are more concerned with the safety and security of air travel than frequent flyers. Business travelers also need prompt, reliable and frequently

---

[59] Stephen Shaw, Airline Marketing & Management 10 (3rd ed. 1990).
[60] Id. at 12.

Chapter 4

scheduled flights. A short-haul business traveler needs conveniently timed frequent flights so as to travel to a city in the morning, conduct business, and return when that business in completed, usually by the end of the working day. More departures enhance flexibility for the business traveler, so it is important for an airline catering to business traffic to have available seats should business plans be changed. Because the flight is of short duration, he or she is generally less concerned about seat pitch or being fed during the flight. Vacation travelers are less concerned with (they don't need) frequent departures—most simply want to travel from A to B on a given day, not a specific hour.[61]

Because major carriers can have similar schedules, fly the same aircraft, and have similar safety records and punctuality performance, wants sometimes become the determinant factor in a consumer's airline choice. Wants can be tangible (e.g., separate check-in a separate cabin, better food, more generous seat pitch, free movies and liquor, and more flight attendants in Business and First Class), or intangible (e.g., the courtesy, friendliness, and helpfulness of the cabin crew). Generally speaking, a long-haul traveler (particularly one crossing an ocean) wants better seat pitch, in-flight entertainment, to fly aboard more spacious wide-bodied aircraft, and to be fed a hot meal. Vacation travelers view the air portion of their journey as part of the holiday, and appreciate a high level of in-flight service. Most travelers prefer jets to turboprop aircraft, because pressurized jets fly above the weather, are much faster, generally do not leave baggage behind because of weight restrictions, and have a superior safety record to prop aircraft. They also prefer nonstop service to one-stop service (because of time considerations), and one-stop service to connections (because of time, convenience, and the greater likelihood that a connection might result in the loss of checked baggage). Business travelers prefer to fly more prestigious airlines with a cleaner and more educated clientele than low-fare airlines filled with the Great Unwashed. So as to expedite exit from the airport, business travelers want spare chech-in, priority boarding, and sufficient storage space in

---

[61] Id. at 32-35.

the cabin so that they can carry their garment bags aboard the plane without having to check them.[62]

The demographic characteristics of demand are also important. Most business travelers are male, although the percentage of female business travelers is growing. Most business travel is undertaken by a younger age group, from the mid-20s to the mid-50s. This is the result of the "business traveler life cycle." Younger executives tend to view travel as a desirable perquisite of the job, until they tire of living out of suitcases, being away from home, and jet lag. Older executives tend to encourage others in the firm to make necessary business trips.[63]

According to one survey, the typical flyer is male (36% have flown in the past twelve months), between 25-34 or 55-64 years old, has a household income of $40,000 or more (46%), and lives in the west (50%). The average flyer took 3.79 trips within the past twelve months. While frequent flyers (individuals taking ten or more trips a year) constitute only 8% of travelers, they account for 45% of trips taken.[64] As a percentage of total passengers, business travelers fell from 47% in 1994, to 41% in 1995.[65]

In designing its product, airline management must also assess competitive alternatives to air travel. For short-haul transportation, the automobile and high-speed rail is a viable alternative, and will become more so as airports become more congested. Moreover, various forms of communication can replace some portion of air travel, particularly as telecommunications technologies improve. Already, video conferencing systems have replaced some intra-corporate communications.

EVOLVING CONSUMER PREFERENCES

The essential task of marketing is to monitor evolving consumer preferences and use this information to influence the airline's other departments to create a competitive array of price/service options consonant with changing consumer tastes, to produce value for consumers and profits for the airline. A *marketing audit* should be performed, which evaluates the external (e.g., economic, demographic,

---

[62] See id. at 32-43.
[63] Id. at 44.
[64] Air Transport Ass'n., Air Travel Survey (1993).
[65] Air Transport Ass'n., Annual Report 11 (1996).

social, regulatory, technological and competitive) and internal (e.g., corporate, organizational, fleet and route) environment and trends, as well as the firm's marketing strategy.[66]

No firm can become sanguine about its market, for consumer preferences evolve over time. For example, IBM, the dominant mainframe computer manufacturer, was left in the dust in the personal computer market by failing to anticipate the robust consumer demand which emerged there. America's tastes change, and change rapidly. At different points in time, America has fallen in love with Frank Sinatra (who, incidentally, sang in the first 747 piano lounge), Elvis Presley, the Beatles, or Michael Jackson. It has listened to them on 45 rpm single records, long-playing 33 1/3 albums, eight track tapes, cassette tapes, and compact discs. Every market is dynamic, and producers must adapt to evolving consumer tastes. Markets mature and decline over time.

Wanting more value for their money, and content to accept fewer service amenities, Americans in large numbers shifted from retailers like Sears, Woolworths, and Montgomery Wards to K-Mart, Wal-Mart, and Target. Responding to the shift in consumer tastes toward value of product at the lowest price over the attractiveness of the shopping environment, many airlines have trimmed both service and price.

ValuJet's Maurice Gallagher expressed the new airline's view of shifting consumer preferences as it launched its low-fare, low-cost airline in the early 1990s:

> The traditional business traffic, the backbone of the majors, was eroding. The peak period for white collar business traffic appears to have been in the late 1980s. However, since the 1990 Gulf War, downsizing has become the trend for corporate America. Downsizing has targeted the airline industry's best traditional customer, the white-collar middle manager. Corporations now were beginning to exert much greater control over variable budgets, such as travel. Video

---

[66] Newal Taneja; Airline Planning: Corporate, Financial, and Marketing (1982).

Planning: Product Development

conferencing was evolving as a viable alternative to a number of business trips.

There are other key trends still at work. The first is value—the consumer of the '90s is very value-conscious. Unlike the 1980s, passengers are reluctant to pay more for a product because of its name. Witness the rise of low-cost generic products. The second trend is leisure travel—the baby boom generation is aging and has substantial wealth. As a result, the leisure component of travel will be increasing in the coming years. And industry statistics support this change. Overall airline traffic has not been decreasing; rather, there has been a change in the mix of passengers—leisure traffic is up and business is down.[67]

Domestically, discretionary traffic appears to be growing at a faster rate than business traffic. This suggests the downward pressure on yields will continue well into the 21st Century. One airline alternative to this long-term trend is the "leisure market strategy," which, according to Stephen Shaw, has its advantages and disadvantages:

A leisure market airline will have the advantage that it will be targeting the part of the total market for air travel where growth prospects are more promising. It should therefore benefit from an increasing share of the total market. Its problem will be that yields from leisure travel will always be low . . . .

The leisure market airline's problem of yield is countered by the fact that it can keep its costs relatively low. The leisure traveler is not usually sensitive to either the frequency or the exact timings of flights. Therefore, airlines can

---

[67] Maurice Gallagher, ValuJet Airlines: An Analysis, in Handbook of Airline Economics 37-39 (D. Jenkins ed. 1996).

serve the denser leisure markets using larger aircraft, thereby gaining access to the greatest economies of scale. They can also work their aircraft hard, obtaining lower costs through high utilization. On board the aircraft, service standards can be lower than those offered to the sophisticated business traveler. Also, many leisure passengers appear willing to make sacrifices in seating comfort in order to gain access to the lowest fares. This allows airlines to reduce seat pitch and thereby to lower unit costs substantially by placing more seats in the aircraft than an airline targeting the business traveler.

Demand fluctuations are an important problem which affect all leisure market airlines. Leisure demand tends to peak at the weekends and to be lower in mid-week, due to passenger preferences in beginning their holidays. To an even greater degree, demand shows seasonal peaking characteristics in almost all leisure markets....

Leisure demand . . . will be affected by a number of factors which will make it relatively unstable. Fluctuations in real disposable income and in exchange rates are good examples of this. Also, civil disturbances and terrorist incidents can cause overnight declines in individual leisure markets.[68]

TRAFFIC AND REVENUE FORECASTING

Revenue from combination carriers is derived primarily from carrying passengers, and secondarily, from carrying cargo and mail. Other revenue streams may come from such sources as computer reservations systems, sale of frequent flyer mileage, sale of alcoholic

---

[68] Stephen Shaw, Airline Marketing & Management 124, 125 (3rd ed. 1990).

Planning: Product Development

beverages and movie head-sets aboard aircraft, and interest earned on investments.

Both passengers and freight have their own demand characteristics. The demand for air travel is highly segmented among business, leisure, and VFR passengers. Domestic and international traffic, first class, business class and coach traffic all have different demand characteristics. Each of these segments may grow at different rates from year-to-year.[69] In particular city-pair markets, demand by each segment of traffic may rise or fall depending on the season (e.g., northeastern U.S.-Florida/Caribbean leisure traffic picks up in the Winter), day of week (e.g., business travel is predominantly east-west, and heaviest on Mondays and Fridays), or time of day. Such factors as rises or declines in personal income (for leisure travelers), or business activity (for business travelers) can also effect demand significantly.

Airline forecasters typically evaluate historical data on such items as boarding volumes and yield, as well as demographic trends, such as age and economic activity.[70] Once trends in the overall economy have been assessed, separate traffic forecasts are made for passengers, freight and mail, taking into account such factors as:

- Expected state of the economy;
- Historic growth rate of airline traffic;
- Known factors causing change (for example, route expansion);
- Elasticity of demand (demand levels vis-à-vis expected changes in price and income levels); and
- Forecast industry capacity.[71]

Then the carrier assesses its anticipated share of capacity and traffic in the market, considering historical market shares, the identity, type and number of competitors, and its planned level of operations in the market. According to Crandall:

> A macro-forecast is then developed by geographic entity. To accomplish this step, passenger

---

[69] See Lee Howard & John Summerfield, Airline Financial Forecasting, in Airline Economics 57, 59, 60 (G. James ed. 1982).
[70] Robert Crandall, Marketing Planning, in Airline Economics 231, 232 (G. James ed. 1982).
[71] Id. at 231,241.

> traffic is estimated by fare basis, by type (business, pleasure), and by length of haul. This traffic is then priced to develop revenue estimates. As a check on this process, we construct a micro-forecast, built up from origin and destination markets. The macro- and micro-forecasts are reconciled to ensure reasonableness.[72]

Among the methodologies used to forecast future demand based on historical data are the growth factor method (an extrapolation of future growth from past growth traffic data), the Gompertz curve (in which market maturity is taken into account), category analysis (which adds behavioral aspects to the analysis, based on each population category's socio-economic characteristics), and multiple regression analysis (which allow comparison of a time series of data with changes in a dependent variable, air transport, and several independent variables, including the price of air travel and the incomes of potential travelers).[73] Howard and Summerfield identified the tools used in traffic forecasting:

> Airline analysts have developed a number of econometric models for forecasting airline traffic. These models differ in detail but include such independent variables as Gross National Product (GNP), Disposable Personal Income, average fare level (yield), and consumer confidence. Each of the models claims a high correlation between forecast traffic and actual traffic for a given year when actual values of the independent variables for that year are inserted in the model. Forecasting errors nonetheless persist with all of these models....
>
> These comments are not intended to convey the impression that the economic variables men-

---

[72] Id. at 231, 241, 242.
[73] Stephen Shaw, Airline Marketing & Management 62-65 (3rd ed. 1990).

tioned have no influence on traffic. Clearly they do or the analysts using the models would not have found such good correlations .... But ... traffic is multidimensional and growth rates of traffic components vary widely in magnitude and often in direction. Hence a more eclectic approach to traffic forecasting is in common use in the airline industry. This approach to short-term forecasting enables the forecaster to analyze recent data that exhibit changes in the structure and operation of the industry as a principal influence on results to be expected in the near future.[74]

Airline profit is but a relatively small difference between revenue and expense, smaller than in most industries. Even a modest underperformance in revenue or a modest increase in costs can result in a substantial loss. An error of one or two percentage points in either can shift the profit position significantly.[75] Thus forecasting is an extremely critical function.

ROUTE STRUCTURES:
HUB-AND-SPOKE vs. LINEAR ROUTE SYSTEMS

Subsequent to deregulation, airlines began consolidating their operations around hubs. Hubs account for 70% of the flights offered by domestic airlines.[76] What are the characteristics of an airport that make it an attractive venue for a hub? A prudent airline seeks these attributes:

1. An interior point geographically situated for flow from several directions, particularly east to west, since that is the routing of most business traffic (the most lucrative share of the market);

---

[74] Lee Howard & John Summerfield, Airline Financial Forecasting, in Airline Economics 57, 62, 63 (G. James ed. 1982).
[75] Id. at 57.
[76] American-Sponsored Study Blasts Criticism of Hubs, Aviation Daily (July 31, 1990), at 197.

2. A large population base to enhance high-yield origin and destination (O&D) traffic, preferably white collar (again, because business travelers pay more for air transportation); and
3. Preferably, no nearby hubs or competing airports dominated by another airline.[77]

According to the 1990 census, the largest metropolitan area population of U.S. cities is shown in Table 4.3, "Largest U.S. Metropolitan Areas". Note that Nashville, Dayton, and Raleigh-Durham had too small a population to create a sufficient O&D traffic base to support sustained hubbing operations by American, USAir, and American Airlines, respectively. Northwest has also downsized its Memphis hub.

Table 4.3—LARGEST U.S. METROPOLITAN AREAS (1990)[78]

Metropolitan Area	Population (millions)
1. New York	18.1
2. Los Angeles	14.5
3. Chicago	8.1
4. San Francisco	6.3
5. Philadelphia	5.9
6. Detroit	4.7
7. Boston	4.2
8. Washington	3.9
9. Dallas	3.9
10. Houston	3.7
11. Miami	3.2
12. Atlanta	2.8
13. Cleveland	2.8
14. Seattle	2.6
15. San Diego	2.5
16. Minneapolis	2.5
17. St. Louis	2.4

---

[77] Paul S. Dempsey, Robert Hardaway & William Thoms, 1 Aviation Law & Regulation § 2.12 (1993). See also J.P. Morgan Securities, The U.S. Airline Industry 17 (1993).
[78] U.S. Statistics 797 (1991).

Table 4.3 (Cont'd.)

Metropolitan Area	Population (millions)
18. Baltimore	2.4
19. Pittsburgh	2.2
20. Phoenix	2.1
21. Tampa	2.0
22. Denver	1.8
23. Cincinnati	1.7
24. Milwaukee	1.6
25. Kansas City	1.6
34. Charlotte	1.2
38. Salt Lake City	1.1
40. Nashville	1.0
41. Memphis	1.0
44. Dayton	1.0
54. Raleigh-Durham	0.7
? Colorado Springs	0.3

Table 4.4, "Ten Largest U.S. Airports", lists the largest airports in the United States. Chicago dominates U.S. air transportation because of geographic proximity and huge metropolitan population (8 million people, compared to Detroit's 4.7 million, St. Louis' 2.4 million, or Minneapolis' 2.5 million). Dallas dominates the south central region, and Atlanta the southeast, for the same reasons—population base and geographic proximity. Atlanta, for example, has but one airport serving a metropolitan population of 2.8 million compared to the surrounding southern hubs of Charlotte, Nashville, Raleigh, and Memphis of less than half the population. The three largest U.S. airports are dominated by the three largest U.S. airlines—American, Delta and United.

Compare these data with the number of passengers and operations at the largest foreign airports as shown in Table 4.5, "Ten Largest Foreign Airports".

Table 4.4—TEN LARGEST U.S. AIRPORTS (1990)[79]

Airport	Total Passengers	Scheduled Operations
Chicago O'Hare	58,775,486	775,687
Dallas/Ft. Worth	48,915,464	713,958
Atlanta	47,629,438	569,438
Los Angeles	45,530,880	612,428
San Francisco	30,355,338	397,524
New York Kennedy	29,428,400	282,126
Denver	27,383,602	305,660
Miami	25,838,398	281,180
New York LaGuardia	22,789,260	333,512
Newark	22,207,200	356,957

Table 4.5—TEN LARGEST FOREIGN AIRPORTS (1990)[80]

Airport	Total Passengers	Scheduled Operations
London Heathrow	42,647,235	388,289
Frankfurt	29,631,427	324,387
Paris Orly	24,205,570	191,421
Paris Charles de Gaulle	22,094,122	233,000
London Gatwick	21,047,089	203,211
Stockholm	14,822,450	257,606
Copenhagen	12,080,978	190,767
Dusseldorf	11,576,506	139,147
Munich	11,218,119	163,282
Vancouver	9,912,429	279,788

---

[79] U.S. Large Airport Traffic, Aviation Daily (Aug. 15, 1990), at 309. Enplaned passenger figures have been doubled to approximate total passengers, the standard used in the chart for foreign airports. However, the reader should beware that a doubling of enplaned passengers may not be precisely the total number of passengers flown through the airport.
[80] Worldwide Airport Traffic, Aviation Daily (Aug. 15, 1991), at 308.

Planning: Product Development

Again, the three largest U.S. airlines—American, Delta and United, have the largest U.S.-flag presence at the two largest foreign airports (Delta has been the largest U.S.-flag carrier at Frankfurt; American and United are the dominant U.S.-flag carriers at Heathrow).

The primary "weapon of war" in the unleashed competition following deregulation was the hub-and-spoke system.[81] Some call them "fortress hubs", where a single airline controls the lion's share of gates, takeoffs and landings, and passengers. James Hirsch notes:

> A product of deregulation, the hub system was initially a great success. It enabled more airlines to envelop huge geographical regions like giant spiderwebs, snare passing traffic and expand market share. By replacing linear routes, it multiplied customers flight options —and customers. American Airlines, for example, [in 1990] had 455 daily departures from Dallas/Fort Worth International Airport compared with 137 in pre-hub 1979. Hubs also integrated remote cities into a national and international route network.[82]

Before deregulation, while Atlanta (for Delta) and Pittsburgh (for Allegheny, now USAirways), were moderately concentrated, no airline dominated more than 45% of the capacity or market share of any major airport in the United States (as measured by gates, passengers, or takeoffs and landings). Today, dominant airlines control more than half the enplanements at more than half of the nation's 50 largest airports (see Table 4.6, "Concentrated Hub Airports).

---

[81] R.L Thornton, Airlines and Agents: Conflict and the Public Welfare, 52 J. of Air Law and Commerce (1986).
[82] James Hirsch, Big Airlines Scale Back Hub-Airport System to Curb Rising Costs, Wall St. J., at 1.

Table 4.6—CONCENTRATED HUB AIRPORTS (1994)[82]

Airport	Carrier	Market Share
Atlanta	Delta	79%
Baltimore	USAirways	50%
Charlotte	USAirways	95%
Chicago (Midway)	Southwest	50%
Cincinnati	Delta	91%
Dallas/Ft. Worth	American	61%
Dallas (Love)	Southwest	100%
Denver	United	63%
Detroit	Northwest	77%
El Paso	Southwest	64%
Houston (Hobby)	Southwest	78%
Houston (Intercontinental)	Continental	81%
Memphis	Northwest	76%
Miami	American	62%
Minneapolis	Northwest	83%
Nashville	American	64%
Newark	Continental	54%
Philadelphia	USAirways	60%
Pittsburgh	USAirways	91%
Raleigh/Durham	American	75%
St. Louis	TWA	65%
Salt Lake City	Delta	72%
San Francisco	United	57%
San Juan	American	66%
Syracuse	USAirways	52%
Washington (Dulles)	United	69%

The infrastructure of gates and landing slots at the major airports has been consumed by the megacarriers, leaving little room for significant new entry.[83] Some upstarts have focused on the remaining, smaller airports. In the early 1980s, America West focused on Phoenix and

---
[82] Julius Maldutis, Airline Competition at the 50 Largest U.S. Airports (May 11, 1994).
[83] 88% of the gates at the nation's 66 largest airports are leased to airlines, and 85% of the leases are for exclusive use. Intelligence, Aviation Daily (Aug. 20, 1990), at 323.

Las Vegas. In the 1990s, WesternPacific began operations at Colorado Springs, and American Trans Air focused operations on Indianapolis.[84] Several major carriers (i.e., TWA, Braniff and Eastern) unsuccessfully attempted to establish a hub at Kansas City. In the 1990s, upstart Vanguard Airlines also focused operations at Kansas City.

Strategically located hubs are designed to allow the carriers to blanket the nation with ubiquitous service. For example, United established hubs at Chicago, Denver, San Francisco, and Washington, D.C. (Dulles). American Airlines developed hubs at Chicago, Dallas/Ft. Worth, Miami, San Juan, San Jose, Nashville, and Raleigh/Durham. Delta built hubs at Atlanta, Dallas/Ft. Worth, Salt Lake City, and Cincinnati. Northwest has hubs at Detroit, Minneapolis/St. Paul and Memphis.

In contrast, TWA has a domestic hub only at St. Louis (and an international gateway at New York-Kennedy). Before its demise, Pan Am dominated no domestic airport. Among the airlines which have fallen into bankruptcy, only Continental had multiple strategically located hubs—at Houston, Denver, Cleveland and Newark (the latter it acquired from People Express on its death bed).[85]

But this is a dynamic process. Hubs have been dismantled or downsized at Washington Dulles Airport (United), Denver (Continental), Dallas/Ft. Worth (Delta), Dayton (USAirways), Kansas City (TWA, Eastern and Braniff), San Jose, Nashville and Raleigh/Durham (American), and Colorado Springs (WesternPacific). Many do not have a sufficient O&D traffic base on which to load fixed costs. Downsizing a hub is a painful process, for every spoke eliminated deprives other spokes of traffic feed, causing the synergies of the hub to unravel.[86] Nevertheless, airline management must be sufficiently agile to withdraw from markets which are producing unsatisfactorily, and re-deploy resources to more lucrative markets.

Hubbing is advantageous for a number of reasons. It allows enhanced marketing opportunities via the geometric proliferation of the number of possible city-pair markets which can be served. The number of passengers enjoys a corresponding exponential growth, while labor

---

[84] Aviation Daily (Jan. 30, 1996), at 150.
[85] Continental no longer maintains a hub in Denver.
[86] James Hirsch, Big Airlines Scale Back Hub-Airport System To Curb Rising Costs, Wall St. J., Jan. 12, 1993, at A1, A6.

Chapter 4

staffing increases at a much more moderate rate.[87] Figure 4.1, "Hub-And-Spoke vs. Linear Route Model", shows the advantages of the hub-and-spoke system over linear routes by increasing the city pairs served (in this particular model) from 6 to 36 through the hub city, "H".

Figure 4.1—HUB-AND-SPOKE vs. LINEAR ROUTE MODEL
(Hypothetical Route Structure To Serve Nine Cities)

Linear Route System (6 City-Pairs)

A ⟷ B
C ⟷ D
E ⟷ H ⟷ F
G ⟷ I

Hub-And-Spoke Network (36 City-Pairs)

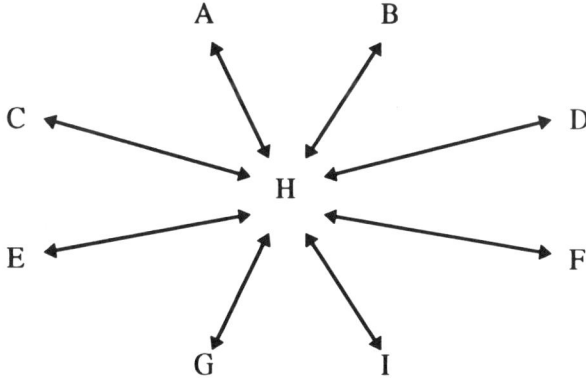

---

[87] Dan Reed, American Eagle 157 (1992).

Planning: Product Development

To work, a hub must have a large number of flights ("banks," as they are called) from a large number of origins converging at an air-port in close time proximity, so that passengers can readily transfer to flights departing to an equally large number of destinations. This re-quires a large number of gates and ground personnel. Mel Olsen, who did the initial planning for American Airlines' hub networks, calculated that adding a new city to an existing bank of flights added 73 new passengers to the network, at an average fare of $180. The $13,140 in additional revenue compared favorably with the projected additional cost of only $560.[88] Thus, significant network economies may be achieved via hubbing.

Both O&D and many connecting passengers pay a yield premium for the frequent service hubbing allows. At the concentrated "fortress hub", consumption of airport infrastructure often translates into higher yields. Yields at concentrated airports are more than 20% higher per mile for passengers who begin or end their trips there than at unconcentrated airports.[89] Hubbing also results in a yield premium for connecting traffic, particularly in the large majority of city-pair markets not served nonstop, for city-pairs less than 1,500 miles in distance, and for smaller cities without multiple hub connections. Some hub carriers have learned to focus on this high-yield connecting traffic, and avoid the local O&D price wars with non-union upstart airlines.[90]

Airlines with more gates, takeoff and landing slots (at capacity constrained airports), and/or code sharing agreements charge significantly higher prices than those without, according to the U.S. General Accounting Office. In fact, flights at airports where majority-in-interest clauses reduce expansion opportunities result in 3% higher fares; flights at slot controlled airports result in 7% higher fares; and carriers with code-sharing arrangements charge 8% higher fares.[91]

In 1988, the eight largest airlines controlled 96% of the landing and takeoff slots at the four slot-constrained airports (i.e., Chicago

---

[88] Thomas Petzinger, Hard Landing 137, 138 (1995).
[89] U.S. General Accounting Office, Airline Competition: Higher Fares and Reduced Competition at Concentrated Airports (1990).
[90] Address by Maurice Myers Before the Salomon Brothers Transportation Conference (New York, N.Y., Nov. 17, 1994).
[91] Paul Dempsey, Robert Hardaway & William Thoms, Aviation Law & Regulation § 5.05 (1993). General Accounting Office, Testimony of Kenneth Mead Before the Aviation Subcomm. of the U.S. Senate Commerce Comm. 6 (Apr. 5, 1990).

O'Hare, Washington National, and New York's Kennedy and LaGuardia). In 1985, before the U.S. Department of Transportation decreed these public resources could be bought and sold in the market, the eight largest airlines controlled only 70% of the slots.[92] An airline which doubles the number of its gates enjoys a 3.5% increase in fares.[93]

These yield advantages are achieved because of a broader economic principle, the "S-Curve", which posits that the dominant carrier in terms of frequency and capacity in any market will enjoy a disproportionate share of the traffic in terms of higher load factors and higher yields.[94]

International carriers also employ their gateways as venues for sixth freedom connecting traffic. For example, KLM puts enough capacity on the North Atlantic to transport the entire population of the Netherlands to the United States in a single Summer. Most of the traffic is funneled through its hub at Amsterdam Shiphol, from or to points beyond.

Several sources have criticized hubbing as inefficient for short-haul operations, because of the increase in delay and congestion, which has a debilitating effect on labor and aircraft productivity. They point to Southwest's average of 20.4 minutes of ground time, compared to American's 50.3 minutes.[95] Southwest's half hour less ground time translates into enhanced aircraft utilization, 22% higher than the industry norm.[96] The absence of banking flights into congested hub airports also results in more efficient use of ground personnel. Table 4.7, "Major Airlines Aircraft Utilization Per Day", provides comparisons of aircraft utilization of selected major carriers.

---

[92] U.S. General Accounting Office, Airline Competition: Industry Operating and Marketing Practices Limit Market Entry 4 (1990).
[93] Id. at 6.
[94] Barbara Beyer, The Curse and Blessing of Hubs 3 (unpublished paper delivered at the International Conference on Aviation & Airport Infrastructure, Denver, Colorado, Dec. 5-9, 1993).
[95] SH&E, The Facts About American vs. Southwest 47 (unpublished study prepared on behalf of APA, Sept. 13, 1993). Southwest's average stage length is 380 miles, compared to American's 807. Id. at 49.
[96] Id. at 48, 49.

Table 4.7—MAJOR AIRLINES AIRCRAFT UTILIZATION PER DAY (1993)[97]

Carrier	Average Stage Length (miles)	Daily Aircraft Utilization (hours flown)
Southwest	380	10:55
America West	637	10:35
United	826	9:44
USAir	518	9:44
Delta	626	9:35
Continental	793	9:29
American	835	9:25
Northwest	705	9:08
TWA	695	9:01

Despite the growth and profitability of Southwest Airlines and its linear route clones, American Airlines' Chairman Robert Crandall argues, "hubs will continue to be the most efficient way, in most markets, of providing the frequent time-of-day choices travelers like even more than they like nonstop service. In fact, intense competition between multiple carriers offering very frequent service to many destinations via multiple hubs tends to make most nonstop service unfeasible."[98] He continues:

> One of our greatest strengths is a huge and well-integrated domestic and international route system centered around our six hubs. This hub-and-spoke system allows us to serve thousands of markets, thus generating a large network revenue benefit....
>
> While a hub-and-spoke system is admittedly more expensive to operate than a com-

---
[97] Mead Jennings, Staying At the Top, Airline Bus. (Mar. 1994), at 28, 31; See also SH&E, The Facts About American vs. Southwest 49 (unpublished study prepared on behalf of APA, Sept. 13, 1993).
[98] Robert Crandall, The Hub Debate, American Way Magazine.

Chapter 4

> parably-sized system of point-to-point routes, the system's incremental costs are more than offset by its enormous revenue benefits. For example, we estimate that there are fewer than 500 city pair markets in the United States big enough to adequately support point-to-point jet service. However, our hub-and-spoke system makes it possible for American to effectively serve over 10,000 markets—and realize a large revenue per available seat mile premium relative to point-to-point carriers.[99]

Nevertheless, hubbing sacrifices equipment and labor utilization and consumes more fuel than a linear route system in markets sufficiently dense to support nonstop service. Clearly also, the United States is over-hubbed by duplicative parallel route networks connecting virtually every conceivable city-pair market. As noted above, to trim costs and reduce capacity, in the 1990s, carriers began to down-size or close selected hubs.

As noted above, the only profitable U.S. major airline, Southwest, embraces a point-to-point linear route system, which allows more productive equipment and labor utilization, and more efficient fuel consumption than does a hubbed operation. Southwest avoids congested airports, focusing instead on secondary airports in many markets, thereby allowing a quick turn around time (15 minutes is the goal).

Think of an aircraft as a $30 million to $180 million factory that produces consumer goods—in this case, seats. A factory that operates more hours per day produces more seats. Southwest's planes sit on the ground between flights only 15-20 minutes. United's sit at its hub airports for 45-55 minutes, during which time they produce no product. Southwest also enjoys enhanced asset utilization by using its gates 10-12 times a day compared to United's six times a day, or American's seven.

By the early 1990s, several of the megacarriers appeared interested in following Southwest's lead, with Continental inaugurating CALite

---

[99] AMR Corporation, 1993 Third Quarter Report 2, 3 (1993).

Planning: Product Development

and United launching U-2, or "United Shuttle", and USAir developing "Operation High Ground." Each retreated, in whole or part. America West tried a different approach to improving daily aircraft utilization—adding banks of discounted "red-eye" trips to Las Vegas (in 1996, these accounted for more than 14% of America West's flights).[100] Barbara Beyer predicts that hubs will continue to dominate air transportation:

> While there is increasing demand for point-to-point services and carriers willing to offer them like Southwest, Continental Lite and a number of new entrants, the actual amount of traffic carried on the flights is only about 6 to 7 percent of the total traffic. Most city pairs are too small to justify point-to-point service so the maximum growth in traffic will probably never exceed 20 percent of the total traffic. Thus, at least 80 percent of all passengers are still expected to utilize hub services into the foreseeable future.[101]

By the mid-1990s, U.S. domestic commercial aviation seems to have divided itself into two dominant types of service providers: (1) the ubiquitous network hub carriers (e.g., United, American, Delta, Northwest) emphasizing connecting traffic; and (2) the short-haul nonstop point-to-point carriers (e.g., Southwest) focusing on O&D traffic. Internationally as well, new long-haul point-to-point carriers have emerged (e.g., Virgin Atlantic) to compete along side the established international network carriers (e.g., British Airways).

---

[100] Fast Growth Hurts America West, Wall St. J., Sept. 10, 1996, at B4.
[101] Barbara Beyer, The Curse and Blessing of Hubs 4 (unpublished paper delivered at the International Conference on Aviation & Airport Infrastructure, Denver, Colorado, Dec. 5-9, 1993).

Chapter 4

INTERNATIONAL ALLIANCES

Although international marketing and equity alliances are discussed later in this book, for present purposes, it is important to mention that the global code-sharing alliances that have emerged provide a wider array of city-pairs to sell to customers (e.g., San Diego to Johannesburg), and interline feed, which can be significant. This may diminish the need to extend a route structure to duplicate the alliance. In essence, this allows a carrier to enjoy market penetration without capital investment—or in other words, realize the joys of commercial intercourse without fear of pregnancy.

ROUTE SELECTION

In selecting routes, a potential entrant into a city-pair market must assess the nature of competition in that market—the size, type and cost structure of its rivals—as well as how well the city-pair integrates with its existing route structure. A carrier with a hub system will evaluate a route on the basis of interdependence with its network so as to strengthen the exchange complexes—what traffic can be expected from a candidate route, and how well will that traffic mesh with the existing or contemplated hub connecting network.[102] A linear route point-to-point carrier will tend to focus on dense markets with sufficient O&D traffic to sustain nonstop operations. Southwest attempts to find underutilized airports within driving distance of major populated areas. For example, it found that Providence, Rhode Island, was the easiest airport to reach from the Boston metropolitan area, and inaugurated northeastern service there.[103]

Traffic density (the quantity of passengers or other traffic in a market) is an important ingredient of route selection,[104] as is the mix of O&D versus connecting passengers, and the mix of business versus leisure passengers in the market. Demand must be adequate to provide adequate load factors for the equipment and frequencies to be flown in the market.

---

[102] Robert Crandall, Marketing Planning, in Airline Economics 231, 232, 238 (G. James ed. 1982).
[103] Scott McCartney, Competitors Quake As Southwest Air Is Set To Invade Northeast, Wall St. J., Oct. 23, 1996, at A1.
[104] Richard Kane & Allan Vose, Air Transportation 14-3 (7th ed. 1979).

Planning: Product Development

Stage length can be important from a cost and revenue perspective. As a rule of thumb, an aircraft enjoys lower ASM costs the longer the stage length, since takeoff and landing burns additional fuel and consumes additional time vis-à-vis the cruise altitude portion of the journey. But the longer the stage length, the more connecting competitive airline alternatives a consumer will have, and carriers willing to sell a seat at a small premium above variable costs. Because of the dearth of competition, yields tend to be higher for trips of less than 1,000 miles. However, very short-haul trips compete with surface modes of transport, including the automobile.

A carrier which inaugurates service in a city-pair market encounters a "ramp-up" period of initially poor, then gradually improving revenue. Commencement of service in new markets is characterized by relatively high initial operating costs and low introductory fares to introduce the new service to the traveling public. Revenues gradually build up over a 60-180 period until the carrier achieves anticipated market penetration.

After a reasonable developmental period, if projected market penetration does not materialize, the carrier must be sufficiently flexible to cut its losses and re-deploy its aircraft elsewhere. Exiting a route can be difficult once marketing and ramp-up costs have been incurred and gate leases signed. But among the most serious errors an airline can make is to mismatch its product pricing in a given market with its cost structure. If it cannot charge an adequate price to assure adequate load factors to cover its costs, it must exit the market.[105]

Evaluated thus far has been the hub network and linear route approach to route selection. The following are two rather nontraditional examples of route selection adopted by upstart airlines Reno Air and Midwest Express.

Reno Air focuses on both the leisure market and the business market. Recognizing the business travelers' preference of frequency and convenient departure times, it adjusts its schedule during weekday peak hours flying predominantly out of San Jose, California, home to Silicon Valley. It configures its aircraft with a large First Class section, and high-quality in-cabin service. It then shifts its fleet to off-peak times and weekends to Reno, Nevada, to satiate the demands of

---

[105] Smith Barney, Northwest Airlines Corp. (Sept. 8, 1994), at 16.

Chapter 4

the leisure market.[106] Thus, Reno Air enhances aircraft utilization by serving these two distinct and different markets.

Midwest Express, created by Kimberly-Clark, focuses on the business travel market. It engages in a self-described "analytical and cautious risk assessment" of routes. It provides single-class premium service, with wide seat pitch, and only 2-2 abreast seat configuration on DC-9s (3-2 seating is the standard for other carriers flying that aircraft). With such low-density seating, it need not focus on dense markets. Instead, Midwest Express focuses on medium-density non-stop high-yield business markets without nonstop jet service, trying to keep out of the cross-hairs of the major airlines. Its focus cities have been Milwaukee and Omaha. It has only had a single market retreat (Detroit).[107]

INTERNATIONAL ROUTES

The economic well being of some airlines appears to be driven disproportionately by profits earned on international routes. For example, between 1987 and 1989, Northwest earned between 68% and 91% of its total operating profit from international markets, while United earned between 24% and 34% from its international routes.[108] In 1993, international markets comprised 35% of United's network, and 38% of its profits.[109] By the mid-1990s, American Airlines was earning 25% of its total operating profit from its Latin American routes.[110]

Table 4.8, "Ten Top Tourist Generating Nations", identifies the source of foreign tourists in the United States.

---

[106] Statement of Reno Air's CEO Robert Redding at the 11th Annual Salomon Bros. Transportation Conference (New York, N.Y., Nov. 13, 1996).
[107] Statement of Midwest Express' Timothy Hoksema at the 11th Annual Salomon Bros. Transportation Conference (New York, N.Y., Nov. 13, 1996).
[108] M. Jedel, Post Deregulation Strategic Employment Relations Response of the Successful, Surviving Major Domestic Airlines: A Story Not Fully Told 42 (unpublished monograph, 1991).
[109] UAL Corporation, First Quarter Report 1 (1993).
[110] Scott McCartney, Latin America Pays Big Dividends for American Airlines, Wall St. J., June 4, 1996, at B4.

Table 4.8—TOP TEN TOURIST GENERATING NATIONS[111]

Country of Residence	Number of Arrivals	Percentage of Total
Canada	6,712,141	53.1
Japan	1,087,298	8.6
United Kingdom	847,244	6.7
Germany	488,452	3.8
Mexico	469,811	3.7
France	271,080	2.1
Australia	166,373	1.3
Brazil	156,342	1.2
Italy	130,193	1.0
China	114,177	0.9

Of course, not all tourists fly. Many tourists traveling between the United States and Canada or Mexico drive their automobiles or travel by cruise ship. A better indication of the nations which are responsible for generating the largest number of airline passengers is provided by Table 4.9, Ten Top Nations Generating Airline Passenger Traffic To And From The United States".

Foreign travel to the U.S. increased by 67% between 1986 and 1991, while U.S. travel abroad rose only 23%.[112] Some 30% of U.S. citizens were expected to travel abroad in 1992, with the most likely group between 45 and 49 years old and family income of more than $40,000 a year.[113]

The global air transport market is growing, and many international markets are quite lucrative. Because there is less competition (resulting from relatively more restrictive bilateral air transport agreements), airlines which serve the North Pacific and Latin American market enjoy the most attractive yields. Many industry analysts predict international markets will grow faster than domestic markets over the next decade or

---

[111] Data shown are from January to May, 1991. Tourist Travel Rebounds in 2d Quarter 1991, Spending Also Up, Aviation Daily (Sept. 24, 1991), at 561.
[112] Id.
[113] Thirty Percent of U.S. adults to Travel Internationally by 1992, Aviation Daily (Feb. 21, 1992), at 317.

two. Observing the devastating impact U.S. deregulation has had on its airlines, many nations have rejected the U.S. policy of "open skies,"[114] though sixth freedom carriers (e.g., Singapore Airlines, KLM) forcefully advocate it.

Table 4.9—TOP TEN NATIONS GENERATING AIRLINE PASSENGER TRAFFIC TO AND FROM THE UNITED STATES[115]

Country	Total Traffic (000)	U.S. Citizens (%)	U.S. Flag (%)
United Kingdom	9,166	50	51
Japan	8,199	24	55
Mexico	7,473	72	55
Germany	4,199	57	51
France	3,064	55	64
Bahama Islands	2,855	75	74
Dominican Republic	1,772	77	77
Jamaica	1,697	72	38
Netherlands	1,467	49	14
Italy	1,440	62	54

With the collapse of Pan Am and Eastern, and the bankruptcy of TWA, the larger domestic U.S. carriers have replaced them in major international markets. Thus, United Airlines purchased Pan Am's trans-Pacific, Latin American and Heathrow routes. American Airlines purchased Eastern's Latin American routes (earlier acquired from Braniff), and TWA's Heathrow authority. Delta bought Pan Am's European routes (absent Heathrow). This has significantly strengthened the U.S.-flag presence in international markets, because United, American and Delta were able to feed these intercontinental routes with traffic generated by their vast and ubiquitous domestic networks. By 1995, the largest U.S. flag carriers in the Trans-Atlantic, Trans-

---

[114] See Paul Dempsey, Law & Foreign Policy in International Aviation (1987).
[115] Data shown are for 1989. Passenger Traffic to and from the U.S. and Other Countries, Aviation Daily (July 18, 1990), at 112.

Pacific and Latin American markets are shown in Table 4.10, "Largest U.S.Flag Carriers In Domestic And International Markets".

Many international markets are more profitable than domestic markets because governments limit the number of carriers which may be designated to serve them. For example, in the third quarter of 1995, American Airlines earned 169% more operating profit per ASM in the Latin American than in the domestic market; Northwest earned 128% more profit in the Trans-Pacific market than in the domestic market; United earned 222% more profit in the Trans-Pacific market than in the U.S. domestic market.[116] American Airlines became the first carrier in the history of aviation to fly to every Latin American country.[117]

Under Stephen Wolf, USAirways began to focus on Philadelphia as an international gateway, recognizing its traditional strength at the city, its size (the fifth largest city in the United States), and the fact that it has a single airport (unlike New York, which has three). Thus, Philadelphia would have higher load factors, comprised of local O&D passengers, as well as domestic and international connecting passengers.[118]

REGIONAL FEEDERS AND FRANCHISEES

Many airlines rely on smaller feeder carriers to bring passengers from smaller communities to connect with their long-haul systems. As a rule, these regional carriers operate smaller turboprop or piston aircraft painted in megacarrier colors and logo, and do not pay union wages. Baggage is interlined, and code-sharing falsely conveys the impression that seamless on-line single-carrier service is being provided. Several of the major carriers have turned over short-haul traffic or thin routes to these regional feeders.[119]

Some carriers have taken equity positions in their regional feeders, both to provide them with essential capital for reliable operations, and to exert managerial influence over them. For example, Delta owns

---

[116] Aviation Daily (Jan. 30, 1996), at 156.
[117] Scott McCartney, Latin America Pays Big Dividends for American Airlines, Wall St. J., June 4, 1996, at B4.
[118] Statement of Stephen Wolf Before the 11th Annual Salomon Bros. Transportation Conference (New York, N.Y., Nov. 14, 1996).
[119] Agis Salpukas, Hurt In Expansion, Airlines Cut Back and May Sell Hubs, N.Y. Times, Apr. 1, 1993, at 1.

23% of ASA, 21% of Comair, and 14% of Skywest.[120] American Airlines purchased 100% of each of its American Eagle feeders.

Table 4.10—LARGEST U.S. FLAG CARRIERS IN DOMESTIC AND INTERNATIONAL MARKETS (1995)[121]

TRANS-ATLANTIC

Carrier	Departures	Enplanements	ASM costs	RPM yield
Delta	32%	27%	9.46	10.79
American	26%	27%	9.06	11.19
United	17%	18%	8.66	9.79

TRANS-PACIFIC

Carrier	Departures	Enplanements	ASM costs	RPM yield
Northwest	45%	43%	9.17	11.64
United	43%	48%	8.23	11.58
Delta	8%	6%	8.32	11.02

LATIN AMERICAN

Carrier	Departures	Enplanements	ASM costs	RPM yield
American	59%	65%	9.00	14.05
Continental	17%	13%	8.67	12.35
United	11%	11%	8.32	11.49

DOMESTIC

Carrier	Departures	Enplanements	ASM costs	RPM yield
Delta	18%	19%	8.49	13.91
United	14%	16%	8.86	12.21
American	13%	15%	8.87	12.62

---

[120] Delta Air Lines, Inc., 10-Q Report (Sept. 28, 1994).
[121] Aviation Daily (Nov. 22, 1995), at 303; Aviation Daily (Feb. 13, 1996), at 242; Aviation Daily (Feb. 14, 1996), at 249; Aviation Daily (Feb. 29, 1996), at 338; Aviation Daily (Jan. 30, 1996), at 156.

Planning: Product Development

These regional code-sharing partners can be a source of passengers and revenue. For example, in 1996, Delta raised the fees its code-sharing partners paid from 2 cents to 2.4 cents per ASM, a 20% increase.[122] Union scope clauses often prohibit management from integrating operations with non-union regional jet carriers. Thus, many large airlines code-share exclusively with high-cost turboprop carriers, thereby depriving many small communities of low-cost jet service they might otherwise be able to support.

FLEET PLANNING

Airlines must select a fleet with the cost, size, and range characteristics which will fit its present and future route structure.[123] Each aircraft type has different plane-mile and seat-mile costs depending upon distance flown, so that airlines must customize the aircraft size and type to fit the market in which it will be flown. New technological advances in engines or airframes may improve operational efficiency.

A fleet must be designed and assembled to meet projected demand in selected city-pair routes. The difficulty is that there are very long lead times between aircraft orders and delivery, during which time the market can change profoundly. Sometimes carriers order aircraft that are only on the drawing board. If demand drops in a high fixed cost industry like commercial aviation, capacity is not easily reduced.

The process of aircraft selection at large airlines involves all major departments of the company. According to Robert Baker:

> Airline departments ranging from maintenance and engineering to marketing, scheduling and finance are involved in analyzing various options; and hours are spent talking with aircraft and engine manufacturers about their product offerings. Fuel efficiency, cost to operate, interior configuration, customer appeal and other factors go into the evaluation of each

---

[122] Aviation Daily (Mar. 1, 1996), at RA2.
[123] Russell Thayer, Airline Fleet and Schedule Planning, in Airline Economics 265, 272 (G. James ed. 1982).

aircraft; airlines even employ trained engineers to validate manufacturers' claims. In the end, the airline team combines all of the technical input with the financial and contractual issues, and a decision is made as to which aircraft should be acquired.[124]

Fuel is a tremendously important component of airline operational costs. A larger fuselage profile imposes more aerodynamic drag, and fuel consumption. Thus, fuel efficiency becomes important in aircraft and engine selection. Generally speaking, newer aircraft are more fuel efficient that older aircraft; thus adding newer aircraft or retiring older planes increases the overall fuel efficiency of the fleet.[125] Older aircraft also pose a problem for satisfying federal and local noise requirements. All U.S. fleets must be 100% Stage 3 by the year 2000, meaning older planes must be retired, or their engines must be fitted with a husk kit.

Commonality in aircraft type effects many other aspects of costs—maintenance, spare parts, inventory levels, training costs, and crew scheduling.[126] As a rule of thumb, the fewer aircraft types an airline operates, the lower its operational costs on an ASM basis, although it will not have a properly sized aircraft for all markets. Fleet simplification allows a reduction in the inventory of spare parts, as well as maintenance and training costs, and thereby improves the cost, speed and efficiency of operations. Southwest flies the 737 exclusively, but limits its operations predominantly to dense short-haul markets. Flying a single aircraft type not only allows Southwest to enjoy enhanced worker productivity vis-à-vis its competitors, it also allows Southwest to realize lower maintenance costs, some 25% less than the industry average.[127] Continental expects to have a fleet which is 60% Boeing 737 by the turn of the century.[128]

---

[124] Robert Baker, Airline Operations, in Handbook of Airline Economics 307 (D. Jenkins ed. 1995).
[125] Lee Howard & John Summerfield, Airline Financial Forecasting, in Airline Economics 57, 74 (G. James ed. 1982).
[126] Russell Thayer, Airline Fleet and Schedule Planning, in Airline Economics 265, 278 (G. James ed. 1982).
[127] James Kling, The Status of Southwest Airlines' Competitive Advantage 17 (unpublished monograph 1993).
[128] Scott McCartney & Stacy Kravetz, Continental Orders 60 Boeing Jetliners, Wall St. J., Oct. 11, 1996, at A4.

However, Southwest focuses its operations on routes with tightly tailored characteristics—short- to medium-haul routes with sufficient density to support frequent non-stop O&D service. Carriers which serve a mix of short and long routes and thick and thin markets must have appropriately sized and stage-length aircraft for each. Thus, the network carriers tend to have several aircraft types in their fleets.

Until recently, United flew predominantly Boeing aircraft. In November 1993, United took delivery of its first Airbus A-320s, acquired under very favorable terms, including a walk-away lease. Not long before, United boasted that buying planes from a single manufacturer, Boeing, promoted "commonalty within the fleet which assures significant long-term operational efficiencies."[129]

The airframe manufacturers (e.g., Boeing, McDonnell-Douglas or Airbus) essentially design and assemble the aircraft shell, or fuselage and wings; the carrier selects the seats, their pitch, galleys, rest rooms, interiors, and engines. ASM costs can be lowered by increasing seat density, reconfiguring aircraft interiors to tighten seat pitch. Of course, tightened seat pitch increases passenger discomfort. Further, as a rule of thumb, larger aircraft have lower ASM costs than smaller aircraft. The mix of large and small aircraft effects average costs per ASM.[130] Unfortunately, all markets are not sufficiently dense to support wide-bodied aircraft. Frequent connecting service deprives many city-pairs (which otherwise might be able to support infrequent non-stop wide-bodied service) of adequate traffic to sustain break-even load factors. Thus, Costs per ASM cannot be the only reference point; costs per aircraft mile are also important.[131]

Newer aircraft have higher acquisition costs, but lower operational costs. Newer aircraft are more fuel efficient, allow enhanced labor productivity, and cost less to maintain. New aircraft with proven technology are also more reliable. High-yield business travelers value punctuality.

But inadequate profitability in the 1980s caused the U.S. fleet to degenerate into the oldest in the developed world. By 1989, thirty-one

---

[129] UAL Corporation, 1990 Annual Report 7 (1990).
[130] Lee Howard & John Summerfield, Airline Financial Forecasting, in Airline Economics 57, 74 (G. James ed. 1982).
[131] Charles Glass, Financial Planning for Fleet Acquisition, in Airline Economics 253, 254 (G. James ed. 1982).

percent of the U.S. fleet exceeded the economic design goals originally set by the manufacturers.[133] By the early 1990s, aircraft more than 20 years old made up a quarter of the U.S. fleet.[134]

Economics now determines when aircraft are retired.[135] Spending $3 million to husk kit a 25-year-old-plane is to some more economically rational than spending $35 million on a new aircraft.[136] As Cole and Carey noted, "with the harrowing airline economics of the early-1990s, the trouble and expense of keeping old planes aloft comes down to a simple maxim: If it's broke, fix it."[137]

Table 4.11, "Average Age Of Fleet", reveals average fleet age for selected major airlines.

Table 4.11—AVERAGE AGE OF FLEET (1996)[138]

Carrier	Number of Aircraft	Average Age (Years)
Alaska	74	7.5
Southwest	243	7.9
American	642	9.0
America West	101	10.5
United	564	10.9
Delta	550	11.5
USAir	390	12.0
Continental	317	14.3
TWA	192	19.0
Northwest	399	19.2

---

[133] General Accounting Office, Testimony of Kenneth Mead Before the Subcomm. on Aviation of the House Comm. on Public Works and Transportation: Meeting the Aging Aircraft Challenge (Oct. 10, 1989).
[134] Jeff Cole & Susan Carey, Airlines Are Keeping Aging Planes Aloft, Testing Repair Rules, Wall St. J., Nov. 3, 1994, at A1.
[135] Id.
[136] Id. at A15.
[137] Id.
[138] Julius Maldutis, The U.S. Airline Industry, 1995-2001 (Mar. 7, 1996); Julius Maldutis, Quarterly Global Aviation Review 2d Quarter 1994 (1994). See also Julius Maldutis, The U.S. Airline Industry 1993-99: Aircraft Fleet Analysis (Jan. 28, 1994); Julius Maldutis, The U.S. Airline Industry, 1996-2002E 4 (Apr. 8, 1997).

Planning: Product Development

By the time Pan Am collapsed in December 1991, its fleet had grown to a geriatric 18 years.[138] In contrast, British Airways fleet is 8.0 years old.[139] Swissair's fleet is 7.3 years old, Qantas maintains a fleet of 5.9 years, while Singapore Airlines is 4.9 years young.[140]

In the United States, deregulation led to an unprecedented number of mergers and acquisitions during its first decade. As a consequence, merged airlines have been forced to deal with the problems of consolidating huge fleets of aircraft of inconsistent types produced by several manufacturers, which increase the cost of maintenance and require multiple inventories of spare parts. Continental, which consolidated Texas International, New York Air, People Express and Frontier under a single roof, experienced this problem of blending an eclectic collection of disparate aircraft fleets and corporate cultures, causing costs to soar and service to disintegrate. Northwest flies the fleets of North Central, Southern and Hughes Airwest, which merged to form Republic, which Northwest acquired.

In contrast, airlines which grow from within (such as, for the most part, United or American) save maintenance cost and aircraft down time by incrementally growing with relatively standardized fleets. Nonetheless, American, Delta, USAirways, and Northwest each fly eight different aircraft types.[141]

The U.S. Congress has mandated the retirement of Stage 2 aircraft by the year 2000.[142] In 1990, the airlines with the highest percentages of aging Stage 2 aircraft were: Eastern (70%), Northwest (65%), Pan Am (58%), USAir (55%), TWA (55%), Continental (52%), and Midway (85%).[143] In contrast, only 31% of American's fleet consisted

---

[138] Paul Dempsey, Robert Hardaway & William Thoms, 1 Aviation Law sec. 2.01 (1993).

[139] Julius Maldutis, British Airways Plc—The Crown Jewel (Aug. 23, 1993), at 5. British Airways is also pursuing a fleet modernization and simplification program. Id.

[140] Address by Otto Loeppe before the Salomon Bros. Transportation Conference (New York, N.Y., November 18, 1994); Address by James Strong before the Salomon Bros. Transportation Conference (New York, N.Y., November 18, 1994).

[141] James Kling, The Status of Southwest Airlines' Competitive Advantage (unpublished monograph 1993).

[142] "Stage 1, 2, or 3" are terms used to describe aircraft (usually jets) meeting certain noise parameters on takeoff and landing as prescribed in 14 CFR Part 36. Stage 3 describes the quietest standard, which all aircraft in the United States must meet by July 1999. See Paul Stephen Dempsey and Laurence E. Gesell, Air Transportation: Foundations for the 21st Century 559 (1997).

[143] Memorandum from Samuel K. Skinner to Congressman James Oberstar, Oct. 25, 1990.

Chapter 4

of Stage 2 aircraft.[144] Table 4.12, "Major Airlines Stage Three Fleet Compositions", reveals the percentage of Stage 3 aircraft in the major airlines' fleets.

Table 4.12—MAJOR AIRLINES STAGE THREE FLEET COMPOSITION (1995)[145]

Carrier	Stage Three
American	88.5%
Southwest	77.7%
America West	77.4%
United	74.3%
Delta	67.7%
USAir	67.2%
Continental	66.7%
TWA	47.1%
Northwest	44.4%

Deregulation also produced the hub-and-spoke phenomenon. Hubbing requires that airlines fly passengers more miles in smaller aircraft with more takeoffs and landings. Indeed, hubbing led many airlines to cancel orders for wide-body aircraft in the early 1980s, and either fly their existing jets or place orders for narrow-bodied planes. The average seat mile costs for a wide-bodied aircraft like a Boeing 747 are significantly lower than that of a narrow-bodied plane like a Boeing 737 or 727. Yet hubbing bleeds off the traffic that might otherwise support more long-distance nonstop service in relatively larger aircraft.

CABIN CONFIGURATION

When ordering a new aircraft from one of the air frame manufacturers such as Boeing, McDonnell-Douglas or Airbus, the purchaser will designate the cabin interior. Will it have one or several

---

[144] AMR Corporation, 1990 Annual Report 27 (1990).
[145] ESG Aviation Services, 8 The Airline Monitor (Mar/Apr 1996).

Planning: Product Development

classes of service? Will it have galleys? What types, fabric and color of seats will be installed, what width, and at what pitch (the distance between two seats as measured from the same point)? What type and color of carpet will be installed? How many lavatories will the cabin hold? Will there be closet space for carry-on garment bags?

A carrier seeking to cater to the business traveler will likely have more than a single class of service (although three classes are generally only viable on long-haul dense international or transcontinental routes), generous seat pitch, a garment bag closet, and a galley. First class will have about a 60 inch seat pitch, business class will have about a 38-40 inch pitch (though TWA has 58 inch seat pitch in international business class),[146] and Economy/Coach will have a pitch of about 31-32 inches. One consumer organization insists that premium seating should include at least 22 inches of width and 34 inches of pitch.[147] However such a configuration, by reducing the number of seats that can be placed in the cabin, cause ASM costs to rise. This is the classic trade-off between yield and cost.[148]

TWA sought to distinguish itself as the carrier with the most leg room, removing 8% of its seats. Generous seat pitch contributed to the decision of J.D. Power & Associates to designate TWA as the best domestic carrier for long flights.[149] But improving seat pitch is not without its costs. Removing four seats from a 141-seat MD-80 aircraft results in an annual $87,603 revenue loss.[150]

A carrier seeking to distinguish itself on the basis of price, rather than service, catering to the leisure rather than the business traveler, will usually have a single-class cabin interior with relatively tighter seat pitch (sometimes about 28 inches). This is the classic trade-off between service quality and cost.

---

[146] Lisa Miller, Fliers Give Business Class Mixed Reviews, Wall St. J., Nov. 22, 1996, at B12.
[147] Better Seats At a Better Price, Consumer Reports Travel Letter (July 1995), at 132.
[148] Stephen Shaw, Airline Marketing & Management 159, 160 (3rd ed. 1990).
[149] Michael McCarthy, TWA, Out of Bankruptcy Court, Struggles to Take Off, Wall St. J., July 27, 1994, at B4.
[150] Michael McCarthy, Airline Squeeze Play: More Seats, Less Leg room, Wall St. J., Apr. 18, 1994, at B1.

Chapter 4

FREQUENT FLYER PROGRAMS

By studying the data, in the early 1980s, American Airlines discovered that 40% of its business was coming from 5% of its customers. Every incremental frequent flyer was 10 times more valuable than an occasional flyer.[151] The fundamental question was, and is, how does an airline build brand loyalty, luring repeat travelers to its product offering. The answer—frequent flyer programs. Fifteen years after their introduction, American Airlines had 28 million members in its AAdvantage program.

Like "Green Stamps" given out at the grocery stores in the 1950s, in which accumulation of books of stamps was rewarded with a toaster or other small appliance, the addicted traveler seeks more and more miles, redeemable for free or discounted travel, hotel, car rentals, and other services. Research reveals that consumers want to be recognized and rewarded for the loyalty they express with repeat business.[152]

The widespread service permitted by multiple hubs allows airlines to enjoy economies of density, and better market their product to the most lucrative customer, the business traveler. For example, for much of the 1980s, United Airlines served all 50 states, not because each was profitable, but because it could hold itself out as satiating the ubiquitous geographic needs of business travelers.

Airlines offer to fill their business needs, while luring them with rewards of free travel to exotic destinations, or if they prefer, upgrades to first or business class, and/or discounts on hotels and automobile rentals. Actually, they encourage businessmen to purchase higher priced goods with company money, for the whole purpose of frequent flyer programs is to inspire business people to purchase a brand product even (perhaps especially) if it costs more than an alternative product.

In another context, such conduct might be considered a cousin to embezzlement. Suppose, for example, a distributor of copying paper offered to sell a company's purchasing manager paper at a price 25% higher than his competitors, but promised him two free first class airline tickets to Hawaii if he bought its paper all year long. Wouldn't

---

[151] Thomas Petzinger, Hard Landing 139 (1995).
[152] Susan Carey, United Air Alters Program Rewards For Frequent Flyers, Wall St. J., Nov. 6, 1996, at A8.

the business executive be defrauding his company if he purchased the higher priced paper? Yet that is precisely the type of inducement that airlines offer business travelers addicted to their frequent flyer programs. Once addicted, many business travelers select (and bill their companies for) the higher priced flight on the airline satiating their desire for free travel. Indeed, 75% of travel agents report that their business customers chose to fly a particular airline more than half the time because of their membership in a frequent flyer program.[153]

Though initially a promotional device designed to stimulate sales by building consumer loyalty for an airline's product line, frequent flyer programs have become an independent revenue source of their own. American Airlines earned approximately $300 million in revenue from sales of frequent flyer mileage in 1995, while United earned $240 million, with a wide variety of companies purchasing them to give to their customers or employees. At two cents per mile, a 25,000 mile round-trip domestic free ticket earns an airline $500, which is a very good fare for a restricted seat, and well above American's costs of $92.50.[154] United Airlines created a Mileage Plus Reward Miles program, offering to sell 60,000 mile books of 500, 1,000 or 5,000 mile coupons to retailers to distribute to their best customers and employees. Today, individuals can earn frequent flyer miles by engaging in activities as diverse as frequenting certain restaurants or money management firms, or purchasing mortgages, shirts, flowers, and mattresses from select vendors. American introduced its own dining card, which offers triple miles for meals eaten at selected restaurants. United upped the ante by offering ten miles per dollar for purchases at selected restaurants with registered credit cards.

While stimulating traffic in the short term, the long-term costs and liability exposure of such programs is significant. By the late 1980s, after a binge of offering travelers double and triple mileage, Wall Street analysts estimated that if all the accumulated miles were redeemed at once, an entire year's revenue could be wiped out.[155]

---

[153] U.S. General Accounting Office, Airline Competition: Industry Operating and Marketing Practices Limit Market Entry 4 (1990).
[154] Scott McCartney, Free Airline Miles Become a Potent Tool For Selling Everything, Wall St. J., at A1.
[155] Id.

Chapter 4

American Airlines' frequent flyer liability was $380 million in 1994.[156] The number of non-revenue passengers have been growing steadily, and by the mid-1990s, comprised 6% of all traffic.[157] The cost of administering the programs is also significant.

Carriers have responded in two ways. First, using inventory management, they have severely constricted the availability of seats for frequent flyer mileage redemption. (For example, try to find a coach seat to Hawaii during December on frequent flyer miles). Second, they have unilaterally changed the award rules, generally increasing the number of miles needed for free travel.[158] For example, United Airlines announced restrictions on use of "saver awards," requiring they be booked 14 days in advance and used only for trips involving a Saturday-night stay-over.[159] Third, airlines have placed expiration dates (typically three years) on accumulated but unredeemed miles. Delta recognized that wiping out the miles of infrequent flyers dissuaded them from booking an occasional Delta flight (building up their miles on a rival carrier), and altered the expiration rules so that a passenger's accumulated mileage could be kept alive by one round-trip flight every three years.

Retroactively imposed redemption restrictions generated some measure of consumer dissatisfaction. What good are all these miles if you can't find a flight to one's destination? Airlines were deriving significant revenue from mileage sales, but were not opening up seats at the rate of accumulation. In 1993, 11 million certificates for free travel were issued by the airlines.[160] Nonetheless, between 1991 and 1996, the number of unused miles grew by 30%. The number of frequent flyer club members jumped from 28 million in 1994 to 38 million in 1996; during the same period, the number of seats set aside

---

[156] James Hirsch, Airlines Will Devalue Frequent-Flyer Miles Next Year, Wall St. J., Apr. 25, 1994, at B1.
[157] James Hirsch, Tracking Travel, Wall St. J., Feb. 14, 1994, at B-1.
[158] James Hirsch, Airlines Will Devalue Frequent flyer Miles Next Year, Wall St. J., Apr. 25, 1994, at B1. Arguably, this is a patent breach of contract with passengers who were encouraged to buy air travel to earn miles under one set of rules, and subsequently be told that the airline has no intention of meeting its commitments.
[159] Susan Carey, United Air Alters Program Rewards For Frequent Flyers, Wall St. J., Nov. 6, 1996, at A8.
[160] Aaron Epstein & Brigid Schulte, Flight for Fliers, Detroit Free Press, Dec. 19, 1994.

by airlines for frequent flyer redemptions grew from about 4% of capacity, to 7%.[161]

With one point issued per mile flown, airlines may actually be rewarding the wrong thing. What they should be rewarding is dollars spent, not miles flown. A passenger paying the Y fare (i.e., the full standard fare) is paying several times more than the advance-purchase, Saturday night stayover, discretionary traveler seated next to him. But both fly the same number of miles, and on most carriers, earn the same travel reward. A reward system focused on dollars spent would likely generate more spending by consumers.

Frequent flyer programs also have been important in generating international traffic. Eighty percent of American Airlines' Latin American passengers are residents of Latin America, where frequent flyer mileage attracts the high-yield business traveler.[162]

Frequent flyer data is also important to airlines seeking to identify their best customers for promotions and perks.[163] For example, United Airlines periodically sends its regular travelers First Class upgrades, or gives them priority in the forward portion of the coach cabin, while leaving unsold seats in the middle so that these passengers can "spread out." Early boarding, separate check-in, free upgrades and bonus mileage are some of the perquisites airlines afford their best customers.[164] The following are interesting trivia about frequent flyer programs:

- Together, all the domestic airlines owe their frequent flyer planholders enough miles for 2.83 million round-trip flights to the moon.
- If they weren't freebies, that mileage would cost travelers $68 billion.
- Travel-industry professionals say frequent flyer miles rank just after dollars as "America's currency of choice."
- An estimated 100,000 frequent fliers have racked up more than one million miles each.

---

[161] Lisa Miller, Still Available: Free Seats to El Salvador, Wall St. J., May 3, 1996, at B6.
[162] Scott McCartney, Latin America Pays Big Dividends for American Airlines, Wall St. J., June 4, 1996, at B4.
[163] Ed Leefeldt, Plane Truth, Bloomberg Personal (Oct. 1994), at 7.
[164] Susan Carey, United Air Alters Program Rewards For Frequent Flyers, Wall St. J., Nov. 6, 1996, at A8.

- With no requirements in force to compel airlines to set aside seats for frequent fliers, 22 percent of readers surveyed told *Frequent Flyer* magazine that they had problems claiming seats.[165]

Unfortunately, the curse of frequent flyer mileage for people who travel often is that at some point, more travel becomes unattractive. While a man lost in the desert may treasure a single drop of water, a man drowning in a lake may not. Charles Kuralt observed:

> I have accumulated many free miles in the airlines' frequent flyer programs. But there is a catch. To use those miles, I have to take another trip on an airline.[166]

DEVELOPING SYNERGIES FROM ECONOMIES OF SCALE AND SCOPE

Just as a meat packer will run an incidental business of selling the hide as leather, many carriers have recognized the revenue potential of converting incidental portions of their vertically integrated enterprises into profit centers. Taking advantage of their economies of scope, passenger carriers transport freight in the belly of their aircraft as an incidental stream of revenue for their primary business. Carriers also have long taken advantage of their economies of scale at various airports in order to sell maintenance, ground-handling, catering, management, and ticketing services for competitors, or sub-lease gates to them. Major airlines sell travel agent bookings to competitors through their ubiquitous computer reservations systems. More recently, major airlines have discovered frequent flyer mileage to be a significant revenue stream.

American Airlines has aggressively pursued customers for its core services. For example, it began processing insurance claims for such HMOs as Blue Cross/Blue Shield at its key-punch center in Barbados. It built a CRS and pricing plan for the French high-speed rail system. It purchased a large share of Canadian Airlines that gave it an

---

[165] Ed Leefeldt, Plane Truth, Bloomberg Personal (Oct. 1994), at 9.
[166] Charles Kuralt, On the Road 251 (1990).

information-services contract worth $2 billion over 20 years for computer reservations, revenue accounting, data-processing and yield management services.[167] Recognizing that the smaller upstart carriers are a phenomenon that won't go away, American sells them a host of management, pricing, revenue and computer services.

One example of creative use of aircraft is a 1996 announcement by United Parcel Service, the world's largest transportation firm, that it was entering the passenger transportation business, by converting 59 Boeing 727 cargo aircraft (which were parked idle during weekends) into weekend charter services for cruise operators.[168] Similarly, World Airways is a passenger carrier (with sort of a scheduled/charter concept) from May to September, then removes the seats and becomes a cargo carrier from September to May.[169]

INNOVATION

Some airline corporate cultures lend themselves to innovation—they encourage and stimulate constructive debate as to alternatives to enhance revenue or curtail costs. In earlier days of commercial aviation, Pan Am and TWA were bastions of innovation. Pan Am blazed new trails by brazenly opening new markets around the world, and pushing the envelope for newer and larger aircraft (such as the 747), flying more seats longer distances. TWA also spurred technological development by pushing the manufacturers to leap-frog ahead of rivals, and developed such essential concepts as efficient scheduling.

The airline which has been most innovative during the last two decades is American Airlines. American was the breeding ground for CRS, frequent flyer programs and yield management—three of the industry's most important developments. ValuJet was innovative too, in out-sourcing so much of core operations, and developing direct distribution.

In its own way, conservative yet unconventional Southwest has developed its own innovations—fly lots of frequencies in short-haul

---

[167] Bridget O'Brian, Tired of Airline Losses, AMR Pushes Its Bid To Diversify Business, Wall St. J., Feb. 18, 1993, at A1, A10.
[168] David Morgan, UPS Considers Entering Air Passenger Market, Rocky Mountain News, May 9, 1996, at 3B.
[169] Address of Henk Guitjens Before the Fifth Annual Phoenix International Aviation Symposium (Apr. 18, 1996).

dense markets without much service or interlining. Southwest comes up with innovative ways to inspire company loyalty and hard work, with a CEO not afraid to dress up like Elvis and be disgracefully silly. Southwest holds a "president for a day" contest among employees, rewarding the employee who comes up with the most innovative or inspirational idea in under 100 days with a chance to spend a day in Dallas (part of which with CEO Herb Kelleher) handing our Spirit Awards to employees and flying in a flight simulator.[170]

Astute CEOs must be sufficiently self-confident not to surround themselves with "yes men," and encourage a healthy debate on fresh ideas from anyone inside or outside the company.[171]

CONSERVATIVE vs. AGGRESSIVE GROWTH STRATEGIES

To grow or not to grow, that is the question. An airline has four alternatives in which to grow: (1) it can grow internally; (2) it can acquire another airline; (3) it can be acquired; or (4) it can enter into a broad marketing and/or equity relationship with another carrier.[172] And it can grow at an accelerated, moderate, or sluggish pace.

An airline can grow too quickly, or too slowly. A small airline is incentivized to add aircraft quickly to spread fixed overhead over more seats, thereby lowering average costs, and achieving "critical mass." Airline costs are disproportionately fixed. Advertising, accounting, and many other corporate headquarters costs do not increase appreciably by adding additional aircraft. Once Reno Air had grown sufficiently large to achieve economies of scale in purchasing, marketing and maintenance, it cut its growth rate, so as to avoid "the great start-up killer: overexpansion."[173]

Growing too fast can be fatal. Recall the Greek myth of Daedalus and his son Icarus. Daedalus fashioned wings of wax for his son to escape from the island on which they were exiled, but warned him not to fly too high. Icarus ignored his father's admonitions and flew so

---

[170] Aviation Daily (May 1, 1996), at 186.
[171] Robert Waterman, Jr., The Renewal Factor: How the Best Get and Keep the Competitive Edge (1987).
[172] Susan Carey, USAir CEO Wold Says Cost Structure Needs an Overhaul, Wall St. J., Apr. 17, 1996.
[173] Scott McCartney, Reno Air Plans to Curtail Growth, Wall St. J., Dec. 1, 1996, at B4.

Planning: Product Development

close to the Sun that his wings melted, sending him spiraling downward to his death. Similarly, few airline executives have been successful in restraining themselves from growing too rapidly.

Braniff International Airlines had been profitable nearly every year prior to deregulation. Immediately after President Jimmy Carter signed the Airline Deregulation Act of 1978 into law, Braniff requested 626 dormant routes. Under Harding Lawrence, Braniff hired hundreds of new pilots, took on scores of additional aircraft (including several 747s and, briefly, the Concorde), and opened routes to Honolulu, Guam, Hong Kong, Seoul, Singapore, London, Paris, Amsterdam, and numerous other exotic destinations. In one twenty-four hour period, Braniff added 32 new routes including 16 cities to which Braniff had never flown.[174] At one point, the joke in Washington was that the Civil Aeronautics Board told Braniff to "Go to Hell", and Braniff promptly applied for the route.[175] The company's costs increased drastically, while its load factors were poor. Routes like Buffalo-Orlando had been abandoned by other carriers for a reason—there was insufficient traffic to warrant non-stop service. Braniff into a crash and burn financial tailspin from which it could not recover.

Sir Freddie Laker started Skytrain, made a bundle of money flying from London to New York, found himself on the cover of *Time* magazine, then bought one DC-10 after another until he found himself in bankruptcy. Donald Burr made a bundle of money flying low-cost low-frills service out of Newark, found himself on the cover of *Time* magazine, then bought Frontier Airlines, Britt, and PBA, until his airlines were so overwhelmed with debt that he was forced to sell out. Corporate raider Frank Lorenzo took over Burr's airlines and, for a short while, had amassed the free world's largest airline empire, which collapsed with the second bankruptcy of Continental Airlines and the liquidation of Eastern Airlines. America West began flying a 747 between Hawaii and Nagoya, Japan, before it collapsed into bankruptcy in June 1991.[176] Seemingly having learned little about the dangers of overly exuberant expansion, once out of bankruptcy, America West launched a plan to increase its size by 29%, creating crew shortages, maintenance problems, flight cancellations, and a

---

[174] John Nance, Splash of Colors 121 (1984).
[175] Id. at 129.
[176] ESG Aviation Services, 9 The Airline Monitor 6 (Dec. 1996).

Chapter 4

sharp deterioration in customer relations.[177] One of the problems is that management, customer service, reservations capacity, and revenue accounting may be unable to keep up with the pace of the company's growth.[178]

In contrast, Southwest Airlines grew by two cities a year with one type of aircraft (the Boeing 737). That was until 1993, when it announced the purchase of Morris Air, hubbed in Salt Lake City, for $128.5 million, and placed a $2.5 billion order for 63 Boeing 737X aircraft to be delivered between 1997 and 2000, the largest order in the 22 year-old carrier's history.[179] Southwest entered seven new cities in 1994, increasing its available seat miles 29% in the fourth quarter of that year.[180] Southwest's management appeared to be concerned that, unless it moved expeditiously, the finite number of short-haul dense city-pairs would be occupied by its competitors. It remains to be seen whether this aggressive growth strategy will in the long run be successful, with the emergence of non-union low cost Southwest clones (e.g., Kiwi and ValuJet), as well as major carriers restructuring to compete in low-cost Southwest-type operations (e.g., United Shuttle).

It took Southwest Airlines 12 years to grow from two aircraft to 50. It took ValuJet only three years to grow so large. Its owners relished describing ValuJet as the "the fastest growing carrier in the country's history."[181] In the week following the 1996 crash of Flight 592 in the Florida Everglades (which killed all 109 people on board), ValuJet operated only 80% of its flights, but saw its load factors drop from 62% down to 51%.[182] Public confidence in ValuJet was shaken because of the age of its fleet (the DC-9 that crashed in the Everglades

---

[177] Scott McCartney & Andy Pasztor, Fast Growth Lands Low-Cost Airline in Trouble, Wall St. J., Sept. 10, 1995, at B1.
[178] Stephen Shaw, Airline Marketing & Management 137, 138 (3rd ed. 1990).
[179] John Keahey & Steven Oberbeck, No-Frills Southwest Airlines Buys Morris Air, Salt Lake Tribune, Dec. 14, 1993, at A-1; Jeff Cole & Bridget O'Brian, Boeing Wins Huge Southwest Air Order, Giving 737 Upgrade Plans a Green Light, Wall St. J., Nov. 18, 1993, at A2. Southwest flew to 37 cities; Morris flew 21 Boeing 737s to 22 cities, and employed 2,000. Bridget O'Brian, Southwest Air to Buy Morris for $129 Million, Wall St. J., Dec. 14, 1993, at A3. Southwest will also take over $50 million in Morris' debt. Southwest has not purchased an airline since it acquired Must Air in 1985 for $40.5 million in cash and $20 million in stock. Id. at A10.
[180] Address by Herb Kelleher before the Salomon Bros. Transportation Conference (New York, N.Y., November 18, 1994).
[181] ValuJet Penny-Pinching Under Scrutiny, Wall St. J., May 15, 1996, at A6.
[182] Martha Brannigan, ValuJet Sees Flights Disrupted Until 4th Quarter, Wall St. J., May 23, 1996, at A3.

was 27 years old), and the fact that it had come from several different sources in different countries, with different avionics and different maintenance schedules.[183] Ultimately, the FAA grounded the entire fleet for several months.

Described as "meticulous and cautious,"[184] Delta Airlines had been the most conservative of airlines until it felt the bandwagon was leaving without it in the late 1980s. Delta jumped on board and purchased Western Airlines and Pan Am's trans-Atlantic routes. Nearly overnight, Delta, which had limited public recognition in Europe, added nearly 50 new routes and 21 new destinations.[185] Delta fell into a financial tailspin. Once it began to suffer from indigestion of this massive route system, conservatism became its curse, for Delta was slow to pare the weakest routes from the system.

Described by its new CEO, Stephen Wolf, as having traditionally been "an underachiever, internally focused and timid," USAirways began to expand significantly across the Atlantic under his reign.[186]

Fast-paced growth of a new airline may irritate its larger rivals, leading them to engage in predatory practices directed toward the upstart airline. Stephen Shaw explained it this way:

> The effect of the new entrant on [a major carrier's] business will be small initially. Matching or undercutting his fares [will dilute the yield of the] traffic they would have carried anyway . . . . Therefore, the initial reaction to the arrival of new competition may be muted.
>
> This sets into play a pattern all too familiar in the airline industry. The new airline achieves notable initial success. Those who run it are blinded by this into believing that the competition is in disarray. New and extremely ambitious expansion plans are immediately

---

[183] ValuJet Penny-Pinching Under Scrutiny, Wall St. J., May 15, 1996, at A6.
[184] Delta's Marketing Guru Is High On Change, Wall St. J., Dec. 12, 1996, at B7.
[185] Robert Goggin, Carrier Executives Share Successful Promotional Strategies, Travel Weekly (Sept. 14, 1992).
[186] Statement of Stephen Wolf Before the 11th Annual Salomon Bros. Transportation Conference (New York, N.Y., Nov. 14, 1996).

Chapter 4

formulated and implemented with all possible speed.

The initial success does not last. The innovating airline begins to run into problems. Staff morale may suffer as the honeymoon period associated with start-up comes to an end. The airline's cost advantages will be reduced. Its own costs will rise as overheads increase and staff members advance along seniority scales. At the same time, the rival airlines will succeed in lowering their costs in response to the competitive threat they are facing. The main problems, though, will stem from the fact that these rivals will no longer face a dilemma in deciding their attitude to the newcomer. The latter's ambitious growth plans will mean that it is no longer a mild irritant. Instead it is threatening the core of the older established airlines' businesses. They must therefore mount a strong response in terms of matching or undercutting its fares, increasing capacity—in fact by using any elements of the marketing mix which will reestablish their dominance.[187]

In order to expand quickly, some carriers have digested rival airlines. For example, Northwest includes North Central, Southern and Hughes Airwest. Continental includes Texas International, New York Air, People Express, and Frontier. In each case, the consuming carrier had a fit of indigestion as service levels deteriorated due to the clash of corporate cultures, procedures and equipment.

But other larger carriers have devised creative means of engaging in fast-paced internal growth successfully. With the two-tiered (B-scale) wage structure American Airlines negotiated with its unions in the early 1980s, it was able to engage in an accelerated growth strategy. With all newly hired employees coming in at significantly lower wages, American was able to lower its average cost by growing the company.

---

[187] Stephen Shaw, Airline Marketing & Management 139, 140 (3rd ed. 1990).

Planning: Product Development

It had little incentive to acquire other airlines, and with the exception of AirCal, did not. Existing employees benefited as they were promoted to better positions (pilots became Captains more expeditiously, for example, and moved up to larger aircraft) and enjoyed improved seniority.

But as the B-scale employees became numerous, union leadership was forced to compel management to integrate the two wage scales. At that point, the aggressive growth strategy had lost its advantages. American Airlines canceled billions of dollars of new aircraft, and like a moving train whose engineer applied the brakes, its growth plan drifted slowly to a halt. Bob Crandall threatened, "Unless the world changes, we will never buy another plane. We won't replace the planes that wear out."[188] Whether posturing for the edification of labor or not, the statement reflects the severity of the loss of the impact of B-scale wages on average costs.

The 1980s were characterized by aggressive growth by nearly all major carriers, each trying to conquer the territories of the others in what one labor leader described as a "malicious addiction to market share."[189] By the 1990s, the carriers were suffering major indigestion from the addition of about one new aircraft per day. By 1994, they had lost $13 billion. Labor and management (and their bankers) came to the abyss and looked over, and were terrified by what they saw.[190] By the mid-1990s, the airlines were much more focused on profit (and its primary ingredients, revenue and costs) than market share. As profitability improved, the major airlines placed billions of dollars in orders for new aircraft. Noting that "the turning radius for a large company is wide," United Airlines CEO Gerald Greenwald expressed adherence to the "wisdom of the buy and replace approach to fleet planning" rather than growth for the sake of achieving an ever-expanding market share.[191] Time will tell whether the airlines have changed their philosophy of growth and competitive collision.

---

[188] Thomas Petzinger, Jr., Hard Landing 415 (1995).
[189] Address of J. Randolph Babbitt Before the Fifth Annual Phoenix International Aviation Symposium (Apr. 18, 1996).
[190] Address of John Harper Before the Fifth Annual Phoenix International Aviation Symposium (Apr. 18, 1996).
[191] Statement of Gerald Greenwald Before the 11th Annual Salomon Bros. Transportation Conference (New York, N.Y., Nov. 14, 1994).

Chapter 4

PERFORMANCE MONITORING AND EVALUATION

TWA inaugurated flight profitability analysis in the 1960s. In 1970, Trans World Airlines instituted a project to computerize its "Flight Profitability Analysis" process for each domestic and international flight segment. It took three years to complete. Once established, monthly flight segment profitability reports were produced. The system was refined over the years into a highly sophisticated and accurate profitability reporting system. Expenses of aircraft depreciation, fuel, landing fees, gate leases, and such were allocated to each flight on a consumption basis, to which was added a reasonable allocation of fixed overhead. Comparing these costs to revenue derived from the flight produced a clearer picture of which flights were successful, and which were not, allowing the carrier to fine tune its route system to maximize profitability.[192]

A *marketing control system* enables a carrier to evaluate its performance in the market, compare such performance with its marketing plan, and if necessary, amend the plan. Marketing control should be attempted both at the macro level (e.g., sales, market share, load factors) and micro level (i.e., profitability of individual services).[193]

Revenue accounting data on a city-pair O&D basis can be derived from the ticket processing function, and with ticketless travel, this function can be accelerated with computer generated information. The more difficult task is both determining how to allocate revenue among flight segments for on-line connecting passengers, and more difficult still, ascribing costs to each segment. Some costs, such as gate leases, station personnel, and such, are easily tagged to the flights which serve the city in question. More difficult is ascribing variable and fixed costs (such as fuel, maintenance, marketing and other overhead costs) to particular flight segments.

Typically, an airline's internally generated monthly flight profitability report will include the following data systemwide, and broken down on a city-pair, flight-by-flight basis:

---

[192] C.E. Meyer, Cabotage, Foreign Ownership and International Marketing Alliances (address before University of Denver/Smithsonian Air & Space Museum Conference on Airlines, Airports & Aviation (Washington, D.C., May 29, 1992).
[193] Newal Taneja, Airline Planning: Corporate, Financial, and Marketing 81 (1982).

Planning: Product Development

- Market profit/(loss)
- Profit/(Loss) Per Trip
- Segment passengers
- Available Seat Miles [ASMs]
- Revenue Passenger Miles [RPMs]
- Load Factor
- Break-Even Load Factor
- Passenger Revenue
- Average Fare
- Yield
- Revenue per Available Seat Mile [RASM]
- Costs per Available Seat Mile [CASM]
- Variable Costs per Available Seat Mile
- Average Passengers per Trip
- Average Seats per Departure
- Break-Even Passengers per Trip
- Number of Frequencies
- Miles

As can be seen, there are a multitude of criteria with which one may compare a carrier's performance from market-to-market, and month-to-month. One of the authors' favorites is the relationship between break-even load factors and actual load factors. Break-even load factor is essentially a function of calculating costs and prices. It reveals how many seats will have to be sold to achieve revenue/cost neutrality on a particular flight. If the break-even load factor is below 60%, target yields are probably high; if above 70%, yields are likely excessively low. Actual load factor is merely a function of sales—how many seats were actually sold. If the difference between break-even and actual load factors is a positive number, the flight is making money. If the difference between the two is a negative number, something is wrong—costs are too high, prices too low, or demand insufficient. If the negative difference is more than a few percentage points, something is very wrong indeed.

Of course, seasonal adjustments must be made. But flight-by-flight and market-by-market comparisons help management identify which routes are performing well, and which are not, so that corrective action may be taken.

American Airlines spent ten years to develop a useful flight profitability system, requiring a restructuring of the accounting system and development of computer software.[194] To assess performance objectively, carriers also compare their revenue and expenses with a benchmark of comparable airlines. Carriers have several means of measuring their performance levels, including consumer complaints, on-time arrivals/departures, questionnaires of frequent flyers, and delay time in answering reservations lines.

After a strategic plan is developed, aircraft acquired, and new service advertised and flown, an airline must engage in post-appraisal evaluation of results—projected versus realized passengers, cargo, mail, and revenue, on a flight-by-flight basis. This allows the company to fine tune its route system, subtracting capacity from weaker markets while adding it to stronger markets.

Each carrier should compare its performance with its peers. *Benchmarking* analysis should include evaluation of indicators of financial performance, including cash, return on assets, labor costs and productivity, cost performance, asset utilization and debt.[195]

Certain governmentally mandated reporting requirements also allow a carrier to monitor its performance vis-à-vis its competitors. For example, the DOT requires that all carriers report on-time performance (within 15 minutes of scheduled arrival). Continental hired an outside firm to audit Southwest's arrival times, which concluded that Southwest mis-reported its data favorably.[196]

TIMING: THE MARKET CYCLE

Rises and falls in the economy and disposable income profoundly effect consumer demand for air travel. For airlines, even modest changes in fuel costs, interest rates, and macro-economic conditions can have a profound effect on the bottom line.[197] They therefore affect

---

[194] Dan Reed, The American Eagle 46 (1992).
[195] Statement of Qantas Airlines' Peter Gregg Before the 11th Annual Salomon Bros. Transportation Conference (New York, N.Y., Nov. 14, 1996).
[196] Scott McCartney, Airline Claims On-Time Data May Be Flawed, Wall St. J., May 13, 1996, at B1.
[197] Thomas Petzinger, Hard Landing 168 (1995).

strategic planning for airlines. Air Canada's Louis Gialloreto has written a book which focuses on this question.[198] His conclusions are summarized here.

Gialloreto divides airlines into three types: (1) traditional high-cost/full-service carriers (e.g., USAirways) ; (2) low-cost/low-service carriers (e.g., ValuJet); and (3) low-cost/low- to medium-differentiated service carriers (e.g., Continental).[199] Many Type One carriers are trying to transform themselves into Type Three carriers. Gaining market share becomes important during the upturn and peak of the market cycle, "the larger the carrier the larger the synergy, network and market share."[200] The ideal time for Type One carriers to purchase or lease aircraft is after the pit and at the beginning of the upturn of the cycle, while the optimum time for Type Twos and Threes is during the downturn and pit of the cycle, when Type One's are shedding themselves of used aircraft at discounted prices.[201] Type Ones and Threes tend to order aircraft at or near the peak of the market cycle, and unfortunately, take delivery during the downturn, thereby making heavy lease and mortgage payments when they can least afford it.[202] But while Type One carriers are unloading excess capacity, Type Two and Three carriers can purchase or lease second-hand aircraft at bargain prices.[203]

The most difficult period for the Type One carrier is during recession, for it cannot defray costs by growing, for the market is contracting, and overhead structures are difficult to disassemble. With a lower cost structure, Type Twos and Threes tend to weather the downturn of the cycle better, complimenting consumers' demands for lower fares during recession, while Type Ones haven't the financial means to wage war for market share,[204] though they do tend to match the price of the low-cost providers, at least, on a capacity-controlled basis. During the upturn and peak of the cycle, consumers focus more on service, for which Type One carriers have an advantage.[205] Though

---

[198] Louis Gialloreto, Strategic Airline Management (1988).
[199] Id. at 47-50.
[200] Id. at 62.
[201] Id. at 83.
[202] Id. at 59.
[203] Id. at 59.
[204] Id. at 77, 78.
[205] See id. at 95.

consumers want more service and workers want wage improvement during good times, the carriers which manage their costs better during the upturn of the cycle have a smoother ride when the cycle turns downward.[206] The roller coaster effect of the cycle, which provides enormous revenue during the upturn and peak of the cycle, often leads to enormous cash flow operating losses during the downturn and pit.[207] The trough is the optimum time for management to seek wage and work rule concessions from labor.[208] Mergers between smaller and medium-size carriers tend to be less successful during the downturn and pit of the cycle, but more successful during the upturn and peak of the market cycle.[209]

This analysis must be tempered somewhat by what occurred since Gialloreto published his book, in 1988. The downturn and pit of the late 1980s and early 1990s was worse than any the airline industry had ever experienced. A vast amount of aircraft capacity was canceled, and new purchase orders were highly conservative, even as the cycle turned upward, in the mid-1990s. Further, the balance sheets of the major airlines have been so polluted with debt that management is constrained either from engaging in the cyclical upturn exuberant expansion to which it was traditionally accustomed, or waging war for market share. Management at the traditional airlines has focused sharply on transforming their companies into Type Three carriers. Further, in the 1990s, a swarm of new Lilliputian Type Two and Three new entrant carriers emerged, and some of the Type One carriers refrained from waging all out war with them, perhaps enabling a few to achieve "critical mass." The lessons of catastrophe appeared to have led management to focus more carefully on profit, and focus less on market share.

COMPETITIVE RESPONSE

Like a game of chess, or the deployment of infantry in a battle, a rival's move may create opportunity or difficulty. The opponent's move and potential alternatives thereto must be studied and evaluated

---

[206] See id. at 105.
[207] Id. at 62.
[208] Id. at 79.
[209] Id. at 62, 78, 79.

Planning: Product Development

in order to best seize the opportunity or minimize the difficulty. The opponent's responses must also be anticipated.

An airline must never, ever, underestimate the actions of its rivals. A competitor seeking to stimulate traffic, improve load factors, enhance market share, or establish market dominance has a number of tools at its disposal, many of a predatory nature. A larger carrier seeking to stifle a smaller rival's profits can slash prices, increase competitive frequencies and the number of seats offered at lower fare buckets, particularly at the time of the target airline's departures, raise travel agent commission overrides, and/or sandwich its competitor's flights with excess capacity. History has proven that management can be emotional and irrational on issues like market share, capacity and pricing. Hubris and testosterone appear in plentiful quantity among airline management.

Like Darwinist beasts, airlines can be quite primordial in responding to intrusions into territory which they perceive as theirs. For example, at different times, Northwest implemented a predatory "scorched earth" approach to People Express' and Reno Air's entry into the Minneapolis market. Ironically, with former consumer advocate Michael Levine as its marketing vice president, Northwest has become among the industry's fiercest carnivores. In 1992, when American Airlines introduced Value Pricing, designed to simplify the unmercifully complex pricing structure which had emerged under deregulation and provide equitable prices to small businesses, Northwest retaliated with "Grownups Fly Free." American counterattacked by slashing fares 50%, which Levine described as a "nuclear-attack"[210]—the pot calling the kettle black, so to speak. Northwest then threw an antitrust bomb at American, in a vicious lawsuit seeking multi-million dollar damages, which the jury expeditiously diffused.

Other examples are abundant. When Southwest airlines entered Baltimore, USAir launched a "blistering counterattack," adding capacity and lowering fares. Southwest was bruised but hung in. Finally USAir retreated.[211] United Airlines engaged in a myriad of anticompetitive activities at Denver, including pricing below costs,

---

[210] Michael Levine, Carrier Executives Share Successful Promotional Strategies, Travel Weekly (Sept. 14, 1992), at 26.
[211] Scott McCartney, Competitors Quake As Southwest Air Is Set To Invade Northeast, Wall St. J., Oct. 23, 1996, at A1.

adding excessive capacity to competitors' markets, awarding travel agents commission overrides to steer business its way, entering into "exclusive dealing" contracts with business purchasers, refusing to allow jet competitors to have non-discriminatory access to its network, and biasing its computer reservations system against competitors' offerings.

As in war, an airline can attack or retreat. With a low pain threshold, American Airlines has exited many markets entered by low-cost rivals, downsized the aircraft, or turned short-haul routes over to its American Eagle turboprop subsidiary.[212] In contrast, United created U-2, or Shuttle by United, as an effort to make a stand against Southwest's penetration into the West Coast markets. Southwest counterattacked to what it described as a "Commencement of Hostilities" by lowering fares and threatening to enter United's long-haul markets.[213] Seeking more peaceful coexistence, United then withdrew to more defensible positions, leaving many of the smaller airports to Southwest.

A major carrier's competitive response to a low-cost rivals entry into its markets depends on several variables beyond psychological: (1) the size of the O&D market; (2) how important the market is to the incumbent's systemwide operation; (3) the existence of service at competing airports; and (4) how much the new entrant under-priced the incumbent and increased the level of service.[214] Of course, the more vigorously a new entrant assaults an incumbent's fares and schedules, and the more vigorously an incumbent meets the competitive threat, the more consumers benefit in terms of new capacity and frequency, and lower fares, at least in the short term. But for the carriers in the market, it can be, and too often is, a financial blood bath.

Many small carriers attempt to stay out of the major airlines' cross-hairs by limiting the number of frequencies they offer, and avoid challenging them to a price war (which of course, the major carrier, with greater resources, would win). Edmund Lawler has studied management at smaller underdog companies, and divided them into

---

[212] Robert Rose & Susan Carey, Money-Losing Routes Prompt Big Carriers To Mull Radical Steps, Wall St. J., Oct. 26, 1994, at A1.
[213] Bridget O'Brian, Southwest Airlines Says It Will Add Longer Flights, Wall St. J., July 5, 1994, at A3.
[214] Aviation Daily (Jan. 3, 1996), at 14, citing study by Linda Perry of Leigh Fisher and Associates.

three categories: (1) "differentiators," who attempt to distinguish themselves from their larger competitors; (2) "re-inventors," who attempt to bypass others by radically changing the industry; and (3) "shadow casters," who cast a larger-than-life shadow in the market in order to build momentum during their inaugural years.

Differentiators include such upstart airlines as WesternPacific, which sold its aircraft livery as advertising billboards, both to generate a new source of revenue and to distinguish itself from its conservative, established major airline competitors. Re-inventors include such carriers as Valujet, which shunned traditional methods of distribution and out-sourced major parts of its operations. Shadow casters show up in the name of deceased airlines, like Braniff II, Braniff III, Midway II, Frontier II, Pan Am II, banking on the good will and name recognition of their predecessors.

Underdogs can use smaller size to motivate employees to give the company their best. Because they are smaller, they can be more agile, for they haven't the tradition and huge bureaucracy to constipate decision-making. Lawler points to Richard Branson's Virgin Atlantic as a "challenger," which established itself with a distinctive (youthful and brash) personality and in a form of corporate jujitsu, turned the gargantuan size of British Airways into a disadvantage. Indeed, adeptly using the press and the courts (with a $975 million antitrust suit) to point out the "dirty tricks" BA played on Virgin, amply tarnished British Airway's public image, and forced it to give Virgin more breathing room.[215] According to *The Economist:* "Far from being a squeaky-clean friend to the consumer, BA now looks, since the Virgin affair, like an anxious, overbearing giant trying to squash a feisty little rival."[216]

In the final analysis, the upstarts can have a difficult go of it if they end up in a megacarrier's cross-hairs. Many passengers welcome the presence of the upstart, for the megacarrier frequently will meet the upstart's prices, at least on a limited bucket of seats on flights in close proximity to those of the upstart. Thus passengers can take advantage of the low fares on the megacarrier, while earning the megacarrier's frequent flyer miles for free travel. Travel agents also welcome the

---

[215] See Edmund Lawler, Underdog Marketing: Successful Strategies for Outmarketing the Leader (1996).
[216] We Are Flying Into Turbulence, The Economist (Mar. 4, 1995), at 64.

upstart's entry, for megacarriers often respond with more generous travel agent commission overrides. Thus, both the passenger and travel agent benefits from the megacarrier's generosity, in the short term, until the upstart is driven from the market, when the megacarrier's low fares and generous commission overrides ordinarily evaporate. This reflects the temporal individualistic view of the world which dominates the species *Homo Sapiens*. We often do what is in our individual short-term interest, rather than what is in our collective long-term interest.

FLEXIBILITY

While successful firms use information as their principal strategic advantage, they employ flexibility as their principal strategic weapon.[217] Successful companies are not paralyzed by analysis; they are flexible, incremental and responsive. They take action in small steps rather than grandiose plans, reversing course quickly if an action turns out to be in error. They adopt the pro-active approach of "do it, fix it, try it."[218]

Airline management must be sufficiently flexible to "cut the losses" and withdraw from strategic plans which are not performing as expected. Several carriers have closed hubs. For example, in the early 1990s, Continental withdrew from Denver, a hub it had built in the 1980s and expanded with the acquisition of Frontier. Continental shifted the aircraft east of the Mississippi to inaugurate CALite, a Southwest-cloned short-haul linear route system. When it became apparent that wasn't working, Continental abandoned it.

Ideally, management develops several contingency, or "fall back" plans to implement should a new strategy fail to meet its expectations, for not only is the future difficult to predict but, as we have seen, many factors influencing demand and costs are wholly beyond the control of management. The product itself will go through a growth phase, maturity phase, and decline phase, requiring that before decline, management either re-launch the product (such as with additional advertising) so that demand resumes, or develop a new product.[219]

---

[217] Robert Waterman, Jr., The Renewal Factor: How the Best Get and Keep the Competitive Edge (1987).
[218] Thomas Peters & Robert Waterman, Jr., In Search of Excellence (1982).
[219] Stephen Shaw, Airline Marketing & Management 145-47 (3rd ed. 1990).

Planning: Product Development

Unable to persuade organized labor to make wage and work rule concessions, and faced with low-cost carriers appearing in many of its major markets, American Airlines launched its "Transition Plan" in 1994, which had three components: (1) make the airline bigger and stronger wherever possible (e.g., adding frequencies in high-yield business markets, building up its hubs at Chicago, Dallas and Miami); (2) withdraw from markets in which it cannot effectively compete (e.g., grounding inefficient aircraft, de-hubbing San Jose, Nashville and Raleigh/Durham); and (3) grow its profitable non-airline businesses (e.g., information technology and management services).[220]

After launching an "airline within an airline," United had to tailor its Shuttle to avoid going head-to-head with Southwest. FedEx had to abandon Zap Mail, after making enormous investments into this public fax service.[221] With a more conservative management style, Delta was slow to improve performance and profitability in the trans-Atlantic routes it purchased from Pan Am.

In the final analysis, flexibility may be the key strategy for airline management in the 21st Century.

---

[220] Robert Crandall, Remarks Before the Salomon Brother Ninth Annual Transportation Conference (Nov. 16, 1994).
[221] See Paul Stephen Dempsey and Laurence E. Gesell, Air Transportation: Foundations for the 21st Century (1997), Chapter 7.

CHAPTER 5.

OPERATIONS: PRODUCT DELIVERY

"It's not a testosterone-driven industry any longer. Success is in making money, not the size of the airline."[1]
Gordon Bethune
CEO, Continental Airlines

SCHEDULING

This Chapter examines the essential components of airline operations—flight scheduling, ground facilities, aircraft maintenance, aviation security, employee training and relations, cabin service, auxiliary in-flight and non-flight services, and bundled travel services. It begins with scheduling and concludes with a review of the various rankings of airlines and their products.

Scheduling is an enormously complicated process. It involves providing aircraft departures to cities at times (supply) to which and when consumers want to fly (demand), in order to convince passengers to exchange economic resources (revenue) for those benefits.[2] One source succinctly identified its principal components:

> Deciding where airplanes should fly, and at what hours of the day, requires four-dimensional thinking, an affinity for solving puzzles

---

[1] Quoted in Carol Hallett, Address Before Salomon Bros. 11th Annual Transportation Conference (New York, N.Y., Nov. 13, 1996), at 3.
[2] Charles Banfe, Airline Management 68 (1992).

> in which the pieces are continually moving. The scheduler analyzes passenger traffic patterns, economic trends, maintenance timetables, fueling requirements, flight times, loading and unloading intervals, noise rules, slot availability, airport curfews, labor costs, fuel prices, and fare levels, among a few dozen other factors, at every location where the airline conducts business. From these variables the scheduler produces a flight plan, from which the airline in turn establishes its financing, staffing, food and beverage requirements, sales strategy, and a series of contingency plans for bad weather, mechanical failure, and every other misery that can befall an airline. The permutations increase arithmetically according to the number of aircraft and geometrically according to the number of aircraft types in any given fleet .... [3]

TWA's Melvin Brenner was the first person to come to grips with the tremendously complicated task of scheduling by linking the essential objective of high aircraft utilization with a more scientific and less intuitive approach to market planning—fitting the right-sized aircraft to a market at times when demand is heaviest.[4] Demand is highly cyclical, with peak and trough periods at certain times of the day, week, or year. The basic objective of scheduling is to increase aircraft utilization, deploy the aircraft in those markets which earn the highest returns and, for network carriers, connect to banks of other arriving and departing aircraft efficiently.[5] One source described the primary ingredients of schedule planning:

> The task of the schedule planner is to serve the cities on the route system in a way that meets the demands of travelers and that return a fair profit to the airline. To accomplish this task

---

[3] Thomas Petzinger, Jr., Hard Landing 122 (1995).
[4] Dan Reed, The American Eagle 91 (1992).
[5] William Waltrip, International Planning, in Airline Economics 281, 283 (G. James ed. 1982).

it is necessary to balance capacity against the demand at the price at which capacity is offered. Selection of the proper aircraft type for each part of the route system is the fulcrum of this scheduling concept. This balance is achieved by operating at a low cost per seat-mile, accomplished in part by high utilization of equipment and high productivity of both equipment and manpower, by frequent service, and by flow-through traffic.[6]

For each flight segment, the scheduler must predict the size of market demand and how it will fluctuate by day of week and hour of day. Curfews and slot requirements may constrict scheduling flexibility. Scheduling also must be done in a way that takes account of routine aircraft maintenance checks. The scheduler also attempts to align through flight numbers, offering nonstop service from A to B, and one-stop service from A to C.

For network carriers, the scheduler evaluates local traffic, through traffic, and connecting traffic, attempting to choreograph efficient complexes with multiple cross-feed of passengers and cargo.[7] The effort is to reduce dwell time (the period of time between aircraft arrival and departure), which can be a challenging task at congested hub airports.[8] For large carriers like United and American, two minutes of additional system-wide utilization is the equivalent of adding another aircraft to the fleet.[9]

Proper scheduling is extremely important to airline profitability. According to William Nesbit, "Fine tuning of seat capacity, scheduling and aircraft ground times, as well as a conscious effort to maximize the productivity of each airplane in the fleet, comprise the direct route

---

[6] Russell Thayer, Airline Fleet and Schedule Planning, in Airline Economics 265, 268, 269 (G. James ed. 1982).
[7] Robert Crandall, Marketing Planning, in Airline Economics 231, 233 (G. James ed. 1982).
[8] See George Pearson & Joan Strahler, Airline Scheduling, in Handbook of Airline Economics 423, 424 (D. Jenkins ed. 1995).
[9] Charles Banfe, Airline Management 119 (1988).

to higher overall productivity, which is the basis for sustained profitability."[10]

Unfortunately, the schedule can be scuttled by unforeseen circumstances causing flight delay, including inclement weather and mechanical problems with the aircraft.[11] This can have a ripple and compounding effect throughout the day, delaying subsequent departures, becoming even worse as flight crew duty time ceilings are approached.

One issue of consumer satisfaction is punctuality. Although with hubbing and airport and air traffic congestion, some schedules have regressed back to the DC-3 era, airlines superficially appear to be punctual by padding their schedules.[12] The DOT requires airlines to report delays of more than 15 minutes, which it makes available to the public. Airlines advertise the fact that they rank higher on the list than their competitors. Again, flying has not become faster; it just appears to be.

Industry expert Ted Harris notes the inherent advantages of aviation vis-à-vis other modes of transportation: (1) it is the only mode of transport that can travel in a straight line from A to B without being impeded by topography; and (2) it is ten times faster than any other mode. Yet under deregulation, trips of 1,500 miles or less can take twice as long.[13]

GROUND FACILITIES

Airlines must negotiate with airports for gates, ticket counters, office space, crew locker and briefing rooms, baggage systems, and maintenance facilities. Many major airports have no available gates, necessitating additional construction (unless majority-in-interest clauses are exercised to prohibit new construction), or the sub-lease of gates from incumbent airlines (often at a monopoly premium). Slot constraints at Chicago O'Hare, Washington National and New York Kennedy and LaGuardia Airports require a purchase of a slot (the right to take-off and land one aircraft per day) from an incumbent,

---

[10] William Nesbit, Airline Productivity—The Key to Sustained Profitability, in Handbook of Airline Economics 379, 384 (D. Jenkins ed. 1995).
[11] Charles Banfe, Airline Management 24 (1992).
[12] See This Is 'On Time'?, U.S. News & World Rep. (May 8, 1995), at 62.
[13] William Terdoslavich, Domestic, International Airline Regulation Debated, Tour & Travel News (Mar. 15, 1993), at 23.

which may require an expenditure of more than $1 million per slot. The airline must purchase or lease ground equipment, or lease such services from a ground services provider, such as another airline. An airline may either internalize or out-source its "above the wing" (e.g., ticketing) or "below the wing" (e.g., baggage handling, maintenance) services. Flight kitchens must be built at hubs, or catering services contracted. Additionally, the airline must make arrangements for hotels and transfers for overnight flight crews. Reservations and communications systems linking each airport served with headquarters must also be developed.

MAINTENANCE

The purpose of a rigorous maintenance program is to ensure safety, obtain high levels of aircraft utilization, efficiency and punctuality, and preserve the value of the airline's most important capital assets.[14] After a designated number of flight hours and pressurization cycles (which vary by aircraft type, according to FAA regulations), each aircraft must undergo a comprehensive check at a maintenance and engineering base. Maintenance checks are of four types:

A-Check—required about every 125-150 flight hours. It consists of a visual examination of the airframe, power plant, avionics, and accessories to ascertain the general condition of the aircraft. The A-Check requires about eight hours of ground time, and about 60 hours of labor.

B-Check—required about every 700 flight hours. It includes an A-Check, plus selected operational checks, fluid servicing, and lubrication, as well as an open inspection of the panels and cowlings during which preventive maintenance is performed. The B-Check requires about eight hours of ground time, and about 200 hours of labor.

C-Check—required about every 3,000 flight hours. It includes an A-Check and a B-Check, and consists of a detailed inspection of the airframe, engines and accessories, heavy lubrication, and a portion of the corrosion prevention program. Flight controls are calibrated, major

---

[14] Michael Lam, An Introduction to Airline Maintenance, in Handbook of Airline Economics 397 (D. Jenkins ed. 1995).

internal mechanisms are tested, and FAA Service Bulletin requirements are fulfilled The C-Check requires about 72 hours of ground time, and about 3,000 hours of labor.

D-Check—required about every 20,000 flight hours. It includes removal of cabin interiors to allow careful structural inspection, in effect, stripping the aircraft to its shell and rebuilding the interior.[15]

These checks are in addition to unscheduled line maintenance, where licensed mechanics meet arriving aircraft to replace any part or system identified in the pilot logbook as not working properly. A and B Checks are considered "line maintenance"; C and D Checks are considered "heavy maintenance."

Robert Baker explains the nature of the heavy maintenance check at American Airlines:

> During that check, which takes between seven and 21 working days, more than 100 mechanics spend a total of 15,000 labor-hours making sure that everything is in perfect working order. They check the aircraft from nose to tail, literally dismantling it, inspecting every piece, and refurbishing or replacing any system, engine part, or structural component that does not measure up to standards, or has reached a pre-scheduled maintenance interval. All told, each aircraft receives approximately 14 hours of maintenance for every hour it flies.[16]

As one would expect, as a fleet ages, its maintenance burden increases. For example, with a fleet more than 18 years old by the mid-1990s, TWA was spending more than 15% of its operating expenses on maintenance.[17] Like a living animal, performance and reliability of

---

[15] Lawrence Crawford, World Forecast of Aircraft Maintenance Capacity, in Handbook of Airline Economics 385, 387 (D. Jenkins ed. 1995); Michael Lam, An Introduction to Airline Maintenance, in Handbook of Airline Economics (D. Jenkins ed. 1995).
[16] Robert Baker, Airline Operations, in Handbook of Airline Economics 307, 308 (D. Jenkins ed. 1995).
[17] Aviation Daily (Jan. 25, 1996), at 129.

an aircraft is relatively poor both during its infancy (during the shake-out period) and in its senior years.

Unless out-sourced, the maintenance function requires significant hangar space in which to park aircraft while they are serviced, storage space for spare parts, and office space, as well as a corps of trained and experienced maintenance personnel.

SECURITY

The emergence of the hijacker and terrorist has made aviation particularly susceptible to attack. The flag an airline flies is a unique identification of its nationality, making it a potential political target. Hijacking and bombing aircraft have become an increasingly popular means for the military weak to advance perceived political or religious objectives.[18] According to international aviation security expert Jalal Haidar:

> An airplane is particularly vulnerable to the threat or use of violence. A small explosion, even a stray shot, can cripple or doom an airborne aircraft. The tight confines and crowded environment of an airplane fuselage enable a single terrorist to control a large number of people with a single small weapon. Concerted or even individual resistance to unarmed and immobilized passengers, among whom are women and children, is not only impracticable but dangerous. If the aircraft is airborne, aid or assistance from the outside world is not possible. If the aircraft is grounded, access to the aircraft is limited and controlled by the small number of exits. The ability of a terrorist to control and harm a large number of people give him substantial leverage in blackmailing and negotiating with political authorities.[19]

---

[18] Paul Dempsey, Law & Foreign Policy in International Aviation 349 (1987).
[19] Jalal Haidar, Airport Security, in Airport Law, Regulation & Public Policy 133 (R. Hardaway ed. 1991).

Airlines serving the United States are subjected to stringent FAA security procedures, including mandatory X-ray searches of all baggage and cross-checks of baggage and passengers to ensure there are no unaccompanied bags in the belly of the aircraft.[20] Airport security entails running passengers through a magnetometer between the ticket counter and the departure gate. Airline employees are trained to identify passengers who fit FAA security profiles. Security is heightened in international travel, and may include individual interviews, positive identification of all ticket holders, and the screening of all checked baggage.[21]

While much of the direct liability costs of aerial terrorism may be covered in aviation insurance policy issued by, for example, the Lloyd's consortium, the more severe economic injury for a carrier lies in deterioration of passenger bookings as potential travelers begin to shy away from a carrier they perceive as unsafe.

After the crash of TWA flight 800 off the coast of Long Island, N.Y., in 1996, President Clinton appointed Vice President Al Gore to head a White House Commission on Aviation Safety and Security to recommend new procedures to deal with aerial terrorism. The Gore Commission recommended the installation of automated passenger screening procedures, the deployment of explosive detection systems, an assessment of airport security vulnerabilities, review of criminal history and finger print check for airline and airport employees, and the use of bomb-sniffing dogs. A trial procedure was inaugurated to determine the cost and feasibility of domestic full passenger/bag correlation.

THE AIRLINE BUSINESS AS A SERVICE INDUSTRY: THE IMPORTANCE OF HUMAN RESOURCES

Well managed companies enjoy enhanced productivity by motivating and stimulating their employees, by giving them autonomy,

---

[20] Jalal Haidar, Airport Security, in Airport Law, Regulation & Public Policy 133, 150 (R. Hardaway ed. 1991).
[21] Robert Baker, Airline Operations, in Handbook of Airline Economics 307, 310, 311 (D. Jenkins ed. 1995).

feedback, recognition and rewards for exemplary performance.[22] Managers are given autonomy to act as entrepreneurs and exercise initiative, and employees are encouraged to work as a team with a common goal.[23] In a labor-intensive service industry like commercial aviation, highly motivated employees are vitally important to an airline's ability to enjoy cost savings via efficiency and productivity, and enhance revenue by pleasing high-yield customers.

Safety first, then punctuality, appear to be the primary objectives of air transport service for most airlines, although economic imperatives may sometimes conflict with these worthy goals. Management must never lose sight of the fact that commercial aviation is a labor-intensive service industry. In an industry with so much human contact between line personnel and consumers as commercial aviation, the attitude, courtesy and friendliness of flight crew, ticketing personnel, and reservationists can be more important to customers than the quality of the food served (particularly as airlines serve less and less food, and spend less and less on what they do serve).

Yet airlines are also among that category of businesses which are 24-hours-a-day, seven-days-a-week, 365-days-a-year enterprises, without a break even for Thanksgiving or Christmas. The hours can be long. The time zone changes between the cities where flight personnel crawled out of bed that morning and fall into bed that evening can be vast. Body temperature reaches a high during mid-day, and a low at night. Sleep-inducing melatonin is not naturally released from the penal gland into the bloodstream when the body is exposed to sunlight. For every one-hour time-zone difference, the body requires one day to adjust its biological clock. Thus jet lag is a serious problem for airline employees. Flight personnel flying across time zones several days in a row may suffer from fatigue.

Flight crews without seniority can be denied the opportunity to spend time with their families on weekends or holidays. That, of course, is why seniority is so dear to flight employees—it determines where and when they fly (whether they layover in Paris or Lubbock), in what aircraft, and in what position on the aircraft. Some senior captains fly fewer than 15 days a month. But any business run on a

---

[22] Thomas Peters & Robert Waterman, Jr., In Search of Excellence (1982).
[23] Robert Waterman, Jr., The Renewal Factor: How the Best Get and Keep the Competitive Edge (1987).

Operations: Product Delivery

24-hour a day basis, day in and day out, is likely to have a discontent work force. Hence, the high rate of unionization in the airline industry, which not only drives up salaries and benefits, but limits cross-utilization of personnel.

Salaries and benefits are important in motivating employees. Dr. Ludwig Lederer, American Airlines' physician in the 1970s, observed, "the pilot's life is founded on three things: sex, seniority, and salary, in that order."[24] Most major airlines pay their employees well, and offer them an attractive health care and retirement package. The fact that new entrants can attract qualified flight crews at significantly less generous levels of wages, and significantly more flexible work rules suggests that established employees at mature airlines are well compensated. Free "space available" travel for an employee and his or her family is also a perquisite of airline employment, and one that costs the airline little. For these things, management tends to believe the employees should give the airline's customers their very best. But while many airline employees like the wage and benefits package enough not to leave the airline (despite the inconveniences described above), their attitude may not reach management's expectations. This requires hiring the right people, and continually motivating employees to give airline customers the highest level of service.

The problem is further compounded because most of the flight personnel with whom passengers will come into contact are largely unsupervised. The Captain may be designated "boss", but he or she sits in the left seat in the cockpit, while the flight attendants distribute food and drink in the cabin (although in larger aircraft, the flight attendants will have a designated supervisor in the cabin). The problem is further compounded because large airlines (like most large corporations) can be vast, impersonal, bureaucratic institutions. One additional problem is that profitability turned sharply south under deregulation, putting pressure on management not only to cap wages, but to lower them. Hypocrisy can elevate the level of labor-management acrimony, as when the CEO's wage and benefits package is in the tens of millions of dollars as he seeks to trim employee salaries. At the negative extreme, with a leverage buy-out or asset cannibalization or an

---

[24] Thomas Petzinger, Jr., Hard Landing 221 (1995).

Chapter 5

effort by management to bust a union, employees can be motivated to sabotage service levels, driving away high-yield business travelers.

Thus, the fundamental challenge of airline management is to motivate these large numbers of somewhat inherently discontent and unsupervised employees to exude courtesy and friendliness to the airline's customers. Culturally, the Asian airline cabin crews are inclined to give business travelers a level of subservient "TLC" (tender loving care) usually not attainable with North American or European cabin crews. Singapore Airlines surveyed consumers to ascertain the dozen or so factors which determined which airline they selected. It found service to be an important factor, particularly among business travelers, or anyone flying very long trips. It introduced the "Singapore Girl," a flight attendant culturally attuned to making her guests feel comfortable. While in the West, many may view such behavior as chauvinistic, the fact remains that business travelers tend to rate Asian airlines as among the very best in the world.

How can management incentivize its employees to give its customers their very best? At the outset, screening potential employees based on their appearance, demeanor, ability to communicate, diligence, dedication, perfection, sense of humor, people skills and such—to place each person hired into the position where they will perform best. Once hired, proper training is essential—training as to safety, distribution of food, beverages, magazines, pillows, head sets, and so on. Safety training is required of airline flight personnel by the FAA on a regular basis. Service training, including attitude, motivation, courtesy, and friendliness, should be coupled with it. Line personnel must also be coached on how to solve their passengers' problems, or if they cannot be solved, to diplomatically placate discontent travelers, and how important it is to bring them back as repeat customers, even the grumpy ones. For example, in 1991 Northwest inaugurated its Northbest University training program for its customer service personnel in an attempt to overcome its "Northworst" service reputation.[25]

Given that there are few means of product differentiation, such subtleties as employee attitude, positive or negative, can be extremely important in the firm's long term success, particularly with higher

---

[25] Morgan Stanley, Northwest Airlines (Oct. 31, 1994), at 2.

yield customers. John Nance, a pilot, lawyer and author, eloquently described the fundamental challenge of airlines on the issue of service:

> Airline customers tend to be fickle. Like a coquettish, adolescent girl, the allegiance of most passengers will shift like the wind in the face of lower fares, different departure times, different aircraft, or indifferent service. A business traveler may fly an airline . . . for years before a problem occurs, but as a result of a lost bag, a botched connection, a lost reservation, or a myriad of other potential problems, only a forceful and professional attempt to make amends will rescue his or her business for the future. Present such a person with indifferent attitudes or lackadaisical, uninterested effort to solve his or her problem and you have created an enemy—a passenger who will consciously avoid your airline and, what's worse, communicate to anyone who will listen how lousy and incompetent and perpetually late, etc. your airline always is . . . . One wave in a sea of smooth service and on-time arrivals can leave an airline's reputation in irreparable ruin with that one customer (and whomever he or she can influence).[26]

Airline studies show that Nance is absolutely right. When passengers receive good service, they may tell as many as five other people about it. But when they receive poor service, they tell an average of 9 to 13 people about it.[27] Thus good service rewards an airline, while poor service harms an airline more.

Of the established old trunk line carriers, Delta managed to keep the peace best, with a kind and gentle corporate culture which, until the 1990s, laid off no employees, and paid them as well or better than their

---

[26] John Nance, Splash of Colors 98 (1984).
[27] Aviation Daily (May 15, 1996), at 265.

counterparts at rival airlines. For this, the employees produced better than average customer service, and except for the pilots, steered clear of unions, enabling the company to enjoy higher levels of efficiency. Few companies enjoyed a work force so proud to be affiliated with it (only Coors beer employees come to mind). Delta's employees worked for Delta Air Lines, and were proud of it. At one point, the employees put a down payment on a Boeing 767 from their own paychecks and presented it to the company.[28] But the imperatives of cost-cutting may well amend that kinder, gentler corporate culture into something different from what it has been.[29]

Southwest Airlines offers almost no in-flight amenities. With its short stage lengths, its customers are handed a cup of cola and a bag of peanuts, or on longer flights, vanilla wafers and peanut butter cookies. Thus, attitude, friendliness and courtesy become even more important. Southwest accomplishes that in a somewhat novel, but effective, way. Southwest will not open a new market until it has the "right" people (people with good attitudes and team spirit) in place. From the moment an individual is selected for a set of interviews, every Southwest employee with whom he or she comes into contact (including reservationists, ticketing personnel, and flight personnel) evaluates the candidate's appearance, demeanor, courtesy, friendliness, and sense of humor. At the end of a series of interviews, the candidate is handed a photograph of Southwest Airlines CEO Herb Kelleher dressed in "drag." If they do not laugh, they are not hired. Kelleher tells this story:

> The People Department came to me one day and said, 'We've interviewed 34 people for this ramp agent's position, and we're getting a little worried about the time and effort and cost that's going into it.' And I said if you have to interview 134 people to get the right person, do it.[30]

---

[28] Thomas Petzinger, Jr., Hard Landing 390 (1995).
[29] See Paul Stephen Dempsey and Laurence E. Gesell, Air Transportation: Foundations for the 21st Century (1997), Chapter 3.
[30] Tim Ferguson, Airline Asks Government for Room to Keep Rising, Wall St. J., Mar. 9, 1993, at A17.

Operations: Product Delivery

Further, once hired, they are introduced to the avant-garde atmosphere of "fun," with Kelleher playing comedian in employee video tapes (sometimes done in rap) and appearances. Flight attendants have been known to sing the safety drill to the tune of the *William Tell Overture*, or to pop out of overhead storage bins to surprise passengers.[31] Every payroll check is inscribed with the words, "From Our Customers," to remind the employee of whom is buttering their bread.[32] Although 84% of Southwest's employees are union members, the company enjoys high productivity and is spared much of the labor-management acrimony that exists at rival airlines.[33]

Donald Burr's People Express attempted a similar strategy. Though its passengers were charged for coffee (fifty cents) and checked bags (three dollars), People Express attempted to provide good service by hiring friendly people and motivating them to be passionate about serving the customer. Warm service arguably costs the airline nothing more to provide, and makes a favorable impression upon the customer. According to Burr, the friendly attitudes would be the ultimate frill when flying his no-frills airline.[34]

Sir Colin Marshall introduced sensitivity training at British Airways with the title "Putting People First." Employees were guided through game and role playing exercises to educate them as to how passengers felt and to take responsibility for solving a passenger's problem. Marshall began distributing buttons which said, "I Fly the World's Favourite Airline," a goal, more than a actual fact. He brought in marketing people from Mars candies to help the company differentiate its first and business class products.[35]

Several airlines have attempted to instill employee dedication by giving them stock in the company. As the value of the stock rises, employee morale improves. As it falls, morale can deteriorate.[36]

Yet another technique is for the airline to give employee "thank you" cards to its frequent flyers. A traveler favorably impressed with

---

[31] Bridget O'Brian, Southwest Airlines Is A Rare Air Carrier: It Still Makes Money, Wall St. J., Oct. 26, 1992, at A1, A7.
[32] Thomas Petzinger, Jr., Hard Landing 288 (1995).
[33] Tim Ferguson, Airline Asks Government for Room to Keep Rising, Wall St. J., Mar. 9, 1993, at A17.
[34] Thomas Petzinger, Jr., Hard Landing 115 (1995).
[35] Id. at 348, 349.
[36] See Paul Stephen Dempsey and Laurence E. Gesell, Air Transportation: Foundations for the 21st Century (1997), Chapter 3.

service gives a card to the employee, who gives it to his or her supervisor. A system of rewards can be installed for accumulating a number of these cards, or unsolicited "Orchid letters" praising service from customers. Supervisors can surreptitiously fly as passengers, observing individual levels of service. Monitoring in large institutions can be difficult; but it is not impossible.

One means of destroying service is to merge airlines, with different corporate cultures, operational etiquette, and fleets. Several carriers have done this. When Northwest acquired Republic (itself the product of mergers of North Central, Republic and Hughes Airwest only a few years before), management had to put together 14 union groups, several incompatible fleets, and corporate cultures. A middle manager observed, "The results of the discontent are pushing us dangerously close to self-destruction."[37] Lorenzo's attempted overnight merger of Continental (which had already absorbed Texas International), New York Air, People Express, Frontier, Britt and PBA was the worst of all:

> Suddenly Continental had 32 different galley configurations in its fleet. Continental meal trays wouldn't fit into Frontier's warming carts. People with tickets on Continental found themselves boarding bright red New York Air planes. Passengers at Newark were herded from gate to gate as cancellations mounted. People Express employees were assigned to Continental flights with no idea how to operate Jetways. Golf bags, skis, and luggage of every shape and variety began to accumulate in a warehouse of lost bags in Houston. The entire system ran late all day long.
>
> Lorenzo had not foreseen the worst problem of all: scheduling the newly swollen and far-flung work force. As with so much else in airlines, crew scheduling creates a reverse economy of scale: the bigger the operation, the more

---

[37] Thomas Petzinger, Jr., Hard Landing 365 (1995).

difficult, costly, and inefficient it becomes. Pilots and flight attendants, calling in for new assignments as flight cancellations worsened, encountered busy signals, meaning they could not be reassigned, causing still more flights to be canceled. There's no such thing as a half-broken airline.[38]

Deteriorating employee morale can be debilitating to passenger service. The Bonderman group, which took Continental Airlines out of its second Chapter 11 bankruptcy filing in 1993, swept senior managerial positions clean of many former Lorenzo managers (as Hollis Harris had done when he became Continental's CEO as Lorenzo departed). When Gordon Bethune (whose resume included senior positions at Piedmont Airlines and Boeing) took over Continental, he sought to turn morale around. He eliminated unprofitable routes, jettisoned CALite, grounded uneconomical jets, closed ground stations, postponed a scheduled raise, and out-sourced maintenance. But by communicating with workers and bringing workers into the decision-making process, focusing on measurable performance standards (e.g., on-time flights), and providing employees with modest financial bonuses when the goals were met ($65 in any month when Continental met on-time performance standards), sick leave dropped 20%, on-the-job injuries fell, and employment applications rose. Employees began to work together, infighting subsided, and performance improved. Morale increased so much, the labor groups chipped in to buy Bethune a $22,000 Harley-Davidson motorcycle as a Christmas present. According to Bethune, "You ever heard of a successful company that doesn't have a good product, that doesn't have employees who like to work there?"[39]

To improve operational and financial performance, Aloha Airlines adopted a bonus program tying compensation based on each managers' performance in its Economic Value Added unit, encouraging managers

---

[38] Id. at 322.
[39] Scott McCartney, Piloted By Bethune, Continental Air Lifts Its Workers' Morale, Wall St. J., May 15, 1996, at A1, A4.

to think and act like owners. If a manager increases his costs without increasing his revenues, he must explain the result to himself.[40]

Stephen Shaw expressed the role of employee morale in the quality of the product delivered in these terms:

> An airline can achieve long-term gains in market share if it is successful in motivating and training its customer service staff to give outstanding levels of personal service. It will also do it if it can achieve 'brand' rather than 'commodity' status . . . . Airlines are service businesses, and the aspects of the product relating to service will therefore be all-important. An airline with poorly motivated staff facing competition from another airline not having this problem will steadily lose market share. Correcting a problem of poor staff motivation will probably take many years. During all that time, the airline will be vulnerable.[41]

CABIN SERVICE

In-flight service opportunities are limited, for with the exception of the Concorde at one end, or the turboprop carriers at the other, airlines fly essentially the same aircraft. How, then, does one carrier distinguish its product from another's? And given the extremely slim historical profit margins the industry has suffered since deregulation, how much service can an airline provide without driving up its costs excessively.

To distinguish itself as "better," the airline can offer passengers multiple-class service, better seat pitch, wider seats, leather upholstery, leg rests, telephones, interactive video, movies, garment bag closets, better food, free liquor, pillows, blankets, newspapers, magazines, separate ticketing, priority boarding and baggage delivery, and a more plentiful supply of charming, gregarious and helpful flight attendants.

---

[40] Statement of Glenn Zander Before the 11th Annual Salomon Bros. Transportation Conference (New York, N.Y., Nov. 13, 1996).
[41] Stephen Shaw, Airline Marketing & Management 155, 156 (3rd ed. 1990).

Operations: Product Delivery

Once they land, a carrier can offer shower, valet, and breakfast facilities, and complimentary access to airport club facilities. Generally speaking, the longer the trip, the more likely a carrier will offer several of these amenities, even for coach passengers, for carriers understand they need to do more to satisfy and entertain a passenger seated for hours and hours. Thus, international service is characterized by more generous pitch and free liquor and movies, even in coach. Conversely, Southwest Airlines offers nearly none of these cabin amenities (except for the friendly flight attendants) on its relatively short stage-lengths.

American Airline's service planning is predicated on a notion that American should attempt to provide a perceptibly superior passenger service than its competitors. According to Crandall, "We seek to convince all travelers that American is the best airline, and to build an image as the standard of excellence in domestic commercial aviation."[42] Recognizing that long-haul international routes accounted for 18% of its revenue and 30% of its profits, American spent $400 million upgrading its international business class to enhance seat pitch (with 75% more space) and comfort (computer-designed lumbar support and padded leg rests), and provide its passengers with interactive video and computer services (personal 8mm Hi-Fi Stereo VCRs, and a variety of movies for personal use), a wider variety of menu choices and eating times, and upon arrival at selected airports, shower facilities.[43] Since the airline industry is a service industry, having service-oriented friendly employees dedicated to customer satisfaction is critical. Each of American Airlines' top managers in its Latin American division is a native of the country in which they work.[44] Focusing on business customer comfort enables it to attract a higher proportion of high-yield business travelers than its rivals. By covering its fixed costs in the first and business classes, it can offer coach class seats at ASM costs competitive with those of its upstart non-union rivals.

Several carriers have redesigned, reconfigured and re-marketed their business class service, particularly on international routes. For

---

[42] Robert Crandall, Marketing Planning, in Airline Economics 231, 245, 246 (George James ed. 1982).
[43] Scott McCartney, American Air To Refurbish Business Class, Wall St. J., Feb. 8, 1996, at B8.
[44] Scott McCartney, Latin America Pays Big Dividends for American Airlines, Wall St. J., June 4, 1996, at B4.

example, USAirways introduced a new business class, called "Envoy."[45]

British Airways also has gone to great lengths to distinguish its upper classes of services. Of course, the British, being very class conscious, would. BA issues First Class passengers cotton pajamas on trans-Atlantic flights. At Heathrow and Gatwick Airports, British Airways established "Club World" in 1993, which at its arrival lounges at Heathrow and Gatwick Airports includes showers, changing rooms, breakfast, clothes pressing, and valet service.[46] (Its competitor, Virgin Airlines, offers its passengers a facial and massage in Virgin's Victorian-style bathhouse).[47] British Airways spent $117 million adding luxurious individual First Class cabins designed by a yacht builder. British Airways offers the "Cradle Seat," claiming it is "the most comfortable international business class seat," and the only bed in the air, offering anyone 25,000 frequent flyer miles who tries it and explains why it is not.[48]

Similarly, Air France added a new first-class cabin named "L'Espace 180," which has 180° reclining seats to make a horizontal bed, and "L'Espace 127," in business class, allowing a 127° recline. British Airways offers a 135° recline in its business class. Air France also focuses on the foods of France's provinces, showing videos of the provinces while the food is presented. In British Airways' first class, passengers can order whatever food they want (from caviar to steak to pasta) whenever they want it. The sauces are specially prepared for high altitude service, where taste buds are 30% less effective.[49]

Of course supersonic Concorde service sets British Airways and Air France apart from other major carriers on the North Atlantic. The major advantage is speed—like Superman, it flies at twice the velocity of a speeding bullet. But the cabin is small, seating is cramped, and the price from New York to London is about $4,500, some $2,400 more than a First Class seat on a sub-sonic flight.[50]

---

[45] David Field, USAir Changes More Than Cosmetic, USA Today, Nov. 13, 1996, at 3B.
[46] Thomas Petzinger, Jr., Hard Landing 398 (1995).
[47] Dana Milbank, Airlines Are Plunging Into Shower Wars, Wall St. J., Mar. 31, 1995, at B9.
[48] Advertisement, Wall St. J., May 16, 1996, at A13.
[49] New Needs, New Service, Air Transport World (Apr. 1996), at 36.
[50] Carl Quintanilla, Unsold Seats Sully Concorde's Snooty Image, Wall St. J., Feb. 23, 1996, at B1.

Seat pitch on American Airlines' international First Class is 62 inches, which is sufficient room for a full horizontal recline, while international business class has been expanded from 40 to 50 inches. Continental's hybrid business class has a 55-inch pitch with French-designed sleeper seats; Delta's trans-Atlantic business class has a 40-42 inch pitch.[51] Continental also upgraded its dining fare in its BusinessFirst cabin, and added a long wine list.

Japan Airlines is spending $95,000 a piece on new bathrooms for its New York-Tokyo flights. The bathrooms will be about 1.5 times as large as existing ones, will have their own windows, softer lighting, background music and better water faucets.[52] UltrAir added a long-stem rose in the lavatory.[53]

UltrAir was an interesting experiment. It attempted to cater to business travelers, offering gourmet meals, free drinks and other amenities for full-fare tickets. Passengers loved the service, but there weren't enough of them to keep the company flying more than six months. Passengers apparently prefer lower ticket prices, frequency, and frequent flyer programs over in-flight service.[54]

While UltrAir collapsed six months after it was born, Midwest Express apparently is succeeding. Launched in 1984 by Kimberly-Clark, Midwest Express is a high cost (10 cents) high yield (16 cents) carrier which offers spacious seating (single class 2-2 abreast seating and 33-34 inch pitch in its DC-9 and MD-80 fleet), and gourmet food (spending $10.24 per meal, compared with the industry's average of $4.61).[55] Fifty-five percent of its customers are business travelers, higher than the industry average.[56] It has been ranked the nation's best airline in consumer polls.

Whatever the improvements for the bourgeoisie in First or Business Class, the proletariat is packed together in Coach like peanut-fed sardines. If the FAA would allow it, many airlines would sell standing room in the aisle, causing aircraft to more closely resemble subway

---

[51] Scott McCartney, American Air To Refurbish Business Class, Wall St. J., Feb. 8, 1996, at B8.
[52] Aviation Daily (May 9, 1996), at 235.
[53] James Hirsch, Airlines Bet That Pampering Passengers Will Build Loyalty, Soften Fare Increases, Wall St. J., Feb. 17, 1993, at B1.
[54] Upscale UltrAir Makes Its Final Flight After 6 Months As a Scheduled Carrier, Wall St. J., July 26, 1993, at B4.
[55] Donna Rosato, Midwest Express Revs Its Engine, USA Today, Sept. 22, 1995, at 3B.
[56] Julius Maldutis, Midwest Express Holdings Inc.—A New Nichee (Nov. 9, 1995).

cars during rush hour commute. While many airlines have upgraded First and Business Class seats, improved seating has not found its way into the coach cabin. Seat manufacturers have squeezed three inches out of the front-to-back profile of coach seats; but this has translated into more seats in the cabin rather than more leg-room for passengers (the exception being TWA, or international flights). Though a new video system can cost $3,000 per seat, or about double the cost of a new seat, airlines invest in video systems rather than seats because video produces revenue.[57]

TWA's service deteriorated horribly with the labor animosity created during Carl Icahn's ownership of the company, and the strike he took with the flight attendant's union in 1986. After Icahn, TWA sought to restore service and differentiate its product by offering enhanced leg room, removing 8% of its seats. The company exchanged common stock for wage and work rule concessions. In 1994, J.D. Power & Associates named TWA the top domestic carrier for long flights.[58]

Nonetheless, for short flights, customers appear willing to forego service. Many major airlines have removed meals for flights of less than two hours. Southwest offers rock bottom fares for short flights with no meals, and has made a profit all but two years in the last quarter century doing it. It tells its customers to "Enjoy a great meal at your favorite restaurant with the money you save."[59]

From 1989-1991, Northwest spent $200 million refurbishing aircraft interiors, improving food service, installing in-seat air phones, improving airport lounges, and enhancing flight punctuality, in an effort to improve its "Northworst" service image.[60]

Aer Lingus changed its interior into a new color scheme, with writings from famous Irish authors embroidered into the seat covers, and an upgraded Premiere (business) class with leather seats and crystal dinnerware. The staff was also retrained to provide better service. Thus, Aer Lingus launched an integrated package of a more distinct

---

[57] Scott McCartney, They Can Build a Better Plane Seat, But Nor for Coach, Wall St. J., June 28, 1996, at B1.
[58] Michael McCarthy, TWA, Out of Bankruptcy Court, Struggles to Take Off, Wall St. J., July 27, 1994, at B4.
[59] Southwest Airlines Co., 1994 Annual Report 5 (1994).
[60] Morgan Stanley, Northwest Airlines (Oct. 31, 1994), at 2.

visual image, upgraded business class, and upgraded service personnel.[61]

When USAir consumed Piedmont, its loyal customers were most concerned with whether USAir would continue Piedmont's practice of giving passengers the full can of Coca-Cola, rather than just a cup. That one example reflects how far consumer expectations have fallen. The point is, today, it does not take much service to stand out as being better.

Air travel is a credence good, meaning that consumers have no opportunity to examine it prior to purchase. While many consumers may not purchase one airline's product over another's based on promises of better service, many will steer clear of an airline that has treated them badly. Consumers can be turned off by late arrivals and departures, dirty planes, inedible food, and embittered employees.

AUXILIARY IN-FLIGHT SERVICES

Movie theaters apparently merely break even on admissions vis-à-vis film rental, making their profit on overpriced soft drinks, pop corn and candy. Hotels also find revenue centers in restaurants, liquor, pay television, telephones, and room and valet services.

Airlines have slowly learned that the captive passenger strapped to a seat can be a source of income, selling passengers alcohol, headsets and movies, duty free products, telephone service, as well as catalog sales. The in-flight magazine and video entertainment also offer a source of advertising revenue. Only Laker Skytrain and People Express explored the possibility of selling food, although this seems a natural source of potential revenue, particularly if the food is good. MarkAir charged $1.00 for a soft drink. People Express also imposed a $3 charge per checked bag, a requirement which caused its price-conscious travelers to cram every nook and cranny of the cabin with carry-on luggage.

Passengers are a trapped and un-tapped audience. They have few opportunities for diversion from boredom—eating, sleeping, or reading. In the future, individualized interactive video will allow carriers to generate revenue from passengers playing video games, scanning com-

---

[61] Douglas Nelms, Imaging's New Demands, Air Transport World (Apr. 1996), at 34-36.

puter libraries, communicating with their offices, word processing, "surfing the net", in-flight shopping, or, on international flights, gambling (though Congress has eliminated the latter option on U.S. flights).[62] With the swipe of a credit card, the passenger may play. If gambling ships can depart from Ft. Lauderdale and sail out beyond the two-mile limit for its patrons to gamble, why cannot airlines offer gambling when flying over international waters? Already, Singapore Airlines, Virgin Atlantic, and British Airways are offering in-flight gambling.[63] One in five passengers would gamble if given the opportunity.[64] It has been estimated that U.S. carriers could earn another $300 million a year in new revenue if the gambling ban were lifted, without imposing any significant safety burden of air travel.[65] There may also be some effort to convert the belly of the aircraft and its upper deck into sleeping berths on long-distance flights.

Interactive communications technologies are increasingly available, including telephone, fax, and e-mail, on an air-to-ground, ground-to-air, seat-to-seat and plane-to-plane basis.[66] It seems there may be no where one may go to get away from the telephone.

AUXILIARY NON-FLIGHT SERVICES

American Airlines has turned to its various non-flight subsidiaries as profit centers, generating revenue from computer reservations systems, education, consulting, and such. The economies of scale associated with aircraft maintenance, ground handling and catering services have long been profit centers for airlines. Additionally, air freight is also a growing profit center for combination carriers.

Airlines have also found the sale of frequent flyer miles to various businesses (from long-distance telephone companies, to hotels, to car rental companies, to florists, and so on) to be a lucrative source of income. Airline miles appear to have replaced green stamps as the public's collection of choice. Airlines also team up with credit card companies to award a mile earned for each dollar charged. American

---

[62] Michael McCarthy, In-Flight Gambling Is Ready To Take Off, Wall St. J., May 24, 1996, at B1.
[63] Aviation Daily (Apr. 15, 1996), at 87.
[64] Timothy Ito, Flying? Consider the Odds, U.S. News & World Rep. (Dec. 23, 1996), at 50.
[65] Aviation Daily (Apr. 17, 1996), at 105.
[66] Calmetta Coleman, Fliers Balk At Taking Calls In the Air, Wall St. J., June 23, 1995, at B1.

Operations: Product Delivery

Airlines inaugurated a diner's card, offering three miles per dollar charged at selected restaurants across the nation.

BUNDLED TRAVEL SERVICES

The tour and travel industry is the largest in the world. Air transportation is one essential component of that industry. Hotels and automobile rentals are two of the other major pieces. On most business or vacation trips, a passenger needs all three—air transportation, a hotel, and, often, a rental car.

Several airlines have purchased hotels in the past (e.g., United owned Westin; American owned Americana; TWA owned Hilton International; Pan Am owned InterContinental; Air France owned Meridien). United Airlines' Richard Ferris blundered by trying to assemble a travel network of hotel chains and car rental chains under a single roof, called "Allegis." Airline people seem not to know how to run hotel and car rental companies any better than hotel and car rental executives know how to run airlines. That was one mistake Ferris made. The other was UAL's wholesale failure to integrate the companies from both a marketing and operational standpoint. Virtually every airline that owned a major hotel chain eventually jettisoned it. In some instances, corporate raiders have seen more value in the liquidation of independent properties exceeding their integrated value.

But conceptually, such vertically integrated "seamless travel" is an intriguing possibility. Suppose one airline had the foresight to bring seamless, vertically integrated travel under a single umbrella, offering integrated one-stop shopping, discounts with affiliated hotel and car rental companies, and seamless service, distributed as a package through computer reservations systems. Newspaper advertisements would offer bundled air-hotel-automobile discounts.

Suppose a customer called an airline's reservations agent to book a flight, and was asked, "Will you also be needing a hotel or rental car? Since you booked your flight on our airline, we can give you a 20% discount at the following hotels, and another 20% discount at the following car rental agencies. Moreover, when you arrive at your destination, you can go straight to your hotel. We will collect your bags at the airport and deliver them later in the afternoon to your hotel room. Or if you prefer, we'll put them into the trunk of your rental car."

A passenger could take advantage of one-stop shopping, thereby lowering his or her transactions costs. Additionally, bundled products would be presented in such a way that the consumer would purchase an integrated travel itinerary with the belief s/he was enjoying a discount on affiliated product lines, and would be free of the enormous hassles of bags. S/he could take the golf clubs or skis, but be spared the burden of heavy lifting.

In the same way that business travelers become addicted to particular product lines because of frequent flyer mileage, business travelers might applaud a system which would permit them to go straight from their destination airport to their business meetings, allowing their bags to catch up with them later that afternoon at the hotel. Convenience and time savings would be the hallmark of such a bundled travel product. Consumers already prefer aviation to other modes of transport because it saves the most valuable commodity a human being has—time.

Charter and tour group operators have long provided bundled products, for many travelers to foreign countries want an experienced provider to assemble the hotel and transfer portion of the itinerary.

All airlines recognize that consumers detest handling bags. Airlines provide as much in-cabin baggage space as possible. They ensure swift and efficient baggage transfer between themselves and their commuter and code-sharing affiliates. Yet remarkably few scheduled airlines have offered baggage transfer from their aircraft to hotels or automobile rental companies.

Integration would have to take place along marketing and operational lines. Joint advertising and joint discounts are easy. The operational dimension is the trickiest and most critical, because passengers also detest lost bags. So, monitoring would be essential, perhaps coupled with performance based employee rewards.

But the economies of scope are manifest. Airlines already employ a platoon of baggage handling personnel at every airport. Computer technology would allow tagging at check-in of those bags going to specific hotels or car rental companies. The tags could be florescent orange, if necessary. Car rental companies already have reservations and operations personnel who could collect bags and put them into the trunks of cars. Hotels already have vans and porters to collect bags. The vans could be sent to meet each incoming flight, and the hotel concierge could guide the passengers to the van in the way tour groups are met.

Like most of the innovations airlines have inaugurated, if successful, it will be copied. Therefore, to get the jump on competitors, the first to embrace seamless travel should identify those hotel chains and car rental companies which business travelers prefer most, and lock those up in an equity and marketing marriage, whereby they trade, say, a block of airline stock for an equally valued block of hotel and/or car rental stock. That would allow each to earn a profit on the other's business, enjoying significant mutual synergistic marketing advantages.

Customers would get what they have always wanted. They could sit back and relax and leave the least pleasant parts of the journey to the airline, for which they would express their gratitude and loyalty in repeat business to increase load factors and core business. The affiliated hotels and car rental companies would also prosper, and the dividends earned on their stock should reflect it.

WHO'S GOT THE BEST PRODUCT?

Most anecdotal evidence suggests a near-universal deterioration of airline service quality since deregulation, as financial collapse has mandated draconian cost cutting. Meals have been eliminated on many flights, and cabin crews have been reduced to FAA minimums. For example, United upped the mileage requirement for a snack from 251 miles to 501 miles, and upped the mileage requirement for a hot meal from 501 miles to 701 miles. Compared with 1992, U.S. airline spending for food dropped $368 million in 1996, from an average of $5.60 per meal to less than $4.50.[67] So, there's less food, and when it's served, it's cheaper food. All of the turbulence in labor/management relations engendered by cost-cutting, mergers and acquisitions has found its way into the cabin as well. One survey revealed that 41% of travelers had experienced a decline in airline service quality.[68]

Several independent organizations rank airlines in order of consumer preference. Perhaps the most important of these is the Zagat

---

[67] Edwin McDowell, How Far Will You Go For a Hot Meal?, N.Y. Times, Aug. 11, 1996.
[68] Moonkyu Lee & Lawrence Cunningham, Customer Loyalty in the Airline Industry, 50 Transp. Q. 57 (1996).

Airline Survey, which polls abut 5,000 business travelers (which, as everyone knows, are the high-yield segment of the market) asking them to rank carriers on comfort, service, on-time performance, food and price. It has ranked the world's airlines as shown in Table 5.1, "Zagat Airline Survey: Foreign Carriers"; and Table 5.2, "Zagat Airline Survey: Domestic Carriers". A score of 26-30 is excellent; 20-25 very good to excellent; 10-19 poor to very good; and 0 to 9, poor to fair. It might be noted that most U.S. carriers rank well below their foreign competitors.

Table 5.1—ZAGAT AIRLINE SURVEY: FOREIGN CARRIERS[69]

	Carrier	1990	1993	1995
1.	Singapore	25.14	25.79	25.85
2.	Swissair	23.95	24.44	23.93
3.	Cathay Pacific	not ranked	23.77	23.39
4.	JAL	22.57	23.29	22.96
5.	Qantas	22.08	22.22	22.41
6.	All Nippon	not ranked	23.03	22.18
7.	Virgin Atlantic	18.52	21.50	21.85
8.	Lufthansa	22.05	22.28	21.49
9.	KLM	21.34	21.52	21.33
10.	Finnair	not ranked	not ranked	21.25
11.	SAS	22.33	22.44	n.a.
12.	British Airways	20.54	20.71	n.a.
13.	Air France	20.50	20.79	n.a.
14.	Varig	19.94	18.92	n.a.
15.	Air Canada	18.39	18.54	n.a.
16.	El Al	16.29	17.09	n.a.
17.	Alitalia	16.74	16.69	n.a.
18.	Air India	not ranked	13.60	n.a.
19.	Olympic	13.43	12.90	n.a.
20.	Aeroflot	7.31	6.16	n.a.

---

[69] Data culled from Fliers Take Turn As Airline Critics, Chicago Tribune, Sept. 7, 1990, at 1C; Carol Smith, Frequent Fliers Are Looking for comfort, Los Angeles Times, Mar. 9, 1995, at D5.

Operations: Product Delivery

Table 5.2—ZAGAT AIRLINE SURVEY: DOMESTIC CARRIERS[70]

Carrier	1990	1993	1995
1. Midwest Express	not ranked	19.05	23.38
2. Alaska	not ranked	21.75	20.95
3. Kiwi International	not ranked	not ranked	18.95
4. American	18.62	18.37	18.16
5. Delta	18.12	18.33	18.10
6. United	16.61	17.09	17.35
7. Reno	not ranked	not ranked	16.97
8. America West	not ranked	16.26	16.49
9. Midway	16.54	--	16.43
10. Northwest	13.95	15.37	16.37
11. Southwest	not ranked	14.78	n.a.
12. USAir	13.73	14.62	n.a.
13. TWA	14.91	13.34	n.a.
14. Piedmont	15.11	--	--
15. Pan Am	14.69	--	--
16. Eastern	10.66	--	--

Consumer Reports magazine has also placed airlines on its annual questionnaire, asking its 100,000 readers to evaluate check-in, seat and leg room, crowding, flight attendant service, baggage handling and on-time arrival. Its 1994 survey ranked U.S. airlines, from best to worst, as shown in Table 5.3, "Consumer Reports Rankings Of Airlines".

One other ranking uses 19 categories of "objective" government data to assess carrier on-time performance, accidents, customer service, the age of each carrier's fleet, lost bags, overbooking and financial stability. The Annual Quality Rating survey is conducted by Brent Bowen of the University of Nebraska's Aviation Institute, and Dean Headley of the National Institute for Aviation Research at Wichita State University. Its results are as shown on Table 5.4, "University of Nebraska/Wichita State Airline Quality Rating".

---

[70] Id.

Table 5.3—CONSUMERS REPORT RANKING OF AIRLINES (1994)[71]

1. Midwest Express
2. Alaska
3. Kiwi International
4. Southwest
5. Reno Air
6. Aloha
7. Delta
8. TWA
9. Horizon Air
10. American
11. Northwest
12. America West
13. USAir
14. United
15. Morris
16. Hawaiian
17. American Trans Air
18. Continental
19. Carnival
20. MarkAir

Table 5.4—UNIVERSITY OF NEBRASKA/WICHITA STATE AIRLINE QUALITY RATING[72]

Carrier	*1991*	*1992*	*1993*	*1994*	*1995*
Southwest	2	2	1	2	1
American	1	1	2	1	2
United	4	3	3	3	3
Delta	3	4	4	4	4
America West	9	7	8	7	5
Northwest	7	6	6	6	6
USAir	5	5	5	5	7
TWA	10	9	7	8	8
Continental	8	8	9	9	9
Pan Am	6	--	--	--	--

Some have criticized the appropriateness of comparing Southwest, which provides relatively little service (it has radically fewer connections and less checked baggage, and provides little food service) with the full-service network carriers—a bit like comparing apples

---

[71] Consumer Reports (June 1995), at 386.
[72] Data culled from Geographic Names, Tampa Tribune, May 21, 1995, at 6; Laura Casaneda, Southwest Airlines First In Quality Survey, Dallas Morning News, Apr. 12, 1994, at 1D; Barbara Curcio, Worldwise, Washington Post, Apr. 18, 1993, at E3; Jesus Sanchez, Study Cites Decline In Air Service, Los Angeles Times, Apr. 13, 1993, at D1; Kristin Jensen, Southwest Is Top Airline In Study, Rocky Mountain News, Apr. 16, 1996, at 8B.

with prunes. With relatively little checked baggage, less gets lost; without connections, flights are less often delayed; with no hot food, passengers cannot complain about how awful it tastes.[73] Thus, statistically Southwest may appear to offer better service, when in reality, it simply offers less of it.

From 1991-1994, Southwest Airlines won the industry's triple crown, with the best numbers on the DOT's rankings of airline on-time performance and baggage handling, and fewest consumer complaints.[74] One other ranking service is J.D. Powers & Associates which sells its results to the airlines. Only the top-ranked firm in each category can advertise the results.

---

[73] See e.g., Airline Quality: Twisted Yardstick, Consumer Reports Travel Letter (July 1994), at 158.
[74] Aviation Daily (Feb. 7, 1996), at 206.

CHAPTER 6.

THE PRICE: REVENUE AND INVENTORY MANAGEMENT

"All people really want is a cheap seat." [1]
Neil Bergt
CEO, MarkAir

"I think when airlines want to set new fares, they put their people into a room without food or water. And when they start to hallucinate, then they make the fares." [2]
Virginia Dean
President, Dean Travel Services

"The key to profitability is to have a good share of premium-class passengers." [3]
Donald Carty
President, American Airlines

---

[1] Statement by Neil Bergt made to Paul Stephen Dempsey in MarkAir's headquarters.
[2] Air-Fare War Goes On and On, Is Proving to Be a Battle of Wits, Wall St. J., June 14, 1994, at B5.
[3] Scott McCartney, American Air To Refurbish Business Class, Wall St. J., Feb. 8, 1996, at B8.

TERMINOLOGY

A discussion of the pricing dimensions of commercial aviation begins with an introduction to basic industry terminology.[4] *Yield* is a term which the industry uses to measure revenue. Yield is calculated by dividing revenue by *revenue-passenger miles* [RPM], (or $/RPM), or in cargo, revenue divided by ton-miles. Typically, yields range between 10-16 cents for the major airlines. Revenue-passengers include those flying on frequent flyer mile redemptions, but do not include gratuitous transportation. Costs are usually calculated on the basis of *available seat miles* [ASM], (or $/ASM), for the basic unit of production is a seat-mile in an individual city-pair market.[5] (For combination carriers, cargo is assumed to be handled on a break-even basis). Ordinarily, ASM costs range between 6-8 cents for new entrants, 8-11 cents for established network carriers, and 15-20 cents for regional or piston turboprop carriers. Revenue is also sometimes calculated on an ASM basis. A *break-even load factor* is the passenger load factor that will result in operating revenue being equal to operating costs. It is calculated on the basis of costs divided by revenue (ASM/RPM). Thus, a carrier with an ASM cost of 9 cents, and RPM yield of 14 cents, would have a break-even load factor of 64%. Both break-even and actual load factors usually have ranged between 60-70% over the last decade on an annualized basis. An increase in costs raises break-even load factors; an increase in yields has the opposite effect.[6]

Lee Howard and John Summerfield summarized the industry's measure of economic performance in these terms:

> Profit is defined as revenue minus expenses. Revenues can be measured or estimated as a product of traffic (for example, revenue passenger-miles) and yield (for example, revenue per revenue passenger-mile). Expenses can be measured or estimated as a product of capacity (for

---

[4] For a comprehensive glossary of air transportation terminology, see Paul Stephen Dempsey and Laurence E. Gesell, Air Transportation: Foundations for the 21st Century (1997), Chapter 10.
[5] Russell Klingaman, Predatory Pricing and Other Exclusionary Conduct in the Airline Industry, 4 DePaul Bus. L. J. 281 (1992).
[6] Air Transport Ass'n., The Airline Handbook (1993).

example, available seat-miles) and unit costs (for example, expenses per available seat-mile). The above relationship is referred to as the earnings equation and can be written in the following form.

Traffic x Yield = Operating Revenue

Capacity x Unit Cost = Operating Expense

Operating Revenue − Operating Expenses = Operating Profit

Operating Revenue ± Nonoperating Items = Net Income[7]

The concept of *price elasticity of demand* describes the enhanced price sensitivity of a leisure traveler vis-à-vis a business traveler. The law of demand suggests consumers will respond to a price decline by buying more of a given product. Consumer sensitivity to price change is referred to as *elasticity*. When price change gives rise to considerable change in consumption, demand is said to be *elastic*. Conversely, if consumers are relatively unresponsive to price change, demand is inelastic.[8] The elasticity coefficient is derived by dividing percentage change in quantity demanded by percentage change in price, to determine elasticity of demand. The result is price elasticity reflected on a continuum from elastic to perfectly elastic on the one end, and inelastic to perfectly inelastic at the other. The mid-point, where a given percentage change in price (either up or down) is exactly offset by the same percentage change in quantity, is *unitary elastic demand*.[9]

By recognizing that the market is segmented among various classes of travelers with differing demand elasiticites, a carrier can tailor a combination of price and service offerings (in this context, travel

---

[7] Lee Howard & John Summerfield, Airline Financial Forecasting, in Airline Economics 57, 58 (G. James ed. 1982). Nonoperating items include interest income and expense, capital gains and losses, taxes, accounting changes and extraordinary items. Id. at 84.
[8] Campbell R. McConnell 417 Economics: Principles, Problems, and Policies (4th ed. 1969).
[9] Martin T. Farris and Stephen K. Happel, Modern Managerial Economics 105-109 (1987).

The Price: Revenue And Inventory Management

restrictions) designed both to increase load factors (filling seats which otherwise would fly empty with discretionary travelers) and maximizing yields (charging less price sensitive, or *demand inelastic,* travelers more). For example, business travelers are less demand elastic than vacation travelers, because the cost of business travel is borne by their employer rather than themselves, it is paid with pre-tax dollars, and the company realizes potential business opportunities if such travel is made. In contrast, vacation travel is paid for with post-tax dollars by an individual, and usually consists of multiple-family members traveling (with associated costs of hotels, meals and surface transportation), and in the final analysis, is a privilege rather than a necessity.[10] Julius Maldutis succinctly summarized the impact of pricing shifts and the business cycle on demand:

> It has been proven, statistically, that total demand for domestic airline travel is price inelastic (-0.3), that is for a 10% decline in airline fares, passenger traffic will increase by 3%. Stated another way, a 10% increase in fares will reduce travel only 3%, and revenue will increase about 7%, *ceteris paribus.* Fare changes for individual markets or airlines have a particularly stimulative effect (elasticity coefficient of more than -1.0) but it is difficult to isolate effects of diversion from other modes or market share gains from other carriers. The more important determinant of air travel is disposable personal income of the consumer. Income elasticity is about 2.7, that is, for every 1% increase in real disposable income, air travel increases 2.7%.[11]

Each of these concepts is extremely important in developing an array of prices composing a regime of yield management, designed to

---

[10] Stephen Shaw, Airline Marketing & Management 46-48 (3rd ed. 1990).
[11] Julius Maldutis, Airline Update - August 1996 (Sept. 9, 1996), at 2.

produce load factors above break-even levels, and aggregate revenue above fully allocated costs.

PRICE AND DEMAND

There is a painful joke in the airline industry: "Fare wars are like city buses; if you miss one, there'll be another in 15 minutes."[12] Alfred Kahn, America's principal deregulation architect, predicted that airline deregulation would produce marginal cost pricing. It has not. Airline pricing appears to only be dimly related to costs. Factors of demand and competition are much more important in determining price.[13] Only a few years after the inauguration of deregulation, Dr. Maldutis wrote:

> In the good old regulated days, the price of an airline seat was directly related to the cost of producing it. Prices were simply based on costs, allowing for a rate of return . . . . The impact of economic recession was blunted by a benevolent Civil Aeronautics Board . . . .
>
> Since deregulation . . . the pricing structure has become much more complex. The linkage between costs and prices has been broken. The price of an airline seat has no relationship to the cost of producing it, but rather reflects the degree and nature of competition. *Costs* and *prices* have gone their separate ways. In fact, the relationship has been reversed. Airline managements are seeking to lower costs in order to match prices . . . .
>
> I respectfully submit that it was the management of airlines that precipitated price wars. Managements have become truly innovative. Fares of every shape, size and color have been developed. And, if that were not enough, product tie-ins with cameras, film,

---

[12] Carl Quintanilla, Air-Fare War Is Proving to Be a Battle of Wits, Wall St. J., June 14, 1994, at B1.
[13] Newal Taneja, Civil Aviation 145-56 (2d ed. 1989).

> breakfast cereals, and autos were brought about .... I, for one, eagerly await the ultimate in airline pricing—where the airline will pay the passenger to travel. Some airlines already provide free travel if you occasionally purchase a ticket.
>
> [L]et me identify the culprits. First, it is clear that some of the financially weak carriers have utilized deep-discount fares, both to generate cash and force the travel agent—who has become increasingly concerned with the financial viability of an airline—to to book on this carrier....
>
> Second, smaller airlines—including new entrants—have played a significant role in lowering airline fares. The lower unit costs, in con-junction with lower fares, have enabled them to obtain substantial market shares from large, established carriers and from other competitors....
>
> It would be grossly unfair to suggest that all the blame lies with the chipmunks, the smaller airlines. The King Kongs, the majors, decided to retaliate....
>
> There is another cause of airline price wars: hubs and spokes .... [They] make it possible for managements to offer competitive low fares against established carriers in the long-haul nonstop market. Someday, some poor soul will get on an airplane and will never reach his destination. He will hub and spoke forever.[14]

Charles Banfe notes, "Of all the Competitive Variables, pricing is perhaps the most complicated and transitory. It is the art of translating into quantitative terms the value of the journey to passengers at a point

---

[14] Julius Maldutis, The Airlines: $99 Forever (Apr. 1983).

in time, relative to competition."[15] Defining the appropriate price requires an assessment of consumer demand, offerings by competitors, and cost, with a keen eye on profitability. One particularly useful reference point is break-even load factor. Lowering prices stimulates demand, but raises the break-even load factor; raising prices dulls demand, but lowers the break-even load factor.

Yet the competition, or the economic cycle, often dictates the price. A competing carrier with lower costs, or needing to fill empty seats, or to secure an immediate cash infusion may well drive prices down for all carriers, for in a high fixed-cost industry like commercial aviation, none can withstand the loss of large numbers of passengers to their rivals, and will follow the price leader down to preserve market share. Yet high load factors do a carrier little good when the break-even load factor is higher still. After the disastrous and prolonged price wars of the late 1980s and early 1990s, some major airlines were willing to surrender the low-fare origin-and-destination discretionary market to low-cost new entrant rivals, recognizing that the low fares were stimulating new traffic (vacations and visiting friends and relatives [VFR] travel not otherwise viable for low-income consumers, or luring consumers out of their automobiles or intercity buses), rather than diverting existing traffic.

The market for air transportation services is highly segmented, and the demand characteristics of each are different. As noted above, the market for passenger air travel can be divided into two primary segments—business and leisure.

The business travel market may be subdivided into several segments. Employees of large corporations often are less sensitive about price than other travelers because the ticket is being paid for by someone other than the customer. However, large corporate travel departments are becoming more astute about exerting their oligopsony power to negotiate a contract rate with airlines on behalf of their employees close to the discretionary travelers' rate, but without the restrictions. Employees of small businesses, which do not have such leverage, may have less price elasticity of demand than leisure travelers, but some small businesses must watch every penny carefully. Thus, the extremely high full coach fares may be prohibitively ex-

---

[15] Charles Banfe, Airline Management 26 (1992).

pensive for some small businesses. However, business travelers are paying for travel with "before tax" dollars, which blunts the full effect of high fares.[16] Yet another segment of the business travel market is the business "trader" in developing international markets, who buys goods abroad and transports them to his home country for sale. They are less concerned with frequency and in-flight amenities than price and excess baggage allowances.[17]

The leisure travel market can also be subdivided into two segments. Leisure travelers can be highly price sensitive, for such travel is paid out of "after tax" disposable income. Individuals have many alternatives other than taking a vacation by air (they could drive to Wally World, for example, or stay home and paint the garage). Moreover, the air travel price is but one component of a vacation that may include hotels, meals and automobile rental costs, for example. Costs can multiply quickly in families with children. VFR traffic can be much less price sensitive than leisure traffic. Again, air transportation is a derived demand product. If a family illness, death, or emotional crisis is the purpose of the trip, price may not stand in the way of making the flight. A VFR traveler can often stay with a friend or relative, and need not rent a hotel room and car, unlike most vacation travelers.[18]

Demand elasticity can be divided demographically among income groups, with higher income groups less concerned about the price of air travel (for it consumes a lower percentage of their income), and having more time for vacations, than lower income groups.[19] In fact, very high income travelers may find a higher price accompanied with elite treatment an appropriate reflection of their upper class status. Thus, demand for first class travel for those who can afford it is relatively inelastic.

For cargo, air freight caters to high-value, time-sensitive shipments, because the cost of moving freight by air is high, and many goods can be routed via another mode of transport. If it is of high-value, the goods can absorb the high cost of air freight in its purchase price. If it

---

[16] Stephen Shaw, Airline Marketing & Management 30 (3rd ed. 1990).
[17] Id. at 32.
[18] Id. at 31.
[19] Id. at 46, 47.

is time-sensitive (such as perishable fish or flowers), it often must move by air or not at all.[20]

Discounted fares are targeted at discretionary (vacation) travelers. So as to dissuade business travelers from using them, they ordinarily come saddled with restrictions—non-refundability, advance purchase requirements, and Saturday night stay over obligations. However, large corporations can often negotiate a contract rate with airlines which includes the discounted fares, but is largely devoid of restrictions.[21]

Demand, and therefore pricing flexibility, can also differ geographically, depending on rates of economic growth and the degree of carrier competition. Though no longer an accurate measure for developed markets, traffic growth tends to grow at 1.5 to 2.0 times the real rate of Gross Domestic Product.[22] Thus, the trans-Pacific market, with high growth rates and restricted capacity (because of conservative bilateral air transport agreements) enjoys the highest yields of all.

Air fares at small and medium sized communities are nine percent higher, on average, than at large communities.[23] Fares are some 21% higher for trips beginning or ending at concentrated hub airports.[24] (Airlines impose the fixed cost burden disproportionately on captive traffic).[25] Fares in monopoly markets (about 10% of the total markets), are about 10% higher than competitive markets.[26] In 1992, the U.S. Department of Justice launched an antitrust investigation of the airline industry for allegedly engaging in price fixing.[27] An American Airlines vice president colorfully rebutted the contention of monopolization, saying, "We're obviously not enjoying monopoly prices because we're all losing our butts."[28]

---

[20] See Paul Stephen Dempsey and Laurence E. Gesell, Air Transportation: Foundations for the 21st Century (1997), Chapter 7.
[21] See Business and the Airlines Play Let's Make a Deal, Bus. Week (Mar. 4, 1991), at 54.
[22] ESG Aviation Services, 9 Airline Monitor 7 (Dec. 1996).
[23] Fares at Smaller Airports Show Greatest Drop Since 1978, Aviation Daily (Dec. 18, 1990), at 520.
[24] GAO, Air Fares and Service At Concentrated Airports (1989).
[25] Andrew Kleit & Stewart Maynes, Airline Networks As Joint Goods: Implications for Competition Policy, Air Law 175 (1992).
[26] The Financial Condition of the Airline Industry and the Adequacy of Competition, Hearings Before the Subcomm. on Aviation of the House Comm. on Public Works and Transportation, 102d Cong., 2d Sess. VII (1991).
[27] Asra Nomani, U.S. Steps Up Probe on Fixing of Air Fares, Wall St. J., Mar. 18, 1992, at A3.
[28] Bridget O'Brian, Airlines Seek to Earn More From an Irritated Clientele, Wall St. J., Mar. 16, 1992, at B1, B10. See Nomani, Airlines Claim Inquiry on Fares Is Unwarranted, Wall St. J., Mar. 19, 1992, at A3.

The Price: Revenue And Inventory Management

At any given time, consumers hold some $3.5 billion in prepaid tickets.[29] Hence, bankruptcies can leave many travelers stranded, literally and financially.

Despite widespread allegations that deregulation resulted in billions of dollars in consumer savings, the truth is that prices were falling faster before deregulation than after it. Inflation adjusted yields declined 2.5% annually from 1950 to 1978; they fell only 1.7 a year after 1978.[30] In the decade preceding 1978, fuel adjusted real yields fell 2.7% annually; in the decade following promulgation of the Airline Deregulation Act of that year, fuel adjusted yields declined only 1.9% a year.[31] Consumer savings allegedly resulting from deregulation are discussed in greater detail below.

Today, the airline industry prices in a highly schizophrenic way—there is evidence of monopoly, monopsony and variable cost based destructive competition side by side, as one would expect to see in a deregulated public utility. The full fare has risen to such prohibitive levels that only those who absolutely must will pay it.[32] Inequitable distortions in the pricing system force tens of thousands of people who would fly at a reasonable price simply to stay home.

---

[29] Intelligence, Aviation Daily (Feb. 25, 1991), at 359.
[30] Edmund Greenslet, World Airline Capital Requirements (address to the Chicago Convention 50th Anniversary Conference, Oct. 31, 1994).
[31] Paul Dempsey & Andrew Goetz, Airline Deregulation & Laissez Faire Mythology 243-63, 281-95 (1992). Moreover, a yield measure of pricing in the post-deregulation era overstates the consumer benefits because hubbing has made traveling more circuitous for most passengers—they fly more miles today to get from A to B through H. The linear route pre-deregulation systems were generally in a somewhat straight line. Plus, the yield number includes frequent flyer redemptions, which did not even exist pre-1978. These factors make it even more remarkable that yields fell more slowly since deregulation than before it.

Prices were falling faster before deregulation than after because costs were not declining the way they were before. In fact, poor profitability led to more leasing, which increased 300% as a portion of operating expenses in the 1980s, while travel agent commissions increased 700% (again, as a percentage of carrier operating expenses). Interest payments ascended because of more debt. Equipment and labor utilization declined because of hubbing. The average size of larger and larger aircraft (with corresponding declining ASM costs) grew until the early 1980s, then plateaued, largely because carriers needed 737 and equivalent stage length and seat capacity aircraft to feed hubs. These changes (plus the lack of a breakthrough technological revolution the equivalent of jets at Boeing and Douglas in the past 15 years) help explain why the decline in yields slowed post-deregulation.
[32] Julius Maldutis, Industry Investment Requirements—Looking Beyond 2000 (address before the 7th IATA High-Level Aviation Symposium, Sept 6-7, 1993, Cairo, Egypt).

By the end of the first decade of deregulation, the full unrestricted "Y" fare had increased 156%, double the inflation rate.[33] With the full fare rising so sharply, relatively few passengers would pay it. In 1981, 71% of all tickets were sold at a discount, with the average discount 46%.[34] A decade later, 95% of all tickets were sold at a discount, with the average discount some 66% off the full fare[35] (see Figure 6.1, "U.S. Airline Discount RPMs And Discount Yields").

Figure 6.1—U.S. AIRLINE DISCOUNT RPMs AND DISCOUNT YIELDS[36]

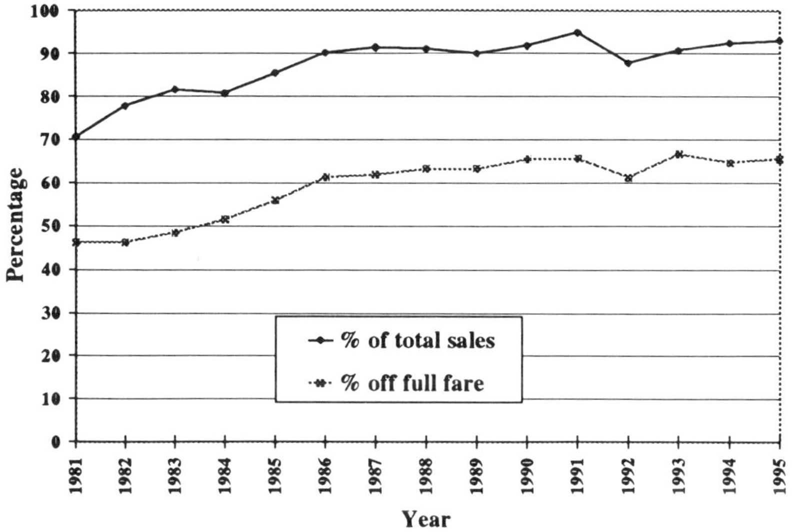

Responding to criticism that the fare structure had grown too complex, and the fact that small business employees and professionals had curtailed travel because of the excessively high price of unrestricted travel, in 1992 American Airlines attempted to simplify the fare structure under the banner of "Value Pricing." The highest fares were lowered, and the lowest raised. Fares were to be limited to four

---

[33] James Ott, Industry Officials Praise Deregulation, But Cite Flaws, Av. Week & Space Tech. (Oct. 31, 1988), at 88.
[34] Charles Banfe, Airline Management 81 (1992).
[35] Few Bright Spots in 1991 for U.S. Carriers, Aviation Daily (Dec. 16, 1991), at 466.
[36] Source: ESG Aviation Services.

tiers: (1) First Class, which would be 20%-50% lower; (2) unrestricted coach, which would be 40% lower; (3) 14-day advance purchase; and (4) 30-day advance purchase. Corporate contractual discount rates were eliminated. Although American anticipated early losses on the program, it believed Value Pricing would stimulate traffic (particularly business and professional traffic) and reduce costs.[37] According to Bob Crandall, "Customers have been alienated and aggravated by a price structure perceived as irrational, unfair and very complex."[38] Airline pricing had become akin to Crazy Eddie Antar's electronics . . . *"in-SAAAANE!"*[39]

Consumers applauded this effort to restore sanity to the chaotic pricing structure which had evolved under deregulation, and to which American Airlines had been no small contributor. But the leadership American attempted to exert to simplify the fare structure evaporated when Northwest Airlines introduced a "Grownups Fly Free" promotion. American slashed fares, halving the price of its cheapest fares, and the result was a financial blood bath for the industry as all carriers spiraled down in a free-fall to the lowest offered price.[40] Ultimately, fare proliferation re-emerged, with all of the complexity and volatility of before. A Galveston, Texas, jury promptly exonerated American Airlines from an antitrust claim brought by Northwest alleging that Value Pricing was a device employed by American to destroy its competitors.

Pricing at concentrated, gate and slot constrained airports is monopolistic, as the U.S. General Accounting Office [GAO] has well documented.[41] But not enough monopolies yet exist to cover the industry's fixed costs and offset steep discounting in competitive markets. Furthermore, the Fortune 500 exert monopsony power to play carriers off against each other for corporate discounts at the discretionary traveler level, without the restrictions, a level which often fails to cover fully allocated costs.

---

[37] Bridget O'Brian, Predatory Pricing Issue Is Due To Be Taken Up In American Air's Trial, Wall St. J., July 12, 1993, at A1, A6.
[38] Id. at A1.
[39] Quoted in It's Crazy Eddie, So the Idea May Be A Little Insane, Wall St. J., June 13, 1996, at A1.
[40] Joan Feldman, The Price of Retribution, Air Transport World (Dec. 1992), at 54.
[41] U.S. General Accounting Office, Airline Competition: Higher Fares and Less Competition Continue At Concentrated Airports (1993).

Chapter 6

Computer reservations systems and computer software will enable increased decoding of the effort of yield managers to obfuscate the availability of the cheapest seats. Carriers will continue to follow each other down as price wars erupt to sell excessive inventory, because of the factors described above.

YIELD MANAGEMENT

Price is a function of both supply and demand. Price is also related to cost and can heavily influence load factors (both actual and break-even). Demand for air transportation services is derived, uncertain, cyclical, directional and highly segmented. Productivity of airline resources is enhanced by a strategy of carrying multidimensional traffic—business, vacation and VFR. Since each group of passengers may have a different demand characteristic, an airline seeking both to sell perishable surplus inventory (increasing load factors) and maximize revenue will develop a yield/inventory (or price/capacity) management system (sometimes referred to as a *revenue management system*). Revenue management may be the better term, for the objective of such a system is not to manage yields, but to optimize total revenue by selling different blocs of capacity at the highest possible price.[42] In essence, this is a capacity-controlled discount fare structure, with yield managers monitoring demand carefully, and altering the size of each fare bucket depending on rises and falls in actual vis-à-vis projected demand on each flight.[43]

Yield/revenue management is the process of combining price and inventory controls to maximize revenue. It requires assessing future passenger demand (usually based on historical sales data), determining the optimal way to price and allocate seat inventory on each flight, and communicating the resulting price/inventory distribution to distribution and sales outlets.[44] It involves selectively accepting or rejecting sales in order to maximize revenue. As Sabre's Ben Vinod put it, yield management is, "selling the right seat, to the right customer, at the

---
[42] Sylvian Daudel & Georges Vialle, Yield Management 29 (1994).
[43] Newal Taneja; Airline Planning: Corporate, Financial, and Marketing 71, 72 (1982); Sylvian Daudel & Georges Vialle, Yield Management 113 (1994).
[44] Robert Cross, An Introduction to Revenue Management, in Handbook of Airline Economics 443 (D. Jenkins ed. 1995).

right price, at the right time to maximize system revenues and profitability."[45]

Price discounting is not a practice that emerged just since deregulation. As early as the 1940s, airlines began offering seats (initially in the front of the aircraft) at a discounted "coach" price (the rear of the aircraft was then believed safer; it still is, but first class was moved forward to get away from the engine noise in the aft cabin). In 1948, Capital Airways inaugurated coach class service between New York and Chicago with a high-density 60-seat configuration in its DC-4s, flying at off-peak times with minimum inflight service. The price was 4 cents per mile, only two-thirds of the prevailing rate.[46]

By the 1970s, airlines were beginning to think creatively about how to fill empty seats with discretionary, leisure or vacation travelers, while not diluting revenue from passengers who would pay more (mostly, business travelers). Charter airlines had begun to offer cheap seats for affinity groups, particularly in international transport, and had demonstrated considerable demand in the leisure market for low-priced service. The scheduled carriers responded with APEX (advance purchase excursion) fares—a discounted ticket purchased 60 days in advance of departure, with length of stay and cancellation penalties.

American Airlines began to study the problem, and recognized two features of vacation travelers: (1) they typically plan their vacations weeks ahead of time; (2) they usually stay for extended periods.[47] American introduced the Super Saver fare program in 1977, offering discounted seats on a capacity controlled basis with certain advance purchase (30 days) and minimum stay (14 days) requirements tailored to the price elastic discretionary traveler, so as to generate increased demand. Such capacity controlled fares were offered to fill seats at off-peak hours (the times of day when demand was soft), as a means of using seat capacity more efficiently.[48] The restrictions were such as to be impractical for business travelers, thus avoiding the revenue dilution which occurs when a seat is sold to a traveler who would be

---

[45] Ben Vinod, Origin-and-Destination Yield Management, in Handbook of Airline Economics 459 (D. Jenkins ed. 1996).
[46] Robert Cross, An Introduction to Revenue Management, in Handbook of Airline Economics 443, 445 (D. Jenkins ed. 1995).
[47] Thomas Petzinger, Jr., Hard Landing 74, 75 (1995).
[48] Melvin Brenner, The Significance of Airline Passenger Load Factors, in Airline Economics (G. James ed. 1982).

willing to pay more for it.[49] Large computer systems were eventually developed to forecast and monitor demand, watched over by a platoon of analysts to tweak the system to account for market shifts.

American Airlines launched a comprehensive plan of flight-specific pricing in the Fall of 1980, raising the number of fares from 8,000 to 280,000, charging different fares for the same class, depending on the day of week or time of day flown.[50] This required a major improvement of the airline's automation ability. American had recognized that different segments of the market have different price elasticities of demand, and that different flights have different load factors. By tailoring the price to respond to consumer demand by passenger category (e.g., leisure or business) and by time, day and seasonal preferences, American began to improve yields.

Over the years, American Airlines refined the process of pricing, adding a Saturday-night stay-over requirement, imposing non-refundability rules, and carefully adjusting the size of the buckets of different fare categories depending on whether sales were running ahead of or behind a predicted level. The net effect was to lure passengers away from the charter carriers as well as the new low-fare entrants.[51]

On January 17, 1985, American Airlines introduced "Ultimate Super Saver Fares," at levels at or below the new low-cost entrants' prices on a capacity controlled basis. Taking only a handful of passengers off each flights can rob a carrier of break-even load factors. Upstart airlines like People Express saw their load factors effectively mutilated by strategic discounting via yield management. By capturing a disproportionate share of fixed costs from their First and (on transcontinental and international flights) Business Class customers, the major carriers could offer seats in the coach cabin at ASM costs closer to those of the low-cost entrants. Computerized revenue management systems enable high-cost carriers to meet the fares of low-cost competitors on a capacity-controlled basis, in city-pairs and on flight departures in direct competition with them, thereby avoiding load-factor deterioration and minimizing revenue loss.[52] Strategic discount-

---

[49] Dan Reed, The American Eagle 99, 148, 49 (1992).
[50] Robert Crandall, Market Planning, in Airline Economics 244 (G. James ed. 1982).
[51] Thomas Petzinger, Hard Landing 270-73 (1995).
[52] Newal Taneja, Civil Aviation 146, 47 (2d ed. 1989).

ing (the pejorative term is predatory pricing) can deprive low-cost rivals of break-even load factors, driving them from the market, after which prices often are raised to monopolistic levels.

By the mid-1990s, yield management was generating more than $600 million year in incremental revenue for American Airlines.[53] The purpose of differential pricing (the pejorative term is discriminatory pricing) is to stimulate additional demand without diluting revenue. Since the demand for air transportation is made up of several customer segments with differing demand elasticities, different fares could be coupled with different restrictions, thereby creating different product offerings.[54] With differential pricing, a carrier is able to impose a higher percentage of fixed costs disproportionately on more price inelastic traffic. From the perspective of the business traveler, this appears unfair, for she is paying more for travel than the fellow wearing the palm tree shirt and straw hat seated next to her. But if vacation travelers were not sprinkled throughout the cabin, the entire fixed cost burden would be placed on the business traveler, which would result in even higher ticket prices and/or less frequent service than business travelers prefer.[55] In some instances, strategic discounting can be used as a competitive weapon to deny smaller rivals of break-even load factors, with losses of the predator suffered as a result of below-cost pricing in competitive markets cross-subsidized with profits earned in monopoly markets.

Given the significant elasticities of demand of the leisure or vacation traveler, a low fare can stimulate significant demand. Southwest learned that when it ran a single radio spot advertising a $10 flight aboard a late-night maintenance flight. To its amazement, the gate was swamped with passengers, many of whom had never flown before. It was so successful, that Southwest decided to charge one fare in the day (a peak price), and a lower (off-peak) fare at night. Revenue exploded.[56] But some airline managers destroyed their companies with indiscriminate fare cuts, focusing on high load factors rather than revenue. Ed Acker, who came to Pan Am from Air Florida,

---

[53] Robert Cross, An Introduction to Revenue Management, in Handbook of Airline Economics 443, 447 (D. Jenkins ed. 1995).
[54] Sylvian Daudel & Georges Vialle, Yield Management 35 (1994).
[55] See Paul Dempsey & William Thoms, Law & Economic Regulation in Transportation 179-83 (1986).
[56] Thomas Petzinger, Jr., Hard Landing 33 (1995).

engaged in such indiscriminate fare slashing, and the results were disastrous.[57]

As deregulation began in the late-1970s, many carriers began to offer lower fares. Texas International introduced "Peanuts Fares," symbolizing the on-board food, and a reflection on then President, Jimmy Carter, a champion of airline deregulation. Texas International's bill-boards showed winged peanuts flying in formation, each with an ear-to-ear tooth-filled smile resembling the former peanut farmer from Plains, Georgia.

Today, the proliferation of discounted fares is nearly beyond comprehension. In 1979, there were 58,000 domestic air fares. A decade later, there were 4,000,000 domestic air fares.[58] Airlines have learned that by watching passenger demand carefully, they can shrewdly manipulate the number of seats for which restricted discounts are offered, and fill seats with passengers paying the maximum price. That explains the phenomenon of tens of thousands of rate changes each day. An average day may have 200,000 new fares inputted into CRS, while during a fare war, 1,500,000 fares may be added.[59]

While airlines invested more information technology resources in upgrading reservations systems in the first half of the 1990s, they began to devote greater resources to yield management in the second half.[60] Professor Newal Taneja described the trends in the industry:

> The airlines are . . . becoming much more market oriented and innovative in developing, pricing, distributing and promoting their products. The direction being followed to develop and implement innovative marketing concepts has been influenced partly by the use of automation (for example, the use of computers to manage seat inventory) and partly by the lessons learned from other industries (for example, the use of frequent-flyer programs to build brand loyalty). Further exploitation of auto-

---

[57] See id. at 188, 190.
[58] Charles Banfe, Airline Management 81 (1992).
[59] Max Hopper, Rattling Sabre—New Ways To Compete On Information (May/June 1990).
[60] Aviation Daily (Feb. 12, 1996), at 225.

mation and experience gained from other industries will continue to shape future marketing programs in the airline industry. Some airlines, for example, have thought about la carte pricing as used in the restaurant industry and have considered pricing policies based on the methods used in the stock market industry, wherein the price of a stock is a function of not only the change in demand but also the rate at which demand is changing.[61]

The yield manager must attempt to identify the different price elasticities of demand between different classes of travelers to stimulate demand from passengers who would not otherwise fly, while attempting to avoid having passengers with low demand elasticity divert to fares set for passengers with high demand elasticity. This is done by coupling the lower fare buckets with restrictions such as advance purchase requirements, day and time of departure, and minimum and maximum stay requirements.[62] Advance purchase restrictions are placed on the lower fares in recognition of the fact that leisure travelers can (and usually do) plan vacations well ahead of time. The carrier will also want to restrict the number of seats in every deeply discounted fare bucket, holding higher-yield inventory in reserve to sell to passengers with less flexibility. By allocating a larger bucket of price discounted seats to off-peak times and days, price-sensitive passengers can be encouraged to shift their demand to off-peak periods, leaving a larger number of high yield seats for peak demand periods.[63]

An alternative approach is to sell as many seats as possible when demanded. This has the advantage of selling out inventory early, and achieving higher overall load factors, albeit at a lower per-passenger yield, since passengers booking earliest tend to be price elastic leisure travelers. Subsequently higher-yield business travelers will have more difficulty finding seats, for many will have been sold. Eventually, the business travel market will begin to move its demand to the airline's

---

[61] Newal Taneja, Civil Aviation 152 (2d ed. 1989).
[62] Newal Taneja, The Commercial Airline Industry 67 (1976).
[63] Sylvian Daudel & Georges Vialle, Yield Management 49 (1994).

competitors, causing significant yield erosion.[64] A strategy which focuses on the leisure market means accepting not only lower yields, but highly seasonal and market cyclical fluctuations in demand. According to Stephen Shaw, to avoid this situation requires that airlines make a "difficult compromise" in order to attract both categories of travelers:

> In order to protect their market position, airlines targeting the business traveler . . . must control when capacity is made available for sale. Modern computer reservations systems enable them to do this with considerable precision. This will probably mean that some of the early demand for a flight will be refused, and seats left unsold at that stage. These seats will then be released for sale near to the departure time of a flight, when business travelers using the highest yielding fares will be seeking bookings.[65]

The danger, of course, is that holding seats back that could have been sold at a lower price for potential future sales at a higher price may result in lower load factors when estimates of higher-yield purchases do not materialize. This is the classic tension between yield and traffic (load factors).

In determining whether to discount the price for travel, whether system-wide or in an individual city-pair market, the yield manager must assess the impact of the discount in terms of *traffic generation* (the number of new passengers stimulated by the low fare, usually measured in terms of higher load factors), and on *dilution* (the amount of revenue lost by giving a lower fare to passengers who would have flown anyway at the higher fare).[66] Where dilution outweighs generation, the discount results in a net revenue loss.

The relationship between yields, bookings and break-even load factors is a complex one. Carriers adept at yield management tend to

---

[64] Stephen Shaw, Airline Marketing & Management 163, 164 (3rd ed. 1990).
[65] Id. at 164.
[66] Robert Crandall, Market Planning, in Airline Economics 243 (G. James ed. 1982).

close out lower fare buckets (e.g., 21-day advance purchase Saturday night stay over) early, particularly during heavy demand periods. This can result in the sale of seats at a higher yield, driving down break-even load factors. Conversely, during poor demand periods (e.g., the first and fourth calendar quarters) carriers tend to seek higher load factors and hold lower fare buckets open longer, thereby reducing yield, and raising break-even load factors. If yield remains constant, the break-even load factor rises with increases in traffic (given the fact that additional passengers do impose modest variable costs on airlines).

One other manipulation of yield management involves holding open larger buckets of discounted seats for connecting traffic than O&D traffic, given the fact that, for flights of more than 1,500 miles, passengers have multiple airlines and multiple hubs over which to connect. Since all carriers view such connecting traffic as incremental revenue, and recognizing that passengers have several competitive alternatives for long-distance journeys, carriers tend to price it on a variable cost basis, attempting to cover fixed costs from the O&D passenger. *Origin-and-destination yield management* is often referred to as itinerary control, which requires a complex assessment of the value of a passenger based on itinerary, departure date, cabin, fare class, published fare, and point of sale, all with the view of holding open seats for high-yield long-distance connecting traffic. Revenue optimization models require valuing each leg of a flight against each other, and assessing the relative value of fare classes on each of its legs. Under a process termed *"nesting,"* as sales build for a flight, the lower-valued itinerary classes are automatically closed, leaving the higher-yield seats open.[67]

Some industry experts have noted the chronic tendency of airlines to focus on traffic rather than yield. According to William Waltrip:

> [T]raffic has a hundred fathers—yield is an orphan.... [T]raffic is seen as created, yield is seen as happening; traffic is personal, yield is impersonal.

---

[67] See Ben Vinod, Origin-and-Destination Yield Management, in Handbook of Airline Economics 459, 461 (D. Jenkins ed. 1996); Sylvian Daudel & Georges Vialle, Yield Management 75 (1994).

[T]raffic is immediate, visible, and concrete; yield is invisible and abstract. The ten passengers you lost because your fare was higher you can see walking over to the counter of your cheaper competitor. Nobody can see the additional revenue derived from ninety passengers retained at a higher fare.

[Y]ou measure traffic a number of different times: prior to the flight on the basis of advance bookings, immediately after departure, then in daily, weekly, and monthly summaries—all on a timely basis and without any doubt about the accuracy. Yield you find out about only once, weeks later and subject to so many influences that, even after the fact, it is more correctly called an estimate than actual.

[T]raffic is measured in a number of different ways: passengers, passenger-miles, seat factor, market share, by sector, by origin and destination, by point of sale, and so on. Yield is measured only one way; cents per passenger-mile or, at best, also as dollars per aircraft-mile.

All in all, the balance between these two forces that should have equal weight is rather lopsided. In almost any conflict, traffic is the victor, with yield (and often revenue, too) second best. With slight exaggeration one could say that some airline executives slash fares, match lower priced competitors, liberalize or violate restrictions on conditions for 365 days a year, then on January first they ask: what happened to the yield?

This phenomenon has a greater potential for threatening the profitability and indeed the viability of our industry than any other factor I can think of.[68]

---

[68] William Waltrip, International Planning, in Airline Economics 281, 291 (G. James ed. 1982).

The Price: Revenue And Inventory Management

Bookings data often precedes revenue data. Thus, load factors can be savored as a measure of success, only to have the bubble burst when the revenue falls short of projections.

Airline pricing relies heavily on computers and computer reservations systems that monitor the impact of price changes and the reactions of competitors in thousands of nonstop and connecting markets.[69] Revenue/inventory management systems require the installation of high-capacity computer hardware and software capable of sifting large databases and automatically optimizing booking limits with sophisticated forecasting models. With six or eight fare classes, the revenue optimization models can be extremely complex, requiring linear programming techniques.[70] Seat inventory management systems enable airlines to decide how many seats to offer at which fares, based on an analysis of historical and contemporary booking patterns, and impose booking limits on lower yield inventory buckets. The proficient use of these systems allows a carrier to balance yield and load factors to maximize net revenue.

The trick is to avoid selling an excessive number of low-yield seats too early, for this may consume inventory and close out later bookings of higher-yield customers, causing *"spill,"* or the inability to accommodate a potential purchase because capacity has been consumed (usually, the loss of sales to later booking customers because earlier booking customers have consumed available inventory). Conversely, holding back an excessive number of seats for potential high-yield customers who may fail to materialize may deprive the carrier of earlier sales to price-sensitive lower-yield customers. This is referred to as *"spoilage,"* a situation where demand for seats exists but, due to misallocation of inventory, they depart empty.[71] As seen below, *overbooking* the flight (or selling more tickets than there are available seats), is one mechanism to reduce the likelihood of spoilage or impact of spoilage, although this increases the likelihood of *denied boardings*, which can impose tangible and intangible costs on carriers.

---

[69] Newal Taneja, Civil Aviation 146 (2d ed. 1989).
[70] Sylvian Daudel & Georges Vialle, Yield Management 49, 114 (1994).
[71] Hugh Dunleavy, Airline Passenger Overbooking, in Handbook of Airline Economics 469, 473 (D. Jenkins ed. 1996); Sylvian Daudel & Georges Vialle, Yield Management 46 (1994).

Yield management has become a principal means of revenue improvement, with some carriers segmenting markets in up to 26 categories.[72] Successful yield management can increase revenue by between 2-5%, and for on-line connections within an airline's hub, up to 7%.[73] Some carriers have been slow to take advantage of the tremendous benefits of revenue management. TWA did not have an automated yield management system until 1995. In 1996, it purchased technology enabling it to automate crew scheduling and market analysis.[74]

Consumer groups complain that by offering cut-rate fares for only a relatively small number of seats, airlines are engaging in "bait-and-switch" advertising.[75] The bewildering array of fares has also increased transactions costs for consumers. There are between 40,000 and 100,000 price changes on a typical day, with the average fare having a life of only 10 days. Pricing complexity costs some airlines up to $25 million annually in administrative costs alone.[76] The public finds airline pricing confusing, irrational and unnecessarily complex. Two people flying to the same destination can pay radically different prices for precisely the same service, the only difference being when they purchased their ticket. Further, the Y fare had grown so high that many business travelers began foregoing travel.

As noted above, American Airlines responded in March 1992 with "Value Pricing," an effort to simplify the coach fare into four categories, lowering the highest fares significantly, and raising the lowest fares somewhat. Many applauded this effort at rationalizing the pricing structure. But soon anarchy ensued as Northwest Airlines introduced "Grownups Fly Free." American was unable to sustain the pricing structure as competitors began to nip at its edges. The price wars which followed were highly destructive to airline balance sheets. Eventually, price simplification became only a sad chapter in the history of post-deregulation era of market Darwinism, and major airline pricing reverted to its chaotic complexity.

---

[72] The Balancing Act, Airline Bus., The Skies in 1992 17 (1992).
[73] Id. at 19.
[74] Aviation Daily (Jan. 22, 1996), at 101.
[75] See Cowan & Gargan, Mirage of Discount Air Fares Is Frustrating to Many Fliers, N.Y. Times, Apr. 22, 1991, at 1.
[76] Robert Cross, An Introduction to Revenue Management, in Handbook of Airline Economics 443, 453 (D. Jenkins ed. 1995).

OVERBOOKING

As a means of selling unsold inventory, and thereby avoiding seat spoilage, overbooking plays an important role in revenue management. Most carriers estimate the number of sales cancellations and "no-shows"—customers who book a flight, but do not show up at departure for boarding—and overbook the flight by that number, selling more tickets than there are seats. Robert Cross has estimated that overbooking generates as much as 40% of the revenue management benefit at some airlines, and that without overbooking, the cost of seat spoilage for the world's airlines would be $3 billion annually.[77]

While overbooking reduces the amount of unsold inventory (spoilage), it increases inconvenience of denied access for customers holding confirmed reservations but denied boarding on those occasions when the airline has overestimated the number of "no-shows." DOT regulations require *de minimus* economic compensation for passengers denied boarding, though usually carriers can skirt even these modest requirements by offering free travel coupons to volunteer passengers willing to de-board the aircraft. When a sufficient number of volunteers step forward, fewer passengers are inconvenienced.

In estimating the number of sales by which to overbook flights, the carrier should calculate its tangible and intangible costs of denied boarding. Tangible costs are cash penalties paid to individuals who hold confirmed reservations but are denied boardings, as well as the cost of transporting them to their destinations by alternative means (sometimes a competitor's flight). Intangible costs are incurred because the "bumped" passengers may by angry at the carrier because they cannot fly to their destination on the agreed upon flight. Public perception of carrier service levels deteriorates. Thus, while inventory management requires a careful balance between spoilage and spill, overbooking requires a balance between spoilage and denied access.[78]

As is the case with discount fare buckets, overbooking limits also need to be carefully adjusted upward or downward in the period preceding the flight. Overbooking allows carriers to improve load factors marginally, and hold seats open for high-yield last-minute

---

[77] Id.
[78] Sylvian Daudel & Georges Vialle, Yield Management 69 (1994).

bookings. Southwest Airlines typically has the largest number of overbooked passengers.

TYPES OF FARES

First Class—During the piston-era of commercial aviation, coach class was carved out of first class and placed in the front of the aircraft. First class was offered in the rear of the aircraft, because that was the safest place to be in the event of a crash. As flying became safer, particularly with the advent of jets, noise in the aft cabin became less tolerable, and first class was moved to the front of the aircraft. The forward cabin also provided more convenient access to the Jetway. First class travel can be quite expensive, the airlines recognizing the price inelasticity of the wealthy and senior corporate executives. The seats are wider, seat pitch more generous (on some carriers' international flights, they permit the seat to become almost a horizontal bed), and food better (on international flights, passengers can be offered a several-course gourmet meal). In-flight amenities, such as alcoholic beverages and movie head-sets, are complimentary.

Business Class—Since many businesses will not allow their mid-level managers to fly in first class, because of the cost, airlines have created "Business Class", which is essentially the equivalent of domestic First Class. It is priced between First and Coach (or as some carriers call it "Economy") Class, includes wide seats, pitch not as generous as in First nor as niggardly as in Coach, free liquor and movie head-sets.

The "Y" Fare—The Y fare refers to an unrestricted, full-coach "walk-up" fare, available for a Coach Class seat on the day of departure. It is generally the highest fare offered in coach, although it has none of the restrictions described below. Generally speaking, all other Coach fares are discounted off the Y, and include some or all of the restrictions listed below. As Figure 6.2, "U.S. Airline Discount And Full Fare Yields", reveals, full fare yields have risen significantly under deregulation, and by the mid-1990s, were approaching 35 cents per mile; the average discounted yield held steady at slightly north of 10 cents per mile:

Figure 6.2—U.S. AIRLINE DISCOUNT AND FULL FARE YIELDS[79]

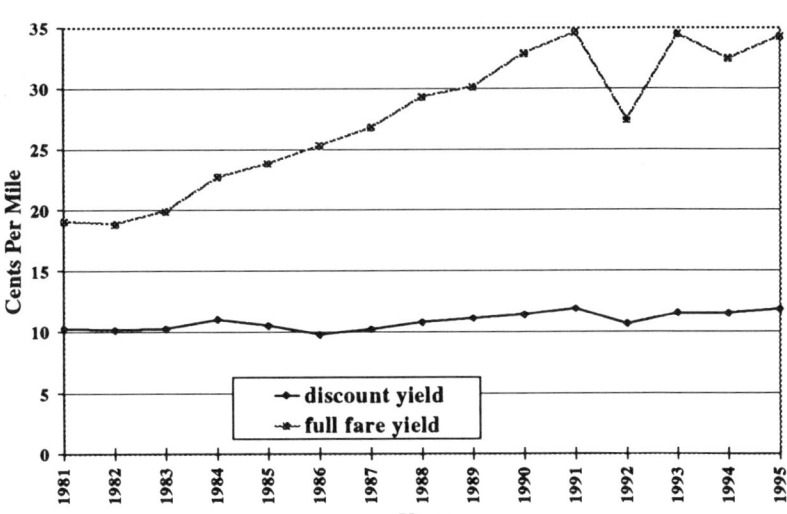

Promotional Fares—A product of yield management, promotional fares are various classes (sometimes referred to as "*buckets*") of fares with various restrictions. Generally, these are the only fares that are advertised, with the restrictions listed in incredibly small type at the bottom of the newspaper page. Among such fare restrictions are the following.

TYPES OF FARE RESTRICTIONS

Introductory Fares—Inventory, or promotional, fares typically are below-cost prices used to stimulate interest in the carrier's new service in a market.

Companion Fares—Airlines sometimes offer a discount of free travel to a passenger accompanying a full-fare passenger. Thus, a business traveler, wanting to take along his or her spouse, may shift a business flight to the carrier offering free or reduced rate travel to a

---

[79] Source: ESG Aviation Services

companion. In the 1980s, TWA inaugurated a "Kids Fly Free" version of this program, encouraging discretionary family travel.

Peak/Off Peak Fares—Some carriers have offered a simplified fare structure consisting of just two fares, peak (for travel during heavy demand periods), and off-peak (a lower fare, for travel at softer demand times). For example, higher fares may exist at peak business traveler demand times (e.g., Monday-Friday 7:00-9:00 a.m., and 4:00-6:00 p.m. departures). Lower fares may be offered on softer demand days (e.g., travel on Tuesdays, Wednesdays and Saturdays), or weaker demand periods, imposing black-out periods on travel during certain peak travel days.

Red-Eye Specials—In order to increase aircraft utilization, and spread fixed costs over a larger number of passengers, carriers may offer late night or early morning departures, offering a discount to travelers willing to fly at such undesirable times. In the 1980s, Eastern Airlines attempted to couple "Moonlight Special" fares out of Houston with a contract to fly belly freight on behalf of a cargo company.[80]

Seasonal Discounts—Airlines can be counted upon to announce sales preceding certain demand troughs or vacation periods. May is a popular time to announce Summer sales. September is a popular time to announce Fall sales.

Advance Purchase Requirements—Generally speaking, many business travelers are unable to plan their trips weeks ahead of time; conversely, individuals do plan vacations several weeks before. In addition, business travelers tend to be much less demand elastic than are vacation travelers. Recognizing these distinctions, many airlines offer lower fares the earlier the ticket is purchased. Thus, 21-day, 14-day, 7-day, or 3-day advance purchase requirements result in progressively higher fares the closer the purchase is to departure.

Immediate Purchase Requirements—Because of the volatility of air fares, airlines often insist that the consumer purchase the ticket within 24-hours of making the reservation. This "locks in" the customer, and "locks in" the fare.

Round-trip Requirements—In order to assure that both the inbound and outbound legs of the journey are made on the same carrier, many airlines insist that the lower fares be offered only if the consumer pur-

---

[80] See Lisa Miller, Leisure Class Finds Late-Night Bargains, Wall St. J., June 7, 1996, at B8.

chases a round-trip ticket. Sometimes these fares are higher than a one-way fare.

Minimum/Maximum Stay Requirements—Minimum stay requirements are another means of differentiating the business from the leisure traveler. For example, business travelers tend to shy away from Saturday-night-stay-over requirements (some airlines have shifted this requirement to Friday night), when they prefer to be home with their families. This particular requirement has been a boon to the hotel business, for the weekend period was traditionally a weak demand period for the hotel industry prior to airline deregulation. Maximum stay requirements (e.g., 30 days) are also imposed by some airlines.

Nonrefundability—Although because of deliberate overbooking, no customer is actually guaranteed a seat (even with a "confirmed reservation"), many airlines refuse to refund a ticket once it is sold, although many will allow it to be exchanged for another ticket with the same restrictions, minus a $50 "service charge." This so-called "service charge" is far higher than the actual costs of rebooking, and itself has become a significant stream of industry revenue.

Senior Saver and Youth Fares—Recognizing that senior citizens travel less than younger people, and that people living on retirement incomes or in school or college have less discretionary income, many airlines offer discounts to stimulate travel among these two groups. Some carriers offer coupon books of discounted travel on a space available basis.

Stand-By, Space-Available Travel—"EEE" fares are often offered to air travel industry professionals on a deeply-discounted space-available basis. In the 1970s, Laker Skytrain sold excess inventory with its "Youth Standby Fares," whereby college students waited in line on Queens Boulevard in Jamaica, New York, for a bus to take them to JFK Airport if there were any empty seats to London.[81]

"Sale Fares"—The "V", or sale, fare is generally a short-lived promotional price designed to stimulate traffic during trough or vacation periods. Thus, sales are typically announced in January, May, and September to stimulate sales.

Non-transferability—Airlines insist that only the person whose name appears on the ticket may use it. Security screening, requiring a

---

[81] Julius Maldutis, The Airlines—The Third Revolution (Apr. 8, 1996), at 5.

positive photo identification, has turned into a means whereby ticket trafficking and arbitrage has been stifled.[82]

Bereavement Fares—Major airlines typically offer 50% discounts off the full coach Y fare for individuals who have to rush to a relative's bedside or funeral. Northwest offers only 30% off. Most require some sort of documentation (e.g., a funeral notice, Doctor's letter, or death certificate).[83]

Other Restrictions—Airlines usually insist "other restrictions may apply," although it is unclear what that means. Perhaps it refers to the airlines' discretionary right to deny boarding to excessively intoxicated, vulgar, unruly, or smelly passengers.

CORPORATE DISCOUNTING

Large volume purchasers of air travel often negotiate a contract price for air travel which may be set as low as the discretionary travel rate, but without the advance purchase and Saturday stay-over restrictions. George James explained the monopsony power of large volume purchasers this way:

> Airlines are especially reactive to the bargaining power of volume purchasers of transportation—whether in the personal travel market (that is, tour operators) or in the business travel market (that is, government agencies or large corporations). This vulnerability stems from the uniquely low marginal cost of selling a seat that would otherwise be empty. The almost zero marginal cost of the otherwise empty seat places carriers in a position where they can seek the larger purchasers of transportation to the point where full-cost economics are ignored.[84]

---

[82] Eleena de Lisser, Airlines Cracking Down On Ticket-Swapping Tactics, Wall St. J., Oct. 13, 1995, at B9.
[83] Compassionate Fares, Consumer Reports Travel Letter (Sept. 1995), at 212.
[84] George James, The Coming Decade in Commercial Aviation, in Airline Economics 185, 205 (G. James ed. 1982).

Some corporate travel departments have become quite innovative. For instance, IBM negotiated still deeper discounts without frequent flyer mileage.[85] Perhaps the largest corporate discounts of all go to the federal government. In 1996, for example, the U.S. General Services Administration negotiated contract rates discounted 62% below the normal unrestricted fare, saving the government approximately $2.4 billion on air travel, with Delta landing the largest number of city-pair contracts.[86] From the taxpayer's perspective, this is an enormous cost savings. But of course, such deep (variable cost based) discounts to one class of patrons (government workers) means that the fixed cost burden is shifted to other classes of patrons—typically nondiscretionary small business traffic. In effect, this is a hidden tax imposed on those firms which create most of the jobs in our economy. From the perspective of its true effect, this is curious public policy indeed.

LIQUIDATING UNSOLD INVENTORY

United Airlines' CEO Gerald Greenwald likened the value of an empty airline seat on a departing aircraft to the value of a banana turning brown to a grocer. Either would sell it for whatever he could get if given the opportunity. The fundamental dilemma is the conflict between supply and demand in the unique way it presents itself in the airline industry.

From the consumer's perspective, an airline seat becomes more valuable the closer in time to departure. Conversely, from the airline's perspective, an airline seat becomes less valuable the closer in time to departure. As seen above, yield management attempts to forego the opportunity to sell all seats by rationing the capacity offered in various fare buckets over time so as to maximize yield. But given the relentless problem of excess and highly perishable inventory, as well as the low variable costs of production, how does an airline fill seats which otherwise would fly empty? Certainly, appropriately crafted yield management goes a long way toward filling seats, and extracting the highest yields for those seats. The question is, can airlines sell unused

---

[85] William McGee, IBM To Swap Air Miles for Discounts, Business Travel News, Mar. 7, 1994, at 1.
[86] Carole Shifrin, Delta Tops U.S. Travel Contract Awards, Aviation Week & Space Tech. (Sept. 30, 1996), at 42.

inventory to individuals who otherwise would not fly? Several airlines have come up with intriguing solutions.

For example, TWA offers its employees "Buddy Passes," which enable friends of employees to purchase stand-by travel on a deeply discounted EEE fare. Additionally, TWA allows employees of other airlines and their family members to purchase deeply discounted space-available travel within its system, including fares to Europe as low as $150. Iberia also sells deeply discounted space-available travel to employees of other airlines. In most cases, black-out dates apply, and large numbers of passengers holding these ticket coupons may be left stranded at the gate. The theory apparently is that employees of other airlines fly quite a lot anyway, can fly on a space-available basis on their own airlines for free, are accustomed to free or reduced-rate transportation, are also accustomed to occasionally being "bumped" from a flight, and are therefore not likely to purchase a TWA ticket without a deeply-discounted promotion. TWA derives revenue from seats which would otherwise fly empty, improving load factors and revenue.

Some carriers have liquidated unsold inventory with "Mystery Trips," whereby a potential traveler shows up at the airport at a designated time and is sold a ticket for an unknown destination. For a deeply discounted fare, it could be a weekend for two in San Francisco or Indianapolis.

Other carriers have begun selling excess inventory by auction over the World Wide Web. Among the pioneers in this innovation, Cathay Pacific offered 50 Los Angeles-Hong Kong Business Class seats to the highest bidder. About 2,400 people bid, and the sale price was about half the list price.[87] Shortly thereafter, Cathay offered a 747 full of seats to the highest bidders. Teaming with IBM, American Airlines launched weekly "Net SAAver Fares" to undersold destinations via e-mail.[88] The World Wide Web began to be a promising medium for the liquidation of perishable inventory. What no one could predict was whether the consumption of leisure demand at distress sale prices would, in the long term, decrease leisure demand at higher prices.

---

[87] Scott McCartney, Poised for Takeoff, Wall St. J., June 17, 1996, at R6.
[88] Wall St. J., Dec. 16, 1996, at B5.

CONSUMER SAVINGS UNDER DEREGULATION: THE TEN BILLION DOLLAR MYTH

Airline expert Edmund Greenslet has calculated pre- and post-deregulation real (inflation adjusted) yields, concluding that yields fell an average of 2.5% per year from 1950 to 1978, then fell at a lower rate (1.9% annually) after 1978.[89] An inflation adjustment is appropriate given the fact that national economic trends have nothing to do with airline deregulation. Fuel adjustments are similarly appropriate, given the high fixed costs of fuel for the airline industry, and the fact that rises and falls in fuel costs are also ungoverned by airline deregulation. While there were significant price reductions in the 1977-1979 period of regulatory reform, fuel adjusted real yields fell 2.7% in the decade preceding deregulation, and only 1.9% in the decade after it.[90] Given the enhanced circuity created by hubbing (a decidedly post-deregulation phenomenon, although there is some dispute over its magnitude), a yield measure of pricing would overstate the downward slope of the post-deregulation trend. Also, it should be noted that yield data are collected only for scheduled carriers. Before deregulation, many travelers flew aboard charter or supplemental carriers, most of which have been eradicated by the competition deregulation unleashed. Thus, the true trends are more profound than even these numbers suggest. Even using real yields as a proxy for ticket prices, *airline prices have fallen at a much slower rate since deregulation than before it* (see Figure 6.3, "U.S. Airline Real Yields").

---

[89] Edmund Greenslet, World Airline Capital Requirements (address to the Chicago Convention 50th Anniversary Conference, Oct. 31, 1994).
[90] Paul Dempsey & Andrew Goetz, Airline Deregulation & Laissez Faire Mythology 243-63 (1992).

Figure 6.3—U.S. AIRLINE REAL YIELDS[91]

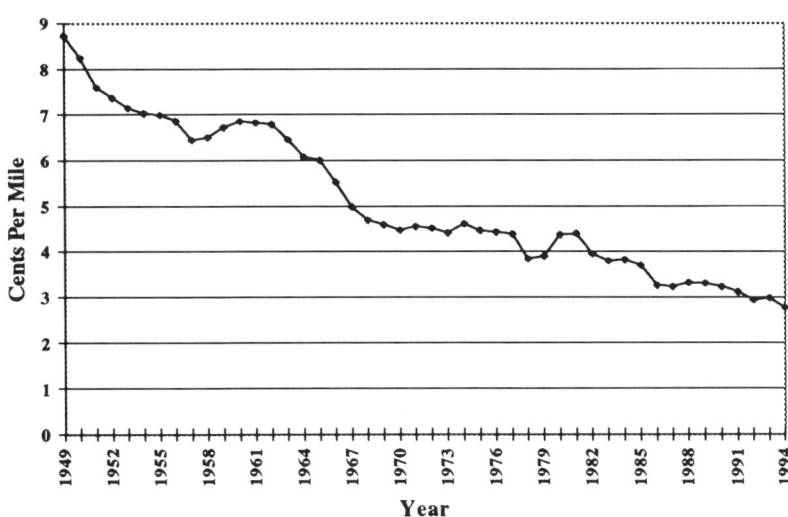

Note: 1967 = 100

Given the competition deregulation unleashed, which has driven carrier profitability to unacceptable low levels, why would this be so? Shouldn't declining profitability translate into a wealth transfer from investors to consumers?

The answer lies on the cost side of the equation, and in the hub-and-spoke phenomenon. Hubbing has been the dominant strategy of airlines during deregulation. While hubbing enables a carrier to enjoy a yield premium (particularly on passengers who begin or end their trips at the hub, or are traveling to non-competitive spokes, or who value frequency), it increases circuity, congestion, and fuel consumption, while reducing labor productivity and equipment utilization. Further, the trend toward larger (lower ASM cost, higher scale economy) aircraft was abated by hub-and-spoke networks which require relatively smaller aircraft flying shorter distances. Moreover, inadequate profitability and LBOs (another phenomenon which would not have been tolerated under regulation) raised the debt burden for carriers, while denying many of them the economic resources to retire older, less fuel

---

[91] Source: ESG Aviation Services.

efficient and productive aircraft. The age of the U.S. fleet grew significantly after deregulation. Carriers also bid up distribution costs significantly after travel agent commissions were deregulated.

Despite these facts, several studies by the Brookings Institution have insisted that consumers have saved billions of dollars because of deregulation.[92] In their first major study of the issue, the authors (Steven Morrison and Clifford Winston) alleged consumer savings of $6 billion, two-thirds of which they attribute to time savings caused by increased scheduling frequency.[93] The myth that consumers have saved billions of dollars under deregulation is largely attributable to the Morrison and Winston study. De-bunking the myth, therefore, must begin with a critical review of the Morrison and Winston report.

Employing a "counterfactual" methodology, Morrison and Winston's estimate of the value of time saved was extraordinary (1.44 times the business traveler's hourly wage). More importantly, they appear to have missed the fact that less than 10% of all travelers fly on unrestricted tickets and enjoy the flexibility to take an earlier flight if their travel plans change; most waste time in a city in which they would prefer not to be in order to satisfy the Saturday-night stay-over restrictions. Hubbing also increases flight and connection time for many travelers. Further problems with the Brookings methodology include the lack of consideration of actual delay time, reliance on 1977-1983 data only, the omission of quality-of-service measures other than time and cost, and the problematic nature of drawing such broad conclusions from deregulated fare data.[94]

Morrison and Winston didn't respond to the criticism directly. But instead, they invented a new methodology to sustain their hypothesis, and raised their prediction of annual consumer savings, this time to $10 billion. The new methodology involved calculating what fares would have been had Congress not deregulated the airline industry and was based on the Standard Industry Fare Level [SIFL], which had been used by the Civil Aeronautics Board for several years after deregulation. They then adjusted this fare upward by subtracting what

---

[92] It comes as no surprise that deregulation architect Elizabeth Bailey serves on Brookings' Board of Trustees.
[93] Steven Morrison & Clifford Winston, The Economic Effects of Airline Deregulation (1986).
[94] Paul Dempsey & Andrew Goetz, Airline Deregulation & Laissez Faire Mythology 281-93 (1992).

they estimated to be the increased industry productivity created by deregulation, concluding that deregulation had produced fares 22% lower than they would have been had deregulation not occurred.[95]

There are several serious problems with the revised Brookings methodology as well as the original. First, the SIFL emerged from the Airline Deregulation Act of 1978 as a reference point to be adjusted annually based on carrier costs. But had Morrison and Winston read that statute, they would have seen that carriers were free to offer prices up to 5% above or 50% below the SIFL without seeking regulatory approval (they had to justify prices above or below this zone of pricing flexibility).[96] Thus, were rates still regulated under that statutory methodology, the price offered to consumers would not be at the SIFL reference point. They would likely be closer to the level provided for in the statute at 50% below the SIFL.

Second, except in adjusting for what they perceive to be the enhanced productivity of higher load factors under deregulation, the SIFL calculation is predicated on post-deregulation costs. Hubbing likely would not have occurred without deregulation, and it has eroded equipment and labor utilization, increased fuel consumption, and abated the trend toward larger (lower ASM cost) aircraft. Further, inadequate profitability (at least some of which must be attributable to deregulation) increased the cost of debt service, while travel agent commission deregulation radically increased distribution costs. To include these additional post-deregulation costs in the calculation of the SIFL is necessarily to drive it up by cost features which would have been significantly different had deregulation not occurred, and grossly overstate the price consumers would have paid. Whatever methodology a regulatory agency might employ today, it is unlikely it would be the SIFL (even with its 5% above and 50% below zones), for in the four decades of airline regulation, no methodology was embraced that long.

There are other, less fundamental, but troublesome problems with the Morrison-Winston methodology. For example, they threw out all tickets that they concluded were unreasonably high, and kept in all free travel tickets.[97]

---

[95] Steven Morrison & Clifford Winston, The Evolution of the Airline Industry 12, 13 (1995).
[96] Paul Dempsey & William Thoms, Law & Economic Regulation in Transportation 198, 199 (1986).
[97] Steven Morrison & Clifford Winston, The Evolution of the Airline Industry 13 (1995).

The Price: Revenue And Inventory Management

Finally, to compare pre-deregulation tickets with post-deregulation tickets is to compare apples and oranges. The pre-deregulation charter and supplemental discounted prices are ignored, and in the post-deregulation era, these carriers account for far less of the service providers. Further, most pre-deregulation tickets were unencumbered by the post-deregulation restrictions—non-refundability, minimum stay, and advance purchase, for example. With Saturday-night stay requirements, the real cost of travel for the overwhelming number of today's passengers includes the additional expenses of meals and lodging—expenses often not required prior to deregulation, before the airlines assumed jurisdiction to regulate the behavior of their patrons. To compare apples to apples—pre-deregulation Y fares to post-deregulation Y fares—reveals that *post-deregulation prices for unrestricted travel have risen far above the inflation rate*. The Consumer Price Index [CPI] for all commodities rose from 58.2 in 1975 to 131.3 in 1993; during the same period the CPI for air fares rose from 38 to 178.7, more than twice the rate of all commodities. The Y fare has grown so monstrously high that less than 10% of the traveling public will pay it.

The real surprise is that coach fares did not fall more in the post-deregulation period given the deterioration in the quality of coach service in the post-deregulation period. Though flight frequency has improved, seat pitch has been tightened, meals have been eliminated, the aircraft have aged, the cabin crew embittered and the cabin more poorly staffed, and (because of hub and spoke circuity) travel times have increased. Comparing apples to apples again, consumers are now purchasing a poorer product for their money than they were prior to deregulation. The pre-deregulation apple was a crisp, juicy Washington state apple. The post-deregulation apple is a bruised crab apple full of worm holes.

There is no doubt that analysts at Brookings are sufficiently creative to find yet another methodology to sustain their allegation that consumer savings attributable to deregulation are enormous, and one might expect the pile of dollars they ascribe to deregulation will be larger still. But one must beware. In reviewing results of studies produced by government-employed think tanks like Brookings, one must keep in mind that what they often conduct is evaluative research (or *program evaluation*). Program evaluation is not objective scientific work. Program evaluation is similar to (scientific) experimental research in that it may employ quantitative data and other empirical methods to produce information. But unlike hypothetico-deductive reasoning (i.e., science) which declares itself to be objective and scientifically neutral, program evaluation is directly involved in policy research, and is, therefore, highly biased by overt, politically-loaded input.[98] It is anything but neutral, and rather, is oftentimes intended to satisfy the interests of the patron saint who paid for the study.

But irrespective of who may have ordered it, the Brookings study should send red flags up to anyone who reads it. It clearly demonstrates a bias, and it unquestionably served the interests of the then current administration by reporting a deregulatory policy success.

The results of evaluative research can be valuable tools in triangulating information. But taken alone, they must always be viewed with suspicion.[99]

---

[98] Laurence E. Gesell, Airline Re-Regulation 12, 13 (1990).

[99] See generally, id.

The Price: Revenue And Inventory Management

CHAPTER 7.

PROMOTION AND DISTRIBUTION

"A sucker is born every minute." [1]
P.T. Barnum
Entertainment Entrepreneur

INTRODUCTION

At the outset, it is important to distinguish between the customer (the individual who purchases the ticket for air travel) and the consumer (the passenger who actually flies on the ticket, or the firm whose freight is in the belly of the aircraft), for they are often not the same person. For example, business travel may be booked by an executive's secretary or his or her corporate travel office. For discretionary travel, a single family member (e.g., the husband or wife) may purchase tickets for the entire family. Vacation packages (consisting of air transportation, ground transfers and hotel rooms) may be assembled by tour operators. For both business and leisure travel, travel agents may significantly influence the purchase. For cargo, an air freight forwarder will purchase air travel on behalf of shippers' consolidated freight. These individuals often have wide discretion as to the airline and flight selected. It is these key individuals to whom an effective marketing program must be targeted.[2]

---

[1] George Selder, The Great Quotations 83 (1983).
[2] See Stephen Shaw, Airline Marketing & Management 14-29 (3rd ed. 1990).

Promotion And Distribution

In the mid-1970s, before deregulation, promotion and sales accounted for about 11% of total operating expenses.[3] Under regulation, travel agent commissions were capped by the Civil Aeronautics Board. Under deregulation, distribution costs have been one of the fastest growing operating expenses, accounting for between 18-20% of a major carrier's costs.[4] Promotion, distribution and sales expenses include expenditures for advertising, publicity, computer reservations system [CRS] fees, credit card fees, ticket stock, travel agent commissions, and commission overrides. In addition to sales via their own internal reservations agents, carriers have begun to embrace creative distribution channels, including direct sales through telephone lines and the world wide web, and ticketing machines.

An airline's distribution system typically has two elements—the sales outlets, and the reservations system. A *sales outlet* is a venue where a customer can purchase a ticket. This may be a sales office of a carrier, its competitor, or a travel agent. Ticketing can be done at airports, at airline ticket offices or by travel agents. Tickets may also be mailed, or with ticketless distribution, the customer may be given a confirmation number over the telephone with no ticket stock and no need to coordinate ticket distribution with a sales outlet. A *reservations system* allows coordination of seats, prices, and sales. A carrier may offer its products in one or all (usually all) of the major computer reservations systems—Sabre, Galileo, Worldspan and System One—and/or it typically also keeps track of bookings in its own internal reservations system, to which its own reservations agents are tied.[5]

THE EVOLUTION OF AIRLINE RESERVATIONS SYSTEMS

The early airline reservations systems were primitive, labor-intensive, endeavors. As air traffic grew, they became incapable of keeping up with demand. The essential problem was one of matching passengers to seats before the seats perished on take-off, in essence, balancing demand with supply, or reservations and sales with inventory. In

---

[3] Newal Taneja, The Commercial Airline Industry 76 (1976).
[4] Address of Al Lenza Before the Fifth Annual Phoenix International Aviation Symposium (Apr. 19, 1996).
[5] Newal Taneja, The Commercial Airline Industry 73 (1976).

Chapter 7

the 1930s, many carriers used a "request and reply" system, whereby a reservations agent would telephone a central control venue where inventory was rationed. A single ledger would be passed from hand to hand as agents wrote reservations in, or erased those which were canceled. A response to the reservations agent would be returned via teletype.

With the introduction of the DC-3, the fleets and schedules of the airlines grew and became more complex. Throughout the 1940s, at some airlines reservations were recorded manually with pencil in books, and at others on different colored index cards, called "Tiffany" cards after the lamps with the cut glass shades. The cards were arranged on a "Lazy Susan," with a half dozen employees sitting around a table, spinning the Lazy Susan to reach the index card that corresponded to a particular flight. Simply by counting the marks on the card, the reservations clerk could determine the availability of seats on a particular flight.

The books and Tiffany cards gave way to chalk and wall-size slate boards, and eventually to electric light boards. As reservations grew, more and more clerks were crammed into these rooms within line of sight of the boards, some peering through opera glasses while teletypes chattered. Single boards gave way to multiple boards, creating the same problems of reconciliation that multiple ledgers had created.[6]

As airline systems grew, and passenger itineraries became more complex, these manual reservations systems became incapable of keeping up. In the early 1940s, American Airlines contacted the makers of adding machines and other computational equipment for help. None would. Needing "real time" data, American undertook to create a system internally. In 1946, American developed the airline industry's first electrical/mechanical device for rationing seat inventory, which it christened the "Availability Reservisor."[7] According to Thomas Petzinger:

> [American created] a grant contraption of tall
> cylinders, each representing a different flight on
> a different day. The cylinders were filled with

---

[6] Sabre, The Sabre Story (1996); Thomas Petzinger, Jr., Hard Landing 52 (1995).
[7] Sabre, The Sabre Story (1996).

> marbles, one for every unsold seat. With each reservation a button was pressed and an electrical signal sent, opening a hatch at the bottom of the cylinder through which one marble was emptied. Conversely, the cancellation of any reservation caused a marble to be electrically released into the top of the cylinder, restoring the seat to the unsold inventory of the flight.[8]

Finally, American enticed Teleregister Corporation to join the project, and develop a random access memory drum with arithmetic capabilities:

> Together the companies developed a phalanx of switches, relays, and plugs, which they called "the brain." The room-sized device in turn was hooked to hundreds of little terminals that looked like adding machines. Reservationists were issued stacks of notched metal plates, which they inserted into their terminals as a way of notifying the brain which flight they were inquiring about. The brain responded with a signal that illuminated a green light, when seats were available, or an amber light, if the flight was sold out. A few years later, in 1952, the ganglia of wires and relays were replaced by a crude, homemade memory device—a giant grinding wheel, covered in aluminum and sprayed with an oxide, on which millions of tiny electrical charges could be deposited.[9]

Still, there was no efficient way to correlate a passenger's name, address and telephone number with her reservation. Meanwhile, IBM developed a Cold War computer to handle nuclear warfare simulations for the defense department called SAGE (Semi-Automatic Ground

---

[8] Thomas Petzinger, Jr., Hard Landing 53 (1995).
[9] Id.

Environment). American and IBM partnered in 1953 to develop an airline reservations system based on that technology. IBM called it SABER (Semi-Automatic Business Environment Research). An American Airlines executive subsequently transposed the last two letters, making it, "in every respect, the weapon that its name implies."[10] Sabre came to life in 1962. American had invested almost $40 million, then the price of four Boeing 707s.

One early consortium of travel agents and airlines, the Automatic Travel Agency Reservations System, attempted to set up a joint CRS. But in 1967, the U.S. Civil Aeronautics Board [CAB] refused to grant it antitrust immunity.[11]

In 1974, the CAB conferred antitrust immunity on the airline industry to combine resources and create a single national CRS. But the project collapsed in 1976 because of insufficient funding and cooperation, and American announced it was going forward individually to create a proprietary CRS.[12] American invested more than $160 million in its Sabre, while United invested $100 million in its Apollo CRS.[13] In 1976, Sabre installed its first computer terminal in a travel agency.[14]

Computer reservations systems enabled reservations to be booked in one third of the time previously required, increasing travel agent productivity 42%.[15] Other systems followed. Delta implemented an internal reservations system in 1968, and TWA implemented one in 1971. TWA's PARs was installed in travel agencies in 1976; Delta's DATAS II was installed in travel agencies in 1982. Eastern Airlines developed System One. But two systems managed to capture the preponderance of the domestic market. By 1986, Sabre was number one with 43% of the market, and United's Apollo was second with 32%. Figure 7.1, "Computer Reservations Systems: U.S. Market Shares", reveals CRSs domestic market shares in the 1980s.

---

[10] Id. at 54.
[11] Marj Leaming, Enlightened Regulation of Computer Reservations Systems Requires a Conscious Balance Between Consumer Protection and Profitable Airline Marketing, 21 Transp. L.J. 469, 471, 472 (1993).
[12] Joseph Callow, Jr., Case Note, U. Cin. L. Rev. 681 (1992).
[13] Note, The Legal and Regulatory Implications of Airline Computer Reservations Systems, 103 Harv. L. Rev. 1930 (1990).
[14] Sabre, The Sabre Story (1996).
[15] Note, The Legal and Regulatory Implications of Airline Computer Reservations Systems, 103 Harv. L. Rev. 1930 (1990).

Figure 7.1—COMPUTER RESERVATIONS SYSTEMS: U.S. MARKET SHARES (1986 and 1988)[16]

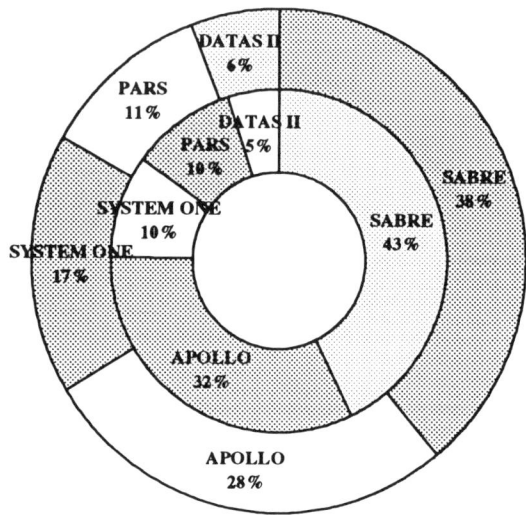

Inner Circle = 1986   Outer Circle = 1988

Customer airlines of thoses systems accused CRS owners of taking unfair advantage, in some cases raising charges 300 and 500 percent, and of generally creating a bias in the systems in favor of those dominant carriers which owned and operated them.

THE AIRLINE TARIFF PUBLISHING COMPANY

The airlines load their fares into CRSs electronically through a clearinghouse, the Airline Tariff Publishing Company [ATPCO]. This function was performed by the Tariffs Department of the Air Transport Association for the 25 years preceding ATPCO's formation in 1965. ATPCO collects and disseminates rules, fares and rate information on behalf of about 200 domestic and international airlines.

---

[16] Source: U.S. Department of Transportation.

Airlines, travel agents and CRSs subscribe to the clearinghouse for passenger fares, cargo rates, and car rental rates.[17]

THE BIG FOUR COMPUTER RESERVATIONS SYSTEMS

The overwhelming majority of sales of air travel (and a huge portion of sales of hotel rooms and automobile rentals) are accomplished through one of the four major computer reservations systems, which offer its users (principally travel agents) enormous capacity, speed, accuracy and reliability:

Sabre—American Airlines pioneered CRSs, with Sabre.[18] It is reputed to be the world's largest computer, outside the Defense Department. Its main frame computer sits in an underground bunker capable of withstanding a nuclear blast.[19] Sabre is connected to 300,000 reservations terminals in 57 countries around the world, and has processed as many as 4,176 transactions per second.[20] It processes up to a quarter billion transactions a day.[21] Sabre has 21% of the world market.

Galileo/Apollo—Owned by United, USAirways, Air Canada, British Airways and several other European carriers, Galileo International Partnership operates and markets the Apollo CRS, developed by United Airlines. Galileo was initially formed by British Airways, Swissair, KLM and Alitalia. Before a 1993 merger, United owned 50% of the Covia Partnership (Apollo's parent) and 25.6% of Galileo; United Airlines now owns 38% of Galileo, and 77% of the Apollo Travel Services Partnership, which markets the Apollo CRS to North American travel agencies.[22] Sabre and Apollo dominate the U.S. market, with a combined market share of 71%.[23] Used by more than

---

[17] Marj Leaming, Enlightened Regulation of Computer Reservations Systems Requires a Conscious Balance Between Consumer Protection and Profitable Airline Marketing, 21 Transp. L.J. 469, 474 (1993).
[18] In 1990, Sabre signed a marketing agreement with the European CRS Amadeus, which is a consortium owned equally by Lufthansa, Iberia, SAS and Air France in 1987. Amadeus, Sabre Sign Long-Term Marketing Agreement, Aviation Daily (Nov. 19, 1990), at 334.
[19] It is oddly comforting that we will still be able to book an airline reservation after a nuclear war.
[20] Sabre, The Sabre Story (1996); Thomas Petzinger, Jr., Hard Landing 407 (1995).
[21] AMR Corporation, Annual Report 22 (1994).
[22] UAL Corporation, Annual Report 34 (1994).
[23] Frank Mulvey, Airline Concentration and Competition At the Nation's Airports 10 (unpublished monograph 1992).

10,000 U.S. travel agencies, Galileo/Apollo has 24% of the world market.

Amadeus/System One—Eastern Airlines developed the System One CRS in the 1980s. With Eastern's LBO by Texas Air, System One was stripped from Eastern for a good deal less than its fair market value, and became a subsidiary of Texas Air (later renamed Continental Airline Holdings). It was subsequently folded it into Amadeus (the European CRS), for a 12.5% interest. In 1995, System One was restructured into a limited liability company (System One Information Management LLC), owned equally by Continental CRS (formerly System One, a Continental Airlines subsidiary), Amadeus (a European CRS), and EDS.[24] Amadeus is owned by Lufthansa, Air France, Iberia and Continental.[25] Amadeus/System One has 27% of the world market.

Worldspan—Delta owns 38% of Worldspan; Northwest owns 32%; TWA owns 25%; Abacus (the Asian CRS) owns 5%.[26] Northwest had purchased 50% of TWA's Pars in 1986. In 1990, Northwest, TWA and Delta agreed to combine Pars with Datas II, developed by Delta, thereby forming Worldspan.[27] Worldspan and Abacus reached an equity-sharing agreement in 1990, and Worldspan, Abacus and Amadeus formed a technical alliance in 1992. The Worldspan data center is located in Atlanta.[28] Generating $400 million in annual revenue, Worldspan has 11% of the world's market.[29]

Other CRSs—Several smaller systems exist. Abacus is owned jointly by Singapore Airlines and Cathay Pacific. Gemini was owned by Air Canada and Canadian.[30]

Figure 7.2, "World-Wide Market Share Of Computer Reservations Systems", reveals the relative market shares of the world's major CRSs.

---

[24] Continental Airlines, Annual Report 24 (1995).
[25] Aviation Daily (Apr. 5, 1996), at 39.
[26] Delta Air Lines, Inc., 10-Q Report (Sept. 28, 1994).
[27] System One, Continental Optimistic About Deal with Worldspan, Aviation Daily (Mar. 20, 1991), at 517.
[28] Worldspan, Net Page Information (1996).
[29] Michael McCartney and Eleena de Lisser, United Studies Merging Its Reservations System, Wall St. J., Mar. 5, 1996, at A3.
[30] The Financial Condition of the Airline Industry and the Adequacy of Competition, Hearings Before the Subcomm. on Aviation of the House Comm. on Public Works and Transportation, 102d Cong., 2d Sess. 489 (1991) (statement of Helane Becker).

Chapter 7

Figure 7.2—WORLD-WIDE MARKET SHARE OF COMPUTER RESERVATIONS SYSTEMS (1996)

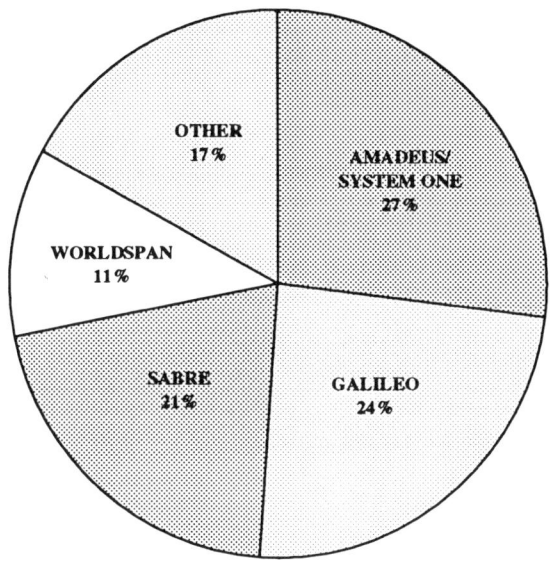

PUBLIC POLICY CONCERNS

According to the GAO, an airline which owns its own computer reservations system stands a significantly better chance of selling its product through its system than does a competitor.[31] A 1990 study of the U.S. General Accounting Office revealed that travel agents subscribing to a particular CRS "choose that airline 41 percent of the time for business travelers and 55 percent of the time for leisure travelers."[32] This phenomenon is referred to as the "halo effect"—a carrier with a disproportionate number of CRS terminals in a given area enjoys a greater number of bookings relative to the capacity it offers in the market.[33]

---

[31] U.S. General Accounting Office, Airline Competition: Impact of Computerized Reservations Systems (1986).
[32] U.S. General Accounting Office, Airline Operating & Marketing Practices 65 (1990).
[33] Thomas Petzinger, Hard Landing 242 (1995).

The disproportionate number of sales reflects several factors. First, the airline which owns a CRS typically services its vendors well, sometimes opening up closed buckets so that agents can satiate the needs of preferred customers. Airlines also offer free travel to agent employees to build good will. Second, airlines offer commission overrides to agents, which book sales above a designated quota (sometimes the quota is 90% of sales in a given market) on it. With capped commissions, overrides have become an increasingly important stream of revenue for travel agencies. Third, a carrier which dominates a CRS market also usually has the most flights in the market. Thus, an agent can save opportunity costs by focusing sales on the dominant carrier, which also happens to own the CRS. Fourth, allegations of CRS display bias persist.

Finally, DOT allows airlines to penalize the display of off-line connections. Code-sharing connections are falsely treated as on-line connections, thereby often pushing them up onto the first page of the CRS screen, or conversely, shoving their competitors off the first page. Eighty-five percent of sales are made from the first page of the CRS screen. Because the largest airlines have the most ubiquitous code-sharing relationships, the competitive offerings of smaller, independent airlines receive poorer display. Through "dual designations" most code-sharing flights are listed three different times, creating enormous "screen clutter," and again, shoving competitive offerings onto the second or third page of the CRS display, where they rarely are sold.

The algorithms which determine which flights receive priority are established by each CRS company. Typically, they involve a formula consisting of the proximity of a flight to the requested departure time (*displacement time*), plus total *elapsed time* from origin to destination, with penalties imposed on flights that require a connection, and those which involve a change in airlines. Code-sharing interlining connections are falsely treated as if they were on-line connections, to which no additional time is added. However, the major CRSs significantly penalize interline connections which do not enjoy a code-share. For example, Galileo adds 1,440 points (the equivalent of 24 hours); Worldspan adds 3,030 points; Sabre adds 999 points. In many instances, this pushes the competitive interline connection off the first page of the CRS screen, even where the interline connection is jet-to-jet, and the CRS preferred code-share alternative is jet-to-turboprop.

Chapter 7

Because of the dearth of competition in the CRS industry, United and American earn more than $300 million per year from weaker airlines beyond the cost of providing the service, according to the GAO.[34] The DOT has concluded that booking fees charged other airlines were approximately double American's or United's average costs in 1988.[35] These carriers enjoy rates of return on their CRSs of between 60% to 100% a year.[36] Sabre earned a 20% operating margin in 1993, and a 24% operating margin in 1994.[37] Critics have argued that CRSs produce extraordinary profits for their owners, far beyond the rents which could be exacted in a fully competitive market. For example, they have asserted that Sabre gives American Airlines fees in excess of costs of approximately $215 million a year, and an advantage of $328 million a year as a result of the "halo" effect.[38] American responds by insisting that Sabre's annual profits are only about $78 million, and it pays some $57 in booking fees to other CRS vendors.[39]

Computer reservations systems have created a sophisticated and expedient means of exchanging pricing proposals, and according to some critics, have facilitated implicit price fixing.[40] Before the U.S. Department of Justice entered into a consent decree with Airline Tariff Publishing Company [ATPCO] in 1994,[41] carriers would sometimes enter a fare into the CRS with an effective date in the future. If it was a higher or lower fare than already offered, the carrier providing price leadership would quickly learn whether other carriers would join in; if other carriers were particularly annoyed by a price drop, they would respond with a below-cost fare labeled "f.u.", and the proposed fare

---

[34] Intelligence, Aviation Daily (Feb. 11, 1991), at 269.
[35] The Financial Condition of the Airline Industry and the Adequacy of Competition, Hearings Before the Subcomm. on Aviation of the House Comm. on Public Works and Transportation, 102d Cong., 2d Sess. XVII (1991). DOT, Study of Computer Reservations Systems 110 (1988).
[36] The Financial Condition of the Airline Industry and the Adequacy of Competition, Hearings Before the Subcomm. on Aviation of the House Comm. on Public Works and Transportation, 102d Cong., 2d Sess. XVIII (1991).
[37] AMR Corporation, Annual Report 21 (1994).
[38] The Financial Condition of the Airline Industry and the Adequacy of Competition, Hearings Before the Subcomm. on Aviation of the House Comm. on Public Works and Transportation, 102d Cong., 2d Sess. 65 (1991) (statement of Edward R. Beauvais).
[39] The Financial Condition of the Airline Industry and the Adequacy of Competition, Hearings Before the Subcomm. on Aviation of the House Comm. on Public Works and Transportation, 102nd Cong., 2d Sess. 595 (1991) (statement of William J. Burhop).
[40] See Asra Nomani, Fare Warning: How Airlines Trade Price Plans, Wall St. J., Oct. 9, 1990, at B1.
[41] 59 Fed. Reg. 33,783 (June 30, 1994).

would be withdrawn. Thus, carriers were engaging in tacit price fixing, a per se violation of section 1 of the Sherman Antitrust Act. It was the equivalent of picking up the telephone to discern whether a competitor would match a price increase. The Justice Department's consent decree attempted to remedy the problem by requiring that fares be effective immediately when filed. But since most tickets are sold Monday through Friday, a carrier can still engage in tacit price fixing by loading a new fare on Friday evening, withdrawing it by Monday morning if other carriers do not follow the price leadership.

CRSs give management access to real-time market demand information with which to engage in yield management—expanding or contracting the low- or high-fare buckets as demand falls or rises, respectively. CRSs allow the accumulation of exceptionally detailed information on consumer travel patterns between any conceivable pair of city-pairs on the planet. However, the exorbitant fees charged by CRS owners for the data tapes are cost prohibitive for small airlines. As a consequence, the megacarriers have detailed data on small carrier sales through their CRSs, while the small carriers are effectively denied access to the same sales data of the major carriers. One wonders whether Wal-Mart would have been snuffed out in its infancy had Sears and Montgomery Ward had proprietary data concerning its sales, offering to divulge their sales data only at a price beyond the ability of their competitors to pay.

CRS REGULATION

Widespread allegations of display bias arose in the mid-1980s, leading to several proposed Congressional bills to regulate CRSs or force their divestiture from the airlines which own them. Because "market forces and competition have relatively little impact on important facets of CRS operations,"[42] the CAB/DOT found regulation necessary to prohibit airlines owning CRSs from manipulating the systems to prejudice other airlines.[43] The CAB began to regulate CRSs in 1984 by (1) prohibiting CRS owners from using airline identity to rank and edit screen display, (2) requiring that each CRS charge the same

---

[42] See Application of Covia Partnership, DOT Order 94-8-5 (1994).
[43] See Study of Airline Marketing Practices, DOT Order 94-9-35 (1994).

booking fee for each airline listed, (3) prohibiting CRSs from tying up travel agencies with contracts longer than five years, and forbidding exclusive contracts, and (4) requiring that CRS owners share marketing, booking and sales data generated by CRS.[44]

Still, a number of airlines, either singly or collectively, filed suit on antitrust grounds against computer reservations systems vendors.[45] The non-vendor airlines alleged that American and United, specifically, were restricting competition in four ways, by: (1) displaying flight information in a biased manner; (2) imposing discriminatory and extraordinarily high fees on competing carriers; (3) using data to identify specific travel agents who could be induced or persuaded to divert their business; and (4) by delaying entry of competing airlines' data into their systems.

American and United responded with a claim that arrangements of computer displays to their advantage on their systems was only fair. It was they who had taken the chance and invested in the computer systems in question, and they were entitled to a favorable return on their investments. Fundamentally, the systems had been designed to serve their companies first, not their competition.[46]

In a 1988 summary judgment, the court declared computer reservations systems subject to essential facilities doctrine. An *essential facility* is one which cannot be reasonably duplicated and to which access is necessary if one wishes to compete. A facility is "essential" when competition must have access to the facility to meaningfully be able to compete with the controlling firm.[47]

American, United, Eastern, TWA, and Delta jointly agreed to eliminate the use of secondary displays biased in favor of their own flights. Subsequently, the International Air Transport Association [IATA] formed an interest group to investigate the establishment of a neutral industry reservations system. Out of the IATA task force evolved a group of twenty-nine U.S. and foreign carriers which attempted to establish what it called the Neutral Industry Booking System. Unfortunately, the proposal was faced with significant monetary and

---

[44] 14 CFR § 255.
[45] See In re Passenger Computer Reservations Systems Antitrust Litigation, CCH 21 AVI 17,732 (1988).
[46] Laurence E. Gesell, Aviation and the Law 350 (2d ed. 1993).
[47] See In re Passenger Computer Reservations Systems Antitrust Litigation, CCH 21 AVI 17,732 (1988).

operational barriers to entry. But what did come out of the initiative was an amalgamation into a number of world-wide systems (as identified above).[48] Still, these almalgamated systems first serve the interests of their collective vendor owners ahead of other airlines.

Today, DOT regulations require that CRS displays of schedules, fares, rules and seat availability be neutral with respect to carrier identity.[49] Any default feature may not give preferential display to CRS owners. Several provisions prevent discrimination against carriers: any service enhancement must be made available to all participating carriers on a non-discriminatory basis;[50] fees charged participating carriers shall be non-discriminatory;[51] marketing, booking and sales data must be made available to all participating carriers on a non-discriminatory basis;[52] and CRSs must not discriminate against code-sharing flights.[53] To encourage travel agent independence, subscriber contracts may not exceed a term of five (and in some instances three) years, nor may they be automatically extended beyond the initial term.[54] It is debatable whether these regulation go far enough to remedy the problems identified in the immediately preceding section.

TRAVEL AGENTS

The origins of today's travel agents goes back to the creation of the Air Traffic Conference [ATC] by the domestic airlines in 1940. Implemented in 1945, ATC standardized agent qualifications, and created a program for selecting and monitoring the activities of accredited travel agents, as well as a system of reporting and remitting ticket sales by agents.[55] The International Air Transport Association [IATA] implemented a similar program shortly after World War II.

Before deregulation, travel agents booked about 40% of flights. But with the enormous complexity of fare restrictions proliferating under deregulation, agents have become an essential intermediary for most

---

[48] Laurence E. Gesell, Aviation and the Law 350 (2d ed. 1993).
[49] 14 CFR § 255.4.
[50] 14 CFR § 255.5.
[51] 14 CFR § 255.6.
[52] 14 CFR § 255.10.
[53] 14 CFR § 256.4.
[54] 14 CFR § 255.8.
[55] Thomas Dickerson, Travel Law § 5.03[2] (1993).

consumers. By the mid-1990s, 80% of flights were booked through one of the United States' 33,000 travel agents, and 95% of tickets were sold through one of the airline-owned computer reservations systems.[56] The nation's largest travel agency is American Express, which has $8 billion in sales and 68 of the Fortune 100 as travel clients.[57] (In air cargo transportation, freight forwarders essentially perform the role that travel agents play for passengers, although forwarders perform other services as well, such as packaging and consolidating small shipments).[58]

Though under regulation, the travel agents were primarily viewed as ticket issuers or dispensers on behalf of airlines, under deregulation, they have increasingly become gathers and disseminators of information on behalf of the consumer. As travel law expert Thomas Dickerson put it, "travel agents are, primarily, information specialists [upon whom consumers rely for the provision of accurate and concise information], and secondarily, order takers and ticket dispensers. The contemporary travel agent is a professional, holds himself or herself out as a travel expert, and is relied upon much like other professionals such as attorneys, doctors and accountants."[59] In 1970, the Civil Aeronautics Board recognized the fiduciary relationship between the travel agent and the consumer:

> The agent, thus, is not a mere dispenser of tickets. Rather, his role is more analogous to that of a fiduciary in whom the client places his trust for the optimum attention to his travel needs."[60]

---

[56] U.S. General Accounting Office, Airline Competition: Higher Fares and Reduced Competition at Concentrated Airports 27 (1990). Airlines attempt to induce travel agents to book flights with them by offering commission overrides, which offer economic inducements for exceeding quotas. A poll of travel agents reveals that more than half of them "usually" or "sometimes" select a carrier in order to obtain override commissions. Id. at 29.
[57] James Hirsch, American Express, the Sleeping Giant, Wakes and Spooks the Travel Industry, Wall St. J., Feb. 24, 1994, at B1.
[58] Newal Taneja, The Commercial Airline Industry 74 (1976).
[59] Thomas Dickerson, Travel Law § 5.03[1] (1993) [citations omitted].
[60] Air Travel Conference of America, Resolution Relating to Travel Agents, 55 C.A.B. 821, 824 (1970).

Promotion And Distribution

The CAB's successor agency, the U.S. Department of Transportation, has used its enforcement powers to impose sanctions against agents which violate DOT's advertising[61] and public charter regulations,[62] both of which were promulgated to protect consumer interests.

Dickerson concludes that the travel agent is an agent of the consumer to whom the agent owes a fiduciary obligation:

> The elements of consumer reliance and professional expertise have served as a basis for many courts to expressly hold travel agents as fiduciaries. The virtue of such a status is that the travel agent's duties to the consumer are independent from the travel agent's relationship with the supplier. Regardless of whether the travel agent has disclosed the identity of the principal, its liability to the consumer is based on the obligations of a fiduciary and agent of the consumer.[63]

The largest agency organization is the American Society of Travel Agents' [ASTA], which has 25,000 members in 136 countries (about half of U.S. travel agencies). ASTA's Code of Ethics also puts the interests of the consumer first, requiring that "ASTA members will not allow any preferred relationship with a supplier to interfere to interfere with the interests of their clients."[64] This suggests, for example, that travel agents have an ethical responsibility to ignore carrier commission overrides when satiating consumer's schedule, price, or service preferences. Of course, if agents ignored overrides, the airlines would stop giving them.

Before deregulation, air fares were relatively simple and standardized. With the increasing complexity of the fare structure created under deregulation, opportunity costs in the retail distribution process have grown sharply. Typically, domestic airlines change about 133,000

---

[61] 14 CFR § 380.30 and 399.84; see American Express Travel Related Services Company, Inc., DOT Order 96-11-19 (1996).
[62] 14 CFR Part 380; see Third-Party Enforcement Complaint of Ground Air Transfer, DOT Order 90-3-47 (1990).
[63] Thomas Dickerson, Travel Law § 5.30[3] (1993) [citations omitted].
[64] ASTA Code of Ethics.

fares and 3,000 flight schedules per day; the size of the discount fare buckets typically will change more than a dozen times during the life of a particular flight.[65] The wide proliferation of fares has made the services of travel agents more essential as consumers rely on agents to find the lowest fares possible. The agents now shops on consumers' behalf from a wide array of scheduled and charter airlines, and (as discussed below) tour operators and consolidators.

As noted above, travel agents rely principally on the airline CRSs to which they subscribe, from which they call up a screen display of airline schedules, fares, seat availability, restrictions, and other essential flight information, and on which they book their customers' flights.[66] But as explained below, additional travel alternatives are also available directly from tour operators and consolidators.

THE AIRLINE REPORTING CORPORATION

Airline ticketing is handled through a huge airline clearinghouse and collection agency between airlines and travel agents, the Airlines Reporting Corporation [ARC], a non-profit Delaware corporation with a principal place of business in Arlington, Virginia. ARC was created in 1984 by a consortium of Air Transport Association [ATA]-member airlines, which are its sole shareholders. In issuing a carrier's ticket, an authorized travel agent binds the carrier to provide the transportation described therein, while binding itself to remit the customer's payment to the carrier through the ARC clearinghouse. One source summarized ARC's principal functions:

> ARC essentially acts as an intermediary in the air transportation industry. Travel agents accredited by ARC are furnished with standard form traffic documents, which the agents issue to their customers as tickets for travel on particular air carriers. The carriers honor these tickets as if issued by themselves directly. In

---

[65] Marj Leaming, Enlightened Regulation of Computer Reservations Systems Requires a Conscious Balance Between Consumer Protection and Profitable Airline Marketing, 21 Transp. L.J. 469, 475 (1993).
[66] Id.

turn the travel agents report their sales and remit the money due for the tickets, minus commissions, to the carriers through ARC. ARC is then responsible for forwarding the sales proceeds to the appropriate air carrier.

One hundred and forty-three air carriers have agreed to participate in this ticket distribution system by executing a "Carrier Services Agreement" [CSA] with ARC. Section XVIII of the CSA grants ARC the power of attorney to enter into contracts with travel agents and to institute legal proceedings against any agent to collect funds owed to the carriers on transactions involving ARC ticket stock. Pursuant to that power of attorney, ARC enters into an "Agent Reporting Agreement" [ARA] with travel agencies on behalf of itself and the carriers. In signing the ARA travel agents explicitly agree to sell tickets on behalf of participating air carriers in the specific manner outlined in the ARA, and to conduct business with these carriers solely through ARC.[67]

The Airlines Reporting Corporation administers and operates the travel agents' standard ticket and area settlement plan, through which agents regularly report sales on ARC ticket stock and make payment therefor. ARC maintains an agency list of agents eligible to participate. Under the Agent Reporting Agreement, eligibility requires compliance with bonding requirements, personnel qualifications, and reports and settlement obligations.[68]

In essence, the travel agent performs several functions for the consumer: (1) shopping for the combination of schedule, itinerary, class of service, price and travel package (including hotels, automobile rentals, cruises, transfers and tours) on reputable and safe travel providers the customer seeks; (2) informing the customers of options

---

[67] Airlines Reporting Corporation v. S and N Travel, 58 F.3d 857, 859 (2d Cir. 1995).
[68] Industry Agents' Handbook § 80.

available to him/her and the restrictions thereon; (3) booking the reservations with the airline and/or other travel providers; (4) collecting revenue to be forwarded to the airline and/or other travel providers; (5) issuing the customer an airline ticket and/or other travel documents; and (6) notifying the consumer of any changes in his/her travel itinerary. To the carrier whose tickets it issues, the travel agent is bound through the ARA to follow its instructions regarding such sales, to report sales and transmit the revenue acquired from the customer to the carrier via the ARC's Central Collection Service; as the carrier's agent, the travel agent also has the power to bind the carrier to provide the transportation described in the ARC ticket. Sometimes, however, the travel agent arranges for the purchase of air travel from a tour operator or consolidator.

TOUR OPERATORS

Before deregulation, the charter airlines transported a large share of the leisure travel market. With scheduled airlines engaging in discriminatory pricing to increase their shares of the vacation market, many charter airlines have disappeared under deregulation. Nonetheless, tour operators still put together vacation "packages," consisting of air travel, hotels and/or transfers. They make advance purchases of various quantities of seats (sometimes in plane-load lots) from scheduled or charter carriers, hotels, cruise lines, bus and van services, restaurants, tour providers, and so on. These are normally combined as one- or two-week package tours, at a price lower than the sum of their component parts, and sold as package or charter tours. Many consumers want a travel expert to put together a complete package so as to avoid the inconvenience of dealing with unknown variables of service quality in a strange land whose inhabitants speak a foreign language.

CONSOLIDATORS

Once derided as "bucket shops," which focused on the ethnic sales in the long-haul international market, consolidators[69] differ from tour operators in that they focus on the airline segment of the travel package. Consolidators function as wholesale ticket distributors, purchasing relatively large blocks of seats from airlines at a discount, then selling the seats to consumers (either directly or via travel agents) at a price usually lower than the retail price offered directly by the carrier itself.[70] The tickets are essentially leftover stock or surplus inventory—what the airline projects would not otherwise be sold. An appropriate analogy would be a garment manufacturer ridding itself of unsold capacity through a factory outlet. Sometimes consolidator seats are sold without frequent flyer mileage attached. Tickets are for regularly scheduled flights but typically are nonrefundable, and dates of travel or classes of service may be limited. Cancellations and last-minute changes usually are prohibited. Travel agents will often act as an intermediary between a consumer and a consolidator. Some ticket distributors are also "rebaters," who will rebate a portion of an inflated commission back to a consumer.[71]

In 1981, the CAB provided an exemption for air carrier distribution of tickets via "contract bulk fare operators," subject to certain disclosure and consumer protection provisions (including clear and conspicuous notice before any payment of any special contractual conditions involving such issues as cancellation penalties, fees for reservations changes, and so on).[72] The DOT summarized the role of these middlemen as follows:

> The blanket exemption allows these direct air carriers to contract to sell a portion of their seats to middlemen (contract bulk fare operators). These contractors are then free to sell

---

[69] The term consolidator may also be used with reference to a freight forwarder.
[70] Consolidators: Sources of Discount Airfares, Consumer Reports Travel Letter (Oct. 1995), at 220.
[71] James Hirsch, Some Clever Fliers Beat Sky-High Fares By Knowing Where To Look On the Ground, Wall St. J., Mar. 12, 1993, at B1; Lisa Miller, Attention, Airline Ticket Shoppers..., Wall St. J., July 7, 1995, at B10.
[72] See CAB Order 81-7-109 (1981); DOT Order 86-9-61 (1986), and DOT Order 88-9-2 (1989).

> individual tickets to customers, either with or without a ground package, at whatever price their business judgments dictate. The contractors generally pay for the seats in advance and are sometimes subject to cancellation penalties for returning unsold seats. The direct air carrier continues to market seats on these flights on its own behalf through the normal air transportation distribution system ....
>
> Although the contractor assumes the risk for those seats that it has purchased from the direct air carrier, the direct air carrier has control over the scheduling of the flights involved, allocation of seat inventory, and ultimate responsibility for safeguarding the passengers' money.[73]

In essence, consolidators are wholesalers of this somewhat fungible product of air transportation, while airlines are retailers (though they often discount retail fares with sale or contract prices). Travel agencies function both as retailers (on behalf of airlines) and discounters (on behalf of consolidators or corporate travel departments), marking up the wholesale price of consolidator tickets, while still offering their customers a price lower than the suggested "list" price of the airlines. Actually, not even the airlines maintain the integrity of their "list," or published, prices, selling discount tickets to consolidators, tour operators, or large corporate or governmental enterprises. While under regulation, the tariffs filed by airlines with the Civil Aeronautics Board contained rates from which there could be no lawful deviation, under deregulation, the "list" price becomes as negotiable as the list price of a car at an automobile dealership, with the dealer sometimes adding destination charges (the equivalent of travel agent service fees) or discounting the price depending upon the buyer's schrewdness or market power.

The increasing demand of consumers for the lowest price coupled with the fiduciary relationship a travel agent has to faithfully serve his

---

[73] Exemption of Persons Who Contract for the Purchase of Blocks of Seats on Scheduled Pursuant To Applicable Tariffs for Resale To the Public, DOT Order 94-9-31 (1994) [citation omitted].

customers' needs is directing a larger share of the market toward consolidators. A 1997 survey of consolidators revealed that they are experiencing robust growth as a distribution channel. Sales increased 14.6% over the previous year, or about 50% more than the increase in airline ticket sales nationally. Since 1990, the number of travel agencies booking with consolidators increased nearly 16%. The average discount on international tickets purchased from consolidators was about 37%. Consolidators typically offer agents a 10% commission on net fares and allow agencies to add their own commissions (or service charges) thereon.[74]

However, arbitrage by individuals of tickets is prohibited by airlines, which often demand a photo ID of passengers before issuing a boarding pass, and impose significant economic penalties upon passengers who must change their travel plans.

DIRECT DISTRIBUTION

Travel agent commissions have risen sharply under deregulation. Part of that reflects the increased time it takes to book a flight, given the enormous complexity of the fare structure, and part reflects the tendency of airlines to bid up the commission in an effort to increase sales. Some low-fare carriers are double trouble for travel agents, for the commissions are lower (both because they consist of a percentage of a lower fare base, and usually do not include overrides), and the bookings sometimes must be made by telephone, for some low-fare carriers do not participate in CRSs.

Although commissions grew sharply during deregulation's first decade, travel agencies were not particularly profitable businesses. A 1990 poll of 1,600 agencies revealed 35% were losing money, 10% broke even, and 23% had a profit margin of 3% or less.[75]

Direct sales to customers allow airlines to avoid certain costs, notably travel agent commissions (which can range from 10% of the ticket price and up domestically, to up to 30% internationally), and CRS booking fees (about $2.70 per segment, whether the passenger actually buys the ticket or not). Delta Air Lines led an industry-wide

---

[74] Airline Consolidator Sales Increasingly Significant, Travel Weekly, Apr. 21, 1997.
[75] James Hirsch, Cuts Hit Travel Agents; Customers May Suffer, Wall St. J., Feb. 14, 1995, at B1, B5.

effort to cap travel agent commissions in the mid-1990s, and they remain a target of management cost-cutting. Since major carriers still rely on travel agents for most sales, the trick is to reduce commissions and increase direct sales without alienating agents, for they have vast influence over which airline tickets are sold (as airlines themselves acknowledge with commission overrides). With commissions capped, commission overrides have become significantly more important to many agencies, thereby increasing the leverage large carriers have on coercing agents to steer their clients' business toward them.

The ticket is the tie that binds the airline to the agent. Ticketless travel (i.e., giving a customer an "e-ticket"—or electronic ticket—consisting of a confirmation number, and perhaps a faxed itinerary, rather than a "red-back" ARC ticket) results in a cost savings and provides the carrier with ad hoc reporting capabilities. To the extent that sales are kept out of the CRSs, an airline retains strategic control of internal sales data. Selling tickets directly means investing more in internal ticketing and reservations personnel, toll-free telephone lines, internal computer systems, and advertising. Prominent advertising of the toll-free telephone number and increasing internal reservations lines and staff and technology are the essential first steps in the transition to direct distribution. For example, Northwest Airlines implores its customers in large type:

> **Save Time and money with one call.**
> You can have tickets mailed to your home or business at no extra charge. It's this easy: Choose your destination and travel dates. Have your credit card available. And have a pencil, paper and calendar handy. Then call Northwest Airlines at 1-800-225-2525. Your tickets will be in the mail in no time. You can also call your travel agent or visit one of our City Ticket Offices.[76]

---

[76] Wall St. J., Apr. 4, 1996, at A11.

Certainly, a consumer can place his or her reservation and purchase a ticket through a travel agent. But this advertisement clearly urges the consumer to purchase a ticket directly from the carrier. The balance between reduced agent commissions and CRS fees on the one hand, and increased internal reservations staff and technology, as well as increased advertising expenses, is the net savings the airline realizes by direct distribution.

Several carriers began interactive World Wide Web internet sites that enable consumers to book flights directly, bypassing CRSs altogether. As an inducement to individuals to book directly, some carriers offer frequent flyer mileage bonuses. Several CRSs are offering access directly to consumers, bypassing travel agents (and agent commissions) altogether. EasySabre is available on America OnLine, and Worldspan is available on CompuServe.[77] Sabre is also available on the Net, at www.travelocity.com. Flights on Southwest Airlines can be booked at www.iflyswa.com. United has its own software, "United Connection," which like the Net, is available via telephone connection. America West began discussions with travel agents to promote booking on the Internet.[78] Reno Air offered travel agents a 2% commission override for direct bookings, outside the CRSs.

In an effort to stem the tide away from CRSs, Sabre developed a new "Basic" service to allow Sabre agents to make bookings directly with cost-conscious carriers at only $1.60 per booking, a price competitive with the internal reservations costs of some carriers.[79]

CORPORATE TRAVEL DEPARTMENTS

Wielding oligopsony power, large corporations which have more than a half-million dollars in travel expenses per year can often negotiate contract rates directly with airlines, providing for discretionary travel fares, but without the pre-purchase and minimum-stay restrictions. Some internalize travel purchasing in a corporate travel department. A few insist that corporate executives rebate frequent flyer mileage to be distributed for future business trips. Others

---

[77] Aviation Daily (Jan. 30, 1996), at 154.
[78] Aviation Daily (Mar. 4, 1996), at 352.
[79] Bridget O'Brian, AMR Designs New Network for Air Tickets, Wall St. J., Jan. 18, 1995, at A4.

"out-source" travel to a local travel agency, often insisting a partial rebate of agent commissions earned on the corporation's sales.

From the corporation's perspective, the advantages of centralized purchasing are several. As noted, negotiating sales as a block enables the corporation to enjoy lower costs for air travel. Centralized purchasing can steer travel to the lowest priced ticket irrespective of the executives' carrier preferences based on frequent flyer affiliations.

CORPORATE COMMUNICATIONS

An airline is a high-profile business. A serious crash or aircraft hijacking will make the front page of many newspapers and covers of many news magazines. Consumers are perpetually concerned with the level of air fares. Thus, many airlines find it beneficial to have a corporate communications, or public relations department, to court and massage the press, creating favorable publicity, and giving newsworthy items the airline's "spin."

An aviation catastrophe in which lives are lost can have a deleterious impact on an airline's internal morale and financial well-being, not to mention the trauma it imposes on the friends and families of the victims. If poorly handled, it can exacerbate the airline's decline in bookings and litigation expense. In such circumstances, the airline must promptly communicate all the information it knows to the families of the victims. It must respond to media requests expeditiously, preferably with a press conference by the CEO expressing compassion for the friends and families of the victims, allaying the public's fears about the carrier's safety, and responding as straightforwardly as possible to all inquiries.[80]

ADVERTISING

Advertising is of two types—institutional and competitive. The purpose of *institutional advertising* is to encourage people to fly more, so as to shift the demand curve to the right. The purpose of *competitive advertising* is to preserve and increase a carrier's market

---

[80] Carl Quintanilla, TWA's Response to Crash Is Viewed As Lesson in How Not to Handle Crisis, Wall St. J., July 22, 1996, at A9.

share relative to its competitors' in the market.[81] The fundamental challenge for an airline is to develop a *brand* which will distinguish it from the widely held perception among many consumers that air transportation is in the nature of a fungible commodity. Branding increases demand and allows a firm to charge a premium for its product. In order to develop a brand, an airline must (1) decide what products, both tangible and psychological, will distinguish it from its rivals, (2) invest heavily in advertising and promotion, (3) consistently deliver what is promised, and (4) stick with it.[82]

Advertising and other promotional efforts are designed to educate potential consumers about an airline, its new routes or fares, or its new class of service, for example. Both service and price form essential components of the carrier's image.[83] Price, destination, schedule and service become the focus of the advertising. A carrier with more destinations enjoys significant economies of scale in advertising multiple product lines with a single ad. Direct distribution depends on the prominent display of the toll-free telephone number as well.

Advertising of airline fares is highly deceptive. First, the price advertised is usually a promotional fare (rather than even the average fare), available only on a small number of seats, and very highly restricted. Moreover, only half the actual lowest price offered is advertised in large print.

"Fares are each way based on round trip purchase," reveals the 4-point mouse type at the bottom of the advertisement for a $79 fare to Orlando. "Seats are limited." These are two restrictions that would be tolerated in no other industry. Could Saks Fifth Avenue or Wall-Mart advertise gloves or pants at only the left glove or right pant leg price, requiring the purchase of the pair? Could Sears offer washing machines at $79, but then only stock a few at that price, and once they were sold, offer its customers the same machine at $499? Yet because of the federal preemption mandated by the Airline Deregulation Act of 1978, states are powerless to enforce their unfair and deceptive advertising laws against airlines. DOT has exhibited little enthusiasm for reigning in these more blatantly misleading (if not fraudulent) anti-consumer practices.

---

[81] Newal Taneja, The Commercial Airline Industry 69 (1976).
[82] Stephen Shaw, Airline Marketing & Management 156-60 (3rd ed. 1990).
[83] See William Pride & O.C. Ferrell, Marketing Concepts and Strategies 28-30 (6th ed. 1989).

Some carriers, such as Northwest, have been notorious for phantom fare sales—raising prices and then declaring a "sale," or declaring a "sale" at prices higher than their prevailing rates.[84] Were he alive, P.T. Barnum would be favorably impressed. Like Pavlov's dog, consumers have been conditioned to salivate (and make discretionary travel purchases) only when they hear the word "sale."[85]

IMAGE

Some carriers have attempted to capitalize on the sex appeal of aviation, and their flight attendants. From its earliest days, Southwest Airlines used the stock symbol LUV, and hired only female flight attendants (until a judge ordered otherwise), requiring them to wear hot pants and clinging tops.[86] National Airlines ran ads with attractive flight attendants saying such provocative lines as, "I'm Jennifer, fly me." Braniff required its flight attendants to do an in-flight "air strip" in which they progressively peeled away layers of their designer uniforms.[87] These ads were run in the days of sexually suggestive books like *Coffee, Tea or Me?*

Several airlines have attempted to transform their image by changing the livery of their aircraft. To increase their visibility, Braniff's jets were painted in seven jellybean colors. Alexander Calder was hired to wrap a DC-8 and 727 planes in swirling colors. Braniff's advertising slogan was "When you've got it, flaunt it!"[88] Both Southwest and All Nippon Airways had killer whales painted on their aircraft. Qantas graces its livery with aboriginal art.[89] American Airlines shuns paint in favor of a polished aluminum fuselage, which, because of lower weight, saves fuel.

To enhance its visibility, Pan Am painted its name across its fuselage like a giant billboard. In its prime, Pan Am's trademark was second only to Coca-Cola in worldwide recognition, "a fixture of pop-

---

[84] Scott McCartney, Why Airline Fare Sales Aren't Always a Bargain, Wall St. J., Mar. 11, 1996, at B1; James Hirsch, Some Air-Fare Sales Are No Sales at All, Wall St. J., Jan. 4, 1995, at B1.
[85] See Air-Fare War Goes On and On, Wall St. J., June 14, 1994, at B5.
[86] Thomas Petzinger, Jr., Hard Landing 29 (1995).
[87] Id at 31.
[88] Id at 134-136.
[89] Douglas Nelms, Imaging's New Demands, Air Transport World (Apr. 1996), at 35.

Promotion And Distribution

ular culture, symbolizing the exotic."[90] In advertising, it emphasized the depth of its experience. One early ad, during the Prohibition era, informed consumers, "Fly with us to Havana, and you can bathe in Bacardi rum four hours from now."[91] The Pan Am name and trademark was purchased for $1.3 million out of Pan Am's bankruptcy estate, and would grace the livery of a new airline by the same name, a low-cost carrier with ASM costs allegedly at an astounding 4.8 cents.[92] Several upstart airlines have attempted to capitalize on the good will of carriers which fell into the deregulation graveyard. Thus, new carriers named Braniff, Midway, PanAm and Frontier have emerged, like the Phoenix, from the ashes.

TWA's advertising firm produced 54 different aircraft livery designs from which management selected one in 1995, to be repainted on its aircraft as they rotate through normal maintenance. This was the first new exterior for the carrier since 1974.[93] In 1996, TWA brought out nostalgic television commercials touting its 50 years of service across the Atlantic. TWA also put its name on a football stadium in St. Louis, while United bought rights to the name of Chicago's coliseum.

Before Lorenzo, the "Proud Bird With the Golden Tail," serving chateaubriand and Chevas Regal in coach. Continental repainted its livery in an attempt to shed an image as a carrier with a poor level of service. United repainted its red and orange striped livery to an industrial gray and blue livery which, unlike any other flying animal, placed the darker color on the belly of the bird, and with a Stealth look, camouflages the aircraft against a gray sky. But then, gray was apparently CEO Stephen Wolf's favorite color (he had Republic's jets repainted gray when he was CEO there). Shortly after he became USAir's CEO, Wolf ordered its fleet repainted deep blue on top and gray on the bottom (like a United Airlines' jet flying upside-down). Northwest Airlines came up with a fuselage painted in a bright red swath above a gray underside, nicknamed the "bowling shoe."[94] America West began repainting its fleet in 1996.[95] Delta began re-

---

[90] Thomas Petzinger, Jr. Hard Landing 17 (1995).
[91] Id. at 7.
[92] Aviation Daily (Jan. 31, 1996), at 159.
[93] Aviation Daily (Sept. 29, 1995).
[94] Carl Quintanilla, United Airlines Goes for the Stealth Look In Coloring Its Planes, Wall St. J., Nov. 21, 1994, at 1A.
[95] Aviation Daily (Jan. 19, 1996), at 92.

Chapter 7

painting its livery in 1997. Typically, the aircraft are repainted over time as they are rotated through normal maintenance checks when they would be repainted anyway, thereby costing the carrier little additional expense. Unfortunately, Southwest refuses to depart from its dreadfully unforgettable gold, red and orange livery.

WesternPacific came up with the novel idea of turning the fuselage into a flying billboard ($125,000 for a two-year display), creating another revenue source, and giving it immediate notoriety as an *avant garde* carrier. Under its Air Logo program, WesternPacific advertised the Fox Network's television program the "Simpson's," on one aircraft, and a garish 39-foot high painting of Aki, a Las Vegas showgirl for the Stardust casino, on another.[96] Actually, the precedent was set in 1927 by Charles Lindbergh, who named his plane the "Spirit of St. Louis" in deference to the wishes of his benefactor, a St. Louis banker.[97] But in WesternPacific's case, it appeared tasteless, obfuscated its market identity, and put it in the consumer's mind as an unprofessional carrier, which cost it sales after the ValuJet crash in the Everglades on May 11, 1996.

Various slogans have been invented by advertising agencies to distinguish one airline from another. United asks consumers to "Come Fly the Friendly Skies," with background music from Gershwin's *Rhapsody In Blue*. With employee ownership, "the employee-owners of United Airlines" implored consumers to "Come Fly *Our* Friendly Skies." American sings, "We're American Airlines, Doing What We Do Best." At different times, Delta insists, "We Love To Fly, And It Shows," "You'll Love the Way We Fly," or "Delta Is Ready When You Are."[98] America West argues it flies the same planes and provides the same service as its larger rivals, then informs the public, "It Seems Silly To Pay More." In response to the sales of its competitors, Southwest ran newspaper advertisements proclaiming, "We'd love to match their new fares, but we'd have to raise our's." Other carrier's tailored their pitch to the high-yield business traveler. SAS proclaimed itself "The Businessman's Airline."[99] Alaska Airlines christened itself "The Last Great Airline," harkening back to the days when gas-station

---

[96] Aviation Daily (Nov. 3, 1995), at 200.
[97] Thomas Petzinger, Jr., Hard Landing 4 (1995).
[98] Delta's Marketing Guru Is High On Change, Wall St. J., Dec 12, 1996, at B7.
[99] Stephen Shaw, Airline Marketing & Management 76 (3rd ed. 1990).

345

attendants washed windshields and checked the oil, although Alaska actually cut back service.[100]

Eastern billed itself as "The Wings of Man." Its CEO, astronaut Frank Borman, would pitch the company personally in television advertisements, an approach Chrysler's Lee Iacocca would later embrace. First Eastern, then Delta, paid for the privilege to be the "Official Airline of Walt Disney World." Atlanta-based Delta also became the "Official Airline of the 1996 Summer Olympic Games," flying livery as the "Spirit of Atlanta."[101] Even the upstart carriers embrace a symbol. Denver-based Frontier Airlines decreed itself "The Spirit of the West," adhering huge decals of Rocky Mountain wildlife on the tails of its 737s.

The cargo carriers also employ advertising slogans. Flying Tigers coined the phrase, "Anything, Anytime, Anywhere." FedEx proclaimed, "When it has to be there, absolutely, positively overnight."

Some carriers have tried to change their image by changing their names. Howard Hughes, who purchased controlling interest in Transcontinental & Western Airways (TWA) changed its name to Trans World Airlines, giving the company a global image (though at the time Pan American World Airways was the only truly trans-world airline). In 1979, Allegheny sought to shed its regional image by changing its name to USAir. In 1997, USAir became USAirways, presumably to position itself as the U.S. equivalent of British Airways on the other side of the Atlantic. Also in 1997, ValuJet jettisoned its name (which had suffered enormous "bad will" after its Everglades' crash) in favor of AirTran after its acquisition of that smaller carrier.

---

[100] Douglas Nelms, Imaging's New Demands, Air Transport World (Apr. 1996), at 34, 36.
[101] Id.

CHAPTER 8.

COST CONTAINMENT

"The most important determinants of carrier success are the abilities to achieve and maintain low costs effectively to provide customers with the value they so clearly seek."[1]
Roberts Roach & Associates
Aviation Consultants

"There have been some morale problems. But so be it. You go back to the question of survival, and it makes the decision very easy."[2]
Ronald Allen
CEO, Delta Airlines

"You can make a pizza so cheap no one will eat it."[3]
Gordon Bethune
CEO, Continental Airlines

THE IMPACT OF THE LOW-COST ENTRANTS

New airlines emerged shortly after the promulgation of the Airline Deregulation Act of 1978—carriers such as Midway Airlines, America West and People Express. Their most singular competitive advantage

---

[1] Roberts Roach & Associates, Scorecard: Airline Industry Cost Management 2Q 1995 (3rd ed. 1996).
[2] Martha Brannigan & Eleena de Lisser, Cost Cutting at Delta Raises the Stock Price But Lowers the Service, Wall St. J., June 20, 1996, at A1, A9.
[3] Quoted in Scott McCartney, Piloted By Bethune, Continental Air Lifts Its Workers' Morale, Wall St. J., May 15, 1996, at A1, A4.

was their cost structure, which enabled them to offer significantly lower fares to consumers. Not saddled with the labor agreements of the established major airlines (which included the generous wage and elaborate work rule provisions which had evolved under regulation, coupled with a relatively senior work force), the new entrants enjoyed a significant comparative advantage in terms of lower base salaries, an entry level work force, and greater flexibility in the utilization of personnel. This enabled the new carriers to 'cream skim' dense routes, offering low-cost, low-fare, no-frills service, allowing them to penetrate the market shares of the established trunk, national and regional airlines. Although this first wave of new entrants never accounted for more then 5% of the total passenger market, and all but America West was liquidated (though it too, stumbled into Chapter 11 bankruptcy), they put enormous pressure on established carriers to cut costs.

Established airlines found the consuming public quite fickle, with little brand loyalty, and willing to purchase air transportation primarily on the basis of schedule and price. There was enormous pent-up demand for low-priced service, and little willingness to pay for in-flight amenities. The large carriers found that the new carriers were diverting traffic, causing load factors to fall below break-even levels. Determined to preserve market shares, the traditional carriers met the low fares, at least on some seats, which caused significant yield erosion. The established carriers attempted to confine the impact of the low fares with revenue and inventory management, and retain high-yield traffic with various manipulations of computer reservations systems display, frequent flyer programs, travel agent commission overrides, and other practices. By the early 1990s, more than 100 airlines had found themselves in bankruptcy, while People Express, Midway and Laker Skytrain were liquidated. Nonetheless, the destructive competition unleashed by deregulation produced the worst economic period in the airline industry's history.

The sharp erosion in carrier profitability led the major carriers to focus on cost containment, efficiency and productivity. Seat pitch was tightened. Hot meals became cold meals, then peanuts, on flights of less than 1,000 miles. But many costs, particularly fuel and equipment costs, as well as interest expenses, are beyond the control of the airlines. (Nor do airlines have adequate control over the demand side of the equation when recession curtails discretionary traffic). Ultimately, management found that it had little choice but to focus on costs that were conceivably pliable—labor costs, and perhaps more importantly, work rules, as well as distribution costs, including travel agent commissions. Labor is the single largest operating expense, accounting for between 34% and 37% of the total operating costs during the 1980s. Again, the new entrants, most operating without labor unions (and those with union contracts significantly less costly and restrictive than those of the established airlines) enjoyed a significant cost advantage.

The first wave of new entrants collapsed into bankruptcy by the mid-1980s, with only America West emerging from Chapter 11 bankruptcy successfully. Even the pre-deregulation airlines lingered on in bankruptcy and there, largely shielded from creditors, began to undercut the fares of their competitors. Pan Am and Eastern were ultimately liquidated, although Continental, TWA and America West lived through Chapter 11 to see another day.

By the early 1990s, a second wave of new entrants would emerge—carriers like Kiwi International, ValuJet, Reno, Morris Air and MarkAir, as well as carriers which borrowed the names of their deceased predecessors, such as Braniff, Midway and Frontier, for example. These were carriers with ASM costs as low as 6.5 cents, in the case of WesternPacific, and 6.7 cents in the case of ValuJet.[4] The glut of capacity had caused the major carriers to ground 700 jets and lay off thousands of skilled workers.

The leasing companies were hungry to derive revenue from their enormous capital investments. By the mid-1990s, a 20 year-old 737-200 with Dash-9 engines could be leased for less than $90,000 a month, while a younger, hush-kitted 737-200 with Dash-17 engines could be leased for about $150,000 per month. A decade old Stage 3 737-300 could be leased for about $215,000, while a new one leased for about $280,000 a month. The 300 was quieter, had greater range, and carried more passengers. And younger aircraft generally are more reliable and have lower maintenance costs than older aircraft. In the 1990s, laid-off pilots were eager to fly, and willing to take a salary at a fraction of their prior pay. At Kiwi, pilots were expected to invest

---

[4] Western Pacific Crows It's Lowest Cost Airline, Rocky Mountain News, Apr. 23, 1996, at 9B.

Cost Containment

$50,000 in the company's stock,[5] making commercial aviation perhaps the only industry in which people will pay for the privilege to work in it. Aircraft and trained personnel were abundant, so off they flew, in the fleets of new carriers with low cost structures and low fares. Table 8.1, "Upstart Airlines", identifies the more prominent post-deregulation start-up airlines.

Table 8.1—UPSTART AIRLINES

Scheduled Carriers Emerging Since Deregulation

Air Atlanta*	Frontier II
Air Florida*	Frontier Horizon**
Air One*	Hawaii Express**
Air Niagara*	Jet America**
Air South	Kiwi International*
Air Train	Leisure Air*
AirTran	MarkAir*
Air21	McClain Air**
Altair*	MGM Grand Air**
America West	Midway Airlines*
American International*	Midway II
Arrow Airways*	Midwest Express
Best Airlines*	Morris Air**
Braniff II*	Muse Air**
Braniff III*	NationsAir
Carnival Air	New York Air**
Discovery Airlines*	Northeastern International
Eastwind Airlines	Pacific Express*
Emerald*	People Express*
Empire Airlines**	Presidential*
Florida Express**	Presidential II

---

[5] Julie Schmit, Small Airline Glides Upward On Loyalty, USA Today, Sept. 22, 1994, at B1; Adam Bryant, Kiwi Works to Redefine a Hostile Airline Culture, N.Y. Times, Feb. 24, 1994, at C-1.

Table 8.1—UPSTART AIRLINES (Cont'd.)

Pride Air*	TriStar
Regent Air*	UltrAir*
Reno Air	USAfrica*
Royal West*	Valujet
Spirit**	Vanguard
Sterling One*	Western Pacific
Sunworld*	

Scheduled/Nonscheduled Startups

American Trans Air	Sun Country
Private Jet/National*	Tower Air

Regional Carriers

Air Wisconsin	Horizon Air
Atlantic Coast Airlines	Mesa
Atlantic Southeast	Mesaba Aviation
Comair	Sky West Airlines

* Liquidated ** Merged into another carrier.

Further, one pre-deregulation airline was achieving fairly consistent profitability—Southwest. Southwest was born in the 1970s as an intrastate Texas airline, and although unionized, was never saddled with the full panoply of restrictive work rules that dominated the contracts of the trunk carriers. Southwest found a niche quite different from the other major carriers. Southwest embraced a linear route system (the dominant route system of all airlines prior to deregulation), flying one type of aircraft (the Boeing 737) in quick turns with frequent service in relatively dense short-haul markets. Southwest shunned hub connections, or interlining, and focused its operations on secondary airports, where available. Its high productivity, measured in equipment and labor utilization, were much admired by carriers with higher cost structures. In 1995, Southwest had the first or second largest market shares in more than half of the 25 largest city-pair markets in the U.S. under 750 miles in length, though in several it was not the low-fare savior it was touted to be, with average yields in some markets it dominated well over 20 cents per RPM.[6]

By the mid-1990s, the non-union, low-cost, low-fare carriers were the driving force in the industry. Borrowing from the wisdom of baseball legend Satchel Paige, Deputy Assistant Secretary of Transportation Patrick Murphy warned the mega-carriers, "Do not look back. A new airline might be gaining on you."[7] In 1993, a record 42 airlines applied for a Certificate of Public Convenience and Necessity to launch commercial air service.[8] From January 1990 until mid-1996, DOT had certificated nearly 50 new airlines.[9] By 1996, 25 of the 39 new carriers certificated since 1993 were still flying (13 were passenger carriers, while 12 were charter and cargo carriers).[10] In 1995, low-cost carriers increased their capacity by 38%.[11] Flying high with 51 aircraft before its 1996 crash in the Florida Everglades, with a $1 billion order, ValuJet became the launch customer for the 100-seat twin-engine MD-95 aircraft.[12] The major carriers had been financially decimated by the anemic profitability deregulation unleashed. Faced with a new round of upstart airlines, the major carriers were no longer able to launch widespread price wars to destroy the new entrants. Although in some markets, the magacarriers targeted the upstarts with predatory practices, dumping capacity and engaging in below-cost pricing.

Though some were predicting a 90% failure rate among the new airline ventures,[13] their yield impact on the majors was real. DOT estimated passengers flying these upstart airlines paid $54 less per

---

[6] Aviation Daily (Apr. 25, 1996), at 154.
[7] Aviation Daily (May 9, 1996), at 232.
[8] Jonathan Dahl, New Airlines Can Leave Fliers Grounded, Wall St. J., June 30, 1995, at B7.
[9] Aviation Daily (Apr. 8, 1996), at 49.
[10] Aviation Daily (May 9, 1996), at 232.
[11] Martha Brannigan & Eleena de Lisser, Delta Air May Try New 'Lite' Service, Wall St. J., Feb. 9, 1996, at B8.
[12] Aviation Daily (Oct. 20, 1995), at 111.
[13] Aviation Daily (Apr. 22, 1996), at 127.

flight.[14] Where major carriers maintained their yields, the new airlines were stimulating new demand. Lower ticket prices were a direct reflection of the new entrants' lower cost structure.

Southwest and Valujet had a 6.5 cent cost per available seat mile [ASM] on 500 mile stage lengths, while American, United and USAir had costs nearly double that. In the short-haul market, Delta's costs were 45% higher than Valujet's, while USAir's costs were 187% higher than Valujet.[15] In the long-haul (1,400 miles) narrow-body aircraft category, American Trans Air had costs of 5.4 cents per ASM (only 60% of USAir's). Adjusted for seating density, America West had the lowest costs in this category, just north of five cents. In the long-haul wide-body aircraft category, American Trans Air had ASM costs of only 4.1 cents (compared with American and United's 8.5 cents per ASM).[16]

And the upstart airlines seemed to be popping up everywhere. Delta was faced with low-fare carriers on 32% of its routes; by 1994, it had grown to 57%; and by 1995, low-fare carriers competed on 60% of its routes.[17] American (which had withdrawn from many markets dominated by low-cost carriers) still had them affecting 40% of its bookings.[18] As a consequence, the established major airlines have been compelled to focus on cost containment and reduction. Revenue must exceed costs by a sufficient margin to attract capital and ensure the industry will be able to meet new equipment needs. Inadequate profitability pushed the industry's debt to "junk" levels. One source predicts, "Unless operating and labor costs can be slashed to 7.0 - 7.5 cents per available seat mile (ASM) and, more importantly, maintained at these levels, the future of most major U.S. airlines will be uncertain at best."[19] One source summarized the trend:

---

[14] Aviation Daily (Apr. 24, 1996), at 139.
[15] Roberts Roach & Associates, Scorecard: Airline Industry Cost Management 2Q 1995 12 (3rd ed. 1996).
[16] Id. at 1, 2.
[17] Delta Air Lines, Annual Report 6 (1995).
[18] Aviation Daily (Apr. 1, 1996), at 1.
[19] Edward Phillips, Lower Costs Key to Airlines' Survival, Aviation Week & Space Tech. (Mar. 13, 1995), at 67.

> Welcome to the new reality of the U.S. airline industry. The big carriers are shrinking—cutting back where they aren't making money, shifting planes and employees to profitable routes....
>
> With union leaders fighting wage cuts and passengers refusing to fly without a discount, airlines have struggled for alternative ways to stop the bleeding.
>
> That means scrapping unprofitable short trips, subbing smaller aircraft for larger ones, and hiring other companies to cook food, train crews, fix engines and even fly the planes.[20]

The major airlines had charted a course to become lean and mean. According to American Airlines' CEO, Robert Crandall:

> Since deregulation, carriers whose costs are far below those of the established industry participants—and whose low costs encourage them to offer very low fares—have become an important part of the industry. In fact, low-cost carriers now provide about one-third of the domestic industry's available seat miles. While many new carriers fail to achieve profitability and leave the industry, the ready availability of airline assets and trained personnel continue to attract more new entrants eager to try their individual approaches to providing low-cost, low-fare transportation. In addition, some who fail are revived by the bankruptcy process and return to the fray. Over the years, several well-established carriers have been unable to meet the challenge and have ceased operations; others have been seriously weakened.

---

[20] America's Airline Industry Adjusts To Harsh New Reality, Denver Post, Apr. 18, 1993, at 7G.

> It is increasingly clear that if American is to be successful in the long term, we must lower airline costs sufficiently so that our revenue advantages can overcome the spread between our costs and those of our low-cost competitors. To do so, we must cut costs across the board and must—particularly—cut our labor costs dramatically, since labor is our single largest expense and the cost category in which our disadvantage is most extreme.[21]

Some low-cost airlines have been the most consistently profitable. Since deregulation, Southwest earned a 10.7% pre-tax operating margin, compared with American Airlines' 1.9%.[22]

OVERVIEW OF OPERATING COSTS

Table 8.2, "Breakdown of Airline Operating Expenses", shows both the relative impact of operating costs, as well as how they changed over the last decade. The airline industry's operating expenses increased 94% during deregulation's first six years.[23] Over the 15 year period from 1980 to 1995, as a percentage of operating expenses, labor costs declined 26% and fuel declined 269%, while rentals soared 861% and commissions increased 238%.[24] Much of rental expense is effectively attributable to off-balance sheet debt.

The largest difference between the major and national carries is the percentage of operating expense attributable to labor, with the majors spending considerably more of operating revenue on this item. This reflects the age of the companies, and the existence or terms of their respective labor agreements. Rentals account for a larger percentage of the national carriers' operating expenses, attributable to new entry

---

[21] AMR Corporation, First Quarter Report 3, 4 (1994).
[22] Roberts Roach & Associates, Scorecard: Airline Industry Cost Management 2Q 1995 7, 8 (3rd ed. 1996).
[23] GAO, Competition: Higher Fares and Reduced Competition At Concentrated Airports 24 (1990).
[24] Salaries Have Doubled Since 1980; Other Expenses Grew Faster, Aviation Daily (July 29, 1991).

Cost Containment

with leased equipment (see Figure 8.1, "U.S. Airlines Operating Expenses Breakdown").

Table 8.2—BREAKDOWN OF AIRLINE OPERATING EXPENSES[25] (in percentage)

Expenses	1969	1973	1980	1990	1994	1995
Labor Salaries & Benefits	40.9	45.6	37.3	33.8	35.6	36.3
Equipment Rentals	n.a.	n.a.	1.8	7.1	15.5	15.5
Aircraft Fuel & Oil	12.4	12.1	31.0	17.7	11.5	11.6
Travel Agent Commissions	2.5	3.2	3.4	10.0	11.0	9.3
Food	3.6	3.9	n.a.	n.a.	3.6	3.4
Landing Fees	1.9	2.6	1.7	1.8	2.2	2.2
Advertising and Other Promotions	2.9	2.4	1.7	2.1	1.7	1.7
Interest On Debt	3.8	3.3	n.a.	n.a.	n.a.	n.a.
All Other	32.0	26.9	21.2	27.2	18.9	20.0

Figure 8.1—U.S. AIRLINE OPERATING EXPENSES BREAKDOWN[26]

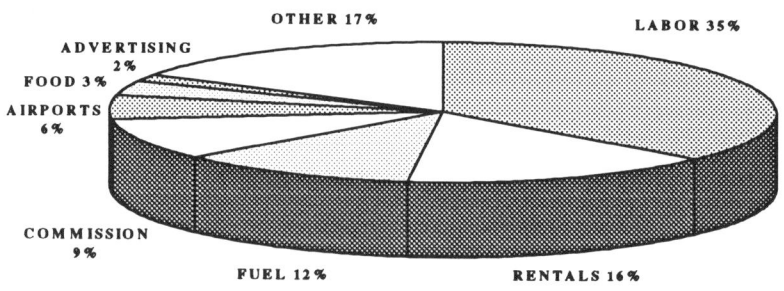

---

[25] Comparison of Selected Airline Industry Expenses, Aviation Daily (July 29, 1991), at 176; Aviation Daily (Jan. 25, 1996), at 127; ESG Aviation Services, 8 Airline Monitor F2 (Mar/Apr 1996): George James, Airline Economics 10 (1982); Newal Taneja, Civil Aviation (2d ed. 1989); ESG Aviation Services, 9 Airline Monitor F2 (June 1996).
[26] Source: ESG Aviation Services and Air Transport Association of America.

Chapter 8

Accounting firms performing independent audits of publicly traded airlines often segregate costs along functional lines. Typically, they divide operating expenses as follows:

- *Flight Operations*—Includes aircraft fuel, aircraft lease and insurance expenses, pilot and flight attendant compensation, in-flight catering, crew overnight expenses, flight dispatch and flight operations administrative expenses.
- *Aircraft and Traffic Servicing*—Includes all expenses incurred at the airport (e.g., baggage handling, catering) as well as station operations, administration, and ground equipment and maintenance thereof.
- *Maintenance*—Includes labor, equipment and parts for repairing aircraft. There are two categories of maintenance and repair—daily or weekly routine service checks, and major engine overhauls and heavy maintenance checks.
- *Promotional and Sales*—Includes travel agent commissions, advertising, and credit card expenses, CRS costs, wages and benefits for reservationists as well as marketing, management and sales personnel.
- *Depreciation and Amortization*—Includes amortization and depreciation of capital leases, office equipment, ground station equipment, and other fixed assets.

It is for each carrier to ascertain its system-wide costs, and compare them with carriers having similar route structures and operational characteristics to determine whether certain cost categories are consuming excessive resources. This is the concept of "benchmarking." It is also imperative for management to break down costs on a route-by-route (or segment-by-segment) basis so as to measure each route's performance. It is a complex, but necessary task, requiring ascribing system-wide overhead to aircraft, crew and ground facilities on some equitable basis.

Some sources maintain that there are three ways to improve carrier profitability—"cutting costs, increasing sales (and market share), and improving yields."[27] To achieve the equivalent bottom line improve-

---

[27] The Balancing Act, Airline Bus., The Skies in 1992 17 (1992).

Cost Containment

ment, an airline would need to slash costs 10%, increase sales by 25%, and improve yields by 5%.[28] Thus, paring costs can be only one tactic among several in attempting to achieve profitability.

The difficulty lies in the fact that most costs are beyond the airlines' control. For example, fuel prices and interest rates are set elsewhere, and can be highly volatile. Airport landing and gate fees are offered on a "take it, or leave it" basis. Aircraft costs are high, and usually negotiable only if purchases are made in large quantities. Labor costs are often locked in by contract, and protected by labor laws from unilateral change until a lengthy process has run its course; and organized labor can exact a huge pound of flesh from any airline wanting to do battle. Nonetheless, according to Air Transport Association [ATA] President Carol Hallett, "Cost-containment has become a way of life for the airline industry."[29] Figure 8.2, "U.S. Airlines Expenses Per Available Seat Mile", reveals the progress that has been made.

Figure 8.2—U.S. AIRLINES EXPENSES PER AVAILABLE SEAT MILE[30]

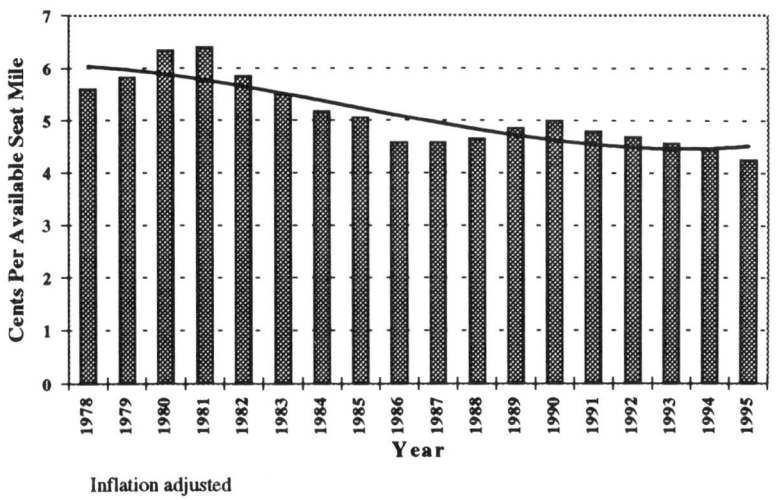

Inflation adjusted

---

[28] Id.
[29] Remarks of Carol Hallett Before the 11th Annual Salomon Bros. Transportation Conference (New York, N.Y., Nov. 13, 1996), at 4.
[30] Source: Air Transport Association.

Chapter 8

OPERATIONAL AND EQUIPMENT COSTS

The real price reductions of the pre-deregulation era were largely spurred by advances in aviation technology, which allowed airlines to enjoy enormous improvements in productivity, and consumers to enjoy faster and more reliable air transportation. Each major change in aircraft and engine technology (e.g., from props to jets, from narrow-body to wide-body aircraft) allowed airlines to enjoy a corresponding reduction in costs.

The dominant megatrend of deregulation—hubbing—robbed the industry of some of those productivity improvements. Hubbing produces greater flight circuity and creates congestion, causing more fuel to be consumed. Hubbing results in more ground time, which has a deleterious impact on equipment and labor utilization. The hub requires scores of gates and huge peaks and valleys in the utilization of ground personnel. Hubbing also requires relatively smaller aircraft, denying airlines the economies of scale of larger aircraft. While the marketing and yield benefits of hubbing are considerable, hubbing pushes costs up and productivity down.

As has been noted, the only major airline which utilizes a pre-deregulation linear route system is Southwest, and it just happens to be the only major carrier which has been consistently profitable. By the mid-1990s, Southwest Airlines was the dominant or second-dominant carrier in most of the 25 largest city-pair markets of less than 750 miles in length.[31] A few major airlines have studied the Southwest Airlines linear route model and have begun to emulate it, at least in part, seeking to improve asset utilization and reduce unit costs. United began "Shuttle by United," in West Coast markets. Continental inaugurated CALite, initially serving 14 cities in the Southeast in a linear route operation.[32] Delta also began a relatively low-cost "express" service. USAir responded with "Project High Ground", designed to increase aircraft utilization by significantly reducing ground time.[33] By reducing ground time from 40 minutes to 20, the "quick turn" strategy (designed to emulate Southwest's 15-minute ground

---

[31] Aviation Daily (Jan. 18, 1996), at 88.
[32] Michael McCarthy & Bridget O'Brian, Lean, Nimble Airlines Head East, Targeting Region's Plump Prices, Wall St. J., Feb. 28, 1994, at A-1.
[33] Id. at A-6.

Cost Containment

turnaround) improved productivity and lowered operational costs. A quick turn of a 737 involves these procedures, many performed simultaneously:

- The ticket agent takes the flight plan to the pilot, who loads the information into the aircraft computer while up to 130 passengers disembark from the aircraft.
- Workers clean trash cans, seat pockets, lavatories, etc.
- Catering personnel board the plane and replenish supply of drinks, ice and snacks.
- A fuel truck loads the wings with 5,300 gallons of aviation fuel.
- Baggage crews unload up to 4,000 pounds of luggage and 2,000 pounds of freight. "Runners" rush the luggage to baggage claim area in the airport terminal.
- Up to 130 passengers are boarded.
- Ramp agents, who helped park the aircraft on arrival, push it back away from the jetway.[34]

Richard Weintraub summarizes how the aircraft de-planing, cleaning, boarding and luggage process of a Boeing 737-200 was streamlined at USAir:

- First, according to company figures, passengers would be unloaded, taking about 6 minutes. Then the cleaning crew would enter, taking 12 minutes to sweep through the plane.
- After the cleaning was completed the gate agents outside would begin the boarding process, taking another 12 minutes. Finally, it took about 8 minutes to ensure the various ticket and passenger counts were reconciled.
- Now, as the cleaning crew makes its way through the plane behind the departing passengers, the pre-boarding process has begun in the lobby. With the cleaning crew off the plane in about eight minutes, passengers, already lined up outside, can begin boarding.
- Below, baggage handlers are getting bags and pre-positioned freight and mail into the plane, trying to use only the forward hold,

---

[34] Carl Quintanilla, New Airline Fad: Faster Airport Turnarounds, Wall St. J., Aug. 4, 1993, at B1.

Chapter 8

which helps with weight distribution on the 737-200. Using the computer system more efficiently, passenger counts are underway as travelers board.[35]

Before landing, flight attendants inventory drinks, ice and snacks, and inform the pilot, who radios the information to the destination airport. Baggage carts and other equipment are lined up before arrival. Like a swarm of bees, six or seven employees (up from three or four) turn around the plane. Cleaners tidy up on an as-needed basis, sometimes skipping emptying the lavatories. Passengers must pass their carry-on luggage through a "sizer box" so that oversized carry-ons won't hold up the boarding process.[36]

Since an aircraft produces RPMs only when it is aloft, reducing ground time enhances equipment utilization, allowing more productive scheduling. Nonetheless, tighter scheduling can cause a ripple effect of departure delays if an aircraft is late, especially if a mechanical problem or inclement weather occurs early in the day.

America West enhances equipment utilization by flying "Red Eye Specials." It built a new nocturnal hub bank at Las Vegas between 10:00 p.m. and 2:00 a.m.[37] It enjoys the highest equipment utilization of any major airline, with an average of 11.36 block hours flown per day.[38]

Like Continental, United formed U-2, or "United Shuttle," as a low-wage short-haul (less than 750 miles) "airline within an airline," threatening that if labor failed to conclude an agreement allowing United to create it, the carrier would turn over short-haul domestic routes to low cost, non-union regional feeders.[39] United estimates the agreement will allow it to reduce operating costs in short-haul markets by about 30%, close to Southwest's approximately seven cents a mile,

---

[35] Richard Weintraub, USAir's High Ground: Flying More—And More Efficiently, Washington Post, Feb. 28, 1994, at D1.
[36] Carl Quintanilla, New Airline Fad: Faster Airport Turnarounds, Wall St. J., Aug. 4, 1993, at B1
[37] Scott McCartney, America West Has Turned Nighttime Into Flight Time, Wall St. J., Jan. 16, 1996, at B4.
[38] Address of John Garel Before the Fifth Annual Phoenix International Aviation Symposium (Apr. 18, 1996).
[39] Robert Rose & Susan Carey, Money-Losing Routes Prompt Big Carriers To Mull Radical Steps, Wall St. J., Oct. 19, 1993, at 1.

though it seems implausible.[40] Quick turns are ensured by boarding window seats first, then middle seats, then aisle seats last.[41] The major carriers' average trip length and average aircraft utilization are shown on Table 8.3, "U.S. Major Airlines Aircraft Trip Length and Utilization".

Table 8.3—U.S. MAJOR AIRLINES AIRCRAFT TRIP LENGTH AND UTILIZATION (1994)[42]

Carrier	Average Flight Stage Length (miles)	Utilization Per Day (hours)
America West	676	11.19
Southwest	389	10.81
Delta	753	9.96
Continental	710	9.95
United	1,062	9.82
American	1,033	9.81
TWA	848	9.60
Northwest	851	9.55
USAir	538	9.10

Long-haul international carriers have quite astounding rates of utilization. For example, Qantas gets 11.8 hours per day out of its jets; Air New Zealand enjoys 14.3 hours of flight time per day.[43]

However, increasing the amount of flying time and number of cycles an aircraft flies accelerates scheduled maintenance, and thus, maintenance costs. Plus it makes no sense to fly aircraft at times of the night incapable of achieving break-even load factors.

Generally speaking, and assuming market demand generates comparable load factors, there are enormous economies of scale and lower

---

[40] Michael McCarthy, UAL Estimates Buyout of United to Hurt Profit at First, Boost It Beginning 1996, Wall St. J., Apr. 13, 1994, at A-4.
[41] Jeffrey Leib, West Coast Air War To Take Friendly Out of California Skies, Denver Post, Sept. 30, 1994, at C1.
[42] ESG Aviation Services, 7 Airline Monitor (Mar/Apr 1995).
[43] Statement of Quantas' Peter Gregg and Air New Zealand's Robert Nuzarian Before the 11th Annual Salomon Bros. Transportation Conference (New York, N.Y., Nov. 14, 1996).

costs achievable for an airline flying relatively larger aircraft longer distances, vis-à-vis flying smaller aircraft shorter distances. In other words, ASM costs ordinarily are lower for larger aircraft than smaller aircraft. And airlines enjoy a cost taper the longer the stage length of the flight. To reduce costs, both USAirways and Reno Air deliberately restructured their route systems to extend their average stage lengths.

Comair and Mesa Airlines, flying turboprop planes with an average stage length of between 150-200 miles, face an ASM cost of between 18-19 cents per mile, far above that of the major airlines.[44] This requires charging higher yields in short-haul markets, which is often achievable because of the dearth of competition.[45] For example, Mesa (a/k/a "United Express," "USAir Express," or "America West Express") earns yields of nearly 35 cents per mile, compared with 12 cents earned by United.[46]

Carriers have also responded to the decline in profitability by slashing new equipment purchases. In the late 1980s and early 1990s, American Airlines cut $5.6 billion in new aircraft, Northwest slashed $3.7 billion in aircraft orders, while United Airlines cut $3.6 billion in aircraft, and $5.5 billion in capital spending overall.[47] To reduce capacity, many U.S. firms began to park existing aircraft in the desert. For example, American Airlines grounded 25 older DC-10s, substituting smaller equipment, thereby improving load factors.

This was a global trend. Even the Pacific Rim (among the few remaining bastions of serious traffic growth, governmental protectionism, and modest profitability), saw its carriers defer or cancel scores of new aircraft. Thai Airlines would take delivery of only 18 of the 23 aircraft it ordered over five years. Philippine Airlines negotiated delayed delivery of six Airbus 340s. Garuda Indonesian Airlines halted plans to purchase 48 wide-bodied Boeing and Airbus aircraft. Malaysian Airlines cut domestic flights, froze hiring, removed surplus aircraft and deferred new deliveries. Only Singapore Airlines (frequently the world's most profitable carrier) did not announced cuts or

---

[44] Address by Larry Risley before the Salomon Bros. Transportation Conference (New York, N.Y., November 17, 1994).
[45] Paul Dempsey, The Social and Economic Consequences of Deregulation 195-216 (1989).
[46] Julius Maldutis, Airline Update—August 1996 (Sept. 8, 1996).
[47] The Balancing Act, Airline Bus., The Skies in 1992 16 (1992); US Cuts With Confidence, Airline Bus. (May 1993), at 11; Julius Maldutis, Northwest Airlines Corp.—More Europe and Less Orient (Apr. 25, 1994).

delays in aircraft orders. But then profitability returned again in the mid-1990s and, predictably, airlines began ordering billions of dollars of new aircraft again.

Despite passenger discomfort, reducing the pitch between seats can enhance carrier capacity and, assuming 100% of seats on some flights are occasionally sold, revenue. For example, both low-cost America West and Southwest squeeze more than 120 seats on their Boeing 737-200s, while Delta puts 105 seats on the same aircraft, adding a first-class section. Southwest's passengers look forward to an average stage length of only 374 miles, while Delta flies the same aircraft 471 miles, and America West 512 miles.[48] More than 500 miles is a long flight in aircraft with thin seat pitch.

The new Frontier Airlines' early 737-200s were initially configured with 108 seats in a single class of service (with a luxurious 34-35" pitch between seats), while later aircraft were added with 122 "slim line" seats (with a still generous 31-32" pitch), improving capacity by 13%. Thus, for every eight additional aircraft, tighter seat configuration added the equivalent of one additional plane.

United added five rows of seats to its DC-10-30s during the last decade, increasing the number of seats from 232 to almost 300.[49] TWA tried to differentiate its service by reducing the number of seats to add leg room, but it was costly. Taking four of the seats off a 141 seat MD-80 results in an $87,603 annual revenue loss.[50] TWA must earn 25% additional revenue (versus Valujet) to offset the generosity it accords to its passengers with liberal seat pitch on its DC-9s, while Reno Air must earn 11% more.[51]

Adding seats to aircraft in order to reduce ASM costs has a long tradition. At the urging of C.R. Smith, Douglas Aircraft added seven seats to the 21-seat DC-2, producing the DC-3. The change increased the cost of operating the aircraft by only 10%, but increased its capacity by 30%.[52] Decades later, Pan Am's Juan Trippe would persuade Boeing to build an aircraft capable of seating 500 passengers, the 747,

---

[48] Boeing 727 and 737, Aviation Daily, June 21, 1995, at 474.
[49] Michael McCarthy, Airline Squeeze Play: More Seats, Less Leg Room, Wall St. J., Apr. 18, 1994, at B1.
[50] Id.
[51] Roberts Roach & Associates, Scorecard: Airline Industry Cost Management 2Q 1995 15 (3rd ed. 1996).
[52] Thomas Petzinger, Jr., Hard Landing 11 (1995).

placing a $550 million order, the single largest commercial purchase that had ever been made by a private firm.[53]

Some carriers have announced they will "hushkit" their aging aircraft (to satiate federal noise requirements), rather than replace them. Thus, Northwest intends to hushkit 40 of its DC-9s whose average age is 24 years, so as to be able to fly them another 15 years.[54] Table 8.4, "U.S. Major Airlines Aircraft", reveals the percentage of Stage 3 aircraft in each major carrier's fleet. The cost of a hush-kit is about $1.5 million per aircraft, or as much as $18 million if new avionics, engines, and cabin interiors are added. This compares favorably with the $30-$35 million cost of a new narrow-body aircraft.[55]

However, aging aircraft have higher maintenance cost and poorer reliability than younger aircraft. Poorer reliability can translate into declining yields as business travelers take their business to airlines better able to meet their published schedules.

Table 8.4—U.S. MAJOR AIRLINES AIRCRAFT (1995)[56]

Carrier	*Number of Aircraft*	*Owned (%)*	*Stage Three (%)*
American	647	53.9	86.4
America West	86	22.1	74.4
Continental	311	14.8	63.7
Delta	543	55.6	67.0
Northwest	382	55.2	43.5
Southwest	199	46.7	74.9
TWA	194	32.0	45.4
United	554	46.9	74.0
USAir	441	52.2	59.2

---

[53] Id. at 19.
[54] Susan Carey, Northwest Airlines Plans to Renovate Some DC-9s Rather Than Replace Them, Wall St. J., Aug. 9, 1994, at A2.
[55] Jeff Cole, McDonnell Embarks On a New Course for Old Planes, Wall St. J., July 26, 1993, at 16A.
[56] ESG Aviation Services, 7 Airline Monitor (Mar./Apr. 1995).

One additional means of rolling back operational costs is fleet simplification. In 1996, TWA announced plans to retire its aging L-1011s and reduce its aircraft groupings to three: DC-9s and MD-80s, 757s and 767s, and 747s.[57] USAirways flew 7 different types in the class of aircraft with fewer than 150 seats, compared with Delta's 5, United's 4 and American's 3, then placed an order with Airbus designed to simplify the fleet.[58]

Commonality in the cockpit can also reduce costs. Southwest Airlines flies the Boeing 737 exclusively, but it insists on an older, basic version of the cockpit in even its new jets so that its pilots can fly any plane in its fleet, thereby enhancing labor utilization and productivity.[59] Air Canada found the Airbus A-319 and A-320 combination desirable, while Reno Air found the DC-9 and MD-80 combination attractive because of cockpit commonality.[60]

During spikes in fuel costs, airlines have trimmed weight by eliminating on-board magazines. American Airlines does not paint its entire fuselage in order to reduce weight, and fuel burn. Carriers also give pilots bonuses for fuel efficiency, which is why, at some airports, the cabin can be uncomfortably hot in the Summer, for the pilots do not want to fuel the generators to work the air conditioning. Finally, some airlines have trimmed costs by removing life rafts from aircraft flying over-water routes within 162 miles from shore, arguing that they can safely glide to a land-based airport.

While there are strategies available to management for trimming certain costs, there are some significant operating costs which are beyond the control of management. Nothing an airline CEO can do will influence the cost of west-Texas crude oil. In the 1980s, fuel accounted for between 17% and 31% of industry operating costs. A $1 increase in the price of a barrel of crude translates into $500 million in additional costs for the airline industry.[61]

---

[57] Aviation Daily (Jan. 22, 1996), at 101.
[58] Address of Stephen Wolf Before the 11th Annual Salomon Bros. Transportation Conference (New York, N.Y., Nov. 14, 1996).
[59] Scott McCartney, Competitors quake As Southwest Air Is Set to Invade Northeast, Wall St. J., Oct. 23, 1996, at A1.
[60] Remarks of Air Canada's Lamar Durett and Reno Air's Robert Redding Before the 11th Annual Salomon Bros. Transportation Conference (New York, N.Y., Nov. 13, 1996).
[61] Edward Phillips, Lower Costs Key to Airlines' Survival, Aviation Week & Space Tech. (Mar. 13, 1995).

The spike in fuel costs precipitated by Saddam Hussein invading Kuwait added about $3.6 billion to the expenses of the world's airlines between August 1990 and March 1991.[62] But while fuel costs rose significantly during the Persian Gulf crisis, average annual aviation fuel prices were nonetheless *lower* in real and nominal terms than they were a decade earlier.

Finally, in comparing carrier operational costs, one must compare apples to apples, and oranges to oranges. Studies by Roberts, Roach & Associates have attempted to do precisely that—compare and contrast the ASM costs on similar aircraft flying similar stage-lengths. The results are fascinating. For example, USAirways and American Airlines have the highest costs for flying a 757 on a 1,400-mile flight: USAirways, 6.72 cents; American, 6.70; Continental, 5.70; Delta, 5.61; and America West, 5.02 cents. The following costs were incurred flying a 767-200 2,450 miles: USAirways, 6.00 cents; American, 5.82; United 5.72; TWA, 4.95; and Delta, 4.67 cents.[63]

In summary, operational costs are directly influenced by efficiency in equipment utilization, including hours flown, seating density, flight stage-length, and appropriately sized aircraft for the market's demand.[64]

SERVICE COSTS

In the U.S. domestic market, the cost cutting mandated by declining profitability under deregulation has caused a nearly universal degeneration of airline service, so consumers have been taught not to expect much. In the post-deregulation era, American Airlines saved $40,000 by removing the olives from its salads. Delta saved $1.5 million by removing the lettuce garnish from its salads. Seat pitch has been tightened, hot food eliminated, new aircraft purchases deferred, and as discussed below, employees embittered.

Major carriers no longer offer meals on flights of less than two hours, and will serve food during traditional meal hours depending on whether its competitors serve food on parallel flights; sometimes all

---

[62] The Balancing Act, The Skies In 1992, Airline Bus. 17 (1992).
[63] Aviation Daily (May 1, 1996), at 186.
[64] See Roberts Roach & Associates, Scorecard: Airline Industry Cost Management 2Q 1995 9 (3rd ed. 1996).

passengers get is a brown-bag lunch at the gate.[65] American introduced "American Bistro" sack lunches, while Delta dubbed its lunch "Sky Deli." Distributing them before boarding saves on labor costs associated with food preparation, a practice already in place in Europe. Northwest introduced "A La Carte" service, where passengers choose among items on the flight attendants' carts, again, saving preparation of a meal tray. Most major carriers are cutting back sharply on meal expenses, which average a little over $4.00 per passenger. As one source aptly noted, "Customers are hungrier because airlines have been starved for profits."[66]

Cutting the number of flight attendants to the FAA minimum (of one per 50 passengers) can cause passengers to wait longer for meals and beverages, and jam the isles with meal carts, blocking access to the lavatories.[67] The more exotic service offerings of the 1970s, including American Airline's piano bars in the upper deck of the 747 (added in the early 1970s because recession coupled with delivery of widebodied aircraft destroyed load factors), United's "happenings" in its 747 lounges (featuring guitarists and wine tastings), and Continental's "Polynesian Pubs" have long since disappeared.[68]

In conclusion, trimming service is a means of cost reduction which can, if done surgically and prudently, improve profitability. But taking a meat cleaver to service can cause yields to plummet. As Continental Airlines' CEO Gordon Bethune observed, "I know of no successful company that has a product no one wants to buy."[69]

LABOR COSTS

Though union members only made up less than 15% of workers in the United States by the mid-1990s (just over 10% if public-sector workers are excluded), unions were still a dominant force in the airline industry. Some credit (or blame, depending on one's perspective) economic regulation with producing high unionization rates in transportation. Yet the fact that commercial aviation is a labor intensive

---

[65] Lisa Miller, Airlines and Hotels Say Nuts to Nourishment, Wall St. J., Oct. 6, 1995, at B1.
[66] Terry Maxon, Starved for Profits, Dallas Morning News, Apr. 30, 1995, at 1H.
[67] James Hirsch, With Fewer Flight Attendants Aboard Jets, Mood of Passengers Turns Turbulent, Wall St. J., July 23, 1993, at B1.
[68] See Thomas Petzinger, Jr., Hard Landing 20 (1995).
[69] Continental Airlines, Inc., 1994 Annual Report (1995).

industry, employees are highly skilled and must be certified as to competence, hours are not 9 to 5, and many employees must be away from home during the week may well have led to high rates of unionization in any event. Even many upstart airlines have found themselves with unions on their property within only a few years of operation.

Some have blamed "bad management" for the airline industry's financial woes, while others blame "greedy labor." As one economist alleged:

> It's not the fault of deregulation, as some critics claim. The basic problem is that, despite a tumultuous 15 years of labor relations since deregulation, very little has really changed. Unions still hold the upper hand in bargaining power at major airlines, leading to high labor costs, low productivity and lots of red ink.[70]

Similarly, deregulation guru Alfred Kahn insists he had anticipated that market forces would correct "out of line" labor wages and work rules: "If the intensified competition of the '90s didn't do it, what will?"[71] But in fact, it did, though apparently not nearly enough to suit Kahn. In the early 1990s, the airlines eliminated 120,000 jobs, while the remaining employees surrendered more than $1 billion annually in wages and benefits.[72]

Many new non-union airlines enjoy significant comparative cost advantages vis-à-vis established carriers in terms of lower, entry wages, and freedom from work rules which impede productivity, enabling them to offer consumers lower ticket prices than the established incumbents. While relatively small, the new entrant low-cost carriers continue their collective Lilliputian erosion of mega-carrier yields. Predation is one response, but a costly one, and appears to be only a short-term solution, for it seems that wherever one upstart airlines is killed, another springs from the earth to take its place.

---

[70] Frank Dooley, Why Airlines Crash, Wall St. J., Mar. 30, 1994, at A16.
[71] Scott McCartney, Why Are Big Airlines Considering Mergers?, Wall St. J., Nov. 9, 1995, at A1.
[72] Remarks of Carol Hallett Before the 11th Annual Salomon Bros. Transportation Conference (New York, N.Y., Nov. 13, 1996), at 4.

Cost Containment

Another solution is cost containment, which appears to be growing in popularity among major airlines. Stated differently, cost reduction is becoming a necessary, albeit painful, ingredient in sustaining survival in a Darwinist economic environment.

Labor costs (including wages, fringes and work rules) account for about a third of carrier operating expenses, more than any other single category (see Figure 8.3, "Airline Labor Costs As A Percentage Of Operating Expenses"). Arguably, labor costs are among the most potentially controllable operating costs,[73] leading troubled airlines to focus on wage and staffing reductions and productivity improvements via work rule changes.

Figure 8.3—AIRLINE LABOR COSTS AS A PERCENTAGE OF OPERATING EXPENSES (1970-1990)[74]

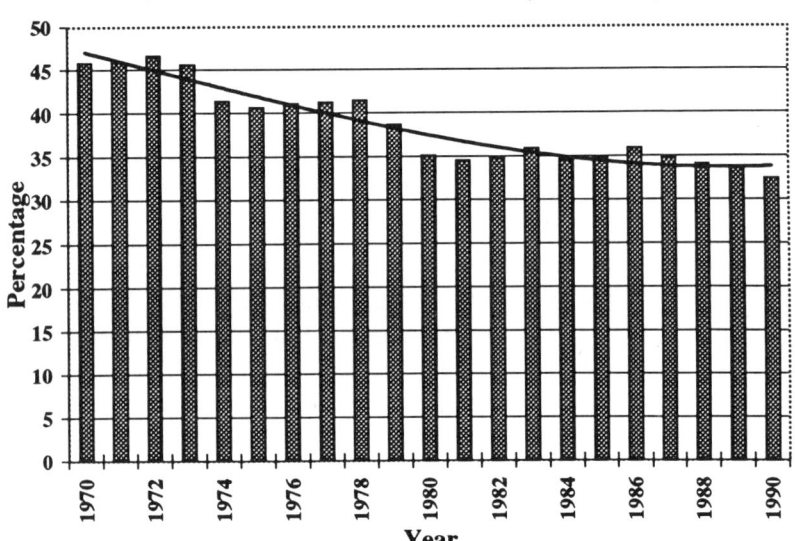

For example, in 1994 Delta announced "Project Leadership 7.5," an ambitious target to reduce ASM costs to 7.5 cents in three years, which would slash its costs by a huge $2 billion annually, or 19% over the three years, much of it achieved by draconian (20%) cuts in its

---

[73] J.P. Morgan Securities, The U.S. Airline Industry 22 (1993).
[74] Source: Air Line Pilots Association.

work force.[75] Delta enjoys more flexibility to outsource work and cut jobs and reduce benefits than many of its rivals because the company is not highly unionized (beyond its pilot's group), although such a radical change will radically alter the traditional Delta corporate culture of labor-management harmony.[76] At one point in the 1980s, Delta's flight attendants pitched in and gave the company a down payment on a new 737. Brannigan and de Lisser described Delta's proud tradition, saying that,

> Over the years, Delta stood out for its pristine planes, plush amenities and a distinctly warm, personalized service. It treated employees exceptionally well, paying top wages and assuring job security. Its proud and stable work force, in turn, delivered Southern hospitality to passengers.[77]

But enormous losses engendered by a bout of indigestion in swallowing Pan Am's trans-Atlantic routes, and the emergence of low-cost ValuJet in its Atlanta back yard, changed all that. According to Jay Lustig, managing director of Drake Capital Securities, "If I didn't know better, I'd swear Delta's executives were trying to earn a degree in the Frank Lorenzo school of management."[78] In 1994 and 1995, Delta eliminated 4,500 full-time customer service employees. However, by 1996, Delta discovered that its customer service had deteriorated intolerably, recalling nearly 500 baggage and cargo handling, fueling, ticket counter, gate agents and administrative support employees at Atlanta to coincide with the Summer Olympic games.[79] Cutting and out-sourcing maintenance, baggage, cabin and ticketing personnel created lines of angry passengers, and mountains of lost

---

[75] Bridget O'Brian, Delta Air to Pare Up to 15,000 Jobs, Or 20% of Staff, in Big Restructuring, Wall St. J., Apr. 29, 1994, at A3.
[76] Id.
[77] Martha Brannigan & Elena de Lisser, Cost Cutting At Delta Raises the Stock Price But Lowers the Service, Wall St. J., June 20, 1996, at A1.
[78] Losing Altitude: Delta Air, Long A Leader, Runs Into Difficulties, Wall St. J., June 25, 1993, at A4.
[79] Aviation Daily (Jan. 31, 1996), at 157.

Cost Containment

luggage. These chaotic conditions are a sharp contrast to the airline Delta once was.

Delta appeared to be in the grips of what has been termed a phenomenon widespread in the 1990s—"corporate anorexia:"

> In corporate America, diet metaphors abound. Companies have trimmed the fat and become lean, fit and ready to compete. Now comes a more disturbing phrase about weight loss: corporate anorexia.
>
> A shrinking company becomes anorexic when it gets so hooked on controlling expenses, closing plants, slashing inventories and eliminating jobs that it neglects the fact that a company should seek to grow, not fade away....
>
> On a more subtle level, excessive cost-cutting tends to strengthen the authority of the financial and accounting departments, which see it as their mandate to control expenses rather than monitor and evaluate opportunities and investments....
>
> But a sea of change may be hitting big corporations. More of their executives are concluding that slashing costs can take a company only so far and that growth must be the paramount goal.[80]

But with ValuJet (operating at 6.7 cents per ASM with a shorter stage length) in its back yard, Delta felt it had little alternative but to cut costs in spite of the unavoidable service deterioration. ValuJet paid its captains $42,000 a year, while the lowest-ranking Delta captain earned $132,000 a year.[81] In 1996, a new ALPA contract gave Delta flexibility to start up a low-cost, short-haul 737 division to compete with the low-fare new entrants. For example, an eight year captain

---

[80] Bernard Wysocki, Jr., Some Companies Cut Costs Too Far, Suffer 'Corporate Anorexia', Wall St. J., July 5, 1995, at A1, A4.
[81] Scott McCartney, Why Are Big Airlines Considering Mergers?, Wall St. J., Nov. 9, 1995, at A1.

earning $150,000 a year would earn only $108,000 flying the budget routes.[82]

Ultimately, however, draconian cost-cutting and outsourcing led to a deterioration of employee morale, an erosion of Delta's traditional reputation of outstanding service, increased efforts to unionize the work force, and the outmigration of senior managers "jumping ship." By May 1997, Delta's Board of Directors had had enough, and refused to renew CEO Ronald Allen's contract.[83]

Table 8.5, "Labor Costs At Major U.S. Airlines", reveals the cost of labor and related expenses (benefits and payroll taxes) on an available seat mile basis at selected carriers.

Table 8.5—LABOR COSTS AT MAJOR U.S. AIRLINES (1993)[84]

Carrier	Cents per ASM	Average Annual Pay ($ U.S.)
USAir	4.54	56,992
Delta	3.49	63,806
TWA	3.24	42,009
American	3.07	50,369
United	3.05	55,781
Northwest	2.88	57,673
Southwest	2.43	47,263
Continental	2.10	33,224
America West	1.67	27,418

By 1995, the average annual salary for pilots of the major U.S. airlines was $58,944.[85] Pilots who fly comparable jets at Southwest, American, Delta and USAirways are paid equivalent salaries—captains at Southwest make as much as $140,000 per year;[86] the

---

[82] Martha Brannigan & Eleena de Lisser, Delta May Try New 'Lite' Service, Wall St. J., Feb. 9, 1996, at B8.
[83] Martha Brannigan & Joseph White, Why Delta Air Lines Decided It Was Time For CEO To Take Off, Wall St. J., May 30, 1997, at A1.
[84] ESG Aviation Services, 7 The Airline Monitor (Mar./Apr. 1995).
[85] ESG Aviation Services, 9 The Airline Monitor (June 1996).
[86] J. Randolph Babbit, Management Marks Its Scapegoat, Air Line Pilot, Jan. 1994, at 13.

Cost Containment

difference is that Southwest's pilots are paid for the hours they fly, and as a consequence clock more than 70 hours in the cockpit, while the pilots at the other airlines clock fewer than 50.[87] The differences are attributable to two factors: (1) Southwest is the only major airline which flies a linear route system exclusively, resulting in significantly higher aircraft, and hence labor, utilization; and (2) Southwest's union contracts were negotiated much later than those of the other majors', and do not include as restrictive work rules. In 1994, Southwest negotiated a 10-year dream contract with its pilots whereby wage increases would be forgone for the first five years, then three 3% increases over the second five years, plus options to acquire as many as 1.4 million shares of Southwest's stock (see Figure 8.4, "U.S. Airline Employee Average Annual Compensation").[88]

Figure 8.4—U.S. AIRLINE EMPLOYEE AVERAGE ANNUAL COMPENSATION (1970-1990)[89]

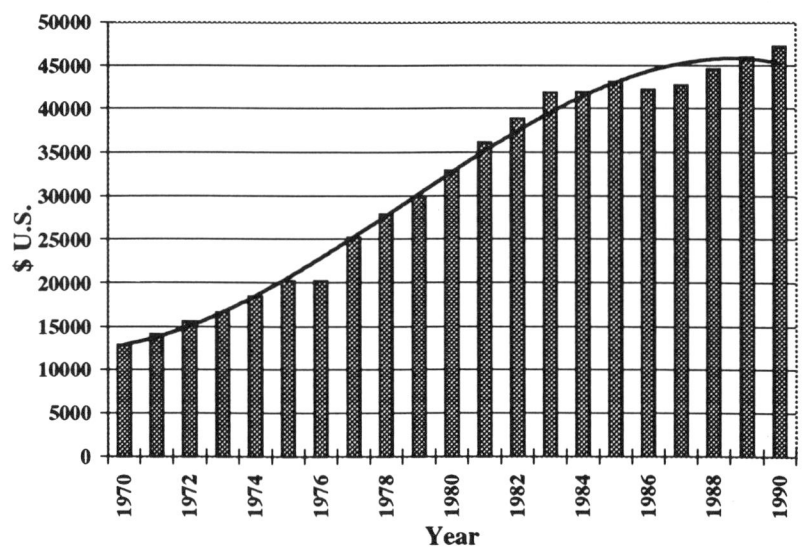

---

[87] Scott McCartney, Pilots in the Driver's Seat With Airlines, Wall St. J., Nov. 12, 1995..
[88] Bridget O'Brian, Southwest Wins Pilots Accord Offering No Wage Boost in First Five of 10 Years, Wall St. J., Nov. 18, 1995, at A2.
[89] Source: Air Line Pilots Association.

Chapter 8

At most major carriers, pilots are paid on the basis of "trip rigs" and "duty rigs," which allow them to be paid on a time-on-duty or time-away-from-home basis. For example, United's pilots are paid for 81 hours of work a month, yet the average flying time is only 53 hours. In 1995, TWA traded equity for work rule concessions increasing pilots to 75 hours of work for 75 hours of pay, compared with 51 hours of work for 75 hours of pay in 1993.[90] Figure 8.5, "U.S. Major Airlines Available Seat Mile Costs", shows a comparison of costs per ASM amongst the major domestic carriers.

Figure 8.5—U.S. MAJOR AIRLINES AVAILABLE SEAT MILE COSTS[91]

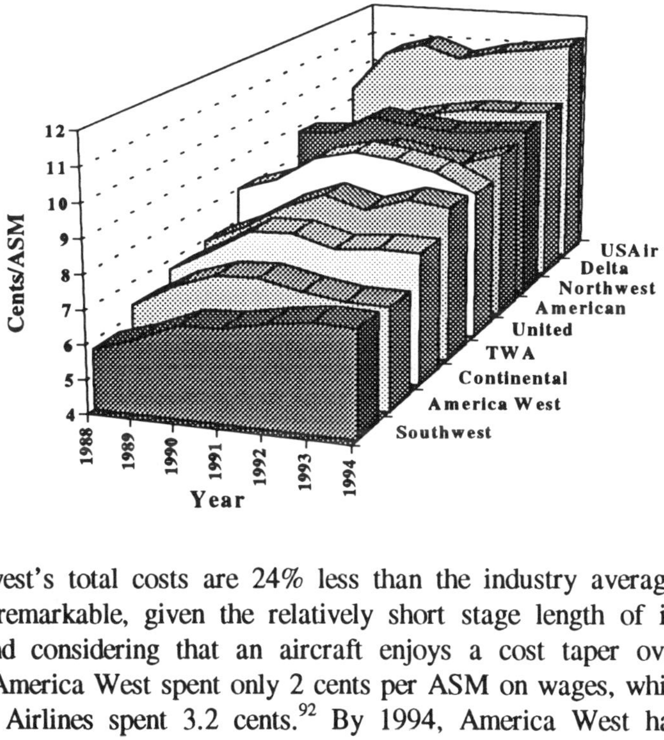

Southwest's total costs are 24% less than the industry average, which is remarkable, given the relatively short stage length of its flights, and considering that an aircraft enjoys a cost taper over distance. America West spent only 2 cents per ASM on wages, while American Airlines spent 3.2 cents.[92] By 1994, America West had

---

[90] Scott McCartney, Why Are Big Airlines Considering Mergers?, Wall St. J., Nov. 9, 1995, at A1, A8.
[91] Source: ESG Aviation Services.
[92] Id.

lowered its ASM costs to 7.03 cents per mile,[93] while Continental had lowered its costs to 7.56 cents per mile.[94] Yet low costs do not guarantee profitability. "If you can't make money at 7.56 cents, there must be something fundamentally and structurally wrong with the system," observed Julius Maldutis. "It's not cost that's Continental's problem. It's a revenue problem."[95]

Another measure of airline productivity is the number of employees per aircraft or per RPM, as shown in Table 8.6, "Employee Productivity Per Aircraft And Per Revenue Passenger Mile". These data suggest Southwest is the most productive airline, and USAir and TWA are least productive, TWA having far too many employees. However, with a short stage length, no in-flight amenities or complicated itineraries, and a single aircraft type, a carrier which offers little in the way of in-cabin or connecting/interline service, and flies a single aircraft type, such as Southwest, need have relatively few employees per aircraft. Thus, although Southwest's annual average salary is some $14,000 higher than Continental's, it employs far fewer people than Continental on a per aircraft or RPM basis.

Another means of comparing airline labor productivity is to assesses the number of RPMs and ASMs produced per employee, as shown on Table 8.7, "Airline Productivity Per Employee". On the basis of RPMs and ASMs, Southwest, United and Northwest appear to be the most productive airlines; USAir, TWA and Continental appear to be least productive.

Still another way is to calculate operating revenue and expense on a per employee basis, as revealed in Table 8.8, "U.S. Airline Operating Revenue And Expenses Per Employee". From an expense perspective, America West, Continental and TWA appear to be the most productive carriers. But from a revenue perspective, Northwest, United and Southwest appear to be the most productive.

Table 8.9, "Airline Costs And Revenues", identifies operating expenses, and operating revenues per available seat mile for selected U.S. carriers.

---

[93] Address by Maurice Myers before the Salomon Bros. Transportation Conference (New York, N.Y., November 17, 1994).
[94] Address by Gordon Bethune before the Salomon Bros. Transportation Conference (New York, N.Y., November 17, 1994).
[95] Bridget O'Brian, Continental Air Ousts Its Chief, a 'Lite' Backer, Wall St. J., Oct. 26, 1994, at A3.

Table 8.6—EMPLOYEE PRODUCTIVITY PER AIRCRAFT AND REVENUE PASSENGER MILE (1993)[96]

Carrier	Employees Per Aircraft	Employees Per Million RPMs
Southwest	86	0.75
Northwest	119	0.75
United	153	0.81
Delta	131	0.88
American West	128	0.98
Continental	126	1.00
American	144	1.00
Alaska	93	1.19
Trans World	158	1.23
USAir	108	1.35

Table 8.7—ARLINE PRODUCTIVITY PER EMPLOYEE (1995)[97]

Carrier	RPMs Per Employee	ASMs Per Employee
Southwest	399	594
United	390	542
Northwest	369	510
Delta	329	496
America West	327	454
American	301	449
Continental	265	386
TWA	258	386
USAir	235	349

---

[96] ESG Aviation Services, 7 Airline Monitor (Mar./Apr. 1995).
[97] Aviation Daily (Nov. 17, 1995), at 275.

Table 8.8—AIRLINE OPERATING REVENUE AND EXPENSES PER EMPLOYEE (1995)[98]

Carrier	Operating Revenue ($000)	Operating Expenses ($000)
America West	38.50	33.44
American	47.49	41.94
Continental	36.36	33.59
Delta	49.31	43.53
Northwest	59.04	48.24
Southwest	50.83	43.40
TWA	38.94	36.89
United	56.78	50.32
USAir	48.35	42.87

Table 8.9—AIRLINE COSTS AND REVENUES (1992)[99]

Carrier	Operating Expenses (cents/ASM)	Operating Revenue (cents/ASM)
America West	7.14	6.84
American	8.81	8.65
Continental	8.26	7.78
Delta	9.39	9.09
Northwest	9.00	8.51
TWA	8.82	8.17
United	9.26	8.76
Southwest	6.95	7.82
USAir	10.79	10.53

---

[98] Aviation Daily (Jan. 8, 1996), at 216.
[99] Adam Bryant, Marketplace Has Big Airlines Charting Unfamiliar Skies, Denver Post, Dec. 5, 1993, at 4H; SH&E, The Facts About American vs. Southwest 23 (unpublished study prepared on behalf of APA, Sept. 13, 1993); James Cling, The Status of Southwest Airlines' Competitive Advantage 14 (unpublished monograph 1993). Operating expense data are for Oct. 1, 1991, to Sept. 30, 1992. For updated data, see Mead Jennings, Staying At the Top, Airline Bus., 28, 31 (Mar. 1994).

By the mid-1990s, the major airlines had engaged in a concerted effort to roll back costs below these levels. To some extent, cost is a function of distance flown, which is revealed in Figure 8.6, "Major U.S. Airlines Yield Compared To Costs".

Figure 8.6—MAJOR U.S. AIRLINES YIELD COMPARED TO COSTS (1995)[100]

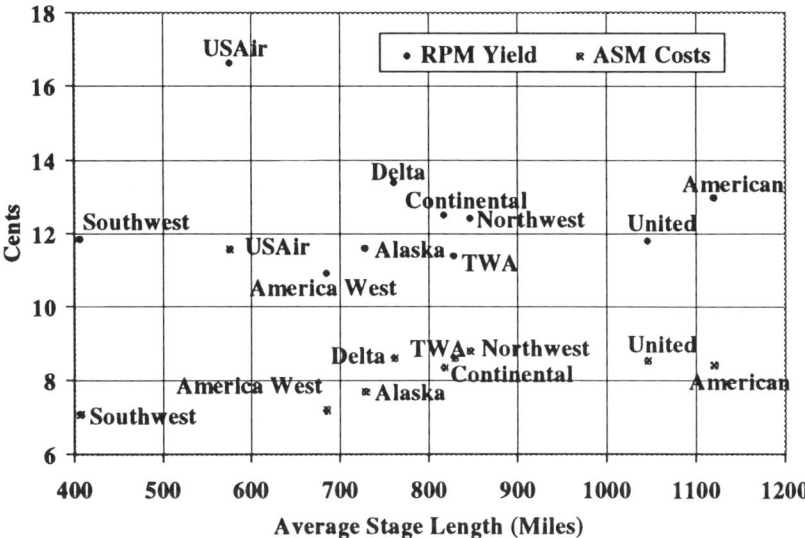

Note these costs are considerably higher than those of the new upstart airlines, whose costs are in the six to eight cents per ASM range. Nonetheless, these costs compare quite favorably with major foreign carriers, as shown in Table 8.10, "Operating Costs Of Selected Foreign Airlines".

Labor costs typically range between 30-40% of total operating expenses for the European carriers. In 1990, labor expenses accounted for 33% at American Airlines and 21.7% at Singapore Airlines.[101] Asia-Pacific airlines are about 30% more productive than European airlines.[102] But one source noted, "The competitive advantage of low labor costs in the Asia-Pacific region, buttressed by higher yields, con-

---

[100] Source: Salomon Brothers.
[101] The Balancing Act, Airline Bus., The Skies in 1992 14 (1992).
[102] Id.

gestion and supportive regulators, is now being eroded by the inflationary pressures of economic growth and the differentials which that growth has generated."[103] Another predicts, "The perennial profit-makers, like Singapore Airlines, Thai International and Cathay Pacific, will see their cost advantage over other world regions eroded as economic growth fosters inflation and living standards and wages spiral upwards."[104]

Table 8.10—OPERATING COSTS OF SELECTED FOREIGN AIRLINES (1993)[105]

Carrier	Operating Costs (cents/ASM)
Qantas Airways	10.6
Air Canada	11.6
British Airways	12.0
Japan Air Lines	18.6

Certain airlines have responded to the burden of wages and employee benefits by contracting out, or "out-sourcing" services. This is by no means a new phenomenon. Carriers have long contracted with other airlines to provide various ground-handling, ticketing, catering and maintenance services in which a larger carrier has such operations, taking advantage of scale economies. Low-wage airlines like Continental and America West have out-sourced such functions as maintenance. ValuJet out-sourced heavy maintenance and reservations.[106] United contracted out sky cap and janitorial services, and sold its flight kitchens to Dobbs, which gave it $120 million, allowing it to avoid a $71 million investment in upgrading and expanding kitchens, and to enjoy a $320 million savings over 7 years. The 5,200 employees could seek a job with Dobbs, albeit at significantly lower wages. American Airlines created a centralized reservations office in low-cost

---

[103] Id.
[104] Success Breeds Its Own Problems, Airline Bus., The Skies in 1992 53 (1992).
[105] Philip Baggaley, Unpublished Address Before the Chicago Convention 50th Anniversary Conference (Oct. 31, 1994).
[106] Aviation Daily (Dec. 19, 1995), at 439.

Dublin, Ireland.[107] Austrian Airlines out-sources revenue accounting in India, and out-sources heavy maintenance as well.[108]

As examples of the contemporary out-sourcing of labor abroad, Japan Airlines [JAL] and All Nippon Airways, burdened with high labor expenses exacerbated by a strong Japanese Yen, have based aircraft abroad to serve regional routes with low cost local cabin crews.[109] With the Japanese currency at historic highs, even German cabin crews are less expensive than Japanese crews. Japan Airlines has frozen new hiring and pay increases while out-sourcing labor from low wage nations like Thailand and Singapore, and relatively lower wage nations like Germany and the United Kingdom. For example, a Thai flight attendant is paid only about 10% of the salary of a Japanese flight attendant, but is well paid compared with comparable jobs in Thailand. So as to ensure that acrimony does not breed between cabin crew members on the same flight, the Thai attendants are given only five-year contracts. In 1996, Japan Airlines announced it would reduce its work force to 17,000 by 1998, transfer more work to outside firms (including a joint-venture maintenance facility in Xiamen, China), and increase contracting out of flight operations. JAL would also achieve additional cost reduction through new lower wage rates and work rules changes.[110] JAL is also abandoning Japan's lifetime employment system by offering its workers as much as $600,000 to quit their jobs. It stopped hiring Japanese flight attendants in 1992. By 1998, 28% of JAL workers will be non-Japanese, up from 4% in 1989. Aircraft overhauling is being shifted from Singapore to Xiamen, China, where labor costs are about one-fourth of those in Singapore.[111] Singapore Airlines also cuts costs by hiring low-wage Malaysian and Indonesian employees.

In the United States, employment-at-will leaves industries free to lay off newly hired employees. Generally, the most recently hired em-

---

[107] Charles Goldsmith, Ireland Offers Green Pastures for Aviation, Wall St. J., Aug. 15, 1996, at A6.
[108] Remarks of Austrian Airlines President Herbert Bammer Before the 11th Annual Salomon Bros. Transportation Conference (New York, N.Y., Nov. 13, 1996).
[109] The Balancing Act, Airline Bus., The Skies in 1992 16 (1992).
[110] Aviation Daily (Jan. 18, 1996), at 85.
[111] Valerie Reitman & Jathon Sapsford, To See Issues Vexing Japanese Business Now, Consider JAL Flight 76, Wall St. J., Aug. 9, 1994, at A1.

ployees are the poorest paid, meaning that layoffs increase average wages per employee.

That flexibility cannot be achieved in Europe, where unions seize airports in protest, or Japan, whose tradition guarantees employment for life. Nonetheless, some foreign airlines have achieved productivity improvements and modest wage concessions. For example, Lufthansa convinced its workers to accept a one year pay freeze and pilots to fly 75 hours per month (as opposed to the prior limit of 53 hours per month).[112]

Before its demise, Pan Am hired low-cost Yugoslavian flight attendants. United Airlines opened bases in Tokyo and Frankfurt.[113] In some instances, employment abroad is not done with a view to lowering wages (although all newly hired employees are hired with entry wage rates, thereby modestly lowering average labor expenditures). But other costs are saved as well, such as high "duty time" costs on international legs, as well as hotel and transportation expenses. Foreign cabin crews also have language skills valued by foreign travelers, and VIP hospitality skills appreciated by business travelers.

Although carrier staffing levels are not always comparable, because of currency valuation, fleet compositions, stage lengths, social welfare benefits, and so on, the data are nonetheless quite interesting (see Table 8.11, "Employees Per 1,000 Revenue Passenger Kilometers Of Selected Foreign Airlines").

These data explain why Air France attempted to lay off 4,000 employees in late 1993 (which led workers to take over Paris Orly and Charles de Gaulle Airports in protest, burning tires on the tarmacs for several days, leading ultimately to the ouster of Air France Chairman Bernard Attali, and retreat from the downsizing plan). As a rule of thumb, most U.S. airlines have about 100 employees per aircraft. Southwest had close to 90. TWA reduced its number of employees to aircraft ratio from 156 in 1993, to 116 in 1994.[114]

---

[112] Robert Rose & Susan Carey, Money-Losing Routes Prompt Big Carriers To Mull Radical Steps, Wall St. J., Oct. 19, 1993, at 1, 6.
[113] United Air To Open Two Foreign Bases for Flight Attendants, Wall St. J., June 10, 1996), at B5B.
[114] Address by Jeffrey Erickson before the Salomon Bros. Transportation Conference (New York, N.Y., November 16, 1994).

Table 8.11—EMPLOYEES PER 1,000 REVENUE PASSENGER KILOMETERS OF SELECTED FOREIGN AIRLINES (1993)

Carrier	Number of employees
Air France	1.22
Lufthansa	1.18
British Airways	.76
American Airlines	.74
Delta Airlines	.66
United Airlines	.60
Singapore Airlines	.41
Japan Airlines	.39
All Nippon Airways	.39

Third-world flight crews are paid far less than those from G-7 industrialized nation airlines. For example, an Air France captain earned about $150,000 a year in the early 1990s, while an Aeromexico captain earned about $4,400.[115] With lower flight attendant wages, a third-world airline can fully staff the cabin, providing a much higher level of service than can a U.S. or Western European carrier.

One may expect to see the trend toward out-sourcing of various airline functions to other firms with lower costs to grow. Organized labor will resist, and use their contract scope clauses to attempt to derail the trend. But the economic motivation to out-source will be powerful. Eventually there may be an emergence of "pseudu-airlines" which provide the good will of the name and certain managerial oversight, but fly wet-leased aircraft, contracting out flight and ground services. Already, code-sharing is a major step in this direction.

One other alternative is creating intercarrier joint-ventures or cooperatives to perform such functions as aircraft maintenance, catering, revenue accounting or reservations, to take advantage of scale economies. While airlines have created joint-venture CRSs for product distribution, few have explored the plethora of joint-venture opportunities which exist.

---

[115] Int'l. Transport Workers' Federation, Working Conditions Survey 3 (1992).

Cost Containment

Other airlines convinced unions to settle for two-tier wage rates, with the "B" scale at entry grade. American, United, and Delta are examples. During the 1980s, more than half of the pilots and flight attendants at American, for example, were on the "B" scale. Some of the flight attendants at the two-tier airlines, earning between $950 and $1,220 a month,[116] qualified for food stamps.

In the 1980s, American Airlines pioneered the concept of two-tiered wage rates, whereby existing employees would continue to receive their existing salaries, but newly hired employees would be hired at a significantly lower wage rate. This produced a radical reduction in costs, from a high of 8.17 cents per ASM in 1983, to 7.28 cents in 1986, and after-tax profit margins of 4%-5% in 1988-1989, a very respectable performance for an airline. American coupled this two-tiered wage system with profit sharing, giving employees a larger bonus check in years when the company did well (while, incidentally, denying shareholders dividends). This enabled American to enjoy relatively low-cost expansion, with significantly declining average costs. That gave it the opportunity to grow into the nation's largest airline, for a time.

But eventually, the newly hired employees made their displeasure with the lower wage rates known to union leaders, and the two-tiered system was eventually shortened, and in 1991, effectively bargained away. American's costs rose 23% from its 1986 low, to 8.93 cents per ASM in 1992. American's growth was abruptly halted, and the newly-hired cockpit crew members were frozen in the right seat of the aircraft. American Airlines CEO Robert Crandall pledged: "Unless the world changes, we will never buy another airplane. We won't replace the airplanes that wear out."[117]

Irrespective, halting growth can push costs up further, for the average seniority rises as workers ascend up the pay scale. Flight attendants now stay on the job an average of 14 years at most airlines.[118] Thus, mature airlines with senior work forces have higher costs than upstart airlines with junior (and non-union) work forces.

---

[116] Flight Attendant Work Force Grows 10 Percent, Salaries Mostly Unchanged, Aviation Daily, Feb. 12, 1991, at 285.
[117] Stephen Solomon, The Bully of the Skies Cries Uncle, N.Y. Times, Sept. 5, 1993, at 6-13.
[118] Tim Ferguson, Settling Process in the Sky, Wall St. J., Nov. 16, 1993, at A23.

Halting growth can have a gradually inflationary impact on average wages, for new entry level wages cease to moderate the average.

Under deregulation, wages of entry-grade employees have been significantly reduced, even among carriers which profess to have a single-tier of wages. While from 1978-1992, wages at the top end of the wage scale declined only at the rate of the economy as a whole, entry-level wages for pilots declined slightly, while wages for machinists and flight attendants declined 17% and 25% more than real wages nationwide.[119] Thus, existing employees by and large have been spared wage reductions, while their newly hired brother and sister employees have paid the price.

Labor resistance to wage reductions and work rule changes is often articulated in terms of blaming management, not labor, as the cause of the company's problems—management that breaks out in irrational price wars, purchases vast route systems that cannot be integrated efficiently, insists on labor-intensive but unproductive hub-and-spoke route systems, and worst of all, pays themselves big bucks while asking rank-and-file workers to share their wallets.[120] They watch with dismay as concessions are transferred through to consumers in yet another round of price wars, with no improvement to the bottom line, and with management eventually returning to labor for more. Eastern Airlines' employees adopted an old acronym for it—BOHICA, or "Bend Over, Here It Comes Again." Yet in those rare instances when profitability improves, management rarely comes forward to offer labor a bonus, though management may be happy to take a bonus themselves. Unfortunately, the environment can degenerate into one of institutionalized hostility, with labor seeking to "partner," and management not willing to share. If things get bad enough, management will open the company's books to labor leaders in order to instill sobriety.

One way to encourage labor productivity and enhance labor-management relations is through profit sharing, among the most important means whereby an airline can position itself with low costs. Southwest implemented the first serious employee profit sharing plan.

---

[119] Nancy B. Johnson, Pay Levels in the Airlines Since Deregulation, in Airline Labor Relations in the Global Era 101, 111, 112 (P. Capelli ed. 1995).

[120] See e.g., Brett Pulley, USAir Strike May Mean Coming Strife for the Industry, Wall St. J., Oct. 19, 1992, at B4.

Profit sharing effectively makes wages variable with the company's performance, allowing it to pay higher wages when the company is performing well, and lower wages when it is performing poorly.[121] In effect, this allows the airline to borrow money at zero interest rates when operating in the red. If the company is profitable, the incentive to unionize is also diminished.

Airline labor unions are formidable institutions. The Air Line Pilots Association [ALPA] has 43,000 pilots at 44 carriers. The International Association of Machinists and Aerospace Workers has 830,000 members.[122] No major carrier can withstand a prolonged pilots' strike (one in which pilots honor the picket line), for the number of replacement workers required would be vast and the FAA training requirements are stringent.

Some carriers have taken advantage of strikes in attempt to coerce labor to surrender concessions in wages and work rules. President Ronald Reagan set the tone early his first term when, in August 1981, he fired 13,000 striking air traffic controllers. The message was clear. The Republican White House would stand by management in its efforts to discipline labor. Frank Lorenzo's Continental Airlines welcomed (and even encouraged) a strike in 1983, and his Eastern Airlines attempted to do the same with a strike in 1989. Lorenzo used Chapter 11 bankruptcy successfully in the 1983 strike to radically roll back wages, causing Congress to subsequently amend the bankruptcy laws to make this option much more difficult. But the reduction in costs was dramatic. In 1982, Continental spent 35% of its operating costs on labor (compared with an industry average of 37%); by 1984, labor costs comprised only 22% of Continental's costs.[123] By busting its unions in its 1983 Chapter 11 bankruptcy, Continental lowered its unit costs to less then 8 cents a mile, although because it created so much labor animosity in the process, it suffered a formidable problem on the pricing side of the equation.[124] Continental would effectively lose the ability to attract significant high-yield passengers, while Eastern's unions were so outraged by Lorenzo's asset stripping that, as a result

---

[121] See Roberts Roach & Associates, Scorecard: Airline Industry Cost Management 2Q 1995 40 (3rd ed. 1996).
[122] Transportation Trades Dep't., The Voice of Transportation Workers (1993).
[123] Newal Taneja, Civil Aviation 148 (2d ed. 1989).
[124] See Bridget O'Brian, Continental Air Ousts Its Chief, A 'Lite' Backer, Wall St. J., Oct. 26, 1994, at A3.

of a highly effective strike honored by most of its employees, the crippled company was ultimately liquidated. Although Continental has lower labor costs than any other major airline (its available seat-mile cost is 8.35 cents, among the lowest in the industry),[125] not even that has kept it out of bankruptcy, as it entered Chapter 11 again in 1990, emerging again in 1993.

Dick Ferris' United Airlines took a machinists' strike in 1981, and a pilots' strike for 29 long days in 1985. Carl Icahn's TWA took a flight attendants' strike in 1986. Bob Crandall's American took a flight attendant's strike in 1993. In each case, the carrier paid a terrible price as embittered employees sabotaged service and thereby dissuaded high-yield business traffic. Even direct costs can be staggering. For example, the five day flight attendant's strike cost American Airlines $190 million in after-tax earnings.[126] Table 8.12, "Major Airline Strikes Since Deregulation", lists several of the major strikes which have taken place in the post-deregulation period.

No major airline can afford a prolonged strike, particularly by its pilots. As Scott McCartney notes:

> Major airlines have grown so large that they can hardly afford a job slowdown by their pilots, much less an outright strike. Fixed costs are so high, and the number of pilots so large (about 9,000 at American), that an airline would be forced out of business long before it could possibly train, certify and deploy replacement pilots. For safety reasons, the government requires exhaustive and expensive pilot training.[127]

---

[125] Jane Levere, Continental's Aim: Profitability, Commercial Aviation News (Aug. 23, 1993), at 3.
[126] Bridget O'Brian, AMR Posts Widened Fourth-Period Loss Largely on Effects of Attendants' Strike, Wall St. J., Jan. 20, 1994, at A2.
[127] Scott McCartney, Pilots in Driver's Seat With Airlines, Wall St. J., Nov. 12, 1995.

Cost Containment

Table 8.12—MAJOR AIRLINE STRIKES SINCE DEREGULATION

Carrier	Date(s)	Labor Union	Victor?
Continental	Sept. 1983 - Nov. 1985	Pilots Mechanics Flight Attendants	Continental
PanAm	Aug. 1984	Mechanics Pilots Ticketing Agents	PanAm
PanAm	Feb.-Mar. 1985	Transport Workers Union	PanAm
United	May-June 1985	Pilots	union
TWA	Mar.-May 1986	Flight Attendants	TWA
Eastern	Mar. 1989 - Jan. 1991	Mechanics	neither
USAir	Oct. 1992	Mechanics	union
American	Nov. 1993	Flight Attendants	draw

The airline industry is a service industry. Happy employees can give passengers a lovely trip, and lure them back for another, and another. Angry, embittered employees can do the opposite. Mark Stevens described Carl Icahn's vision at TWA as myopic: "By focusing almost exclusively on the numbers, he has failed to consider the human element that is the basic building block of quality service and that gives the top-notch airlines a critical edge in winning and retaining passenger loyalty . . . . Given Icahn's devout faith in financial engineering, as opposed to building a business brick by brick, he cannot see the connections among motivated flight attendants, quality service, and the bottom line."[128] The same, of course, could be said of Frank Lorenzo.

In most service industries, salaries account for a disproportionate share of operating costs. But low wages do not guarantee survival. People Express collapsed despite its rock bottom wages. Continental,

---

[128] Mark Stevens, King Icahn 210 (1993).

America West, and Midway, also with relatively low wages, fell into bankruptcy.[129]

The contemporary trend is to attempt to resolve these matters consensually, or in the term preferred by organized labor, "partnering". Airline management has attempted to persuade labor to take wage and work rule concessions for equity. This is not a new concept, for in 1984 Frank Borman gave labor three seats on Eastern Air Lines' board of directors and 25% of the company's stock in exchange for wage and work rule concessions. Eastern negotiated a "variable earnings plan" with labor, tying wages to the company's profitability. If earnings failed to reach a designated level, employees would earn only 96.5% of their salaries; if earnings exceeded a specified threshold, they would earn 103.5%. In essence, this created a new source of capital for the company, unsecured, and without interest, sort of like shareholder equity.[130] For a short while, the employees began to go the extra mile on behalf of the airline; but as earnings projections failed to materialize, morale plummeted, and labor-management acrimony grew.[131] The improved environment after Eastern's employees became equity owners gradually disintegrated, for it lacked real support by union leaders and rank-and-file workers.[132]

A number of Employee Stock Ownership Plans [ESOP] were attempted in the 1980s, albeit unsuccessfully, at carriers such as Frontier and United. In the 1980s, employee stock ownership stood at the levels shown in Table 8.13, "Airline Employee Stock Ownership In The 1980s".

But the drastic losses of the late 1980s and early 1990s brought a new momentum to the process. As a result, by the mid-1990s, labor owned 45% of TWA,[133] 33% of Northwest, and 55% of United.[134] (see Table 8.14, "Wage And Work Rules Exchanged For Equity At Major Airlines"). United Airlines became the largest employee-owned com-

---

[129] Continental has the lowest labor costs, as a percentage of operating expenses, of any major U.S. airline. Aviation Daily, Feb. 11, 1991, at 276.
[130] Thomas Petzinger, Hard Landing 168 (1995).
[131] Id. at 247-49.
[132] Robert Rose, Employee Ownership Is Catching On in Airline Industry, Wall St. J., July 23, 1993, at B3.
[133] Michael McCarthy, TWA, Seeking Savings, to Cut Up to 3,000 Jobs, Wall St. J., Aug. 4, 1994, at A3.
[134] Carl Quintanilla, United Airlines To Hire 1,700 By Year End, Wall St. J., Aug. 17, 1994, at A3, A4.

pany in the world (though the fact that the flight attendants were not included in the ESOP has caused a deterioration in cabin service).[135] Management at American and USAir tried to do the same.[136]

Table 8.13—AIRLINE EMPLOYEE STOCK OWNERSHIP IN THE 1980s[137]

Carrier	Percentage Employee Ownership
Western Airlines	33%
Eastern Air Lines	25%
Pacific Southwest Airlines	15%
Republic Airlines	15%
Pan American World Airways	13%
Continental	9%

Table 8.14—WAGE AND WORK RULES EXCHANGED FOR EQUITY AT MAJOR AIRLINES[138]

Carrier	Value of Concessions	Equity
Northwest (1993)	$883 million over 3 years	33%
TWA (1993)	$600 million over 3 years	45%*
United (1994)	$8 billion over 12 years	55%

* Reduced to 30% by a prepackaged bankruptcy in 1995.

By the mid-1990s, Southwest's employees owned nearly half of its stock, while America West's owned about 30%.[139] Chapter 11 bankruptcy caused the employees' stock at America West to be wiped out, creating labor-management acrimony, and votes by several of the employee groups to unionize. As a consequence of union busting and

---

[135] Susan Carey, Contract Negotiations Divide United's Workers, Wall St. J., Aug. 28, 1996, at B1.
[136] Richard Gibson, USAir Pilots' Plan to Trade Pay Cuts For an Equity Stake Draws Resistance, Wall St. J., Aug. 4, 1994, at A5.
[137] Paul Caver, Employee-Owned Airlines: The Cure for An Ailing Industry?, 61 J. Air L. & Com. 639, 648 (1996).
[138] AMR Corporation, Second Quarter Report 2-3 (1994).
[139] J. Randolph Babbitt, Management Marks Its Scapegoat, Air Line Pilot, Jan. 1994, at 15.

union "partnering," most of the U.S. airline industry is now dominated by relatively low-cost lean-and-mean flying machines. Table 8.15, "Ownership Alternatives", lists the advantages and disadvantages of labor ownership.

Table 8.15—OWNERSHIP ALTERNATIVES[140]

Advantages of Labor Ownership

- It lowers labor costs, which account for about a third of airline operating costs;
- It can result in productivity gains;
- It can result in a higher level of service; and
- It can improve employee relations.

Disadvantages of Labor Ownership

- It requires compromise among different employee groups;
- It limits the options available to management;
- It enhances employee risk, due to the relative volatility of the value of stock vis-à-vis wages; and
- It creates complex regulatory and tax issues.

By the mid-1990s, American Airlines, which faced low-cost competitors on 40% of its routes, sought $750 million in wage cuts and productivity gains from its unionized employees, and restructured 16,000 non-union workers by offering early retirement to some, and contracting out services.[141] In January 1994, low-cost rivals competed on 25% of American's routes; a year earlier, the figure was 8%.[142] American Airlines claimed that if it had the same labor costs as Continental, it would have saved $1.7 billion in 1992; if its labor costs were as low as Southwest's, it would have saved $1.1 billion that

---

[140] Paul Caver, Employee-Owned Airlines: The Cure for An Ailing Industry?, 61 J. Air L. & Com. 639 (1996).
[141] Bridget O'Brian, AMR's Profit In 3rd Quarter Jumped 74%, Wall Street J., Oct. 21, 1994, at A8.
[142] Bridget O'Brian, AMR's Bid for Savings from Unions Faces Rocky Flight, Wall St. J., Oct. 19, 1994, at B4.

year.[143] American offered to re-enter abandoned markets, purchase long-range aircraft, and increase the number of first officer and captain positions for concessions similar to those given by Delta's pilots.[144]

In late 1995, Delta's pilots agreed to accept low pay in low-fare markets, in exchange for the recall of nearly 500 furloughed pilots and a 70-seat maximum on aircraft used in domestic code-sharing. Pilots could earn more by flying more.[145] They also demanded a 5% pay raise (after Delta achieved an annual profit of more than $400 million) and 20% of the company's stock, a proposal Delta's management labeled predictable, inappropriate and embarrassing.[146] Ultimately, Delta signed a contract with its pilots calling for greater job security and growth opportunities for pilots in exchange for a 2% pay cut, longer working hours and other productivity gains worth $760 million over four years, plus the opportunity for the carrier to launch a low-cost service with 737s, whose pilots would be paid 32% less than existing pilots.[147] In order to create labor harmony and improve communications with management, Delta allows labor representatives to hold non-voting seats on its Board of Directors.[148] In 1996, USAir's management rejected an offer by pilots for $2.5 billion in concessions over five years in exchange for 25% of the airline's common stock and $700 million in new preferred stock.[149]

Management seeks deep, long-term concessions on wages and work rules. Labor wants job security, stock, and seats on the boards of directors. As Air Line Pilot Association President Randy Babbitt said:

> [C]onvincing employees that serious wage and work rules are necessary is awfully difficult when upper management enjoys bonuses and stock options in the multiple millions of dollars in the good years, and then in the bad

---

[143] Commercial Aviation News, Sept. 20, 1993, at 4.
[144] Aviation Daily (Apr. 24, 1996), at 141.
[145] Aviation Daily (Dec. 12, 1995), at 395.
[146] Aviation Daily (Jan. 19, 1995), at 89.
[147] Martha Brannigan, Delta Expects Four-Year Savings of $760 Million from Pilots' Pact, Wall St. J., May 3, 1996, at B3.
[148] Address of Delta Air Lines' CEO Ron Allen At the 11th Annual Salomon Bros. Transportation Conference (New York, N.Y., Nov. 13, 1996).
[149] Carl Quintanilla & Judith Valente, USAir Labor Talks Will Be Restarted By a Facilitator, Wall St. J., Oct. 26, 1994, at A12.

> times, turns to the employees time and time again for wage reductions and concessions.
>
> The employees have stepped up to the plate time and time again, with the full knowledge that their long-term success and their long-term security come from healthy corporations. But the time has come . . . to acknowledge the contributions labor has made in the past to their corporations.
>
> Union members will no longer make the types of monetary concessions that have been requested in the past without receiving some acknowledgment in the form of ownership, corporate governance, or future reward.[150]

Labor's presence on the board of directors is by no means an anathema to capitalism. German law requires that its major corporations allocate half the seats on their boards to labor, and Germany is among the world's most competitive and strongest economies.

In the United States, the largest and most successful transportation company in the world, United Parcel Service, is wholly owned by its existing full and part-time employees. Employee ownership can motivate employees to give the company their best effort. At TWA, for example, employee task forces were formed to focus on service improvement and cost reduction.

Assuming that employee ownership can motivate airline workers to "go the extra mile" for their companies, then many of the airlines will find their level of employee ownership eroding over time, for the airline labor ownership structures allow the employees to sell their stock in the market upon retirement, death, or termination of employment. In contrast, if a UPS employee wants to sell his stock, UPS has first right of refusal, and requires mandatory sell-back after retirement or departure. Several decades ago, the Chicago & Northwestern Railroad was employee-owned. But as stock was sold and transferred to decedent employees' heirs, employee-ownership was lost.

---

[150] J. Randolph Babbitt, Management Marks Its Scapegoat, Air Line Pilot, Jan. 1994, at 14, 15.

On the other side of the equation, as labor begins to share the driver's seat, several questions arise: Will carriers continue to compete away profits? If so, will workers continue to be as enthused about labor ownership? While employee-owners may be delighted as the value of their stock ascends (United Airlines employees' stock grew by more than $2 billion in value from 1994 to 1996, more than the concessions they surrendered for their 55% stake),[151] what will be their perception when it falls? Will airline directors protect the interests of non-labor shareholders? Can management resist worker's demands for fleet expansion (With 55% of its stock held by employees, United has placed billions of dollars in orders for new aircraft, despite a poor balance sheet), or salary increases (United's management agreed to raise its employees' wages to their 1994 level by 2000 in a series of "snap backs", essentially restoring what labor had surrendered to purchase its 55% controlling share)?[152] Will management be able to out-source services to lower-cost non-union providers?

In its 1994 Annual Report, UAL Corporation (parent of United Airlines) conceded, "The new labor agreements and governance structure could inhibit management's ability to alter strategy in a volatile, competitive industry by restricting certain operating and financing activities, including the sale of assets and the issuance of equity securities and the ability to furlough employees."[153]

Nonetheless, with labor sitting on the airline boards, several changes in airline management practices were anticipated. Some believed that airline CEOs might be dissuaded from flying blind with intuitively attractive route acquisitions or fare wars, or would be for-bidden from pocketing multi-million dollar salaries and stock options in years when their companies perform poorly. They were wrong. United Airlines' CEO Stephen Wolf earned $18.3 million in salary, stock and benefits in 1990, despite the fact that UAL's profits plum-meted by 60% that year.[154] TWA's top three executives took a $250,000 bonus each for a

---

[151] Ann Imse, Good Deal for UAL Employees, Rocky Mountain News, Apr. 24, 1996, at 1B.
[152] See Jeff Cole & Michael McCarthy, United To Place $3 Billion Order For Boeing Jets, Wall St. J., May 16, 1996, at A2.
[153] UAL Corporation, Annual Report 17, 18 (1994).
[154] Robert Rose, United Airlines Plans Layoff To Trim Costs, Wall St. J., Jan. 7, 1993, at A3; Paul Dempsey & Andrew Goetz, Airline Deregulation & Laissez Faire Mythology 21 (1992).

prepackaged bankruptcy filing which diluted labor's equity.[155] In 1995, Northwest's John Dasburg pocketed a salary and bonus of more than $800,000, and $8.7 million in stock options.[156]

Paradoxically, in the Brave New World of airline deregulation, labor appears to be both the major victim, and victor.

MARKETING AND DISTRIBUTION COSTS

In the mid-1990s, carriers were vigorous in their attempts to contain marketing and distribution costs by rolling back travel agent commissions, increasing direct distribution of the product (thereby reducing travel agency sales and CRS booking fees) via Internet bookings, ticketing machines, and airline telephone reservations, and curtailing costs via ticketless travel.

Some sources maintain that distribution costs comprise nearly 19% of industry operating expenses—less than labor costs, but more than fuel.[157] Marketing costs increased 20% among the world's airlines during the 1980s.[158] Travel agent commissions have grown enormously, rising more than 300% as a percentage of U.S. airlines' operating expenses during the 1980s.[159] Before deregulation, travel agent commissions consumed 4.2% of airline operating expenses, or a total of $883 million; by 1993, commissions had grown to 11.3%, for a total of $7.5 billion.[160] In 1991, Northwest reported average commissions of 38% in the trans-Pacific market.[161]

Before deregulation, total marketing and distribution costs (including reservations, sales, advertising, promotion and commissions) totaled only about 11% of operating expenses.[162] But since deregulation, these costs rose to more than 17%, though they have since subsided

---

[155] Michael McCarthy, TWA Could Shed Bankruptcy Shield Today, Wall St. J., Aug. 23, 1995, at A5.
[156] Susan Carey, Northwest Air's Chief Got $8.7 Million From Exercising Stock Options in 1995, Wall St. J., Apr. 8, 1996, at 4A.
[157] Julius Maldutis, The Airlines—The Third Revolution (Apr. 8, 1996), at 3.
[158] The Balancing Act, Airline Bus., The Skies in 1992 16 (1992).
[159] Paul Dempsey, Robert Hardaway & William Thoms, 1 Aviation Law & Regulation § 2.12 (1993).
[160] Randolph Babbitt, Saving the Golden Goose, Air Line Pilot (Feb. 1995), at 10, 12.
[161] The Balancing Act, Airline Bus., The Skies in 1992 16 (1992).
[162] Roberts Roach & Associates, Scorecard: Airline Industry Cost Management 2Q 1995 34 (3rd ed. 1996).

modestly. Figure 8.7, "U.S. Airline Industry Marketing Expenses", shows the industry's marketing expenses as a percentage of total operating expenses.

Figure 8.7—U.S. AIRLINE INDUSTRY MARKETING EXPENSES[163]

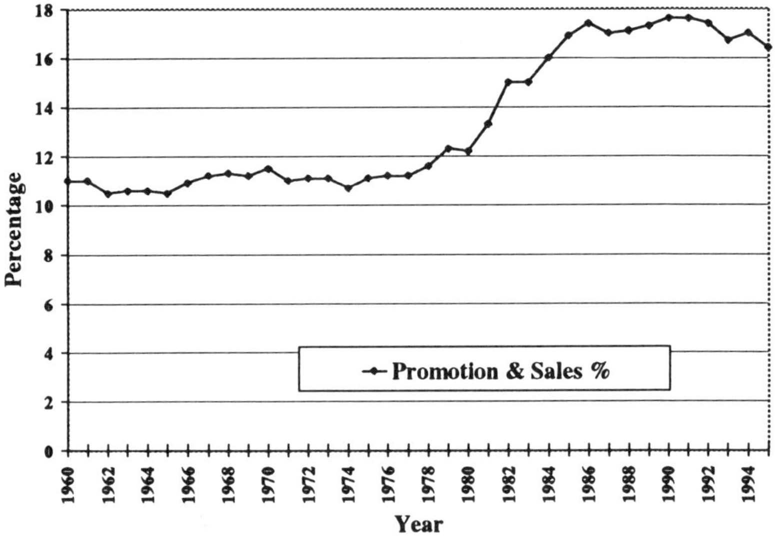

One source observed:

> The lesson of deregulation—that carriers compete on fares rather than quality—has an inherent contradiction. The pressures to lower costs to compete on price run counter to the rise in marketing costs to retain and expand the customer base. This has generated a new school of thought, which says that cost-cutting cannot be a priority when the increasingly sophisticated marketing carries such an inflated price tag.[164]

---

[163] Source: Roberts Roach & Associates.
[164] The Balancing Act, Airline Bus., The Skies in 1992 16 (1992).

Chapter 8

To improve load factors, carriers find themselves competing vigorously on prices (which results in yield dilution) or travel agency commissions (cost inflation). As noted in the preceding chapter, some carriers, such as Delta and Southwest, have taken the "bull by the horns" and unilaterally rolled back travel agent commissions to $50 on round-trip tickets costing more than $500, and/or embraced ticketless travel.[165] Delta also rolled back commissions (from 10% down to 8%) on full-fare international flights.[166] The downside risk was that travel agents might collectively retaliate by steering passengers to more generous carriers, although Northwest, American, United and USAir promptly followed Delta's lead, negating the likelihood of business shifting. TWA balked, briefly, and attempted to cut a deal with agencies to steer business its way.[167] A number of the low-cost carriers have not capped commissions, but their fares rarely pierce the $500 ceiling anyway.

Average commissions fell sharply, from 10.7% in 1994 to 9.1% in 1995.[168] The cap saved several major airlines more than $100 million annually each. The major carriers as a whole saved an estimated half a billion dollars as a result of this program.[169]

Some travel agents did retaliate, by teaching passengers how to purchase inexpensive travel without staying over a Saturday night (i.e., by purchasing two back-to-back round-trip tickets and using only the first coupon in each), and steering travel to rival low-cost airlines.[170] Travel agents will be forced to charge consumers directly for their services, and many marginal ticket agents have gone belly up. Until consumers have direct access to CRSs, they will incur significant transactions costs in calling around to find which airline offers the most convenient flight at the lowest price.

CRS fees are also a significant part of distribution costs. Each reservation booked and re-booked imposes an additional nearly $3.00 in cost. When prices or schedules change, consumers cancel and re-

---

[165] James Hirsch, Delta Air Caps Its Commission On Ticket Sales, Wall St. J., Feb. 10, 1995, at A2; Jane Levere, Paperless Journey, Airline Bus. (Jan. 1995), at 18.
[166] Delta Air Lines Reduces Travel-Agent Commissions, Wall St. J., Oct. 25, 1994, at A4.
[167] James Hirsch, TWA Drops Commission Cap for Agents, Wall St. J., May 10, 1995, at A3.
[168] Travel & Tourism (Jan. 11, 1996).
[169] Aviation Daily (Apr. 12, 1996), at 81.
[170] Lisa Miller, Stung By Fee Cuts, Travel Agents Declare War On Big Airlines, Wall St. J., Mar. 27, 1995, at B1.

book flights, creating "passive segments," accelerating these costs. Many carriers have asked CRSs to roll back these fees, threatening to depart if they do not.[171]

By the mid-1990s, airlines were issuing half a billion tickets a year, at a cost of $15-$20 each for labor, printing, delivery, and agency commissions. About $9.00 is attributable to the cost of ticket processing—clearing house fees, revenue accounting and back office processing. About $3.00 more is charged by CRS for every booking, even those not flown, so the per-ticket sold cost exceeds that number. Then, travel agents take about 10% off the top (up to a maximum of $50.00, and more than that for large airlines which offer agents commission overrides). By eliminating tickets, analysts predict the industry could save approximately $1 billion a year.[172] The cost of processing a ticket at United Airlines drops from $8.00 down to fifty cents with ticketless travel.[173] Tickets are the tie that binds passengers to travel agents, and without a ticket, the need for an agent is diminished. Moreover, moving reservations in-house removes sales data from the eyes of competitors, reduces (but ordinarily does not eliminate) travel agent commissions, and provides real-time data to an airline seeking to make yield, scheduling, or route adjustments.

Ticketless travel will put airlines on par with hotels or car rental companies, which take the customer's credit card number over the telephone, and give them an oral confirmation number, often with no written supplementation. Airlines are increasing the comfort level of consumers by sending them a confirmation itinerary and expensable receipt via mail or fax. They present themselves at the airport for a boarding pass with the confirmation number and a photo I.D.

For airlines, removing travel agents will enable them to direct their passengers away from the lowest fare, or a competitor's service. In addition, directly selling ticketless travel to consumers over the telephone enables airlines to enjoy several cost advantages:

---

[171] Aviation Daily (Jan. 4, 1996), at 18.
[172] Jonathan Dahl, Airlines Try Ticketless Systems, Giving Passengers New Gripes, Wall St. J., Nov. 30, 1994, at B1.
[173] Michael McCarthy, For Fliers, No Ticket Can Mean No Sweat, Wall St. J., Sept. 15, 1995, at B6.

Chapter 8

1. Direct sales eliminate travel agent commissions, which range between 8% - 12% or more (in some international markets, more than 30%) of the cost of a ticket;
2. The airline saves on CRS booking fees;
3. The airline saves money in not having to produce or process "red back" ticket stock;
4. The revenue stream is accelerated since the credit card number is taken over the telephone and the ticket need not pass through the industry clearing house before the airline is paid; and
5. By automating check-in procedures, passengers can pick up a boarding pass at a machine, allowing the carrier to reduce the number of airport ticketing personnel.

Ticketless travel does pose potential legal liability problems. Traditionally, a ticket has been evidence of the conditions of contract of carriage between a carrier and the passenger, an expression of limitations on legal liability, a receipt, and a summary of the travel itinerary. Disagreements may arise between carriers and passengers over misunderstandings surrounding ticket prices or incorrect reservations. But airlines save money in ticket stock, while passengers avoid the $65 fee some airlines charge in replacing lost tickets. Furthermore, by advertising 1-800 telephone numbers, carriers encourage consumers to book directly, thereby eliminating commission expenses and CRS booking fees (although increasing internal reservations costs relatively modestly). By going to direct distribution, carriers also deny competitors access to real-time booking information available on CRS.

As pointed out in the preceding chapter, another means of both curbing costs and improving revenues is via direct distribution, and new information technologies are making that more feasible. Airlines have begun to experiment in auctioning surplus inventory closer to the day of departure so as to improve load factors and generate revenue for seats which would otherwise fly empty.[174] In fact, the cost benefits of new information age technologies have yet to be realized. More information will be available from more sources—the telephone, mail, faxes, computers, and cable and satellite television. Scott McCartney identifies air travel as a "natural" for sale on the Internet:

---

[174] Julius Maldutis, The Airlines—The Third Revolution (Apr. 8, 1996), at 5.

Cost Containment

> Travel is a global industry, one whose products—tickets and itineraries—are easy to deliver to customers. Also, because it's a perishable product—one that can't be sent back if unsatisfactory—travelers demand as much information as possible when purchasing trips, from flight schedules and fares to tidbits about weather and special events.
>
> All that means its tailor-made for the Internet. Skilled cybersurfers can find much more information than the typical travel agent can deliver, and can even "test drive" a vacation before buying it. Through the Internet, potential customers not only have access to the giant airline-reservations computer systems, but also to all kinds of local information.[175]

As yet, Internet bookings are more complicated than telephone reservations. Surfers of the World Wide Web tend to use airline home pages as information sources or a research instrument, and then call the airline or a travel agent for a reservation. But as the airline home pages on the Internet become more consumer friendly, they will become a growing and important area of direct sales. Electronic access to CRS and individual in-house carrier reservations systems will erode the position of the travel agent as an intermediary in the distribution network over time.[176]

Enhanced communications technologies impose both a risk and an opportunity for airlines. On the down side, interactive video conferencing may reduce business travel (though it is unlikely to create a virtual sand, ocean and palm tree experience so real as to curtail vacation travel). On the positive side, enhanced communications technologies may stimulate more sales by providing more information, and simplifying the direct sales process. More communications interactions may also stimulate more business contacts requiring travel to consummate business relationships.

---

[175] Scott McCartney, Poised for Takeoff, Wall St. J., June 17, 1996, at R6.
[176] Roberts Roach & Associates, Scorecard: Airline Industry Cost Management 2Q 1995 33 (3rd ed. 1996).

Airlines can encourage direct bookings (bypassing the travel agents and their commissions, and CRS fees) in several ways. They can prominently advertise their toll free numbers. They can make themselves available on the Internet, or establish ticketing machines in the cities they dominate. And they can encourage consumers to book directly with direct booking rebates, frequent flyer mileage bonuses, and holding back a larger pool of discounted seats from CRSs for direct distribution. If they want to leave travel agents in the loop but by-pass CRS fees, they can offer agents enhanced commissions for direct telephone bookings. Truly low fares cause passengers to insist their agents book flights directly with low-fare airlines. For example, ValuJet, which shunned CRSs and sold its product directly, still had about 25% of sales from travel agents.[177]

Dr. Maldutis described his vision of how such direct distribution would take place:

- Business travelers will continue to book in advance through travel agents that use regular reservations systems.
- Airlines would begin to auction off seats on low load factor flights—during off-peak days, weeks and months—through the Internet and other distribution systems.
- Auctions typically will take place on day of departure or several days in advance, when airline managers can be certain of the number of unsold seats.
- The trick for management will be to prevent large-scale dilution of yields....
- In an ideally functioning market, 50 unsold seats for this evening's 9:00 p.m. flight may go on sale at 1:00 p.m. for $150, at 2:00 p.m. for $125, at 3:00 p.m. for $100, until all tickets are sold.
- All auction tickets are nonrefundable, payable by credit card number only. Travel agents will play a major role by obtaining new low fares for travelers for a fee.[178]

American Airlines was quick to jump aboard. It began offering fares as low as $59 round trip to e-mail subscribers every Wednesday

---

[177] Julius Maldutis, The Airlines—The Third Revolution (Apr. 8, 1996), at 3.
[178] Id. at 6.

for the upcoming weekend, and interactive silent auctions of first-class tickets to international destinations.[179]

THE TAX BURDEN

The airline industry has long argued that it is excessively taxed. Taxes on the industry rose 81% from 1981 to 1991, costing the industry some $6 billion a year. Among the taxes the industry and/or their passengers pay are the following:

- 10% domestic ticket tax that generates $4.8 billion annually.
- 4.3 cents a gallon excise tax that generates $500 million annually.
- $6.00 international departure tax that generates $225 million annually.
- $6.50 Customs fee for travelers entering the United States that generates $284 million annually.
- $6.00 Immigration fee for international arrivals that generates $262 million annually.
- $1.45 Agriculture fee for arriving international passengers and $61 aircraft fee that generate $70 million annually.
- 6.26% air freight tax that generates $225 million annually.
- $3 passenger facility charge per airport used, up to a maximum of $12 round-trip, that generates more than $1.3 billion annually for airports.[180]

From 1988 through 1993, governmentally-imposed taxes and charges rose at the following average annual rates:

- Benefits, many mandated by the government, increased by 8.4% per year.
- Landing fees went up at a 7.4% per year.
- Federal ticket and passenger taxes rose at . . . 12.6% per year.[181]

---

[179] Travel & Tourism (May 9, 1996).
[180] J. Randolph Babbitt, Saving the Golden Goose (address before Salomon Brothers Ninth Annual Transportation Conference, Nov. 17, 1994). James Hirsch, Delta Air Caps Its Commission On Ticket Sales, Wall St. J., Feb. 10, 1995, at A2; Jane Levere, Paperless Journey, Airline Bus. (Jan. 1995), at 18; Remarks of Carol Hallett Before the 11th Annual Salomon Bros. Transportation Conference (New York, N.Y., Nov. 13, 1996), at 7.

Chapter 8

In the early 1990s, several airlines proposed that the U.S. government allow the industry to borrow the 10% ticket tax it collects from passengers, which generates about $4 billion a year.[182] U.S. airlines pointed out that the government of France had provided approximately $400 million to Air France, the Belgian government had given about $300 million to Sabena, and the Italian government had given more than $300 million to Alitalia.[183]

In August 1993, the U.S. government imposed an additional 4.3¢ per gallon excise tax on fuel, to be paid in to the general (and not the trust) fund. Fortunately, the airline industry was successful in persuading Congress to defer imposition of the tax on it. Had that tax been in effect in 1994, the U.S. airline industry's $200 million profit would have been a $300 million loss. Airlines were exempt from this tax until October 1, 1995. The 10% ticket tax expired in January 1996 because of a budget impasse between the Republican Congress and the Democratic White House, then re-imposed on August 27, 1996. At this writing, Congress has several proposals before it to restructure and increase the airline tax burden, a burden which is ultimately borne by consumers.

FUEL COSTS

Every cent a gallon increase in jet fuel costs the industry about $170 million.[184] It costs more than $32,000 to fill up the tank of a Boeing 747. Much of the industry's economic anemia occurring in 1990-1991 was blamed in the spike in fuel costs precipitated by Operation Desert Storm. Actually, aviation fuel cost more per gallon between 1981 and 1984 (when it ranged between $0.79 and $1.04 per gallon, or adjusted for inflation, between $1.40 and $1.47), than in 1990 (when it sold for only $0.80 per gallon).[185] Fuel costs dropped

---

[181] John Dasburg, A Taxing Drag On the Airlines, Wall St. J., Mar. 21, 1995, at A14.
[182] Asra Nomani & Laurie McGinley, Airlines Weigh Plans to Seek Federal Help, Wall St. J., Feb. 19, 1991; Little Support Shown in Washington for Ticket Tax Proposal, Aviation Daily (Feb. 25, 1991), at 361.
[183] DOT Says 'Hands Off' Best Approach to Helping Competition, Aviation Daily (Mar. 6, 1991), at 427.
[184] Plummeting Jet Fuel Prices to Have Little Effect on Air Ticket Prices, Aviation Daily (Dec. 30, 1991), at 545; Remarks of Carol Hallett Before the 11th Annual Salomon Bros. Transportation Conference (New York, N.Y., Nov. 13, 1996), at 7.
[185] Perry Flint, Don't Blame It All On Fuel, Air Transport World (Feb. 1991), at 32.

31% between 1985 and 1986.[186] Though fuel spiked at 77 cents a gallon for 1990, annual fuel costs declined nearly 30% from 1990 to 1995 (to about 54 cents a gallon).[187]

AIR TRAFFIC COSTS

Delays imposed on the air traffic system cost airlines and their passengers approximately $3.5 billion a year.[188] Many have argued that airline productivity could be improved dramatically if pilots were freer of FAA air traffic controller circuitous routing. The existing air traffic control system funnels flights into circuitous, narrow and crowded flight corridors. The alternative is "free flight," allowing pilots to chose the best route, taking advantage of favorable winds and avoiding storms. While there is widespread agreement that "free flight" is desirable, the FAA insists it will take a decade to implement, because complex navigational technology (and perhaps a geostationary satellite Global Positioning System, developed by the Defense Department) must first be installed and integrated.[189]

Its most tenacious proponent, Michael Baiada, president of RMB Associates, describes free flight as the "No. 1 controllable expense facing the airline industry."[190] According to Baiada, "The airlines currently run a 'waste of time' production line controlled by the government, instead of a 'just in time' production line controlled by the airlines."[191] Free flight would cut fuel costs, and allow passengers to reach their destinations more expeditiously. The DOT estimates it could save U.S. carriers as much as $5 billion a year by 2010, and reduce flight time by up to 20%.[192] The major airlines have proposed a user fee to fund operation of the air traffic control system, replacing the federal airline ticket tax. But the U.S. General Accounting Office

---

[186] Id.
[187] Julius Maldutis, Airline Update—November 1996 (Dec. 10, 1996), at 5.
[188] Remarks of Carol Hallett Before the 11th Annual Salomon Bros. Transportation Conference (New York, N.Y., Nov. 13, 1996), at 9.
[189] Randolph Schmid, 'Free Flight' May Take Off In 10 Years, Rocky Mountain News, Mar. 16, 1996, at 2A.
[190] Michael McCarthy, Airplanes May Soon Crisscross the Skies Unfettered by FAA Lane Restrictions, Wall St. J., Aug. 7, 1995, at B1.
[191] R. Michael Baiada, Southwest Airlines: Below the Surface, Air Line Pilot (July/Aug. 1994), at 12, 14.
[192] Asra Nomani, FAA To Let Pilots Change Flight Paths, Wall St. J., Mar. 15, 1996, at A3.

contends this plan will give the large airlines a $600 million annual windfall to the detriment of the discount carriers.[193]

AIRPORT COSTS

Airport costs are the airlines' fastest growing expense item. Landing fees and terminal space rentals cost the airline industry $3.5 billion a year. They have risen 76% since 1982, or twice the rate of the consumer price index.[194] The Air Transport Association has lobbied against increases in Passenger Facility Charges [PFCs], insisting that airport capital improvement projects are overly ambitious.[195] ATA estimated the annual capital expenditures for U.S. airports at $5 billion. But airport associations estimate their needs at $10 billion a year.[196] Consumer prices rose 58% between 1982 and 1995. But as shown in Figure 8.8, "Airport Charges", landing fees and rent rose 90% during this period. Coupled with PFCs, airport charges rose 139%.

Figure 8.8—AIRPORT CHARGES (1982-1995)[197]

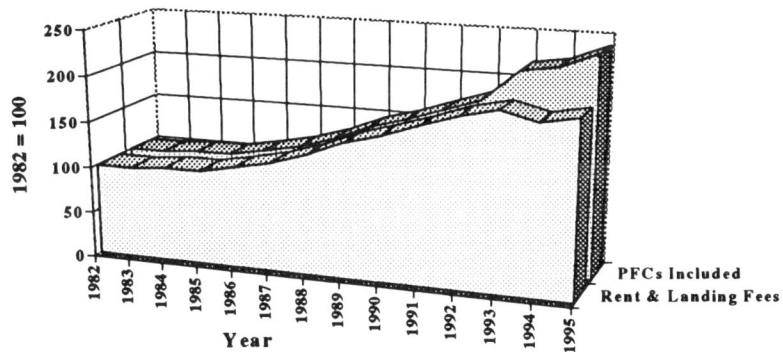

---

[193] Scott McCartney, GAO Says Fees Would Favor Big Airlines, Wall St. J., Dec. 9, 1996, at A3.
[194] Laurie McGinley, Airlines Pressure Airports to Scale Back Expansion Plans in Bid to Reduce Costs, Wall St. J., Sept 25, 1992, at B1.
[195] Aviation Daily (Mar. 21, 1996), at 460.
[196] Remarks of Carol Hallett Before the 11th Annual Salomon Bros. Transportation Conference (New York, N.Y., Nov. 13, 1996), at 8.
[197] Source: Air Transport Association.

RISK MANAGEMENT

To protect against increases in fuel costs, some carriers adopt a fuel price hedging program, whereby they enter into fuel swap contracts and the carrier makes or receives payments based on the difference between a variable price and a fixed price for aviation fuel. Many carriers purchase fuel wherever it is cheapest and ferry it across their systems. Carriers with international routes also need to be concerned with fluctuations in currency valuation. To hedge against this risk, some carriers enter into foreign currency exchange agreements, whereby the change in the value of the agreement caused by currency fluctuations is offset by changes in the value of foreign currency denominated lease and debt obligations at the current rate.[198]

America West staggers termination dates on its aircraft leases, so that when the market cycle turns downward and passenger demand declines, it can painlessly reduce capacity by returning those aircraft whose leases are expiring back to the lessors.[199] Reno Air leases 100% of its aircraft, arguably as a safety net during a down-turn in the market cycle, for it can pare its fleet by returning aircraft to lessors when demand turns south.[200]

CONCLUSION

British Airways' CEO Robert Ayling stated his company's goal with respect to unsatisfactory lines of business (such as unprofitable routes): turn it around, franchise it, sell or close it.[201] Established airlines tend to focus on cost-containment as a principal means of achieving long-term profitability. Yet cost reduction can translate into service disintegration, which can result in yield dilution. Upstart airlines, which by-and-large have low costs, find they need to focus on improving yields as a means of surviving. Success in the airline industry requires an appropriate balance of cost, service and price.

---

[198] AMR Corporation, Annual Report 60 (1994).
[199] Address of John Garel Before the Fifth Annual Phoenix International Aviation Symposium (Apr. 18, 1996).
[200] Address of Reno Air's Robert Redding Before the 11th Annual Salomon Bros. Transportation Conference (New York, N.Y., Nov. 13, 1996).
[201] Address of Robert Ayling Before the 11th Annual Salomon Bros. Transportation Conference (New York, N.Y., Nov. 13, 1996).

CHAPTER 9.

GLOBAL MARKETING AND EQUITY ALLIANCES

"The hardest thing in working on an alliance is to coordinate the activities of people who have different instincts and a different language, and maybe worship slightly different travel gods, to get them to work together in a culture that allows them to respect each other's habits and convictions, and yet work productively together in an environment in which you can't specify everything in advance."[1]
Michael E. Levine
Executive VP-Marketing, Northwest Airlines

"Beware a pact with the devil."[2]
Martin Shugrue
CEO, Pan American World Airways

THE EVOLVING ENVIRONMENT IN INTERNATIONAL AVIATION

As World War II drew to a close, the United States invited Allied world powers to attend the Convention on International Civil Aviation, subsequently referred to as the Chicago Convention of 1944.[3] The U.S. had hoped to have adopted at the convention a multilateral international air transport agreement, wherein, with the exception of cabo-

---
[1] Interview, Air Transport World (Jan. 1993), at 69.
[2] Aviation Daily (Mar. 12, 1996), at 401.
[3] See Paul Dempsey, Law & Foreign Policy in International Aviation 7-13 (1987).

tage (the right to carry air traffic originating and destined to two points within the boundaries of a given country), all nations would have complete freedom to fly commercially between nations. By the end of World War II, the United States was well-positioned to dominate global air transportation. It had air bases situated around the world; it had available air transports that were excess from the war, easily convertible to civilian use; and it had an aircraft manufacturing industry untouched by war-time activities, and, in fact, one which had been geared up by the war effort.

Growth in air passenger demand was stimulated during the war. Demands upon the airlines for the transportation of military personnel and property and of civilians engaged in the war effort brought greatly increased volumes of traffic to the airlines, some of it transported under special contract with the government. The stimulus of wartime activity was felt beyond the close of the war.[4] In short, the U.S. was well-positioned for expansion following WW II, and adoption of an open skies policy by all parties would have been to the United States' advantage.

The United States was successful in convincing 25 nations to sign a multilateral agreement exchanging traffic rights, but the overwhelming majority of the convention delegates were strongly opposed. Fearing the prospect of U.S. dominance in civil aviation, the United Kingdom led the opposition, advocating the concept of national sovereignty for all countries, which would have the effect of creating aerial borders around nations. As Ott and Neidl point out, national sovereignty in the air has been a predominant issue to countries with state-owned airlines. And, most airlines outside of the United States are owned, wholly or in part, by their governments.[5]

Though a multilateral agreement creating the International Civil Aviation Organization was signed at Chicago, the transfer of air rights would be via a contractual, or bilateral format to be used as the basis for air transport agreements between nations. In 1946, representatives of the United States and the United Kingdom met at Bermuda to negotiate an exchange of air rights between the two nations. Named after the place where it was signed, the Bermuda Agreement was the first of

---

[4] D. Philip Locklin, Economics of Transportation 771 (7th ed. 1972).
[5] James Ott & Raymond Neidl, Airline Odyssey 135 (1995).

hundreds of so-called bilateral agreements. It became the standard for other bilateral agreements subsequently written, and incorporated in the Bermuda Agreement was a guiding balance of benefits philosophy. The bilateral system is designed to provide an equal exchange of trade rights between partners which are often of unequal statures. Seldom has the bilateral system been the means to meet actual market demands, or to prepare markets for growth.[6] Nor has the system always provided the "equal exchange" hoped for. The bilateral system has been racked with protests, including a breakdown of the original Bermuda I agreement, replaced with a Bermuda II Agreement, and a subsequent challenge to the latter.

Compounding problems with the bilateral system were abrupt policy changes brought on by deregulation, including the threatened withdrawal of antitrust immunity and a challenge to the rate-setting practices of the International Air Transport Association [IATA]. As a follow-up to deregulation in the United States, Jimmy Carter issued new foreign policy objectives in line with recently adopted domestic deregulatory policy. Carter's policy gave rise to the International Air Transportation Competition Act of 1979 [IATCA]. It became the vehicle for implementing U.S. deregulatory policy abroad, and for increasing international competition. By-and-large, IATCA was designed to promote, among other things, open competition, consumer-oriented fares, and elimination of market restrictions. Included in the policy was a unilateral offer by the United States to provide more opportunity for foreign carriers to obtain access to the U.S. market, in exchange for increased gateways overseas for U.S. carriers.[7]

Rights to cabotage within the United States are of particular value because of the vast distances between U.S. hubs and the well-developed nature of the air transport market in America. Typically there is nothing to be gained by the United States in exchanging cabotage rights with a much smaller country. Access for a U.S. carrier to a port-of-entry is usually sufficient to attract passengers from within the country, where international passengers need travel only short distances, usually by surface transportation, to access the airport. The same is not true in the United States, where (absent code-sharing) a carrier

---

[6] Id.
[7] Laurence E. Gesell, Aviation and the Law 711 (2d ed. 1993).

with internally connected routes has the advantage in capturing the passenger for the overseas leg of an international journey.

Airline deregulation in the United States has yielded mixed results, but for whatever reason, the airline industry has been troubled financially since its outset. To help the beleaguered airline industry, in 1993 President Bill Clinton created The National Commission To Ensure A Strong Competitive Airline Industry [Baliles Commission], to investigate, study and make policy recommendations about the financial health and future competitiveness of the U.S. airline and aerospace industries. The airline industry, by that time, had lost $10 billion in the previous three years. Amongst its findings, the Commission determined that "The principle challenge for our country is to fashion a new, growth-oriented international aviation framework . . .," requiring ". . . a clear and decisive shift in policy by the U.S. away from the present system of bilateral regulation of air services to one based on multinational arrangements . . . ."

Formed about the same time as the Baliles Commission to study airline conditions, was *le Comite des Sages* (the European Wise Men Committee) to study the causes of the on-going air transport crisis in Europe. Their report of February 1994 criticized the air carriers' slow response to the changing air transportation market.[8] Suggesting that in the liberalization of the European Union [EU] (formerly the European Economic Community [EEC]), "There is no way back to the previous era of nationalistic protectionism." The source of the crisis in Europe, they said, was government protection of nationalized carriers.

Despite U.S. foreign policy advocating deregulation on a global scale, few nations followed the U.S. lead in the 1970s and 1980s. As the deregulation trend picked up speed, interest quickened in the privatization of nationalized airlines in order to remain competitive. As Europe has followed its path to liberalization under the EU, free-trade advocates battle with protectionists for an open skies policy. Likewise, in Latin America a highly regulated industry of national carriers has shifted to a more competitive marketplace of largely private airlines.[9] In Asia, highly nationalized (albeit privatized) carriers like Japan Airlines [JAL] and All Nippon Airlines [ANA] are battling low-cost

---

[8] James Ott & Raymond Neidl, Airline Odyssey 122 (1995).
[9] Id. at 123.

carriers such as Korean Airlines, Singapore Air, Cathay Pacific, and Thai International. Japan is among the most protectionist of the world's great economic powers, yet it is having to examine the prospects of liberalization as well.

Although nationalism remains an issue with most countries, global market forces, aided by U.S. policy, are moving the industry closer to an open skies policy worldwide. An overriding trend has been toward alliances or partnerships among the world's airlines through code-sharing agreements. Code-sharing allows two carriers to display a single, joint code on the computer reservations system. It differs from the old system of "interlining," where each carrier would have its own code identifier. Traditionally, passengers were handed off to the succeeding carrier for completion of a journey to a destination not served by the original carrier. Code-sharing, on the other hand, allows the two carriers to act as one, thus providing what is referred to as "seamless travel." Code-sharing began subsequent to deregulation, when the majors began aligning themselves with their commuter counterparts (e.g., American Eagle with American; United Express with United, Delta Connection with Delta, and so forth). The agreements allowed the smaller carriers to share the two-letter code used to identify their larger partner. Code-sharing has since spread to include international partners.

In 1992, the Dutch concluded an open skies agreement with the United States, which permitted airlines from both countries to fly to any point in either country with no restrictions. The alliance between KLM Royal Dutch Airlines and Northwest Airlines [NWA] was one of the first international partnerships to emerge from deregulation. In 1992, the United States and the Netherlands signed an open skies agreement which opened the way for the KLM/NWA partnership. The Dutch had hoped for cabotage rights which the United States could not grant under current U.S. law. Instead, KLM would have to reach internal U.S. markets through its partner NWA. However, the U.S. government granted antitrust immunity to the KLM/Northwest merger. The United States now regards the issuance of antitrust immunity as an incentive for other nations to join the few that favor free trade in the air.[10] The Netherlands has been a long-time advocate of open markets.

---

[10] Id. at 125.

The Netherlands was one of the few countries which supported the multilateral concept presented by the United States at the Chicago Convention in 1944, and it was the Netherlands which signed the first open skies agreement with the United States. As a nation whose airline depends on sixth freedom traffic funneled over its Amsterdam gateway from and to interior continental European points to and from points in North America, it is understandable that the Netherlands would favor "open skies."

The KLM/Northwest alliance was motivated in no small measure by the need of the weaker partner (Northwest), for a cash infusion. KLM owns a major interest in Northwest Airlines. KLM Royal Dutch Airlines and Northwest Airlines merged in every way except adoption of a common name. Nevertheless, Northwest remains a U.S.-based airline and KLM is a Dutch carrier.[11] KLM's interest in Northwest also has a lot to do with North Atlantic cargo feed and Northwest's Pacific operations. Some 30% of KLM's system revenue derives from cargo. Northwest is the only U.S. combination (passengers and cargo) carrier with pure freighters. On the North Atlantic routes, the KLM/NWA alliance has about 10% of the market. In the Asian market, the alliance provided eastbound routes out of Japan to the U.S. by Northwest and westbound flights to Europe by KLM.[12]

The U.S.-Netherlands "open skies" air transportation agreement signaled the start of a new era in world commercial aviation. Former Department of Transportation Secretary Andrew Card hoped that the U.S.-Dutch Open Skies bilateral agreement and the KLM/Northwest Airlines operation would set the stage for a "truly global aviation environment."[13] Until a marital rift in 1996 over KLM's ability to increase its equity in Northwest, the alliance between them was an example of how closely two separate companies with different nationalities could operate. It was the paradigmatic partnership of the, now many, alliances approved by the U.S. government, because it included an equity investment, and because of the antitrust immunity granted to the partnership, and the pooling of revenue and costs, the two companies may operate as nearly like one company as possible. For the U.S. government, and in particular the Clinton administration, the

---

[11] Id.
[12] Joan Feldman, Straining The Family Ties, Air Transport World (June 1993), at 33-37.
[13] Id. at 38.

Chapter 9

KLM/NWA partnership comes closest to fostering its "open skies" international aviation policy objectives than any other strategic alliance.

The next watershed in international alliances occurred between British Airways and USAir. Following closely on the heels of the KLM/NWA approval, came a petition asking the United States to authorize an operational agreement between USAir and British Airways. But unlike the Netherlands, the United Kingdom has been opposed to liberalizing international air travel, and, as noted above, led the opposition against U.S. policy objectives during the 1944 Chicago Convention. International air transportation objectives of the United States and of Great Britain have been diabolically opposed since the end of World War II. Following the War, the United States had adopted a liberal policy to encourage expansion and unlimited capacity. Conversely, the British wished for a more conservative policy of limited expansion and government control of rates and charges. In the give-and-take of negotiating the Bermuda I agreement in 1946, the United States made a major concession to its adopted policy by allowing international rates and fares to be subject to International Air Transport Association (IATA) agreement. In exchange, the British made concessions by accepting no predetermined limitations on capacity, and no pooling of revenue.

Bermuda I broke down in the early 1960s when the United States granted permanent certificates of Public Convenience and Necessity to Supplemental and Charter carriers, thereby flooding a North Atlantic market which already had excess capacity. As a consequence of the resulting price competition, by the early 1970s only 20% of the North Atlantic passengers were paying full IATA fares. For the British, the Bermuda agreement had become completely ineffective, and they announced their intention to terminate the agreement because of the destructively excess capacity offered by U.S. carriers on the North Atlantic routes.[14] A compromise was reached, and Bermuda II was signed in 1977, providing for more governmental involvement in approving routes and subjecting fares to governmental approval. By then, the United States was preparing for airline deregulation, placing the United States and Great Britain at even greater odds.

---

[14] Laurence E. Gesell, Aviation and the Law 710 (2d ed., 1993).

On July 21, 1992, British Airways [BA] announced plans to purchase a substantial share of USAir and to enter into a code-sharing agreement between the two airlines. The United States resisted the BA/USAir proposal, but caught up in its own concerns about the deteriorating financial condition of USAir, the government hesitatingly approved code-sharing agreements linking USAir with British Airways' global network, and granting British Airways a minority interest in an American carrier. After several years of anemic performance, USAir was in dire need of BA's $400 million cash infusion. Begrudgingly approving the agreement, Transportation Secretary Federico Peña placed a few limitations on the alliance and hinged its expansion to removing (capacity-related) restrictions in the Bermuda II agreement. The government then hoped to move directly into negotiations of a new U.S./UK bilateral agreement.

Irrespective of the government's rationale for approving the alliance, other U.S airlines resolutely objected to the administration's approval of the BA/USAir alliance, suggesting that the decision cemented British Airways' status as the preeminent global megacarrier, and provided the British with unlimited access to the U.S., the world's largest air travel market.[15] Nevertheless, Peña maintained that the U.S. was obligated by an earlier (1991) agreement with the United Kingdom to permit code-sharing by the two carriers. And, according to outside observers, the U.S. already was facing considerable opposition to its policies, particularly coming from the French and the Germans, both of which were seeking capacity-restricting agreements to replace their then current bilateral agreements.[16] Re-negotiations with the Germans led to the third watershed alliance between a U.S. carrier and a foreign airline.

In light of the BA/USAir and KLM/NWA deals, Lufthansa at the time was also seeking a U.S. partner. But unlike KLM or British Airways, Lufthansa, itself going through restructuring, could not afford to buy a stake in another airline. Although Lufthansa had nearly three times the capacity of its nearest four European competitors combined,[17] it was bloated and loosing money. Until recently, Lufthansa

---

[15] James Ott & Raymond Neidl, Airline Odyssey 32, 33 (1995).
[16] Id. at 37.
[17] Anthony L. Velocci, Getting Competitive At Lufthansa, Aviation Week and Space Technology (March 8, 1993).

Chapter 9

was totally owned by of the German Government. Battered by competition, the airline was reeling from losses in the hundreds of millions of dollars. The airline was under pressure to reduce its cost structure, improve revenue and yields, and to forge strategic links with Asian and U.S. airlines. As a result, Lufthansa began restructuring in the early 1990s through privatization, downsizing and seeking a U.S. partner in which it did not have to invest. In an ambitious effort called "Project 93," Lufthansa began slashing expenses and boosting revenues. Simultaneously, the German carrier entered into talks with both United and American to select one of them for development of joint marketing efforts, flight code sharing, and coordination of frequent-flyer programs. Lufthansa received competitive bids from both U.S. carriers, but held up making a final decision until after then on-going bilateral negotiations between the United States and Germany were concluded.

The revised U.S./German bilateral was a give-and-take negotiation, but undergirding the agreement was consideration of the administration's Open Skies policy and an expansion of air services between the two countries. German objectives were to have what they considered to be an equal chance of competition on the North Atlantic, which, in their view, necessitated a restraint on additional capacity growth for the U.S. airlines. This condition was met by freezing U.S. airline growth for two years, and allowing only moderate growth for the succeeding two years. According to Jurgen Weber, chairman of Lufthansa's executive committee, the bilateral gave the German airline "the first opportunity to engage in competition with U.S. carriers in conditions that are fair to both sides." Another German objective was to obtain code-sharing rights in the United States, thereby clearing the way for an alliance between Lufthansa and a U.S. carrier. The Germans would have preferred no restrictions on code-sharing. Instead, Germany was granted unlimited points of service in the United States, but with a cap on the frequency of service.[18] The U.S.-Germany bilateral included one significant reservation—Germany would not sign unless Lufthansa was given antitrust immunity to partner with a U.S. carrier.

---

[18] Jeffrey Lenorovitz, Lufthansa, United To Link Efforts, Aviation Week and Space Technology (October 4, 1993), at 22, 23.

Lufthansa chose United. The selection of United Airlines as Lufthansa's strategic partner was a serious blow to American Airlines, which was seemingly left with no other compatible European carrier with which to link. Most of the major European airlines had already worked out alliances with U.S. partners. Not only was the choice a blow to American, the linking of the two huge airlines posed potential competition problems for all world carriers. From a global market perspective, the link-up between United Airlines [UAL] and Lufthansa German Airlines [DLH] was the strongest alliance to have been created. And, interestingly, it did not involve any exchange of ownership. The UAL/DLH code sharing agreement is purely a marketing arrangement. Nevertheless, the shared market between the two airlines is enormous. Measured in either revenue passenger miles or in operating revenues, the United/Lufthansa partnership accounted for almost twice as much business as any other combination of world carriers—that is, until American forged an agreement with British Airways.

On June 11, 1996, American Airlines [AA] and British Airways announced their proposal for the biggest alliance ever. As with the United/Lufthansa arrangement, the American/British Airways alliance was done without an exchange of equity.[19] In addition, it didn't require any changes in British Air's partnership with USAir, although it did leave open many questions as to the future of USAir. Stephen Wolf has a reputation for arranging buyouts of companies for which he is in charge. Was Wolf hired as USAir's CEO to prepare it for takeover? Was American once again considering acquisition of USAir? American's Robert Crandall tried to put such questions to rest by stating American wasn't interested in purchasing USAir or British Air's 24.6% stake in the airline. However, it had been less than a year since USAir had announced its availability for sale. American had previously rejected the opportunity to buy the troubled airline, but the alliance with British Air put a new twist on the prospect. The addition of USAir's market to the AA/BA partnership made the specter of the global alliance even larger.

As of this writing the AA/BA deal was yet to be approved by the U.S. and British governments, but the outlook for sanction by each

---

[19] Scott McCartney, AMR and British Air to Share Profits, As Well as Passengers, From Alliance, The Wall Street Journal, June 12, 1996.

Chapter 9

government looked promising—assuming a new bilateral agreement could be reached. Before the alliance could be approved, the British and the Americans would have to once again negotiate their different perspectives on global air transportation and the exchange of air rights. Robert Crandall warned that there would be no American/British Air deal unless the alliance were to receive antitrust immunity to coordinate schedules and fares.[20] The Clinton administration, in turn, said it would not grant such immunity without a liberal "open skies" treaty with Britain.

Whereas theretofore the United/Lufthansa partnership had accounted for almost twice as much business as any other combination of world carriers, the AA/BA linkage took industry concentration a step further, especially in the North Atlantic market. American and British Air are the two largest trans-Atlantic carriers. Combined, they carried over 60% of the traffic in 1966 between the U.S. and Great Britain—one of the world's most lucrative markets.[21] Opponents argued that the combination of these two mega-carriers could only result in seriously diminished competition, although American and British Airways contended they were just trying to keep pace with others which had already teamed up, such as United Airlines and Lufthansa German Airlines. Said Bob Ayling of British Air, "This is an alliance for now and into the 21st century." In the face antitrust related issues, Ayling maintained competition would increase, not decrease as a result of the AA/BA marketing arrangement. And, rather than resulting in price-gouging by a supposed "Atlantic cartel," fares would fall.[22]

Antitrust is a major issue, but it is only one of the concerns associated with world alliances. Nations and airlines are leaping headlong into these so-called "strategic alliances." In particular, the United States may be repeating the merger-mania experience of the mid-eighties. Just like then, when the Department of Transportation and the Department of Justice [DOJ] were under the pressures of airline deregulation policy, DOJ, now under political pressure of Open Skies policy, may be repeating the merger frenzy of 1985 and 1986 when DOT approved the mergers of airlines with remarkably few restric-

---

[20] Id.
[21] The Associated Press, Trans-Atlantic Merger Plan Alarms Rivals, Tribune Newspapers (June 12, 1996).
[22] Id.

tions. The result then was to re-concentrate the market to pre-deregulation levels. In like manner, by the beginning of 1996, the Justice Department had acted in only one international code sharing case. Yet, the alliances between UAL/Lufthansa, BA/USAir, and KLM/NWA, have created giant mega-carriers and equally large antitrust concerns about concentration, this time on a global level.

Critics of international code-sharing agreements question why there is such excitement when the benefits, if there are any, have not been quantified, or at least not made public. Because of access to the rich U.S. domestic market, the economic benefits of code-sharing appear to be greater for foreign carriers than their U.S. partners. But there is no hard data available to quantify the increased profits result from international code-sharing. Without sufficient data, it may be impossible to determine if there is any net economic gain. Where there is a demonstrable increase in traffic, there is no way of knowing whether it might have occurred irrespective of any code-sharing agreements. Unless any of the airlines are maintaining a proprietary secret, the lack of available information may be one of the consequences of reduced data collection due to airline and budget pressures. Publicly, neither DOT nor the EU Commission have sufficient data to defend their decisions in support of global alliances, yet both are blindly promoting code-sharing agreements. Obtaining code-sharing rights has seemingly become more important than achievement of more liberal bilateral route provisions, and the result has been to undermine the bilateral agenda and statutory prohibitions of foreign ownership.

In addition to concerns about insufficient data to make such sweeping changes in the international air transport scheme of things, there are concerns about consumer rights, cabotage, regulatory enforcement, and threats to organized labor. Labor questions deals made with foreign carriers because they may be job eliminators. Alliances compound enforcement of a given nation's regulatory provisions. The U.S.-related alliances thus far have not provided cabotage rights in the strictest sense. But in certain respects they circumvent cabotage laws by providing unlimited access to the U.S. market through the code sharing partner. And, passengers prefer to stay on the same airline when they are making connections (although the degree of this preference is accentuated by the CRS algorithms which strongly favor on-line and code-share connections interline connections). Alliances offer the appearance of a "seamless travel experience." Consumers may perceive code-sharing to mean travel on the same airline, when, in fact, two or more carriers are giving the false appearance of single-airline service. As a result, truth in advertising becomes an issue, and code-sharing may precipitate consumer complaints. Some airline analysts have gone so far as to call code-sharing "a consumer rip off."

The foregoing concerns add to the overriding issue of antitrust. To make the pacts more perfect requires the granting of antitrust immunity, glaringly pointing to the inherent potential for anticompetitive activity. Required of alliances is that the participating carriers must plan together, sell together and compete together—even to set prices together, all of which, of course, is contrary to antitrust law. Industry concentration anywhere, the international market not excluded, suggests there is the potential for abuse and the reduction of competition.

A strategic alliance may be a vehicle for unfair competition, for it grants code-sharing partners artificial advantages over non-alliance carriers. For example, code sharing biases the computer reservations system by presenting code-sharing connections before it displays other equally convenient interline connections. Additionally, there are concerns that partners in restricted markets will reduce capacity and push prices up while keeping other competitors or potential competition out.

A basic premise of airline deregulation was that there were no economies of scale to be derived from growth beyond a certain level of efficiency. Scale economies refer to combined production resources which can be used in reducing the cost of the marginal unit of production. However, one of the lessons learned from airline deregulation is that while some may insist there are no economies of "scale" in the airline industry, there may well be economies of "size" or "scope" which can provide incumbent carriers with unfair competitive advantages. Not recognized beforehand was that there are economies of size which can provide dominant carriers with market advantages such as barriers to entry.[23]

Proponents, on the other hand, argue that international alliances will have the positive effect of preventing a three or four-carrier oligopoly in the United States. Listed as the primary reason for strategic alliances is access to otherwise restricted markets. Global alli-

---

[23] Laurence E. Gesell, Airline Re-Regulation 46, 77 (1990).

ances permit carriers to compete where they couldn't before due to border restrictions or lack of resources. Many claim that code sharing actually does create new traffic, increases revenues and lowers costs. As Rakesh Gangwal, a former United senior vice president for planning, suggests, "Very few alliances that code share don't make money."[24]

Irrespective of what the empirical data might suggest, "Feed has value." British Airways knows that, and it is why it continued to support their alliance with USAir in spite of the latter's potentially devastating losses. As BA's Sir Colin Marshall stated, combined codeshare and USAir interline connecting traffic grew 104% in 1995 over the previous year, with USAir feed to and from BA then accounting for 42% of all BA's connecting traffic in the U.S.[25] As James Ott points out, "Although a loser from a strict investment standpoint, the USAir connection allowed the British carrier to tap deeply into the U.S. market for lucrative transatlantic passenger feed."[26]

Proponents argue that these alliances provide a "new, growth-oriented international aviation framework," which was a goal identified by The National Commission To Ensure A Strong Competitive Airline Industry. The U.S. government has long sought more liberal, competitive aviation agreements, and strategic alliances provide an opportunity for change. Other than a truly Open Skies environment, it is argued that the next best thing may be international code-sharing rights. Code-sharing could be the catalyst that breaks down protectionist attitudes and the ever-fervent flag mentality that has existed since the close of World War I and the beginning of air transportation service. There may, indeed, be a change in airline corporate culture that has been brought about through implementation of Open Skies policy, further attesting to the power of government, the market, and the leaders of industry to influence cultural change.[27]

---

[24] Joan Feldman, Alliances: Cross-boarder Airline Links, Air Transport World (June 1994), at 174.
[25] Carole A. Shifrin, USAir Write-Down Hits British Airways Profits, Aviation Week and Space Technology (May 29, 1995), at 30.
[26] James Ott, USAir Hoists "For Sale" Sign, Aviation Week and Space Technology (October 9, 1995), at 33.
[27] See Paul Stephen Dempsey and Laurence E. Gesell, Air Transportation: Foundations for the 21st Century, Ch. 3.

Chapter 9

INTERCARRIER RELATIONSHIPS

Traditionally, domestic and international intercarrier agreements have covered a multitude of issues essential to providing the passenger with seamless interline service. *Ticketing-and-baggage agreements* allow one carrier to cut a ticket on the stock of the other, and to transfer baggage efficiently between them. *Joint-fare agreements* enable carriers to agree on the through connecting interline fare, which is usually lower than the sum of their respective point-to-point fares, though the carrier may squabble about the pro-rates between them. A more recent phenomenon is *code-sharing*, which essentially allows one carrier to market its product as another's. Two carriers will share designator codes in the CRSs, so that an interline flight falsely appears to be an on-line connection.

Under regulation, carriers were required to interline passengers between them. Today, carriers no longer are, with the result that large, dominant carriers often refuse to facilitate connections with competing smaller jet carriers. Other intercarrier relationships include *dry* and *wet leases*, the former consisting of aircraft leases, while the latter consisting of the lease of an aircraft and its crew.

INTERNATIONAL MARKETING ALLIANCES

Cabotage restrictions prohibit foreign airlines from plying the domestic trade. They may be avoided in various ways, including code-sharing, blocked space arrangements, and other marketing alliances."[28] Among the major international marketing alliances which have emerged are: (1) code sharing; (2) blocked space relationships; (3) computer reservations systems [CRS]; and (4) frequent flyer programs.

CODE-SHARING, BLOCKED SPACE AND FUNNEL FLIGHTS

Code-sharing has become an increasingly popular means of connecting airline networks in a way to enhance marketing opportunities and, it has been argued, provide a seamless product. For example, a pas-

---

[28] Schraft & Rosen, supra at 29.

senger seeking to travel from Ithaca, New York, to Brasilia, Brazil, could fly on a series of United Airlines through flight numbers under a code-sharing relationship whereby TW Express would pick the passenger up in Ithaca and deliver him to New York Kennedy Airport, United would pick him up at Kennedy and fly him to Rio de Janeiro, and TransBrasil Airways would take him on to Brasilia.[29] Only one passenger every other month takes such a journey, but they can do it all under the United code-sharing umbrella.

Airlines argue these practices are consumer friendly, for they allow two carriers to act as one, simplifying baggage transfers and boarding passes. They also provide more nonstop service between allied carriers hubs than would otherwise exist (e.g., Minneapolis-Amsterdam, Cincinnati-Zurich). Critics argue that baggage transfers have always been handled adequately under interline agreements, that code-sharing deceive consumers into believing they are purchasing one airline's product when they are actually purchasing another, and that by listing the combination three times, they create CRS clutter, and shove competitive alternatives off the first page of the CRS screen, where 85% of all flights are sold. Added to this, some code-sharing connections are less than consumer friendly. For example, a passenger transferring between United Airlines and its code-sharing partner Air Canada at Chicago O'Hare must exit United's terminal and walk outside (sometimes through the rain, sleet or snow) to the American Airlines terminal, where Air Canada leases gates.

Blocked space arrangements involve the leasing or reservation of a specific number of seats by one airline for its passengers to be flown in aircraft operated by another airline. They allow airlines the advantage of offering on-line connections and the potential to draw greater traffic as a result of having one carrier listed in the computer reservations systems, on timetables, and in advertisements, rather than two connecting carriers. For example, Northwest might enter into a blocked space agreement with KLM whereby Northwest would sell up to a specified number of seats on the KLM Minneapolis-Amsterdam flight to Northwest's customers.

Funnel flights involve a single flight number and ticket coupon for change-of-gauge operations, whereby passengers are transferred from

---

[29] See UAL, Second Quarter Report 2 (1993).

Chapter 9

one aircraft to another (in international operations, usually from a larger aircraft to a smaller one, or vice versa). A single flight number falsely conveys the impression of single-aircraft service.

Code sharing[30] and "funnel flights" are two airline practices which have become more widespread in recent years, and more widely condemned in the press. As early as 1988, Thomas Plaskett, chairman of Pan Am, prophetically described "code sharing" as an "ominous trend" that could be injurious to consumers and to airline competition.[31] *The Wall Street Journal* observed, "a growing number of critics claim that network arrangements actually deceive consumers, narrow their choices and possibly raise ticket prices."[32] Both of these practices are driven by the opportunities for consumer deception afforded by fraudulently manipulating the computer reservations systems.

Among the most powerful and ubiquitous computer systems in the world are those owned by the airlines. They reduce the planet to microbits of electrons, allowing everyone to move about Mother Earth with

---

[30] Air Canada has a marketing alliance with United, which increased passenger connections between the two airlines by 171% in its first four months. Canada's Airline Conundrum, Airline Bus. (May 1993), at 50. KLM has a code-sharing agreement with Northwest, acquired as a result of a $400 million investment in the U.S. carrier, which because of Northwest's anemic performance, has been written down on KLM's books to zero. British Airways has a code-sharing agreement with USAir, acquired as a result of its $300 million investment in the carrier. United has entered into a code sharing relationship with Lufthansa.

Iberia signed a code-sharing and block sheet agreement with Carnival Airlines, effectively giving it one-stop service from Spain to New York, Chicago, Los Angeles, Houston and New Orleans through a Miami hub. Iberia Turns Florida Keys, Airline Bus. (May 1993), at 10. Yet soon after creating it, Iberia announced it was retrenching, and considering eliminating the Miami hub. Carlta Vitzthum, Iberia Air Lines Realizes Limitations, Cutting Costs After Years of Expansion, Wall St. J., Sept. 24, 1993, at B5D. Nonetheless, it plans to continue participation in the fast growing Latin American market, where it enjoys a 35% market share and equity interest in three local carriers. Carlta Vitzthum, Iberia Air Lines Realizes Limitations, Cutting Costs After Years of Expansion, Wall St. J., Sept. 24, 1993, at B5D. Iberia owns 30% of Aerolinas Argentinas, 37.5% of Ladeco Chilean Airlines, and 45% of Viasa Venezuelan International Airways. Ian Verchere, Iberia Airlines' Shakeup Extends to South America, Commercial Aviation News (Sept. 13, 1993), at 11. Since 1992, Iberia has trimmed its work force by 5,000, to 24,000 employees. Carlta Vitzthum, Iberia Air Lines Realizes Limitations, Cutting Costs After Years of Expansion, Wall St. J., Sept. 24, 1993, at B5D.

China Airlines has a code sharing relationship with TWA allowing through ticketing from Asia through the gateways of San Francisco and Los Angeles to New York. Qantas has a similar relationship with Canadian Airlines.

[31] Jennifer Dorsey, Plaskett Sees Threat from Foreign Code-Sharing, Travel Weekly (June 20, 1988), at 8.

[32] Susan Carey, Cross-Border Linkups Bring Airlines Range But Uncertain Benefits, Wall St. J., June 7, 1994, at 1.

ease, and book a flight, hotel room, or rental car anywhere one can imagine.[33]

An extremely limited number of consumers have direct access to one of the major computer reservations systems—Sabre, Apollo, Worldspan, or System One. Instead, most consumers must rely on an intermediary in purchasing an airline ticket, usually a travel agent, to render accurate, complete and objective information regarding the schedule, price, availability and routing of specific flights. The travel agent, in turn, must rely on the integrity of the computer reservation system to which he or she is connected. The CRS must rely on the integrity of the information supplied by the scores of participating domestic and international airlines.[34]

The upstream polluter poisons the river for those who drink downstream. Corruption of the information provided by the carriers distorts the CRSs, which in turn, causes the travel agents to provide erroneous information to consumers, who are thereby deprived of choices they prefer, creating a dysfunctional market injuring not only to consumers, but also competing airlines offering equivalent or superior service alternatives. DOT approval of "code sharing" and "funnel flights" legitimates such carrier corruption of flight information.[35]

Even before price, most consumers choose an airline, first, based on scheduling convenience (i.e., which airline offers a flight on the date and time the consumer wants to travel to his or her selected destination).[36] Once date, time and place are established, the consumer turns to convenience, usually with the following priorities:

1. *Nonstop Service*—Nonstop flights are preferred over flights with one or more stops (because flights which stop inevitably consume more origin-destination travel time);
2. *Through-Plane Service*—Single plane service is preferred over connecting flights (because of the inconvenience and delay of

---

[33] Paul Dempsey, Airlines' Polluted Information Stream Harmful to Consumers, Houston Chronicle, Oct. 2, 1994, at 5C.
[34] Thomas Dickerson, Travel Law § 2.05[6] (1993).
[35] Paul Dempsey, Airline Code-Sharing Flying Out of Control, Rocky Mountain News, Oct. 10, 1994; Paul Dempsey, Airlines' Polluted Information Stream Harmful to Consumers, Houston Chronicle, Oct. 2, 1994, at 5C.
[36] 20.3% of U.S. residents select a carrier based on schedule, while only 13.8% choose one based on price. Aviation Daily (Oct. 3, 1991), at 23.

changing planes, often at a crowded hub airport, coupled with the increased possibility of missed connections and lost baggage);
3. *On-Line Connecting Service*—Single carrier connecting service is preferred over connecting carrier service (for all the reasons stated above, as well as the uncertainty of the quality of service on the connecting carrier, and the possibility of being transferred to inferior aircraft);
4. *Interline Service*—Connecting carrier service is preferred over non-interline connecting service (because interline agreements allow "seamless service"—through joint-line ticketing and baggage transfers); and
5. *Non-Interline Connecting Service*—Non-interline connecting carrier service is the least desirable of all (because absent an interline agreement between the carriers, passengers are forced independently to book their connections, with no joint rates or through ticketing, and must collect their own bags and transfer them between connecting aircraft).[37]

Yet the practices of "code sharing" and "funnel flights" obfuscate the service actually being provided, inducing consumers to purchase an inferior product instead of that which they prefer. "Funnel flights" deceive consumers into believing they are purchasing product #2 (through-plane service), when they are actually being sold product #3 (on-line connecting service). "Code sharing" deceives consumers into believing they are purchasing product #3 (on-line connecting service), when they are in fact being deceptively sold product #4 (interline service). By giving the appearance of an on-line connection, it appears to be a superior travel option. And although the DOT has promulgated rules requiring "code sharing" flights be listed with an asterisk and that passengers be so informed, at least a third of consumers are not told which airline they are actually flying.[38]

Compounding the issue, the computer reservations systems are programmed by their megacarrier owners to give a significant display preference to an on-line connection over an interline connection—in

---

[37] See El Al Asks DOT to Resist Northwest's Call for Trade Sanctions, 53 Travel Weekly (Feb. 7, 1994), at 1.
[38] Mead Jennings, US Tries to Clarify Codes, Airline Bus. (June 1994), at 12.

effect, superior shelf space.[39] This is true even for a pseudo on-line connection, such as a code sharing arrangement with an independent airline. As one source noted, "Even with an asterisk, it beats being consigned to the third screen."[40]

By listing the same flight several times, "code sharing" and "funnel flights" consume the finite number of lines available on the computer reservations screen—valuable shelf space.[41] Multiple listings of the same flight combinations squeeze out superior service offerings on each of the major CRSs—Sabre, Apollo, Worldspan and System One. International code shares show up on the CRSs once under the U.S. flag carrier's code (e.g., Northwest's, or NW), once under the foreign-flag carrier's code (e.g., KLM, or KL), and once again as an asterisked interline trip in which the two connect, with all three sometimes consuming the entire first page of the CRS display screen.[42] As an example, on Apollo, a request for 5:00 p.m. flights from Chicago to Dusseldorf pulls up an American Airlines flight, a United flight with a stop in Frankfurt, a Lufthansa flight with a stop in Frankfurt, and a United flight connecting with a Lufthansa flight in Frankfurt.[43] In reality, these are but two flights—the American Airlines nonstop, and a United/Lufthansa connection in Frankfurt. Though travel agents are required to identify the actual carrier to consumers, delimiters provided in the CRS to unravel the deception are easy to miss, and time consuming.[44] Funnel flights show up in the CRS as many as three separate times as well, shoving alternative competitive offerings onto the second page of the CRS screen, where they collect computer dust. Because of the pressure of time, most airline ticket sales are made by travel agents from the first page of the computer reservations screen—it is widely acknowledged that about 85% of all flights are sold from the first page

---

[39] See Code Sharing Threaten Survival of Commuter Airlines, Av. Week & Space Tech. (Apr. 27, 1987), at 57.
[40] Bill Poling, International Code Sharing Heats Up, Travel Weekly (Apr. 7, 1988), at 59.
[41] See Daniel Pearl, Airlines Squawk Over Screen-Hogging, Wall St. J., June 14, 1994, at B1.
[42] It would be the equivalent of Coca-Cola and Pepsi agreeing to sell a joint Pepsi-Coke mix, with Coca-Cola selling it as Coke2, Pepsi-Cola selling it as Pepsi2, and both selling it as Pepsi-Coke, consuming three times the super market shelf space of competing products, and squeezing some of those competitors off the shelf. Thus, even though many consumers might prefer pedigree "Big K" Cola to the cross-bred Pepsi-Coke combination, "Big K" may be nowhere to be found.
[43] Daniel Pearl, Tracking Travel, Wall St. J., June 14, 1994, at B1. For other examples, see Gary Stoller, flight Swapping, Conde Nast Traveler (Oct. 1994), at 29.
[44] James Hirsch, Code Sharing Leaves Fliers Up in the Air, Wall St. J., Mar. 11, 1993, at B3.

of the screen. By relegating competitive service offerings to inferior display on computer reservations systems (the second or third page of the CRS), these practices deceive consumers and damage competing airlines, even though their "interlining" options, or even "on-line" options, may be as good as, or in some respects superior to, the "code sharing" and "funnel flight" alternatives with which they compete.

Code-sharing raises not only consumer deception problems, it poses significant competition problems as well. Domestically, most megacarriers refuse to code-share or enter into joint fare relationships with independent jet carriers, instead insisting their code-share partners fly no jet equipment.[45] Their refusal has relegated numerous small and medium sized communities across America to inferior turboprop or piston air service. The U.S. Department of Transportation has found that 34 small communities have lost all service since promulgation of the Airline Deregulation Act of 1978; many communities which had jet service lost it to turboprop or piston aircraft; out of 320 small communities, the number served by major carriers declined from 213 in 1978 to 33 in 1995; the number of small communities receiving multiple carrier service declined from 135 in 1978 to 122 in 1995. But the DOT studies severely understate the magnitude of the problem. When one examines small community service levels in 1978 and compares them with such service one decade later, one sees a sharp deterioration. Of the 514 non-hub communities receiving air service in 1978, 313 (60.8%) had suffered declines in flight frequency, and 144 (28%) had lost all service; only 32 (6.2%) enjoyed the inauguration of new service.[46] By 1995, things were even worse. According to Professor Andrew Goetz, the 514 non-hub communities receiving air service in 1978, 167 (32.5%) had been terminated by 1995, while only 26 (5.1%) gained new service.[47]

The DOT studies were unable to comment meaningfully about pricing of air service to small communities, for commuter carriers gen-

---

[45] Continental Airlines is the notable exception, which has entered into a major code-sharing relationship with America West Airlines.

[46] Andrew Goetz & Paul Dempsey, Airline Deregulation Ten Years After: Something Foul in the Air, 54 J. Air L. & Com. 927, 947 (1989); Paul Dempsey & Andrew Goetz, Airline Deregulation & Laissez-Faire Mythology 265-76 (1993).

[47] Unpublished research by Professor Andrew Goetz, University of Denver Department of Geography. Professor Goetz has produced some of the most revealing research of the impact of airline deregulation on small communities; See e.g., Andrew Goetz, Air Passenger Transportation and Growth In the U.S. Urban System, 23 Growth & Change 217 (1992).

erally do not report pricing data. But the U.S. General Accounting Office has found that passengers flying from small-city airports to major airports paid 34% more if the major airport was concentrated, and 42% more if both the small-city and major airports were concentrated.

In those small community city-pair markets with sufficient volume to support jet service by a low-cost carrier, the code-sharing phenomenon insures they will instead be relegated to relatively higher-cost/less safe turboprop service. For example, one of the nation's largest connecting turboprop carriers, Mesa Airlines (which in some parts of America operates as a United Airlines code-sharing affiliate—"United Express"), charges yields of nearly 35 cents per mile, compared with about 12 cents a mile by United Airlines. Even USAirways, which operates short-haul high-cost jet service, charges only about 18 cents a mile—about half that charged by a turboprop carrier.[48] A low-cost jet entrant typically charges consumers average prices which are significantly less than the major airlines. Aside from the social consequences of the deterioration of rural air service, such discriminatory treatment by megacarriers in favor of turboprop code-sharing affiliates and against independent regional jet carriers also raises serious antitrust concerns under the "essential facilities doctrine."[49]

"Funnel flights" raise similar concerns. For example, TWA's departure screens in its international terminal at John F. Kennedy Airport in New York displays two or three flights boarding simultaneously (at precisely the same gate and time) to various nonstop destinations across the Atlantic, notwithstanding the laws of physics (see Table 9.1, "TWA Funnel Flights Via New York JFK Airport").

There are probably more, and TWA is probably not the most egregious of the abusers. But it may be at least dismaying for a passenger in San Antonio, who is issued a single ticket coupon for flight 880 to Athens, Greece, to be not only stopping in New Orleans, but also changing planes in New York. Before funnel flights, the passenger would have received two ticket coupons for two separate flights (designated by two separate flight numbers), one from San Antonio to New York, and the other from New York to Athens. For its part, TWA

---

[48] 1996 data: Julius Maldutis, Airline Update—August 1996 (Sept. 8, 1996).
[49] See Robert Hardaway & Paul Dempsey, Airlines, Airports and Antitrust: A Proposed Strategy for Enhanced Competition, 58 J. Air L. & Com. 455, 498-506 (1993).

can pretend to offer single-plane service straight through from San Antonio to Athens. If a passenger does end up connecting to flight 800 from New York to Athens, s/he will be stopping in Paris en route, perhaps changing aircraft again.

Table 9.1—TWA FUNNEL FLIGHTS VIA NEW YORK JFK AIRPORT (1994)[50]

Destination	Flight number	Origin
Athens (via Paris)	800	New York
Athens	880	New York
Athens	880	San Antonio (via New Orleans)
Frankfurt	740	New York
Frankfurt	740	Seattle
Frankfurt	758	St. Louis
Frankfurt	742	Kansas City
Lisbon	900	New York
Lisbon	910	San Francisco
Lisbon	912	Kansas City
Madrid	904	New York
Madrid	914	Los Angeles
Madrid	905	Washington, DC (Nat'l. Airport)
Milan	842	New York
Milan	842	San Francisco
Milan	850	Los Angeles
Rome	840	New York
Rome	886	San Francisco
Rome	844	St. Louis
Rome	854	Kansas City

It may also be a bit surprising for a Seattle passenger on flight 740 bound for Frankfurt, to find herself in New York not only changing airline terminals and planes, but boarding at a gate with three other flights at precisely the same departure time on to the same wide-bodied

---

[50] Data are taken from TWA's May 1, 1994, timetable.

aircraft bound for Frankfurt.[51] For its part, TWA can hold itself out as providing single-plane service to Frankfurt from New York, Seattle, St. Louis, and Kansas City, when in fact, only the New York-Rome service is single-aircraft. More importantly, TWA fills valuable shelf space in the computer reservations systems with four separate flights and flight numbers to Rome, when in fact, it flies only a single jet across the Atlantic to Rome. Again, that is not to say that TWA is the worst perpetrator of such practices. Even airlines which would prefer not to, find they must commit such false and misleading practices to remain competitive with other airlines which engage in them.

Many consumers have traditionally assumed that a single ticket coupon with a single flight number means flying in a single aircraft (with or without stops), but without changing planes. For the overwhelming majority of flights, each change of plane carries a separate flight number and separate ticket coupon. Many consumers prefer not to have to get off the plane and sit and wait, and wait, and wait, at a crowded hub airport, while the airline gets another chance to lose their bags or cause the passenger to miss a connecting flight.

Only a very limited number of consumers enjoy direct access to the CRSs; the overwhelming majority do not. If they did have direct access to one of the computer reservations systems, they would not have to rely on a frazzled travel agent to peel through the several pages of the displays (now cluttered with multiple code sharing and funnel flight listings) to determine whether what fictitiously appears to be the single-plane service in fact connects with other aircraft or airline, how long and where the connection transpires, to what kind of aircraft they will be transferred, and (in a code-sharing situation), the identity of the connecting carrier. More importantly, they could determine whether there was a real nonstop or single-plane alternative on another airline. But direct CRS access is probably years away for many consumers.

Not only do code sharing and funnel flights deceive consumers, they also injure competing airlines. In reviewing the impact code sharing had on small competing independent regional airlines, Professor Clinton Oster found "there seem to be few, if any, markets where an independent [carrier] can maintain its market share in compe-

---

[51] Richard J. Newman, Direct Flight? Hah!, U.S. News & World Rep. (Aug. 15, 1994), at 58.

tition with the code-sharing partner of a major jet carrier."[52] He further found that "when a code-sharing partner prevails in a market, service levels generally seem to drop."[53] William Britt, founder of Britt Airways (at one time the nation's largest regional airline), complained that independent regional air carriers cannot survive when their competitors adopt the codes of the major airlines.[54]

In fact, since the dawn of commercial aviation, all of the purported consumer advantages of "code sharing" have been available under traditional forms of carrier interlining—scheduling, ticketing and baggage coordination—all the essential elements of so-called "seamless service."[55] "Code sharing" merely advances interlining to the point of producing consumer deception, purporting to offer consumers something more than they are actually being sold. "Funnel flights" deceive consumers into believing they will not have to change planes, when in fact, they must. Many consumers are thereby denied the competitive alternative of a nonstop flight via a competing airline.

Additionally, interlining to a code share partner may lead to travel via a carrier or type of aircraft consumers would otherwise prefer to avoid. Domestically, a "code sharing" relationship typically funnels consumers into commuter affiliates flying small aircraft below the weather.[56] Internationally, it can result in being funneled into a third-world airline flying old Soviet aircraft.[57]

Among the parties which have pointed out the pernicious effects of "code sharing" and "funnel flights" to both the Civil Aeronautics Board and the U.S. Department of Transportation during the past decade have been the following:

- American Airlines: The funnel flight "masquerade means that many passengers who will in fact be required to change planes are induced to purchase a product in the belief that they will not be re-

---

[52] Bill Poling, Code Sharing Threatens Independents, Travel Weekly (Jan. 5, 1987), at 2.
[53] Id. See also Robert Moorman, Dilemma of Independent, Non-Aligned Regionals, Air Transport World (July 1988), at 89.
[54] Bill Poling, DOT Adviser Revises Data On Ill Effects of Code Sharing, Travel Weekly (Dec. 25, 1986), at 1.
[55] See Robert Moorman, Dilemma of Independent, Non-Aligned Regionals, Air Transport World (July 1988), at 89.
[56] See Richard Newman, How Safe Are Small Planes?, U.S. News & World Rep., Nov. 14, 1994, at 68.
[57] See Alex McWhirter, Codes of Misconduct, Business Traveler (Mar. 1994), at 16.

quired to do so . . . . It is surprising that a practice so deceptive on its face has been tolerated for so long."[58]
- American Airlines: Code-sharing is an "unfair practice that deceives, misleads, and confuses consumers in violation of Section 411 of the Federal Aviation Act."[59]
- American Airlines: "The purpose and effect of [code-sharing] is to clutter CRS display screens and relegate competitive travel alternatives to lower screen positions than those they would otherwise occupy."[60]
- Association of Retail Travel Agents: The DOT should promulgate a rule prohibiting "screen padding."[61]
- American Society of Travel Agents: "The effect of double or sometimes even triple listing the same flight option is to clutter CRS screens."[62]
- British Airways: "it is intrinsically deceptive for two carriers to share a designator code."[63]
- European Civil Aviation Conference: Code-sharing is "screen padding" and "manipulation of flight categorization."[64]
- Senator Wendell Ford: Code-sharing is "inherently dishonest," and "a legal way of advertising one product, but then selling another."[65]
- North American Airlines: "code-sharing relationships preclude smaller carriers from competing for important international feed traffic."[66]
- Consumer advocate Donald L. Pevsner: "all single-coupon ticketing for two or more flight sectors is inherently deceptive."[67]
- TACA International: "Funnel flights are deceptive and unfair methods of competition."[68]

---

[58] DOT Docket 47546, 1991. This petition was supported by British Airways and Lufthansa. See also American Airlines petition in CAB Docket 41875, 1983.
[59] DOT Docket 49223, 1994.
[60] DOT Docket 49260, 1994.
[61] 57 Fed. Reg. 43780, 1992.
[62] DOT Docket 49260, 1994.
[63] DOT Docket 42199, 1984. See also comments of KLM in Docket 42199, 1984.
[64] Letter to DOT Ass't. Sec. Jeffrey Shane (April. 16, 1987).
[65] Letter to DOT Secretary Pena (Nov. 3, 1993).
[66] Letter to DOT Office of International Aviation, (Jan. 28, 1994).
[67] DOT Docket 47546, 1993. Mr. Pevsner first called for truth in flight listings in 1983, CAB Docket 41217, 1983.

- United Airlines: "the sharing of designators is misleading and deceptive and should not be permitted."[69]
- USAir: Multiple listing reduces "the proportion of competitive flights displayed."[70]

Notwithstanding these widespread concerns and despite the broad-based nature of the opposition, including formal petitions for rulemaking, the DOT has taken little meaningful action to protect the consuming public or injured competitors from these unfair and deceptive practices. Remarkably, the Clinton Administration's DOT appears more inclined to support these practices than its predecessors, with its continued rhetorical praise of such practices.

DOT approved 39 international code-sharing arrangements between 1987 and February 1993. Between February 1993 and March 1994, the DOT approved 89 such agreements.[71] The international integration made possible by "code sharing" promises to reduce competition in international markets, transforming the airline industry into a small number of global megacarrier alliances.

Globalization is a euphemism for cartelization. There was no meaningful competition between Continental and Eastern when Frank Lorenzo dragged them under a single roof. Nor is there meaningful competition between Northwest and KLM now that they are commonly owned and blending marketing under a bilateral which confers unprecedented antitrust immunity, condoning unprecedented pooling—a bilateral air transport agreement concluded only months after Northwest executives gave George Bush's committee to re-elect the President $100,000.

In summary, the fundamental problems of such marketing alliances as code-sharing and funnel flights are, (1) their success relies upon their ability to flood the computer reservations system screens with duplicative information so as to deceive the consumer into purchasing a product that may be different than that s/he prefers; and (2) discriminatory alliances between airlines reduces or eliminates competi-

---

[68] DOT Dockets 49512 and 49513, 1994. These petitions were supported by Aviateca and NICA.
[69] CAB Docket 42199, 1984. See also comments of United Air Lines in CAB Docket 41875, 1983.
[70] DOT Docket 43918, 1986.
[71] DOT Assesses International Code Sharing, Plans Rulemaking On Notification, Aviation Daily (May 6, 1994), at 203.

tion between them and diverts traffic from competitors, thereby leading to higher levels of concentration.

Two major international aviation organizations have provided leadership in this area. The European Civil Aviation Conference has adopted a CRS code of conduct requiring all "code sharing" or "funnel flight" trips specifically be designated as such, rather than on-line and direct flights, respectively, and required the listing of flights on the basis of elapsed time from origin to destination.[72]

The U.N. International Civil Aviation Organization has finalized a CRS code of conduct which requires that:

- "Funnel flights" be treated as connections;
- "Code sharing" trips be listed as off-line connections;
- Such combinations should not be listed more than once under different codes or flight numbers; and
- Displays should clearly indicate when a single flight number itinerary involves a change in aircraft, change in airport, or involves "code sharing."[73]

---

[72] European Aviation Group Expected to Adopt Code on Res Displays, Travel Weekly (Mar. 9, 1989), at 10; ECAC To Issue CRS Regulations, Travel Weekly (Apr. 21, 1988), at 1. All of this could be rectified very simply. All DOT need do is promulgate a common sense rule under section 411 of the Federal Aviation Act requiring that every separate flight have a separate flight number and separate ticket coupon, and that there be no multiple listing of flights in the computer reservations systems. The U.S. Department of Transportation has a statutory responsibility to protect the public against unfair and deceptive competitive practices and unfair methods of competition. 49 U.S.C. sec. 41712. This responsibility makes it imperative that the DOT immediately inaugurate a rulemaking which, at minimum, should:
1. Eliminate all multiple-listing of flights in computer reservations systems; and
2. Require that all consumers be fully informed, orally by the travel agent, and in writing (preferably with the issuance of a separate ticket coupon for each flight in the itinerary), of the true identity of the actual carrier providing the service, the number of stops, changes of aircraft, and types of aircraft.

Continued inaction will cause a cancerous proliferation of such fraudulent practices as even more carriers (even those which philosophically oppose "code sharing" and "funnel flights") clutter the CRSs with multiple flight listings of their own as a competitive defense mechanism, thereby causing inordinate traffic congestion on the Information Superhighway.

[73] Nadine Godwin, ICAO Finalizes CRS Code of Conduct, Travel Weekly (Dec. 22, 1988), at 4.

Chapter 9

COMPUTER RESERVATIONS SYSTEMS

Foreign alliances with U.S. airlines began in the 1980s with shared frequent flyer programs, then entered computer reservations systems, code-sharing, and finally turned to outright equity ownership. Table 9.2, "European Computer Reservations Systems Partners, and Table 9.3, "Asian Computer Reservations Systems Partners", reveal the alliances of the two dominant European computer reservations systems, and a major Asian CRS.

Table 9.2—EUROPEAN COMPUTER RESERVATIONS SYSTEMS PARTNERS

Galileo	*Amadeus*
United (38.0%)	Continental Airlines
British Airways (14.7%)	Air France
KLM (12.1%)	Lufthansa
Swissair (13.2%)	Iberia
Alitalia (8.7%)	SAS
USAir (11.0%)	
Air Canada (1%)	
Olympic (1%)	

Table 9.3—ASIAN COMPUTER RESERVATIONS SYSTEMS PARTNERS

Abacus

ANA
Cathay Pacific
Malaysia Airlines
Singapore Airlines
China Airlines
Royal Brunei
(and a small share of Worldspan)

FREQUENT FLYER PROGRAMS

Like most marketing relationships, partnerships are fluid. Some of the major U.S. airline frequent flyer relationships with foreign carriers in the 1990s are shown in Table 9.4, "Frequent Flyer Relationships".

Table 9.4—FREQUENT FLYER RELATIONSHIPS

American Airlines	TWA
Canadian Airlines International	Air India
Cathay Pacific	Air New Zealand
Qantas	Philippine Airlines
Singapore Airlines	
Continental Airlines	United Airlines
Aer Lingus	Air France
Alitalia	Alitalia
Austrian	British Midland
Cayman Airways	Iberia
Iberia	KLM
KLM	Lufthansa
LanChile	Sabena
SAS	Swissair
Delta Air Lines	USAir
Air New Zealand	Air France
Japan Airlines	British Airways
KLM	Finnair
Lufthansa	Lufthansa
Singapore Airlines	Philippine Airlines
Swissair	Swissair

Several Asian frequent flyer alliances have emerged, including one between Korean Air Lines, China Airlines and Philippine Airlines. Cathay Pacific, Singapore Airlines, and Malaysia Airlines also announced plans to launch a joint Asia Frequent Flyer program.[74] Ansett

---

[74] Ansett Welds Asian FFPs, Airline Bus. (May 1993), at 16.

is affiliated with Singapore Airlines, All Nippon Airways, and United Airlines.[75]

INTERNATIONAL EQUITY ALLIANCES

DATING VERSUS MARRIAGE

A marketing alliance is the equivalent of dating. If the relationship sours, the parties are free (within specified contractual limits) to break it off. An equity investment is the equivalent of marriage. If the relationship sours, the investor cannot easily extricate himself from his investment. In dating, one can be less discriminate in the appearance or health of one's partner. But selecting a marital partner is a more serious endeavor. Usually, one would not seek a marital partner with a terminal disease, for example.

The distinction has been lost on several airlines. Hundreds of millions of dollars of investments in U.S. airlines by SAS, KLM and British Airways have been written down on their books to zero because of the deteriorating health of their mates. Marital spats have erupted between KLM and Northwest over money and between USAirways and British Airways over infidelity. They have been treated in the aviation trade press almost like spats between Lady Di and Prince Charles were in the British tabloids.

Using the dating and marriage analogy, it is appropriate to note the widespread adultery and incest that transpires in the contemporary airline industry. For example, British Airways owns about 25% of USAir, and USAir owns about 15% of United's CRS (Galileo). United has a code-sharing relationship with Lufthansa, coordinating operations under antitrust immunity. USAir had a code-share with British Airways. At this writing BA was seeking code-sharing and antitrust immunity with American Airlines, which owns 33% of Canadian Airlines.

Similarly Delta Air Lines jointly owns the Worldspan CRS with TWA and Northwest. Delta holds equity in both Singapore Airlines and Swissair, and the latter owns a 10% slice of Austrian Airlines (Air France and ANA also own pieces of Austrian Airlines), and nearly half

---

[75] Id.

of Sabena. Northwest and Japan Airlines own a chunk of Hawaiian Airlines, while KLM owns 25% of Northwest, with which it codeshares, under antitrust immunity. These are more than kissing cousins. Globalization appears to be a euphemism for commercial adultery and incest, particularly where carriers lie together under a blanket of antitrust immunity.

U.S. EQUITY ALLIANCES

Foreign airlines have exhibited a tenacious interest in penetrating the U.S. passenger market—the largest market in the world. In the last few years, KLM bought a huge piece of Northwest; SAS purchased a chunk of Continental; Singapore Airlines and Swissair each acquired a slice of Delta; and British Airways unsuccessfully sought a share of United Airlines, and purchased a large slice of USAir. Table 9.5, "Foreign Carrier Ownership Of U.S. Airlines", depicts the substantial foreign airline interests in U.S. flag carriers.

Table 9.5—FOREIGN CARRIER OWNERSHIP OF U.S. AIRLINES (1996)

Foreign Airline	*Percentage Ownership*	*U.S. Airline*
SAS	18.4	Continental*
Swissair	4.6	Delta
Singapore Airlines	5.0	Delta
Ansett Airlines	17.0	America West*
Japan Air Lines	8.5	Hawaiian Airlines*
KLM	25.0	Northwest*
British Air	15.0	United **
British Air	24.6	USAir*
Air Canada	19.6	Continental

* investment written down to zero
** proposed; later withdrawn

The equity interests by Scandinavian Airline System [SAS] in Continental Airline Holdings was inspired by the U.S. carrier's need for a substantial infusion of new capital. From SAS's perspective, the Texas Air alliance gave it new feed into its trans-Atlantic routes; SAS moved its international hub from New York Kennedy Airport to Newark, where Texas Air's Continental and Eastern could provide domestic feed.[76] Swissair's and Singapore Airlines' interest in Delta appears to have been inspired by different reasons—the desire of Delta to have friendly partners poised to fend off potential LBOs, and to align itself with two of the world's carriers renowned for a high quality product.

But most such investments are motivated by foreign airlines' interests in creating operating and market alliances. Thus, they invest "dumb equity," accepting sub-optimal returns because they anticipate synergistic revenue on the passenger feed U.S. airlines promise them, and the diminution of competition thereby created.

As a practical matter, however, much of the foreign investment in U.S. airlines has been an economic failure. SAS wrote its investment in Continental down to zero. KLM has watched its investment in Northwest deteriorate, writing it down on its books to zero. British Airways did the same with respect to most of its investment in USAir, as did Japan Airlines with its investment in Hawaiian Airlines.

In the 1980s, Frank Lorenzo's Texas Air Empire included Texas International, Continental, Eastern, People Express, Frontier, Britt, PBA and New York Air (ultimately all but Eastern folded into Continental), American acquired Air Cal, Delta acquired Western, Northwest acquired Republic (itself a product of the mergers of Southern, North Central and Hughes Airwest), USAir acquired Piedmont and PSA, TWA acquired Ozark, and Southwest acquired Muse and Morris Air.

U.S. carriers have also acquired equity interests in other airlines. Table 9.6, "U.S. Airline Equity Interests In Other Carriers", reveals the equity interests of U.S. airlines in other carriers by the mid-1990s.

---

[76] Repeating Mistakes, Journal of Commerce, Aug. 30, 1989, at 8A.

Table 9.6—U.S. AIRLINE EQUITY INTERESTS IN OTHER CARRIERS (1995)[77]

Purchaser	Percentage Ownership	Target
AMR (American)	33.0	Canadian Airlines
Continental	17.7	America West
Delta Air Lines	2.7	Singapore Airlines
Delta Air Lines	4.5	Swissair
Mesa Air Group	7.6	America West
Northwest Airlines	25.0	Hawaiian Air

FOREIGN EQUITY ALLIANCES

Not only are foreign airlines affiliating with U.S. carriers. Other international aviation alliances and acquisitions are emerging, including British Airway's acquisition of British Caledonian, and Air France's purchase of UTA. Although Table 9.7, "Major Equity Investment Between Foreign Airlines", is rather incomplete, it nevertheless reveals several of the major ownership interests of foreign airlines in the mid-1990s.

Table 9.7—MAJOR EQUITY INVESTMENTS BETWEEN FOREIGN AIRLINES (1995)[78]

Purchaser	Percentage Ownership	Target
Aeromexico	47.0	AeroPeru
Air France	16.0	Air Afrique
Air France	11.2	Air Gabon
Air France	72.3	Air Inter

---

[77] A Question of Give and Take, Airline Bus. (June 1995), at 57-60.
[78] Id. See also Testimony of Helane Becker (vice president, Lehman Brothers) Before the Subcomm. on Aviation of the House Comm. on Public Works and Transportation (Feb. 6, 1991), at 5; Going Steady, Economist (July 22, 1989), at 39; and Overlapping Airlines: Recent Investments, Wall St. J., July 23, 1991, at A6.

Table 9.7—MAJOR EQUITY INVESTMENTS BETWEEN FOREIGN AIRLINES (Cont'd.)

Air France	1.5	Austrian Airlines
Air New Zealand	49.0	Ansett
Alitalia	30.0	Malev
ANA	9.0	Austrian Airlines
British Airways	49.0	Qantas
Cathay Pacific	43.0	Dragonair
Iberia	45.0	Viasa
Japan Air Lines	8.2	Japan Air System
KLM	40.0	ALM Antillian
KLM	45.0	Air UK
Lufthansa	100.0	Condor
Lufthansa	39.7	Lauda Air
Lufthansa	13.0	Luxair
Qantas	19.9	Air New Zealand
SAS	40.0	British Midland
Singapore	100.0	Silkair
Singapore	2.7	Swissair
Swissair	10.0	Austrian
Swissair	49.5	Sabena
Taca Group	30.0	Aviateca
Taca Group	10.0	Lacsa

EUROPEAN CONSOLIDATION

Dr. Maldutis predicts that the "European airline industry will consolidate into four, perhaps five, large systems to achieve economies of scale and to successfully compete against other global airline combines."[79] Market Darwinism has led each airline to fear for its survival, and to extend its route network via alliances to insure it will be one of the remaining megacarriers in the next century.

---

[79] Julius Maldutis, Industry Investment Requirements—Looking Beyond 2000 (address before the 7th IATA High-Level Aviation Symposium, Sept 6-7, 1993, Cairo, Egypt).

THE BRITISH AIR GROUP

Geographically, British Airways [BA] is the world's largest scheduled international passenger airline, serving 72 nations with a total of 155 destinations and transporting 28 million passengers.[80] It was fully privatized in 1987. British Airways is the leading carrier in the U.S.-U.K. market, flying nearly 40% of the seats (up from 29% in 1985).[81] Table 9.8, "The British Air Group", lists the airlines aligned with British Airways.

Table 9.8—THE BRITISH AIR GROUP

British Airways	
Air Mauritius (12.8%)	Deutsch BA (49%)
Air Russia (31%)	GB Airways (49%)
British Caledonian (absorbed)	Qantas (25%)
Brymon (40%)	TAT (49.9%)
Dan Air (100%)	USAir (25%)

British Airways has been consistently profitable since the 1980s. Various sources have attributed its success, vis-à-vis its European cousins, to BA's:

1. protected position under the U.S.-U.K. bilateral;
2. superior origin and destination market, resulting in better yields;
3. superior route structure;
4. pre-privatization write off of the Concorde;
5. greater flexibility as a privatized company;
6. culture of cost-consciousness;
7. enhanced labor and asset utilization; and
8. targeted marketing.[82]

British Airways has been on a major expansion program, purchasing equity in a host of regional carriers around the world. BA spent $400 million for 24.6% voting stock in USAir, and is implemen-

---

[80] Julius Maldutis, British Airways Plc—The Crown Jewel (Aug. 23, 1993), at 2.
[81] Id. at 9.
[82] Ron Katz, The Fine Art of Profit, Airline Bus. (Jan. 1994), at 24.

ting code sharing arrangements, to give it access to 65 U.S. destinations via ten U.S. gateways.[83] However, it declined to invest another $200 million in 1996 without U.S. approval for it to exert more control over USAir.[84]

With code-sharing, British Airways could turn USAir into essentially a feeder system for BA's long-haul, wide-bodied, trans-Atlantic system. Together British Airways and USAir served 339 cities around the world. The alliance was estimated by BA to be worth 70 million Pounds Sterling in additional revenue in 1994 alone.[85] One study estimated that the benefit to British Airways of the alliance was $27.2 million, while the benefit to USAir was only $5.6 million. Another estimated the benefit to British Airways at $100 million.[86] To gain leverage, it was anticipated the two carriers could participate in fuel purchases and aircraft service agreements.[87] With wet leases between Baltimore, Charlotte, and Pittsburgh on the one hand, and London (Gatwick) on the other, flights were operated with USAir-owned aircraft and BA codes, painted in British Airways livery, operated by USAir cabin and flight crews wearing British Airways uniforms.[88] This is nearly as odd as the Continental/Alitalia alliance in which the livery on one side of the Newark-Rome aircraft was painted in Continental colors, and the other side was painted in Alitalia colors. Some joked that the two carriers didn't know whether they were going or coming.

In 1993, British Airways spent $666 million for 25% of Qantas Airways (which absorbed Australian Airlines, and invested in Air New Zealand and Air Pacific).[89] BA owns nearly half (and holds an option to buy the other half) of TAT, France's largest independent airline, with 20% of the landing slots at Orly Airport, Paris' principal domestic airport, and routes to 32 domestic and four international destinations.[90] BA also acquired the assets of Dan-Air, based at London Gatwick Airport, and entered into a new franchising agreement with

---

[83] Julius Maldutis, British Airways Plc—The Crown Jewel (Aug. 23, 1993), at 3.
[84] Aviation Daily (Jan. 22, 1996), at 99.
[85] Thomas Petzinger, Jr., Hard Landing 388-401 (1995).
[86] A Question of Give and Take, Airline Bus. (June 1995), at 54.
[87] Richard Weintraub, Rebuilding USAir, Washington Bus., Mar. 22, 1993, at 21.
[88] Aviation Daily, May 4, 1993, at 187.
[89] Julius Maldutis, British Airways Plc—The Crown Jewel (Aug. 23, 1993), at 3; Richard Evans, Why the World's Airlines Can't Seem to Get Enough Cash, Global Finance (May 1993), at 48, 53.
[90] Julius Maldutis, British Airways Plc—The Crown Jewel (Aug. 23, 1993), at 3, 7.

CityFlyer Express, both of which will operate under the British Airways name.[91] In 1992, British Airways acquired nearly half of Delta Air, renamed Deutsche BA.[92] In addition to the carrier's regional routes, it has been given authority to fly from Berlin to Munich, Stuttgart, Cologne, Dusseldorf, and Moscow.[93] BA owns nearly a third of Air Russia, which was to begin service from Moscow by 1995 or 1996.[94] As a Qantas executive observed, "You can expect us to hunt as a pack."[95] The airlines combine business lounges and check-in counters.

BA has been described as having one of the best management teams in the airline industry: "Management can be characterized as aggressive and demanding. It will, however, be challenged to integrate its far flung airline investments into a cohesive integrated operating entity."[96] Another source observed, "The real test will be whether BA's internal cost discipline, and its competitive edge, will be transposed onto its partnerships."[97]

But BA also inherited a route system from a paternalistic British government historically intent on protecting a BOAC which unified a far flung colonial Empire. This included a dominant position at London's slot-constrained Heathrow Airport, at which only two U.S. carriers have been permitted entry. As Guy Kekwick observed, "The incumbents at Heathrow do enjoy near-monopoly profits from their positions at what is the leading international airport in Europe, if not the world."[98]

In 1996, the British Airways empire was extended further with an agreement to consummate an alliance with American Airlines. These two largest trans-Atlantic airlines, British Airways and American Airlines, sought antitrust immunity to form a code-sharing and revenue pooling alliance. The alliance was predicted to generate as much as $4

---

[91] Id. at 4.
[92] Richard Evans, Why the World's Airlines Can't Seem to Get Enough Cash, Global Finance (May 1993), at 48, 53.
[93] Julius Maldutis, British Airways Plc—The Crown Jewel (Aug. 23, 1993), at 7.
[94] Id.
[95] Address by James Strong before the Salomon Bros. Transportation Conference (New York, N.Y., November 17, 1994).
[96] Julius Maldutis, British Airways Plc—The Crown Jewel (Aug. 23, 1993), at 17.
[97] Ron Katz, The Fine Art of Profit, Airline Bus. (Jan. 1994), at 24.
[98] Erik Ipsen, British Airways Is Flying High, But Troubles Loom, International Herald Tribune, May 24, 1994, at 9.

billion in annual revenue.[99] That causes a rift with BA's partner USAir, which filed suit to block the BA/AA wedding, and announced its divorce from polygamous BA.[100]

THE ALCAZAR GROUP

In 1989, SAS, Swissair and Austrian Airlines created a loose confederation called European Quality Alliance.[101] With KLM, they reached tentative agreements to form a single system, with KLM, SAS and Swissair each owning 30%, and Austrian Airlines owning 10%. The system would revolve around the hubs of Amsterdam, Copenhagen, Geneva, Zurich, Oslo, Stockholm and Vienna. In 1992, the four carriers had revenues of $16 billion (making it the world's largest airline in terms of total sales), but lost a combined $365 million.[102] It was estimated a merger would save the carriers about $1.12 billion a year.[103]

However, merger talks collapsed in late 1993, with Swissair preferring a U.S. partnership with Delta Airlines, and KLM preferring Northwest.[104] KLM had invested $400 million in Northwest in the mid-1980s.[105] Swissair also owns about 5% of Delta Air Lines, and Delta owns about 5% of Swissair. Despite the collapse of the merger, Swissair, Sabena and Austrian Airlines have partnered in what Swissair's CEO Philippe Bruggisser described as the "most extensive inter-carrier collaboration to date among airlines anywhere in the world."[106] The three companies began joint fleet purchases (to take advantage of the volume discount), joint sales offices, and joint

---

[99] Asra Nomani, Justice Agency Probes Implications of Pact Between American, British Air, Wall St. J., July 8, 1996, at A4.
[100] Susan Carey & Charles Goldsmith, USAir Files Suit To Block Alliance of British Airways and American, Wall St. J., July 31, 1996, at B2.
[101] Richard Evans, Why the World's Airlines Can't Seem to Get Enough Cash, Global Finance (May 1993), at 48, 53.
[102] Jacqueline Gallacher, Alcazar: A Fortress in the Sky?, Commercial Aviation News (Aug. 23, 1993), at 3, 21.
[103] Brian Coleman, Four Airlines' Bid in Europe to Unite Fails, Wall St. J., Nov. 22, 1993, at A8.
[104] Id.
[105] David Phelps & John Oslund, Can High-Stakes Game Save Northwest?, Minneapolis Star Tribune, Nov. 16, 1992.
[106] Charles Goldsmith & Margaret Studer, Swissair, Sabena, Austrian Airlines Will Buy Jets, Wall St. J., Dec. 20, 1996, at A11B.

reservations, and announced plans for joint operations across the Atlantic with Delta Air Lines.[107]

THE AIR FRANCE GROUP

Air France merged with UTA and integrated domestic service though Air Inter, allowing it to dominate the hub at Charles de Gaulle Airport in Paris. It invested equity in Sabena (Air France and other private investors bought 37.5%, blocking any rival at Brussels) and CSA (among the more promising east European carriers), and entered into marketing agreements with Air Canada, Aeromexico and Vietnam Airlines, thereby avoiding "the pitfall of equity involvement in heavily loss-making but well positioned carriers."[108] It entered into an agreement with Delta and Continental Airlines for cooperative sales, CRS and passenger hand-ling.[109] Air France sold its Meridien Hotel group. Table 9.9, "The Air France Group", lists the Air France airlines.

Table 9.9—THE AIR FRANCE GROUP

Air France	Air Tchad (33.7%)
Aeropostale (20%)	Austrian Airlines (1.5%)
Air Afrique (16%)	Cameroon Airlines (3.6%)
Air Austral (34%)	Middle East Airlines (28,5%)
Air Caledonie (2.7%)	Royal Air Maroc (4%)
Air Charter (80%)	Sabena (33.3%)
Air Comores (6.3%)	Tunisair (5.6%)
Air Gabon (11.2%)	UTA (absorbed)
Air Inter (72.3%)	Air Canada (marketing alliance)
Air Madagascar (3.5%)	Aeromexico (marketing alliance)
Air Mauritius (12.8%)	Vietnam Airlines (marketing alliance)
Air Tahiti (7.5%)	Servair (catering)

---

[107] Id.
[108] French Polish, Airline Bus. (May 1993), at 25-27
[109] Charles Goldsmith & Scott McCartney, Air France Signs Pact With Delta, Continental Air, Wall St. J., Oct. 17, 1996, at A16.

Chapter 9

THE LUFTHANSA GROUP

Prior to its privatization, Lufthansa's operating costs per kilometer were second only to Swissair's.[110] Lufthansa negotiated new contracts with its pilots in which they agreed to fly at least 75 hours a month (up from 53 hours previously) in return for keeping jobs at its intra-German subsidiary, Lufthansa Express.[111]

Lufthansa owns Condor, its charter arm, established Lufthansa Express, a low cost no-frills subsidiary, and Lufthansa CityLine, a regional operation, and purchased equity in Austrian based Lauda Air (26%) and Luxembourg based Luxair.[112] Lauda Air's costs are just 14% of total revenue (compared with 30% for Austrian Airlines). Lauda has begun operating at London Gatwick Airport, serves Sydney, Melbourne, Hong Kong, and Bangkok, and operates code sharing services with Lufthansa into Los Angeles and Miami.[113] In late 1993, Lufthansa concluded a code-sharing relationship with United,[114] In 1996, the U.S. Department of Transportation gave the alliance anti-trust immunity. In 1995, Lufthansa concluded an alliance with SAS to coordinate flight schedules, merge frequent-flyer programs, and combine check-in facilities and other ground services.[115] Table 9.10, "The Lufthansa Group", lists the Lufthansa airlines.

Table 9.10—THE LUFTHANSA GROUP

Lufthansa	Lauda Air (39.7%)
Cargolux (24.5%)	Luxair (13%)
Condor (100%)	Sun Express (40%)
DHL International (25%)	United Airlines (marketing alliance)

---

[110] Crash Marriage, The Economist (Oct. 9, 1993), at 76.
[111] The Frugal Skies: Major Airlines Mull Radical Steps to Curb Costs, Wall St. J., Oct. 19, 1993, at A6.
[112] Richard Evans, Why the World's Airlines Can't Seem to Get Enough Cash, Global Finance (May 1993), at 48, 53; Jacqueline Gallacher, Austrian Waltzes Lufthansa, Commercial Aviation News, Sept. 13, 1993, at 4.
[113] Jacqueline Gallacher, Austrian Waltzes Lufthansa, Commercial Aviation News, Sept. 13, 1993, at 4.
[114] Jane Levere, Wall St. Doubts Delta's Trans-Atlantic Projections, Commercial Aviation News (Sept. 13, 1993), at 16.
[115] Brian Coleman, Lufthansa, SAS Unveil Plans for an Alliance, Wall St. J., May 12, 1995, at B5B.

NORTH AMERICAN ALLIANCES

In Canada, carrier profitability has plummeted since the Mulrooney Administration imposed deregulation.[116] PWA lost a record $748 million in 1992.[117] Air Canada's long term debt-to-equity ratio rose to 9:1, and was expected to reach 25:1 by the end of 1993.[118] Nationair, a Montreal based charter carrier went bankrupt.[119]

Air Canada has purchased 27.5% of Continental Airlines.[120] AMR (American Airlines) invested $195 million to purchase 25% of the voting stock and 33% of the equity of Canadian Airlines.[121] AMR expects to earn $15 billion in services from the relationship over the next 20 years.[122]

ANTITRUST IMMUNITY

In the last days of the Bush Administration, antitrust immunity was conferred to the alliance between Northwest Airlines and KLM, while statutory foreign ownership restrictions effectively were diluted. Some speculated the decision was predicated on the $100,000 contribution Northwest co-chairman Gary Wilson had made to Bush's committee to re-elect the President in August 1992 (four years earlier he had contributed to Democrat Michael Dukakis' Presidential campaign). In September 1992, the Bush Administration approved a somewhat more liberal bilateral agreement with the Netherlands (a very liberal bilateral had been concluded with the Dutch during the Carter Administration), allowing Dutch carriers to fly anywhere they chose in the United States, while allowing U.S. carriers to fly anywhere they chose in the Netherlands (a charming little country about the size of West Virginia). In November 1992, DOT gave Northwest-KLM preliminary

---

[116] See Paul Dempsey, William Thoms & Sonja Clapp, Canadian Transport Liberalization, 19 Transp. L.J. 113 (1990).
[117] Canada's Airline Conundrum, Airline Bus. (May 1993), at 50, 53.
[118] Id.
[119] Id. at 50.
[120] Id.
[121] Id.; Larry Greenberg & James Hirsch, AMR To Invest $195 Million in PWA Unit, Wall St. J., Dec. 30, 1992, at A3.
[122] Canada's Airline Conundrum, Airline Bus. (May 1993), at 50.

Chapter 9

antitrust immunity.[123] Final approval was given only days before the inauguration of Bill Clinton as President.[124]

One of the most remarkable practices which emerged between the two carriers was pooling of revenue and profits, a practice widespread in international aviation, but steadfastly objected to by the United States in each and every bilateral air transport agreement it signed since the Bermuda I prototype bilateral in 1946. The benefits appeared to be imbalanced. KLM realized $150 million profit annually from the alliance; Northwest realized about $50 million.[125] Further, consumer prices in the U.S.-Netherlands market appeared to increase under the alliance.[126]

To level the playing field, several other carriers sought antitrust immunity as well, including Delta-Swissair-Austrian-Sabena-Virgin, American-Canadian, and United-Lufthansa. But the Clinton Administration's Justice Department took the view that "It is not necessary for code share partners to receive antitrust immunity for any agreement that would not violate the antitrust laws; and conduct that would violate the antitrust laws should not be permitted."[127] Antitrust immunity for the Northwest-KLM alliance was set to expire in 1998. Some anticipated it would not be renewed.

But Clinton's Department of Transportation saw things differently. In order to persuade the government of Germany to sign a liberal "open skies" bilateral, DOT Secretary Federico Peña conferred antitrust immunity to a United-Lufthansa alliance. Shortly thereafter, DOT also conferred antitrust immunity to a Delta-Swissair-Sabena-Austrian Airlines and the American-Canadian alliances. At this writing, American Airlines seeks antitrust immunity with British Airways, an alliance expected to generate up to $4 billion in annual revenue.[128] Pandora's box is open. It seems inequitable to deny American Airlines its proposed alliance with British Airways, having conferred it to United/Lufthansa, the world's first and seventh largest airlines meas-

---

[123] Airline Official Gave $100,000 to GOP, Washington Post, Dec. 6, 1992, at A8; Northwest Co-Chair Gave to GOP Prior to Airline Rules, Denver Post, Dec. 6, 1992, at 15A.
[124] DOT Order 91-1-11 (1993).
[125] Susan Carey, Northwest To Buy Back Preferred from KLM, Wall St. J., July 1, 1996, at A3.
[126] Asra Nomani, Airlines Hope To Get Around Antitrust Laws, Wall St. J., May 8, 1996, at B1.
[127] Anne Bingaman, Consolidation and Code Sharing: Antitrust Enforcement In the Airline Industry (address before ABA Forum on Air and Space Law, Washington, D.C., Jan. 25, 1996).
[128] Asra Nomani, Justice Agency Probes Implications of Pact Between American, British Air, Wall St. J., July 8, 1996.

ured by RPKs. American/British Airways are the world's second and fourth largest carriers, respectively, by the same measure.

DOT officials privately confess they are using code-sharing and antitrust immunity to facilitate international megacarrier alliances because direct consolidation of airlines on a global scale is prohibited by statutory foreign ownership restrictions. While DOT has significantly liberalized those restrictions (allowing, for example, up to 49% equity investment in U.S. airlines so long as voting stock is limited to 25%), they stand as a barrier to outright mergers of airlines across national boundaries (as do the "significant ownership and control" requirements in many bilateral air transport agreement). SAS appears to be an example of the multinational airline DOT would like to see emerge on a de facto basis. In other words, DOT is using antitrust immunity to allow carriers to breach U.S. antitrust laws; it is using antitrust immunity and code-sharing to allow carriers effectively to breach the purpose behind explicit statutory foreign ownership and cabotage prohibitions.

What's worse is the competitive impact of code-sharing and antitrust immunity. After the Delta/Swissair alliance was given antitrust immunity, American abandoned its long-standing New York-Zurich route. After the United/Lufthansa alliance was given antitrust immunity, American abandoned the Miami-Frankfurt route. Business fares rose 18%. Delta has closed its Frankfurt hub, and TWA dropped its New York-Frankfurt flights.[129] The competition and national security concerns of the U.S. Congress appear to be of little concern to the DOT.

EMERGENCE OF THE GLOBAL MEGACARRIERS

By the mid-1990s, four major global airline systems had emerged—the United/Lufthansa alliance, the British/American alliance, the Delta/Dwarfs alliance, and the Northwest/KLM alliance. The assets of each of the alliances are shown on Table 9.11, "The Global Megacarriers".

---

[129] Scott McCartney, Are Airline Alliances Bad News for Consumers? Wall St. J., June 17, 1997, at B1.

Table 9.11—THE GLOBAL MEGACARRIERS

THE UNITED/LUFTHANSA("STAR") ALLIANCE

- Members: United Airlines, Atlantic Coast, Air Wisconsin, Lufthansa, Lauda Air Luxair, South African Airways, SAS, British Midland, Air Canada, Varig, Thai Airways
- Sales: $46 billion
- Fleet: 1,522 aircraft
- Employees: 243,000
- RPKs: 377 billion
- Passengers: 189 million

THE BRITISH/AMERICAN ALLIANCE

- Members: American Airlines, Canadian Airlines, British Airways, USAir, Qantas
- Sales: $44 billion
- Fleet: 1,706 aircraft
- Employees: 252,000
- RPKs: 399 billion
- Passengers: 195 million

THE DELTA/DWARFS ALLIANCE

- Members: Delta Air Lines, Comair, Atlantic Southeast, Skywest, Swissair, Sabena, Austrian, Virgin, Singapore
- Sales: $27 billion
- Fleet: 1,004 aircraft
- Employees: 123,000
- RPKs: 227 billion
- Passengers: 127 million

Table 9.11—THE GLOBAL MEGACARRIERS (Cont'd.)

THE NORTHWEST/KLM ALLIANCE

- Members: Northwest, Mesaba, Express, KLM, Martinair-Holland, Air UK, Kenya Airways
- Sales: $17 billion
- Fleet: 654 aircraft
- Employees: 80,000
- RPKs: 160 billion
- Passengers: 71 million[130]

But the dance partners are constantly shifting, and a photograph taken of the party is soon obsolete. Since this listing was compiled (in the fall of 1996), USAir announced its divorce with British Airways, Air France began an affair with Delta and Continental, and Continental Airlines announced it had proposed to Delta. United wants to add Japan Airlines. In July 1997, the American/BA alliance began a code-share agreement with Iberia. And, American purchased 10% of Aerolinas Argentinas and a domestic Argentine carrier. All seems fair in love, war, and perhaps, airline alliances.

---

[130] Emerging Mega-Alliances, Airline Bus. (Sept. 1996), at 31.

CHAPTER 10.

PUBLIC POLICY IN AVIATION

"Whether you blame it on deregulation and excessive competition, recession, poor management, recalcitrant unions, or just plain bad luck, the reality is that the U.S. airline industry is in terrible trouble. In my view the state of our airline industry is a national embarrassment." [1]
Thomas Plaskett
CEO, Pan American World Airways

"Between bureaucracy and the jungle, there must be compromise." [2]
Bernard Attali
CEO, Air France

INTRODUCTION

The final quarter of the 20th Century was strongly influenced by several major phenomena which converged to convince the American body politic that the market can do no wrong, and government can do no good. This anti-government template was formed on the left by the war in Vietnam and the Nixon Watergate scandal; on the right, it was influenced by the tax-and-spend Great Society programs of President Lyndon Johnson, and an intrusive government aimed at social engineering. Political leaders on the left (notably President Jimmy Carter and Senator Edward Kennedy) and right (e.g., President Ronald Reagan

---

[1] Quoted in Thomas Petzinger, Jr., Hard Landing 394 (1995).
[2] Unclear for Takeoff, U.S. Airlines Hit Barriers Over Foreign Routes, WSJ, May 14, 1993, at A6.

and Senator Bob Packwood) converged on a common path which perceived government as the enemy. Transportation deregulation was but one by-product of that broader social and political movement, which in the United States spilled over into deregulation of savings-and-loan institutions, banking, telecommunications, broadcasting and electric power production.

Despite the tens of thousands of employees who have lost their jobs, and investors, lenders and equipment manufacturers who have been stiffed, and a growing number of consumers disenchanted by inequitable pricing and deteriorating service, at this writing, the political will for reform of airline deregulation is weak. It has become politically incorrect to challenge deregulation, or advocate increased government oversight.

Thus, any discussion of what government should do to rectify some of the more serious problems which have emerged from too free a market seems an intellectual activity of futility, for there is at present no consensus that the market can be too free, or that any important social and economic goals can be achieved by governmental intervention of any kind. Though the seductive rhetoric about perfect competition, contestable markets, the absence of economies of scale and barriers to entry—which in the 1970s served as the intellectual justification for deregulation[3]—has now all but been abandoned by serious students of airline economics, the prevailing wisdom is that government only harms, not helps, and managed economies are inferior to *laissez-faire* economies.

But recall the title of this book—*Strategies for the 21st Century*. Every generation develops its own view of the appropriate relationship between government and the market. Virtually every generation sees a need for government to play an essential role in the economy (at the very least, it prints money, and maintains the highways and national defense). The fundamental issue is not whether government will play a role in the economy. It is instead, precisely what role will the government play? Ideally, the government should play as little a role as possible, allowing the free market to work its wonders in stimulating innovation, efficiency and productivity, but gently correcting in areas

---

[3] See Paul Dempsey, Robert Hardaway & William Thoms, 1 Aviation Law & Regulation § 1.06 (1993); Paul Dempsey & Andrew Goetz, Airline Deregulation & Laissez-Faire Mythology (1992); Paul Dempsey, The Social & Economic Consequences of Deregulation (1989).

Chapter 10

of market failure. Perfect competition is the ideal, and where the market can produce it (or can at least come as close as imperfect markets can) government should step aside. But deregulation clearly has not produced the model of perfect competition its proponents predicted it would. Instead, deregulation has produced an odd environment in which, depending on the market, airlines alternatively engage in destructive competition, predatory pricing, or monopolistic exploitation. Some consumers enjoy below-cost pricing, while others suffer extortionate prices for air transportation.

Transportation is a fundamental component of the nation's infrastructure—like energy and communications, the foundation upon which economic growth and prosperity is built. A weak infrastructure denies the broader national and global economy of the productivity of which it is capable. Like a tariff wall, monopolistic pricing and/or poor service imposes negative externalities upon businesses and communities subjected to it, distorts inherent comparative advantage and specialization, and constricts the broader market of the free flow of goods to their highest valued use. For aviation, government is already deeply involved, in maintaining the airports, airways and navigational systems, and ensuring aircraft, the crew, and the traveling public are safe to fly, for example. In the 21st Century, what more should it do?

DESTRUCTIVE COMPETITION

In the early 1990s, as the airline industry lost all the profit it had earned since the dawn of commercial aviation in the 1920s, and 97% of the airline industry's securities were downgraded by Wall Street to "junk" status, President Clinton appointed a National Commission to Ensure a Strong and Competitive Airline Industry, headed by former Virginia Governor Gerald Baliles. (One major airline CEO testified, paradoxically, that he was "increasingly pessimistic that the airline industry can be *both* strong *and* competitive"). Unfortunately, that commission was dominated by several of the architects of deregulation,[4] and was therefore unwilling to ask the essential question—

---

[4] Pro-deregulation members of the Baliles Commission included American Association of Airport Executives president Charles "Chip" Barclay, who had worked on airline deregulation bills as a Senate Aviation Subcommittee staffer, Dan Kasper, a former protégé to CAB Board member Elizabeth Bailey, Herb Kelleher, embittered at regulation because the CAB had denied his

whether deregulatory policy had anything to do with the industry's financial collapse under deregulation. The Commission instead focused on issues of fuel spikes and recession, as if they had never read history and never realized that these phenomena occurred before. To recommend a taxpayer bail out (i.e., tax relief) and selling off the airlines to foreign citizens, as that Commission did, would seem a confession that aviation policy had been a dismal failure.

In the mid-1980s, the industry and conservative think-tanks turned on a tremendously effective propaganda machine which convinced much of the public that airline deregulation was a phenomenal success, largely because of grossly overstated estimations of consumer benefits. Airline executives had a marvelous opportunity to request meaningful oversight before the Baliles Commission, but declined, insisting it focus instead largely on peripheral issues, rather than on the central causes of the industry's collapse. This stems from a distrust of government, a failure to understand that a model other than classic price and entry regulation is possible, and frankly, a dose of hubris.

The Baliles Commission's report emphasized that, adjusted for inflation, airline ticket prices have fallen during the last 15 years, and that more people were flying than ever before.[5] Of course, that could be said for any 15 year period since the inauguration of commercial aviation in the 1920s. Allegations of consumer savings resulting from deregulation have been grossly overstated.[6] Airline yields were falling at a significantly faster rate before deregulation than after it, and passenger growth rates were higher before than after deregulation. It is remarkable that deregulation's proponents find a solid correlation between falling prices and deregulation, but find no relationship whatsoever between deregulation and falling profits.

The 1975 Kennedy Subcommittee Report was the first comprehensive attack on economic regulation of the airline industry. Unfortunately, it reached a number of erroneous conclusions, including "there is no substantial historical, empirical or logical reason for believing that increased reliance on competition would lead to pred-

---

Southwest Airlines to fly beyond Texas, and John Robson, who had been CAB Chairman prior to Alfred Kahn and rather remarkably claimed to be the "Father of Deregulation."

[5] See National Commission To Ensure a Strong Competitive Airline Industry, Change, Challenge and Competition 1 (1993).

[6] See Paul Dempsey & Andrew Goetz, Airline Deregulation & Laissez Faire Mythology 243-63, 281-95 (1992).

atory pricing, destructive competition, or risk of monopolization."[7] A decade and a half after deregulation, Alfred Kahn as much as conceded that the economic theories upon which deregulation was predicated (including the perceived absence of economies of scale or barriers to entry, contestability and perfect competition) were simply wrong, the predictions of deregulation's proponents were therefore wrong, and the industry may well exhibit a tendency to engage in destructive competition.[8] While economic regulation was imperfectly administered and created some distortions (including excessive service competition and bloated labor costs),[9] it nevertheless created an environment in which destructive competition was avoided. Profits were by no means robust (the industry's average profit margin averaged 2.4% from 1960-1977, below that of all manufacturers, which typically earn between 4-6%), but they were significantly better then than they were during the 15 years after deregulation (when they fell to a negative 0.4%). Though the Civil Aeronautics Board identified 12% as an appropriate rate of return on investment for the airline industry, under deregulation, the industry has never achieved it (see Figure 10.1, "Rate Of Return On Investment"). In the early-1970s, neither the infusion of tremendous

---

[7] Civil Aeronautics Board Practices and Procedures, Report of the Subcomm. on Administrative Practice and Procedure of the Senate Judiciary Comm., 94th Cong., 1st Sess. 4 (1975). The report was penned in part by Stephen Breyer, who went on to become a U.S. Supreme Court Justice, and Phil Bakes, who went on to become a senior executive at Continental Airlines and Eastern Airlines under Frank Lorenzo.

[8] Anthony Velocci, Jr., Kahn Tells Airlines: Sit Tight, Cut Costs, Av. Week & Space Tech. (Aug. 16, 1993). When asked what he might have done differently if he could turn back the clock, Kahn said, "I would recognize the danger of excessively exuberant investment, overcapacity and destructive competition was greater than we evaluated it at the time." Id. "I knew a lot about communications and not much about airlines. That was the main reason I tried to proceed very gradually with deregulation. I read studies by serious academic scholars of the industry, and it was clear to me they underestimated the benefits of airline deregulation, including the advantages of scale and the advantages of hub-and-spoke operations. Id. at 44. For a more recent assessment of the theories upon which deregulation was predicated, see Paul Dempsey & Andrew Goetz, Airline Deregulation & Laissez Faire Mythology (1992); Paul Dempsey, The Social & Economic Consequences of Deregulation (1989). In fact, Kahn did *not* proceed gradually with deregulation. See Paul Dempsey, The Rise and Fall of the Civil Aeronautics Board—Opening Wide the Floodgates of Entry 91 (1979).

[9] In 1972, the Air Transport Association observed "airline wages continue to be among the highest in private industry and continue to increase at a rapid rate." Air Transport Ass'n., Annual Report 10 (1972). The following year, it noted, "Between 1967 and 1972, the average annual airline employee salary gained 53.1%, compared with a national average of 38.6%." Air Transport Ass'n., Annual Report 11 (1973). In 1976, ATA observed, "Since 1967, average airline employee compensation has increased 102 per cent, compared to an increase of 58 percent in the average airline fare . . . ." Air Transport Ass'n., Annual Report 6 (1976).

wide bodied capacity, recession, nor the sharp and unprecedented rise in fuel costs precipitated by the Arab Oil Embargo of 1973 bankrupted a single airline. Before deregulation, there was "unanimous agreement ... that the U.S. air transportation system is the best in the world."[10]

Figure 10.1—RATE OF RETURN ON INVESTMENT

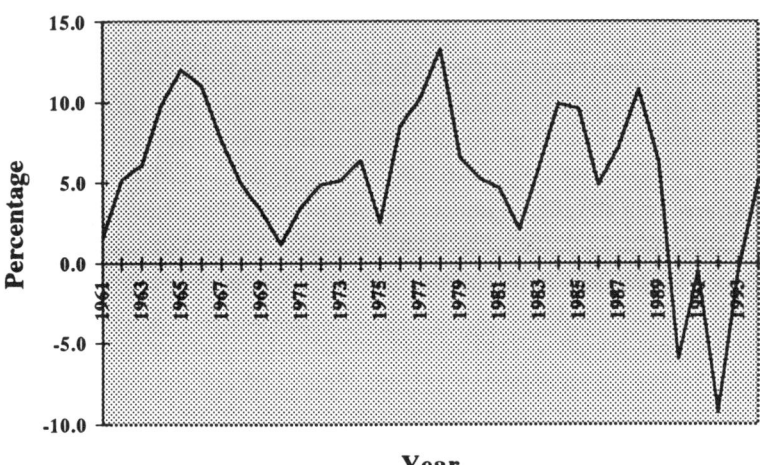

Again, regulation was imperfect. But some forget that under regulation, real consumer prices were falling (inflation-adjusted air fares fell 63% from 1938 to 1975)[11] as more consumers took advantage of promotional fares ("such as excursion, family, military and youth discounts and other fares designed to broaden the base of the air travel market"),[12] wages and productivity were rising, safety was improving, traffic was growing, concentration was declining, and profit, by no means robust, kept balance sheets respectable and equipment new. In the mid-1970s, regulatory reform was well on the way to curing many of the distortions in the system—enhanced pricing and entry flexibility allowed carriers to rationalize operations, tap the elasticities of demand to fill seats which otherwise would have flown

---

[10] Air Transport Ass'n., Annual Report 1 (1977). U.S. commercial aviation was described as a "system in which people fly or ship at lower cost and with better performance than on any other air system in the world." Air Transport Ass'n., Annual Report 3 (1975).
[11] Air Transport Ass'n., Annual Report 6 (1975).
[12] Air Transport Ass'n., Annual Report 10 (1972).

empty, and enjoy respectable profitability. But full deregulation has unleashed the industry's inherent primordial tendency to engage in destructive competition.

THE UNIQUE CHARACTERISTICS OF COMMERCIAL AVIATION

Why does the airline industry exhibit a tendency to engage in destructive competition, a phenomenon uncommon to most major industries? The answer lies in first describing the unique attributes of commercial aviation. The airline industry is a service industry which is capital intensive, labor intensive, and fuel intensive. Because it confines people in canisters of aluminum and steel, propelling them through the skies at speeds of hundreds of miles an hour at elevations of several miles above sea level, it is potentially a highly dangerous industry. For that reason, it is highly regulated, and requires highly skilled (and therefore, adequately trained and paid) employees.

The airline industry is extremely susceptible to events outside its control, particularly fuel costs and the market cycle. Demand for air transportation is derived. In other words, air transport is a means to an end—typically either a business meeting, a vacation, or a trip to visit friends or relatives. Demand therefore is highly influenced by recessionary and inflationary swings in the market cycle and their impact on consumer confidence and discretionary spending. And it is becoming more susceptible as the discretionary travel market share grows relative to the business travel market.

The airline industry also has a chronic tendency to produce excess capacity, because demand is highly cyclical, depending on the time of day, day of week, or month of year, or macro-economic inflationary or recessionary swings. The industry also produces excess capacity because of the S-curve relationship between flight frequency and capacity on one axis, and demand and revenue on the other. The high-yield discretionary market disproportionately makes product selection based on schedule (frequency) over price. Schedule is also one of the few means of product differentiation of what is otherwise a relatively fungible product. Therefore, airlines are incentivized to provide capacity in excess of demand (historically, by about a third).

The product of air transportation is in the nature of a credence good. One may not examine its quality before its consumption. There is relatively little brand loyalty among consumers (except those addicted to a particular carrier's frequent flyer program). Therefore, the primary means of product differentiation are schedule and price.

Because airlines produce a largely fungible and highly perishable commodity relentlessly in excess supply, they have a tendency to fall into variable cost pricing in competitive markets. But variable costs (when measured by the incremental cost of adding one passenger to a scheduled flight) are "peanuts," a relatively small percentage (perhaps only 15-20%) of fully allocated costs. Airlines attempt to cover fixed costs from relatively price-inelastic business travelers (typically paying for travel with someone else's pre-tax dollars) or persons flying on monopoly routes (particularly to or from Fortress Hubs). Yet not enough of these monopoly routes exist to cross-subsidize predatory below-cost battles for market share in competitive markets, and the industry's profit margin remains well below most other industries.

One industry expert who has succinctly summarized the essential characteristics of commercial aviation which propel airline management to behave in an individually rational, but collectively irrational, manner is Bob Crandall, CEO of American Airlines. Crandall distilled the governing economic factors to five:

> In the first place, we offer a product for which there is very soft brand loyalty, and we offer it in a market which is as close to a perfect marketplace from the consumer's perspective as that of any product I know. Many consumers have a favorite airline, but because of this very soft brand loyalty are quite willing to change it at a moment's notice for either a very small fare differential or for a flight which is 30 minutes more convenient than the one they had planned to take.
>
> As to the perfect marketplace . . . in the airline industry . . . a consumer need make only a single phone call to [a travel agent] using any one of the major CRSs and will be able

instantaneously . . . to know the availability of seats and the price of each of those seats on all competing carriers. . . .

Number two, you've got an industry where marginal costs are always substantially below full costs. The cost of operating one additional flight is always dramatically lower than the average cost of any other flight, and on a per-seat basis, the cost of selling one more seat is a small fraction . . . of the fully allocated cost of selling any average seat. . . .

Third, you have in industry in which supply and demand never have been, will never be, and should not ever be fully balanced. . . . [I]f supply and demand were ever balanced, that is to the extent that demand represents 100 percent of supply, the system would be so unavailable to consumers, and particularly to consumers who want a seat on demand, that it would no longer be functioning as a scheduled transportation business.

Fourth, you have a market which is fragmented into thousands of individual origins and destinations and in which each additional fight represents a completely unique product. That is, one additional flight between Chicago and New York at 2:00 in the afternoon is an entirely different product than a flight between Chicago and New York offered at 12:00 noon. As a consequence, individual carriers are incentivized . . . to compete in that new market . . . by offering a new product, a flight between Chicago and New York at 2:00 in the afternoon, a market for which they cannot compete at all if they offer flights only at 12:00 and 4:00.

And finally, you have a business in which the entry costs are very low. The cost of entering the airline business is very small. You need only go out and acquire secondhand airplanes, used airplanes. In today's marketplace, for example, there are examples of people acquiring airplanes at very low cost and operating them with people who actually pay for the privilege of working at the airline. And thus, the . . . entry cost, is very low, and the production cost of the new entrant, particularly in periods when the market is depressed, as it is today, are likely to be a small fraction of the operating cost of the existing carriers.

For all of those reasons, there are very, very powerful incentives for airlines to continue to add capacity to compete . . . . [A]n airline has no ability to reduce its capacity by shaving 2% off the whole tennis ball or the whole apple. If demand declines by 3%, I cannot, and no airline can, reduce capacity by 3% on all flights. You can reduce capacity only by withdrawing from one or more of those individual market segments and thus giving up all of the revenue associated with that withdrawal.

As a consequence of all those factors, individual airlines, following their own interests in a completely rational way, act in a way which is collectively irrational. That's why the airline business has lost a lot of money over many years.[13]

As a consequence, profitability in the post-deregulation era has been woefully inadequate, airline balance sheets have been polluted with enormous debt, bankruptcies have wiped out billions of dollars of investment, and employees have seen wages cut and tens of thousands of jobs lost.

---

[13] Testimony of Robert Crandall Before the National Commission to Ensure a Strong Competitive Airline Industry (June 3, 1993).

Chapter 10

CONSUMER WELFARE

The Congressional Declaration of Purpose set forth in the 1966 legislation which created the U.S. Department of Transportation, insisted DOT give "full and appropriate consideration to the needs of the public, users, carriers, industry, labor and national defense." Though deregulation proponents like Alfred Kahn predicted that airline employees, stockholders and creditors would benefit from deregulation,[14] no serious observer of the airline industry today would claim that either the air carriers, their lenders, investors or workers have fared well, as a whole, since deregulation in 1978. Yet some do allege that deregulation has advanced consumer welfare and economic efficiency (and some insist it is politically incorrect to suggest otherwise).

Neo-classical economists tend to measure consumer welfare based on consumer prices in the marketplace. Though price is a relatively easy thing to measure, price-based assessments of consumer welfare may be an unduly myopic way of viewing the world.

Infamous studies of airline deregulation published by Steven Morrison and Clifford Winston of the Brookings Institution allege consumers save billions of dollars a year as a result of airline deregulation.[15] In their first "counter-factual" study,[16] they calculated these savings at $6 billion a year. About $4 billion of that was attributed to the value of enhanced flight frequency for business travelers (with their time calculated by the authors at an implausible 1.5 times their hourly wages). But only about 7% of passengers fly on an unrestricted coach ticket (and are therefore able to fly on short notice as business needs change), and they pay a price for air transportation which is radically higher than before deregulation, even adjusted for inflation. Ninety-three percent of passengers are saddled with advance-purchase, Saturday night stay-over restrictions, which cause an enor-

---

[14] "I am confident that . . . consumers will benefit; that the communities throughout the nation—large and small—which benefit upon air transportation for their economic well being will benefit, and that the people most closely connected with the airlines—their employees, their stockholders, their creditors—will benefit as well." Statement of Alfred E. Kahn before the Aviation Subcommittee of the House Public Works and Transportation Committee no H.R. 11145, 8 (Mar. 6, 1978).

[15] See. e.g., Steven Morrison & Clifford Winston, The Evolution of the Airline Industry (1995).

[16] Steven Morrison & Clifford Winston, The Economic Effects of Airline Deregulation (1986).

mous waste of opportunity costs and additional weekend hotel and meal expenses which have never been taken account of by Brookings.

Morrison and Winston's conclusions were soundly criticized,[17] though rather than responding to the criticism, the Brookings' authors quietly expunged their earlier methodology in favor of a wholly new methodology capable of reaching an even more astounding conclusion. This time the Brookings' authors insisted consumers were saving $10 billion a year.

To get there, they used something called the "Standard Industry Fare Level" [SIFL]. The SIFL was something Congress had placed in the Airline Deregulation Act of 1978 to provide a cost-based benchmark for a "zone of reasonableness" while the Civil Aeronautics Board was winding up the business of regulating airline rates.[18] Under that legislation, an airline could freely price up to 5% above the SIFL, and up to 50% below the SIFL in any fare category, while the CAB could allow an airline to pierce the ceiling or floor only if it deemed it in the public interest. The Brookings' authors insisted that the SIFL is the point at which prices would be set if regulation were still in effect today. By calculating the difference between the SIFL and real average fares in the post-deregulation period, they came up with the $10 billion number. But they apparently had not read the legislation. Under the Airline Deregulation Act, if regulation were still alive, carriers would be free to price up to 50% below the SIFL without regulatory intervention (and could seek permission to offer prices lower still). Since air fares fell at a faster rate under regulation than under deregulation, average regulated fares would likely be somewhere nearer the bottom than the top of that zone, if not below that zone.

Though a fatal flaw, that wasn't even the most serious shortcoming the Brookings' new "counter-factual" methodology. It was using post-deregulation cost to calculate hypothetical regulatory rates. Some costs have declined in the post-deregulation period. It must be conceded that labor wages and benefits are not what they would have been had deregulation not occurred. Many urge they were excessively bloated

---

[17] For an early criticism of the Brookings methodology, see a chapter entitled "The Economic Effects of Deregulation: The Six Billion Dollar Myth," in Paul Dempsey & Andrew Goetz, Airline Deregulation & Laissez-Faire Mythology 281-95 (1992). For a more recent criticism of the Brookings study, see Robert Kuttner, Everything for Sale: The Virtues and Limits of Markets 259 (1997).
[18] See e.g., Standard Industry Fare Level, Interim Methodology, 82 C.A.B. 1752 (1979).

under, and because of, regulation (though many levy the same criticism of labor costs under deregulation as well). The deferral of new aircraft capital expenditures have also saved the airline industry money (though newer technology would be more fuel efficient and more maintenance free, and therefore would have allowed the industry to achieve lower operating costs and higher productivity). In 1970, the average age of the U.S. fleet was four years.[19] By the 1990s, not a single U.S. major carrier had a fleet so young, and U.S. airlines were flying the oldest fleet of any industrialized G-7 nation. Finally, ASM costs have been reduced by squeezing the seats together, tightening seat pitch, reducing the number of flight crew members per passenger, and eliminating meals.

However, certain costs have skyrocketed under deregulation. Debt service has grown enormously, both on-balance, and off—in the form of aircraft leases (see Figure 10.2, "Interest On Long-Term Debt"). Distribution costs have also become bloated, including CRS fees and travel agency commissions. Fuel prices have been significantly higher since deregulation (see Figure 10.3, "Domestic Fuel Prices").

Figure 10.2—INTEREST ON LONG-TERM DEBT[20]

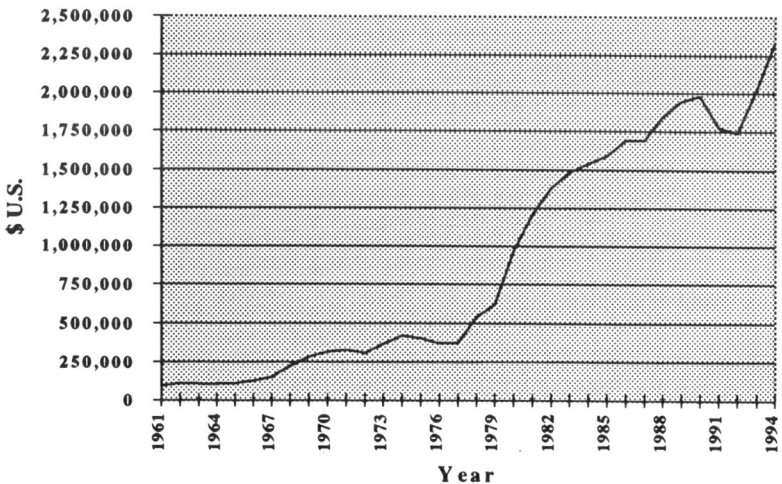

---

[19] Air Transport Ass'n., Annual Report 3 (1977).
[20] Source: Air Transport Association.

Figure 10.3—DOMESTIC FUEL PRICE[21]

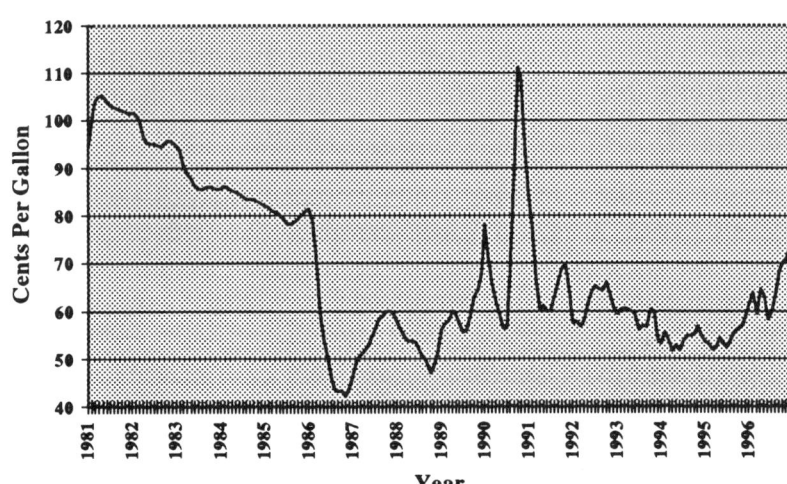

Finally, the hub-and-spoke system, the dominant route structure during the deregulatory era, has mutilated equipment, gate and labor utilization, diluted fuel efficiency, and eroded consumer welfare in terms of convenience and time consumption. Hubbing also created massive congestion which necessitated enormous public expenditures in expansions in airport infrastructure.[22]

Economist Harvey Wexler, former Senior Vice-President at Continental Airlines, insists that hubbing has sharply eroded operational efficiency in the airline industry:

> Efficiency is a measure of how effectively a given factor of production is utilized, and in this case, it is the airplane. The utility of the plane is speed. Under regulation, the plane's natural advantage was maximized by providing the public with a maximum of non-stop and single plane service. Such service, unlike change of plane service, minimizes the elapsed

---

[21] Source: Salomon Brothers.
[22] See Paul Dempsey, Andrew Goetz & Joseph Szyliowicz, Denver International Airport: Lessons Learned (1997).

> travel time Under deregulation, the advantage of the plane is inhibited since change of plane service is regarded as "the norm." Thus, the efficiency of the plane is reduced under deregulation.
>
> For distances of less than 1,000 miles, today's change of plane service . . . results in elapsed travel time approximating the non-stop travel time in the piston era. For a very substantial portion of air travel, deregulation has resulted in reducing efficiency back to the state of the art thirty years ago![23]

Thus, hubbing creates severe costs in terms of delay and circuity (which impose significant opportunity costs on consumers), use of relatively smaller and higher-ASM cost equipment with attendant inefficiency in the consumption of fuel, labor, airport infrastructure and passenger time, and with higher noise pollution and engine emissions. Hubbing is hardly a paradigm of economic efficiency. Though it has its benefits in increasing yields and establishing market dominance at Fortress Hubs, and offering passengers more and more frequency (albeit with more and more excess capacity) the deregulated air transportation system is far more costly than the linear-route system it replaced. It is telling that only one major airline has been consistently profitable since deregulation—Southwest—and it alone maintains a linear route system.

To insert higher post-deregulation costs into a regulatory methodology in order to try to discern what regulated prices would be today is like filling a chicken with lead in order to fetch a higher price in the market. To calculate what regulatory prices would have been, it would be necessary to know what airline costs would have been without hubbing, inadequate profitability which created enormous debt (and debt service), and without airlines scrambling to bribe travel agents to steer business their way with ever higher commission overrides.

One must lay aside the "counter-factual," hypothetical, results-driven methodology and take a look at the *factual* results of pricing

---

[23] Harvey Wexler, Deregulation: The Political Environment 20, Transp. L.J. 135 (1991).

pre- and post-deregulation. Yields are a poor measure of pricing in the post-deregulation period, for they overstate consumer savings because hubbing has increased travel circuity somewhat (how much is disputed). But looking at real (inflation adjusted) yields, they were falling an average of 2.5% annually between 1955 and 1978. They fell an average of only 1.9% after deregulation (see Figure 10.4, Yields Per Revenue Passenger Mile", and Figure 10.5, "Domestic Passenger Yields).

Figure 10.4—YIELDS PER REVENUE PASSENGER MILE[24]

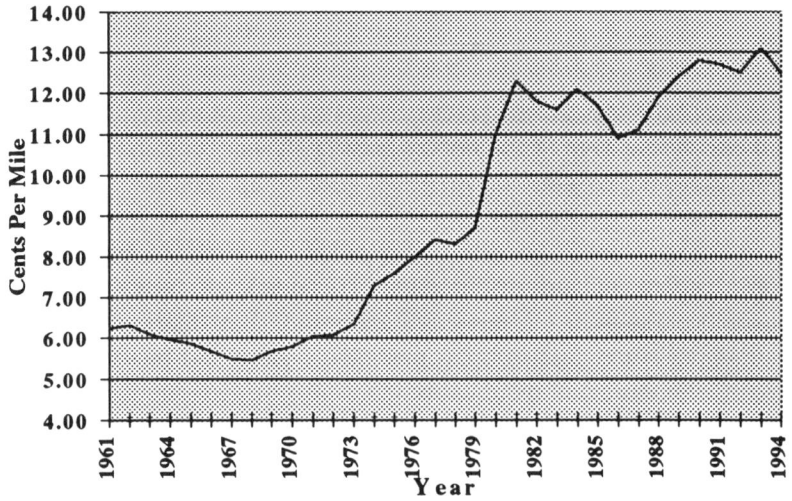

CONSUMER EQUITY

It is appropriate to assess equity in terms of the post-deregulation consumer experience. There are winners and loser among consumer groups. The winners are Fortune 500 companies and government agencies (both of which, because of oligopsony power enjoy steep corporate contractual discounts), and leisure/vacation travelers (who will not fly unless the price is right).

---

[24] Source: Air Transport Association.

Figure 10.5—DOMESTIC PASSENGER YIELDS[25]

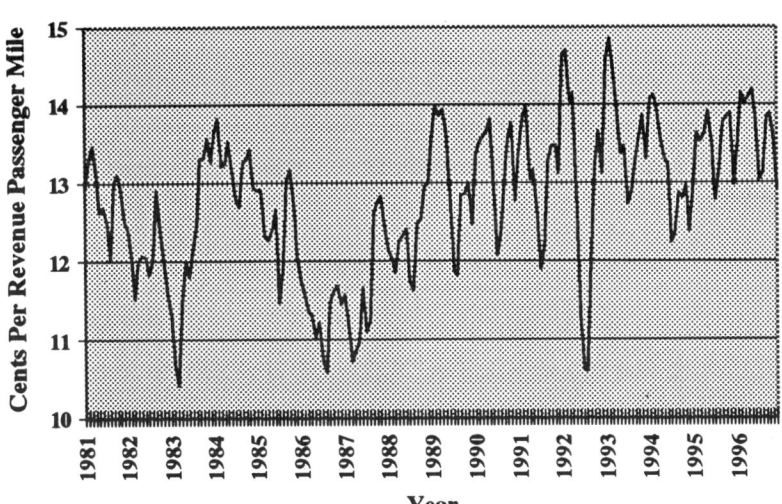

Yet some have argued that even the so-called "winners" are disadvantaged by the contemporary air transportation system. Ted Harris, Chairman of Airline Industry Resources, said this:

> The goal of air transportation, as a branch of transportation science, is the increasingly efficient movement of people, products, and ideas—through the air—over time and space. Efficiency is measured not just in terms of cost, but also in terms of time—man's most perishable commodity.
>
> This incredible time component of air transportation has proven to be an important catalyst in the rapid social and economic development of the United States. And yet we are throwing it away with high fares and circuitous routings through choking hubs operated by what is now

---

[25] Source: Salomon Brothers.

> the oldest fleet of geriatric jets in the developed world.
>
> Air travel speed, the correlative of time, has effectively been cut in half—compromised by hub-and-spoke operations that can double travel time on almost all but nonstop routings . . . . The added landings and takeoffs in hub rotations are not only expensive, they create severe peaking congestion of airways, runways, and gates—and cries for new airports.[26]

The losers of deregulation are many small communities, small businesses, and people who live in concentrated hub airports (though the latter's high prices are somewhat offset by the advantage of having frequent non-stop service). Since small businesses create 90% of the nation's jobs, any nation which values job creation as a matter of public policy would not want its finest job-creators challenged with discriminatory access (vis-à-vis their larger competitors) to the nation's air transportation infrastructure. After all, the public built the airports and owns the airways.

Small communities have been hard hit by deregulation, despite a federally-subsidized skeletal essential air services program for them. Deregulation has not been kind to small communities across the United States. Senator Robert Byrd has lamented only two of the 14,000 votes he has cast—a vote against the Civil Rights Act of 1964, and a vote in favor of the Airline Deregulation Act of 1978 (because of the deterioration of service and escalation of prices his home state of West Virginia has suffered since deregulation began).[27]

The U.S. Department of Transportation has found that 34 small communities have lost all service since promulgation of the Airline Deregulation Act of 1978; many communities which had jet service lost it to turboprop or piston aircraft; out of 320 small communities, the number served by major carriers declined from 213 in 1978 to 33 in 1995; the number of small communities receiving multiple carriers has decreased from 135 in 1978 to 122 in 1995.

---

[26] Ted Harris, The Disaster of Deregulation, 20 Transp. L.J. 87-89 (1991).

[27] Aviation Daily, July 31, 1995, at 153. Senator Byrd was Majority Leader of the Senate at the time; had he fought airline deregulation, it likely would not have passed.

The DOT studies *severely understate* the problem. Of the 514 non-hub communities receiving air service in 1978, by 1987 (a decade after deregulation began) 313 (60.8%) had suffered declines in flight frequency, and 144 (28%) had lost all service; only 32 (6.2%) enjoyed the inauguration of new service.[28] By 1995, things were even worse. Of the 514 non-hub communities receiving air service in 1978, 167 (32.5%) had been terminated by 1995, while only 26 (5.1%) gained new service.[29]

The DOT's studies were unable to comment meaningfully about pricing of air service to small communities, for commuter carriers generally do not report pricing data. But the General Accounting Office has found that passengers flying from small-city airports to major airports paid 34% more if the major airport was concentrated and 42% more if both the small-city and major airport were concentrated.

Moreover, in those small community city-pair markets with sufficient volume to support jet service by a low-cost carrier, the code-sharing phenomenon insures that they will instead be relegated to relatively higher-cost/higher-priced turboprop service. For example, one of the nation's largest connecting turboprop carriers, Mesa Airlines (which in some parts of the country operates as a United Airlines code-sharing affiliate—"United Express"), charges yields of nearly 35 cents per mile, compared with about 12 cents a mile by United Airlines. Even USAir, which operates short-haul high-cost jet service, charges only about 18 cents a mile—about half that charged by a turboprop or piston carrier.[30] A low-cost jet entrant typically charges consumers significantly less than do the major airlines.

INTERNATIONAL AVIATION

U.S. international aviation policy purports to be both "pro-consumer" and "pro-competitive." Yet how can a policy that pretends to be pro-consumer embrace institutionalized consumer deception in the

---

[28] Andrew Goetz & Paul Dempsey, Airline Deregulation Ten Years After: Something Foul in the Air, 54 J. Air L. & Com. 927, 947 (1989). See also, Paul Dempsey & Andrew Goetz, Airline Deregulation & Laissez Faire Mythology (1991).
[29] Unpublished study by Dr. Andrew Goetz, University of Denver.
[30] 1996 data from Julius Maldutis, Airline Update-August 1996 (Sept. 8, 1996).

form of code-sharing? Code-sharing is nothing more than fraudulently selling one company's product as another's, and biasing computer reservations systems to shove competitive interline offerings off the first page of the CRS screen. And how can a policy that pretends to be pro-competitive authorize patently anti-competitive activity, such as carrier pooling of revenue and profits? In not a single bilateral air transport agreement concluded by the U.S. since Bermuda I has the U.S. allowed pooling. Yet antitrust immunity has been conferred to several inter-carrier agreements so that the parties between them can coordinate activities and cease competing.

U.S. international aviation policy is neither pro-consumer nor pro-competitive. It is instead highly ideological. Code-sharing and antitrust immunity are necessary, DOT officials privately admit, because statutory restrictions on foreign ownership and prohibitions against cabotage prohibit the creation of multinational airlines. So it is necessary to thwart the consumer protection laws and the competition laws so as to thwart the national security laws. U.S. international aviation policy is devoid of law.

The ideology is predicated on the belief that "open skies" will bring the same benefits to international aviation that deregulation brought to domestic aviation. Certainly, the benefits of domestic deregulation have not inured to airline investors, lenders, management or employees. The benefit is purported to be that of enhancing economic efficiency and consumer welfare.

Estimates of consumer price savings under deregulation have been grossly overstated. In fact, air fares have fallen at a significantly slower pace in the post-deregulation period than before deregulation. And as to economic efficiency, clearly hub-and-spoke networks—the predominant system since deregulation—are far from ideal efficiency. In the final analysis, globalization is a euphemism for cartelization, and the emergence of a global airline cartel is proceeding apace.

Foreign markets are growing steadily and at a faster rate than U.S. domestic markets. Foreign governments view U.S. firms as dumping excess capacity abroad and endangering their national flag carriers. For example, while the U.S. may not care about Pan Am's survival, the government of France cares dearly about the survival of Air France. On grounds that U.S. airlines were providing excessive capacity in the market, France renounced the U.S.-France bilateral air transport agreement on May 4, 1992, and it expired one year later. Thailand renounced its bilateral for similar reasons.[31] The Australian Department of Transport moved to restrict the number of fifth-freedom passengers Northwest could carry between Osaka and Sydney. Friction has also erupted in U.S.-Japanese aviation relations, a market dominated by Japanese passengers by a 6 to 1 margin, but where U.S.-flag carriers fly 60%-70% of the capacity.[32]

Increased privatization and mergers will enhance the competitive prowess of foreign carriers. Many emerge from privatization with relatively clean balance sheets and route structures built by decades of paternalistic care. More than 40 foreign airlines have proposed or completed partial or full privatization.[33]

The U.S. Department of Transportation has steadfastly insisted that "open skies" (a/k/a exporting deregulation abroad) ought ubiquitously to govern air transport. Some foreign governments view this as naive,[34] for they perceive deregulation as the catalyst for the financial collapse of much of the U.S. airline industry. Further, U.S. negotiators often trade hard rights (e.g., routes to valuable U.S. markets) for soft rights (e.g., vague promises of free competition). Professor Taneja addressed the weakness of the open skies policy in international aviation:

> Most foreign-flag airlines are not privately owned; air-transportation policies of most governments include non-economic objectives; and different nations have different antitrust philosophies. Given the existence of almost universal government subsidy, the absence of a common regulatory framework, and the operations of fifth-freedom carriers, the probability of predatory pricing is high. Also, air transportation is

---

[31] For a discussion of conflict resolution under bilateral air transport agreements see Paul Dempsey, Law & Foreign Policy in International Aviation (1987).
[32] Jennifer Cody, Japan, U.S. Tussle Over Airlines' Rights, Wall St. J., June 7, 1994, at B1.
[33] Julius Maldutis, Industry Investment Requirements—Looking Beyond 2000 (address before the 7th IATA High-Level Aviation Symposium, Sept. 6, 7, 1993, Cairo, Egypt).
[34] Most sensible nations look at U.S. government transport ministers as hopelessly naive, and they are right. While the U.S. government may care little about the well being of Pan Am or Eastern, the government of France cares dearly about the survival of Air France. Hence, renunciation of bilaterals is the response to a perception that U.S. carriers can make no money in their deregulated domestic markets, and are dumping capacity in international markets.

> both a public service and an integral part of the nation's economy and, as in the case of public utilities, requires appropriate protection from uncontrolled competition. Free competition is sensible and succeeds only when all participants operate under the same rules. Thus, present U.S. aviation policy—both domestic and international—ignores basic economic principles; and, more crucially, U.S. aviation policy goals are inconsistent with other policy objectives, including national security.[35]

Consistent with its philosophical devotion to "open skies," DOT has approved code-sharing (despite the manifest consumer deception and the deleterious impact on independent regional airlines) and facilitated foreign ownership as a means of providing capital to U.S. airlines financially ravaged by deregulation and LBOs—both caused by a bankrupt U.S. aviation policy. The *quid pro quo* for signing an "open skies" bilateral air transport agreement is code-sharing (giving foreign airlines indirect access to rich domestic U.S. feed), liberal bilateral rights of access (with direct non-stop access to interior U.S. points, and generous fifth-freedom rights), and antitrust immunity so that partner carriers can agree to merge marketing, cease competing, and pool traffic and revenue. Foreign investment is far more attractive to foreign airlines if the foreign carrier can control the North American feed into their relatively lucrative wide-bodied long haul networks.

Foreign carriers secure adequate access to the world's largest passenger market (the U.S.) via code-sharing, risking only a few hundred million dollars if they decide to buy control. They invest dumb equity, expecting synergistic revenue on the feed the U.S. carriers provide into their wide-bodied long-haul networks.

While propping up airlines collapsing because of the failure of U.S. domestic aviation policy, foreign ownership poses four potential problems:

---

[35] Newal Taneja, Airline Planning: Corporate, Financial, and Marketing 113 (1982).

Chapter 10

1. Given that the U.S. relies on the civilian commercial airline fleet for needed lift capacity in time of international conflict under the Civil Reserve Air Fleet [CRAF] program, it may have a deleterious effect on national security;
2. It eliminates competition in foreign markets;
3. It undermines the integrity of bilateral air transport negotiations; and
4. It may potentially endanger domestic aircraft production.[36]

U.S. aviation labor unions have declared war against lifting of the cabotage prohibition. They are fighting the wrong battle. Even if the United States gave away cabotage tomorrow and received nothing in return, little would change. The foreign airlines are not so foolish to invest billions of dollars setting up a route network in a nation where almost every airline suffers from chronic economic anemia. Moreover, the most desirable airport infrastructure in the United States has been consumed.

All that would likely happen from elimination of cabotage would be the elimination of some closed door restrictions on foreign carrier flights that serve two points in the U.S. Thus, a European carrier with a through flight from Europe to Los Angeles via New York could pick up a few passengers in New York. The competitive impact would be but marginal, as is the U.S.-flag competitive impact on fifth freedom flights in Europe. The trans-oceanic schedule does not allow much in terms of threatening competition.

As a rule, U.S. airlines enjoy their highest load factors, highest yields, and highest profits in the most heavily regulated international markets, and suffer their lowest load factors, lowest yields, and lowest profits in the "open skies" domestic markets. U.S. flag carriers perform best in the Latin America and Pacific markets, which are relatively tightly regulated. U.S. carriers transport only about 15% of the passengers in the open skies U.S.-Netherlands market, and about 20% in the open skies U.S.-Korea market. Exporting "open skies" to the international arena will, in the long term, export the severe overcapacity U.S. airlines face domestically, created by overlapping hub

---

[36] Paul Dempsey, The Disintegration of the U.S. Airline Industry, 20 Transp. L.J. 9, 36-42 (1991); Paul Dempsey, The Sky Ought to Be the Limit, N.Y. Times, Jan. 26, 1991, at 19.

and spoke networks, while profitability is eroded by new entrants. Open skies will result in that duplicative network capacity played out on a global scale, coupled with low-cost Laker Skytrain-, Virgin Atlantic-, and People Express-type carriers emerging in a host of international markets.

In the short term, U.S. airlines might eat the lunch of some of the foreign-flag carriers (although airport capacity constraints in Europe will themselves deny U.S. carriers the opportunity for significant new entry). In the early 1990s, U.S. carriers enjoyed a comparative labor cost advantage in both arenas, much enhanced by a weak U.S. dollar.

But in the long-term, in an open skies environment, the Asian tigers might well eat the lunch of the U.S. flag carriers because of their comparative cost advantage, as well as their relatively higher service levels. Business travelers already rate Asian carriers among the world's best. This results from a cultural and attitudinal difference in the level and type of cabin service that U.S. airline management cannot expect to exact from U.S. cabin crews. For obvious reasons, employee-owned companies will have a difficult time hiring third world cabin and cockpit employees. As a means of achieving essential cost reductions, most of the major U.S. airlines likely will succumb to some degree of employee ownership.

Code-sharing will deprive U.S. carriers of the comparative advantage of on-line domestic feed from the world's largest market—North America. But over the next two decades, Asia will become the largest passenger market. In an open skies regime, Asia inherits the earth, as it has in most major industrial sectors.

Regarding state-aid, the objection of the United States seems somewhat hypocritical. For example, the U.S. objects to the government of France pouring billions of francs into Air France, and yet the Air Transport Association of America repeatedly calls for rolling back taxes. Whether the government hands airlines the money, or takes less away, the net effect is the same.[37] The 4.3% per gallon exemption in aviation excise fuel taxes, as well as the expiration of the 10% ticket

---

[37] Moreover, the airline industry is sucking at the state and local teats in North Carolina, Minnesota, Indiana, Missouri and Colorado.

tax, coupled with low fuel costs, was an enormous factor in producing profitability in the mid-1990s.[38]

Certainly, subsidized airlines need not make a profit in order to survive. Nor are they vigorous price competitors. Many subsidized and government-owned carriers are lethargic and inefficient. But, as is the case with British Airways, paternalistic governments have established ubiquitous global route networks, and are willing to engage in subtle forms of protectionism (e.g., capacity restrictions at Heathrow).

Privatization of industry is a global phenomenon driven in part by ideology, and in part by the fiscal needs of governments having a more difficult time satiating the social welfare needs of their constituents. In most western industrialized nations, the aging population is growing and consuming more resources, while the number of working taxpayers is declining. Flushing out capital from state-owned indus-tries via privatization offers politicians a Band-Aid, which postpones the higher taxes and lower benefits which must eventually come. In the airline sector, the privatized airlines usually proceed through a downsizing of employment, a streamlining of operations, and (perhaps most significantly), emerge triumphant with a clean balance sheet.

After 15 years of deregulation (a/k/a domestic open skies), the balance sheets of U.S. carriers have been polluted with enormous debt. If British Airways wants to raise $400 million on the capital markets to control USAir, no problem. If USAir entered the capital markets to find $400 million on its own, the junk interest rate would be prohibitive. From a purely Machiavellian perspective, U.S. carriers are better off with sluggish governmentally owned and subsidized competitors than with more privatized British Airways.

With most major airlines suffering chronic economic malaise, some have bemoaned the absence of a U.S. aviation policy. With commendable dedication, Transportation Secretary Federico Peña attempted to chart a new course in aviation policy. Unfortunately, the path he chose suffers from two fundamental misunderstandings and misconceptions,

---

[38] Samuel Buttrick of Kidder, Peabody, pointed out that 70% of U.S. airline gains in the first half of 1994 were attributable to lower fuel prices. Julius Maldutis of Salomon Brothers observed that in spite of the $313 million profit the industry earned in the third quarter of 1994, they posted only a $68 million profit for the first nine months, and would likely lose $300 or more for the year. Randolph Babbitt, Saving the Golden Goose, Air Line Pilot (Feb. 1995), at 10.

and a generous dose of naiveté. In the long term, these policies may do serious harm to U.S. airlines.

First, Mr. Peña spent much time negotiating "open skies" bilateral agreements with nations the size of their postage stamps, offering them virtually unlimited access to the United States (the largest and richest source of passenger and freight traffic in the world) in exchange for ... the opportunity for U.S. carriers to fly to any airport in countries like Luxembourg, Iceland, Switzerland, and Austria. While these are splendid nations, the air traffic opportunities they offer U.S. carriers are minuscule compared to the opportunities the vast U.S. passenger and cargo market offer their airlines. Small countries, with airlines focusing on sixth-freedom traffic, with little domestic passenger feed, are more than happy to trade access to a little for access to a lot.

Further, Mr. Peña offered foreign carriers direct access to U.S. traffic via anticompetitive marketing and equity relationships with U.S. carriers, which feed traffic into the lucrative long-haul, wide-bodied foreign carrier networks.

Such an approach is arguably inconsistent with Congressional policy as expressed in the International Air Transportation Competition Act of 1979, which provides that, in negotiating bilaterals, the Department of Transportation may allow "opportunities for carriers of foreign countries to increase their access to United States points *if exchanged for benefits of similar magnitude* for United States carriers . . . ." The opportunity for a U.S.-flag airline to fly to Luxembourg is hardly the equivalent of allowing a Luxembourg carrier to fly to New York, Chicago and Los Angeles.

Second, there is, has been, and continues to be a long standing priority given to the interests of the passenger carriers vis-à-vis the cargo carriers. Since World War II, the entire framework of bilateral air transport agreements negotiated between the United States and foreign nations has been predicated on a route structure designed to move people.

Freight has always taken a back seat to passengers in U.S. bilateral negotiations. The international aviation system was designed primarily to accommodate bilateral passenger aviation needs. But the routings are vastly different. People prefer to move from A to B nonstop if they can. Most bilaterals focus on point-to-point passenger routings.

Although highly time sensitive, air freight is less particular about its routing. A circuitous movement from A to hub to B annoys cargo less than it does passengers. Freight will sit obediently on tarmacs, and needs little entertainment, food, or warmth. Cargo doesn't mind overnight circuity in the flight path. While a passenger would be loathe to fly from Dublin to New York via Frankfurt, freight does not seem to mind.

Consolidating freight from numerous origins allows aggregate load factors to take advantage of the economies of scale of larger aircraft. Thus, an A to B route structure (e.g., Dublin to New York) is antithetical to the efficiency of air cargo operations.

Additionally, the economies of scope in the movement of freight are profound. Thus, a U.S. cargo jet flying from Dublin to Frankfurt (where packages coming from all over Europe headed for the United States are consolidated) can easily accommodate another package or two to Rome, or Budapest, or Copenhagen. The additional costs are nil. The additional revenue goes straight to the bottom line. But the necessary seventh freedom rights are absent from most bilateral air transport agreements.

Freight is also much less sensitive to price than about half of the passenger market, which consists of discretionary traffic. Freight *must* move to market. People do not have to fly to vacation destinations, and if the price is too dear, they stay home, or drive the kids to Wally World.

The all-cargo carriers do compete with the passenger combination airlines, which carry freight, along luggage and mail, in the belly of their planes. But given their route structures, the passenger carriers are a somewhat poor competitor for the large cargo carriers, which are well integrated with surface carriers for a seamless movement from origin to destination.

The only way to responsibly pursue international aviation negotiations is pragmatically, with hard bargaining for meaningful rights of access for U.S. airlines. The International Air Transportation Competition Act of 1979 calls for "the *strengthening of the competitive position* of United States air carriers to at least assure equality with foreign air carriers, including the attainment of opportunities for United States air carriers to *maintain and increase their profitability*, in foreign air transportation . . . [and] opportunities for carriers of foreign countries to increase their access to United States points if exchanged for *benefits of similar magnitude for United States carriers* or the traveling public with permanent linkage between rights granted and rights given away."[39] What, then, should drive U.S. international aviation policy?

First, pragmatism. Bilateral negotiations should be pursued pragmatically, as the law requires, rather than ideologically. The United States should bargain hard for access by U.S. carriers, and surrender only that for which there is a roughly equivalent quid-pro-quo. Platitudes about "open skies" coupled with signing new one-sided bilaterals with small nations with little traffic potentially erodes the long-term vitality of U.S. airlines.

Further, the U.S. Department of Transportation could do more to address the day-to-day operational barriers in foreign markets, including limited airport access, inadequate terminals and hangar space, restrictions and delays in processing cargo, restrictions on ground handling and currency remittances, and discriminatory charges, fees and taxes. DOT should aggressively defend the rights of U.S. airlines to compete abroad, with the threat of imposing sanctions on the airlines of nations which discriminate against U.S. carriers, and where necessary, the implementation of the threat.[40]

Air cargo rights should be negotiated separately from passenger rights, and preferably on a multilateral basis, in which the U.S. sits down with all the major nations in a region and hammers out an agreement which creates a multidirectional distribution network geared to the way freight moves most efficiently, allowing the carriers to take advantage of their inherent economies of scale and scope with a maximum of efficiency and productivity.

All that requires a fundamental re-thinking of U.S. aviation policy, embracing pragmatism and common sense over ideology. Transportation is the fundamental catalyst for shrinking the planet, allowing the economic system to fulfill its global destiny. Prudent government policy can much enhance both the free flow of commerce and the economic well being of the U.S. airlines.

---

[39] Paul Dempsey, Robert Hardaway & William Thoms, 2 Aviation Law & Regulation § 10.18 (1993).
[40] See Paul Dempsey, Law & Foreign Policy in International Aviation (1987).

Chapter 10

In the final analysis, the U.S. Department of Transportation is entrusted with protecting the public interest. The public interest should be broadly defined, to include the interest of shippers, passengers, airlines and their employees, lenders, creditors and investors. With that as its goal, a course correction along the lines succinctly described here would be in the best national interest.

THE RELATIONSHIP BETWEEN GOVERNMENT AND THE AIRLINE INDUSTRY IN THE 21st CENTURY

WHY MANAGED COMPETITION MAY BE SUPERIOR TO LAISSEZ-FAIRE

Ultimately, unless the government provides the oversight necessary to enhance pricing stability and rationalize capacity, when all the dust settles, the United States will be left with fewer, but horribly injured, airlines.[41] Several major airlines will gradually collapse into liquidation, but the process likely will be so slow and the few survivors so weak that a Penn Central or Amtrak-type public bail-out will not be implausible. However, the federal government's ability to provide a bail out will be circumscribed by its own excessive debt burden and a reluctance to repeat the catastrophic bail out of the deregulated savings and loan [S&L] industry, which itself cost the public half a trillion dollars. If the survivors are able to reap monopoly rents on a widespread basis, the public outcry will be for imposition of public utility type regulation. Alternatively, the free marketeers will call for surrender of cabotage to allow foreign entrants to discipline the few surviving U.S. carriers, and the cycle will begin anew.

Some contend that the success of Southwest is proof positive that good management will harness costs and resolve these problems without the need for governmental intervention. Southwest thrives on a comparative advantage that other airlines cannot achieve because of existing labor agreements and their tenacious commitment to hubbing, CRS, travel agents, and other costly overhead. The success of about 5% of the U.S. industry, predicated in part on artificial comparative

---

[41] See Richard Gritta, Garland Chow & Todd Shank, Business and Financial Risk in Air Transportation on Carrier Rates of Return (unpublished monograph 1993).

advantages created by the labor laws, and the Wright Amendment (for example, yields in the Southwest dominated Dallas-Houston market exceed 20 cents a mile),[42] should not dictate national policy for the 95% of the industry upon which most Americans must rely. If one could wave a magic wand and give all airlines Southwest's cost structure, the industry eventually would compete away its profit, for all the reasons described above.

Government is a highly imperfect institution, but one must reluctantly concede it is sometimes a necessary companion, particularly to correct for market failure in industries essential to the vitality of the nation as a whole.[43] With more competitors, there can be less government; but with fewer competitors, there will undoubtedly be a need for more government. Thus, injecting modest governmental oversight now to provide some measure of stability to pricing and allow a rationalization of capacity will stem the implosion of this important infrastructure industry, so vital to commerce, communications and national defense.

After deregulation, the U.S. airline industry found itself bleeding from a thousand cuts, losing more than twice the accumulated profit earned since it began commercial service in the 1920s.[44] Name another major industry in the history of our republic that has lost all the money it ever made. Wall Street downgraded virtually all of the industry's crushing debt to "junk bond" status.[45] As Wall Street analyst Julius Maldutis aptly noted, if the airlines were S&Ls, the government would put them into receivership and liquidate them. In a desperate attempt to stay aloft, airlines shelved new aircraft orders, trimmed and abandoned hubs, and fired more than 100,000 employees. The ripple effect on Boeing and McDonnell-Douglas, producers of our nation's single most important manufacturing export, was devastating. Boeing alone slashed 26,000 jobs from its work force.

---

[42] Aviation Daily (Sept. 23, 1994), at 493. In the Southwest dominated Chicago-Detroit market, yields are nearly 30 cents. Id.

[43] Paul Dempsey, Market Failure and Regulatory Failure As Catalysts for Political Change: The Choice Between Imperfect Regulation and Imperfect Competition, 46 Washington & Lee L. Rev.. 1 (1988).

[44] "The nine U.S. major airline companies had a combined net loss of $5.14 billion last year, which is more than double the $1.89 billion the same companies lost in 1991." U.S. Major Carriers Lost $5.1 Billion in 1992, Aviation Daily (Mar. 30, 1993), at 495.

[45] See Big Three Placed On CreditWatch By Standard & Poor's, Aviation Daily (Jan. 15, 1993), at 77.

Anemic McDonnell-Douglas sold out to Boeing. Paradoxically, airlines are now more highly concentrated, and less profitable, than ever. Clearly, this is a dysfunctional market, reflecting dysfunctional economic policies.

The airline industry has always flown through the turbulence caused by the updrafts and downdrafts of the market cycle. Before promulgation of the Airline Deregulation Act of 1978, at a time when it was taking delivery of tremendous wide-body capacity, the industry suffered recession, dampened consumer demand, and soaring fuel costs. But under regulation, never was a Pan Am or Eastern liquidated, nor a TWA or Continental cast into bankruptcy.

Not to be confused by the facts, laissez-faire theologians tenaciously point to consumer savings and declare victory. Never mind the tremendous losses of investors, creditors and workers, or the opportunity costs squandered by imprisoning business travelers in canisters of aluminum and steel and flying them circuitously through constipated hubs, or that Americans now fly the oldest fleet of aircraft of any G-7 nation, or that bankruptcies and concentration have grown. Many market economists suffer from a severe methodological handicap by insisting that competition is perfect and a uni-dimensional assessment of consumer prices is the only salient measure of sound public policy.[46]

True, some consumers do save, paying rates which fail to cover the fully allocated costs of providing service. Of course, below-cost-pricing contributes to the industry's insolvency. It is tantamount to cutting the orchard's trees to harvest the fruit.

Moreover, post-deregulation pricing is hideously discriminatory. Many consumers pay fares which have soared well above the inflation rate. As noted above, small businesses, which create 90% of the nation's jobs, pay obscenely higher prices (vis-à-vis the Fortune 500), causing many reluctantly to boycott air transportation. No nation which values job creation would willfully endorse such a regressive pricing structure.

---

[46] Even the purported consumer benefits of airline deregulation, such as the $6 billion that the Brookings Institution claims has been saved as a consequence of deregulation, have been controverted. See Paul Dempsey & Andrew Goetz, Airline Deregulation & Laissez-Faire Mythology 281-95 (1992). Most studies fail to account for the long-term pre-existing trend of declining prices that preceded deregulation. Id. at 243-63. A recent study by Morton Beyer reveals that consumer savings would have tens of billions of dollars *greater* had deregulation not occurred.

But under deregulation, Americans no longer have any say over how their airports and airways—public resources developed with taxpayer dollars—serve them. Deregulation traded public interest regulation of the airline industry for airline regulation of the public. To get a decent fare, consumers must surrender their freedom of how far in advance they plan their trips, how long they stay, and where they sleep on Saturday nights. If consumers are so happy, why does Ralph Nader describe the airline system as a "public utility"?[47] Why does *Consumer Reports* describe airline deregulation as "anti-consumer"?[48] Why do polls of frequent flyers reveal a majority would prefer re-regulation?

Market failure has always been an appropriate catalyst for governmental intervention, particularly in infrastructure industries as vital to commerce, communications and national defense as transportation. The airlines need not be returned to the tight fisted regime of New Deal public utility regulation, not if Congress acts to save the industry from the concentration levels which will mandate such a draconian result. And there are clearly better solutions than selling off the U.S. airline industry to foreign nationals and their governments.

Unfortunately, the public policy debate has degenerated into the polarized extremes of public utility regulation or *laissez-faire* deregulation. The appropriate solution probably lies between, or beyond, them. But a proper cure will never be found for the disease unless it is diagnosed correctly, casting aside blind faith in the curative powers of market alchemists, and moving promptly to restore the public interest in safe, dependable, and reasonably priced transportation service. Only then can the nation regain what was, before deregulation, universally applauded as the "world's finest system of transportation."[49]

Tragically, Alfred Kahn was true to his promise. The eggs have been so scrambled that they can never be put back into their shells again. Neither can the proud airlines that have been lost be resurrected, nor can the emotional and economic injury suffered by hundreds of thousands of loyal employees who have lost their jobs be

---

[47] Martin Tolchin, Clinton To Focus On Helping U.S. Airlines, N.Y. Times, Dec. 27, 1992, at 11.
[48] Dear President Clinton, Consumer Reports (Jan. 1993), at 6.
[49] See Dempsey, The Bitter Fruits of Airline Deregulation, Wall St. J., Apr. 8, 1993, at A 15.

rectified. Nor can the investors and creditors who have been stiffed be reimbursed.

This is not to suggest that the U. S. Civil Aeronautics Board should be resurrected in its 1938 clothes to fix what went wrong. That approach may have been appropriate then, but not now. Regulatory reform was a prudent dose of course correction that the CAB clearly needed.[50] Unfortunately, the successes of regulatory reform in the late 1970s became the political catalyst for deregulation, persuading Congress to throw the baby out with the bath water.

If Congress does nothing, the airline industry will likely become more highly concentrated than it now is. Unless human nature has changed in the 21st Century, because airline managers are rational wealth maximizers, prices will eventually rise and grow even more discriminatory.

OBJECTIVES OF SOUND PUBLIC POLICY

If a nation is to have prudent public policy in transportation, it must begin with an understanding of four major premises:

First, *transportation is an industry in which the public interest is paramount.* Like the public utilities, transportation is a necessity. Transportation comprises the very veins and arteries of the nation. It is an integral part of the national infrastructure, essential for commerce, communications and national defense. For that reason, the public has a strong and compelling interest in how it performs its mission on behalf of the public. The public interest should be holistically defined as including all constituencies—consumers, investors, creditors, workers, and taxpayers.

Second, *transportation is an industry which has a chronic tendency to engage in below-cost and highly discriminatory pricing, at least until oligopoly or monopoly is achieved.* Where carriers compete head-to-head, they tend to price at levels adequate to cover

---

[50] Alfred Kahn sometimes makes the argument that deregulation began in the mid-1970s, well before he was appointed Chairman of the Civil Aeronautics Board. The modest rate and entry liberalization implemented in that period were actually a process of regulatory reform, clearly warranted by the state of the industry and the times, and permitted under the Federal Aviation Act, a regulatory statute. In fact, full deregulation probably did not actually occur until much later, and one might argue not until the Civil Aeronautics Board was sunset, in 1985.

short-term marginal costs, leaving their fixed costs to be recovered, if at all, in those markets in which they enjoy market power. This is true because transportation firms sell what is, in essence, an instantly perishable commodity, the short-term variable costs of operation are both low and somewhat obfuscated,[51] and every firm prices at the margin in order to fill capacity that otherwise would be lost, and there-by preserve market share. Individually rational behavior becomes collective irrational behavior. In the short term, consumers enjoy a wind-fall, at the expense of investors, creditors and workers, while equipment ages, bankruptcies soar, and all the while, the industry becomes more highly concentrated. Left to its own devices, the industry tends toward concentration in the long term.

This was true of the railroads in the 19th Century, before regulation, and true of the airlines and motor carriers in the 1920s and 1930s, again, before regulation.[52] In those days, this industry wide propensity to charge rates below fully allocated costs was referred to as "destructive competition." It is true of airlines and motor carriers since deregulation.[53]

Third, *the airline industry suffers from serious cost and capacity problems.* Hub-and-spoking (in attempt to re-rationalize the deregulated environment to the individual airline's advantage), ironically, has created largely duplicative ubiquitous, high-cost transport networks. The excessive capacity created thereby exacerbated the principle described above, of carriers to engage in below-cost pricing to preserve market share. Escalating costs have pushed the envelope of prices to the outer limit of demand elasticity.[54]

---

[51] Most costs are joint costs, spread over origin, intermediate, destination, and connecting points, causing calculations of fully allocated costs to be quite difficult to achieve. Moreover, the enormous cash flow of the industry leads to a hand-to-mouth behavior, postponing the day of recovering fully allocated costs.

[52] See Paul Dempsey, The Social & Economic Consequences of Deregulation 5-25 (1989); Paul Dempsey & Andrew Goetz, Airline Deregulation & Laissez-Faire Mythology 159-66 (1992); Paul Dempsey, Robert Hardaway & William Thoms, 1 Aviation Law & Regulation §§ 1.02-1.08 (1993).

[53] Airlines were deregulated with the promulgation of the Airline Deregulation Act of 1978. Motor carriers were deregulated with the Motor Carrier Act of 1980. Busses were deregulated with the Bus Regulatory Reform Act of 1982. Railroads, deregulated with the Staggers Rail Act of 1980, are now so highly concentrated and have largely been freed discriminate against captive customers that they have somewhat escaped this downward spiral. Air cargo carriers, deregulated with the Air Cargo Deregulation Act of 1977, are also highly concentrated, and relatively profitable.

[54] Hubs are high cost methods of distributing passengers in terms of aircraft and labor utilization and fuel consumption. Cargo doesn't seem to object to the inconvenience, but passengers detest it.

Fourth, *the domestic air passenger market may be approaching maturity.* Domestic passenger demand appears to be leveling, and many analysts anticipate that such demand will grow at a much slower rate in the new millennium, and a significantly slower rate than the international market. In part this is attributable to age and income shifts in the population base, a saturation of the leisure market, and the current and future technological strides in the telecommunications industry, an alternative for business communications. In part, this is attributable to consumer attitudes developed during the unrealistic airline price wars as to the appropriate price for the product. In part, this is attributable to escalating costs, pushing price against the envelope of demand elasticity.

With these essential premises in mind, potential solutions to the crisis in the airline industry need to be examined. As noted at the outset of this chapter, this may be a futile academic exercise as the 21st Century dawns. But the public's needs and problems, as well as their willingness to find solutions thereto, are quite fluid and may evolve over the course of the 21st Century. Any list of solutions may stimulate creative improvements to the alternatives proffered. In the authors' view, any comprehensive legislative effort to solve the problems in commercial aviation optimally should have four primary substantive objectives:

1. It must attempt to rectify the financial crisis in the airline industry;
2. It must promote consumer equity;
3. It must allow new firms equitable entry opportunities; and
4. Finally, it must also address the procedural question of what sort of government agency should oversee the managed competition this regime requires.

OVERCOMING THE FINANCIAL MORASS

Addressing the financial crisis in commercial aviation must be a high priority for an enlightened regime of aviation public policy.

Perhaps carriers seeking to serve nonstop routes not currently being served should be awarded limited-term exclusive nonstop route franchises as a means of stimulating nonstop service, thereby providing some collateral for lending. If price ceilings are imposed, the attractiveness of hubs diminishes, for they will no longer produce monopoly rents.

Creative means to rebuild the nation's aviation system need to be explored.

There are four paths to improved balance sheets and potential profitability in the airline industry: (1) a government financial bailout; (2) selling off the airlines to foreign citizens and their governments; (3) reformation of the labor, bankruptcy and antitrust laws; or (4) regulatory reform.

Recognizing the importance of transportation to commerce, communications and national defense, Congress in earlier periods of American history appropriated direct federal subsidies to bail out failing transportation firms such as Conrail, Chrysler, Lockheed, and Amtrak. But the contemporary realities of a multi-trillion dollar federal debt probably preclude direct subsidies to ameliorate the contemporary crisis in the transportation industry. Various proposals to provide direct or indirect taxpayer assistance (from outright grants, to rolling back taxes, to federal loan guarantees) so as to improve airline balance sheets are Band-Aids, likely to provide some short-term relief without addressing the fundamental structural problems in the industry. Any such relief must be coupled with a more comprehensive set of remedies to assure that the taxpayer's investment will not be lost.

The problem is not just industry debt, of course, it is also the endless hemorrhaging caused by pricing the product below cost. Lowering costs can only be achieved in a limited number of ways—cutting labor expenditures, abandoning hubs, and removing taxes and costly regulations, for example. Labor costs have declined as a percentage of operating expenses since 1978. Further reductions would require a restructuring of the Railway Labor Act. More importantly, the real problem appears to be the industry's chronic inability to price its product above costs. So further wage reductions might well only be a temporary respite from unprofitability.

Foreign control potentially jeopardizes national security. More than half of the U.S. wide-bodied fleet is committed to the CRAF program, and military dependence on civilian lift capacity will likely increase in the post-cold war era. Two-thirds of the soldiers and a quarter of the supplies flown to the Middle East during Operation Desert Shield/Storm were flown aboard U.S. CRAF aircraft. Certainly, although the United States fought wars with Britain in two centuries, and British soldiers burned down the White House, nations like the United Kingdom do not appear today to be a military threat to the United States. But recall that the Shah of Iran proposed to buy Pan Am in 1974, at a time when Iran was the United States' closest ally in the Middle East. And recall that not one of the nation's loyal NATO allies in continental Europe would give the U.S. permission to use their air space when President Reagan decided to bomb Libya. If they wouldn't be comfortable with the United States using their air space in a time of military conflict, how would they feel about the U.S. using their aircraft?[55]

Domestically, the airline industry is more highly concentrated than at any time in its history. Nonetheless, duplicative hub networks assure that most long-haul markets suffer from excess capacity. The elimination of some of the weaker airlines will reduce the number of duplicative networks, and thereby enhance profitability of the surviving airlines. But the concentration imperative which deregulation has unleashed has been somewhat stymied by the bankruptcy laws, which cause airlines to linger on in Chapter 11 with one foot in the grave. A more highly concentrated industry would likely be more profitable. Nonetheless, monopoly or oligopoly control of an essential infrastructure industry like aviation may lead to the exertion of market power, manifested by more highly discriminatory pricing, and the loss of competitive discipline in pricing and service. Ultimately, such abuses could lead to the imposition of public utility regulation on the few remaining firms.[56]

The final alternative is regulatory reform, or if one prefers, managed competition. It need not embrace economic regulation of the nature created in the 1930s.

---

[55] At any given point in time, about half of our wide-bodied fleet is flying over an ocean, or sitting on the tarmac in a foreign airport.

[56] Eventually, Congress may be faced with the prospect of introducing public utility regulation to the few surviving firms, or failing that, nationalizing the industry. In the author's view regulated competition is preferable to regulated monopoly; regulated monopoly is preferable to nationalization; nationalization is preferable to unregulated monopoly. Neither of the extremes of nationalization nor the contemporary environment of Market Darwinism are desirable. Public policy in this essential infrastructure industry might best be enhanced by preserving the level of competition which now exists and imposing light-handed regulation upon it, while there are still a sufficient number of competitors to preserve.

LESSONS TO BE LEARNED

One characteristic of mankind is that we would hope to learn the lessons of the past, not only to avoid repeating the same mistakes, but also to develop a better way. The way humans learn and progress seems to follow an evolutionary pattern which resembles a series of synergistic loops. As the authors have stated in the companion volume to this text,[57] rather than a linear model where information is added to "A", and "B" follows "A", "C" follows "B", and so forth, the model is a "synergistic loop" where "B" is pulled back through, and combined with "A" to form a "C" which is not exactly the same but still resembles "A", as follows:

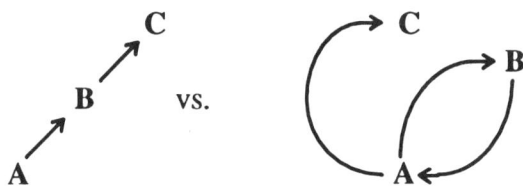

The synergistic model resembles patterns in nature. Michael Lauderdale contends that parallels can be drawn from biological to social evolution, and he equates societal development to an undersea creature, the nautilus. The chambered nautilus, he says,

> ... grows by adding a spiral of a shell around a central axis so that, as it grows, it slowly revolves about the axis. It grows by becoming different and yet remaining the same. What it once was is a part of what it now is, and what it will become will be, in part, what now is.[58]

To Lauderdale, the growth of the nautilus is "the pattern of individual psychological and cultural evolution." Time and reality can be thought of as curvilinear, not linear. The past is not behind us, but

---

[57] See Paul Stephen Dempsey and Laurence E. Gesell, Air Transportation: Foundations for the 21st Century 197 (1997).
[58] Michael L. Lauderdale, Burnout: Strategies for Personal and Organizational Life 172, 183 (1982).

Chapter 10

rather, is wrapped around us like "thread wound around a spool", with the past just adjacent to the present.[59]

The synergistic model, like Lauderdale's metaphor of the nautilus, suggests that the future is not only predicated upon the past, but that old clichés are only partially correct. The "pendulum" of historical development not only swings back and forth, but the whole mechanism is elevated simultaneously so that the pendulum bob never returns to the exact same place. Similarly, history doesn't "repeat itself", it only mirrors reflections from the past.[60]

If the synergistic, reiterative model is an accurate depiction of the natural evolutionary development of social skills, then perhaps regulatory reform ought not only to conform to that social evolutionary model, but, in fact, can be expected to follow a natural, recognizable pattern. The future of regulatory reform, therefore, will likely resemble the model in Figure 10.6, "The Evolution of Economic Regulation"; where the negative experiences gained from strict economic regulation led to a desire for its opposite, complete deregulation. The failure of airline deregulation, in turn, is prompting a call for some type of regulatory reform—that, ostensible, lies somewhere between the two regulatory extremes of regulation and deregulation.

Figure 10.6—THE EVOLUTION OF ECONOMIC REGULATION

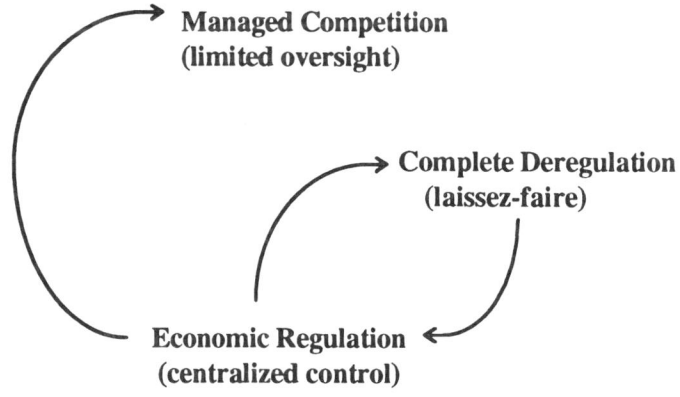

---

[59] Id. at 173, 188.
[60] Laurence E. Gesell, Airline Re-Regulation 123 (1990).

The synergistic, reiterative model is a natural form which can be seen repeatedly in social development.[61] As such, it provides a perspective on what the future regulatory model in air transportation will probably look like.

Looking back upon the early railroad industry, when left to their own ends to compete, the inevitable result was collusion, merger, and monopoly.[62] It was because of monopoly and its associated consumer abuses that Congress first instituted economic regulation in the United States.[63] Against this historical backdrop, according to Melton, "Regulation was instituted for good and sufficient reasons . . .," because ". . . the public was unwilling to tolerate uncontrolled monopoly and equally reluctant to endure the vicissitudes of rigorous competition, even if it could be compelled."[64]

As a consequence, economic regulation was tried, but it eventually resulted in what was perceived as a collusion between government, big business and organized labor. Then the "pendulum" swung to the opposite extreme when the cry went out in the 1970s for regulatory relief and complete deregulation.

In transportation deregulation, Congress adopted different goals and meanings with respect to each of the acts deregulating the various transportation modes. From the outset, and even among those who favored deregulation, complete deregulation (i.e., the elimination of all economic regulation) was less popular than was partial deregulation.[65] Nevertheless, under two successive (Carter and Reagan) administrations, airline deregulation was to be complete. And, the legacy has languished on in successive administrations.

In all of the acts deregulating transportation, the common thread was greater reliance upon market mechanisms and less upon government social controls. The Airline Deregulation Act of 1978, in particular, was oriented to the consumer, with a thrust toward improving

---

[61] See Laurence E. Gesell, Airline Re-Regulation Chapter 4 (1990).

[62] L. J. Melton Jr., Transportation Regulation: An Effective Tool Of Public Policy, 17 Transportation J. (Spring 1978), at 87.

[63] Laurence E. Gesell and Martin T. Farris, Antitrust Irrelevance In Air Transportation and the Redefining of price Discrimination, 57 J. of Air Law and Commerce (Fall 1991).

[64] L. J. Melton Jr., Transportation Regulation: An Effective Tool Of Public Policy, 17 Transportation. J. (Spring 1978), at 93.

[65] J. C. Johnson and D.V. Harper, The Potential Consequences Of Deregulation Of Transportation, in G. M. Davis, Transportation Regulation: A Pragmatic Assessment (1976).

the lot of the passenger.[66] However, as evaluated by attainment (or non-attainment) of the stated objectives of the Airline Deregulation Act, airline deregulatory policy failed to measure up to its expected outcomes.[67] As Alfred Kahn stated it, deregulation held some "unpleasant surprises."[68] Total deregulation allowed the market to be rationalized to the advantage of the capitalist alone, at the expense of both labor and the consumer. The rationalization led to mergers and a market more concentrated than before deregulation, giving the perception that deregulation, too, resulted in a collusion between government and big business.

Hence, economic regulation through centralized government control was tried and rejected. And its opposite, laissez-faire deregulation (defined as "complete deregulation"), was also tried and equally found wanting. At this juncture, just as in 1978 (when there was a general desire for regulatory reform), there are still but three alternative choices when it comes to social control: regulate, deregulate, or choose something in-between which reflects added emphasis on competition and/or simplified rules and procedures that restore effectiveness to the regulatory process.[69]

STATUTORY PROPOSALS

The imminent problem is to discover an effective way to regulate, one that might "balance" the marketplace forces of capital, labor and the consumer. Effective regulatory reform would seem to lie somewhere along a continuum between the extremes of highly centralized economic regulation at one end, and total, or "complete", deregulation at the other.

One purpose of this final chapter is to present a suggested model for air transportation regulation, and a starting point for continued discourse on regulatory reform. Whereas Figure 10.6, above, provides

---

[66] See 49 U.S.C. §1302, Declaration of Policy.
[67] Laurence E. Gesell and Martin T. Farris, Airline Deregulation: An Evaluation of Goals and Objectives, 21 Transportation Law J. (1992).
[68] Alfred E. Kahn, Surprises Of Airline Deregulation, 78 The American Economic Review (May 1988), at 316.
[69] L. J. Melton Jr., Transportation Regulation: An Effective Tool Of Public Policy, 17 Transportation. J. (Spring 1978), at 88.

a visualization of the evolutionary process, presented below is a narrative description of what regulatory reform (defined as "managed competition") might look like.

MANAGED COMPETITION

At a minimum the new regulatory model should encourage healthy competition amongst carriers; it ought to express concern for the welfare of consumers; and it should ensure equity in the marketplace. It should include more vigorous antitrust enforcement, with a focus on local, terminal markets and competition between city-pairs. Consideration might also be given to the introduction of price controls—or, more ideally, price oversight, with the power to impose controls where prevailing air fares might exceed reasonable industry-wide parameters.

- *Regulatory reform*—All regulations must survive cost/benefit review, and unnecessary regulatory burdens must be eliminated. Any changes must be implemented in a way least likely to cause injury to existing airlines. Equity demands that all airlines be treated equally. And as to taxes, they should be lowered. But any taxpayer investment, direct or indirect, must be protected by a comprehensive program to insure that such contribution is not wasted away in a new round of below-cost pricing.
- *Airline agreements*—Much could be done to alleviate congestion and excessive capacity problems by allowing airlines to sit down and talk about solutions thereto. Cooperation between airlines can sometimes reduce industry costs while providing better service to the public. The government should, of course, monitor such discussions so as to protect consumers and other airlines from anti-competitive behavior. But antitrust immunity might be conferred for those arrangements which serve the public interest by better rationalizing the air transport system, to the benefit of all stake-holders—capitalists, labor, and consumers. This could help alleviate wasted capacity, ease airport congestion and delay, reduce fuel consumption, and improve the economic health of airlines. Mandatory retirement of old, noisy, fuel-inefficient aircraft should be required.

- *Fitness*—Congress should pass legislation imposing fitness standards prospectively prohibiting any future LBO or other excessive enhancement of carrier debt, force airlines to wean themselves of existing debt over a period of time, and prohibit public assets (such as international routes, landing slots and gates) to be sold off to enhance the personal wealth of corporate raiders. Fitness scrutiny might be exerted against any airline either entering bankruptcy, having an excessive debt-to-equity ratio, or having an excessively aging or inadequately maintained fleet. New accounting standards should be adopted to give a clearer picture of debt, requiring capitalization of leases, frequent flyer obligations, and other liabilities. Debt/equity targets should be announced, to be phased in over time.
- *Bankruptcy reform*—The bankruptcy laws should be amended to prevent Chapter 11 carriers from pricing below fully allocated costs, assuming no bankruptcy, with an exception allowed for meeting the lower fares of a competitor. A specific time limitation should also be imposed on carriers entering Chapter 11, requiring them to emerge or liquidate within a specified number of months. Nine months might be an appropriate gestation period. To deter a company from entering Chapter 11, its top management should be replaced promptly by the bankruptcy judge.
- *International aviation*—New capital from any source should be welcome, particularly to shore up failing U.S. airlines. But foreign control should be avoided, for foreign control tends to reduce competition in international markets, endangers national security by diluting the loyalty of the CRAF fleet, jeopardizes the integrity of the bilateral negotiating process, and creates an unlevel playing field because of the foreign regime of government ownership, subsidies and regulation. All bartering of international aviation rights should be done on the basis of an equal exchange of opportunities. Access to the U.S. market, either through marketing alliances, equity ownership, or route authority should be given only to those nations offering equivalent market opportunities. Carriers should be selected to serve international routes on the basis of which carrier is best able to

provide vigorous competition to the foreign carriers in the market, and best able to serve consumers.

- *Loan guarantees*—The capital requirements of the U.S. airline industry are enormous. With today's deficit, a government bailout, a la Conrail and Lockheed, is probably not feasible. Neither probably are tax credits for new equipment purchases. However, using some slice of the Airport and Airway Trust Fund might be explored to provide federal loan guarantees to domestic airlines for new aircraft, provided old aircraft are retired. Some have suggested requiring the elimination of two seats for every one acquired under such a program. But again, any public contribution to the industry must be encompassed within a comprehensive package of remedies to the more fundamental and long-term industry problems, such as those suggested herein, so as to protect the taxpayer's investment. If the U.S. government dedicates itself firmly and forcefully to shoring up the financial health and financial prospects of the industry, the private capital markets will become available quite quickly, creating stronger airlines better positioned economically and efficiently to serve the public interest.

ENHANCING CONSUMER EQUITY

- *Pricing Simplification*—With hundreds of thousands of price changes every day, information costs have soared. Consumers deserve to have pricing information which allows them to compare alternatives rationally. The European Community adopted four fare categories, with restrictions tied to each alternative.[70] Such a tiered price structure would make the labyrinth navigable. Some have suggested resurrecting the old statutory "just and reasonable" rate provisions of the Federal Aviation Act, but that may be difficult given the heterogeneous nature of airline cost structures. Perhaps some of the regulatory reform pricing provisions of the Airline Deregulation Act or the European rules might be appropriate. Pricing standardization would much en-

---

[70] See Dempsey, European Aviation Regulation: Flying Through the Liberalization Labyrinth, 15 Bos. College Int'l. & Comp. L. Rev. 311 (1992).

Chapter 10

hance consumer equity and hopefully provide the industry with some opportunity for pricing stability.
- *Pricing Discrimination*—Both airline profitability and consumer equity will be enhanced by eliminating pernicious forms of pricing discrimination, such as corporate and governmental discounting. Small businesses create the lion's share of the nation's jobs, and they are seriously disadvantaged by the contemporary transportation pricing structure. If job creation is an important national policy, this type of discrimination might be challenged on both equity and economic grounds. Of course, pricing differentials ought to be allowed for discretionary traffic, so as to allow airlines the flexibility to tap the elasticities of demand to fill seats which otherwise might fly empty.
- *Monopoly Pricing*—As a general rule, the government should stay out of the business of setting fares where sufficient competition exists to discipline airlines. Take some appropriate measure of competition at airports or in nonstop city-pair markets (say, some appropriate point on the Herfindahl-Hirshman Index, or some other definition of market dominance),[71] and let airlines price as they will. But in markets dominated by only one or two carriers, a price ceiling should be imposed to prevent the extraction of monopoly rents. The ceiling could be based on average industry fares for similar stage lengths, or carrier costs.
- *Unfair and Deceptive Competitive Practices*—Code sharing, bait and switch advertising, misleading scheduling, travel agent commission overrides, exclusive dealing arrangements with corporate purchasers or interlining carriers, demand based flight cancellations and other deceptive practices should be prohibited. Congress should adopt a Code of Fair Competitive Practices defining what is not permitted and providing penalties for violations. Alternatively, Congress could eliminate federal preemption over such questions, letting the state Attorney Generals loose.
- *Mergers and Acquisitions*—Anticompetitive mergers and acquisitions can injure consumers. Any merger or acquisition should require pre-consummation governmental review to determine the transaction's impact on competition, service, pricing, and the

---

[71] See Staggers Rail Act of 1980, Pub. L. No. 96-448, 94 Stat. 1895, 49 U.S.C. § 10701(a)(b)(1).

financial condition of the surviving airline. In order to enhance the financial viability of the industry and reduce redundant capacity, stronger airlines should be encouraged to acquire weaker carriers. In order to preserve competition in international markets and the ability of the U.S. commercial fleet to facilitate national defense needs under the Civil Reserve Air Fleet program, foreign control restrictions should be maintained, if not strengthened.

STIMULATING COMPETITIVE ACCESS

Ultimately, any comprehensive statutory proposals have to address in some way the entry barriers of access to slots and gates, as well as computer reservations systems bias, but do so delicately, so that the established airlines aren't financially injured in the process.

- *Airport Access*—Majority in interest clauses should be examined to determine whether incumbent airlines use them to restrict entry unduly. Airports should be free to exercise eminent domain powers to recapture underutilized gates or landing slots, at fair market failure, and lease them to new entrants, or convert gates to multiple carrier use.
- *Airport Capacity*—Airports are public resources. Federal preemption of noise and other environmental issues might well enable the needed additional infrastructure development. Peak period pricing could flatten congestion. Encouraging liner route structures might re-distribute demand to underutilized airport facilities where service has either been diminished or lost altogether under deregulation.
- *Frequent Flyer Programs*—To give smaller airlines a better chance to compete, frequent flyer awards should be taxed. Proceeds from such a tax should be dedicated to fund airport and airway infrastructure expansion and improvement.
- *Nonstop Route Certificates*—Hubbing-and-spoking is choking the air transport system, reducing aircraft and labor utilization, and burning excessive fuel. New nonstop service overflying hubs might be inaugurated if airlines could receive a protected franchise for a term of years. A franchise to serve any city-pair not

now receiving nonstop service ought to be available to an airline promising to provide at least one round-trip a day. It would receive an exclusive franchise to serve the market for say, 3-5 years.
- *Predatory Practices*—Carriers, and consumers, who have heretofore been disenfranchised from antitrust proceedings, equally should be able to file a complaint and have a hearing against rivals which engage in predatory pricing, capacity dumping, and airport monopolization. More specifically, in order to protect upstart airlines against predatory behavior, the practice ought to be prohibited. But first the antitrust laws need to be strengthened and made enforceable. Historically, antitrust violations have been difficult to prove, and nearly impossible to enforce. This needs to be corrected.

ANTITRUST ENFORCEMENT

It should be declared an "unfair and deceptive practice," and an "unfair method of competition" under 49 U.S.C. § 41712, and constitute unlawful monopolization under section 2 of the Sherman Act, 15 U.S.C. § 2, for any major airline which dominates (i.e., possesses more than a 60% market share, as measured by passengers, capacity or frequency) a nonstop city-pair market, or a U.S. airport, to engage in any of the following practices:

- Increasing flight frequency or seat capacity over a 12-month period by more than 50% of any regional or national carrier's flight or seat capacity in any city-pair market the major airline dominates, after the announcement of entry therein by a regional or national airline;
- Selling air transportation at average fares lower than 85% of its distance-adjusted fully allocated costs in any dominated non-stop city-pair market, unless the dominant carrier is matching a currently available lower price offered by a competitor in that market on a number of seats no larger than the total seats flown in the market by the airline whose price is matched;

- Offering "hidden-city" connecting or one-stop fares which match the prices of any regional or national airline in any non-stop city-pair market it serves;
- "Locking down" a competitor's fares by failing to raise prices in the dominated non-stop city-pair market once a smaller competitor raises its prices in that same market, unless raising prices would elevate them above the dominant carrier's costs;
- Raising average fares more than 50% within a year after a competing regional or national airline ceases to serve any non-stop city-pair market it dominates;
- Entering into "exclusive dealing" arrangements with corporate purchasers in any metropolitan area served by a large airport it dominates;
- Entering into "exclusive dealing" agreements, or exclusive joint-fare or code-sharing relationships with other airlines applicable to or from any major airport it dominates;
- Refusing to enter into a ticketing-and-baggage or joint-fare agreement with a competitor seeking such an agreement on such terms as are at least as favorable as those already offered to other carriers to or from a major airport it dominates;
- Offering travel agents commission overrides triggered by a percentage of sales of its product in city-pair markets it dominates; or
- Refusing to sell access to its frequent flyer program at a reasonable price (defined as not more than the average price it sells such access to other carriers) to a competitor which operates in a city-pair market or major airport it dominates.
- It could also be declared an "unfair and deceptive practice," and an "unfair method of competition" under 49 U.S.C. § 41712 for any computer reservations system to give superior screen display to interline connections between code-sharing partners vis-à-vis interline connections between airlines which do not have a code-sharing or other alliance.

PRUDENT PROCEDURE AND PROCESS

Article 1, section 8, of the U.S. Constitution vests in Congress to power to regulate interstate and foreign commerce. Since 1985, however, such powers over commercial aviation have been vested in the Executive Branch.

As the Reagan and Bush Administrations revealed, excessive White House influence can lead to a highly ideological result. Economic regulatory functions over aviation should be placed in an independent agency, shielded from the political winds that blow down Pennsylvania Avenue. Autonomy, responsibility and fair-mindedness are essential to good government.

This agency should be modeled after the Federal Reserve Board, with individuals appointed having high levels of airline industry expertise, appointed for long, but nonrenewable terms, held to the highest ethical standards, and removable from office only for malfeasance. So as to prohibit radical policy shifts, and manage the work load, the new commission should be a collegial body, with five or seven members, no more than a simple majority of whom could be members of a single political party. In order to facilitate creation of a seamless intermodal transportation network, all the regulatory functions over all modes of transport (air, rail, motor, bus and domestic and international water carriers) could be vested in a new Intermodal Transportation Commission, into which would be folded jurisdiction now held by the DOT, the Surface Transportation Board (formerly the Interstate Commerce Commission), and the Federal Maritime Commission. Congress recognized a need for industry expertise and autonomy among members of the Surface Transportation Board. The qualifications for public servants at the helm of a transportation agency must be expertise in the transportation industry.

SHOULD MORE BE DONE?

Where possible, transportation firms should be privately owned, and publicly supervised only insofar as is absolutely necessary to protect important public interest values which do not find a high priority in a regime of *laissez-faire.* Yet some readers will conclude that this package of remedies goes too far, and exerts the government too deeply into the affairs of private enterprise. Others will conclude that this smorgasbord of remedies does not go far enough. Upon reading an earlier draft of these cures, economist Harvey Wexler wrote:

> It is impossible to have a rational pricing—one devoid of both destructive and monopolistic pricing as well as the critical undue discrimination—without regulation. As long as some carriers are willing (perhaps required) to price on an incremental basis, there cannot be a rational pricing system, and regulation is the *only* solution.
>
> In order to regulate pricing in a rational manner, the government must also regulate one of the following three: routes (entry), or capacity (schedules), or investment base and capitalization (a la classic styled utility regulation). It has to be *one* of these three and the first is the least oppressive, by a wide margin.[72]

Another economist who has attempted to come to grips with what a new regulatory regime would include is Robert Kuttner, who suggested the following regime:

> Regulators could set a zone of tolerable prices, to reflect actual costs more nearly. The same computers that make it possible for unregulated airlines to price-discriminate could enable regulators to calculate appropriate pricing zones, just a public-utility regulators do in other industries. Floors on prices would prevent cross-subsidy and ruinous competition. Ceilings would prevent opportunistic price-gouging. In between there could be a range of price and quality competition.[73]

Finally, we should ask, what would the most influential economist of the western world—Adam Smith—think of all this were he alive today? There is much economic mythology which equates Smith's views with those of *laissez-faire*. In fact, Smith believed that govern-

---

[72] Letter by Harvey Wexler to Paul Stephen Dempsey (May 5, 1995).
[73] Robert Kuttner, Everything For Sale: The Virtues and Limits of Markets 268 (1997).

ment could do quite a bit of good in improving the market's efficiency. In his enormously influential treatise, *Wealth of Nations,* Smith revealed that he believed government could legitimately protect the merchant marine, provide public goods (such as highways, harbors, bridges and canals), give a temporary monopoly to a firm developing commerce in a new and risky region, and punish and prevent dishonesty, violence and fraud.[74] While Smith lived before the dawn of commercial aviation, we can infer from much of what he endorsed that he might well find at least a few of the remedies suggested above acceptable.

THE DYNAMICS OF COMMERCIAL AVIATION IN THE NEW MILLENNIUM

One must caution any gaze into the crystal ball by recalling the words of Wilbur Wright: "I confess that in 1901, I said to my brother Orville that man would not fly for fifty years . . . . Ever since, I have distrusted myself and avoided all predictions."[75] Though predicting the future is a fool's game, current trends suggest several possible results in the 21st Century:

- Improved communications technologies will erode the business traffic base of airlines, leaving them gradually, but increasingly, more reliant on discretionary traffic, which is highly price sensitive.
- Both the number and market share of Southwest-clone low-cost, low-priced, linear route carriers will grow, although these carriers ultimately will not account for more than a fifth of the total U.S. air passenger market. Such growth will plateau, for the number of city-pair markets which can support nonstop service is finite.
- The United States will be served by many fewer than its current two dozen interior hubs.
- The surrender of wage and work rules by labor for equity at Northwest, TWA and United may give them a competitive cost advantage that the remaining major airlines will be forced to

---

[74] Herbert Stein, Remembering Adam Smith, Wall St. J., Apr. 6, 1994, at A20.
[75] Statement of Wilbur Wright in 1908, quoted in Newsweek (Jan. 27, 1997), at 86.

replicate. Labor will control or own significant equity in most of the major network U.S. carriers, which must restructure their costs if they are to grow, and survive. But workers will be disappointed if they expect to earn meaningful dividends from their airline stock portfolios. Paradoxically, employee ownership of the means of production is pure Marxism, hardly what free market neo-classical economists anticipated when they unleashed deregulation.
- Several major domestic network carriers will collapse or merge, leaving the industry more highly concentrated. This trend will be accelerated should fuel costs or interest rates rise significantly, or recession be prolonged.
- While the U.S. domestic market will not grow at the rates at which it grew in the 1980s, international aviation will grow robustly, particularly in the Pacific Rim.
- With mergers and bankruptcies, the number of major international carriers will shrink, each survivor having strategic alliances with network carriers and pseudo-carriers on other continents. Many regional carriers unable to join the surviving global megacarrier alliances will find survival challenging, if not impossible.
- The U.S. government will have to face up to its obligation to provide responsible oversight of this essential infrastructure industry to enable it to rationalize capacity and stabilize pricing. History is prologue.

These words were said by a former President of the Air Transport Association:

> Since air transport was launched into meteoric growth . . . of [the] private capital devoted to it . . . there remains today scarcely 50 percent. Since the beginning of air transport, a hundred scheduled lines have traversed the airways in a struggle to build this newest avenue of the sky. But today scarcely more than a score of those companies remain. The industry has been reduced to the very rock bottom of its financial resources . . . .

> There are only two ways whereby the necessary capital can be provided to this industry. One is the way toward which the governments of foreign lands increasingly tend—the way of mounting governmental subsidies, whereby public funds are poured without stint into air transport. The other way is the traditional American way, a way which invites the confidence of the investing public by providing a basic economic charter that promises the hope of stability and security, and orderly and intelligent growth under watchful governmental supervision.[76]

These words are as true today as when they were first spoken, only a few months before Congress passed the Civil Aeronautics Act of 1938, which for four decades allowed the U.S. airline industry to grow and prosper, and establish what was once universally acclaimed as the "world's finest system of transportation."

---

[76] Quoted in Paul Dempsey, Robert Hardaway & William Thoms, 1 Aviation Law & Regulation § 1.03 (1993).

INDEX

Abacus, 324, 435
Acker, Ed, 295
acquisitions; See market consolidation
administrative costs, 96, 302
administrative expenses, 357
advance purchase excursion fares [APEX], 293
advance purchase requirements, 297, 306
advertising, 23, 54, 61, 63, 72, 80, 83, 96, 167, 175, 178, 233, 246, 247, 270, 273, 295, 302, 318, 332, 339-346, 356, 357, 395, 399, 419, 432, 497
Aer Lingus, 164, 269, 436
Aero Sun International, 115
Aero Virgin Islands, 115
Aeroamerica, 114
Aeroflot, 276
Aeromexico, 383, 440, 446
agent reporting agreement [ARA], 334
aging aircraft, 15, 39, 110, 111, 123, 125, 155, 166, 173, 221, 223, 349, 365, 465
agriculture fee, 402
Air 21 Airlines, 118
Air Afrique, 440, 446
Air Atlanta, 116, 350
Air Austral, 446
Air Bahia, 114
Air Cal, 123, 128, 439
Air Caledonie, 446
Air Canada, 12, 44, 125, 162, 242, 275, 323, 324, 366, 380, 422, 423, 435, 438, 446, 448, 451
air cargo, 1, 2, 5-7, 21, 23, 27, 59, 61, 63, 64, 96, 137, 176, 188, 197, 232, 241, 251, 281, 287, 306, 317, 323, 331, 346, 352, 371, 412, 447, 478-480, 486, 487
  freight; See air freight
  mail; See air mail
  express; 64
air carriers, defined, 6
Air Charter, 446

Air Comores, 446
air express, See air cargo
Air Florida, 115, 120, 172, 295, 350
Air France, 19, 21, 23, 160, 164, 267, 272, 275, 323, 324, 382, 383, 403, 435-437, 440, 441, 446, 452, 453, 472, 473, 476
air freight, 5, 23, 27, 60, 64, 152, 161, 180, 184, 188, 190, 198, 231, 271, 287, 306, 317, 331, 336, 360, 402, 412, 478, 479, 480; See also air cargo
Air Gabon, 440, 446
Air India, 275, 436
Air Inter, 440, 446
Air Line Pilots Association [ALPA], 48, 386, 392
Air Madagascar, 446
air mail, 64, 96, 132, 192, 197, 198, 241, 255, 271, 310, 318, 339, 360, 398, 399, 401, 479; See also air cargo
Air Mauritius, 442, 446
Air New Orleans, 116
Air New Zealand, 362, 436, 441, 443
Air Niagara, 350
Air North, 115
Air One, 116, 350
Air Pacific, 443
Air Partners, 125, 161
Air Pennsylvania, 115
Air Russia, 442, 444
Air South, 115, 116, 350
Air Tahiti, 446
Air Tchad, 446
Air Traffic Conference [ATC], 330
air traffic and air space congestion, 25, 61, 62, 112, 190, 194, 209, 251, 252, 312, 434, 466, 470, 494, 498
air traffic control system, 68, 155, 404
air traffic system cost, 404
Air Train, 350
Air Transport Association [ATA], 3, 4, 6, 33, 49, 50, 52, 96, 97, 98, 101, 105, 106, 109, 111, 139, 154, 289, 321, 329,

330, 322, 329, 330, 333, 356, 358, 405, 409, 413, 441, 457, 465, 468, 473, 476, 504
air transportation, defined, 6
Air UK, 441, 452
Air Vermont, 115
Air Wisconsin, 16, 129, 351, 451
Air21, 350
Airbus aircraft,
A-340, 363
A-319, 366
A-320, 222, 366
Airbus Industrie, 110, 154, 160, 222, 225, 363, 366
AirCal, 238
aircraft leases; See leases
aircraft utilization, 155, 209, 215, 250, 253, 306; See also utilization of personnel and equipment
Airline Deregulation Act of 1978 [ADA], 108, 113, 119, 234, 289, 314, 342, 347, 427, 464, 470, 483, 486, 492, 493, 496
Airline Industry Resources, 469
airline industry's annual financing need, 157
Airline Tariff Publishing Company [ATPCO], 322, 327
Airlines Reporting Corporation [ARC], 333
airport and airway trust fund, 162, 496
airports, 3, 10, 11, 14, 15, 21, 32, 35, 38, 61, 63, 68, 76, 77, 79, 80, 88, 93, 102, 112, 119, 155, 163, 171, 192-194, 200-206, 208, 209, 211, 213, 218, 231, 245, 250-253, 256, 266, 269, 272, 273, 288, 291, 310, 352, 357, 360, 361, 366, 382, 398, 399, 402, 405, 409, 425, 428, 430, 434, 443, 444, 455, 466, 467, 470, 471, 475, 476, 478, 480, 484, 489, 494, 497-500
access, 498
capacity; See air traffic and air space capacity
gates; See gates
fees; See landing fees; see also costs
facilities; See terminals
leases; See leases
operations, 3
slots; See landing slots
AirTran, 129, 346
Alaska Airlines, 9, 10, 116, 140, 143, 156, 223, 276, 278, 345, 346, 377
Alitalia, 22, 164, 275, 323, 435, 436, 441, 443
modes of transport; See alternative modes of transportation

All Nippon Airways [ANA], 20, 21, 52, 143, 176, 275, 280, 292, 343, 381, 383, 406, 411, 435, 437, 441
Allegheny Airlines, 7, 17, 204, 346
Allegis, 16, 126, 272
Allen, Ronald, 147, 347, 373, 392
alliances, 13, 14, 17, 27, 42, 74, 168, 187, 213, 239, 324, 407, 411-423, 433, 435, 436, 439-441, 443- 450, 452, 495, 500, 504; See also international alliances
Allied Pilots Association, 95
allocated cost, 34, 42, 57-59, 64-66, 76, 89, 90, 284, 291, 460, 461, 483, 486, 495, 499
ALM Antillian Airlines, 441
Aloha Airlines, 9, 264, 278
Altair, 115, 350
alternative modes of transportation, 25, 58, 181, 194, 231, 252
Amadeus, 323, 324, 435
America OnLine, 340
America West Airlines [AmWest], 9, 10, 19, 101, 113, 117-119, 125, 129, 130, 139, 140, 143, 145, 156, 161, 205, 210, 212, 223, 225, 234, 276, 278, 340, 344, 345, 347-350, 353, 361, 362, 364, 365, 367, 373, 375-378, 380, 389, 390, 406, 427, 438, 440
America West Express, 363
American Airlines [AMR], 3, 7-11, 14, 16-22, 35, 36, 44, 47- 49, 51, 52, 58, 66, 68, 85, 95, 100-102, 109, 110, 113-116, 123, 124, 127-130, 139, 140, 143, 145, 151, 153, 154, 156, 163, 172, 176, 190, 195, 200-202, 204-212, 215-219, 223-225, 227-232, 237, 238, 241, 244, 245, 248, 250, 251, 254, 258, 259, 266, 268, 271, 272, 276, 278, 280, 288, 290, 291, 293-295, 302, 310, 319-321, 323, 327, 329, 331-346, 350, 351, 353-355, 362, 363, 365-368, 373, 375, 377-380, 383, 384, 387, 388, 390-392, 397, 401, 407, 411, 414-417, 422, 423, 426, 431, 432, 436, 437, 439, 440, 444, 445, 448-453, 455, 460, 482-484, 488, 493, 505
American Airlines' Value Pricing, 109, 244, 290, 291, 302
American Automobile Association [AAA], 190
American Eagle, 219, 245
American International Airlines, 115, 350
American Society of Travel Agents [ASTA], 332, 432
American Trans Air [ATA], 9, 351, 353

Index

amortization, 96, 135, 149, 357
Amsterdam Shiphol Airport, 209
Amtrak, 481, 488
AmWest Partners L.P., 125, 129
annual quality rating, 276
annual report, 14, 28, 52, 67, 106, 132, 133, 153, 162, 194, 222, 225, 269, 323, 324, 327, 457, 458, 465
Ansett, 161, 436-438, 441
anti-government protest; See distrust of government
antitrust, 24, 119, 244, 246, 288, 291, 321, 328, 329, 409, 411, 412, 416, 417, 419, 428, 433, 437, 448-450, 473, 488, 494, 499
antitrust enforcement, 494
antitrust immunity, 409, 411, 416, 437, 438, 444, 447, 449, 450, 472, 474
Apollo, 17, 190, 321, 424, 426
Apollo Travel Services Partnership, 323
Arab Oil Embargo of 1973, 103, 108, 458
Arrow Airways, 116, 350
Arthur, Brian, 73
Asian market, 13, 49, 155, 216, 324, 410, 412, 415, 423, 435, 436, 476
assetless airlines, 159
assets, 12, 41, 119-123, 126, 131, 133-135, 143, 145, 152, 159-161, 163, 241, 253, 443, 450, 495
Association of Retail Travel Agents, 432
Astec Air East, 115
Atlantic Coast Airlines, 351
Atlantic Gulf, 115
Atlantic Southeast, 351, 451
Atlantic Southeast Airlines [ASA], 162, 219
Attali, Bernard, 382, 453
attributes of commercial aviation, 459
Australian Airlines, 443
Austrian Airlines, 70, 89, 164, 381, 436, 437, 441, 445-447, 449, 451
automatic travel agency reservations system, 321
available seat mile [ASM], 18, 19, 60, 61, 63, 80, 112, 150, 170, 176, 214, 218-222, 226, 235, 240, 266, 281, 289, 294, 312, 314, 344, 349, 353, 363, 364, 367, 370, 372, 373, 375-380, 384, 465
Aviateca Airlines, 433, 441
aviation fuel, 11, 24, 25, 27, 43, 47, 59-62, 65, 67, 68, 70, 96, 103, 108, 109, 111, 112, 144, 153, 155, 159, 163, 179-181, 211, 214, 220-222, 239, 241, 250, 289, 311, 312, 314, 343, 348, 355-360, 366, 367, 371, 395, 403, 404, 406, 443, 456, 458, 459, 465, 467, 476, 477, 487, 494, 498
fuel consumption, 60, 62, 112, 155, 180, 211, 221, 312, 314, 487, 494
fuel cost, 24, 25, 47, 103, 108, 109, 153, 181, 250, 311, 366, 367, 403, 406, 458, 459, 465, 477, 483, 504
fuel efficiency, 11, 27, 220-222, 313, 366, 466
fuel swapping contracts, 153
aviation policy, 69, 413, 456, 471, 472, 474, 477, 480
aviation security; See security
Ayling, Robert, 110, 406, 417

Babbitt, Randy, 48, 134, 238, 390, 392, 393, 395, 402, 477
baggage, 23, 28, 63, 67, 79, 109, 110, 189, 192, 193, 218, 252, 253, 256, 263, 265, 270, 273, 276, 278, 279, 287, 357, 360, 361, 371, 372, 421, 422, 425, 431, 479, 500
baggage handling, 23, 276, 279, 357, 360
checked baggage, 193, 256, 278
lost luggage, 372
Baggaley, Philip, 47, 61, 99, 100, 102, 138, 146, 149, 150, 152, 154, 165
Baiada, Michael, 404
Bailey, Elizabeth, 69, 72, 74-76, 83, 313, 455
Baker, Robert, 220, 221, 254, 256
Bakes, Phillip, 85
balance sheet, 13, 26, 122, 125, 131-133, 138-142, 145-150, 152, 157, 160, 165, 243, 302, 355, 394, 458, 462, 473, 477, 488
Baliles Commission; See National Commission To Ensure A Strong Competitive Airline Industry
Baliles, Gerald, 410, 455, 456
Banfe, Charles, 25, 26, 131, 133-135, 171, 174, 177-179, 181, 182, 249, 251, 252, 285, 286, 290, 296
bankruptcy, 10-12, 16, 44, 47, 48, 65, 93, 102, 113, 114, 118, 119, 121, 122, 126, 127, 130, 145, 147, 150, 152, 154, 160, 161, 166, 206, 217, 234, 264, 289, 344, 348, 349, 354, 386, 389, 390, 395, 448, 458, 462, 474, 483, 486, 488, 489, 495, 504
chapter 7, 114-118
chapter 11, 10, 12, 15, 44, 48, 102, 113, 114, 115, 116, 117, 118, 119, 121,

509

122, 124, 126, 147, 154, 160, 264, 348, 349, 386, 390, 489, 495
chapter "22", 12
section 1110 of the bankruptcy code, 152
Bar Harbor Airlines, 117
Barnum, P.T., 317, 343
barriers to market entry and exit, 32, 61, 69, 71, 72, 74, 76, 80, 330, 419, 454, 457
Bates, Dave, 95
the Beatles, 195
belly cargo, 59, 61, 231, 256, 271, 306, 317, 344, 479
below-cost pricing, 66, 352, 486, 494
benchmarking, 241, 357
bereavement fares, 308
Bermuda Agreement, 408, 409, 413, 414, 449, 472
Best Airlines, 350
Bethune, Gordon, 12, 249, 264, 347, 368, 376
Beyer, Barbara, 212
Big Sky Airlines, 117
bilateral agreements, 89, 216, 288, 408-410, 412, 414, 415, 417, 418, 433, 442, 448-450, 472-475, 478-480, 495
blocked space, 422
board of directors, 175, 187, 373, 392
boarding process, 193, 198, 230, 263, 265, 301, 303, 308, 338, 360-362, 368, 398, 399, 422, 428, 430
Boeing aircraft,
  B-707, 108, 141, 321
  B-727, 61, 107, 132, 225, 232, 343
  B-737, 14, 16, 28, 39, 61, 62, 82, 221, 225, 235, 289, 346, 349, 351, 360, 361, 364, 366, 371, 372, 392
  B-747, 5, 17, 39, 60, 61, 62, 103, 108, 195, 225, 232, 234, 310, 365, 366, 368, 403
  B-757, 366, 367
  B-767, 160, 203, 261, 366, 367
  B-777, 17
Boeing Air Transport Company, 5, 14, 17, 28, 33, 61, 107, 108, 110, 132, 154, 155, 160, 221, 222, 225, 232, 235, 261, 264, 289, 321, 482, 483
Bonderman group, 10, 161, 264
Bonderman, David, 10, 12, 119, 125, 161, 264
Borenstein, Severin, 38, 77, 83
Borman, Frank, 346
Boston Logan Field, 18
Bowen, Brent, 276

brand loyalty, 58, 227, 265, 296, 342, 348, 460
Braniff Airways, 7, 11, 115, 117, 121, 127, 140, 206, 217, 234, 246, 343, 344, 349, 350
Brannigan, Martha, 130, 235, 347, 352, 371, 373, 392
Branson, Richard, 246
break-even load factor, 41, 66, 76, 137, 222, 240, 281, 286, 294, 295, 298, 299, 362
Brenner, Melvin, 34, 36, 38, 45, 62, 65, 80, 98, 250, 293
Breyer, Stephen, 85
British Air; See British Airways
British Airways [BA], 12, 17-23, 44, 52, 110, 124, 140, 160, 161, 164, 165, 212, 224, 246, 262, 263, 267, 271, 275, 323, 346, 380, 383, 406, 413, 414, 416-418, 420, 423, 432, 435-445, 449-452, 477
British Caledonian Airlines, 440, 442
British Midland Airlines, 436, 441, 451
British Overseas Airways Corporation [BOAC], 444
British/American alliance, 451
Britt Airways, 12, 117, 234, 263, 431, 439
Brookings Institute, 313-316, 463, 464, 483
Bruggisser, Philippe, 445
B-scale wage rates; See two tier wage structure
buddy passes, 310
bundled services, 249, 272, 273
Bureau of Pricing and Domestic Aviation, 69
bureaucracies, 22
Burr, Donald, 121, 234, 262
Bush, George, 433, 448, 501
business class, 52, 54, 96, 170, 174, 198, 226, 227, 262, 266-268, 270, 280, 294, 304, 310
Business Express Airlines, 118
business travel, 38, 39, 48, 51, 52, 56-60, 68, 81, 169, 170, 188, 189, 193, 194, 197, 198, 214, 215, 222, 226-228, 230, 259, 266, 268, 273-275, 282, 283, 286-288, 292-295, 297, 298, 302, 305-308, 313, 317, 325, 345, 365, 382, 400, 401, 459, 460, 463, 476, 483
Byrd, Robert, 470

CAB/DOT Handbook of Airline Statistics, 190
cabotage, 42, 239, 408, 409, 411, 418, 421, 450, 475, 481

Index

defined, 408
CALite, 170, 211, 247, 264, 359
Cameroon Airlines, 446
Canadian Airlines, 231, 423, 436, 437, 440, 448, 451
Canadian market, 128, 129
Canteen Corporation, 15, 126
capacity, 24, 32-35, 38-44, 48, 57, 58, 60-62, 64-68, 70, 72, 77, 84-87, 89, 91, 92, 97, 103, 108, 109, 111, 140, 176-178, 183, 190, 198, 204, 208, 209, 211, 220, 235, 237, 241-245, 251, 282, 288, 289, 292-294, 298, 301, 309, 323, 325, 349, 352, 364, 406, 413-415, 419, 457-459, 462, 467, 472, 473, 475-477, 481-483, 486, 488, 489, 494, 498, 499, 502, 504; See also excess capacity
Capital Airways, 293
capital investment, 11, 12, 65, 124, 125, 132, 143, 213, 349, 353, 412, 462; See also equity
capital leases, 141, 142
capitalization, 134, 138-140, 142, 148
Capitol Air, 116
car rental, 18, 227, 271-274, 323
Card, Andrew, 412
cargo; See air cargo
cargo air carriers, 352, 479; See belly cargo; See also combination air carriers
Cargolux, 447
Caribbean Express, 117
Carlzon, Jan, 189
Carnival Air, 350, 423
carrier services agreement [CSA], 334
cartel, 93, 417, 433, 472
Carter, Jimmy, 69, 234, 296, 409, 448, 453
Cascade Airways, 116
cash flow, 44, 119, 125, 126, 132, 133, 136, 148, 149, 156, 157, 181, 243, 486
categories of aviation, 6
Cathay Pacific, 20, 22, 275, 310, 324, 380, 411, 435, 436, 441
Cayman Airways, 436
CC Air, 117
Century 21, 15, 126, 160
certificate of public convenience and necessity [PC&N], 6, 89, 130, 352, 413
characteristics of major airlines, 9
charter air carriers, 7, 293, 335, 413
charter and tour group operations, 6, 7, 232, 273, 294, 311, 315, 332, 333, 335, 447, 448, 505
Checchi, Alfred, 119, 122, 123, 128, 161
Chicago & Northwestern Railroad, 393

Chicago Airlines, 116
Chicago Convention of 1944, 146, 154, 157, 289, 311, 380, 407, 412, 413
Chicago O'Hare Airport, 11, 15, 16, 203, 209, 252, 422
Chief Executive Officer [CEO], 12, 17, 31, 35, 42, 66, 78, 95, 120, 121, 124, 132, 147, 167, 174-176, 186, 215, 233, 236, 238, 249, 258, 261, 264, 280, 309, 341, 344, 346, 347, 354, 366, 368, 373, 384, 392, 394, 406, 407, 416, 445, 453, 455, 460
Chief Financial Officer [CFO], 175
Chief Operating Officer [COO], 175, 186
China Airlines, 423, 435, 436
Chrysler Corporation, 346, 488
CityFlyer Express, 444
city-pair markets, 20, 35, 39, 40, 42, 61, 63, 65, 67, 72, 74-76, 80-83, 88, 170, 172-174, 180, 190, 198, 206, 208, 211, 213, 214, 220, 222, 235, 239, 281, 294, 298, 309, 328-430, 352, 359, 428-430, 439, 444, 450, 461, 471, 473, 479, 482, 494, 497, 499, 500, 503
Civil Aeronautics Act of 1938, 505
Civil Aeronautics Board [CAB], 16, 69, 85, 95, 108, 114, 120, 142, 234, 284, 313, 318, 321, 331, 337, 431, 457, 464, 485
Civil Reserve Air Fleet [CRAF], 140, 210, 362, 365, 377, 475, 488, 495, 498
Civil Rights Act of 1964, 470
Clark, Kimberly, 215
classes of service, 56, 173, 174, 226, 267, 336; See also first class; business class; coach class
clearinghouse, 322, 333
Clinton, Bill, 110, 256, 410, 413, 417, 433, 449, 455, 484
coach class, 96, 198, 226, 266, 293, 304, 463
Cochise Airlines, 115
code-sharing, 79, 81, 170, 208, 213, 218, 220, 273, 326, 330, 383, 392, 410, 411, 414, 415, 418-428, 430, 432-435, 437, 443, 444, 447, 450, 471, 472, 474, 497, 500
Comair, 219, 351, 363, 451
combination air carriers, 61, 63, 197, 271, 281, 412; See cargo air carriers
Combs Airways, 115
commerce, 2, 480, 482, 484, 485, 488, 500, 503
commodity, 41, 54, 64, 66, 153, 159, 167-169, 265, 273, 342, 460, 469, 486

511

common carrier, 6
communications, 2, 40, 52, 194, 271, 341, 454, 455, 457, 482, 484, 485, 487, 503
commuter air carriers, 7, 9, 18, 273, 411, 428, 431, 471
commuter aircraft, 7, 9
companion fares, 305
competitive advertising, 341
competitive equilibrium, 90, 92
complete deregulation, 491-493
CompuServe, 340
computer reservations systems [CRS], 10, 17, 25, 27, 28, 67, 72, 73, 76, 80, 82, 83, 96, 126-128, 168, 172-174, 190, 197, 231, 232, 245, 272, 296, 298, 318, 321-331, 333, 338-340, 348, 357, 383, 395, 397-401, 411, 419, 421-427, 430, 432, 434, 435, 437, 446, 460, 465, 472, 481, 498, 500
Condor Airlines, 441, 447
Connectaire, 116
Conquest Airlines, 118
Conrail, 488, 496
consolidators, 180, 333, 336-338
constant costs, 59, 148
consumers, 3, 15, 21, 23, 25, 28, 31, 36, 38, 40, 47, 54, 55, 61, 64, 66, 70-72, 74, 76, 82-84, 88, 89, 92, 102, 107, 108, 153, 168-172, 176, 178, 181, 187-189, 196, 199, 211, 214, 226-230, 241, 242, 244-246, 249, 252, 257, 259, 268, 270, 273, 279, 282, 283, 286, 289, 291, 294, 302, 306, 309, 312-315, 328, 331-337, 340-345, 348, 359, 367, 369, 385, 397- 401, 403, 409, 418, 419, 422-428, 430-434, 449, 450, 454-456, 458-461, 463, 464, 467, 468, 471, 472, 474, 483-487, 492-494, 496, 497, 499
abuses, 492
benefits, 102, 289, 456, 483
complaints, 15, 172, 241, 279, 419
confidence, 22, 47, 107, 153, 186, 235, 459, 505
demand, 35, 39, 171, 195, 241, 286, 294, 483
groups, 302, 468
preference, 170, 189, 191, 192, 194, 195
satisfaction, 178, 252
spending, 3
welfare, 463, 466, 472, 494
Consumer Price Index [CPI], 315
contestable market theory, 31, 32, 68, 70, 72, 74, 75, 77, 79, 83, 84, 454

Continental Airlines, 7-12, 18-20, 22, 28, 44, 101, 113, 115, 117-121, 125-130, 139, 140, 143, 145, 147, 154, 156, 160-162, 170, 172, 173, 176, 205, 206, 210-212, 219, 221, 223-225, 234, 237, 241, 242, 247, 249, 263, 264, 268, 272, 278, 324, 344, 347, 349, 359, 361, 362, 365, 367, 368, 373, 376-378, 380, 386-391, 427, 433, 435, 436, 438-440, 443, 446, 448, 452, 457, 466, 483
Continental Lite, 28
Convention on International Civil Aviation, 407
Coral Air, 114
core theory, 32, 90, 91, 92, 93
corporate culture, 11, 21, 130, 175, 176, 224, 232, 237, 260, 263, 420
corporate downsizing, 44, 52, 195, 415
corporate raiders, 16, 119, 121, 125, 126, 136, 161, 272, 495
costs, 11, 14, 15, 17, 18, 23-25, 28, 31, 32, 34, 36, 38, 40- 44, 47, 53, 54, 57-66, 68, 70, 72-80, 82, 85, 87, 91-93, 95, 97, 103, 108-112, 119, 124, 127, 130, 132, 135, 138, 141, 143, 146-148, 150, 151, 153, 155, 159, 163, 167, 168, 173, 178, 181, 183, 187, 190, 195, 196, 200, 206, 208, 211, 213, 214, 219-222, 224-228, 230, 232-235, 237-242, 244, 245, 247, 248, 250, 251, 256-258, 261, 262, 264, 265, 266, 268, 269, 273, 274, 281-289, 291, 292, 294, 295, 299, 301-309, 311-315, 318, 326-328, 332, 338-341, 344, 345, 411, 412, 415, 419, 420, 428, 442, 444, 447, 455, 457-461, 464, 465, 467, 469, 471, 476, 477, 479, 481, 483, 485- 488, 494-497, 499, 500, 502-504
available seat mile cost, 467
cost allocation; See allocated costs
cost containment, 168, 358, 406
direct costs, 130
indirect costs, 130
interest expenses, 12, 123, 144, 150, 161
joint costs, 60, 486
minimum average costs, 92
non-operating costs; See fixed costs
operating costs; See operating expenses; see also variable costs
sunk costs, 74, 76, 86, 91
Covia Partnership, 323, 328
Crandall, Robert L., 35, 42, 44, 48, 56, 57, 63, 65, 66, 95, 102, 176, 180, 198, 210,

Index

213, 238, 248, 251, 266, 291, 294, 298, 354, 384, 387, 416, 417, 460, 462
credence good, 54, 169, 270, 460
Cross, Robert, 303
cross-subsidization, 68
CSA Airlines, 334, 446
current liabilities, 134
current ratio, 134
customer relations, 26, 28, 40, 77, 81, 135, 173, 178, 180, 188, 204, 213, 227, 228, 230, 231, 235, 257-263, 268-270, 274, 291, 294, 301, 303, 326, 333, 335, 337-339, 342, 368, 422, 486
customer satisfaction, 28, 172, 189, 266
customer service, 175

Daedalus, 233
Dallas Love Field, 14
Dallas/Fort Worth International Airport, 204
Dan Air, 442, 443
DATAS II, 321
Davies, Ron, 176
Davis, Marvin, 124
de Lisser, Eleena, 324, 347, 352, 371, 373
debt, 12, 15, 18, 21, 27, 39, 44, 48, 97, 100, 102, 113, 119, 120, 122-125, 127, 133-135, 138-143, 145-153, 157, 158, 160, 162-165, 167, 181, 234, 235, 241, 243, 289, 312, 314, 356, 448, 462, 465, 467, 477, 481, 482, 488, 495
  debt service, 121, 467
  debt-to-capital ratio, 134, 139
  debt-to-equity ratio, 121, 134, 139, 146, 495
  long-term obligations, 12
delay, 62, 64, 209, 241, 252, 279, 313, 424, 467, 480, 494
Delta Air Lines, 7-9, 12, 13, 18-22, 44, 58, 83, 100-102, 113, 114, 122-125, 128-130, 139-141, 143, 145-147, 151, 156, 172, 176, 202, 204-206, 210, 212, 217-220, 223-225, 229, 236, 248, 260, 261, 268, 276, 278, 309, 321, 324, 329, 338, 344-347, 352, 353, 359, 362, 364-368, 370-373, 377, 378, 383, 384, 392, 397, 402, 411, 436-440, 444-447, 449-452
Delta/Dwarfs alliance, 451
demand, 4, 24, 28, 31-36, 39-41, 43, 45, 47, 49, 52, 53, 56, 58, 60, 64, 65, 68, 71, 81, 91-93, 97, 107-109, 111, 119, 144, 148, 167, 168, 170, 171, 173, 176, 177, 183, 187, 188, 194, 195, 197-199, 212, 214, 220, 240-242, 247, 249-251, 282, 284, 286, 287, 292- 299, 301, 306, 307, 309, 310, 318, 328, 337, 338, 341, 348, 353, 362, 392, 394, 400, 406, 408, 444, 459, 462, 483, 486, 487, 497, 498
  cyclical, 24, 34, 91, 107, 250
  derived, 24, 56, 168, 188, 459
  growth, 5
  passenger, 4
  demand curve, 68, 71
denied boarding, 276, 301, 303, 307
Department of Defense [DOD], 162
Department of Justice [DOJ], 417
Department of Transportation [DOT], 7, 9, 76, 80, 102, 113, 114, 119, 122, 123, 125, 130, 132, 162, 190, 209, 241, 252, 279, 303, 322, 326-328, 330, 332, 336, 337, 342, 352, 403, 404, 412, 417, 418, 424, 425, 427, 428, 431-434, 447-450, 463, 470-474, 478, 480, 481, 501
depreciation, 96, 135, 136, 144, 149, 239, 357
destructive competition, 13, 32, 68, 70, 84-86, 92, 457, 459, 486; See predation
Deutsch BA, 442
DHL International, 447
Dickerson, Thomas, 331
Digman, Lester, 179, 185
dilution, 298
direct air carriers, 6
direct sales, 338, 399
discounted fare, 72, 288, 296, 297, 310
Discovery Airlines, 350
discretionary spending, 54, 459
discretionary travelers, 38, 45, 56, 64, 159, 189, 283, 286
displacement time, 326
disposable personal income, 199
distribution, 27, 65, 82, 90, 96, 132, 159, 167, 168, 172, 173, 177, 178, 181, 184, 246, 259, 292, 313, 314, 318, 332, 334, 336-340, 342, 480
  distribution costs, 349, 395, 397, 465
  distribution systems, 401
distrust of government, 453, 456
Dobbs Kitchens, 380
Dodd, Graham, 136
Dolphin Airlines, 115
domestic market, 3-5, 7-11, 13, 18, 24, 31, 32, 36, 41, 44, 45, 47, 49-53, 69, 89, 97, 100, 103, 109, 122, 139, 141, 159, 180, 190, 192, 196, 198, 200, 206, 210, 212, 215-218, 228, 230, 239, 245, 252, 256, 266, 269, 275, 283, 296, 321, 322, 330, 333, 338, 354, 361, 363, 367, 375, 392, 402, 418, 421, 427, 431, 439, 443,

513

446, 465, 468, 472-476, 478, 487, 496, 501, 504
Dorgan, Byron, 114
Douglas aircraft,
  DC-10, 103, 108, 141, 234, 363, 364
  DC-2, 364
  DC-3, 252, 319, 364
  DC-4, 293
  DC-8, 108, 343
  DC-9, 44, 107, 215, 235, 268, 364, 365, 366
Douglas Aircraft Company, 52, 364
Dragonair, 441
dry lease; See leases
Dukakis, Michael, 448
dumb equity, 439, 474
duty rigs, 375

early railroad industry, 492
Eastern Airlines, 7, 8, 11-13, 15, 18, 20, 44, 101, 113, 117, 119-121, 123, 124, 126-130, 132, 139-141, 147, 150, 156, 160-162, 176, 206, 217, 224, 234, 276, 306, 321, 324, 329, 346, 349, 385-390, 433, 439, 457, 473, 483
Eastwind Airlines, 350
economic concentration, 83, 86, 87, 97, 204, 208, 288, 291, 428, 470, 471, 483, 485, 486, 489, 493, 504; See also market consolidation
economic characteristics of the airline industry, 31, 32, 66
economic growth, 1, 2, 13, 52, 53, 90, 288, 455
economic multiplier, 53, 112
economic rationalization, 39, 112, 462, 493, 494, 502
economic regulation, 4, 7, 26, 32, 69, 84, 86, 89, 92, 97, 109, 130, 368, 456, 466, 489, 491-493, 501
economic theory, 69
economies of density, 61, 63, 227
economies of scale and scope, 32, 36, 61, 62, 69, 70, 74, 80-82, 91, 111, 182, 187, 197, 220, 231, 233, 271, 273, 342, 359, 362, 383, 419, 441, 454, 457, 479, 480
economies of size, 61, 63, 419
economy class, 174
EEE fares, 307, 310
efficiency, 2, 11, 27, 62, 68, 89, 90, 92, 112, 135, 175, 220, 221, 253, 257, 261, 348, 366, 367, 419, 454, 463, 466, 467, 472, 479, 480, 503
Eisenhower, Dwight D., 185

El Al, 275, 425
elapsed time, 326
elasticity of demand, 24, 48, 49, 53, 56, 58, 64, 97, 108, 170, 188, 189, 282, 283, 286, 287, 294, 295, 297, 304, 459, 487, 497
Elders IXL, 123
Emerald Airlines, 115, 350
eminent domain, 498
Empire Airlines, 350
Employee Stock Ownership Plan [ESOP], 17, 162, 389, 390, 393
employment, 3, 11-13, 15, 17, 28, 47, 51, 57, 58, 71, 73, 76, 121, 123, 124, 132, 133, 149, 154, 161, 163, 175, 181, 187-189, 192, 209, 221, 228, 233, 235, 237, 238, 246, 247, 249, 256-266, 270, 273, 283, 290, 291, 310, 314-316, 319, 326, 345, 346, 348, 354, 361, 363, 367, 369, 371, 373, 376, 380-385, 387-394, 418, 423, 454, 457, 459, 462, 463, 472, 476, 477, 481, 482, 484, 504
entrepreneurship, 74, 131, 148, 176, 257
environmental regulation, 32, 93
equipment utilization, 312, 361, 367
equity, 12, 14, 17, 21, 39, 90, 119, 120, 122, 123, 125, 130-135, 138, 139, 145, 146, 148, 149, 154, 159-162, 165, 167, 168, 181, 213, 218, 233, 274, 324, 375, 389, 390, 394, 395, 412, 416, 423, 435, 437, 439, 440, 442, 446-448, 450, 468, 474, 478, 487, 494, 495, 497, 503
equity alliances, 168; See also alliances
ESG Aviation Services, 22, 62, 98, 105, 109, 111, 112, 125, 139, 141, 144, 155, 170, 225, 234, 288, 290, 305, 312
essential air services program [EAS], 470
essential facility, 329
e-ticket, 339
European carriers, 323, 379, 446
European Civil Aviation Conference, 432, 434
European Economic Community [EEC], 162, 410, 496
European market, 49, 50, 129, 236, 476
European Quality Alliance, 445
European Union [EU], 13, 164, 410, 418
European Wise Men Committee (*le Comite des Sages*), 410
evaluative research, 315
Excellair Airlines, 115
excess capacity, 33-35, 39-42, 44, 58, 62, 64, 65, 68, 70, 84-87, 89, 92, 97, 242, 244, 245, 413, 459, 467, 472, 486, 489, 494

Index

exclusive dealing arrangements, 245, 497, 500
Exec Express, 117
Express Airlines, 452

Far West Airlines, 116
fare buckets, 244, 297, 299, 303, 309, 328, 333
fare restrictions, 305, 330
fare wars, 41, 47, 54, 109, 296
fares, 2, 28, 32, 47, 49, 56, 58-60, 67, 76, 77, 83, 96, 102, 108, 171, 190, 197, 208, 209, 214, 236, 237, 242, 244-246, 260, 269, 280, 283, 285, 286, 288, 290, 291, 293-298, 300-302, 304-307, 310, 313, 315, 322, 328, 330, 332, 333, 336-338, 340-342, 345, 348-350, 354, 396, 397, 400, 401, 409, 413, 417, 421, 450, 458, 464, 469, 472, 483, 494, 495, 497, 499, 500
  low fares, 28, 53, 64, 72, 76, 108, 119, 197, 245, 285, 288, 292, 294, 297, 305, 308, 310, 311, 314, 337, 340, 348, 353, 409, 428, 456, 463, 484, 495, 496, 499, 502
Federal Aviation Act of 1958, 102, 113, 432, 434, 485, 496
Federal Aviation Administration [FAA], 76, 113, 236, 253, 254, 256, 259, 268, 274, 368, 386, 404
Federal Aviation Regulations [FARs], 178, 253
  Part 121, 7, 118
  Part 135, 9
  Part 241, 130
Federal Express [FedEx], 21-23, 64, 128, 248, 346
feeder air carriers, 18, 154, 161, 173, 218, 219, 361, 443
Feldman, Alvin, 120, 121, 291, 412, 420
Ferris, Richard, 16, 121, 272, 387
Fidelity Investments, 161
fifth-freedom rights, 16, 473, 474
finance, 50, 124, 125, 141, 142, 151, 152, 156-160, 162, 163, 165, 175, 178, 220
Financial Accounting Standards Board, 142
  SFAS No. 13, 142
Finnair, 275, 436
first class, 54, 90, 96, 170, 171, 174, 193, 198, 214, 226, 227, 230, 267, 268, 287, 291, 293, 294, 304, 364, 402
fitness, 76, 102, 113, 119, 122, 125, 495
fixed costs, 34, 40-42, 47, 57, 59, 65-67, 68, 85, 91, 148, 206, 220, 239, 266, 288, 291, 294, 295, 299, 306, 309, 311, 387, 460, 486
flag air carriers, 134, 160, 164, 204, 217, 255, 316, 420, 426, 438, 472, 473, 475, 476, 478
Flagship Express Airlines, 118
flight attendants, 113, 136, 169, 193, 258, 259, 262, 264, 265, 269, 276, 343, 357, 361, 368, 371, 381, 382, 383, 384, 385, 387, 388, 390
flight crews, 54, 59, 63, 113, 159, 177, 193, 221, 234, 252, 253, 257-259, 263, 274, 302, 315, 354, 357, 360, 381-384, 421, 443, 455, 465, 476; See also pilots
flight dispatch, 357
flight operations, 28, 96, 175, 177, 178, 357, 381
flight standards, 175
Florida Airlines, 114
Florida Express, 350
Florida West, 118
Flying Tigers Airline, 127, 128, 346
food and beverage service, 15, 23, 27, 28, 54, 55, 63, 64, 67, 96, 126, 152, 160, 169, 172-175, 192, 193, 226, 228, 231, 250, 253, 257-259, 263, 265, 267-271, 274, 275, 278- 280, 283, 287, 296, 304, 315, 348, 354, 356, 357, 360, 361, 367, 368, 380, 446, 465, 479
Ford, Wendell, 432
forecasting, 177, 180, 182, 183, 198-222, 282, 294, 301, 389
foreign air carriers, 119, 161, 162, 329, 379, 382, 409, 418, 421, 436, 439, 440, 473-475, 478, 496
foreign ownership, 418, 448, 450, 472, 474
foreign travel, 216
form 41 reports, 130, 142, 190; See Uniform System of Accounts and Reports
fortress hubs, 204, 208, 460, 467
Fortune 500 companies, 291, 468, 483
Fortune 1000 companies, 57, 72
four major premises of sound regulation, 485
France's Institute of Air Transport, 24
free flight, 404
free-trade, 410
freight; See air freight; See also air cargo
freight forwarders, 331
frequency of service, 24, 28, 34, 35, 39, 40, 61, 64, 81, 88, 173, 180, 190, 196, 209, 213, 214, 245, 268, 287, 312, 313, 315, 415, 427, 459, 463, 467, 471, 499
Frequent Flyer magazine, 231

frequent flyer mile, 228, 229, 281, 401
frequent flyer programs, 10, 27, 36, 38, 51, 56, 58, 81, 82, 96, 140, 146, 170, 171, 173, 191-194, 197, 227-232, 241, 246, 262, 267, 268, 271, 273, 289, 309, 336, 340, 341, 348, 415, 421, 435, 436, 460, 484, 495, 498, 500
Frontier Airlines, 7, 12, 116, 121, 126, 127, 129, 131, 172, 224, 234, 237, 246, 247, 263, 344, 346, 439
Fruhan, William, 36
fuel, See aviation fuel
full service carrier, 173
fungible commodity, 40, 54, 55, 64, 159, 168-170, 337, 342, 459, 460
funnel flights, 422-426, 428, 430, 431, 433, 434

G-7 nations, 383, 465, 483
Galileo, 318, 323, 326, 435, 437
Galileo International Partnership, 323
Gallagher, Maurice, 195
Gallagher, Thomas, 52, 53, 111, 112, 156, 196
game theory, 90
Gangwal, Rakesh, 22, 420
Garuda Indonesian Airlines, 363
gates, 11, 23, 44, 61, 62, 76, 77, 79, 80, 82, 108, 113, 114, 126, 128, 129, 138, 155, 172, 175, 180, 192, 204-206, 208, 209, 211, 214, 218, 231, 239, 252, 256, 263, 284, 291, 295, 310, 329, 332, 410, 422, 423, 428, 430, 432, 434, 457, 466, 470, 471, 479, 495, 498
gateways, 409, 412, 443
GB Airways, 442
GE Capital Corp., 166
Gemini, 324
Gialloreto, Louis, 242, 243
Glass, Charles, 159, 222
global alliances; See international alliances
global positioning system [GPS], 404
globalization, 472
Goetz, Andrew, 14, 54, 70, 75, 97, 112, 120, 122, 124, 127, 138, 152, 160, 161, 185, 289, 311, 313, 394, 427, 454, 456, 457, 464, 466, 471, 483, 486
Golden Gate Airlines, 115
Golden West Airlines, 115
Gompertz curve, 199
Gore, Al, 256
Government Accounting Office [GAO], 8, 288, 291, 325, 327
government intervention, 454, 464, 481, 484

government paternalism, 2, 114, 163, 444, 473, 477
governmental subsidies; See subsidies
GP Express Airlines, 118
GPA Group, 161, 165, 166
Grand Airways, 117
Great Society programs, 453
Greenslet, Edmund, 125, 143, 157, 169, 289, 311
Greenwald, Gerald, 161, 238, 309
Gritta, Richard, 140-142, 148, 481
Gross Domestic Product, 288
gross domestic product [GDP], 3, 47, 49, 53, 97, 111, 287
gross national product [GNP], 3, 199
ground facilities, 253
ground operations, 177, 178
grownups fly free, 109, 244, 291, 302
Grumbridge, J.L., 168
Gulf War, 103, 195, 367, 403, 488
Gull Air, 116

Haidar, Jalal, 255, 256
Hallett, Carol, 249, 358, 369, 402-405
halo effect of computer reservations system, 73
Hammonds Commuter Airline, 115
Hardin, Garrett, 87
Harding, Lawrence, 234
Harris, Hollis, 264
Harris, Ted, 252, 469
Hawaii Express, 350
Hawaiian Airlines, 9, 118, 278, 438, 439, 440
Headley, Dean, 276
heavy maintenance, 254
Herfindahl-Hirshman Index [HHI], 497
Hermans/Markair Express Airlines, 118
high fare, full service network carriers, 171
high fare, high service point-to-point carriers, 172
hijackers; See international terrorism
Hilton International, 15, 16, 126, 128, 160, 272
Hirsch, James, 204
Hobson's choice, 65
Horizon Air, 9, 10, 25, 91, 92, 126, 278, 351
hostile takeovers, 11, 16, 120, 122
Houston Hobby Airport, 14
Howard, Lee, 199, 281
hub-and-spoke networks, 10-14, 16, 18, 26, 27, 35, 36, 39, 43, 44, 53, 58-62, 64, 68, 72, 74, 79-82, 84, 90, 111, 112, 161, 200-202, 204, 206-214, 225, 227,

235, 247, 248, 251-253, 285, 288, 289, 299, 302, 311, 312, 315, 352, 359, 361, 385, 409, 422, 423, 425, 427, 430, 439, 445, 446, 450, 457, 466-472, 476, 479, 481-483, 487-489, 498, 503
Hughes Airwest, 7, 13, 224, 237, 263, 439
Hughes, Howard, 15, 176, 346
hush kit, 155, 221, 223, 349, 365
Hussein, Saddam, 109, 367
hypothetico-deductive reasoning (i.e., science), 316

Iberia Airlines, 164, 310, 323, 324, 423, 435, 436, 441, 452
Icahn, Carl, 15, 111, 119, 121, 122, 128, 136, 147, 161, 269, 387, 388
Icarus, 233
immediate purchase requirements, 306
Imperial Airlines, 116
income statement, 131, 135
Indiana Airways, 114
indirect air carriers, 6
industry concentration; See market consolidation; See also economic concentration
inflation, 24, 39, 59, 86, 97, 103, 181, 290, 311, 315, 456, 458, 459, 463, 468
in-flight services, 27, 71, 96, 172, 174, 175, 192, 193, 249, 261, 265, 268, 270, 271, 287, 343, 348, 357, 376
infrastructure, 2, 68, 102, 155, 163, 183, 205, 208, 455, 466, 467, 470, 475, 482, 484, 485, 489, 498, 504
initial public offering [IPO], 131, 132
insurance, 153, 231, 256, 357
intercarrier agreements, 421
Intercontinental Hotel, 160
interest rates, 153, 158, 181, 241, 358, 386, 504
interline service, 28, 173, 213, 218, 233, 326, 352, 376, 411, 419-422, 425, 426, 431, 472, 497, 500
Intermodal Transportation Commission, 501
international air carriers, 10, 362, 504
International Air Transport Association [IATA], 3, 49, 50, 52, 97, 105, 106, 109, 154, 289, 329, 330, 409, 413, 441, 473
International Air Transportation Competition Act of 1979 [IATCA], 409, 478, 479
international alliances, 13, 14, 27, 74, 213, 411, 416, 418, 419

International Association of Machinists and Aerospace Workers [IAM], 386
International Business Machines [IBM], 51, 195, 309, 310, 320, 321
International Civil Aviation Organization [ICAO], 155, 408, 434
international markets, 7, 10, 11, 13, 16-18, 24, 32, 44, 45, 47, 51, 56, 74, 89, 100, 149, 163, 168, 171, 180, 192, 198, 204, 206, 210, 212, 213, 215-218, 226, 230, 239, 255, 256, 266-269, 271, 287, 293, 294, 304, 322, 336, 338, 362, 382, 397, 399, 402, 406, 409-411, 413, 418-420, 423, 424, 428, 432, 433, 439, 440, 442-444, 449, 450, 471-473, 475, 478-480, 487, 495, 498, 501, 504
international routes, 7, 13, 16, 27, 74, 100, 149, 163, 215, 266, 495
international terrorism, 47, 197, 255
internet, 310, 340, 395, 399-401
interstate air carriers, 10
intra-Asia market, 155
intrastate air carriers, 14, 351
introductory fares, 305
inventory, 1, 21, 33, 41, 64-66, 72, 85, 91, 124, 221, 229, 292, 296, 297, 301, 303, 307, 309, 310, 318-320, 336, 337
inventory costs, 91
inventory management, 301, 348
surplus inventory, 292, 336, 399
investment houses, 131-134, 144, 150, 161, 166
Island Empire, 115

J.D. Power & Associates, 226, 269
Jackson, Michael, 195
Japan Air Lines[JAL], 19, 21-23, 52, 268, 380, 381, 383, 411, 436, 438, 439, 441, 452
Japan Air System, 441
Jet America, 350
Jet Aspen, 118
Jet Express, 117
jetway, 40, 360
Johnson, Lyndon, 385, 453, 492
joint product, 59
joint-fare, 79, 81, 425, 500
joint-fare agreements, 421
junk bonds, 114, 122, 126, 138, 149, 353, 455, 477, 482
just-in-time, 1, 21, 64

Kahn, Alfred, 69, 70, 74, 75, 78, 81, 85-87, 95, 161, 284, 369, 455, 457, 463, 484, 485, 493

517

Kawasaki Leasing, 161
Kekwick, Guy, 444
Kelleher, Herb, 14, 233, 235, 261, 262, 455
Kennedy, Edward, 85, 453, 456
Kennedy, John F., 2
Kenya Airways, 452
Keynes, John Maynard, 73
Kimberly-Clark, 215, 268
Kiwi International Airlines, 118, 235, 276, 278, 349, 350
KLM Royal Dutch Airlies, 14, 22, 23, 44, 52, 122, 160, 162, 164, 209, 217, 275, 323, 411-414, 418, 422, 423, 426, 432, 433, 435-439, 441, 445, 448-450, 452
Korean Air Lines, 22, 23, 411, 436
Krattenmaker, Thomas, 79
Kuralt, Charles, 231
Kuttner, Robert, 89, 464, 502

L'Express Airlines, 117
labor, 15, 17, 18, 21, 24, 31, 41, 44, 45, 47, 48, 52, 59, 61-63, 65, 96, 112, 121, 124, 126, 127, 130, 132, 148, 152, 154, 162, 164, 168, 181, 187, 207, 209, 211, 222, 238, 241, 243, 248, 250, 253, 254, 257, 258, 262, 264, 269, 274, 289, 312, 314, 318, 348, 349, 352, 353, 355-359, 361, 366, 368-371, 373, 374, 376, 379, 381-383, 385, 386, 388-395, 398, 418, 442, 445, 457, 459, 463, 464, 466, 467, 475, 476, 481, 487, 488, 492-494, 498, 503, 504
 labor agreements, 21, 481
 labor costs, 47, 63, 349, 353, 355, 358, 368-370, 379, 381, 386, 389, 391, 395, 465
 labor unions, 18, 63, 126, 187, 235, 248, 349, 352, 354, 358, 361, 368, 382, 384, 386, 389, 391, 393, 418, 475, 481, 492
Lacsa Airlines, 441
Lady Di and Prince Charles, 437
LaGuardia Airport, 18, 128, 129, 203, 209, 252
laissez-faire economics, 32, 48, 69, 70, 73, 77, 454, 474, 481, 483, 484, 491, 493, 501, 502, 504
Laker Skytrain, 270, 307, 348, 476
Laker, Sir Freddie, 234
LanChile Airlines, 436
landing fees, 96, 239, 356, 402, 405
landing slots, 15, 16, 18, 77, 80, 122, 128, 129, 163, 205, 208, 209, 443, 495, 498
LANICA Airlines, 114

Latin America market, 11, 17, 113, 127-129, 215-218, 230, 266, 410, 423, 475
Lauda Air, 441, 447, 451
Lauderdale, Michael, 271, 490, 491
Lawler, Edmund, 245, 246
leases, 15, 16, 21, 40, 79, 82, 122, 124, 126, 132-134, 138, 140-146, 149, 150, 152, 155, 159-161, 165, 181, 190, 192, 205, 214, 222, 231, 239, 242, 252, 257, 298, 320, 349, 356, 357, 383, 406, 421, 422, 443, 465, 495, 498
 dry leases, 421
 leasebacks, 145
 wet leases, 159, 383, 421, 443
Lederer, Ludwig, 258
Leisure Air, 350
leisure travel, 45, 48, 52, 56, 60, 169, 188, 189, 192, 196, 198, 282, 286, 294, 297, 307
leveraged buy out [LBO], 11, 13, 15, 119-126, 138, 148, 157, 312, 324, 439, 474, 495
Levine, Michael, 32, 38, 59, 69, 70, 75-79, 81-84, 120, 244, 407
liabilities, 131, 133-135, 495
liberalization, 2, 13, 97, 108, 122, 160, 300, 364, 410, 411, 413, 417, 418, 420, 448-450, 474, 485
Lindbergh, Charles A., 1, 345
line maintenance, 254
line personnel, 192, 257, 259
linear route systems, 14, 27, 28, 61, 62, 74, 204, 207, 210, 211, 213, 214, 247, 289, 351, 359, 374, 467, 498, 503
liquidation of assets, 26, 44, 80, 132, 163, 234, 310
load factors, 32-34, 36, 41, 45, 47, 60, 66, 68, 70, 76, 89, 119, 137, 180, 209, 213, 214, 218, 222, 234, 235, 239, 240, 244, 274, 281, 283, 284, 286, 292-295, 297-299, 301, 303, 310, 314, 348, 362, 363, 368, 397, 399, 475, 479
loan guarantees, 496
Lockheed Corporation, 108, 160, 488, 496
Lockheed L-1011, 103, 108, 160, 366
London Gatwick Airport, 443, 447
London Heathrow Airport, 11, 15, 16, 129, 160, 162, 203, 204, 217, 267, 444, 477
long haul markets, 16-18, 27, 39, 44, 54, 111, 162, 173, 193, 212, 218, 226, 245, 266, 285, 336, 353, 362, 443, 474, 478, 489
Long, Jeffrey, 144

Index

Lorenzo, Frank, 11, 12, 15, 69, 85, 119-121, 126, 161, 172, 234, 263, 264, 344, 371, 386, 388, 433, 439, 457
Los Angeles International Airport [LAX], 129
low fares, 28, 53, 77, 193, 195, 246, 285, 286, 294, 338, 348, 350, 352-354, 372, 392, 401
low-cost airlines, 14, 44, 66, 110, 119, 195, 196, 220, 234, 235, 242, 245, 248, 286, 294, 295, 305, 327, 344, 348, 352-355, 359, 364, 369, 371, 372, 380, 382, 391, 392, 397, 411, 428, 455, 460, 471, 476, 483, 485, 486, 494, 503
low-cost,low- to medium-differentiated service carriers, 242
low-cost,low-service carriers, 242
low fare, high service network carriers, 172
low fare, high service point-to-point carriers, 172
low fare, low service network carriers, 172
low fare, low service point-to-point carriers, 172
Lufthansa CityLine, 447
Lufthansa Express, 447
Lufthansa German Airlines [DLH], 19-23, 128, 164, 275, 323, 324, 382, 383, 414-418, 423, 426, 432, 435-437, 441, 447, 449-451
luggage; See baggage
Lustig, Jay, 371
Luxair, 441, 447, 451

Machiavellian perspective, 477
mail, See cargo
maintenance, 21, 23, 28, 47, 76, 80, 96, 131, 132, 159, 163, 175, 177, 178, 180, 221, 224, 231, 233, 234, 236, 239, 249-255, 264, 271, 295, 344, 345, 349, 357, 362, 365, 371, 380, 381, 383, 465
maintenance checks, 251, 253
maintenance costs, 80, 221
major air carriers (Majors), 7-16, 26-28, 31, 35, 44, 47, 53, 56, 61, 63, 66, 73, 74, 78-80, 82, 85, 86, 90, 97, 100, 102, 110, 111, 113, 114, 118, 121, 122, 127, 131, 132, 136-141, 144, 146, 153, 154, 158, 161, 164-166, 174-176, 186, 193, 195, 204-206, 208, 209, 211, 213, 215, 217, 218, 220, 223, 225, 231, 235, 236, 238, 243, 245, 246, 248, 252, 253, 258, 267, 269, 272, 281, 285, 286, 294, 302, 308, 313, 318, 323, 324, 326, 328, 339, 348, 349, 351-355, 359, 361-363, 365, 367-370, 373-375, 379, 383, 386, 387, 389, 395, 397, 401, 404, 412, 413, 416, 426-428, 430, 431, 435, 436, 440, 442, 460, 465, 467, 470, 471, 476, 477, 481, 482, 499, 503, 504
Malaysian Airline Service [MAS], 363, 381, 435, 436
Maldutis, Julius, 3, 32, 50, 52, 97, 101, 106, 139, 140, 154, 156, 176, 205, 223, 224, 268, 283-285, 289, 307, 363, 376, 395, 399, 401, 404, 428, 441-444, 471, 473, 477, 482
Malek, Frederic, 122
Malev Airlines, 441
managed competition, 487, 489, 494
management goals, 153
marginal and average costs of production, 32, 42, 43, 70, 71, 86, 284, 308, 419, 461, 485
MarkAir, 9, 118, 172, 270, 278, 280, 349, 350
market capitalization, 138
market consolidation, 8, 70, 72, 83, 86, 127, 224, 243, 274, 414, 417-419, 434, 440, 441, 450, 458, 483, 484, 486, 489; See also economic concentration
market Darwinism, 2, 26, 244, 302, 370, 441, 489
market maturity, 487
marketing, 14, 17, 23, 25, 26, 36, 42, 61, 63, 76, 80, 131, 137, 138, 148, 156, 160, 167, 168, 175-184, 186-189, 192, 194, 195, 197-199, 206, 209, 213, 214, 220, 226, 228, 233, 235-237, 239, 244, 246, 247, 251, 262, 265, 266, 272-274, 283, 287, 292, 296, 298, 317, 321, 323, 325, 328, 330, 333, 342, 345, 357, 359, 395, 407, 415-417, 421, 423, 433, 436, 442, 446, 448, 474, 478, 495
marketing 4Ps, 177
marketing alliance, 421, 437
marketing audit, 194
marketing control system, 239
marketing costs, 396
marketplace forces, 493, 494
market research, 177, 178
Marshall, Sir Colin, 262, 420
Martinair-Holland Airlines, 452
McCartney, Scott, 110, 130, 132, 213, 215, 218, 221, 228, 230, 233, 235, 241, 244, 264, 266, 268, 269, 280, 310, 324, 343, 347, 361, 366, 369, 372, 374, 375, 387, 399, 400, 405, 416, 446, 450
McClain Air, 116, 350

McDonnell-Douglas Corporation, 49, 52, 107, 108, 154, 222, 225, 270, 289, 343, 346, 482, 483
McDonnell-Douglas aircraft,
 MD-80, 82, 226, 268, 364, 366
 MD-95, 352
McWilliams, Abagail, 91, 92
mechanics, 254, 388
megacarriers, 14, 205, 211, 218, 246, 328, 414, 425, 428, 433, 441, 450, 504
Melton, L.J., 492
mergers, 11-13, 17, 26, 39, 44, 82, 92, 113, 118, 123, 130, 168, 176, 195, 212, 213, 224, 235, 243, 244, 255, 263, 274, 291, 293, 314, 323, 344, 347, 349, 371, 383, 411, 412, 417, 418, 421, 436, 439, 445-447, 449, 450, 472-474, 477, 492, 493, 497, 504; See market consolidation; See also economic concentration
Meridien Hotels, 160, 446
Mesa Airlines, 161, 173, 351, 363, 428, 440, 471
Mesaba Airlines, 351, 452
Metro Airlines Northeast, 117
Meyer, Ed, 42
MGM Grand Air, 350
Mid Pacific Airlines, 117
Middle East Airlines, 446
Midway Airlines, 15, 18, 113, 117, 118, 128, 156, 205, 224, 246, 276, 344, 347-350, 389
Midwest Express, 9, 55, 172, 214, 215, 268, 276, 278, 350
minimum/maximum stay requirements, 307
Minneapolis/St. Paul Airport, 163
modes of transportation; See alternative modes of transportation
Mohawk Airlines, 117
monopoly power, 14, 32, 68, 72, 75, 79, 82-84, 91-93, 252, 288, 289, 291 295, 444, 455, 460, 481, 485, 487, 489, 492, 497, 499, 502, 503
monopsony power, 92, 291, 308
morale, 181, 237, 262, 264, 265, 341, 347, 373, 389
Morris Air, 129, 235, 349, 350, 439
Morrison, Steven, 83, 102, 130, 313, 314, 463, 464
Mountain West Airlines, 114
Mullan, Homi, 50, 112, 157, 158
Mulrooney, Prime Minister, 448
multilateral agreements, 408, 410
Murphy, Kevin, 73, 74
Murphy, Patrick, 352

Muse Air, 127, 350

Nader, Ralph, 484
Nance, John, 234, 260
narrow-body aircraft, 353, 359, 365
Nationair, 448
national air carriers (Nationals), 7, 8, 348, 355, 499
National Airlines, 8, 9, 120, 127, 140, 343
National Commission To Ensure A Strong Competitive Airline Industry, 154, 163, 410, 420, 455, 456
national defense, 2, 454, 463, 482, 484, 485, 488, 498
National Florida Airlines, 115
National Institute for Aviation Research at Wichita State University, 277
national protectionism, 410, 411, 420, 477
NationsAir, 350
Neidl, Raymond, 103, 124, 153, 159, 408, 410, 414
nesting, 299
Net, 340
net income, defined, 135, 282
net worth, 131, 135
neutral industry booking system, 329
New Deal, 484
New York Air, 78, 114, 126, 224, 237, 263, 350, 439
New York Airways, 114
New York Helicopter Airlines, 115
New York John F. Kennedy Airport [JFK], 16, 129, 203, 209, 252, 307, 422, 428, 429, 439
New York LaGuardia Airport, 18
niche markets, 23, 28, 132, 171, 177, 351
Nixon, Richard, 453
non-flight services, 96, 249
non-interline connecting service, 425
nonrefundable tickets, 306
nonstop service, 35, 54, 64, 72, 74, 75, 80, 193, 208, 210-213, 215, 225, 251, 285, 301, 422, 424, 426, 428, 430, 431, 470, 478, 487, 497-499, 503
non-transferable tickets, 307
non-union, 126, 208, 220, 235, 266, 352, 361, 369, 384, 391, 394
North American Airlines, 432
North Atlantic routes, 15, 209, 267, 412, 413, 415, 417
North Central Airlines, 7, 13, 224, 237, 263, 439
Northcoast Executive Airlines, 117
Northeast Airlines, 140

Index

Northeastern International Airlines, 116, 350
Northwest Airlines, 7-9, 13, 14, 19-23, 44, 52, 58, 69, 78, 101, 109, 119, 122-125, 127, 128, 130, 139-141, 145, 147, 151, 154, 156, 160-163, 172, 201, 205, 206, 210, 212, 214, 215, 218, 219, 223-225, 237, 244, 259, 263, 269, 276, 278, 291, 302, 308, 324, 339, 343, 344, 362, 363, 365, 368, 373, 376-378, 389, 390, 395, 397, 407, 411, 412, 422, 423, 425, 426, 433, 437-440, 445, 448-450, 452, 473, 503
Northwest/KLM alliance, 452
Nyrop, Donald, 141

O'Connor, William E., 36, 45, 49, 55, 56, 59, 60, 80
Oceanaire Lines, 115
Official Airline Guide [OAG], 190
oligopoly power, 72, 420, 485, 489
oligopsony power, 57, 63, 72, 286, 340, 468
Olsen, Mel, 208
Olympic Airways, 164, 276, 346, 435
on-line connecting service, 425
on-time performance, 15, 241, 264, 275, 276, 279
open skies, 217, 408, 410-412, 415, 417, 420, 449, 472-478, 480
operating expenses, 15, 76, 91, 96, 105, 135, 141, 144, 149, 150, 154, 155, 178, 214, 221, 222, 254, 281, 289, 318, 349, 355, 357, 361, 366, 370, 376, 379, 380, 386, 388, 389, 391, 395, 447, 462, 465, 488
defined, 282
operating leases, 133, 138, 141, 142, 149, 150
operating loss, 135
operating margin, 135
operating margins, 50, 112, 146, 157
operating profit, 21, 22, 108, 135, 282
defined, 282
operating ratio [OR], 2, 6, 9, 13, 14, 21, 33, 37, 46, 101, 104, 108, 149, 151, 191, 197, 203, 205, 210, 225, 278, 325, 429, 441
operating revenue, 96, 104, 105, 135, 157, 188, 281, 282, 355, 376, 378, 416
defined, 282
Operation Desert Shield/Storm; See Gulf War
operations, 3, 11, 16-18, 28, 61, 82, 96, 102, 103, 113, 133, 135, 149, 167, 175-178, 184, 186, 198, 201, 202, 206, 209, 213, 218, 220-222, 232, 235, 246, 249, 273, 328, 412, 422, 446, 457, 458, 470, 473, 477, 479
organization, 12, 25, 84, 102, 113, 118, 119, 160, 161, 174, 177, 179, 185, 186, 195, 226, 275, 332
organized labor; See labor
origin and destination traffic [O&D], 14, 35, 36, 68, 79, 174, 199, 201, 206, 208, 212, 213, 218, 222, 239, 245, 286, 299, 442
Oster, Clinton, 430
Ott, James, 103, 124, 159, 224, 290, 408, 410, 414, 420
Oum, Tae, 33, 35, 36, 49, 57, 60, 63, 64
outsource, 132, 246, 253, 255, 264, 341
overbooking; See denied boarding
Ozark Airlines, 7, 15, 123, 128, 439

Pacific Express Airlines, 115, 530
Pacific markets, 475
Pacific Rim markets, 11, 363, 504
Pacific Southwest Airlines [PSA], 17, 128, 390, 439
Packwood, Bob, 454
Paige, Satchel, 352
Pan Am flight 103, 109
Pan American World Airways [Pan Am], 7, 8, 13, 15, 16, 44, 101, 109, 113, 117, 120, 123, 127-130, 132, 139, 140, 147, 156, 160, 161, 206, 217, 224, 232, 236, 246, 248, 272, 276, 278, 295, 343, 344, 346, 349, 364, 371, 382, 388, 390, 407, 423, 453, 472, 473, 483, 489
Pareto optimalization, 90, 188
Paris Charles de Gaulle Airport, 382, 446
Paris Orly Airport, 203, 382, 443
PARS computer reservations system, 128, 321
passenger facility charge [PFC], 155, 402, 405
passengers, totals carried, 2, 4, 5
peak/off peak fares, 306
Peña, Frederico, 414, 449, 477, 478
Penn Central Railroad, 481
Pension Benefit Guarantee Corporation [PBGC], 147
People Express Airlines, 12, 78, 121, 123, 126-128, 140, 161, 171, 172, 206, 224, 237, 244, 262, 263, 270, 294, 347, 348, 350, 388, 439, 476
perfect competition, 32, 68, 70, 71, 74, 75, 84, 89, 90, 454, 455, 457

521

perishable products, 40, 41, 64-66, 85, 91, 288, 292, 309, 310, 460, 486
Persian Gulf crisis; See Gulf War
Petzinger, Thomas, 2, 95, 208, 227, 238, 241, 250, 258, 261-263, 267, 293, 294, 295, 319, 320, 323, 325, 343-345, 443, 453
Pevsner, Donald L., 432
Philippine Airlines, 165, 363, 436
Phoenix lenders, 161
Piedmont Airlines, 7, 17, 18, 128, 264, 270, 276, 439
Pikarski, Adam, 52
pilots, 47, 95, 124, 126, 154, 176, 234, 238, 254, 258, 260, 261, 264, 349, 357, 360, 361, 366, 370, 371, 373-375, 382, 384-388, 390, 392, 404, 447; See also flight crews
Pinehurst Airlines, 115
Pitcairn Aviation, 113
planning, 23, 25, 137, 138, 148, 156, 159, 160, 167, 175, 177-187, 195, 198, 208, 213, 220-222, 238, 239, 242, 250, 251, 266, 292, 294, 298, 300, 420, 474
Plaskett, Thomas, 423, 453
Pocono Airlines, 117
point-to-point service, 28, 61, 172, 173, 180, 211-213, 421, 478
Pompano Airways, 116
pooling, 412, 413, 433, 444, 449, 472
postal service, 64
predation, 13, 22, 60, 77-79, 82, 236, 244, 289, 295, 348, 352, 369, 455, 460, 474, 497, 499, 502; See also destructive competition
pre-operating costs, 76, 149
president, 2, 48, 69, 110, 117, 174-176, 186, 256, 280, 410, 455, 484
Presidential Airlines, 117, 350
Presley, Elvis, 195, 233
price, 1, 2, 8, 24, 25, 28, 31, 32, 38, 39, 41-43, 50, 52-58, 60, 62, 64-68, 70-72, 74-79, 82, 83, 85-87, 89, 90, 92, 97, 108, 109, 112, 119, 123, 126, 131, 132, 137, 138, 153, 167, 168, 170-174, 178, 180, 181, 184, 189, 190, 192, 194, 195, 198, 199, 208, 214, 226, 227, 240, 242, 244-246, 250, 251, 267, 268, 270, 275, 282-302, 304, 305, 307, 308, 310, 311, 314, 315, 318, 321, 327, 328, 332, 334-338, 340-343, 413, 417, 419, 423, 424, 428, 449, 455, 456, 458-461, 463-465, 467, 468, 470-472, 477, 479, 483, 485-488, 492, 494, 496, 497, 499, 500, 502, 503
options, 25
price and entry regulation, 456
price and service options, 28, 167
price wars, 54, 89, 110, 284, 286, 302, 352, 385
price-earnings ratio, 137
pricing, 38, 40, 60, 65-67, 72, 77-79, 83, 84, 89, 92, 108, 178, 190, 214, 231, 244, 281, 283-285, 288, 289, 291, 294-296, 301, 302, 311, 314, 327, 335, 428, 454, 455, 457, 458, 460, 467, 471, 474, 481-483, 485, 486, 488, 489, 494-499, 502, 504
differential pricing, 295
price discounting, 293
pricing discrimination, 68, 78, 295, 335, 485, 489, 497, 502
pricing simplification, 496
Pride Air, 116, 351
Princeton Air Link Corp, 117
Private Jet/National, 351
privatization, 93, 147, 165, 410, 415, 442, 447, 473, 477
product differentiation, 38, 40, 55, 56, 72, 167, 168, 170, 171, 173, 259, 459, 460
profits, 11, 13-15, 17, 18, 20, 21, 23, 25-27, 39, 44, 47- 49, 65, 66, 68, 70, 75, 78-80, 84-86, 89, 93, 95, 97, 99, 100, 103-111, 113, 121, 122, 124, 126, 127, 130, 131, 133-135, 137, 138, 142, 145, 148, 154, 157-159, 161, 167, 168, 171, 177, 181, 182, 187-189, 194, 200, 210, 211, 215, 218, 222, 227, 231, 234, 238-241, 243, 244, 248, 250, 251, 258, 264-266, 269-271, 274, 280, 286, 289, 293, 295, 300, 312, 314, 327, 333, 338, 348, 351-355, 357, 359, 363, 367, 368, 376, 380, 384, 385, 389, 392, 394, 403, 406, 418, 442, 444, 448, 449, 455-457, 459, 467, 472, 475, 477, 482, 486, 488, 489, 497
profit and loss statement, 131
profit margins, 97, 99, 105-108, 111, 135, 157, 338, 460
profitability, 20, 25, 26, 84, 100, 107, 110, 158, 238, 239, 252, 312, 348, 351-354, 357, 363, 367, 368, 376, 385, 389, 406, 462, 476, 477, 479, 488
program evaluation, 315
projected price earnings ratio, 138
promotion and sales, 76, 77, 96, 175, 177, 178, 184, 228, 230, 236, 244, 296, 305, 307, 310, 318, 342, 356, 357, 395, 458
promotional fares, 76, 305, 342, 458
prospectus, 131, 133

Providence-Boston Airlines [PBA], 12, 116, 234, 263, 439
public interest, 114, 464, 481, 484, 485, 494, 496, 501
public policy, 24, 31, 58, 76, 92, 93, 187, 217, 309, 409, 410, 413, 415, 470, 474, 483-485, 487, 489
public utility, 289, 481, 474, 484, 485, 489, 502
PWA Airlines, 448

Qantas Airlines, 22, 165, 224, 241, 275, 343, 362, 380, 423, 436, 441-444, 451
quality of service, 25, 26, 54, 55, 71, 149, 168, 214, 226, 257, 265, 274, 313, 315, 335, 388, 396, 425, 439, 460, 479, 502
quarterly reports, 132
quick ratio, 134
quick turnaround, 351, 362
Qwest Air, 117

Railway Labor Act of 1926, 488
ramp agents, 360
Reagan, Ronald, 386, 453, 489, 492, 501
recession, 24, 25, 39, 42, 47, 49, 50, 103, 104, 107-109, 112, 159, 181, 242, 284, 453, 456, 458, 459, 483, 504
red eye specials, 306, 361
Reed, Dan, 47, 67
Regent Air, 171, 351
regional air carriers (Regionals), 7, 118, 137, 348, 361, 430, 474, 499, 504
regulatory reform, 69, 108, 311, 458, 485, 488, 489, 491, 493, 494, 496
Reno Air, 214, 215, 233, 244, 276, 278, 340, 349, 351, 363-366, 406
Republic Airlines, 13, 32, 122, 127, 140, 217, 224, 263, 344, 390, 439
research and development [R&D], 2, 162
reservations agent, 272, 318, 319
reservations system, 10, 17, 27, 28, 67, 72, 76, 80, 82, 126, 168, 172, 190, 197, 231, 245, 272, 292, 296, 298, 318, 319, 321, 323, 329, 331, 411, 419, 421-425, 427, 430, 433- 435, 472, 498, 500
Resort Commuter Airline, 117
return on assets, 135
return on equity, 135
revenue, 3, 4, 8, 10, 12, 18, 20, 23, 24, 34, 36, 38, 42, 43, 52, 58, 61, 63, 65, 66, 68, 72, 78, 81, 83, 95, 97, 102, 104, 105, 111, 129, 131, 132, 134-136, 142, 148, 157, 165, 167, 170, 177, 178, 181, 183, 187, 188, 197, 199, 200, 208, 210, 211, 214, 220, 226, 228, 229, 231, 232, 235, 238-241, 243, 246, 249, 257, 265, 266, 269-271, 281, 283, 284, 292-295, 298-303, 307, 310, 324, 326, 335, 345, 348, 349, 355, 364, 376, 381, 383, 398, 399, 412, 413, 415, 416, 420, 439, 443-445, 447, 449, 459, 462, 472, 474, 479
revenue passenger mile [RPM], 4, 5, 8, 18, 19, 219, 240, 281, 290, 352, 361, 376, 377
Rickenbacker, Eddie, 176
Rio Airways, 116
risk assessment, 182
Roberts, Roach & Associates, 347, 353, 355, 364, 367, 386, 395, 396, 400
Robinson, Joan, 84
Rocky Mountain Airways, 12, 117
Rohatyn, Felix, 134
Rolls Royce, 160
Roper Organization, 190
round-trip requirements, 306
Royal Air Maroc, 446
Royal Brunei Airlines, 435
Royal West Airlines, 116, 351
Royale Airlines, 116
Rule, Charles, 84
rural air service; See small community air service

Sabena Airlines, 164, 403, 436, 438, 441, 445, 446, 449, 451
Sabre, 10, 27, 127, 190, 292, 296, 318, 319, 321, 323, 326, 327, 340, 424, 426
safety, 24, 32, 37, 55, 76, 93, 153, 175, 190-193, 253, 257, 259, 262, 271, 341, 387, 406, 458
safety regulation, 32
salaries, 96, 181, 258, 348, 349, 355, 356, 373, 376, 381, 383, 384, 388, 389, 394, 395, 457
sale fares, 307
sales outlet, 292, 318
Salop, Steven, 79
San Francisco Oakland Helicopter Airline [SFO], 116
saturday night stayover, 230
savings and loan industry [S&L], 481, 482
Scandanavian Air Services [SAS], 12, 22, 44, 162, 164, 189, 275, 323, 345, 435-439, 441, 445, 447, 450, 451
scanning, 189
schedule, 2, 4, 6, 10, 14, 34, 36, 38-40, 54-56, 59, 64, 65, 67, 71, 72, 76, 100, 124, 170, 176, 177, 179, 189, 193, 214, 232, 236, 241, 245, 250-252, 264, 273, 293,

311, 319, 330, 332-336, 342, 417, 424, 442, 447, 459-461, 475, 502, 504
schedule frequency, 34, 39, 64
scheduling, 20, 28, 36, 55, 61, 167, 175, 177, 181, 220, 221, 232, 249, 250, 251, 263, 302, 313, 337, 361, 398, 424, 431, 497
Scherer, F.M., 68, 71, 89
Schumpeter, Joseph, 70, 89
Scocozza, Matthew, 80
S-curve phenomenon, 24, 36, 38, 170, 209, 459
Sea Airmotive, 116
Seaboard Airlines, 127
seamless travel, 40, 218, 272, 274, 411, 419, 421, 425, 431, 479, 501
seasonal discounts, 306
seasonal variation, 45
seat pitch, 55, 63, 112, 174, 193, 197, 215, 222, 226, 265, 266, 268, 304, 315, 348, 364, 367, 465
section 401 of the Federal Aviation Act, 23, 109, 113, 118, 162, 407, 443
section 411 of the Federal Aviation Act, 432
Securities and Exchange Commission [SEC], 130, 133
SEC forms,
    10-K, 133
    10-Q, 133
    SB-2, 133
security, 22, 75, 85, 145, 175, 193, 249, 255, 256, 307, 472, 474, 475, 488, 495, 505
semi-automatic business environment research [SABER], 321
semi-automatic ground environment [SAGE], 321
senior saver and youth fares, 307
sensitivity analysis, 183
Servair Catering, 446
shareholders, 26, 131, 132, 134, 162, 333
Shaw, Stephen, 26, 138, 183, 187, 188, 192, 196, 197, 199, 226, 235, 236, 237, 247, 265, 283, 287, 298, 317, 342, 345
Sherman Antitrust Act, 328
short-haul markets, 16, 27, 28, 53, 54, 61, 111, 154, 161, 173, 193, 194, 209, 212, 214, 218, 221, 232, 235, 245, 247, 351, 353, 361, 363, 372, 428, 471
Shugrue, Martin, 407
shuttle air service, 13, 18, 124, 128, 129
Shuttle by United, 212, 245, 359, 361
shuttle market, 18
Silver State Airlines, 115

Simon, Herbert, 73
Sinatra, Frank, 195
Singapore Airlines, 13, 20, 22, 23, 125, 217, 224, 234, 259, 271, 275, 324, 363, 379-381, 383, 411, 435- 441, 451
situation analysis, 180
sizer box, 361
Sjostrom, William, 92
Sky West Airlines, 351
small business, 52, 57, 68, 244, 286, 290, 309, 470, 483
small community air service, 220, 427, 428, 470, 471
Smart, Edwin, 120
Smith, Adam, 502
Smith, C.R., 364
South African Airways, 451
Southern Airways, 7, 13, 69, 83, 116, 117, 224, 237, 439
Southwest Airlines, 9, 14, 17-20, 22, 27, 28, 53, 54, 61, 83, 101, 127-130, 139, 140, 143, 145, 150, 156, 170, 172, 173, 205, 209-213, 221-225, 232, 233, 235, 241, 244, 245, 247, 248, 261, 262, 266, 269, 276, 278, 279, 295, 304, 340, 343, 345, 351-353, 355, 359, 361, 362, 364-366, 373-378, 382, 385, 390, 392, 397, 404, 439, 455, 467, 481, 482, 503
sovereignty, 408
space-available, 310
spare parts, 122, 221, 224, 255
Spartan Foods, 15, 126, 160
spill, 301, 303
Spirit Airlines, 233, 345, 346, 351
Spirit of St. Louis, 345
spoilage, 85, 301, 303
St. Louis Lambert International Airport, 15
Stage 2 noise requirements, 146, 155, 224, 225
Stage 3 noise requirements, 123, 180, 221, 224, 225, 349, 365
stage length, 20, 60, 62, 111, 180, 209, 214, 222, 261, 266, 289, 353, 363, 364, 367, 372, 375, 376, 382, 497
Standard and Poor's index, 99, 148, 150
standard industry fare level [SIFL], 313, 314, 464
stand-by, space-available travel, 307
State Airlines, 115
statement of cash flow, 135
States West Airlines, 118
station operations, 357
Sterling One Airlines, 351
Stevens, Mark, 388

Index

stock, 13, 120, 122, 124, 125, 131, 132, 136-138, 148, 153, 161, 162, 235, 262, 269, 274, 297, 318, 334, 336, 342, 343, 421, 442, 448, 450, 463, 504
stock value, 137
stockholder's equity; See equity
strategic alliances, 417, 419, 420, 504
strategic petroleum reserve, 163
strategic planning, 23, 25, 131, 133, 167, 177, 179, 182, 185-187, 241, 242, 247, 311
subsidies, 163, 295, 470, 473, 477, 502
Summerfield, John, 198-200, 221, 222, 281, 282
Sun Coast Airlines, 116
Sun Country Airlines, 351
Sun Express, 447
Sun Jet International, 118
Sun West Airlines, 116
Sunworld Airlines, 351
supplemental air carriers, 7
supply, 31-33, 35, 40, 48, 92, 125, 167, 176-178, 249, 265, 292, 309, 318, 460, 461
Swift Aire Line, 115
Swissair, 13, 125, 164, 224, 275, 323, 435-441, 445, 447, 449-451
synergistic loops, 490
System One, 126, 190, 318, 321, 324, 424, 426
System One Information Management LLC, 324

TACA Group, 441
TACA International Airlines, 433
Taneja, Nawal, 34, 41, 45, 65, 68, 137, 138, 148, 156, 160, 168, 171, 180-184, 186, 187, 195, 239, 284, 292, 294, 296, 297, 301, 318, 331, 342, 473, 474
TAP Air Portugal, 164
TAT Airlines, 2, 217, 278, 442, 443
taxes, 24, 56, 68, 104, 105, 110, 111, 135, 136, 141, 143, 144, 147, 154-156, 162-164, 170, 282, 283, 287, 309, 373, 402, 403, 453, 456, 460, 476, 477, 480, 484, 485, 488, 494, 496, 498
    customs fee, 402
    departure tax, 402
    excise tax, 402, 403
    freight tax, 402
    fuel tax, 163, 403
    pfc tax; See passenger facility tax
    ticket tax, 110, 154, 402-404, 477
technology, 24, 25, 51, 62, 68, 74, 81, 82, 89, 108, 161, 179, 181, 220, 222, 248, 273, 296, 302, 321, 339, 340, 359, 400, 404, 415, 420, 465
Tejas Airlines, 114
Teleregister Corporation, 320
Telser, Lester, 91, 92, 93
terminals, 16, 18, 129, 320, 321, 323, 325, 360, 405, 422, 428, 430, 480, 494
territorial air carriers, 9
terrorists; See international terrorism
Texas Air, 69, 85, 123, 126, 128, 324, 439
Texas International Airlines, 7, 11, 120, 127, 224, 237, 263, 296, 439
Thai International Airlines, 22, 363, 380, 411, 451
theoretical economics, 31
think tanks, 456
Thomas, Paul, 52
through-plane service, 424
Thorton, R.L., 204
ticketing agents, 360, 371, 397, 388
ticketless travel, 25, 27, 28, 239, 318, 339, 395, 397-399
Tiffany cards, 319
tour and travel industry, 1, 3, 16, 272
tour group operators, 180, 273, 274, 308, 317, 333, 335, 336
Tower Air, 9, 351
traditional high-cost/full-service carriers, 242
traffic generation, 298
training, 23, 28, 76, 132, 175, 177, 181, 189, 221, 234, 249, 259, 262, 265, 412
tragedy of the commons, 87
Trans Air, 116
Trans World Airlines [TWA], 7-9, 11, 14-17, 19, 42, 44, 58, 101, 111, 113, 118-123, 125, 126, 128-130, 136, 139-141, 145, 147, 154, 156, 160-162, 176, 205, 206, 210, 217, 223-226, 232, 239, 250, 254, 256, 269, 272, 276, 278, 302, 306, 310, 321, 324, 329, 341, 344, 346, 349, 362, 364-367, 373, 375-378, 382, 387-390, 393-395, 397, 423, 428-430, 436, 437, 439, 450, 483, 503
trans-Atlantic markets, 49, 162, 236, 248, 267, 268, 371, 417, 439, 443, 444
TransBrasil Airways, 422
Transcontinental & Western Airways, 346; See also Trans World Airlines
trans-Pacific markets, 14, 123, 127, 155, 160, 217, 218, 288
Transportation Research Board [TRB], 3, 9, 10, 103, 122, 139, 141, 148, 158, 159

525

travel agents, 63, 73, 81, 82, 154, 168, 172, 180, 188, 228, 231, 244-247, 285, 289, 313, 314, 317, 318, 321, 323, 325, 326, 329-334, 336-340, 348, 349, 395, 397-401, 424, 426, 430, 434, 460, 467, 481
travel agent commission overrides, 81 82, 244, 247, 332, 348, 497, 500
travel agent commissions, 338, 349, 356, 357, 395, 398
Tretheway, Michael, 33, 35, 36, 49, 57, 60, 63, 64
trip rigs, 375
Trippe, Juan, 364
TriStar Airlines, 351
Trump Shuttle, 9, 18, 129
Trump, Donald, 9, 18, 114, 124, 128, 129
trunk air carriers, 348
trust fund; See airport and airway trust fund
Tunisair, 446
turboprop service, 170, 173, 193, 218, 220, 245, 265, 281, 326, 363, 427, 428, 470, 471
TW Express, 422
Twain, Mark, 16
two-tier wage structure, 10, 18, 237, 238, 384

U.S. Constitution, 500
U.S. Department of Defense [DOD], 162, 323, 404
U.S. Department of Justice [DOJ], 288, 327, 328
U.S. Department of Transportation [DOT], 9, 162, 190, 209, 322, 332, 427, 431, 434, 447, 463, 470, 473, 480, 481
U.S. Federal Maritime Commission, 501
U.S. Federal Reserve Board, 501
U.S. General Accounting Office [GAO], 139, 146, 208, 209, 223, 228, 291, 325, 331, 404, 428, 471
U.S. General Services Administration [GSA], 309
U.S. Interstate Commerce Commission [ICC], 501; See also U.S. Surface Transportation Board
U.S. Surface Transportation Board, 501
U-2; See Shuttle by United
ubiquitous service, 2, 39, 62, 171, 206, 212, 217, 227, 231, 326, 423, 473, 477, 486
UltrAir, 268, 351
unfair and deceptive competitive practices, 497; See predation

Uniform System of Accounts and Reports [USAR], 130, 131, 241
union busting, 391
United Airlines [UAL], 7-9, 16, 18, 20, 22, 23, 31, 44, 48, 58, 100-102, 121, 124, 126-130, 139, 140, 143, 145-147, 151, 152, 154, 156, 162, 163, 167, 173, 204, 205, 210-212, 215, 217, 219, 222-225, 227-230, 238, 244, 272, 274, 276, 278, 309, 323, 327, 329, 344, 345, 353, 359, 361-363, 365-368, 373, 375-378, 380, 382-384, 387-390, 394, 398, 411, 416-418, 422, 426, 428, 433, 435-438, 447, 451, 471
United Connection, 340
United Express, 363, 411, 428, 471
United Parcel Service [UPS], 23, 232, 350, 351, 393
United Shuttle; See Shuttle by United
United/Lufthansa("Star") alliance, 451
University of Nebraska Aviation Institute, 276
upstart airlines, 173, 190, 208, 214, 246, 344, 352, 353, 369, 370, 379, 384, 406, 499
US Airways, 17, 18, 139, 346, 367; See USAir
USAfrica Airways, 118, 351
USAir, 8, 9, 17-20, 22, 44, 58, 100, 101, 110, 121, 128-130, 139, 140, 143, 145, 146, 151, 154, 156, 160, 161, 165, 201, 204-206, 210, 212, 218, 223-225, 233, 236, 242, 244, 267, 270, 276, 278, 323, 344, 346, 353, 359-363, 365-367, 373, 376-378, 385, 388, 390, 392, 397, 413, 414, 416, 418, 420, 423, 428, 433, 435-439, 442, 443, 445, 451, 452, 471, 477
USAir Express, 363
UTA Airlines, 440, 446
utilization of personnel and equipment, 28, 61, 62, 112, 155, 167, 197, 209, 211, 215, 241, 250, 251, 253, 258, 289, 306, 312, 314, 348, 352, 359, 361, 362, 366, 367, 374, 442, 466, 487, 498

V fare, 307
vacation travel, 56, 283, 287, 292, 293, 295, 306, 468
ValuJet, 44, 129, 172, 195, 196, 232, 235, 236, 242, 246, 345, 346, 349, 351-353, 364, 371, 372, 380, 401
Vanguard Airlines, 206, 351

Index

variable costs, 34, 42, 43, 57-59, 63, 65-67, 87, 91, 214, 240, 289, 299, 309, 460, 486
Varig, 275, 451
vertical integration, 82, 96, 231, 272
Viasa Airlines, 423, 441
Vietnam Airlines, 446
Vietnam War, 453
Vinod, Ben, 292, 293, 299
Virgin Atlantic Airlines, 115-118, 212, 246, 267, 271, 275, 280, 333, 448, 449, 451, 476
Virgin Island Seaplane, 118
Virginia Island Seaplane, 117
visiting friends and relatives [VFR], 56, 188, 198, 286, 287, 292

wage and work rule concessions, 162
wages, 10, 17, 18, 27, 43, 63, 121, 124, 126, 132, 154, 218, 237, 238, 242, 243, 248, 258, 269, 313, 348, 354, 357, 361, 369-371, 374, 375, 380-386, 388, 389, 391-394, 457, 458, 462-464, 488, 503; See also salaries
wage concessions, 17
Waltrip, William, 250, 299, 300
Washington Dulles Airport, 206
Washington National Airport, 18, 209, 252
Watergate scandal, 453
weapons of war, 204
weather, 25, 62, 64, 134, 168, 193, 242, 250, 252, 361, 400, 431
Weintraub, Richard, 360, 361, 443
Westair, 9
Western Airlines, 7, 12, 13, 123, 128, 129, 140, 172, 206, 236, 345, 390, 439
Western Pacific Airlines, 246, 345, 349, 351
Westin Hotels, 16, 126
Wexler, Harvey, 466, 467, 501, 502
White House Commission on Aviation Safety and Security, 256
Whitman, Marty, 136
wide-bodied aircraft, 17, 18, 44, 60, 108, 162, 193, 222, 225, 359, 363, 368, 430, 443, 474, 478, 483, 488, 489
Wien Air Alaska, 116
Will's Air, 115
Wilson, Gary, 122, 448
Wings Holdings, 122, 123
Winston, Clifford, 83, 102, 130, 313, 314, 463, 464
Wise Airlines, 116
Wolf, Stephen, 17, 31, 40, 41, 48, 124, 167, 218, 236, 344, 366, 394, 416

Woolman, C.E., 176
work rules, 27, 63, 258, 349, 351, 369, 370, 374, 381, 386, 389, 392, 503
World Airways, 117, 232, 346, 390, 407
World War I [WWI], 107, 330, 407, 408, 413, 420, 478
World War II [WWII], 107, 330, 407, 408, 413, 478
world wide web; See internet
Worldspan, 190, 318, 324, 326, 340, 424, 426, 435, 437
Wright Air Lines, 115
Wright Amendment, 14, 482
Wright Brothers, 100, 503

Y fare, 230, 290, 302, 304, 308, 315
yield, 11, 24, 26, 38, 39, 41, 47, 48, 52, 56, 58, 59, 62, 68, 74, 76, 79, 81, 89, 109, 111, 112, 137, 167, 173, 180, 181, 189, 196, 198, 199, 201, 208, 209, 214-216, 219, 222, 226, 230, 232, 236, 240, 248, 257, 259, 260, 266, 268, 275, 281-283, 288-290, 292-305, 309, 311, 312, 328, 345, 348, 352, 357, 359, 363, 365, 368, 369, 379, 386, 387, 397, 398, 401, 406, 410, 415, 428, 442, 456, 459, 467, 468, 471, 475, 482
defined, 137
real yield, 62, 111, 112, 289, 311
yield management, 11, 26, 52, 58, 68, 76, 167, 181, 232, 283, 292, 294-299, 302, 305, 309, 328
defined, 292

Zagat Airline Survey, 191, 275

ABOUT THE AUTHORS

PAUL STEPHEN DEMPSEY

Paul Stephen Dempsey is Professor of Law and Director of the Transportation Law Program at the University of Denver, and Vice Chairman and Director of Frontier Airlines, Inc. He formerly served as an attorney with the Civil Aeronautics Board and the Interstate Commerce Commission in Washington, D.C.

Professor Dempsey has written more than fifty law review and professional journal articles, scores of newspaper and news magazine editorials, and several books:

- Denver International Airport: Lessons Learned (McGraw-Hill 1997).
- Aviation Law & Regulation (two volumes, Butterworth 1993).
- Airline Deregulation & Laissez-Faire Mythology (Quorum Books 1992).
- Flying Blind: The Failure of Airline Deregulation (Economic Policy Institute, 1990).
- The Social & Economic Consequences of Deregulation (Quorum Books 1989).
- Law & Foreign Policy in International Aviation (Transnational 1987).
- Law & Economic Regulation in Transportation (Quorum Books 1986).

Dr. Dempsey holds the following degrees: ABJ (1972) and JD (1975) University of Georgia; LLM (1978) George Washington University; DCL (1987) Institute of Air & Space Law, McGill

University. He is admitted to practice law in Colorado, Georgia and the District of Columbia.

LAURENCE E. GESELL

Laurence E. Gesell is Professor of Air Transportation Management in the Department of Aeronautical Management Technology at Arizona State University. Additional faculty appointments have included Adjunct Professor in the Extended Campus of Embry-Riddle Aeronautical University (1986-1989); Lecturer in the College of Business at California Polytechnic University, San Luis Obispo (1983-1984); and Instructor in the Department of Aviation at Northern Virginia Community College (1976-1979). Prior to accepting an appointment at ASU, he was the Airports Manager for the County of San Luis Obispo, California (1979-1984). He is an Accredited Airport Executive (AAE) with the American Association of Airport Executives, and Certified Airport Executive (CAE) with the Southwest Chapter of the American Association of Airport Executives. He was an aviation consultant and airport planning project manager with Howard, Needles, Tammen and Bergendoff, a leading design firm of architects, engineers and planners (1973-1979). And, he is a commercially rated pilot, retired Lieutenant Colonel, and Master Army Aviator.

Professor Gesell has authored numerous professional papers, journal articles, final consultant reports, and the following books:

- Aviation and the Law (2d ed. 1993).
- The Administration of Public Airports (3rd ed. 1992).
- Airline Re-Regulation (1990).
- Air Traffic Control: An Invitation To a Career (1989).

Dr. Gesell holds the following degrees: BA (1976) Upper Iowa University; MPA (1982) University of San Francisco; PhD (1990) Arizona State University.